THE
BOOK ®

D1374664

Saab 9000
Service and Repair Manual

A K Legg LAE MIMI and Spencer Drayton

(256-1686-11AG3)

Models covered
Saab 9000 models with 4-cylinder engines, including special/limited editions
1985 cc & 2290 cc

Does NOT cover V6 engines

70003563705X

Printed in the USA

ABCD

Haynes Publishing
Sparkford, Yeovil, Somerset BA22 7JJ, England

Haynes North America, Inc
861 Lawrence Drive, Newbury Park, California 91320, USA

Editions Haynes
4, Rue de l'Abreuvoir
92415 COURBEVOIE CEDEX, France

Haynes Publishing Nordiska AB
Box 1504, 751 45 Uppsala, Sweden

ISBN **1 85960 764 0**

British Library Cataloguing in Publication Data
A catalogue record for this book is available from the British Library.

Contents

LIVING WITH YOUR SAAB 9000

Roadside Repairs

MOT Test Checks

MAINTENANCE

Routine Maintenance and Servicing

Contents

REPAIRS & OVERHAUL

Engine and Associated Systems

Transmission

Brakes and Suspension

Body Equipment

Wiring Diagrams

REFERENCE

Index

Introduction to the Saab 9000

The Saab 9000 was introduced in the UK in October 1985 as a 5-door Hatchback, with a turbocharged fuel-injected 16-valve 1985 cc engine. The normally-aspirated engine followed in early 1986, and an automatic transmission version in late 1986. A 4-door booted Saloon version was introduced in early 1991.

All engines are of 16-valve double overhead camshaft design, the 2290 cc version being introduced in late 1989 on the 9000i and CDi. This engine is fitted with the Saab Direct Ignition system, with separate ignition coils for each spark plug together with a system ECU, instead of the previous Hall-effect/distributor ignition system. Initially, a Bosch LH-Jetronic fuel injection system was fitted. The Saab-manufactured "Trionic" system fitted to the 2290 cc engine in 1993 is a full engine management system, controlling the fuel injection, ignition and turbocharger. This system was later fitted to non-turbo models. All engines are fitted with hydraulic tappets, and later engines are fitted with balancer shafts.

The engine is mounted transversely, with the transmission mounted on the left-hand side. A five-speed manual transmission or four-speed automatic transmission is available.

All models have fully-independent front and rear suspension. The rear suspension incorporates leading and trailing arms, shock absorbers and a low-level Panhard rod.

A wide range of standard and optional equipment is available within the Saab 9000 range to suit most tastes, including central locking and electric windows. An anti-lock braking system, traction control system and air conditioning system are available on certain models.

Provided that regular servicing is carried out in accordance with the manufacturer's recommendations, the Saab 9000 should prove reliable and economical.

Saab 9000 Turbo 16

Saab 9000 CDi

Acknowledgements

Thanks are due to Draper Tools Limited, who provided some of the workshop tools, and to all those people at Sparkford who helped in the production of this manual.

We take great pride in the accuracy of information given in this manual, but vehicle manufacturers make alterations and design changes during the production run of a particular vehicle of which they do not inform us. No liability can be accepted by the authors or publishers for loss, damage or injury caused by errors in, or omissions from, the information given.

General dimensions and weights

Note: *All figures are approximate, and may vary according to model. Refer to manufacturer's data for exact figures.*

Dimensions

Overall length:
9000 5-door	4620 mm
9000 CD	4794 mm
9000 CS	4761 mm

Overall width:
9000 5-door	1806 mm
9000 CD	1806 mm
9000 CS	1788 mm

Overall height (unladen):
9000 5-door	1430 mm
9000 CD	1420 mm
9000 CS	1420 mm

Wheelbase	2672 mm

Front track:
5.5 inch wheels	1510 mm
6.0 inch wheels	1522 mm
6.5 inch wheels	1534 mm
7.0 inch wheels	1538 mm

Rear track:
5.5 inch wheels	1480 mm
6.0 inch wheels	1492 mm
6.5 inch wheels	1504 mm
7.0 inch wheels	1508 mm

Weights

Kerb weight:
9000 5-door	1390 to 1550 kg
9000 CD	1395 to 1550 kg
9000 CS	1410 to 1570 kg

Maximum gross vehicle weight:
9000 5-door	1780 to 1960 kg
9000 CD	1780 to 1960 kg
9000 CS	1830 to 1960 kg

Maximum roof rack load	100 kg

Maximum towing weight:
Braked trailer:
Except 9000 CS	1600 kg
9000 CS	1800 kg
Unbraked trailer	750 kg

Working on your car can be dangerous. This page shows just some of the potential risks and hazards, with the aim of creating a safety-conscious attitude.

General hazards

Scalding

• Don't remove the radiator or expansion tank cap while the engine is hot.
• Engine oil, automatic transmission fluid or power steering fluid may also be dangerously hot if the engine has recently been running.

Burning

• Beware of burns from the exhaust system and from any part of the engine. Brake discs and drums can also be extremely hot immediately after use.

Crushing

• When working under or near a raise vehicle, always supplement the jack with axle stands, or use drive-on ramps. *Never venture under a car which is only supported by a jack.*
• Take care if loosening or tightening high-torque nuts when the vehicle is on stands. Initial loosening and final tightening should be done with the wheels on the ground.

Fire

• Fuel is highly flammable; fuel vapour is explosive.
• Don't let fuel spill onto a hot engine.
• Do not smoke or allow naked lights (including pilot lights) anywhere near a vehicle being worked on. Also beware of creating sparks (electrically or by use of tools).
• Fuel vapour is heavier than air, so don't work on the fuel system with the vehicle over an inspection pit.
• Another cause of fire is an electrical overload or short-circuit. Take care when repairing or modifying the vehicle wiring.
• Keep a fire extinguisher handy, of a type suitable for use on fuel and electrical fires.

Electric shock

• Ignition HT voltage can be dangerous, especially to people with heart problems or a pacemaker. Don't work on or near the ignition system with the engine running or the ignition switched on.

• Mains voltage is also dangerous. Make sure that any mains-operated equipment is correctly earthed. Mains power points should be protected by a residual current device (RCD) circuit breaker.

Fume or gas intoxication

• Exhaust fumes are poisonous; they often contain carbon monoxide, which is rapidly fatal if inhaled. Never run the engine in a confined space such as a garage with the doors shut.
• Fuel vapour is also poisonous, as are the vapours from some cleaning solvents and paint thinners.

Poisonous or irritant substances

• Avoid skin contact with battery acid and with any fuel, fluid or lubricant, especially antifreeze, brake hydraulic fluid and Diesel fuel. Don't syphon them by mouth. If such a substance is swallowed or gets into the eyes, seek medical advice.
• Prolonged contact with used engine oil can cause skin cancer. Wear gloves or use a barrier cream if necessary. Change out of oil-soaked clothes and do not keep oily rags in your pocket.
• Air conditioning refrigerant forms a poisonous gas if exposed to a naked flame (including a cigarette). It can also cause skin burns on contact.

Asbestos

• Asbestos dust can cause cancer if inhaled or swallowed. Asbestos may be found in gaskets and in brake and clutch linings. When dealing with such components it is safest to assume that they contain asbestos.

Special hazards

Hydrofluoric acid

• This extremely corrosive acid is formed when certain types of synthetic rubber, found in some O-rings, oil seals, fuel hoses etc, are exposed to temperatures above 400°C. The rubber changes into a charred or sticky substance containing the acid. *Once formed, the acid remains dangerous for years. If it gets onto the skin, it may be necessary to amputate the limb concerned.*
• When dealing with a vehicle which has suffered a fire, or with components salvaged from such a vehicle, wear protective gloves and discard them after use.

The battery

• Batteries contain sulphuric acid, which attacks clothing, eyes and skin. Take care when topping-up or carrying the battery.
• The hydrogen gas given off by the battery is highly explosive. Never cause a spark or allow a naked light nearby. Be careful when connecting and disconnecting battery chargers or jump leads.

Air bags

• Air bags can cause injury if they go off accidentally. Take care when removing the steering wheel and/or facia. Special storage instructions may apply.

Diesel injection equipment

• Diesel injection pumps supply fuel at very high pressure. Take care when working on the fuel injectors and fuel pipes.

⚠️ *Warning: Never expose the hands, face or any other part of the body to injector spray; the fuel can penetrate the skin with potentially fatal results.*

Remember...

DO

• Do use eye protection when using power tools, and when working under the vehicle.

• Do wear gloves or use barrier cream to protect your hands when necessary.

• Do get someone to check periodically that all is well when working alone on the vehicle.

• Do keep loose clothing and long hair well out of the way of moving mechanical parts.

• Do remove rings, wristwatch etc, before working on the vehicle – especially the electrical system.

• Do ensure that any lifting or jacking equipment has a safe working load rating adequate for the job.

DON'T

• Don't attempt to lift a heavy component which may be beyond your capability – get assistance.

• Don't rush to finish a job, or take unverified short cuts.

• Don't use ill-fitting tools which may slip and cause injury.

• Don't leave tools or parts lying around where someone can trip over them. Mop up oil and fuel spills at once.

• Don't allow children or pets to play in or near a vehicle being worked on.

Jacking

The jack supplied with the vehicle tool kit should only be used for changing the roadwheels - see *"Wheel changing"* later in this Section. When carrying out any other kind of work, raise the vehicle using a hydraulic (or "trolley") jack, and always supplement the jack with axle stands positioned under the vehicle jacking points at the front and rear of the sills on each side of the car **(see illustration)**.

To raise the front of the vehicle, position the trolley jack head beneath the reinforced subframe for the engine compartment. **Do not** jack the vehicle under the sump, or any of the steering or suspension components.

To raise the rear of the vehicle, position the jack head beneath the reinforced member adjacent to the rear towing eye. **Do not** jack the vehicle under the rear axle.

The jack supplied with the vehicle locates in the jacking points positioned at the front and rear of the body sills on each side of the car. Ensure that the jack head is correctly engaged before attempting to raise the vehicle **(see illustration)**.

Never work under, around, or near a raised vehicle, unless it is adequately supported in at least two places.

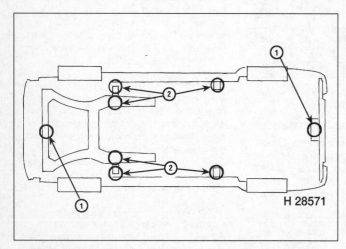

Hydraulic jack lifting points (1) and axle stand positions (2)

Using the vehicle jack to raise the rear of the car

Towing

Towing eyes are fitted to the front and rear of the vehicle for attachment of a tow rope **(see illustrations)**. The front towing eye is accessed by prising out the plastic cover. Always turn the ignition key to the "OFF" (accessory) position when the vehicle is being towed, so that the steering lock is released, and the direction indicators and brake lights are working.

Before being towed, release the handbrake, and select neutral on manual transmission

models, or "N" on automatic transmission models. Note that greater-than-usual pedal pressure will be required to operate the brakes, since the vacuum servo unit is only operational with the engine running. Similarly, on models with power steering, greater-than-usual steering effort will be required.

Where possible, models with automatic transmission should ideally be towed with the front wheels off the ground, particularly if a transmission fault is suspected. If the vehicle

is to be towed with its front wheels on the ground, it must always be towed forwards at speeds not exceeding 30 mph (50 km/h) or for a distance no further than 30 miles (50 km). Also note that, to avoid damaging the automatic transmission, the fluid level must be topped-up to the dipstick maximum mark as described in Chapter 1, then an extra 2.0 litres of fluid added. Note that the excess fluid must be drained off before the vehicle is driven again.

Front towing eye location

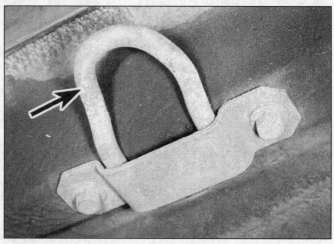

Rear towing eye location

Wheel changing

The spare wheel is located beneath a panel in the luggage compartment floor. The jack and jack handle are stored together with the spare wheel; the wheel brace is stored in the tool kit located on the right-hand side trim. For access to the spare wheel, proceed as follows:

a) *Lift the luggage compartment floor panel, and hold it in its raised position by hooking the rubber strap to the peg on the right-hand side of the panel.*

b) *Unscrew the plastic retainer, and lift the spare wheel out of the floor well. On some models, the brace may be used to unscrew the spare wheel retainer.*

c) *The jack and handle are located beneath the spare wheel.*

To change a wheel, remove the spare wheel, jack and wheel brace, as described previously, then proceed as follows.

Apply the handbrake, and place chocks at the front and rear of the wheel diagonally opposite the one to be changed. Select first or reverse gear on manual transmission models, or select "P" on automatic transmission models. Make sure that the vehicle is located on firm, level ground. Prise off, and remove, the trim from the centre of the wheel, using a screwdriver. Slightly loosen the wheel bolts with the brace provided **(see illustrations)**. Locate the jack head in the jacking point nearest the wheel to be removed, and raise the jack by turning the handle. When the wheel is clear of the ground, remove the bolts and lift off the wheel. On some models, a plastic bag is provided in the tool kit to store the removed wheel. Fit the spare wheel, and moderately tighten the bolts. Lower the vehicle, and then tighten the bolts fully in a diagonal sequence. Refit the wheel trim. If possible, check the tyre pressure on the spare wheel, and adjust as necessary. Remove the chocks, and stow the jack, tools and the punctured tyre in the floor well. Release the rubber strap, and lower the floor panel.

On later models, the spare wheel is of lightweight compact design, and should only be used in an emergency situation. **Do not** drive at speeds exceeding 50 mph, and **do not** drive further than 2000 miles with the compact spare wheel fitted.

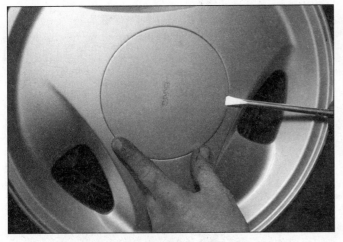

Prising off the trim from the centre of the wheel

Loosening the wheel bolts with the brace provided in the tool kit

Radio/cassette unit anti-theft system - precaution

On later models, the radio/cassette unit fitted as standard equipment by Saab has a built-in security code, to deter thieves. If the power source to the unit is cut, the anti-theft system will activate. Even if the power source is immediately reconnected, the radio/cassette unit will not function until the correct security code has been entered. Therefore, if you do not know the correct security code for the radio/cassette unit, **do not** disconnect the battery negative terminal of the battery, nor remove the radio/cassette unit from the vehicle.

To enter the correct security code, follow the instructions provided with the radio/cassette player handbook.

If an incorrect code is entered, the unit will become locked, and cannot be operated.

If this happens, or if the security code is lost or forgotten, seek the advice of your Saab dealer.

Jump starting

When jump-starting a car using a booster battery, observe the following precautions:

✔ Before connecting the booster battery, make sure that the ignition is switched off.

✔ Ensure that all electrical equipment (lights, heater, wipers, etc) is switched off.

✔ Take note of any special precautions printed on the battery case.

✔ Make sure that the booster battery is the same voltage as the discharged one in the vehicle.

✔ If the battery is being jump-started from the battery in another vehicle, the two vehicles MUST NOT TOUCH each other.

✔ Make sure that the transmission is in neutral (or PARK, in the case of automatic transmission).

 HAYNES HiNT *Jump starting will get you out of trouble, but you must correct whatever made the battery go flat in the first place. There are three possibilities:*

1 *The battery has been drained by repeated attempts to start, or by leaving the lights on.*

2 *The charging system is not working properly (alternator drivebelt slack or broken, alternator wiring fault or alternator itself faulty).*

3 *The battery itself is at fault (electrolyte low, or battery worn out).*

1 Connect one end of the red jump lead to the positive (+) terminal of the flat battery

2 Connect the other end of the red lead to the positive (+) terminal of the booster battery.

3 Connect one end of the black jump lead to the negative (-) terminal of the booster battery

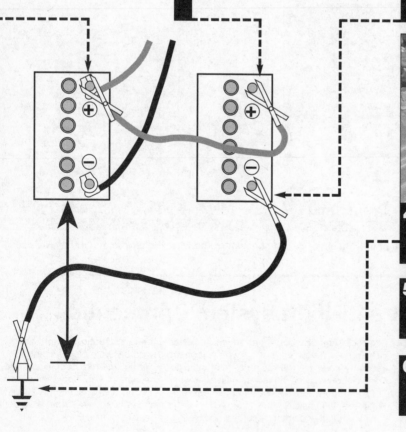

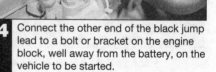

4 Connect the other end of the black jump lead to a bolt or bracket on the engine block, well away from the battery, on the vehicle to be started.

5 Make sure that the jump leads will not come into contact with the fan, drive-belts or other moving parts of the engine.

6 Start the engine using the booster battery and run it at idle speed. Switch on the lights, rear window demister and heater blower motor, then disconnect the jump leads in the reverse order of connection. Turn off the lights etc.

Identifying leaks

Puddles on the garage floor or drive, or obvious wetness under the bonnet or underneath the car, suggest a leak that needs investigating. It can sometimes be difficult to decide where the leak is coming from, especially if the engine bay is very dirty already. Leaking oil or fluid can also be blown rearwards by the passage of air under the car, giving a false impression of where the problem lies.

 Warning: Most automotive oils and fluids are poisonous. Wash them off skin, and change out of contaminated clothing, without delay.

HAYNES HiNT *The smell of a fluid leaking from the car may provide a clue to what's leaking. Some fluids are distictively coloured. It may help to clean the car carefully and to park it over some clean paper overnight as an aid to locating the source of the leak.*
Remember that some leaks may only occur while the engine is running.

Sump oil

Engine oil may leak from the drain plug...

Oil from filter

...or from the base of the oil filter.

Gearbox oil

Gearbox oil can leak from the seals at the inboard ends of the driveshafts.

Antifreeze

Leaking antifreeze often leaves a crystalline deposit like this.

Brake fluid

A leak occurring at a wheel is almost certainly brake fluid.

Power steering fluid

Power steering fluid may leak from the pipe connectors on the steering rack.

Buying spare parts

Spare parts are available from many sources, including maker's appointed garages, accessory shops, and motor factors. To be sure of obtaining the correct parts, it will sometimes be necessary to quote the vehicle identification number. If possible, it can also be useful to take the old parts along for positive identification. Items such as starter motors and alternators may be available under a service exchange scheme - any parts returned should always be clean.

Our advice regarding spare part sources is as follows.

Officially-appointed garages

This is the best source of parts which are peculiar to your car, and which are not otherwise generally available (eg badges, interior trim, certain body panels, etc). It is also the only place at which you should buy parts if the vehicle is still under warranty.

Accessory shops

These are very good places to buy materials and components needed for the maintenance of your car (oil, air and fuel filters, spark plugs, light bulbs, drivebelts, oils and greases, brake pads, touch-up paint, etc). Components of this nature sold by a reputable shop are of the same standard as those used by the car manufacturer.

Besides components, these shops also sell tools and general accessories, usually have convenient opening hours, charge lower prices, and can often be found not far from home. Some accessory shops have parts counters where the components needed for almost any repair job can be purchased or ordered.

Motor factors

Good factors will stock all the more important components which wear out comparatively quickly, and can sometimes supply individual components needed for the overhaul of a larger assembly (eg brake seals and hydraulic parts, bearing shells, pistons, valves, alternator brushes). They may also handle work such as cylinder block reboring, crankshaft regrinding and balancing, etc.

Tyre and exhaust specialists

These outlets may be independent, or members of a local or national chain. They frequently offer competitive prices when compared with a main dealer or local garage, but it will pay to obtain several quotes before making a decision. When researching prices, also ask what "extras" may be added - for instance, fitting a new valve and balancing the wheel are both commonly charged on top of the price of a new tyre.

Other sources

Beware of parts or materials obtained from market stalls, car boot sales or similar outlets. Such items are not invariably sub-standard, but there is little chance of compensation if they do prove unsatisfactory. In the case of safety-critical components such as brake pads, there is the risk not only of financial loss but also of an accident causing injury or death.

Second-hand components or assemblies obtained from a car breaker can be a good buy in some circumstances, but this sort of purchase is best made by the experienced DIY mechanic.

Vehicle identification numbers

Modifications are a continuing and unpublicised process in vehicle manufacture, quite apart from major model changes. Spare parts lists are compiled upon a numerical basis, the individual vehicle identification numbers being essential to correct identification of the component concerned.

When ordering spare parts, always give as much information as possible. Quote the car model, year of manufacture, body and engine numbers, as appropriate.

The *Vehicle Identification Number (VIN)* plate is located on the right-hand side of the bulkhead in the engine compartment **(see illustration)**. It is also stamped in the body, to the left of the right-hand rear light. On pre-1989 models, it is on the crosspanel to the rear of the luggage compartment: on 1989-on models, it is on the crossmember inside the spare wheel well. On 1994-on models, it is etched into the windscreen and rear window.

The *engine number* is situated on the left-hand rear face of the cylinder block on 2.0 litre models up to 1993, or on the left-hand front face of the cylinder block on 1994-on 2.0 litre and all 2.3 litre models.

The *transmission number* is situated on the top of the transmission casing.

The *body trim and colour code* is stamped on a plate located on the right-hand side of the bulkhead in the engine compartment on 1985 models, on the panel at the rear of the luggage area on models up to 1990, and on the left-hand rear door pillar on models from 1991 onwards.

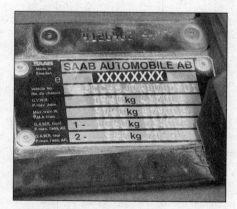

The VIN plate is located on the right-hand side of the bulkhead

This is a guide to getting your vehicle through the MOT test. Obviously it will not be possible to examine the vehicle to the same standard as the professional MOT tester. However, working through the following checks will enable you to identify any problem areas before submitting the vehicle for the test.

Where a testable component is in borderline condition, the tester has discretion in deciding whether to pass or fail it. The basis of such discretion is whether the tester would be happy for a close relative or friend to use the vehicle with the component in that condition. If the vehicle presented is clean and evidently well cared for, the tester may be more inclined to pass a borderline component than if the vehicle is scruffy and apparently neglected.

It has only been possible to summarise the test requirements here, based on the regulations in force at the time of printing. Test standards are becoming increasingly stringent, although there are some exemptions for older vehicles.

An assistant will be needed to help carry out some of these checks.

The checks have been sub-divided into four categories, as follows:

1 Checks carried out **FROM THE DRIVER'S SEAT**

2 Checks carried out **WITH THE VEHICLE ON THE GROUND**

3 Checks carried out **WITH THE VEHICLE RAISED AND THE WHEELS FREE TO TURN**

4 Checks carried out on **YOUR VEHICLE'S EXHAUST EMISSION SYSTEM**

---

1 Checks carried out **FROM THE DRIVER'S SEAT**

Handbrake

☐ Test the operation of the handbrake. Excessive travel (too many clicks) indicates incorrect brake or cable adjustment.

☐ Check that the handbrake cannot be released by tapping the lever sideways. Check the security of the lever mountings.

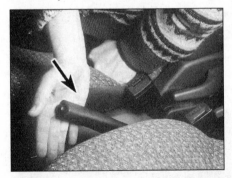

Footbrake

☐ Depress the brake pedal and check that it does not creep down to the floor, indicating a master cylinder fault. Release the pedal, wait a few seconds, then depress it again. If the pedal travels nearly to the floor before firm resistance is felt, brake adjustment or repair is necessary. If the pedal feels spongy, there is air in the hydraulic system which must be removed by bleeding.

☐ Check that the brake pedal is secure and in good condition. Check also for signs of fluid leaks on the pedal, floor or carpets, which would indicate failed seals in the brake master cylinder.

☐ Check the servo unit (when applicable) by operating the brake pedal several times, then keeping the pedal depressed and starting the engine. As the engine starts, the pedal will move down slightly. If not, the vacuum hose or the servo itself may be faulty.

Steering wheel and column

☐ Examine the steering wheel for fractures or looseness of the hub, spokes or rim.

☐ Move the steering wheel from side to side and then up and down. Check that the steering wheel is not loose on the column, indicating wear or a loose retaining nut. Continue moving the steering wheel as before, but also turn it slightly from left to right.

☐ Check that the steering wheel is not loose on the column, and that there is no abnormal

movement of the steering wheel, indicating wear in the column support bearings or couplings.

Windscreen, mirrors and sunvisor

☐ The windscreen must be free of cracks or other significant damage within the driver's field of view. (Small stone chips are acceptable.) Rear view mirrors must be secure, intact, and capable of being adjusted.

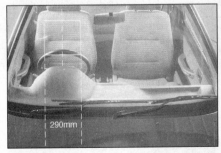

☐ The driver's sunvisor must be capable of being stored in the "up" position.

MOT Test Checks

Seat belts and seats

Note: *The following checks are applicable to all seat belts, front and rear.*

☐ Examine the webbing of all the belts (including rear belts if fitted) for cuts, serious fraying or deterioration. Fasten and unfasten each belt to check the buckles. If applicable, check the retracting mechanism. Check the security of all seat belt mountings accessible from inside the vehicle.

☐ Seat belts with pre-tensioners, once activated, have a "flag" or similar showing on the seat belt stalk. This, in itself, is not a reason for test failure.

☐ The front seats themselves must be securely attached and the backrests must lock in the upright position.

Doors

☐ Both front doors must be able to be opened and closed from outside and inside, and must latch securely when closed.

2 Checks carried out WITH THE VEHICLE ON THE GROUND

Vehicle identification

☐ Number plates must be in good condition, secure and legible, with letters and numbers correctly spaced – spacing at (A) should be at least twice that at (B).

☐ The VIN plate and/or homologation plate must be legible.

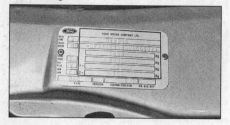

Electrical equipment

☐ Switch on the ignition and check the operation of the horn.

☐ Check the windscreen washers and wipers, examining the wiper blades; renew damaged or perished blades. Also check the operation of the stop-lights.

☐ Check the operation of the sidelights and number plate lights. The lenses and reflectors must be secure, clean and undamaged.

☐ Check the operation and alignment of the headlights. The headlight reflectors must not be tarnished and the lenses must be undamaged.

☐ Switch on the ignition and check the operation of the direction indicators (including the instrument panel tell-tale) and the hazard warning lights. Operation of the sidelights and stop-lights must not affect the indicators - if it does, the cause is usually a bad earth at the rear light cluster.

☐ Check the operation of the rear foglight(s), including the warning light on the instrument panel or in the switch.

☐ The ABS warning light must illuminate in accordance with the manufacturers' design. For most vehicles, the ABS warning light should illuminate when the ignition is switched on, and (if the system is operating properly) extinguish after a few seconds. Refer to the owner's handbook.

Footbrake

☐ Examine the master cylinder, brake pipes and servo unit for leaks, loose mountings, corrosion or other damage.

☐ The fluid reservoir must be secure and the fluid level must be between the upper (**A**) and lower (**B**) markings.

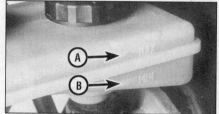

☐ Inspect both front brake flexible hoses for cracks or deterioration of the rubber. Turn the steering from lock to lock, and ensure that the hoses do not contact the wheel, tyre, or any part of the steering or suspension mechanism. With the brake pedal firmly depressed, check the hoses for bulges or leaks under pressure.

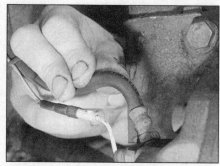

Steering and suspension

☐ Have your assistant turn the steering wheel from side to side slightly, up to the point where the steering gear just begins to transmit this movement to the roadwheels. Check for excessive free play between the steering wheel and the steering gear, indicating wear or insecurity of the steering column joints, the column-to-steering gear coupling, or the steering gear itself.

☐ Have your assistant turn the steering wheel more vigorously in each direction, so that the roadwheels just begin to turn. As this is done, examine all the steering joints, linkages, fittings and attachments. Renew any component that shows signs of wear or damage. On vehicles with power steering, check the security and condition of the steering pump, drivebelt and hoses.

☐ Check that the vehicle is standing level, and at approximately the correct ride height.

Shock absorbers

☐ Depress each corner of the vehicle in turn, then release it. The vehicle should rise and then settle in its normal position. If the vehicle continues to rise and fall, the shock absorber is defective. A shock absorber which has seized will also cause the vehicle to fail.

Exhaust system

☐ Start the engine. With your assistant holding a rag over the tailpipe, check the entire system for leaks. Repair or renew leaking sections.

3 Checks carried out **WITH THE VEHICLE RAISED AND THE WHEELS FREE TO TURN**

Jack up the front and rear of the vehicle, and securely support it on axle stands. Position the stands clear of the suspension assemblies. Ensure that the wheels are clear of the ground and that the steering can be turned from lock to lock.

Steering mechanism

☐ Have your assistant turn the steering from lock to lock. Check that the steering turns smoothly, and that no part of the steering mechanism, including a wheel or tyre, fouls any brake hose or pipe or any part of the body structure.
☐ Examine the steering rack rubber gaiters for damage or insecurity of the retaining clips. If power steering is fitted, check for signs of damage or leakage of the fluid hoses, pipes or connections. Also check for excessive stiffness or binding of the steering, a missing split pin or locking device, or severe corrosion of the body structure within 30 cm of any steering component attachment point.

Front and rear suspension and wheel bearings

☐ Starting at the front right-hand side, grasp the roadwheel at the 3 o'clock and 9 o'clock positions and rock gently but firmly. Check for free play or insecurity at the wheel bearings, suspension balljoints, or suspension mountings, pivots and attachments.
☐ Now grasp the wheel at the 12 o'clock and 6 o'clock positions and repeat the previous inspection. Spin the wheel, and check for roughness or tightness of the front wheel bearing.

☐ If excess free play is suspected at a component pivot point, this can be confirmed by using a large screwdriver or similar tool and levering between the mounting and the component attachment. This will confirm whether the wear is in the pivot bush, its retaining bolt, or in the mounting itself (the bolt holes can often become elongated).

☐ Carry out all the above checks at the other front wheel, and then at both rear wheels.

Springs and shock absorbers

☐ Examine the suspension struts (when applicable) for serious fluid leakage, corrosion, or damage to the casing. Also check the security of the mounting points.
☐ If coil springs are fitted, check that the spring ends locate in their seats, and that the spring is not corroded, cracked or broken.
☐ If leaf springs are fitted, check that all leaves are intact, that the axle is securely attached to each spring, and that there is no deterioration of the spring eye mountings, bushes, and shackles.

☐ The same general checks apply to vehicles fitted with other suspension types, such as torsion bars, hydraulic displacer units, etc. Ensure that all mountings and attachments are secure, that there are no signs of excessive wear, corrosion or damage, and (on hydraulic types) that there are no fluid leaks or damaged pipes.
☐ Inspect the shock absorbers for signs of serious fluid leakage. Check for wear of the mounting bushes or attachments, or damage to the body of the unit.

Driveshafts (fwd vehicles only)

☐ Rotate each front wheel in turn and inspect the constant velocity joint gaiters for splits or damage. Also check that each driveshaft is straight and undamaged.

Braking system

☐ If possible without dismantling, check brake pad wear and disc condition. Ensure that the friction lining material has not worn excessively, (A) and that the discs are not fractured, pitted, scored or badly worn (B).

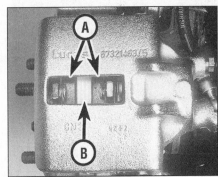

☐ Examine all the rigid brake pipes underneath the vehicle, and the flexible hose(s) at the rear. Look for corrosion, chafing or insecurity of the pipes, and for signs of bulging under pressure, chafing, splits or deterioration of the flexible hoses.
☐ Look for signs of fluid leaks at the brake calipers or on the brake backplates. Repair or renew leaking components.
☐ Slowly spin each wheel, while your assistant depresses and releases the footbrake. Ensure that each brake is operating and does not bind when the pedal is released.

MOT Test Checks

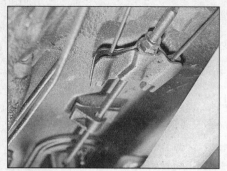

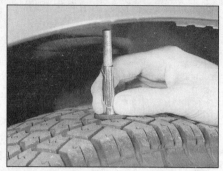

☐ Examine the handbrake mechanism, checking for frayed or broken cables, excessive corrosion, or wear or insecurity of the linkage. Check that the mechanism works on each relevant wheel, and releases fully, without binding.

☐ It is not possible to test brake efficiency without special equipment, but a road test can be carried out later to check that the vehicle pulls up in a straight line.

Fuel and exhaust systems

☐ Inspect the fuel tank (including the filler cap), fuel pipes, hoses and unions. All components must be secure and free from leaks.

☐ Examine the exhaust system over its entire length, checking for any damaged, broken or missing mountings, security of the retaining clamps and rust or corrosion.

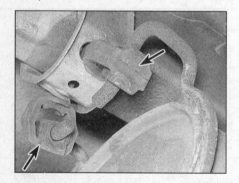

Wheels and tyres

☐ Examine the sidewalls and tread area of each tyre in turn. Check for cuts, tears, lumps, bulges, separation of the tread, and exposure of the ply or cord due to wear or damage. Check that the tyre bead is correctly seated on the wheel rim, that the valve is sound and properly seated, and that the wheel is not distorted or damaged.

☐ Check that the tyres are of the correct size for the vehicle, that they are of the same size and type on each axle, and that the pressures are correct.

☐ Check the tyre tread depth. The legal minimum at the time of writing is 1.6 mm over at least three-quarters of the tread width. Abnormal tread wear may indicate incorrect front wheel alignment.

Body corrosion

☐ Check the condition of the entire vehicle structure for signs of corrosion in load-bearing areas. (These include chassis box sections, side sills, cross-members, pillars, and all suspension, steering, braking system and seat belt mountings and anchorages.) Any corrosion which has seriously reduced the thickness of a load-bearing area is likely to cause the vehicle to fail. In this case professional repairs are likely to be needed.

☐ Damage or corrosion which causes sharp or otherwise dangerous edges to be exposed will also cause the vehicle to fail.

4 Checks carried out on YOUR VEHICLE'S EXHAUST EMISSION SYSTEM

Petrol models

☐ Have the engine at normal operating temperature, and make sure that it is in good tune (ignition system in good order, air filter element clean, etc).

☐ Before any measurements are carried out, raise the engine speed to around 2500 rpm, and hold it at this speed for 20 seconds. Allow the engine speed to return to idle, and watch for smoke emissions from the exhaust tailpipe. If the idle speed is obviously much too high, or if dense blue or clearly-visible black smoke comes from the tailpipe for more than 5 seconds, the vehicle will fail. As a rule of thumb, blue smoke signifies oil being burnt (engine wear) while black smoke signifies unburnt fuel (dirty air cleaner element, or other carburettor or fuel system fault).

☐ An exhaust gas analyser capable of measuring carbon monoxide (CO) and hydrocarbons (HC) is now needed. If such an instrument cannot be hired or borrowed, a local garage may agree to perform the check for a small fee.

CO emissions (mixture)

☐ At the time of writing, for vehicles first used between 1st August 1975 and 31st July 1986 (P to C registration), the CO level must not exceed 4.5% by volume. For vehicles first used between 1st August 1986 and 31st July 1992 (D to J registration), the CO level must not exceed 3.5% by volume. Vehicles first

used after 1st August 1992 (K registration) must conform to the manufacturer's specification. The MOT tester has access to a DOT database or emissions handbook, which lists the CO and HC limits for each make and model of vehicle. The CO level is measured with the engine at idle speed, and at "fast idle". The following limits are given as a general guide:

> At idle speed -
> CO level no more than 0.5%
> At "fast idle" (2500 to 3000 rpm) -
> CO level no more than 0.3%
> (Minimum oil temperature 60°C)

☐ If the CO level cannot be reduced far enough to pass the test (and the fuel and ignition systems are otherwise in good condition) then the carburettor is badly worn, or there is some problem in the fuel injection system or catalytic converter (as applicable).

HC emissions

☐ With the CO within limits, HC emissions for vehicles first used between 1st August 1975 and 31st July 1992 (P to J registration) must not exceed 1200 ppm. Vehicles first used after 1st August 1992 (K registration) must conform to the manufacturer's specification. The MOT tester has access to a DOT database or emissions handbook, which lists the CO and HC limits for each make and model of vehicle. The HC level is measured with the engine at "fast idle". The following is given as a general guide:

> At "fast idle" (2500 to 3000 rpm) -
> HC level no more than 200 ppm
> (Minimum oil temperature 60°C)

☐ Excessive HC emissions are caused by incomplete combustion, the causes of which can include oil being burnt, mechanical wear and ignition/fuel system malfunction.

Diesel models

☐ The only emission test applicable to Diesel engines is the measuring of exhaust smoke density. The test involves accelerating the engine several times to its maximum unloaded speed.

Note: *It is of the utmost importance that the engine timing belt is in good condition before the test is carried out.*

☐ The limits for Diesel engine exhaust smoke, introduced in September 1995 are:

Vehicles first used before 1st August 1979: Exempt from metered smoke testing, but must not emit "dense blue or clearly visible black smoke for a period of more than 5 seconds at idle" or "dense blue or clearly visible black smoke during acceleration which would obscure the view of other road users".

Non-turbocharged vehicles first used after 1st August 1979: $2.5m^{-1}$

Turbocharged vehicles first used after 1st August 1979: $3.0m^{-1}$

☐ Excessive smoke can be caused by a dirty air cleaner element. Otherwise, professional advice may be needed to find the cause.

Chapter 1
Routine maintenance and servicing

Contents

Degrees of difficulty

| Easy, suitable for novice with little experience | Fairly easy, suitable for beginner with some experience | Fairly difficult, suitable for competent DIY mechanic | Difficult, suitable for experienced DIY mechanic | Very difficult, suitable for expert DIY or professional |

Saab 9000 maintenance schedule

1 The maintenance intervals in this manual are provided with the assumption that you will be carrying out the work yourself. These are the minimum maintenance intervals recommended by the manufacturer for vehicles driven daily. If you wish to keep your vehicle in peak condition at all times, you may wish to perform some of these procedures more often. We encourage frequent maintenance, because it enhances the efficiency, performance and resale value of your vehicle.

2 If the vehicle is driven in dusty areas, used to tow a trailer, or driven frequently at slow speeds (idling in traffic) or on short journeys, more frequent maintenance intervals are recommended.

3 When the vehicle is new, it should be serviced by a factory-authorised dealer service department, in order to preserve the factory warranty.

Every 250 miles (400 km) or weekly

- ☐ Check the engine oil level (Section 3).
- ☐ Check the engine coolant level (Section 3).
- ☐ Check the brake fluid level (Section 4).
- ☐ Check the screen washer fluid level (Section 5).
- ☐ Visually examine the tyres for tread depth, and wear or damage (Section 6).
- ☐ Check and if necessary adjust the tyre pressures (Section 6).
- ☐ Check and if necessary top-up the battery electrolyte level - where applicable (Section 8).
- ☐ Check the operation of the horn, all lights, and the wipers and washers (Sections 7 and 9).

Every 6000 miles (10 000 km) or 6 months – whichever comes sooner

- ☐ Change the engine oil and filter (Section 10)

Maintenance Schedule

Every 12 000 miles (20 000 km) or 12 months – whichever comes sooner

- ☐ Check the crankcase ventilation system (Section 20)
- ☐ Check all hoses (Section 21)
- ☐ Check and if necessary adjust the coolant antifreeze concentration (Section 11)
- ☐ Check and if necessary adjust the auxiliary drivebelt tension (Section 22)
- ☐ Check the air conditioning refrigerant (Section 23)
- ☐ Renew the ventilation air filter (Section 32) *(after first renewal, every 24 000 miles)*
- ☐ Check and if necessary top-up the power steering fluid level (Section 13)
- ☐ Check the exhaust system (Section 24)
- ☐ Renew the spark plugs (leaded petrol models only) (Section 25)
- ☐ Check and if necessary top-up the manual transmission oil level (Section 26)
- ☐ Check and if necessary top-up the automatic transmission fluid level (Section 27)
- ☐ Check the driveshaft rubber gaiters (Section 28)
- ☐ Check the front and rear brake pads and discs (Section 29)
- ☐ Check all brake lines and flexible hoses (Section 30)
- ☐ Check the suspension and shock absorbers (Section 31)
- ☐ Visually check the airbag system (Section 15)
- ☐ Lubricate all hinges and locks (Section 16)
- ☐ Check the seat belts for operation and damage (Section 14)
- ☐ Clean the battery terminals (Section 17)
- ☐ Check the headlight and foglight beam alignment (Section 18)
- ☐ Road test (Section 19)

Every 24 000 miles (40 000 km) or 2 years – whichever comes sooner

In addition to all the items listed in the previous Section, carry out the following:

- ☐ Renew the air cleaner filter element (Section 33)
- ☐ Renew the spark plugs (unleaded petrol models only) (Section 25)
- ☐ Change the automatic transmission fluid and filter (Section 34)
- ☐ Check and if necessary adjust the front wheel alignment (Section 12)

Every 48 000 miles (80 000 km) or 3 years – whichever comes sooner

- ☐ Renew the coolant/antifreeze (Section 35)

Every 96 000 miles (160 000 km)

- ☐ Renew the fuel filter (Section 36)

Every 2 years (regardless of mileage)

- ☐ Renew the brake fluid (Section 37)

Lubricants and fluids

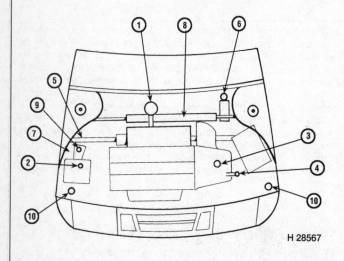

H 28567

Component or system	Lubricant type/specification
1 Engine	Multigrade engine oil, viscosity SAE 10W/30, 10W/40, 5W/30 or 5W/40, to API SG and CCMC G4/G5 specifications*
2 Cooling system	Ethylene glycol-based antifreeze
3 Manual transmission	10W/30 or 10W/40 **(synthetic oil not to be used)**
4 Automatic transmission	Dexron type II ATF
5 Driveshaft CV joints	Outer driveshaft: Molycote VN 2461C Inner driveshaft: Mobil grease GS 57C
6 Brake and clutch hydraulic systems	Hydraulic fluid to DOT 4
7 Hub/wheel bearings	Multi-purpose lithium-based grease
8 Steering rack	Multi-purpose lithium-based grease
9 Power steering	Saab or GM power steering fluid
10 Washer fluid reservoir	-

*5W grade oils should be synthetic or semi-synthetic

Capacities

Engine oil

Including filter:
B202 engine	4.2 litres
B234 engine (up to 1993)	4.3 litres
B204 and B234 engines (1994 onwards)	5.5 litres
Difference between MAX and MIN dipstick marks	1.0 litre

Cooling system

All engines .... 9.0 litres (approximate)

Manual transmission

Up to 1993	2.5 litres
1994 onwards	1.8 litres

Automatic transmission

Including torque converter and fluid cooler:
2.0 litre models	8.2 litres (approximate)
2.3 litre models	8.7 litres (approximate)
Service fluid change	3.0 to 3.5 litres

Fuel tank

1985 to 1989 models	68 litres (15 gallons)
1990 and 1992-on models	66 litres (14.5 gallons)
1991 models	62 litres (13.6 gallons)

Power steering

All models .... 0.75 litre

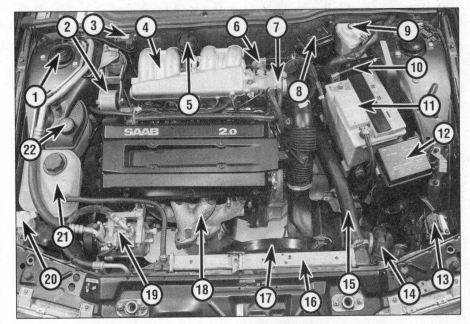

Underbonnet view of the engine compartment (1994 Saab 9000 CSE)

1 Front suspension top mounting
2 Top engine mounting
3 Manifold absolute pressure (MAP) sensor
4 Inlet manifold (double section)
5 Engine oil filler cap and dipstick (com bined)
6 Throttle lever
7 Throttle housing
8 ABS fuse and relay box
9 Brake fluid reservoir
10 ABS ECU
11 Battery
12 Auxiliary fuse and relay box
13 Left-hand front crash sensor
14 Air cleaner cover and housing
15 Top hose
16 Radiator
17 Electric cooling fan
18 Exhaust manifold
19 Air conditioning compressor
20 Washer fluid reservoir
21 Coolant expansion tank
22 Power steering fluid reservoir

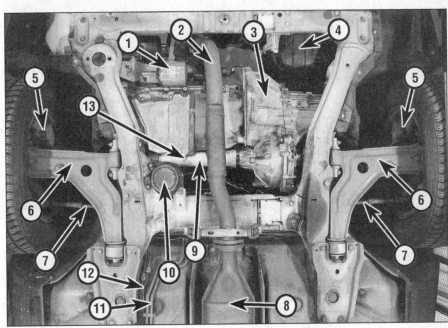

Front underbody view (1994 Saab 9000 CSE)

1 Oil filter
2 Exhaust downpipe
3 Manual transmission
4 Air inlet ducting assembly
5 Front brake caliper
6 Front suspension lower arm
7 Steering track rod
8 Catalytic converter
9 Driveshaft intermediate tube
10 Engine mounting
11 Fuel feed and return lines
12 Brake hydraulic pipes
13 Engine oil drain plug

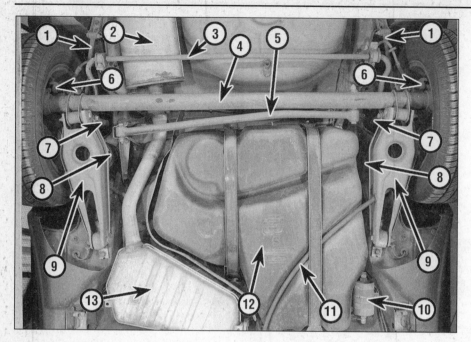

Rear underbody view (1994 Saab 9000 CSE)

1 Rear suspension torque arm
2 Rear silencer
3 Rear anti-roll bar
4 Rear axle tube
5 Panhard rod
6 Rear brake caliper
7 Rear shock absorber
8 Rear coil spring
9 Rear suspension lower arm
10 Fuel filter
11 Handbrake cable
12 Fuel tank
13 Intermediate silencer

Maintenance procedures

1 General information

1 This Chapter is designed to help the home mechanic maintain his/her vehicle for safety, economy, long life and peak performance.
2 The Chapter contains a master maintenance schedule, followed by Sections dealing specifically with each task in the schedule. Visual checks, adjustments, component renewal and other helpful items are included. Refer to the accompanying illustrations of the engine compartment and the underside of the vehicle for the locations of the various components.
3 Servicing your vehicle in accordance with the mileage/time maintenance schedule and the following Sections will provide a planned maintenance programme, which should result in a long and reliable service life. This is a comprehensive plan, so maintaining some items but not others at the specified service intervals, will not produce the same results.
4 As you service your vehicle, you will discover that many of the procedures can - and should - be grouped together, because of the particular procedure being performed, or because of the close proximity of two otherwise-unrelated components to one another. For example, if the vehicle is raised for any reason, the exhaust can be inspected at the same time as the suspension and steering components.
5 The first step in this maintenance programme is to prepare yourself before the

actual work begins. Read through all the Sections relevant to the work to be carried out, then make a list and gather together all the parts and tools required. If a problem is encountered, seek advice from a parts specialist, or a dealer service department.

2 Intensive maintenance

1 If, from the time the vehicle is new, the routine maintenance schedule is followed closely, and frequent checks are made of fluid levels and high-wear items, as suggested throughout this manual, the engine will be kept in relatively good running condition, and the need for additional work will be minimised.
2 It is possible that there will be times when the engine is running poorly due to the lack of regular maintenance. This is even more likely if a used vehicle, which has not received regular and frequent maintenance checks, is purchased. In such cases, additional work may need to be carried out, outside of the regular maintenance intervals.
3 If engine wear is suspected, a compression test (refer to the relevant Part of Chapter 2) will provide valuable information regarding the overall performance of the main internal components. Such a test can be used as a basis to decide on the extent of the work to be carried out. If, for example, a compression test indicates serious internal engine wear, conventional maintenance as described in this Chapter will not greatly improve the

performance of the engine, and may prove a waste of time and money, unless extensive overhaul work (Chapter 2B) is carried out first.
4 The following series of operations are those most often required to improve the performance of a generally poor-running engine:

Primary operations
a) Clean, inspect and test the battery (Section 8)
b) Check all the engine-related fluids (Section 3).
c) Check the condition and tension of the auxiliary drivebelt (Section 22).
d) Renew the spark plugs (Section 25).
e) Inspect the distributor cap, rotor arm and HT leads - as applicable (Chapter 5B).
f) Check the condition of the air cleaner filter element, and renew if necessary (Section 33).
g) Renew the fuel filter (Section 36).
h) Check the condition of all hoses, and check for fluid leaks (Section 21).
i) Check the idle speed and mixture settings - as applicable (Chapter 4A).

5 If the above operations do not prove fully effective, carry out the following secondary operations:

Secondary operations
a) Check the charging system (Chapter 5A).
b) Check the ignition system (Chapter 5B).
c) Check the fuel system (Chapter 4).
d) Renew the distributor cap and rotor arm - as applicable (Chapter 5B).
f) Renew the ignition HT leads - as applicable (Chapter 5B).

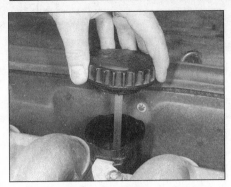

3.3a Removing the engine oil filler cap

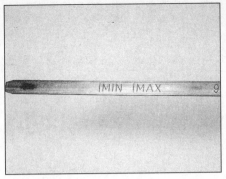

3.3b Markings on the engine oil level dipstick

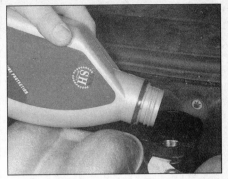

3.3c Topping-up the engine oil level

Weekly checks

3 Engine-related fluid level checks

Engine oil

1 The engine oil level is checked with a dipstick that extends through the dipstick/oil filler tube on the rear of the cylinder block and into the sump at the bottom of the engine. Depress and turn the cap anti-clockwise to remove it. The dipstick is attached to the cap.

2 The oil level should be checked with the vehicle standing on level ground with the engine still warm, between 2 and 5 minutes after the engine has been switched off.

3 Release the oil filler cap and withdraw the dipstick from the tube, then wipe all the oil from the end with a clean rag or paper towel. Insert the clean dipstick back into the tube as far as it will go, then withdraw it once more. Note the oil level on the end of the dipstick. Add oil as necessary until the level is on the upper ("MAX") mark on the dipstick **(see illustrations)**. Note that 1.0 litre of oil will be required to raise the level from the lower ("MIN") mark to the upper mark.

4 Always maintain the level between the two dipstick marks. If the level is allowed to fall below the lower mark, oil starvation may result, which could lead to severe engine damage. If the engine is overfilled by adding too much oil, this may result in oil leaks or oil seal failures.

5 Oil is added via the dipstick/filler cap on the rear of the engine, behind the inlet manifold. Remove the filler cap and dipstick completely before topping-up the oil level. Always use the correct grade and type of oil as shown in "Lubricants, fluids and capacities".

Coolant

 Warning: DO NOT attempt to remove the expansion tank pressure cap when the engine is hot, as there is a very great risk of scalding.

6 All vehicles covered by this manual have a pressurised cooling system. An expansion tank is incorporated in cooling system, and is located on the right-hand side of the engine compartment. As engine temperature increases, the coolant expands, and the level in the expansion tank rises. As the engine cools, the coolant level drops. Circulation of coolant through the expansion tank occurs at all times that the engine is running, and in this way, any accumulation of air in any part of the engine is purged continually.

7 The coolant level in the expansion tank should be checked regularly. The level in the tank varies with the temperature of the engine. When the engine is cold, the coolant level should be on or slightly below the "MAX" mark on the side of the tank. When the engine is hot, the level may rise slightly above the "MAX" mark.

8 If topping-up is necessary, wait until the engine is cold, then unscrew the pressure cap on the expansion tank one or two turns. Wait until any pressure remaining in the system is released, then fully unscrew the cap and remove it.

9 Add a mixture of water and antifreeze (see Section 35) through the expansion tank filler neck until the coolant is on the "MAX" mark on the side of the tank **(see illustrations)**. Refit the cap, and tighten it clockwise as far as it will go to secure.

10 With a sealed type cooling system like this, the addition of coolant should only be necessary at very infrequent intervals. If frequent topping-up is required, it is likely there is a leak in the system. Check the radiator, all hoses and joint faces for any sign of staining or actual wetness, and rectify as necessary. If no leaks can be found, it is advisable to have the pressure cap and the entire system pressure-tested by a dealer or suitably-equipped garage, as this will often show up a small leak not previously apparent.

4 Brake and clutch fluid level checks

Brake and clutch fluid

1 The brake and clutch fluid reservoir is mounted on the left-hand side of the engine compartment, behind the battery. The "MAX" and "MIN" marks are indicated on the side of the reservoir **(see illustrations)**, and the fluid level

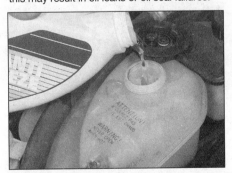

3.9a Topping-up the coolant level in the expansion tank

3.9b "MIN" and "MAX" marks on the side of the coolant expansion tank

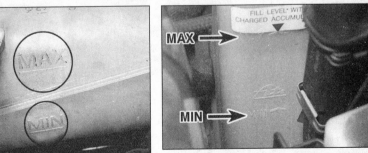

4.1a "MIN" and "MAX" marks on the side of the brake/clutch fluid reservoir (early models)

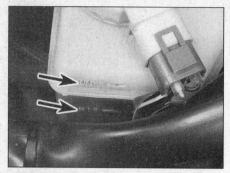

4.1b "MIN" and "MAX" marks on the side of the brake/clutch fluid reservoir (later models)

4.2a Unscrew the cap . . .

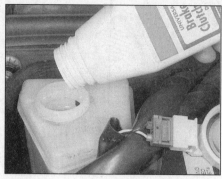

4.2b . . . and top-up the brake/clutch fluid reservoir with the specified fluid

should be maintained at or just below the "MAX" mark at all times. With wear of the brake pads the brake fluid level will drop slightly, however it must never be allowed to reach the "MIN" mark.

2 If topping-up is necessary, first wipe the area around the filler cap with a clean rag before removing the cap. If necessary, disconnect the low fluid level warning switch wiring. When adding fluid, pour it carefully into the reservoir, to avoid spilling it on surrounding painted surfaces **(see illustrations)**. Be sure to use only the specified brake hydraulic fluid, since mixing different types of fluid can cause damage to the system. See "Lubricants, fluids and capacities" at the beginning of this Chapter.

3 When adding fluid, it is a good idea to

⚠️ *Warning: Brake hydraulic fluid can harm your eyes and damage painted surfaces, so use extreme caution when handling and pouring it. Do not use fluid that has been standing open for some time, as it absorbs moisture from the air. Excess moisture can cause a dangerous loss of braking effectiveness.*

inspect the reservoir for contamination. The system should be drained and refilled if deposits, dirt particles or contamination are seen in the fluid.

4 After filling the reservoir to the correct level, make sure that the cap is refitted securely, to avoid leaks and the entry of foreign matter. If necessary, reconnect the wiring for the low fluid level warning switch.

5 The fluid level in the reservoir will drop slightly as the brake pads wear down during normal operation. If the reservoir requires repeated replenishment to maintain the proper level, this is an indication of a hydraulic leak somewhere in the system, which should be investigated immediately.

5 Washer fluid level check

Washer fluid

1 The windscreen/tailgate washer fluid reservoir filler is located at the front left-hand corner (early models) or front right-hand corner (later models) of the engine compartment, behind the headlight unit.

2 When topping-up the reservoir, a screenwash additive should be added in the quantities recommended on the bottle **(see illustration)**.

6 Tyre checks

1 On later models the tyres have tread wear safety bands, which will appear when the tread depth reaches approximately 1.6 mm. Tread wear can be monitored with a simple, inexpensive device known as a tread depth indicator gauge **(see illustration)**.

2 Wheels and tyres should give no real

problems in use, provided that a close eye is kept on them with regard to excessive wear or damage. To this end, the following points should be noted.

3 Ensure that the tyre pressures are checked regularly and maintained correctly **(see illustration)**. Checking should be carried out with the tyres cold, not immediately after the vehicle has been in use. If the pressures are checked with the tyres hot, an apparently-high reading will be obtained, owing to heat expansion. **Under no circumstances** should an attempt be made to reduce the pressures to the quoted cold reading in this instance, or effective under-inflation will result. Note that on later models, the emergency spare wheel is of special lightweight construction, and the tyre pressure is higher than normal (see "Specifications"). This spare wheel must only be used in an emergency, and at speeds not exceeding 50 mph.

4 Note any abnormal tread wear **(see illustration)**. Tread pattern irregularities such as feathering, flat spots, and more wear on one side than the other, are indications of front wheel alignment and/or balance problems. If any of these conditions are noted, they should be rectified as soon as possible.

5 Under-inflation will cause overheating of the tyre, owing to excessive flexing of the casing, and the tread will not sit correctly on the road surface. This will cause excessive wear, not to mention the danger of sudden tyre failure due to heat build-up.

6 Over-inflation will cause rapid wear of the centre part of the tyre tread, coupled with

5.3 Topping-up the windscreen washer fluid level

6.1 Checking a tyre tread depth with a depth gauge

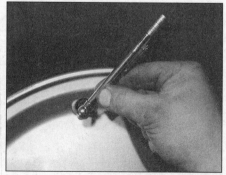

6.3 Checking a tyre pressure with a tyre pressure gauge

Tyre Tread Wear Patterns

Shoulder Wear

Underinflation
(wear on both sides)
Check and adjust pressures

Incorrect wheel camber
(wear on one side)
Repair or renew suspension parts

Hard cornering
Reduce speed!

Centre Wear

Overinflation
Check and adjust pressures

If you sometimes have to inflate your car's tyres to the higher pressures specified for maximum load or sustained high speed, don't forget to reduce the pressures to normal afterwards.

Toe Wear

Incorrect toe setting
Adjust front wheel alignment

Note: The feathered edge of the tread which characterises toe wear is best checked by feel.

Uneven Wear

Incorrect camber or castor
Repair or renew suspension parts

Malfunctioning suspension
Repair or renew suspension parts

Unbalanced wheel
Balance tyres

Out-of-round brake disc/drum
Machine or renew

---

reduced adhesion, harsher ride, and the danger of shock damage occurring in the tyre casing.

7 Regularly check the tyres for damage in the form of cuts or bulges, especially in the sidewalls. Remove any nails or stones embedded in the tread before they penetrate the tyre to cause deflation. If removal of a nail does reveal that the tyre has been punctured, refit the nail so that its point of penetration is marked. Then immediately change the wheel, and have the tyre repaired by a tyre dealer. Do not drive on a tyre in such a condition. If in any doubt as to the possible consequences of any damage found, consult your local tyre dealer for advice.

8 Periodically remove the wheels, and clean any dirt or mud from the inside and outside surfaces. Examine the wheel rims for signs of rusting, corrosion or other damage. Light alloy wheels are easily damaged by "kerbing" whilst parking, and similarly steel wheels may become dented or buckled. Renewal of the wheel is very often the only course of remedial action possible.

9 The balance of each wheel and tyre assembly should be maintained to avoid excessive wear, not only to the tyres but also to the steering and suspension components. Wheel imbalance is normally signified by vibration through the vehicle's bodyshell, although in many cases it is particularly noticeable through the steering wheel. Conversely, it should be noted that wear or

damage in suspension or steering components may cause excessive tyre wear. Out-of-round or out-of-true tyres, damaged wheels, and wheel bearing wear also fall into this category. Balancing will not usually cure vibration caused by such wear.

10 Wheel balancing may be carried out with the wheel either on or off the vehicle. If balanced on the vehicle, ensure that the wheel-to-hub relationship is marked in some way prior to subsequent wheel removal, so that it may be refitted in its original position.

11 General tyre wear is influenced to a large degree by driving style - harsh braking and acceleration, or fast cornering, will all produce more rapid tyre wear. Interchanging of tyres may result in more even wear. However, if this is completely effective, the added expense is incurred of replacing all four tyres at once, which may prove financially-restrictive for many owners.

12 Front tyres may wear unevenly as a result of wheel misalignment. The front wheels should always be correctly aligned according to the settings specified by the vehicle manufacturer.

13 Legal restrictions apply to many aspects of tyre fitting and usage, and in the UK this information is contained in the Motor Vehicle Construction and Use Regulations. It is suggested that a copy of these regulations is obtained from your local police, if in doubt as to current legal requirements with regard to tyre type and condition, minimum tread depth, etc.

7 Electrical system check

1 Check the operation of all the electrical equipment, ie lights, direction indicators, horn, washers, etc. Refer to the appropriate Sections of Chapter 12 for details if any of the circuits are found to be inoperative.

2 Stop-light switch adjustment is described in Chapter 9.

3 Visually check all accessible wiring connectors, harnesses and retaining clips for security, and for signs of chafing or damage. Rectify any faults found.

8 Battery electrolyte level check

 Caution: Before carrying out any work on the vehicle battery, read through the precautions given in "Safety first!" at the beginning of this manual.

1 The battery is located on the left-hand side of the engine compartment. If the battery is of standard or low-maintenance type, the electrolyte level may be checked, and if necessary topped-up. If it is of maintenance-free type, it is not possible to check the electrolyte level.

2 Remove the cell covers from the top of the battery.

3 Check that the level of electrolyte is approximately 15 mm above the tops of the cell plates.
4 If necessary top-up the level, using only distilled or demineralised water.
5 Refit the cell covers.
6 Further information on the battery, charging and jump-starting can be found in Chapter 5, and in the preliminary Sections of this manual.

9 Wiper blade check

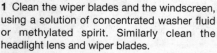

1 Clean the wiper blades and the windscreen, using a solution of concentrated washer fluid or methylated spirit. Similarly clean the headlight lens and wiper blades.
2 Check the condition of the wiper blades; if they are cracked or show any signs of deterioration, or if the glass swept area is smeared, renew them. For maximum clarity of vision, windscreen wiper blades should be renewed annually, as a matter of course. At the same time, check the headlight wiper blades (where fitted) for condition, and renew if necessary.

9.3 Removing the wiper blade from the windscreen wiper arm

3 To remove a windscreen or tailgate wiper blade, pull the arm fully away from the glass until it locks. Swivel the blade through 90°, press the locking tab with your fingers, and slide the blade out of the arm's hooked end **(see illustration)**. On refitting, ensure that the blade locks securely into the arm.
4 To remove a headlight wiper blade, pull the arm fully away from the headlight glass, then

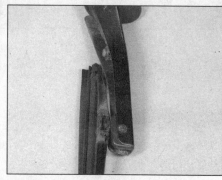

9.4 Headlight wiper blade separated from wiper arm

move it downwards until it is separated from the arm **(see illustration)**. On refitting, check that the blade locks securely into the arm.
5 Check that the windscreen washer jets operate correctly, and direct the washer fluid towards the upper area of the wiper blade stroke. If necessary, use a pin to reposition the washer jets.

Every 6000 miles or 6 months

10 Engine oil and filter renewal

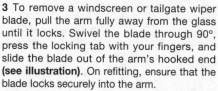

Note: *Owners of high-mileage non-turbo vehicles, or those who do a lot of stop-start driving, may prefer to carry out engine oil and filter renewal at 6000 mile/10 000 km intervals, as specified for turbos, instead of at the normal 12 000 mile/20 000 km interval.*

HAYNES HiNT *Frequent oil and filter changes are the most important preventative maintenance procedures which can be undertaken by the DIY owner. As engine oil ages, it becomes diluted and contaminated, which leads to premature engine wear.*

1 Before starting this procedure, gather together all the necessary tools and materials. Also make sure that you have plenty of clean rags and newspapers handy, to mop up any spills. Ideally, the engine oil should be warm, as it will drain better, and more built-up sludge will be removed with it. Take care, however, not to touch the exhaust or any other hot parts of the engine when working under the vehicle.
2 To avoid any possibility of scalding, and to protect yourself from possible skin irritants and other harmful contaminants in used engine oils,

it is advisable to wear gloves when carrying out this work. Access to the underside of the vehicle will be greatly improved if it can be raised on a lift, driven onto ramps, or jacked up and supported on axle stands (see *"Jacking, towing and wheel changing"*). Whichever method is chosen, make sure that the vehicle remains level, or if it is at an angle, that the drain plug is at the lowest point.
3 Slacken the drain plug about half a turn **(see illustration)**. Position the draining container under the drain plug, then remove the plug completely. If possible, try to keep the plug pressed into the sump while unscrewing it by hand the last couple of turns. As the plug releases from the threads, move it away sharply so the stream of oil issuing from the sump runs into the container, not up your

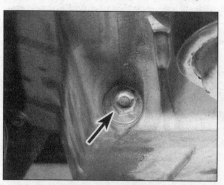

10.3 Engine oil drain plug on the sump

sleeve! Recover the sealing washer from the drain plug.
4 Allow some time for the old oil to drain, noting that it may be necessary to reposition the container as the oil flow slows to a trickle.
5 After all the oil has drained, wipe off the drain plug with a clean rag. Check the sealing washer for condition, and renew it if necessary. Clean the area around the drain plug opening, and refit the plug. Tighten the plug to the specified torque.
6 Move the container into position under the oil filter. On the B202 engine (without balance shafts) the filter is located on the rear right-hand side of the cylinder block **(see illustration)**. On B204 and B234 engines (with balance shafts) the filter is located on the front right-hand side of the cylinder block.

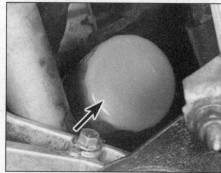

10.6 The oil filter is located on the rear of the cylinder block on the B202 engine

10.7 Removing the oil filter on a B204 engine

7 Using an oil filter removal tool if necessary, slacken the filter initially, then unscrew it by hand the rest of the way **(see illustration)**. Note that on the B204 and B234 engines, the oil filter is located very close to the sump, and it may not be possible to use a chain-type removal tool to remove the filter. Use of a strap-type removal tool is possible on these engines. Empty the oil from the old filter into the container, and discard the filter.

8 Use a clean rag to remove all oil, dirt and sludge from the filter sealing area on the engine. Check the old filter to make sure that the rubber sealing ring hasn't stuck to the engine. If it has, carefully remove it.

9 Apply a light coating of clean engine oil to the sealing ring on the new filter, then screw it into position on the engine. Tighten the filter firmly by hand only - **do not** use any tools. Wipe clean the filter and sump drain plug.

10 Remove the old oil and all tools from under the car, then lower the car to the ground (if applicable).

11 Remove the oil filler cap and withdraw the dipstick from the top of the filler tube. Fill the engine, using the correct grade and type of oil (see "Lubricants, fluids and capacities"). An oil can spout or funnel may help to reduce spillage. Pour in half the specified quantity of oil first, then wait a few minutes for the oil to fall to the sump. Continue adding oil a small quantity at a time until the level is up to the lower mark on the dipstick. Adding a further 1.0 litre will bring the level up to the upper mark on the dipstick. Insert the dipstick, and refit the filler cap.

12 Start the engine and run it for a few minutes; check for leaks around the oil filter seal and the sump drain plug. Note that there may be a delay of a few seconds before the oil pressure warning light goes out when the engine is first started, as the oil circulates through the engine oil galleries and the new oil filter, before the pressure builds up.

13 Switch off the engine, and wait a few minutes for the oil to settle in the sump once more. With the new oil circulated and the filter completely full, recheck the level on the dipstick, and add more oil as necessary.

14 Dispose of the used engine oil safely, with reference to "General repair procedures" in the reference Sections of this manual.

Every 12 000 miles or 12 months

11 Antifreeze concentration check

1 The antifreeze should always be maintained at the specified concentration. This is necessary not only to maintain the antifreeze properties, but also to prevent corrosion which would otherwise occur as the corrosion inhibitors become progressively less effective.

2 The check should be made with the engine cold, and it will be necessary to obtain an antifreeze tester from a car accessory shop.

3 Slowly unscrew the cap from the top of the coolant expansion tank, then draw coolant into the tester. Check the concentration of the antifreeze according to the manufacturer's instructions. The most common tester consists of three coloured balls of varying density - a high concentration will cause all three balls to float, whereas a low concentration may only cause one ball to float.

4 If the concentration is incorrect, slight adjustments may be made by drawing some of the coolant out of the expansion tank and replacing it with undiluted antifreeze. If the concentration is excessively out, it will be necessary to completely drain the system and renew the solution (refer to Section 35).

5 Tighten the cap onto the expansion tank on completion.

12 Front wheel alignment check

1 Due to the special measuring equipment necessary to check the wheel alignment accurately, checking and adjustment is best left to a Saab dealer or similar expert. Note that most tyre-fitting shops now possess sophisticated checking equipment. Refer to Chapter 10 for more information.

2 Before having the front wheel alignment checked, all tyre pressures should be checked and if necessary adjusted (see Section 4).

13 Power steering fluid level check

1 The power steering fluid reservoir is located on the right-hand side of the engine compartment, behind the cooling system expansion tank.

2 For the check, the front wheels should be pointing straight-ahead and the engine should be stopped. The car should be positioned on level ground.

3 On some models, the markings on the side of the reservoir indicate the "HOT" and "COLD" checking levels. With the engine hot, the level should be on the "HOT" mark, and vice-versa. On other models, a "MIN" mark indicates the effective cold level mark **(see illustration)**.

4 Before removing the filler cap, use a clean rag to wipe the cap and the surrounding area, to prevent any foreign matter from entering the reservoir. Unscrew and remove the filler cap **(see illustration)**.

5 Top-up if necessary with the specified power steering fluid **(see illustration)**. Be careful not to introduce dirt into the system, and do not overfill. Frequent topping-up indicates a leak which should be investigated.

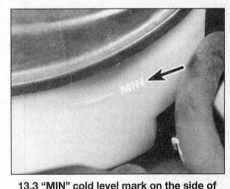

13.3 "MIN" cold level mark on the side of the power steering fluid reservoir

13.4 Unscrewing the power steering fluid reservoir filler cap

13.5 Topping-up the power steering fluid level

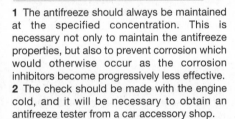

14 Seat belt check
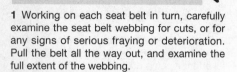

1 Working on each seat belt in turn, carefully examine the seat belt webbing for cuts, or for any signs of serious fraying or deterioration. Pull the belt all the way out, and examine the full extent of the webbing.

2 Fasten and unfasten the belt, ensuring that the locking mechanism holds securely, and releases properly when intended. Check also that the retracting mechanism operates correctly when the belt is released.

3 Check the security of all seat belt mountings and attachments which are accessible, without removing any trim or other components, from inside the vehicle.

15 Airbag system check
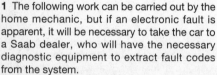

1 The following work can be carried out by the home mechanic, but if an electronic fault is apparent, it will be necessary to take the car to a Saab dealer, who will have the necessary diagnostic equipment to extract fault codes from the system.

2 Turn the ignition switch to the drive position (warning lights on), and check that the SRS (Supplementary Restraint System) warning light is illuminated for six seconds. After this period the light should go out, indicating that the system has been checked and is functioning correctly.

3 If the warning light remains on or refuses to light, have the system checked by a Saab dealer.

4 Visually examine the steering wheel centre pad and the passenger airbag module for external damage. If there is any doubt if damage is evident, consult a Saab dealer.

5 In the interests of safety, make sure that there are no loose items inside the car which could be thrown onto the airbag modules in the event of an accident.

16 Hinge and lock lubrication
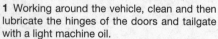

1 Working around the vehicle, clean and then lubricate the hinges of the doors and tailgate with a light machine oil.

2 Lubricate the bonnet release mechanism, hinges and safety locks with a smear of petroleum jelly.

3 Check carefully the security and operation of all hinges, latches and locks, adjusting them where required. Check the operation of the central locking system (if fitted).

4 Check the condition and operation of the tailgate struts, renewing them if either is leaking or no longer able to support the tailgate securely when raised.

5 On completion, check the operation of all door locks, tailgate/boot locks and the fuel filler flap. Check that the child safety catches on the rear doors operate correctly.

17 Battery terminal check

⚠ **Caution: Before carrying out any work on the vehicle battery, read through the precautions given in "Safety first!" at the beginning of this manual.**

1 The battery is located on the left-hand side of the engine compartment. The exterior of the battery should be inspected periodically for damage such as a cracked case or cover.

2 Check the tightness of the battery cable clamps to ensure good electrical connections, and check the entire length of each cable for cracks and frayed conductors. Check the positive cable between the battery and the starter motor.

3 If corrosion (visible as white, fluffy deposits) is evident, remove the cables from the battery terminals, clean them with a small wire brush, then refit them. Corrosion can be kept to a minimum by applying a layer of petroleum jelly to the clamps and terminals after they are reconnected.

4 Make sure that the battery retaining clamp is secure. On later models, check that the retaining bolt is tight.

5 Corrosion on the retaining clamp and the battery terminals can be removed with a solution of water and baking soda. Thoroughly rinse all cleaned areas with plain water.

6 Any metal parts of the vehicle damaged by corrosion should be covered with a zinc-based primer, then painted.

7 Periodically (approximately every three months), check the charge condition of the battery as described in Chapter 5A.

8 Further information on the battery, charging and jump-starting can be found in Chapter 5 and in the preliminary Sections of this manual.

18 Headlight and foglight beam alignment

1 Check the headlights and front foglights for damage such as stone chipping.

2 Check the headlight beam adjustment with reference to Chapter 12, noting that the tyres must be correctly inflated for an accurate setting. Where a headlight beam adjustment switch is fitted, make sure that it is set to zero before making any alterations to the beam alignment.

3 If necessary, adjust the front foglight beam alignment at the adjustment screws either on the top front corners of the unit, or underneath the unit. An approximate adjustment can be made by directing the beam vertically parallel to the ground and horizontally parallel to the centre-line of the car.

19 Road test

Instruments and electrical equipment

1 Check the operation of all instruments and electrical equipment.

2 Make sure that all instruments read correctly, and switch on all electrical equipment in turn to check that it functions properly. Check the function of the heating, air conditioning and automatic climate control systems.

Steering and suspension

3 Check for any abnormalities in the steering, suspension, handling or road "feel".

4 Drive the vehicle, and check that there are no unusual vibrations or noises.

5 Check that the steering feels positive, with no excessive "sloppiness", or roughness, and check for any suspension noises when cornering, or when driving over bumps. Check that the power steering system operates correctly. Check that the cruise control system (where fitted) operates correctly.

Drivetrain

6 Check the performance of the engine, clutch (manual transmission), transmission and driveshafts. On Turbo models, check that the boost pressure needle moves up to the red zone briefly during sharp acceleration.

7 Listen for any unusual noises from the engine, clutch (manual transmission) and transmission.

8 Make sure that the engine runs smoothly when idling, and that there is no hesitation when accelerating.

9 On manual transmission models, check that the clutch action is smooth and progressive, that the drive is taken up smoothly, and that the pedal travel is correct. Also listen for any noises when the clutch pedal is depressed. Check that all gears can be engaged smoothly, without noise, and that the gear lever action is not abnormally vague or "notchy".

10 On automatic transmission models, make sure that all gearchanges occur smoothly without snatching, and without an increase in engine speed between changes. Check that all the gear positions can be selected with the vehicle at rest. If any problems are found, they should be referred to a Saab dealer.

11 Listen for a metallic clicking sound from the front of the vehicle, as the vehicle is driven slowly in a circle with the steering on full lock.

Carry out this check in both directions. If a clicking noise is heard, this indicates wear in a driveshaft joint, in which case, refer to Chapter 8.

Check the operation and performance of the braking system

12 Make sure that the vehicle does not pull to one side when braking, and that the wheels do not lock prematurely when braking hard.

13 Check that there is no vibration through the steering when braking.

14 Check that the handbrake operates correctly, without excessive movement of the lever, and that it holds the vehicle stationary on a slope.

15 Test the operation of the brake servo unit (where applicable) as follows. With the engine off, depress the footbrake four or five times to exhaust the vacuum. Start the engine, holding the brake pedal depressed. As the engine starts, there should be a noticeable "give" in the brake pedal as vacuum builds up. Allow the engine to run for at least two minutes, and then switch it off. If the brake pedal is depressed now, it should be possible to detect a hiss from the servo as the pedal is depressed. After about four or five applications, no further hissing should be heard.

20 Crankcase ventilation system check

1 Check all crankcase ventilation and vacuum hoses for damage and leakage (refer to Chapter 4). Where necessary, remove the hoses and clear them of any blockage.

21 Hose and fluid leak check

1 Visually inspect the engine joint faces, gaskets and seals for any signs of water or oil leaks. Pay particular attention to the areas around the camshaft cover, cylinder head, oil filter and sump joint faces. Bear in mind that, over a period of time, some very slight seepage from these areas is to be expected - what you are really looking for is any indication of a serious leak. Should a leak be found, renew the offending gasket or oil seal by referring to the appropriate Chapters in this manual.

2 Also check the security and condition of all the engine-related pipes and hoses. Ensure that all cable-ties or securing clips are in place, and in good condition. Clips which are broken or missing can lead to chafing of the hoses, pipes or wiring, which could cause more serious problems in the future.

3 Carefully check the radiator hoses and heater hoses along their entire length. Renew any hose which is cracked, swollen or deteriorated. Cracks will show up better if the hose is squeezed. Pay close attention to the

hose clips that secure the hoses to the cooling system components. Hose clips can pinch and puncture hoses, resulting in cooling system leaks.

4 Inspect all the cooling system components (hoses, joint faces etc.) for leaks. A leak in the cooling system will usually show up as white- or rust-coloured deposits on the area adjoining the leak. Where any problems of this nature are found on system components, renew the component or gasket with reference to Chapter 3.

5 Check that the pressure cap on the expansion tank is fully tightened, and shows no sign of coolant leakage.

6 With the car raised, inspect the petrol tank and filler neck for punctures, cracks and other damage. The connection between the filler neck and tank is especially critical. Sometimes, a rubber filler neck or connecting hose will leak due to loose retaining clamps or deteriorated rubber.

7 Carefully check all rubber hoses and metal fuel lines leading away from the petrol tank. Check for loose connections, deteriorated hoses, crimped lines, and other damage. Pay particular attention to the vent pipes and hoses, which often loop up around the filler neck and can become blocked or crimped. Follow the lines to the front of the vehicle, carefully inspecting them all the way. Renew damaged sections as necessary.

8 From within the engine compartment, check the security of all fuel hose attachments and pipe unions, and inspect the fuel hoses and vacuum hoses for kinks, chafing and deterioration.

22 Auxiliary drivebelt check and renewal

1 On the B202 (non-balance shaft) engine, the main (multi-grooved) drivebelt is used to drive the water pump, alternator and power steering pump from the crankshaft pulley. On models fitted with air conditioning, a further crankshaft pulley drives the air conditioning compressor via a V-type drivebelt **(see illustration)**. The main drivebelt is tensioned either manually or automatically - the air conditioning drivebelt is manually adjusted using an adjustable idler pulley.

2 On B204 and B234 (balance shaft) engines, a single (multi-grooved) drivebelt is used to drive the water pump, alternator and power steering pump from the crankshaft pulley. A single drivebelt is also used on models fitted with air conditioning, but it is longer in order to include the air conditioning compressor pulley. The drivebelt is automatically tensioned, using two idler pulleys and a tension spring.

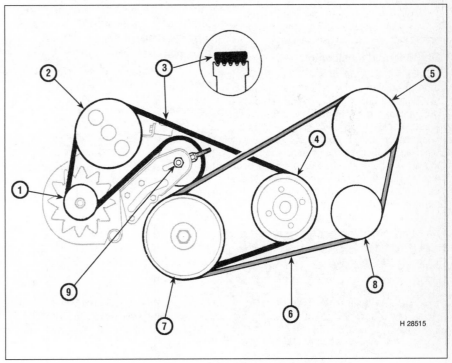

22.1 Auxiliary drivebelt configuration on the B202 engine

1 Alternator pulley (multi-groove belt)
2 Power steering pump pulley (multi-groove belt)
3 Multi-groove belt
4 Water pump pulley (multi-groove belt)
5 Air conditioning compressor pulley (V-type belt)
6 Air conditioning compressor drivebelt (V-type belt)
7 Crankshaft pulley
8 Idler pulley (V-type belt)
9 Idler pulley (multi-groove belt)

Checking the auxiliary drivebelt(s) condition

3 For better access to the drivebelt, apply the handbrake then jack up the front of the car and support it on axle stands. Remove the right-hand front roadwheel, then remove the front wing plastic moulding, followed by the front section of the wing liner from under the right-hand wheelarch.

4 Using a suitable socket and extension bar fitted to the crankshaft pulley bolt, rotate the crankshaft so that the entire length of the drivebelt(s) can be examined. Examine the drivebelt for cracks, splitting, fraying, or other damage. Check also for signs of glazing (shiny patches) and for separation of the belt plies. Renew the belt if worn or damaged.

5 On the B202 engine, if the condition of the A/C compressor drivebelt is satisfactory, check the drivebelt tension as described below under the relevant sub-heading.

Auxiliary (air conditioning compressor) drivebelt (B202 engine) - removal, refitting and tensioning

Removal

6 If not already done, carry out the operations described in paragraph 3.

7 Unscrew the locknut on the tensioner pulley 90°, then use a further spanner on the inner nut to slide the pulley to its inner position on the tensioning arm. Re-tighten the locknut.

8 Slip the drivebelt from the tensioner, crankshaft and compressor pulleys.

Refitting and tensioning

9 Locate the drivebelt on all three pulleys, then re-position the idler using a spanner on the inner nut until it is possible to depress the belt approximately 15 mm under firm thumb pressure midway between the crankshaft and compressor pulleys. Tighten the locknut. Note that Saab technicians use a special tensioning tool to set the drivebelt tension - if any doubt exists about the tension of the belt, it should be checked by a Saab dealer.

10 Refit the wing liner and plastic moulding, and lower the car to the ground.

22.13 Auxiliary drivebelt adjustment nut (arrowed) on the B202 engine

Auxiliary (multi-grooved) drivebelt (B202 engine with manual adjustment) - removal, refitting and tensioning

Removal

11 If not already done, carry out the operations described in paragraph 3.

12 On models fitted with air conditioning, remove the compressor drivebelt as previously described (paragraphs 6 to 8).

13 Loosen the idler pulley centre bolt a quarter to a half a turn, then loosen the adjustment nut until it is possible to slip the drivebelt from the tensioner, crankshaft, alternator, power steering pump and water pump pulleys **(see illustration)**.

Refitting and tensioning

14 Locate the drivebelt on all the pulleys, then tighten the adjustment nut until it is possible to depress the belt approximately 15 mm under firm thumb pressure approximately a quarter of the way along its upper run near the power steering pump pulley. Tighten the idler pulley centre bolt. Note that Saab technicians use a special tensioning tool to set the drivebelt tension - if any doubt exists about the tension of the belt, it should be checked by a Saab dealer.

15 Refit the wing liner and plastic moulding, and lower the car to the ground.

Auxiliary (multi-grooved) drivebelt (non-balance shaft engines with automatic tensioning) - removal and refitting

Removal

16 If not already done, carry out the operations described in paragraph 3.

17 On early B202 engines with air conditioning, remove the compressor drivebelt as previously described (paragraphs 6 to 8).

18 Using a socket on the tensioner pulley nut,

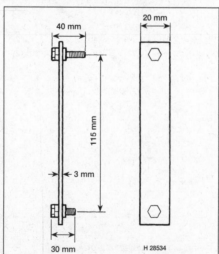

22.25a Dimensions of the home-made tool for retaining the auxiliary drivebelt tensioner spring

press the tensioner pulley down to release the tension from the drivebelt.

19 Slip the drivebelt from the water pump pulley (and where applicable, from the compressor pulley). Release the tensioner pulley.

20 Remove the drivebelt from the remaining pulleys.

Refitting

21 Locate the drivebelt on all the pulleys except the water pump (and where applicable, the compressor pulley). Make sure that the multi-grooves are all correctly seated.

22 Using the socket on the tensioner pulley nut, press the tensioner pulley down until it is possible to locate the drivebelt on the water pump/compressor pulleys. Release the tensioner pulley. The drivebelt tension will be adjusted automatically with the engine running.

23 Refit the wing liner and plastic moulding, and lower the car to the ground.

Auxiliary (multi-grooved) drivebelt (balance shaft engines with automatic tensioning) - removal and refitting

Removal

24 If not already done, carry out the operations described in paragraph 3.

25 The tensioner spring must now be compressed and held in compression using a home-made tool. Cut a length of flat metal bar to the dimensions shown in the accompanying illustration, then drill two holes and fit the bolts as shown. First pull down the drivebelt on the upper run to compress the spring, then position the retaining tool over the cut-outs on the tensioner bracket. Release the drivebelt, and check that the tensioner is held in its compressed position **(see illustrations)**. Note that the tensioner spring is very strong, and considerable pressure is required to compress it.

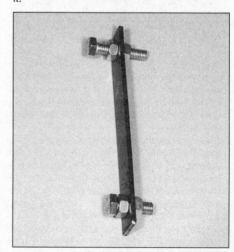

22.25b Completed home-made tool for retaining the auxiliary drivebelt tensioner retainer

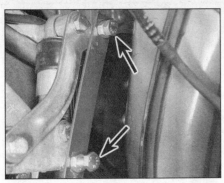

22.25c Auxiliary drivebelt tensioner retainer tool in position

22.27 Remove the auxiliary drivebelt tensioner pulley, followed by the drivebelt

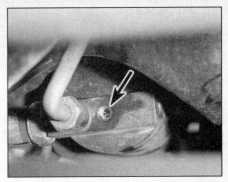

23.1 Air conditioning system sight glass

26 Slip the drivebelt from the water pump, power steering pump, crankshaft (and where applicable, the compressor) pulleys.

27 Unscrew and remove the bolt securing the tensioner pulley to the bracket, then remove the pulley and drivebelt from the engine compartment **(see illustration)**. Note: *The tensioner pulley bolt has a* **left-hand thread,** *so it must be turned clockwise to unscrew it.*

Refitting

28 Locate the drivebelt in the tensioner bracket, then refit the pulley and tighten the retaining bolt.

29 Locate the drivebelt over all the pulleys, making sure that the multi-groove side is correctly engaged with the grooves on the pulleys.

30 Pull down on the drivebelt to compress the tensioner spring, then remove the retaining tool and release the drivebelt. The drivebelt tension will be finally adjusted automatically with the engine running.

31 Refit the wing liner and plastic moulding, and lower the car to the ground.

23 Air conditioning system refrigerant check

> ⚠️ **Warning: Do not attempt to open the refrigerant circuit. Refer to the precautions given in Chapter 3.**

1 A sight glass is fitted to the air conditioning system, in order to check the quantity of fluid in the system. It is located on the top of the receiver at the front right-hand corner of the engine compartment on right-hand drive models **(see illustration)**, or on top of the evaporator on the right-hand side of the bulkhead in the engine compartment on left-hand drive models.

2 Run the engine, and switch on the air conditioning.

3 After a few minutes, inspect the sight glass, and check the fluid flow. Clear fluid should be visible - if not, the following will help to diagnose the problem:

a) *Clear fluid flow - the system is functioning correctly.*

b) *No fluid flow - have the system checked for leaks by a Saab dealer or air conditioning specialist.*

c) *Continuous stream of clear air bubbles in fluid - refrigerant level low - have the system recharged by a Saab dealer or air conditioning specialist.*

24 Exhaust system check

> ⚠️ **Warning: If the engine has been running take care not to touch the exhaust system, especially the front section, as it may still be hot.**

1 Position the car over an inspection pit, or on car ramps. Alternatively, raise the front and rear of the car and support on axle stands (see *"Jacking, towing and wheel changing"*).

2 Examine the exhaust system over its entire length, checking for any damaged, broken or missing mountings, security of the pipe retaining clamps, and condition of the system with regard to rust and corrosion.

3 Look for signs of leakage - a leak normally shows up as a black sooty stain. With the engine running, have an assistant place a wad of rag over the exhaust tailpipe, while you listen for the rhythmic "fluffing" sound characteristic of an exhaust leak.

4 It may be possible to repair a minor leak yourself, using one of the proprietary exhaust sealing products available, but more serious damage will require the replacement of one or more sections of the exhaust system - refer to Chapter 4A.

5 Lower the vehicle to the ground on completion.

25 Spark plug renewal

1 The correct functioning of the spark plugs is vital for the correct running and efficiency of the engine. It is essential that the plugs fitted are appropriate for the engine. If this type is used and the engine is in good condition, the spark plugs should not need attention between scheduled replacement intervals.

Spark plug cleaning is rarely necessary, and should not be attempted unless specialised equipment is available, as damage can easily be caused to the firing ends.

Models without Direct Ignition

2 Remove the screws, and lift the inspection cover from the centre of the camshaft cover.

3 If the marks on the spark plug (HT) leads cannot be seen, mark the leads "1" to "4", to correspond to the cylinder the lead serves (No 1 cylinder is at the timing chain end of the engine).

4 Pull the leads from the plugs by gripping the end fitting, not the lead, otherwise the lead connection may be fractured. With all the leads disconnected, lift the rubber grommet from the distributor end of the cylinder head, and position the leads to one side.

Models with Direct Ignition

5 Disconnect the wiring multi-plug from the flywheel end of the ignition cartridge.

6 Unscrew the four screws securing the ignition cartridge to the top of the cylinder head. An Allen key will be required for this.

7 Where applicable, unscrew the bolt and release the cartridge wiring support clip.

8 Where applicable, unscrew the bolt and disconnect the earth lead.

9 Carefully lift the ignition cartridge, at the same time releasing it from the tops of the spark plugs.

All models

10 It is advisable to remove the dirt from the spark plug recesses using a clean brush, vacuum cleaner or compressed air before removing the plugs, to prevent dirt dropping into the cylinders.

11 Unscrew the plugs using a spark plug spanner, suitable box spanner or a deep socket and extension bar **(see illustrations)**. Keep the socket aligned with the spark plug - if it is forcibly moved to one side, the ceramic insulator may be broken off. As each plug is removed, examine it as follows.

12 Examination of the spark plugs will give a good indication of the condition of the engine. If the insulator nose of the spark plug is clean and white, with no deposits, this is indicative

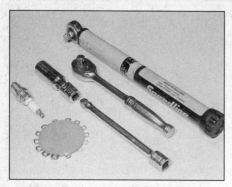

25.11a Tools required for spark plug removal, gap adjustment and refitting

25.11b Removing a spark plug

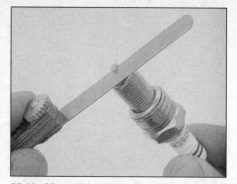

25.16a Measuring the spark plug gap with a feeler blade

of a weak mixture or too hot a plug (a hot plug transfers heat away from the electrode slowly, a cold plug transfers heat away quickly).

13 If the tip and insulator nose are covered with hard black-looking deposits, then this is indicative that the mixture is too rich. Should the plug be black and oily, then it is likely that the engine is fairly worn, as well as the mixture being too rich.

14 If the insulator nose is covered with light tan to greyish-brown deposits, then the mixture is correct, and it is likely that the engine is in good condition.

15 The electrode gap is of considerable importance as, if it is too large or too small, the size of the spark and its efficiency will be seriously impaired. The gap should be set to the value given in the Specifications.

16 To set the gap, measure it with a feeler blade or wire gauge and then bend open, or close, the outer plug electrode until the correct gap is achieved **(see illustrations)**. The centre electrode should never be bent, as this will crack the insulator and cause plug failure, if nothing worse. If using feeler blades, the gap is correct when the appropriate-size blade is a firm sliding fit.

17 Special spark plug electrode gap adjusting tools are available from most motor accessory shops, or from some spark plug manufacturers.

18 Before fitting the spark plugs, check that the threaded connector sleeves are tight, and that the plug exterior surfaces and threads are clean.

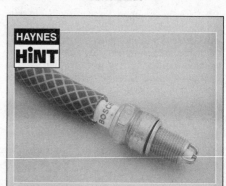

It is very often difficult to insert spark plugs into their holes without cross-threading them. To avoid this possibility, fit a short length of 5/16-inch internal diameter rubber hose over the end of the spark plug. The flexible hose acts as a universal joint to help align the plug with the plug hole. Should the plug begin to cross-thread, the hose will slip on the spark plug, preventing thread damage to the aluminium cylinder head. Remove the rubber hose, and tighten the plug to the specified torque using the spark plug socket and a torque wrench. Fit the remaining spark plugs in the same manner.

Models with Direct Ignition

19 Refit the ignition cartridge using a reversal of the removal procedure. Tighten the four screws to the specified torque.

Models without Direct Ignition

20 Connect the HT leads in their correct order, and refit the rubber grommet.
21 Refit the inspection cover, and tighten the retaining screws.

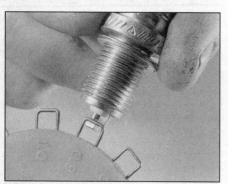

25.16b Measuring the spark plug gap with a wire gauge . . .

25.16c . . . and adjusting the gap using a special adjusting tool

26 Manual transmission oil level check

Note: *A suitable Allen key will be required to unscrew the manual transmission filler and level plugs (as applicable). This can be obtained from most motor factors, or from your Saab dealer.*

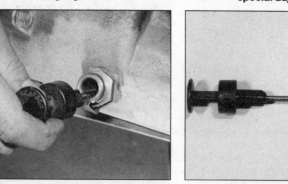

26.1a Withdrawing the dipstick from the front of the gearbox

26.1b Upper and lower level marks on the gearbox oil level dipstick

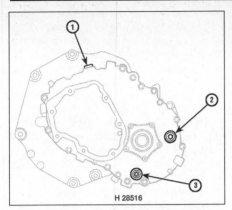

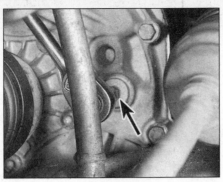

26.2b Unscrewing the manual transmission level plug (arrowed)

26.2a Location of manual transmission filler, level and drain plugs (later models)

1 Filler plug   2 Level plug   3 Drain plug

26.4 Topping-up the manual gearbox oil level (later model shown)

1 On early models, an oil level dipstick is provided on the front of the gearbox, and there is no need to jack up the vehicle. Push the spring clip to one side, then pull out the dipstick. Wipe clean the dipstick, then re-insert it fully again. Withdraw it, and check that the oil level is between the upper and lower limits **(see illustrations)**.

2 On later models, jack up the front and rear of the car, and support on axle stands (see *"Jacking, towing and wheel changing")*. Make sure that the car is level. Remove the left-hand front wheel in order to view the level plug on the side of the transmission. Wipe clean the area around the level plug, which is located on the side of the transmission behind the left-hand driveshaft. Unscrew the plug, and wipe it clean **(see illustrations)**. The oil level should reach the lower edge of the level hole. A certain amount of oil will have gathered behind the level plug, and will trickle out when it is removed; this does **not** necessarily indicate that the level is correct. To ensure that a true level is established, wait until the initial trickle has stopped.

3 If the oil level requires topping-up, wipe clean the area around the filler plug, which is located on top of the transmission. Unscrew the plug, and wipe it clean.

4 Add oil as necessary until the level is up to the upper mark on the dipstick on early models, or until a steady trickle of oil can be seen emerging from the level hole on later

models **(see illustration)**. Use only good-quality oil of the specified type. A funnel will be helpful when adding oil to the transmission through the filler plug aperture.

5 When the level is correct, refit and tighten the filler plug (and where necessary, the level plug) to the specified torque wrench setting. Wipe off any spilt oil.

6 Where necessary, refit the left-hand front wheel, and lower the car to the ground.

27 Automatic transmission fluid level check

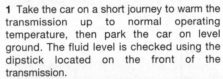

1 Take the car on a short journey to warm the transmission up to normal operating temperature, then park the car on level ground. The fluid level is checked using the dipstick located on the front of the transmission.

2 With the engine idling, select "D" for approximately 15 seconds, then engage "R" and wait a further 15 seconds. Do this again in position "P", and leave the engine idling.

3 Withdraw the dipstick from the tube, and wipe all the fluid from its end with a clean rag or paper towel. Insert the clean dipstick back into the tube as far as it will go, then withdraw it once more. Note the fluid level on the end of the dipstick - there are two sets of level marks, the lower ones are for a fluid temperature of 40°C, and the upper ones are for a temperature of 80°C **(see illustration)**. If the engine is at normal operating temperature, use the upper level marks.

4 If topping-up is necessary, add fluid as necessary via the dipstick tube until the level is on the upper mark on the dipstick. **Note:** *Never overfill the transmission so that the fluid level is above the upper mark. Use a funnel with a fine mesh gauze, to avoid spillage and to ensure that no foreign matter enters the transmission.*

5 After topping-up, take the car on a short run to distribute the fresh fluid, then recheck the level again, topping-up if necessary.

6 Always maintain the level between the two dipstick marks. If the level is allowed to fall below the lower mark, fluid starvation may result, which could lead to severe transmission damage.

28 Driveshaft rubber gaiter check

1 With the vehicle raised and securely supported on stands, turn the steering onto full lock, then slowly rotate the roadwheel. Inspect the condition of the outer constant velocity (CV) joint rubber gaiters, squeezing the gaiters to open out the folds. Check for signs of cracking, splits or deterioration of the rubber, which may allow the grease to escape, and lead to water and grit entry into the joint. Also check the security and condition of the retaining clips. Repeat these checks on the inner CV joints. If any damage or deterioration is found, the gaiters should be renewed as described in Chapter 8.

2 At the same time, check the general condition of the CV joints themselves by first holding the driveshaft and attempting to rotate the wheel. Repeat this check by holding the inner joint and attempting to rotate the driveshaft. Any appreciable movement indicates wear in the joints, wear in the driveshaft splines, or possibly a loose driveshaft retaining nut.

29 Front and rear brake pad and disc check

1 Firmly apply the handbrake, then jack up the front and rear of the car and support it securely on axle stands (see *"Jacking, towing and wheel changing"*). Remove the front and rear roadwheels.

2 For a quick check, the thickness of friction material remaining on each brake pad can be measured through the aperture in the caliper body. If any pad's friction material is worn to the specified thickness or less, all four pads on that axle must be renewed as a set.

3 For a comprehensive check, the brake pads should be removed and cleaned. The operation of the caliper can then also be checked, and the condition of the brake discs can be fully examined on both sides. Refer to Chapter 9 for further information.

4 On completion, refit the wheels and lower the car to the ground.

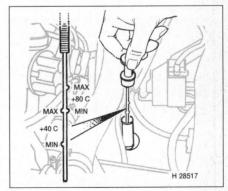

27.3 Fluid level dipstick on the automatic transmission

31.3 Rocking the roadwheel to check steering /suspension components

30 Brake line and flexible hose check

1 Apply the handbrake, then raise the front and rear of the car and securely support on axle stands. Remove all wheels.
2 Thoroughly examine all brake lines and brake flexible hoses for security and damage. To check the flexible hoses, bend them slightly in order to show up any cracking of the rubber.
3 Check the complete braking system for any signs of brake fluid leakage.
4 Where necessary, carry out repairs to the braking system with reference to Chapter 9.

31 Steering, suspension and shock absorber check

1 Apply the handbrake, then raise the front and rear of the car, and securely support it on axle stands.

2 Visually inspect all balljoint dust covers and the steering rack-and-pinion gaiters for splits, chafing or deterioration. Any wear of these components will cause loss of lubricant, together with dirt and water entry, resulting in rapid deterioration of the balljoints or steering gear.
3 Grasp each front roadwheel in turn at the 12 o'clock and 6 o'clock positions, and try to rock it **(see illustration)**. Very slight freeplay may be felt, but if the movement is appreciable, further investigation is necessary to determine the source. Continue rocking the wheel while an assistant depresses the footbrake. If the movement is now eliminated or significantly reduced, it is likely that the hub bearings are at fault. If the freeplay is still evident with the footbrake depressed, then there is wear in the suspension joints or mountings.
4 Now grasp the wheel at the 9 o'clock and 3 o'clock positions, and try to rock it as before. Any movement felt now may again be caused by wear in the hub bearings or the steering track-rod balljoints. If the inner or outer balljoint is worn, the visual movement will be obvious.
5 Using a large screwdriver or flat bar, check for wear in the suspension mounting bushes by levering between the relevant suspension component and its attachment point. Some movement is to be expected, as the mountings are made of rubber, but excessive wear should be obvious. Also check the condition of any visible rubber bushes, looking for splits, cracks or contamination of the rubber.
6 Check for any signs of fluid leakage around the front suspension struts and rear shock absorbers. Should any fluid be noticed, the suspension strut/shock absorber is defective

internally, and should be renewed. **Note:** *Suspension struts/shock absorbers should always be renewed in pairs on the same axle.*
7 Lower the car to the ground.
8 The efficiency of the suspension struts and shock absorbers may be checked by depressing each corner of the car in turn. If the struts/shock absorbers are in good condition, the body will rise and then settle in its normal position. If it continues to rise and fall, the suspension strut or shock absorber is probably suspect. Examine also the suspension strut/shock absorber upper and lower mountings for any signs of wear.
9 With the car standing on its wheels, have an assistant turn the steering wheel back and forth about an eighth of a turn each way. There should be very little, if any, lost movement between the steering wheel and roadwheels. If this is not the case, closely observe the joints and mountings previously described, but in addition, check the steering column universal joints for wear, and the rack-and-pinion steering gear itself.

32 Ventilation air filter renewal

Note: *If the car is used in a dusty or extremely polluted environment, the ventilation air filter should be renewed more frequently.*
1 Unscrew the screw, and remove the cover from the top of the evaporator/heater housing.
2 Slide out the ventilation air filter, then insert the new filter.
3 Refit the cover and tighten the screw.

Every 24 000 miles or 2 years

33 Air cleaner filter element renewal

1 The air cleaner is located on the front left-hand corner of the engine compartment, and the air inlet is taken from the front of the car behind the radiator grille area. On early models with the LH-Jetronic fuel injection system, the air cleaner element is rectangular in shape, whereas on later models with the Trionic engine management system, the air cleaner element is cylindrical in shape.

Models with LH-Jetronic fuel injection system

2 Remove the washer fluid reservoir from the front left-hand corner of the engine compartment (see Chapter 12). If preferred, the reservoir may be positioned to one side, leaving the fluid inside.
3 Loosen the clip and disconnect the air ducting from the air cleaner. On some models, it will be necessary to completely remove the airflow meter. On Turbo models, also

disconnect the rubber socket from the turbocharger.
4 Release the toggle clips, and remove the top cover from the air cleaner filter housing.
5 Lift out the air cleaner filter element, noting which way round it is fitted.
6 Wipe clean the inner surfaces of the cover and main housing, then locate the new element in the housing, making sure that the sealing lip is at the bottom, and correctly engaged with the edge of the housing.
7 Refit the cover, and secure with the toggle clips.
8 Reconnect the air ducting/airflow meter, as applicable.
9 Refit the washer fluid reservoir to the front left-hand corner of the engine compartment.

Models with Trionic engine management system

10 Disconnect the air ducting from the air cleaner. Where necessary to provide additional room, remove the air ducting complete, by releasing the support strut and

disconnecting the wiring from the air temperature sensor (refer to Chapter 4A) **(see illustrations)**.
11 Release the toggle clips and remove the cover from the air cleaner housing **(see illustrations)**.
12 Pull out the element from the housing **(see illustration)**.

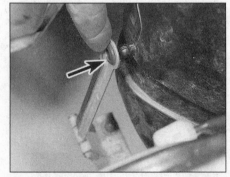

33.10a Release the air ducting support strut . . .

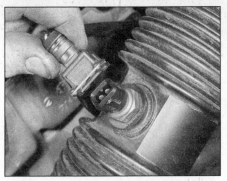

33.10b . . . and disconnect the wiring from the air temperature sensor . . .

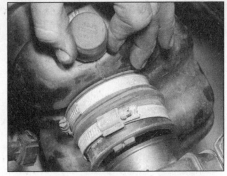

33.10c . . . then loosen the clips and disconnect the air ducting (Trionic)

33.11a Release the toggle clips . . .

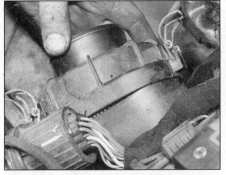

33.11b . . . and remove the cover from the air cleaner housing (Trionic)

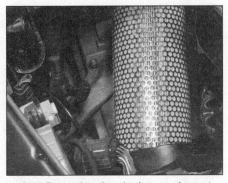

33.12 Removing the air cleaner element from the housing (Trionic)

33.14 "UP" facing mark on the air cleaner housing cover

13 Wipe clean the inner surfaces of the cover and housing, then insert the new element.

14 Refit the cover, and secure with the toggle clips. Note that the "UP" facing arrow must point upwards (see illustration).

15 Reconnect/refit the air ducting.

34 Automatic transmission fluid and filter renewal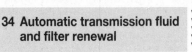

1 Take the car on a short journey to warm the transmission up to normal operating temperature. Position the car over an inspection pit, or alternatively jack up the front and rear of the car and support on axle stands (see "*Jacking, towing and wheel changing*"). Whichever method is used, make sure that the car is level for checking the fluid level later.

2 Position a suitable container beneath the transmission, then unscrew the drain plug and allow the fluid to drain. Note that a special key is required to unscrew the plug.

⚠️ *Warning: The fluid will be very hot, so take necessary precautions to prevent scalding. The use of thick waterproof gloves is recommended.*

3 With all the fluid drained, wipe clean the plug and refit it to the automatic transmission housing. Tighten the plug to the specified torque.

4 Unscrew the three bolts, and remove the filter cover from the bottom of the transmission (see illustration).

5 Remove the filter from its location. Remove the O-rings, and obtain new ones.

6 Wipe clean the filter location and the cover, then fit the new filter using new O-rings. Tighten the cover bolts securely.

7 Fill the automatic transmission with the

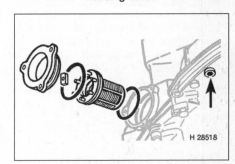

34.4 Automatic transmission filter components, and drain plug (arrowed)

specified grade and quantity of fluid. Referring to Section 27, top it up to the correct level. Use the lower set of dipstick markings first, then take the car for a run. With the fluid at operating temperature, re-check the fluid level using the upper set of dipstick markings.

Every 48 000 miles or 3 years

⚠️ *Warning: Wait until the engine is cold before starting this procedure. Do not allow antifreeze to come in contact with your skin, or with the painted surfaces of the vehicle. Rinse off spills immediately, with plenty of water. Never leave antifreeze lying around in an open container - antifreeze can be fatal if ingested.*

35 Coolant renewal

Cooling system draining

1 With the engine completely cold, unscrew and remove the expansion tank filler cap. Turn the cap a few turns anti-clockwise, then wait until any pressure remaining in the system is released. Fully unscrew the cap and remove it.

2 Apply the handbrake, then jack up the front of the car and support on axle stands (see "*Jacking, towing and wheel changing*").

3 Remove the centre panel from beneath the radiator. Unscrew the retaining bolts, then release the panel from the clips.

4 Position a suitable container beneath the lower right-hand side of the radiator.

5 Loosen the drain plug in the radiator bottom tank, and allow the coolant to drain into the container.

6 When the flow of coolant stops, reposition the container below the cylinder block drain plug. On balance shaft engines, there are two cylinder block drain plugs, one located on the front left-hand side, and the other located on the rear left-hand side. With the plug(s) removed, allow the coolant to drain from the cylinder block.

7 Refit and tighten the radiator and cylinder block drain plugs.

8 If the coolant has been drained for a reason other than renewal, then provided it is clean and less than three years old, it can be re-used.

Cooling system flushing

9 If coolant renewal has been neglected, or if the antifreeze mixture has become diluted, then in time, the cooling system may gradually lose efficiency, as the coolant passages become restricted due to rust, scale deposits, and other sediment. The cooling system efficiency can be restored by flushing the system clean.

10 The radiator should be flushed independently of the engine, to avoid unnecessary contamination.

Radiator flushing

11 To flush the radiator, first disconnect the top and bottom hoses from the radiator.

12 Insert a garden hose into the radiator top inlet. Direct a flow of clean water through the radiator, and continue flushing until clean water emerges from the radiator bottom outlet.

13 If after a reasonable period, the water still does not run clear, the radiator can be flushed with a good proprietary cleaning agent. It is important that their manufacturer's instructions are followed carefully. If the contamination is particularly bad, remove the radiator then insert the hose in the radiator bottom outlet, and reverse-flush the radiator.

Engine flushing

15 To flush the engine, first remove the thermostat as described in Chapter 3, then temporarily refit the thermostat cover.

16 With the top and bottom hoses disconnected from the radiator, insert a garden hose into the radiator top hose. Direct a clean flow of water through the engine, and continue flushing until clean water emerges from the radiator bottom hose.

17 On completion of flushing, refit the thermostat and reconnect the hoses with reference to Chapter 3.

18 Check that the radiator and cylinder block drain plugs are in place and tight.

19 Remove the container from under the car, then refit the centre panel beneath the radiator, and lower the car to the ground.

Cooling system filling

20 Before attempting to fill the cooling system, make sure that all hoses and clips are in good condition, and that the clips are tight. Note that an antifreeze mixture must be used all year round, to prevent corrosion of the engine components (see following sub-Section).

21 Pour the correct amount of antifreeze (see *"Lubricants, fluids and capacities"*) into a container, then add water until the total amount is approximately 6.5 litres.

22 Slowly fill the system through the expansion tank filler neck, allowing time for trapped air to escape through the purge line.

Top-up to the "MAX" mark on the side of the expansion tank.

23 Refit and tighten the filler cap.

24 Start the engine, and run it at a fast idle speed until the cooling fan cuts in, and then cuts out. This will purge any remaining air from the system. Stop the engine.

25 Allow the engine to cool, then check the coolant level with reference to Section 3 of this Chapter. Top-up the level if necessary. Saab recommend that the level be checked again after a few days, and topped-up as necessary.

Antifreeze mixture

26 The antifreeze should always be renewed at the specified intervals. This is necessary not only to maintain the antifreeze properties, but also to prevent corrosion which would otherwise occur as the corrosion inhibitors become progressively less effective.

27 Always use an ethylene-glycol based antifreeze which is suitable for use in mixed-metal cooling systems. The percentage of antifreeze and levels of protection are indicated in the Specifications.

28 Before adding antifreeze, the cooling system should be completely drained, preferably flushed, and all hoses checked for condition and security.

29 After filling with antifreeze, a label should be attached to the expansion tank filler neck, stating the type and concentration of antifreeze used, and the date installed. Any subsequent topping-up should be made with the same type and concentration of antifreeze.

30 Do not use engine antifreeze in the windscreen/tailgate washer system, as it will cause damage to the vehicle paintwork. A screenwash additive should be added to the washer system, in the quantities stated on the bottle.

Every 96 000 miles

| 36 Fuel filter renewal |

⚠ **Warning: Before carrying out the following operation, refer to the precautions given in "Safety first!" at the beginning of this manual, and follow them implicitly. Petrol is a highly-dangerous and volatile liquid, and the precautions necessary when handling it cannot be overstressed.**

1 On some early models with the LH-Jetronic fuel injection system, the fuel filter is located in the engine compartment between the battery and the false bulkhead. On later models with both the LH-Jetronic and Trionic fuel injection systems, the filter is adjacent to the fuel tank underneath the rear of the car.

2 Depressurise the fuel system with reference to Chapter 4A, Section 9.

Early models with LH-Jetronic fuel injection system

3 Clean the areas around the fuel filter inlet and outlet unions.

4 Position a small container or cloth rags beneath the filter, to catch spilt fuel.

5 Unscrew the banjo coupling bolt on the bottom of the filter, while holding the coupling with a further spanner. Recover the sealing washers.

6 Unscrew the banjo coupling bolt on the top of the filter, using the same procedure.

7 Noting the direction of the arrow marked on the filter body, loosen the retaining clip and withdraw the filter from the engine compartment.

8 Locate the new filter in the retaining clip, and tighten the clip. Make sure that the flow arrow on the filter body is pointing towards the outlet which leads to the fuel injection rail.

9 Check the condition of the sealing washers, and renew them if necessary.

10 Refit the banjo couplings and hoses to the top and bottom of the filter, together with the sealing washers. Tighten the bolts securely, while holding the couplings with a further spanner.

11 Wipe away any excess fuel.

Later models with LH-Jetronic or Trionic systems

12 Chock the front wheels, then jack up the rear of the car and support on axle stands (see *"Jacking, towing and wheel changing"*).

13 Pull off the plastic guard where fitted **(see illustration)**, then clean the areas around the fuel filter inlet and outlet unions.

14 Position a small container or cloth rags beneath the filter to catch spilt fuel.

15 Unscrew the banjo coupling bolts from each end of the filter **(see illustration)**, while holding the coupling with a further spanner. Recover the sealing washers.

16 Noting the direction of the arrow marked on the filter body, loosen the retaining clip and withdraw the filter from under the car.

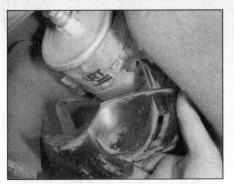

36.13 Removing the plastic guard from the bottom of the fuel filter

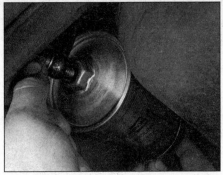

36.15 Unscrewing the banjo bolts from the ends of the filter

36.17 Note the direction of the arrow on the filter body

17 Locate the new filter in the retaining clip, and tighten the clip. Make sure that the flow arrow on the filter body is pointing towards the outlet which leads to the engine compartment **(see illustration)**.
18 Check the condition of the sealing washers, and renew them if necessary.

19 Refit the banjo couplings and hoses to each end of the filter, together with the sealing washers. Tighten the bolts securely, while holding the couplings with a further spanner.
20 Wipe away any excess fuel, refit the plastic cover where fitted, then lower the car to the ground.

All models

21 Start the engine, and check the filter hose connections for leaks.
22 The old filter should be disposed of safely, bearing in mind that it will be highly inflammable.

Every 2 years

37 Brake fluid renewal

Note: *Refer to Chapter 9 for models with ABS.*

⚠ *Warning: Brake hydraulic fluid can harm your eyes and damage painted surfaces, so use extreme caution when handling and pouring it. Do not use fluid that has been standing open for some time, as it absorbs moisture from the air. Excess moisture content can cause a dangerous loss of braking effectiveness.*

1 The procedure is similar to that for the bleeding of the hydraulic system as described in Chapter 9, except that the brake fluid reservoir should be emptied by syphoning, using a clean poultry baster or similar before starting, and allowance should be made for the old fluid to be expelled when bleeding a section of the circuit. To prevent contamination from the fluid in the clutch hydraulic system (which uses the same reservoir) the latter system should be bled as described in Chapter 6 after bleeding the brake system.

2 Working as described in Chapter 9, open the first bleed screw in the sequence, and pump the brake pedal gently until nearly all the old fluid has been emptied from the fluid reservoir. Top-up to the "MAX" level with new fluid, and continue pumping until only the new fluid remains in the reservoir, and new fluid can be seen emerging from the bleed screw.

Tighten the screw, and top the reservoir level up to the "MAX" level line.
3 Old hydraulic fluid is invariably much darker in colour than the new, making it easy to distinguish the two.
4 Work through all the remaining bleed screws in the sequence, until new fluid can be seen at all of them. Be careful to keep the master cylinder reservoir topped-up to above the "MIN" level at all times, or air may enter the system and greatly increase the length of the task.
5 When the operation is complete, check that all bleed screws are securely tightened, and that their dust caps are refitted. Wash off all traces of spilt fluid, and recheck the reservoir fluid level.
6 Check the operation of the brakes before taking the car on the road.

Specifications

Engine
Difference between MIN and MAX marks on dipstick . . . .   1.0 litre

Cooling system
Antifreeze mixture:
    28% antifreeze . . . .   Protection down to -15°C (5°F)
    50% antifreeze . . . .   Protection down to -30°C (-22°F)
Note: *Refer to antifreeze manufacturer for latest recommendations.*

Specifications

Ignition system

Spark plugs:

Engine code:	Type	Electrode gap
B202L	Bosch FR 5 DCX	1.0 mm
B202i	Bosch FR 8 D+	0.8 mm
B204i	Bosch FR 7 D+X	1.1 mm
B234L, B234E and B234R	Bosch FR 5 DCX	1.1 mm
B234i	Bosch FR 7 D+X	1.1 mm
Ignition HT lead resistance	Approximately 600 ohms per 100 mm length	

Brakes

Brake pad friction material minimum thickness .... 4.0 mm

Tyres

Tyre size .... 195/65 R15T, 195/65 VR15, 205/60 ZR15, 205/50 ZR16, or 205/55 ZR16

Pressures (tyres cold) - psi (bars):	Front	Rear
1 to 3 persons:		
195/65 R15T	30 (2.1)	30 (2.1)
195/65 VR15	30 (2.1)	30 (2.1)
205/60 ZR15	32 (2.2)	32 (2.2)
205/50 ZR16	35 (2.4)	35 (2.4)
205/55 ZR16	35 (2.4)	35 (2.4)
Maximum load (up to 99 mph) - where different to above:		
205/50 ZR16	38 (2.6)	38 (2.6)
Maximum load (over 99 mph):		
195/65 R15T	33 (2.3)	33 (2.3)
195/65 VR15	38 (2.6)	38 (2.6)
205/60 ZR15	39 (2.7)	39 (2.7)
205/50 ZR16	43 (3.0)	43 (3.0)
205/55 ZR16	41 (2.8)	41 (2.8)
Spare wheel (maximum 50 mph):		
115/70 R16	60 (4.2)	60 (4.2)
175/70 R15T	36 (2.5)	36 (2.5)

Note: *The pressures quoted are for 1992-on models. Consult manufacturers handbook for other models.*

Note: *Pressures apply only to original-equipment tyres, and may vary if any other make or type is fitted; check with the tyre manufacturer or supplier for correct pressures if necessary.*

Torque wrench settings

	Nm	lbf ft
Automatic transmission drain plug	45	33
Engine oil drain plug	25	19
Ignition cartridge (models with Direct Ignition)	12	9
Manual transmission filler, level and drain plugs	50	37
Roadwheel bolts	115	85
Spark plugs	28	21

Chapter 2 Part A:
Engine in-car repair procedures

Contents

Degrees of difficulty

Easy, suitable for novice with little experience	**Fairly easy,** suitable for beginner with some experience	**Fairly difficult,** suitable for competent DIY mechanic	**Difficult,** suitable for experienced DIY mechanic	**Very difficult,** suitable for expert DIY or professional

Specifications

Engine (general)

Designation:
1985 cc engine (without balance shafts)	B202
1985 cc engine (with balance shafts)	B204
2290 cc engine (with balance shafts)	B234
Bore	90.00 mm

Stroke:
1985 cc engine	78.00 mm
2290 cc engine	90.00 mm
Direction of crankshaft rotation	Clockwise (viewed from right-hand side of vehicle)
No 1 cylinder location	At timing chain end of engine

Compression ratio:
  Models up to 1993:
B202i and B202 cat	10 : 1
B202 Turbo and B202 Turbo cat	9 : 1
B234i	10 : 1
B234L and B234R	8.5 : 1
B202S	9.0 : 1

  Models from 1994:
B204i	10 : 1
B204S	8.8 : 1
B204L	9.2 : 1
B234i	10.5 : 1
B234E, B234LM, B234LA, and B234R	9.25 : 1

Maximum power / torque:
  Models up to 1993:
B202i, B202i cat	125 to 135 bhp (93 to 101 kW) / 170 to 173 Nm
B202 Turbo, B202 Turbo cat	160 to 175 bhp (119 to 131 kW) / 255 to 270 Nm
B202S, B234i	150 bhp (112 kW) / 212 to 215 Nm
B234L (1991 to 1993)	200 bhp (149 kW) / 330 Nm (manual) or 300 Nm (automatic)
B234R	225 bhp (168 kW) / 350 Nm

  Models from 1994:
B204i	130 bhp (97 kW) / 177 Nm
B204S	150 bhp (112 kW) / 210 Nm
B204L	185 bhp (138 kW) / 283 Nm
B234i	146 bhp (109 kW) / 205 Nm
B234E	170 bhp (127 kW) / 260 Nm
B234LM (manual) and B234LA (automatic)	200 bhp (149 kW) / 323 Nm (manual) or 294 Nm (automatic)
B234R	225 bhp (168 kW) / 342 Nm

Engine codes

The engine code is situated on the left-hand rear of the cylinder block on models manufactured up to 1993, and on the left-hand front of the cylinder block on models manufactured from 1994. The code is stamped directly on the cylinder block.

B = Petrol engine
L = Turbocharged engine with intercooler, power output 1
R = Turbocharged engine with intercooler, power output 2
S = Turbocharged engine
E = Turbocharged engine with intercooler, light-pressure turbocharger
LM = L specification, Manual transmission model
LA = L specification, Automatic transmission model

Camshafts

Drive	Chain from crankshaft
Number of bearings	5 per camshaft
Camshaft bearing journal diameter (outside diameter)	28.922 to 28.935 mm
Endfloat:	
Up to 1993	0.14 to 0.35 mm
1994 on	0.08 to 0.35 mm

Lubrication system

Oil pump type	Bi-rotor type, driven off the crankshaft
Minimum oil pressure at 80°C	2.7 bars at 2000 rpm
Oil pressure warning switch operating pressure	0.3 to 0.5 bars
Clearance between pump outer rotor and timing cover housing	0.03 to 0.08 mm
Oil cooler thermostat opens at:	
B202	90 °C
B234 up to 1993	75 °C
B204 and B234 from 1994	107 °C

Torque wrench settings

	Nm	lbf ft
Automatic transmission driveplate:		
Models up to 1990 (17 mm head)	60	44
Models from 1991 to 1993 (19 mm head)	85	63
Models from 1994 on	95	70
Balance shaft chain idler sprocket	25	18
Balance shaft sprocket	42	31
Big-end bearing cap nuts:		
B202/B204 engines	55	41
B234 engines	48	35
Camshaft bearing cap	15	11
Camshaft sprocket	63	47
Crankshaft pulley bolt:		
1985 to 1990	190	140
1991 on	175	129
Cylinder head bolts:		
Stage 1	60	44
Stage 2	80	59
Stage 3	Angle-tighten a further 90°	Angle-tighten a further 90°
Cylinder head cover	15	11
Engine oil drain plug	25	18
Engine-to-transmission bolts	70	52
Flywheel:		
Models up to 1993 (17 mm head)	60	44
Models up to 1993 (19 mm head)	85	63
Models from 1994 on	80	59
Main bearing cap bolts	110	81
Oil cooler hose unions	18	13
Oil pump on B202 engine (except through-bolts)	8	6
Oil pump on B202 engine (though-bolts)	Same as timing cover bolts - see below	
Piston cooling jet:		
Up to 1993	23	17
1994 on	18	13
Plug for camshaft chain tensioner	22	16
Plug for oil cooler thermostat	60	44
Plug for oil pressure reducing valve	30	22
Sump bolts	22	16
Timing chain tensioner body	63	47
Timing chain tensioner spring plug (1989 on)	22	16
Timing cover bolts:		
Models up to 1993	20	15
Models from 1994 on	25	18

1 General information

How to use this Chapter

This Part of Chapter 2 describes those repair procedures that can reasonably be carried out on the engine while it remains in the car. If the engine has been removed from the car, and is being dismantled as described in Part B, any preliminary dismantling procedures can be ignored.

Note that, while it may be possible physically to overhaul items such as the piston/connecting rod assemblies while the engine is in the car, such tasks are not normally carried out as separate operations. Usually, several additional procedures (not to mention the cleaning of components and of oilways) have to be carried out. For this reason, all such tasks are classed as major overhaul procedures, and are described in Part B of this Chapter.

Part B describes the removal of the engine/transmission from the vehicle, and the full overhaul procedures that can then be carried out.

Engine description

The engine is of in-line four-cylinder, double-overhead camshaft (DOHC), 16-valve type, mounted transversely at the front of the car. The transmission is attached to its left-hand end. The Saab 9000 is fitted with 1985 cc or 2290 cc versions of the engine; later versions of the 1985 cc engine and all 2290 cc engines are fitted with balance shafts in the cylinder block, to smooth out vibrations. All engines are fuel-injected; a Bosch LH-Jetronic fuel injection system is fitted to early models, and a Saab-manufactured "Trionic" engine management system is fitted from 1993 (2290 cc engines) or 1994 (1985 cc engines).

The crankshaft runs in five main bearings. Thrustwashers are fitted to the centre main bearing (upper half only) to control crankshaft endfloat.

The connecting rods rotate on horizontally-split bearing shells at their big-ends. The pistons are attached to the connecting rods by fully-floating gudgeon pins, which are retained in the pistons by circlips. The aluminium-alloy pistons are fitted with three piston rings - two compression rings and an oil control ring.

The cylinder block is of cast-iron, and the cylinder bores are an integral part of the cylinder block. The inlet and exhaust valves are closed by coil springs, and operate in guides pressed into the cylinder head; the valve seat inserts are also pressed into the cylinder head, and can be renewed separately if worn. There are four valves per cylinder.

The camshafts are driven by a single-row timing chain, and they operate the 16 valves via hydraulic cam followers. The hydraulic cam followers maintain a predetermined clearance between the low point of the cam lobe and the end of the valve stem, using hydraulic chambers and a tension spring. The followers are fed with oil from the main engine lubrication circuit.

The balance shafts (fitted to later engines) are driven by a small single-row chain from a sprocket on the front of the crankshaft. The balance shaft chain is located on the outside of the main timing chain.

The engine mountings are of hydraulic type, and provide a progressive damping action.

Lubrication is by means of a bi-rotor oil pump, driven from the front of the crankshaft and located in the timing cover. A relief valve in the timing cover limits the oil pressure at high engine speeds by returning excess oil to the sump. Oil is drawn from the sump through a strainer and, after passing through the oil pump, is forced through an externally-mounted full-flow filter and oil cooler into galleries in the cylinder block/crankcase. From there, the oil is distributed to the crankshaft (main bearings), camshaft bearings and hydraulic cam followers. On Turbo models, it also lubricates the turbocharger. The big-end bearings are supplied with oil via internal drillings in the crankshaft, while the camshaft lobes and valves are lubricated by splash, as are all other engine components. On the B202 (non-balance shaft) engine, the oil filter is located on the rear of the cylinder block. On B204/B234 (balance shaft) engines, the oil filter is located on the front of the cylinder block.

Repair operations possible with the engine in the car

The following work can be carried out with the engine in the car:

a) Compression pressure - testing.
b) Cylinder head cover - removal and refitting.
c) Timing cover - removal and refitting.
d) Timing chain, balance shaft chain (later models), guides and tensioner - removal and refitting.
e) Camshaft oil seals - renewal.
f) Camshafts - removal, inspection and refitting.
g) Cylinder head - removal and refitting.
h) Cylinder head and pistons - decarbonising (refer to Part B of this Chapter).
i) Sump - removal and refitting.
j) Oil pump - removal, overhaul and refitting.
k) Crankshaft oil seals - renewal.
l) Flywheel/driveplate - removal, inspection and refitting.
m) Engine/transmission mountings - inspection and renewal.

2 Compression test - description and interpretation

1 When engine performance is down, or if misfiring occurs which cannot be attributed to the ignition or fuel systems, a compression test can provide diagnostic clues as to the engine's condition. If the test is performed regularly, it can give warning of trouble before any other symptoms become apparent.

2 The engine must be fully warmed-up to normal operating temperature, the battery must be fully charged, and all the spark plugs must be removed (Chapter 1). The aid of an assistant will also be required.

3 On models with an ignition system incorporating a distributor, disable the ignition system by disconnecting the ignition HT coil lead from the distributor cap, and earthing it on the cylinder block. Use a jumper lead or similar wire, to make a good connection. Alternatively, disconnect the low-tension wiring plug from the distributor.

4 On models with Direct Ignition, disable the ignition system by disconnecting the wiring plug from the DI ignition cartridge, referring to Chapter 5B for further information. On models with a catalytic converter, the fuel pump must also be disabled by removing the relevant fuse.

5 Fit a compression tester to the No 1 cylinder spark plug hole - the type of tester which screws into the plug thread is to be preferred.

6 Have the assistant hold the throttle wide open, and crank the engine on the starter motor; after one or two revolutions, the compression pressure should build up to a maximum figure, and then stabilise. Record the highest reading obtained.

7 Repeat the test on the remaining cylinders, recording the pressure in each.

8 All cylinders should produce very similar pressures; a difference of more than 2 bars between any two cylinders indicates a fault. Note that the compression should build up quickly in a healthy engine; low compression on the first stroke, followed by gradually-increasing pressure on successive strokes, indicates worn piston rings. A low compression reading on the first stroke, which does not build up during successive strokes, indicates leaking valves or a blown head gasket (a cracked head could also be the cause). Deposits on the undersides of the valve heads can also cause low compression.

9 Although Saab do not specify exact compression pressures, as a guide, any cylinder pressure of below 10 bars can be considered as less than healthy. Refer to a Saab dealer or other specialist if in doubt as to whether a particular pressure reading is acceptable.

10 If the pressure in any cylinder is low, carry out the following test to isolate the cause. Introduce a teaspoonful of clean oil into that cylinder through its spark plug hole, and repeat the test.

11 If the addition of oil temporarily improves the compression pressure, this indicates that bore or piston wear is responsible for the pressure loss. No improvement suggests that leaking or burnt valves, or a blown head gasket, may be to blame.

12 A low reading only from two adjacent cylinders is almost certainly due to the head gasket having blown between them; the

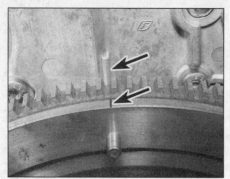

3.1 TDC timing marks (arrowed) on the flywheel and engine backplate

4.1 Disconnecting the wiring connector from the DI ignition cartridge

4.3a Removing the cylinder head cover retaining screws

presence of coolant in the engine oil will confirm this.

13 If one cylinder is about 20 percent lower than the others and the engine has a slightly rough idle, a worn camshaft lobe could be the cause.

14 On completion of the test, refit the spark plugs and reconnect the ignition system and fuel pump as necessary.

3 Top dead centre (TDC) for No 1 piston - locating

1 Timing marks are provided on the flywheel/driveplate perimeter (through the transmission timing hole) and on the sprocket ends of the camshafts. On some later models, the hole in the transmission is blanked off, but on these models, a TDC slot is provided in the crankshaft pulley, together with a timing bar on the timing cover. Also on these later models, TDC marks are provided on the flywheel and engine backplate (rear oil seal housing) - this is helpful if the engine is being dismantled on the bench (see illustration). Note: *With the timing marks correctly aligned, No 1 piston (at the timing chain end of the engine) will be at top dead centre (TDC).*

2 For access to the crankshaft pulley bolt, jack up the front of the car and support on axle stands (see *"Jacking, towing and wheel changing"*). Remove the right-hand front wheel, then remove the front wing moulding, followed by the front wheelarch liner, from under the right-hand front wing. On later models, it will only be necessary to pull out the rubber insert for access to the crankshaft pulley.

3 Using a socket on the crankshaft pulley, turn the engine until the TDC "0" mark on the flywheel/driveplate is aligned with the timing mark on the transmission, or the TDC slot in the crankshaft pulley is aligned with the bar on the timing cover. No 1 piston (at the timing chain end of the engine) will be at the top of its compression stroke. The compression stroke can be confirmed by removing the No 1 spark plug, and checking for compression with a finger over the plug hole as the piston nears

the top of its stroke. As the spark plugs are recessed, the handle end of a screwdriver or suitable tool may be inserted through the plug hole, and used to check for compression instead of your finger.

4 Remove the cylinder head cover with reference to Section 4.

5 Check that the TDC marks on the sprocket ends of the camshafts are aligned with the corresponding TDC marks on the camshaft bearing caps. If necessary, turn the crankshaft to align the marks.

4 Cylinder head cover - removal and refitting

Removal

1 Unscrew the screws and remove the inspection cover or DI ignition cartridge from the centre of the cylinder head cover (refer to Chapter 5B if necessary) (see illustration).

2 On models not fitted with DI ignition, disconnect the HT leads from the spark plugs.

3 Unbolt and remove the cylinder head cover, and remove the gaskets and special split rubber plugs. Note on early models, the split rubber plugs are separate, whereas on later models they are incorporated into the outer gasket (see illustrations). If the cover is stuck, tap it gently with the palm of your hand to free it.

4.3b On later models, the split rubber plugs are incorporated into the outer gasket

Refitting

4 Clean the contact surfaces of the cylinder head cover and cylinder head. On early models, locate the special split rubber plugs on the cylinder head, then apply a 4 mm thick bead of silicone sealant to the corners of the head and over the rubber plugs as shown (see illustration 8.31). On later models, locate the combined rubber ring in the groove in the cylinder head cover.

5 Refit the cylinder head cover, and insert the securing bolts. Tighten the bolts progressively to the specified torque, starting with the bolts at the distributor end, and the central bolt at the timing end.

6 Where applicable, reconnect the HT leads to the spark plugs.

7 Refit the inspection cover or DI ignition cartridge to the centre of the cylinder head cover, and tighten the screws.

5 Timing cover - removal and refitting

Note: *This procedure describes removal of the timing cover, leaving the cylinder head in position. The alternative method (which is less likely to damage the cylinder head gasket) is to remove the cylinder head first.*

Removal

1 Disconnect the battery negative lead. To prevent accidental shorting of the battery

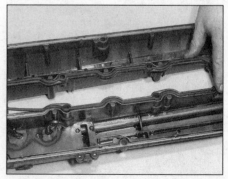

4.3c Removing the cylinder head cover inner gasket

5.9a Unscrewing the lower bracket bolt

5.9b Extract the circlip . . .

5.9c . . . and slide the assembly from the stub

terminals with spanners etc, place a piece of cardboard on top of the battery.

2 On B202 engines, unbolt the bracket for the engine oil dipstick tube on the rear of the cylinder block, and bend the tube to one side.

3 Where applicable, unscrew the bolt securing the coolant pipe above the knock sensor.

4 Apply the handbrake, then jack up the front of the car and support on axle stands (see *"Jacking, towing and wheel changing"*). Remove the right-hand front wheel.

5 Drain the engine oil and coolant, with reference to Chapter 1.

6 Unscrew the retaining screws, and remove the right-hand front wing moulding and front wheelarch liner.

7 Where applicable, remove the separate air

conditioning compressor drivebelt, with reference to Chapter 1.

8 Remove the auxiliary drivebelt with reference to Chapter 1.

9 Unbolt and remove the drivebelt tensioner unit (and where applicable, the mounting bracket). To do this on B204 and B234 engines, first unscrew the lower bracket and upper mounting bolts, then extract the circlip, and slide the assembly from the stub. Unbolt the mounting bracket for access to one of the timing cover retaining bolts **(see illustrations)**.

10 Have an assistant hold the crankshaft stationary, by inserting a wide-bladed screwdriver through the timing hole on the top of the transmission, and jamming the starter ring gear. On later models where the hole is blanked off, engage 4th gear and apply the

handbrake (manual transmission models) or remove the starter motor with reference to Chapter 5A and engage the starter ring gear.

11 Loosen the crankshaft pulley bolt using a long socket bar **(see illustration)**. The bolt is tightened to a high torque.

12 Fully unscrew the crankshaft pulley bolt, and slide the pulley off the end of the crankshaft **(see illustrations)**.

13 Unscrew the coolant pipe and oil cooler pipe supports (as applicable) from the timing cover **(see illustration)**. Withdraw the coolant pipe from the rear of the water pump, where applicable.

14 Unscrew the bolt securing the power steering pump steady bar to the timing cover. Recover the nut from the rear of the timing cover.

5.9d Unscrew the bolts/screws (arrowed) . . .

5.9e . . . and remove the mounting bracket

5.11 Loosening the crankshaft pulley bolt

5.12a Remove the crankshaft pulley bolt . . .

5.12b . . . and slide the pulley off the crankshaft

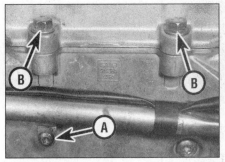

5.13 Pipe support screw (A). Also note two upper bolts (B) securing the timing cover to the cylinder head

5.20a View of the bolts securing the timing cover to the cylinder block

5.20b Removing one of the bolts securing the timing cover to the sump

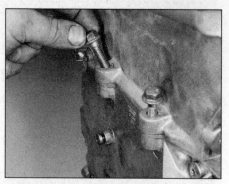

5.20c Removing the upper bolts securing the timing cover to the cylinder head

15 Unscrew the upper bolt for the alternator, and the two securing bolts for the power steering pump, then withdraw the bracket and the steady bar.

16 Loosen the alternator lower mounting bolt, and swivel the alternator to one side.

17 Unscrew the mounting bolts, and remove the alternator and power steering pump mounting bracket from the timing cover.

18 On B202 engines, place a suitable container beneath the oil filter to catch spilt oil, then wipe clean the oil cooler pipe unions on the filter housing. Identify the pipes for position. Unscrew the unions, and disconnect the oil cooler pipes from the housing. Position the pipes clear of the timing cover.

19 On B202 engines, unscrew the bolts and remove the pulley from the water pump drive flange. Lever the coolant pipe away from the rear of the cylinder block, so that it is disconnected from the water pump housing. Position the pipe well clear of the timing cover, and remove the sealing O-ring.

20 Unscrew and remove the bolts securing the timing cover to the cylinder block, sump and cylinder head. Note that the bolts are of different lengths. Note the two upper bolts on the cylinder head and the two lower bolts in the sump (see illustrations).

21 Taking care not to damage the cylinder head gasket, carefully withdraw the timing cover complete with the oil pump from the nose of the crankshaft. Where fitted, remove the gaskets from the cylinder block.

22 Thoroughly clean all traces of gasket and sealant from the contact faces of the timing cover, sump, cylinder head and block. Make sure that the groove in the sump is free of all sealant.

23 Remove the oil pump from the timing cover, with reference to Section 11.

Refitting

24 Apply a bead of suitable sealant to the sump. Locate new gaskets on the cylinder block - if necessary, hold the gaskets in position using a little grease. Where there are no gaskets fitted, apply a bead of suitable sealant to the timing cover flanges (see illustration).

25 Carefully locate the timing cover on the cylinder block, at the same time engaging the oil supply pipe from the block with the hole near the bottom of the timing cover, where applicable.

26 Insert and tighten the timing cover retaining bolts to the specified torque. On B202 engines, do not fit the oil cooler pipe clip retaining bolts at this stage. Insert loosely the upper and lower bolts securing the timing cover to the cylinder head and sump. Check the dimension from the end of the oil supply pipe to the oil pump flange is 25 ± 1 mm (see illustration). Use vernier calipers to make the check

27 On B202 engines, fit a new O-ring to the end of the coolant pipe, then locate it in the water pump housing.

28 Refit the oil pump with reference to Section 11.

29 Tighten the two upper and two lower timing cover bolts to the specified torque.

30 On B202 engines, refit the pulley to the water pump drive flange, and tighten the bolts. Check that the O-rings on the oil cooler pipe unions are in good condition, then reconnect the pipes to the oil filter housing, and tighten the unions to the specified torque.

31 Refit the alternator and power steering pump mounting bracket, and tighten the bolts.

32 Swivel the alternator towards the engine, then refit the alternator/power steering pump bracket and the steady bar, and tighten all bolts to the specified torque.

33 On B202 engines, locate the clips on the oil cooler pipes, then insert the retaining bolts and tighten securely. Insert and tighten the bolt securing the coolant pipe to the top of the timing cover.

34 Slide the crankshaft pulley onto the crankshaft, then insert the pulley bolt. Tighten the bolt to the specified torque, while an assistant holds the crankshaft stationary using a wide-bladed screwdriver inserted in the starter ring gear.

35 On B202 engines, refit the idler pulley and backplate. Insert the centre bolt, but leave it finger-tight at this stage.

36 Refit the drivebelt tensioner assembly, and tighten the bolts. Before locating the assembly on the stub, apply a little grease to the bearing surfaces (see illustration).

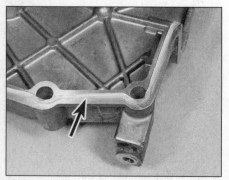

5.24 Sealant on the timing cover flanges

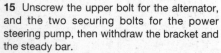
5.26 Oil supply pipe fitting dimension on the B202 engine

25±1 mm   H 28519

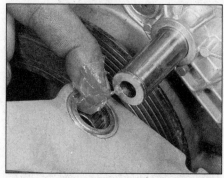

5.36 Apply a little grease to the bearing surfaces

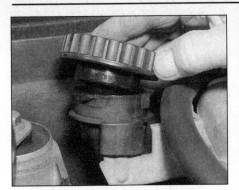

5.46 Removing the engine oil filler cap (model with LH fuel injection)

6.2 Removing the oil pump drive dog from the crankshaft

6.3a "INL" mark on the inlet balance shaft front bearing

37 On B202 engines, fully tighten the idler pulley centre bolt.
38 Refit the auxiliary drivebelt with reference to Chapter 1.
39 Where applicable, refit and tension the air conditioning compressor drivebelt with reference to Chapter 1.
40 Refit the moulding and front wheelarch liner under the right-hand front wing, and tighten the retaining screws.
41 Check that the sump drain plug and the coolant drain plug are tight, and that the splash guard is fitted under the radiator. Refit the right-hand front wheel, and lower the car to the ground.
42 Where applicable, refit and tighten the bolt securing the coolant pipe above the knock sensor.

43 On B202 engines, refit the engine oil dipstick tube bracket, and tighten the bolt.
44 Where applicable, refit the starter motor.
45 Reconnect the battery negative lead.
46 Fill the engine with the correct grade and quantity of oil **(see illustration)**.
47 Refill the cooling system, with reference to Chapter 1.
48 Start the engine, and run it to normal operating temperature. Check for oil and coolant leaks.

6 Timing chain and sprockets - removal, inspection and refitting

Note: *This Section includes the removal of the balance shaft drive chain on later engines.*

Removal

1 Position the crankshaft at TDC compression for No 1 piston (timing chain end of the engine) as described in Section 3.
2 Remove the timing cover as described in Section 5. Also remove the oil pump drive dog from the crankshaft **(see illustration)**.

B204/B234 (balance shaft) engines

3 The balance shafts are "timed" at TDC, but since they rotate at twice the speed of the crankshaft, they may also be correctly "timed" at BDC. Check that the timing marks on the shafts are correctly aligned with the marks on the front of the cylinder block.

> **HAYNES HiNT** *Apply dabs of paint to the chain and sprockets, to ensure correct refitting.*

Note that the balance shaft sprockets are marked "inlet" and "exhaust" for their positions, but both front bearings are marked identically. However, as the bearings are located with single bolts, the "inlet" and "exhaust" marks will always be correctly located at the top of the bearings **(see illustrations)**.
4 Unbolt the balance shaft chain upper guide, then remove the tensioner and side guide **(see illustrations)**.
5 Unbolt the idler from the block, then release the chain from the balance shaft sprockets and crankshaft sprocket. Note that the idler is in two parts **(see illustrations)**.

6.3b "EXH" mark on the exhaust balance shaft front bearing

6.4a Unscrew the bolts . . .

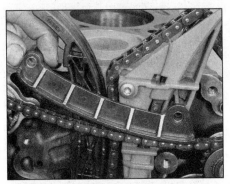

6.4b . . . and remove the balance shaft chain upper guide

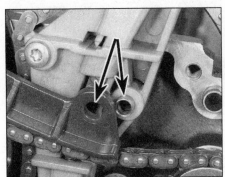

6.4c Note how the upper guide locates on the dowel

6.4d Removing the balance shaft chain tensioner . . .

6.4e . . . and side guide

6.5a Loosen . . .

6.5b . . . and remove the idler retaining bolt (note alignment marks between idler and chain) . . .

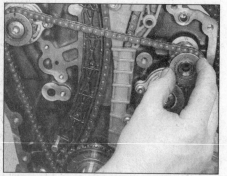

6.5c . . . then withdraw the idler and remove the balance shaft chain

6.5d The idler is in two parts

6 Slide the balance shaft chain sprocket from the front of the crankshaft (see illustration). Note that the word "Saab" is facing outwards.

7 Unscrew the retaining bolts, and remove the sprockets from the ends of the balance shafts. To do this, hold the sprockets stationary with a chain-type oil filter removal tool or similar. Keep the sprockets identified for position.

All engines

8 Remove the cylinder head cover as described in Section 4.

9 Unscrew and remove the timing chain tensioner from the rear of the cylinder head. To do this, first unscrew the centre bolt and remove the spring, then unscrew and remove the tensioner from the cylinder head (see illustrations).

6.6 Removing the balance shaft chain sprocket from the front of the crankshaft

6.9a Unscrew the centre bolt . . .

6.9b . . . and remove the spring . . .

6.9c . . . then unscrew the tensioner . . .

6.9d . . . and remove it from the cylinder head

6.9e The timing chain tensioner components

6.11 Removing the sprocket from the end of the inlet camshaft

6.13a Remove the retaining bolt . . .

6.13b . . . then disengage the sprocket from the chain

10 While holding each camshaft stationary with a spanner on the flats at the flywheel/driveplate end of the camshaft, loosen (but do not remove) the camshaft sprocket securing bolts.

11 Unscrew and remove the bolt, and withdraw the sprocket from the end of the inlet camshaft **(see illustration)**. Hold the timing chain with one hand, and release the sprocket from it with the other hand.

12 Identify each sprocket for position. Note that each sprocket has a projection which engages with a cut-out in the end of the camshaft.

13 Unscrew the bolt and withdraw the sprocket from the end of the exhaust camshaft, then disengage it from the chain **(see illustrations)**.

14 Unscrew the bolts, and remove the timing chain fixed guide from the cylinder block **(see illustrations)**.

15 Disengage the timing chain, then remove the sprocket from the end of the crankshaft. On balance shaft engines, first unbolt the retainer from the cylinder block **(see illustrations)**. If necessary, remove the Woodruff key from the groove in the crankshaft using a screwdriver.

Inspection

16 The timing chain **(see illustration)** (and where applicable, the balance shaft chain) should be renewed if the sprockets are worn, or if the chain is loose and noisy in operation.

It's a good idea to renew the chain as a matter of course if the engine is stripped down for overhaul. The rollers on a very badly worn chain may be slightly grooved. To avoid future problems, if there's any doubt at all about the chain's condition, renew it. The chain tensioner and guides should be examined and if necessary renewed at the same time (refer to Section 7).

17 Examine the teeth on the crankshaft sprocket, camshaft sprockets (and where applicable, the balance shaft sprockets) for wear. Each tooth forms an inverted "V". If worn, the side of each tooth under tension will be slightly concave ("hooked") in shape, when compared with the other side of the tooth (ie one side of the inverted "V" will be concave when compared with the other). If the teeth appear to be worn, the sprockets must be renewed.

Refitting

18 Locate the Woodruff key in the groove in the crankshaft. Tap it fully into the groove, making sure that it is parallel to the crankshaft.

19 Engage the timing chain with the crankshaft sprocket, then locate the crankshaft sprocket on the end of the crankshaft, making sure that it locates correctly on the Woodruff key. Where the timing chain has bright links, locate the single bright link at the bottom of the sprocket, aligned with the slot in the sprocket. On

6.14a Unscrew the bolts . . .

6.14b . . . and remove the timing chain fixed guide

6.15a Removing the timing chain retainer (arrowed) from the cylinder block

6.15b Removing the crankshaft sprocket from the end of the crankshaft

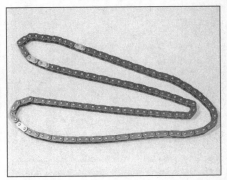

6.16 Timing chain removed from the engine

6.19a The bright link on the timing chain must be aligned with the slot in the sprocket (arrowed)

6.19b Tightening the timing chain retainer bolts

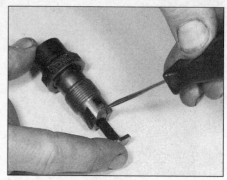

6.25 Setting the timing chain tensioner (B204 engine)

balance shaft engines, refit the retainer and tighten the bolts **(see illustrations)**.

20 Locate the timing chain in the fixed guide, then refit the guide and tighten the bolts.

21 Refit the sprocket to the end of the exhaust camshaft, insert the bolt and finger-tighten it at this stage. **Do not** apply thread-locking fluid to the threads of the bolt.

22 Check that the crankshaft and camshafts are still at their TDC positions.

23 Feed the timing chain up through the cylinder head aperture, and locate it on the exhaust camshaft sprocket, making sure that it is taut between the two sprockets. Check that it is correctly located on the guides. Where the chain has a bright link, make sure that it is aligned with the timing mark.

24 Engage the inlet sprocket with the timing chain so that the engagement cut-out and projection are in alignment, then locate the sprocket on the inlet camshaft, and insert the bolt. Finger-tighten the bolt at this stage. **Do not** apply thread-locking fluid to the threads of the bolt. Where the chain has a bright link, make sure that it is aligned with the timing mark.

25 Set the timing chain tensioner as follows. On models manufactured before 1988, push the plunger fully into the tensioner body, and

turn it to lock it. On later models, use a screwdriver to press down the ratchet, then push the plunger fully into the tensioner, and release the ratchet **(see illustration)**. Check the tensioner washer for condition and renew it if necessary.

26 Insert the tensioner body in the cylinder head, and tighten to the specified torque.

27 On models manufactured up to 1988, trigger the tensioner by pressing the pivoting chain guide against the tensioner, then press the guide against the chain to provide it with its basic tension. When the engine is started, hydraulic pressure will take up any remaining slack.

28 On models manufactured after 1988, insert the spring and plastic guide pin in the tensioner, then fit the plug together with a new O-ring, and tighten it to the specified torque. **Note:** *New tensioners are supplied with the tensioner spring held pre-tensioned with a pin.* **Do not** *remove this pin until after the tensioner has been tightened into the cylinder head. When the engine is started, hydraulic pressure will take up any remaining slack.*

29 Temporarily refit the crankshaft pulley bolt, and rotate the engine two complete turns clockwise. Check that the timing marks still

align correctly. Remove the pulley bolt. Where the chain has bright links, note that these will not now be aligned with the timing marks.

30 Fully tighten the camshaft sprocket bolts to the specified torque, while holding the camshafts with a spanner on the flats.

31 Refit the cylinder head cover with reference to Section 4.

B204/B234 (balance shaft) engines

32 Refit the sprockets to the ends of the balance shafts, and tighten the retaining bolts.

33 Locate the balance shaft chain sprocket on the front of the crankshaft, with the word "Saab" facing outwards.

34 Fit the chain to the sprockets, making sure that the timing marks are aligned correctly **(see illustration)**.

35 Refit the idler to the front of the block, and tighten the retaining bolt.

36 Refit the side guide, tensioner and upper guide to the balance shaft chain **(see illustration)**.

37 Rotate the crankshaft one turn, and check that the balance shaft timing marks are still correctly aligned.

All engines

38 Refit the timing cover with reference to Section 5.

6.34 The balance shaft timing marks must be correctly aligned before refitting the chain

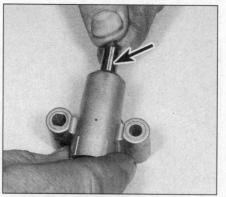

6.36 Depress the balance shaft chain tensioner plunger (arrowed) and retain with a plastic cable-tie

TOOL TiP

Before refitting the tensioner, hold its plunger depressed by fitting a plastic cable-tie around it. Cut the tie after refitting.

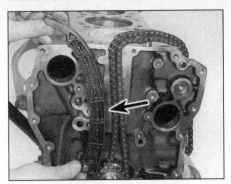

7.2 Removing the pivoting guide from the pin on the cylinder block (B204 engine)

7 Timing chain guides and tensioner - removal, inspection and refitting

Removal

1 Remove the timing chain as described in Section 6. On balance shaft engines, this procedure includes removal of the fixed guide and balance shaft chain guides. On the balance shaft engine, the timing chain need not be removed from the crankshaft sprocket.
2 Unbolt and remove the fixed timing chain guide (B202 engine), and release the pivoting guide from the pin on the cylinder block **(see illustration)**.

Inspection

3 Inspect the chain guides for damage and excessive wear, and renew them if necessary.
4 Clean the tensioner plunger and body, and examine them for damage and wear **(see illustrations)**. On models manufactured after 1988, the plunger may be removed by depressing the ratchet against the spring. If the plunger or body is excessively scored, the complete tensioner should be renewed.

Refitting

5 Locate the pivoting guide on the pin on the cylinder block, then refit the fixed guide and tighten the retaining bolts.
6 Refit the timing chain with reference to Section 6.

8.13 The camshaft bearing caps are marked for position here (arrowed)

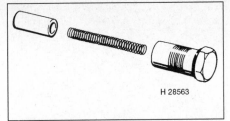

7.4a Timing chain tensioner components on pre-1988 models

8 Camshaft(s) and hydraulic cam followers - removal, inspection and refitting

Note: The following procedure describes removal and refitting of the camshafts and hydraulic cam followers with the cylinder head in position in the car. If it is required to remove the cylinder head for other reasons, the work can be carried out on the bench. In this case, start the procedure at paragraph 12, after removing the cylinder head.

Removal

1 Open the bonnet, and clean the engine around the cylinder head.
2 Apply the handbrake, then jack up the front of the car and support on axle stands (see *"Jacking, towing and wheel changing"*). Remove the right-hand front wheel.
3 Remove the screws, and withdraw the front wing moulding and wheelarch liner from under the right-hand front wing.
4 Disconnect the battery negative lead, and position the lead away from the battery terminal.
5 Disconnect the crankcase breather hose (and where applicable, the vacuum control unit hose), and position them to one side.
5 Unscrew the screws, and remove the inspection cover or DI ignition cartridge from the centre of the cylinder head cover (refer to Chapter 5B if necessary).

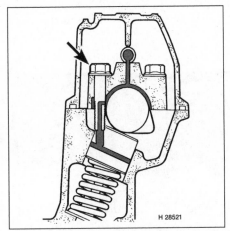

8.14a The camshaft bearing cap inner bolts (arrowed) are hollow for the oil supply to the hydraulic cam followers

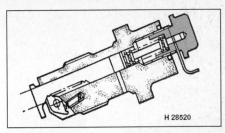

7.4b Cross-section of the timing chain tensioner on 1988-on models

6 Where applicable, disconnect the HT leads from the spark plugs.
7 Where applicable, remove the distributor as described in Chapter 5B, and position it to one side.
8 Unbolt and remove the cylinder head cover, and remove the special split rubber plugs or combined ring. If the cover is stuck, tap it gently with the palm of your hand to free it.
9 Using a socket on the crankshaft pulley, turn the engine until the TDC mark on the flywheel/driveplate is aligned with the timing mark on the transmission, and No 1 piston (at the timing chain end of the engine) is at the top of its compression stroke. On later models, align the slot in the crankshaft pulley with the timing bar on the timing cover. If necessary, refer to Section 3 for more information. Check also that the TDC marks on the sprocket ends of the camshafts are aligned with the corresponding TDC marks on the camshaft bearing caps.
10 Unscrew and remove the timing chain tensioner from the rear of the cylinder head.
11 While holding each camshaft stationary with a spanner on the special flats at the flywheel/driveplate end of the camshaft, unscrew the bolts, then withdraw the sprockets and allow them to rest on the timing chain guides. Note that the sprockets have projections which engage with cut-outs in the ends of the camshafts. The timing chain cannot come off the crankshaft sprocket, since there is a guide located below the sprocket.
12 On B202 engines up to number J082586, remove the oil supply pipes from the camshaft bearing caps; identify them for position, to ensure correct refitting.
13 Check that the camshaft bearing caps and the camshafts are identified for position. The bearing caps are stamped "1" to "5" on the inlet side, and "6" to "10" on the exhaust side - do not confuse these marks with the moulded markings on each cap **(see illustration)**. The inlet camshaft is marked with blue or orange paint, and the letter "G" on the turned surface behind the front bearing journal. The exhaust camshaft is marked with green paint, and the letter "A" on the turned surface behind the front bearing journal.
14 Progressively unscrew the bearing cap bolts, so that the caps are not stressed unduly by the valve springs. Fully remove the bolts and lift off the caps, then lift the camshafts

8.14b Locations (arrowed) of the black-headed inner bearing cap bolts incorporating oil drillings

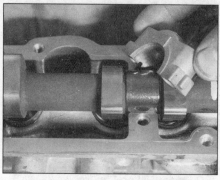

8.14c Removing a camshaft bearing cap

8.15a Removing a hydraulic cam follower

from the cylinder head. Note that the bearing cap inner bolts (except at the timing chain end) have black heads, and incorporate drillings for the oil supply to the hydraulic cam followers; always make sure that the correct bolts are fitted **(see illustrations)**. Keep the camshafts identified for location.

15 Obtain sixteen small, clean plastic containers, and number them "1I" to "8I" (inlet) and "1E" to "8E" (exhaust). Alternatively, divide a larger container into sixteen compartments, similarly marked for the inlet and exhaust camshafts. Using a rubber sucker or a magnet, withdraw each hydraulic cam follower in turn, and place it in its respective container **(see illustrations)**. **Do not** interchange the cam followers. To prevent the oil draining from the hydraulic cam followers, pour fresh oil into the containers until it covers them.

Inspection

16 Examine the camshaft bearing surfaces and cam lobes for signs of wear ridges and scoring. Renew the camshaft if any of these conditions are apparent. Examine the condition of the bearing surfaces on the camshaft journals, in the camshaft bearing caps, and in the cylinder head. If the head or cap bearing surfaces are worn excessively, the cylinder head will need to be renewed. If the necessary measuring equipment is available, camshaft bearing journal wear can be checked

by direct measurement and comparison with the specifications given.

17 Camshaft endfloat can be measured by locating each camshaft in the cylinder head, refitting the sprockets, and using feeler blades between the shoulder on the front of the camshaft and the front bearing surface on the cylinder head.

18 Check the hydraulic cam followers where they contact the bores in the cylinder head for wear, scoring and pitting. Occasionally, a hydraulic cam follower may be noisy and require renewal, and this will have been noticed when the engine was running. It is not easy to check a cam follower for internal damage or wear once it has been removed; if there is any doubt, the complete set of cam followers should be renewed.

19 Clean the internal drillings of the hollow camshaft bearing cap bolts, to ensure oil supply to the hydraulic cam followers.

Refitting

20 Lubricate the bores for the hydraulic cam followers in the cylinder head, and the followers themselves, then insert them in their original positions **(see illustration)**.

21 Lubricate the bearing surfaces of the camshafts in the cylinder head.

22 Locate the camshafts in their correct positions in the cylinder head, so that the valves of No 1 cylinder (timing chain end) are closed, and the valves of No 4 cylinder are "rocking". The timing marks on the sprocket ends of the camshafts should be pointing upwards.

23 Lubricate the bearing surfaces in the

bearing caps, then locate them in their correct positions and insert the retaining bolts. Make sure that the oil supply bolts are in their correct positions (see illustration 8.14b). Progressively tighten the bolts to the specified torque.

24 On B202 engines up to number J082586, refit the oil supply pipes to their correct positions on the camshaft bearing caps.

25 Check that each camshaft is at its TDC position - the timing marks are located on the front of the camshafts, and must be aligned with the mark on the bearing caps.

26 Check that the TDC "0" mark on the flywheel/driveplate is still aligned with the timing mark on the transmission. On later models, check that the TDC slot in the crankshaft pulley is aligned with the timing bar on the timing cover.

27 Locate the sprockets on the camshafts, fitting the exhaust one first, followed by the inlet one. Do not fully tighten the bolts at this stage. Check that the timing chain is correctly located on the guides and sprockets.

28 Refit the timing chain tensioner, with reference to Section 6.

29 Using a socket on the crankshaft pulley, rotate the engine two complete turns clockwise, then check that the TDC timing marks are still correctly aligned.

30 Fully tighten the camshaft sprocket retaining bolts to the specified torque, while holding them stationary with a spanner on the special flats provided **(see illustration)**.

8.15b Hydraulic cam follower removed from the cylinder head. Cam followers should be stored in an oil bath while removed

8.20 Oiling a hydraulic cam follower prior to fitting

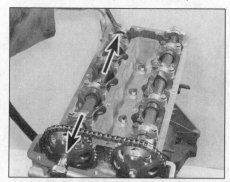

8.30 Tightening the camshaft sprocket retaining bolts, using a spanner on the camshaft flats to hold it stationary

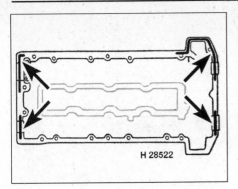

8.31 Areas to apply silicone sealant on the cylinder head cover

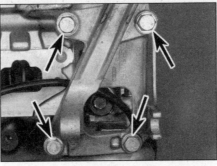

9.8 The bolts (arrowed) securing the right-hand engine mounting bracket to the cylinder head

9.13a Unscrew the mounting bolts . . .

9.13b . . . and remove the air conditioning compressor mounting bracket

31 Clean the contact surfaces of the cylinder head cover and cylinder head. On early models, locate the special split rubber plugs on the cylinder head, then apply a 4 mm thick bead of silicone sealant to the corners of the head and over the rubber plugs as shown **(see illustration)**. On later models, fit the rubber ring on the special groove in the cylinder head cover.

32 Refit the cylinder head cover, and insert the securing bolts. Tighten the bolts progressively to the specified torque, starting with the bolts at the flywheel/driveplate end, and the central bolt at the timing end.

33 Where applicable, check that the distributor rotor is aligned with the timing mark, then refit the distributor and cap with reference to Chapter 5B. Check that the vacuum hose is fitted correctly.

34 Where applicable, reconnect the HT leads to the spark plugs.

35 Refit the inspection cover or DI ignition cartridge to the centre of the cylinder head cover, and tighten the securing screws.

36 Reconnect the crankcase breather hose.

37 Refit the front wing moulding and wheelarch liner under the right-hand front wing, and tighten the screws.

38 Refit the right-hand front wheel, and lower the car to the ground.

39 Reconnect the battery negative lead.

9 Cylinder head - removal and refitting

Removal

1 Open the bonnet, and clean the engine around the cylinder head.

2 Apply the handbrake, then jack up the front of the car and support on axle stands (see *"Jacking, towing and wheel changing"*). Remove the right-hand front wheel.

3 Remove the screws, and withdraw the front wing moulding and wheelarch liner from under the right-hand front wing.

4 Remove the central panel from under the radiator, then drain the cooling system with reference to Chapter 1. Refit and tighten the drain plug.

5 Unscrew and remove the electric cooling fan housing lower mounting bolt.

6 Disconnect the battery negative lead, and position the lead away from the battery terminal.

7 On early models, loosen the clips and disconnect the hoses from the coolant expansion tank on the right-hand side of the engine compartment. Unscrew the mounting bolt, then release the cable-tie and separate the connector. Remove the expansion tank from the engine compartment.

8 Unbolt and remove the torque arm (and where necessary, the mounting) from the upper right-hand end of the engine **(see illustration)**.

9 Where necessary, remove the screws for the power steering reservoir, and move it to one side. Release any cable-ties from the hoses.

10 On early models, remove the separate air conditioning compressor drivebelt with reference to Chapter 1. On later models, remove the auxiliary drivebelt with reference to Chapter 1.

11 Disconnect the wiring plug from the air conditioning compressor (where applicable), then unscrew the mounting bolt and remove the compressor from the bracket.

12 Position a cloth on the radiator crossmember, then disconnect the bottom hose from the water pump, and place the compressor and hose on the crossmember.

13 Unbolt and remove the air conditioning compressor mounting bracket from the cylinder head **(see illustrations)**.

14 Where applicable, disconnect the wiring from the lambda sensor, at the connecting plug beneath the inlet manifold. Release the wiring from the clips on the cylinder head, and place the wiring to one side on the engine subframe.

15 On non-Turbo models, unscrew the nuts securing the exhaust downpipe to the exhaust manifold, and lower the pipe.

16 On Turbo models, remove the turbocharger as described in Chapter 4A. Remove the turbo solenoid valve, and position it to one side by the airflow meter. Loosen the hose clips, and remove the turbo delivery pipe. Loosen the hose clips and remove the turbo inlet hose from the compressor, and also

disconnect the solenoid valve hoses. The hoses should be marked "C" for the compressor and "W" for the wastegate.

17 Disconnect the electric cooling fan wiring, then unscrew the upper mounting nuts and withdraw the cooling fan assembly from the rear of the radiator.

18 Loosen the clip and disconnect the radiator top hose from the thermostat housing on the left-hand end of the cylinder head.

19 Disconnect the crankcase breather hose and the vacuum control unit hose (where applicable), and position them to one side.

20 Unscrew the screws, and remove the inspection cover or DI ignition cartridge from the centre of the cylinder head cover.

21 Where applicable, disconnect the HT leads from the spark plugs.

22 Where applicable, remove the distributor with reference to Chapter 5B, and position to one side.

23 Disconnect the wiring from the temperature sensor on the thermostat housing.

24 Loosen the clip, and disconnect the heater hose from the thermostat housing.

25 Unscrew the mounting bolts for the fuel pressure regulator bracket, and swivel the bracket, complete with sensor and hoses, out of the way.

26 Unbolt the right-hand engine mounting bracket torque arm from the cylinder head.

27 Where applicable, unscrew the upper bolts for the inlet manifold steady bars on each side of the manifold.

9.35 Removing a cylinder head bolt

9.37 Removing a cylinder head locating dowel

9.45 Position a new cylinder head gasket on the cylinder block

28 On models fitted with a two-section inlet manifold, disconnect the air conditioning valve hose and the crankcase breather hose, and (where applicable) unbolt the dipstick tube bracket. Detach the upper inlet manifold from the hoses, then tilt it to one side and secure the hoses with cable-ties.

29 Unscrew the inlet manifold-to-cylinder head mounting bolts, and move the complete manifold assembly to the rear of the engine compartment. Recover the gasket. Leave all wiring, hoses and cables (as applicable) connected to the inlet manifold assembly.

30 Unbolt and remove the cylinder head cover, and remove the special split rubber plugs from the cylinder head. If it is stuck, tap it gently with the palm of your hand to free it.

31 Using a socket on the crankshaft pulley, turn the engine until the TDC mark on the flywheel/driveplate or crankshaft pulley is aligned with the timing mark on the transmission or timing cover, and No 1 piston (at the timing chain end of the engine) is at the top of its compression stroke. If necessary, refer to Section 3 for more information. Check also that the TDC marks on the sprocket ends of the camshafts are aligned with the corresponding TDC marks on the camshaft bearing caps.

32 Unscrew and remove the timing chain tensioner from the rear of the cylinder head.

33 While holding each camshaft stationary with a spanner on the special flats at the flywheel/driveplate end of the camshaft, unscrew the bolts, then withdraw the sprockets and allow them to rest on the timing chain guides. Alternatively, remove the sprockets, after identifying them for position. Note that on B204/B234 engines, the timing chain will not come off the crankshaft sprocket, as there is a retainer located near the bottom of the sprocket. On B202 engines, keep the chain on the sprocket by tying it at the top of the guides.

34 Unscrew and remove the two bolts securing the timing cover to the cylinder head. The bolts screw into the bottom of the head.

35 Working in the reverse of the sequence shown in illustration 9.50a, progressively slacken the ten cylinder head bolts by half a turn at a time, until all bolts can be unscrewed by hand **(see illustration)**. The bolts require

the use of a Torx socket to unscrew them, as they have six external splines.

36 With all the cylinder head bolts removed, check that the timing chain is positioned so that the pivoting chain guide will not obstruct removal of the head. Lift the cylinder head directly from the top of the cylinder block, and place it on the workbench. If necessary, enlist the help of an assistant, since the cylinder head is quite heavy. If the cylinder head is stuck, try rocking it slightly to free it from the gasket - **do not** insert a screwdriver or similar tool between the gasket joint, otherwise the contact faces will be damaged. The head is located on dowels, so do not try to free it by tapping it sideways.

37 Remove the gasket from the top of the block, noting the two locating dowels. If the locating dowels are a loose fit, remove them and store them with the head for safe-keeping **(see illustration)**. Do not discard the gasket - it may be needed for identification purposes.

38 If the cylinder head is to be dismantled for overhaul, remove the camshafts as described in Section 8.

Preparation for refitting

39 The mating faces of the cylinder head and cylinder block must be perfectly clean before refitting the head. Use a hard plastic or wood scraper to remove all traces of gasket and carbon; also clean the piston crowns. Take particular care during the cleaning operations, as the soft aluminium alloy is damaged easily. Also, make sure that the carbon is not allowed to enter the oil and water passages - this is particularly important for the lubrication system, as carbon could block the oil supply to the engine's components. Using adhesive tape and paper, seal the water, oil and bolt holes in the cylinder block.

 HAYNES HiNT *To prevent carbon entering the gap between the pistons and bores, smear a little grease in the gap. After cleaning each piston, use a small brush to remove all traces of grease and carbon from the gap, then wipe away the remainder with a clean rag.*

Clean all the pistons in the same way.

40 Check the mating surfaces of the cylinder block and the cylinder head for nicks, deep scratches and other damage. If slight, they may be removed carefully with a file, but if excessive, machining may be the only alternative to renewal.

41 If warpage of the cylinder head gasket surface is suspected, use a straight-edge to check it for distortion. Refer to Part B of this Chapter if necessary.

42 Check the condition of the cylinder head bolts, and particularly their threads, whenever they are removed. Wash the bolts in suitable solvent, and wipe them dry. Check each for any sign of visible wear or damage, renewing any bolt if necessary. Measure the length of each bolt, and compare with the length of a new bolt. Although Saab do not actually specify that the bolts must be renewed, it is strongly recommended that the bolts are renewed as a complete set if the engine has completed a high mileage.

Refitting

43 Where removed, refit the camshafts with reference to Section 8.

44 Wipe clean the mating surfaces of the cylinder head and cylinder block/crankcase. Check that the two locating dowels are in position on the cylinder block.

45 Position a new gasket on the cylinder block surface, making sure that it is fitted the correct way round **(see illustration)**.

46 Check that each camshaft is at its TDC position - the timing marks are located on the front of the camshaft, and must be aligned with the marks on the bearing caps.

47 Check that the TDC "0" mark on the flywheel/driveplate is still aligned with timing mark on the transmission.

48 Check that the timing chain is located correctly on the chain guides, then carefully lower the cylinder head onto the block, aligning it with the locating dowels.

49 Apply a smear of grease to the threads, and to the underside of the heads, of the cylinder head bolts. Insert the bolts, and screw them in finger-tight.

50 Working progressively and in the sequence shown, tighten the cylinder head

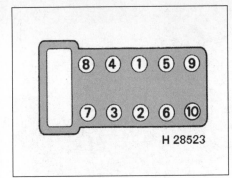

9.50a Cylinder head bolt tightening sequence

9.50b Tightening the cylinder head bolts with a torque wrench

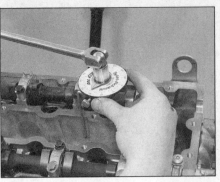

9.52 Using an angle-measuring gauge to tighten the cylinder head bolts through their Stage 3 angle

bolts to their Stage 1 torque setting, using a torque wrench **(see illustrations)**.

51 Using the same sequence, tighten the cylinder head bolts to their Stage 2 torque setting.

52 With all the cylinder head bolts tightened to their Stage 2 setting, working again in the given sequence, angle-tighten the bolts further through the specified Stage 3 angle, using a socket and extension bar. It is recommended that an angle-measuring gauge is used during this stage of the tightening, to ensure accuracy **(see illustration)**.

> **HAYNES HINT**
> *If a gauge is not available, use white paint to make alignment marks between the bolt head and cylinder head prior to tightening; the marks can then be used to check that the bolt has been rotated through the correct angle during tightening.*

53 Insert and tighten the two bolts securing the timing cover to the cylinder head.

54 Locate the sprockets on the camshafts, fitting the exhaust one first, followed by the inlet one. Do not fully tighten the bolts at this stage. Check that the timing chain is correctly located on the guides and sprockets.

55 Refit the timing chain tensioner with reference to Section 6.

56 Using a socket on the crankshaft pulley, rotate the engine two complete turns clockwise, then check that the TDC timing marks are still correctly aligned.

57 Fully tighten the camshaft sprocket retaining bolts to the specified torque, while holding each camshaft stationary using a spanner on the special flats.

58 Clean the contact surfaces of the cylinder head cover and cylinder head. Locate the special split rubber plugs on the cylinder head, then apply a 4 mm thick bead of silicone sealant to the corners of the head and over the rubber plugs as shown (see illustration 8.31).

59 Refit the cylinder head cover, and insert the securing bolts. Tighten the bolts progressively to the specified torque, starting

with the bolts at the flywheel/driveplate end, and the central bolt at the timing end.

60 Refit the inlet manifold to the cylinder head, together with a new gasket, and tighten the mounting bolts.

61 On models with a two-section inlet manifold, refit the manifold to the hoses, then refit the dipstick tube bracket, and reconnect the crankcase breather hose and air conditioning valve hose.

62 Where applicable, insert and tighten the upper bolts for the inlet manifold steady bars on each side of the manifold.

63 Refit the right-hand engine mounting bracket torque arm to the cylinder head, and tighten the bolts.

64 Refit the fuel pressure regulator bracket, complete with sensor, and tighten the mounting bolts.

65 Reconnect the heater hose to the thermostat housing, and tighten the clip.

66 Reconnect the wiring to the temperature sensor on the thermostat housing.

67 Where applicable, refit the distributor with reference to Chapter 5B.

68 Where applicable, reconnect the HT leads to the spark plugs.

69 Refit the inspection cover or DI ignition cartridge to the centre of the cylinder head cover, and tighten the securing screws.

70 Reconnect the crankcase breather hose and the vacuum control unit hose (where applicable).

71 Reconnect the radiator top hose to the thermostat housing, and tighten the clip,

72 Refit the electric cooling fan assembly to the rear of the radiator, and tighten the mounting nuts. Reconnect the wiring.

73 On Turbo models, refit the turbocharger and associated components, with reference to Chapter 4A.

74 On non-Turbo models, refit the exhaust downpipe to the exhaust manifold, together with a new gasket, and tighten the nuts.

75 Reconnect the lambda sensor wiring to the connecting plug beneath the inlet manifold. Secure the wiring in the clips on the cylinder head, and use a cable-tie to secure the wiring to the engine lifting eye.

76 Refit the air conditioning compressor mounting bracket and compressor, and

tighten the mounting bolts. Reconnect the bottom hose to the water pump, and tighten the clip. Reconnect the wiring plug, making sure that it is located well clear of the compressor pulley.

77 Refit the auxiliary drivebelt with reference to Chapter 1.

78 On early models, refit the air conditioning drivebelt with reference to Chapter 1.

79 Where necessary, refit the power steering reservoir, and tighten the mounting screws. Reconnect the cable-ties to the hoses.

80 Refit the torque arm/mounting to the upper right-hand end of the engine, and tighten the mounting bolts.

81 On early models, refit the coolant expansion tank to the right-hand side of the engine compartment, and tighten the bolt. Reconnect the hoses and tighten the clips. Plug in the wiring connector, and use a cable-tie to secure the wiring to the hoses.

82 Reconnect the battery negative lead.

83 Refit the central panel under the radiator, followed by the right-hand front wing wheelarch liner and moulding.

84 Refit the right-hand front wheel, and lower the car to the ground.

85 Refill the cooling system, with reference to Chapter 1.

86 Start the engine, observing the precautions given in Chapter 2B, Section 20.

10 Sump - removal and refitting

Removal

1 Firmly apply the handbrake, then jack up the front of the car and support it on axle stands (see *"Jacking, towing and wheel changing"*). Disconnect the battery negative lead.

2 Drain the engine oil, then clean and refit the engine oil drain plug, tightening it to the specified torque. If the engine is nearing its service interval when the oil and filter are due for renewal, it is recommended that the filter is also removed, and a new one fitted. After reassembly, the engine can then be refilled with fresh oil. Refer to Chapter 1 for further information.

10.9 Engine rear steady bar (arrowed)

10.20a Remove the screws and withdraw the baffle plate from the sump . . .

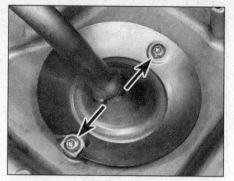

10.20b . . . then unscrew the screws (arrowed) . . .

3 Remove the right-hand front wheel, then remove the front wing moulding, followed by the front section of the wheelarch liner.

4 Working under the wheelarch, unscrew and remove the right-hand front and rear engine mounting nuts.

5 Refer to Chapter 4, and remove the lambda sensor and the exhaust front downpipe.

6 Unscrew and remove the through-bolt securing the torque arm to the right-hand upper engine mounting.

7 Attach a hoist to the engine lifting eyes, then raise the right-hand side of the engine until it is clear of the mountings. Make sure that the hoist is strong enough to support the weight of the engine while the sump is removed.

8 Unscrew and remove the lower bolt and stud securing the sump to the transmission.

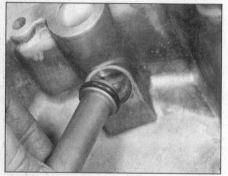

10.20c . . . and remove the pick-up strainer and tube from the sump

To remove the stud, first loosen the nut several threads, then tighten a further nut onto the stud, and unscrew the stud by loosening the inner nut.

9 Where applicable, working under the car, unbolt and remove the bracket for the rear engine mounting and steady bar **(see illustration)**.

10 Where applicable on early models, unbolt the dipstick tube bracket, and pull the tube and seal from the rear of the sump.

11 Where fitted, disconnect the wiring from the oil level sensor, then unscrew the mounting bolts and remove the sensor from the sump. Recover the gasket.

12 Where applicable, unscrew the bolts, and remove the bracket and oil return pipe for the turbo unit from the sump.

13 Under the car, pull down the splash plate for access to the two rubber plugs in the bottom of the transmission. Prise out the plugs, then use an extension bar and socket to unscrew the rear bolts securing the sump to the cylinder block.

14 Working under the right-hand wing, remove the front and rear panels for access to the rear of the engine.

15 Using a socket through the right-hand subframe, unscrew the bolt securing the right-hand wheelarch steady bar to the subframe.

16 Unscrew and remove the two bolts securing the front right-hand corner of the subframe to the underbody.

17 Using a lever, force the corner of the

subframe down, and insert a wooden block about 3 cm thick between the subframe and underbody.

18 Progressively unscrew and remove the bolts securing the sump to the cylinder block, leaving one or two bolts in position to prevent the sump falling. On some models, it may be necessary to remove an exhaust heat shield first.

19 Remove the remaining bolts, and lower the sump to the ground. If necessary, break the joint between the sump and crankcase by striking the sump with the palm of your hand.

20 While the sump is removed, take the opportunity to remove and check the oil pump pick-up/strainer for signs of clogging or damage - also check the O-ring on balance shaft engines. If necessary, unbolt the pick-up/strainer, and clean or renew it. On B204 and B234 (balance shaft) engines, remove the transfer tube by pulling it down from the crankcase, then pulling it sideways from the oil filter housing. Remove the O-ring seals from each end of the tube **(see illustrations)**.

Refitting

21 Clean all traces of sealant from the mating surfaces of the cylinder block/crankcase and sump, then use a clean rag to wipe out the sump and the engine's interior. Refit the oil pump pick-up/strainer on the B202 engine, or the transfer tube (together with new O-rings) on balance shaft engines.

22 Ensure that the sump and cylinder block/crankcase mating surfaces are clean

10.20d On balance shaft engines, pull the transfer tube down from the crankcase . . .

10.20e . . . and pull it sideways from the oil filter housing

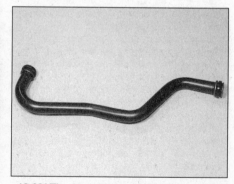

10.20f The transfer tube on balance shaft engines

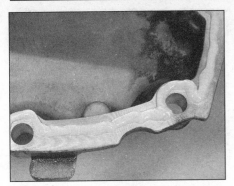

10.22 Apply a bead of sealant to the sump flange

11.8a Using circlip pliers to remove the oil pump cover circlip

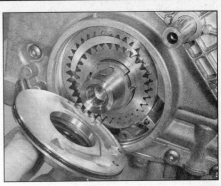

11.8b Withdrawing the oil pump cover from the timing cover

and dry, then apply a bead of suitable sealant to the sump flange **(see illustration)**.

23 Offer up the sump and refit its retaining bolts, tightening them progressively to the specified torque.

24 Refit the rubber plugs to the transmission case, and bend the splash plate to its original position. Where necessary, refit the exhaust heat shield.

25 Remove the wooden block, then refit the two bolts securing the front right-hand corner of the subframe to the underbody. Tighten the bolts.

26 Refit and tighten the bolt securing the right-hand wheelarch steady bar to the subframe.

27 Refit the bracket and oil return pipe for the turbo unit to the sump, and tighten the mounting bolts. Make sure that the seal is correctly positioned on the pipe.

28 Clean the contact surfaces, then refit the oil level sensor to the sump, together with a new gasket. Tighten the screws securely.

29 Check the seal and if necessary renew it, then refit the dipstick tube to the rear of the sump, and tighten the bracket bolts.

30 Refit the bracket for the rear engine mounting and steady bar, and tighten the mounting bolts.

31 Refit and tighten the lower bolt and stud securing the sump to the transmission.

32 Lower the engine onto the mounting studs, and remove the hoist.

33 Where applicable, refit the bracket to the cylinder head, then insert and tighten the

through-bolt securing the torque arm to the right-hand upper engine mounting.

34 Refit the exhaust front downpipe and lambda sensor, with reference to Chapter 4.

35 Refit and tighten the engine mounting nuts.

36 Refit the rear panel and front section of the wheelarch liner and moulding under the right-hand front wheelarch.

37 Refit the right-hand front wheel, and lower the car to the ground.

38 Fill the engine with the correct quantity and grade of oil as described in Chapter 1.

39 Start the engine, and run it to normal operating temperature. Check the joint between the sump and crankcase for signs of oil leaks.

11 Oil pump - removal, inspection and refitting

Removal

1 Apply the handbrake, then jack up the front of the car and support on axle stands (see *"Jacking, towing and wheel changing"*). Remove the right-hand front wheel.

2 Remove the screws, and remove the front wing moulding followed by the front wheelarch liner.

3 Where applicable (B202 engines with separate air conditioning compressor drivebelt) remove the air conditioning compressor drivebelt, with reference to Chapter 1.

4 Remove the auxiliary drivebelt with reference to Chapter 1.

5 Unscrew and remove the centre bolt from

the crankshaft pulley. To do this, the crankshaft must be held stationary using one of the following methods. On manual transmission models, have an assistant depress the brake pedal and engage 4th gear. Alternatively, insert a wide-bladed screwdriver through the timing aperture (early models) on the top of the transmission, and engage it with the starter ring gear to prevent the crankshaft turning. On automatic transmission models, use the latter method only. Where the timing aperture is blanked off, remove the **starter motor** with reference to Chapter 5A for access to the starter ring gear.

6 Pull the crankshaft pulley and hub from the end of the crankshaft. If it is tight, careful use of two levers may be required.

7 On B202 engines, progressively unscrew the bolts securing the oil pump to the cylinder block, and withdraw it over the nose of the crankshaft. Prise the O-ring seal from the groove in the rear of the oil pump casing.

8 On B204/B234 engines, extract the large circlip, then withdraw the oil pump cover from the timing cover. Note that the circlip has a high tension, and a large pair of circlip pliers will be required to compress it. Also note the alignment arrows on the cover and timing cover **(see illustrations)**.

9 Remove the O-ring seal from the groove in the cover **(see illustration)**.

10 Note the position of the crankshaft oil seal in the oil pump cover, then prise it out with a screwdriver **(see illustration)**.

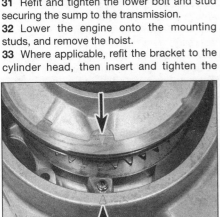

11.8c Alignment arrows on the oil pump cover

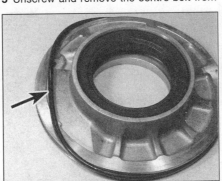

11.9 Removing the O-ring seal from the groove in the oil pump cover

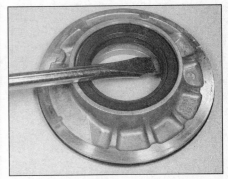

11.10 Prising out the crankshaft oil seal from the oil pump cover

11.12a Removing the inner rotor . . .

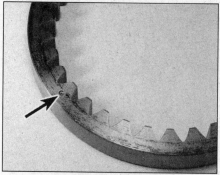

11.12b . . . and outer rotor from the timing cover. Note that the position mark (arrowed) is facing outwards

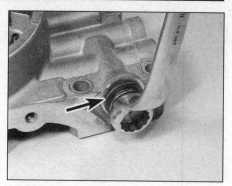

11.13a Unscrew the plug (arrowed) . . .

Inspection

11 Wipe clean the inner faces of the pump rotors, and identify them for position with a marker pen. It is important that the rotors remain in their correct original positions on reassembly. Note that on balance shaft engines, the outer rotor position is identified by the punch hole facing outwards.

12 Remove the rotors from the timing cover (oil pump body), keeping them identified for position **(see illustrations)**.

13 Unscrew the plug, and remove the relief valve spring and plunger, noting which way round they are fitted **(see illustrations)**. Recover the plug washer.

14 Clean all components, and examine them for wear and damage. Examine the pump rotors and body for signs of wear ridges and scoring. Using a feeler blade check the clearance between the outer rotor and the timing cover, with reference to the Specifications **(see illustration)**. If worn excessively, the complete pump assembly must be renewed.

15 Examine the relief valve plunger for signs of wear or damage, and renew if necessary. The condition of the relief valve spring can only be measured by comparing it with a new one; if there is any doubt about its condition, it should also be renewed.

16 If there are any signs of dirt or sediment in the oil pump, it will be necessary to remove the sump, and clean the pick-up/strainer (see Section 11).

17 Insert the relief valve plunger and spring, then refit the plug together with a new washer, and tighten the plug.

18 Lubricate the rotors with fresh engine oil, then insert them in the oil pump body in their original positions. The outer rotor must be positioned with the identification mark facing outwards.

Refitting

19 Wipe clean the oil seal seating in the oil pump casing, then drive a new oil seal into the casing, making sure that it enters squarely and is fitted in the previously-noted position.

20 On B204/B234 engines, fit a new O-ring seal, then insert the oil pump in the timing cover, making sure that the alignment arrows point to each other. Refit the large circlip in the groove with its chamfer facing outwards, and the opening facing downwards.

21 On B202 engines, locate a new O-ring seal in the oil pump groove, then clean the contact surfaces of the oil pump and cylinder block. Locate the oil pump over the nose of the crankshaft, and onto the dowels. Insert the bolts, and tighten them progressively to the specified torque. Note that two of the bolts are through-bolts into the cylinder block, and are tightened to the same torque as the timing cover bolts.

22 Locate the crankshaft pulley and hub on the end of the crankshaft. Insert the centre bolt and tighten it to the specified torque, holding the crankshaft stationary using one of

the methods described in paragraph 5.

23 Refit the auxiliary drivebelt with reference to Chapter 1.

24 Where applicable, refit the air conditioning compressor drivebelt, with reference to Chapter 3.

25 Refit the wing liner and moulding, and tighten the screws.

26 Refit the right-hand front wheel, and lower the car to the ground.

27 Before running the engine, disconnect the ignition wiring harness to the distributor or DI ignition cartridge to disable the ignition system, then spin the engine on the starter motor until oil pressure is restored and the oil pressure warning light is extinguished. Reconnect the wiring harness, and run the engine to check for oil leaks.

12 Oil cooler - removal and refitting

Removal

1 An oil cooler is fitted to Turbo models only. It is connected to ports on an adapter fitted to the oil filter, and the adapter also incorporates an oil thermostat.

2 To remove the oil cooler, first jack up the front of the car and support on axle stands (see *"Jacking, towing and wheel changing"*). If necessary, drain the engine oil as described in Chapter 1, then refit and tighten the drain plug.

3 Position a suitable container beneath the oil cooler on the right-hand side of the engine compartment. Unscrew the unions from the top and bottom of the oil cooler, and disconnect the oil supply and return hoses. Allow any oil to drain into the container.

4 Unscrew the mounting bolts and remove the oil cooler. On early models, the lower mounting bolt holes are slotted, and therefore the lower bolts need only be loosened. Lift the oil cooler from engine compartment.

Refitting

5 Refitting is a reversal of removal, but tighten the unions to the specified torque. Fill the engine with oil with reference to Chapter 1. On completion, start the engine and run it at a fast

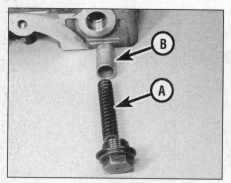

11.13b . . . and remove the relief valve spring (A) and plunger (B)

11.14 Checking the clearance between the oil pump outer rotor and the timing cover

13.2 Disconnecting the wiring from the oil pressure switch

15.8 Fitting a new oil seal to the oil pump cover

idle speed for several minutes, to allow the oil to fill the oil cooler. Check and if necessary top-up the engine oil level with reference to Chapter 1.

13 Oil pressure warning light switch - removal and refitting

Removal

1 On non-balance shaft engines, the switch is screwed into the top of the oil filter adapter on the rear of the cylinder block. On balance shaft engines, the switch is screwed into the rear of the cylinder block, beneath the inlet manifold. First jack up the front of the car, and support on axle stands (see "Jacking, towing and wheel changing").
2 Disconnect the wiring from the switch terminal (see illustration).
3 Unscrew the switch from the oil filter adapter or cylinder block. Be prepared for slight loss of oil. If the switch is to be left removed for any length of time, plug the hole, to prevent the entry of dust and dirt.

Refitting

4 Wipe clean the threads of the switch and the location aperture, then insert the switch and tighten securely.
5 Reconnect the wiring to the switch terminal.
6 Start the engine and check for leakage, then lower the car to the ground.

14 Oil level sensor - removal and refitting

Removal

1 An oil level sensor is fitted to models with a trip computer. The sensor is located on the rear of the sump, and consists of a float and transducer. A warning light on the instrument panel is illuminated when the ignition is switched on and the engine oil level is low. After illuminating the warning light, the sensor will not operate again until the ignition has been switched off for at least 5 minutes.
2 Apply the handbrake, then jack up the front

of the car and support on axle stands (see "Jacking, towing and wheel changing").
3 Drain the engine oil with reference to Chapter 1.
4 Disconnect the wiring from the oil level sensor on the rear of the sump.
5 Wipe clean the area around the sensor, then unscrew the mounting screws and withdraw the sensor from the sump. Remove the gasket.

Refitting

6 Refitting is a reversal of the removal procedure, but clean the contact surfaces and fit a new gasket. Tighten the mounting screws progressively.

15 Crankshaft oil seals - renewal

Right-hand oil seal

1 Apply the handbrake, then jack up the front of the car and support on axle stands (see "Jacking, towing and wheel changing"). Remove the right-hand front wheel.
2 Remove the front wing plastic moulding, followed by the front wheelarch liner.
3 Where applicable (early models with separate air conditioning compressor drivebelt) remove the air conditioning compressor drivebelt with reference to Chapter 3.
4 Remove the auxiliary drivebelt with reference to Chapter 1.
5 Unscrew and remove the centre bolt from the crankshaft pulley. To do this, the crankshaft must be held stationary using one of the following methods. On manual transmission models, have an assistant depress the brake pedal and engage 4th gear. Alternatively, insert a wide-bladed screwdriver through the timing aperture (where applicable) on the top of the transmission, and jam the starter ring gear to prevent the crankshaft turning. On automatic transmission models, use the latter method only. Where the timing aperture is blanked off, it will be necessary to remove the starter motor as described in Chapter 5A for access to the starter ring gear.
6 Pull the crankshaft pulley and hub from the

end of the crankshaft. If it is tight, careful use of two levers may be required.
7 Note the fitted depth of the oil seal, then using a screwdriver, carefully prise the oil seal from the oil pump casing. Alternatively, punch or drill two small holes opposite each other in the seal. Screw a self-tapping screw into each, and pull on the screws with pliers to extract the seal. Another method is to remove the oil pump cover as described in Section 11, and remove the oil seal on the bench.
8 Clean the seating in the oil pump casing, then lubricate the lips of the new oil seal with clean engine oil, and locate it squarely on the oil pump casing. Make sure that the closed side is facing outwards. Using a suitable tubular drift (such as a socket) which bears only on the hard outer edge of the seal, tap the seal into position, to the same depth in the casing as the original was prior to removal (see illustration).
9 Locate the crankshaft pulley and hub on the end of the crankshaft. Insert the centre bolt and tighten it to the specified torque, holding the crankshaft stationary using one of the methods described in paragraph 5.
10 Refit the auxiliary drivebelt with reference to Chapter 1.
11 Where applicable, refit the air conditioning compressor drivebelt with reference to Chapter 1.
12 Refit the wheelarch liner front section and moulding, and tighten the screws.
13 Refit the right-hand front wheel, and lower the car to the ground.

Left-hand oil seal

14 Remove the flywheel/driveplate as described in Section 16.
15 Make a note of the fitted depth of the seal in its housing. Punch or drill two small holes opposite each other in the seal. Screw a self-tapping screw into each, and pull on the screws with pliers to extract the seal. Alternatively, use a screwdriver to prise out the oil seal.
16 Clean the seal housing, then lubricate the lips of the new seal with clean engine oil, and carefully locate the seal on the end of the crankshaft.
17 Using a suitable tubular drift, which bears only on the hard outer edge of the seal, drive the seal into position, to the same depth in the housing as the original was prior to removal.
18 Wipe clean the oil seal, then refit the flywheel/driveplate as described in Section 16.

16 Flywheel/driveplate - removal, inspection and refitting

Removal

1 Remove the transmission as described in Chapter 7A or 7B.
2 On manual transmission models, remove the clutch assembly as described in Chapter 6.
3 Prevent the flywheel/driveplate from turning

16.10 Apply locking fluid to the bolt threads, and tighten to the specified torque

17.11a Unscrew the bolts . . .

17.11b . . . and remove the engine mounting bracket from the cylinder block

by jamming the ring gear teeth with a wide-bladed screwdriver or similar tool. Alternatively, bolt a metal link between the flywheel/driveplate (using the clutch or torque converter bolt holes) and the cylinder block/crankcase.

4 Unscrew and remove the retaining bolts, remove the locking tool, then remove the flywheel/driveplate from the crankshaft flange. Note that the unit is located by a single dowel pin, and cannot be fitted incorrectly.

Inspection

5 If the flywheel's clutch mating surface is deeply scored, cracked or otherwise damaged, the flywheel must be renewed. However, it may be possible to have it surface-ground; seek the advice of a Saab dealer or engine reconditioning specialist.

6 Similarly check the condition of the driveplate on automatic transmission models.

7 If the ring gear is badly worn or has missing teeth, it may be possible to renew it. This job is best left to a Saab dealer or engine reconditioning specialist. The temperature to which the new ring gear must be heated for installation is critical and, if not done accurately, the hardness of the teeth will be destroyed.

Refitting

8 Clean the mating surfaces of the flywheel/driveplate and crankshaft. Clean the threads of the retaining bolts and the crankshaft holes.

 HAYNES HiNT *If a suitable tap is not available, cut two slots into the threads of an old flywheel bolt, and use the bolt to clean the threads.*

9 Ensure that the locating dowel is in position, then offer up the flywheel and locate it on the dowel.

10 Apply locking fluid to the threads of the retaining bolts. Insert and tighten them to the specified torque, holding the flywheel/driveplate stationary using one of the methods described in paragraph 3 **(see illustration)**.

11 On manual transmission models, refit the clutch assembly as described in Chapter 6.

12 Refit the transmission with reference to Chapter 7A or 7B.

17 Engine/transmission mountings - inspection and renewal

Inspection

1 For improved access, raise the front of the car and support it securely on axle stands (see *"Jacking, towing and wheel changing"*).

2 The engine mountings are located at the front and rear on the right-hand side, beneath the left-hand side of the transmission, and at the upper right-hand side of the engine. With the exception of the upper right-hand mounting, all mountings are of hydraulic type, incorporating an inner chamber filled with oil. Vibration damping is progressive depending on the load applied, and works for both horizontal and vertical movement.

3 Check the mounting rubbers to see if they are cracked, hardened or separated from the metal at any point; renew the mounting if any such damage or deterioration is evident.

4 Check that all the mounting's fasteners are securely tightened.

5 Using a large screwdriver or a crowbar, check for wear in the mounting by carefully levering against it to check for freeplay. Where this is not possible, enlist the aid of an assistant to move the engine/transmission back and forth, or from side to side, while you watch the mounting. While some freeplay is to be expected even from new components, excessive wear should be obvious. If excessive freeplay is found, check first that the fasteners are securely tightened, then if necessary renew any worn components as described below.

Renewal

Right-hand lower mountings

6 Apply the handbrake, then jack up the front of the car and support on axle stands (see *"Jacking, towing and wheel changing"*). Remove the right-hand front wheel.

7 Remove the screws, and withdraw the right-hand front wing plastic moulding and front wheelarch liner.

8 Unscrew the nuts from the tops of the right-hand engine mountings. Access is possible from the right-hand side of the engine compartment, using a socket and long extension. It may be necessary to unbolt the coolant expansion tank and the power steering hydraulic fluid reservoir, and move them to one side for access.

9 Attach an engine lifting hoist to the lifting brackets bolted onto the cylinder head, then raise the engine until it is clear of the right-hand engine mountings.

10 Remove the anti-rotation washers from the tops of the mountings, then unscrew the bolts and remove the mountings from the subframe.

11 If necessary, the engine mounting brackets may be unbolted from the cylinder block **(see illustrations)**.

12 Fit the new mountings using a reversal of the removal procedure, making sure that the anti-rotation washers are correctly positioned and the nuts fully tightened.

Left-hand lower mounting

13 Apply the handbrake, then jack up the front of the car and support on axle stands (see *"Jacking, towing and wheel changing"*).

14 Loosen the nut on the left-hand engine mounting bolt under the transmission (the mounting bracket is slotted).

15 Attach an engine lifting hoist to the left-hand lifting bracket on the cylinder head, then raise the transmission until the left-hand mounting is clear of the bracket.

16 Unbolt the engine mounting from the transmission, and remove it from the engine compartment.

17 Fit the new mounting using a reversal of the removal procedure, making sure that the weight of the engine/transmission is on the bracket before tightening the nut on the mounting bolt.

Right-hand upper mounting

18 Unscrew the bolts from the torque arm and upper right-hand engine mounting bracket, and remove the torque arm from the engine.

19 Unbolt the mounting bracket from the cylinder head.

20 Fit the new mountings using a reversal of the removal procedure.

Chapter 2 Part B:
Engine removal and general overhaul procedures

Contents

Degrees of difficulty

Easy, suitable for novice with little experience	Fairly easy, suitable for beginner with some experience	Fairly difficult, suitable for competent DIY mechanic	Difficult, suitable for experienced DIY mechanic	Very difficult, suitable for expert DIY or professional

Specifications

Cylinder head

Height (new):
Models up to 1993 .... 140.5 ± 0.1 mm
Models from 1994 on .... 139.4 to 139.6 mm
Height (minimum):
Models up to 1993 .... 140.1 mm
Models from 1994 on .... 139.0 mm
Valve guide to valve stem clearance (max) .... 0.50 mm (measured on valve head raised 3 mm above seat)

Valves

Valve head diameter:
Inlet .... 33.0 mm
Exhaust .... 29.0 mm
Valve head machining angle (inlet valve only) .... 44.34° to 44.67°
Valve seat cutting angle .... 45°
Valve stem diameter:
Inlet .... 6.960 to 6.975 mm
Exhaust .... 6.965 to 6.980 mm
Valve spring free length .... 45.5 ±1.5 mm
Depth of valve stem below the camshaft bearing surface:
Checking .... 19.5 ± 0.05 mm min to 20.5 ± 0.05 mm max
Setting .... 20.0 mm min to 20.4 mm max (20.2 mm nominal)

Cylinder block

Cylinder bore diameter:
B202 engine:
Standard (A) .... 90.000 to 90.010 mm
Standard (B) .... 90.010 to 90.020 mm
First oversize .... 90.500 mm
Second oversize .... 91.000 mm
B204 and B234 engines:
Standard (A) .... 90.000 to 90.012 mm
Standard (B) .... 90.003 to 90.020 mm
Standard (B+) .... 90.011 to 90.030 mm
First oversize .... 90.500 to 90.512 mm
Second oversize .... 91.000 to 91.012 mm

Balance shafts

Endfloat	0.050 to 0.450 mm
Diameter of journal:	
Larger, inner	39.900 ± 0.008 mm
Smaller, outer	19.947 to 19.960 mm
Diameter of bearing:	
Larger, inner	39.988 to 40.043 mm
Smaller, outer	20.000 to 20.021 mm
Bearing running clearance (maximum)	0.080 to 0.151 mm

Pistons

Note: *Piston diameter is measured at right-angles to the piston boss, at the specified distance from the bottom of the skirt.*

Distance from bottom of skirt	
B202	16.00 mm
B234, models up to 1993	9.0 mm
B204L/S, B234L/R/E, 1994-on models	9.3 mm
B204i and B234i, 1994-on models	11.0 mm
Piston diameter:	
B202i:	
Standard A......................................	89.971 to 89.980 mm
Standard AB	89.980 to 89.989 mm
Standard B	89.989 to 90.000 mm
Standard C	90.000 to 90.008 mm
First oversize (0.5 mm)	90.470 to 90.485 mm
Second oversize (1.0 mm)	90.970 to 90.985 mm
Nominal piston clearance (new)	0.010 to 0.039 mm
B202 Turbo and B202S:	
Standard A......................................	89.967 to 89.977 mm
Standard AB	89.977 to 89.985 mm
Standard B	89.985 to 89.993 mm
Standard C	89.993 to 90.009 mm
First oversize (0.5 mm)	90.470 to 90.485 mm
Second oversize (1.0 mm)	90.970 to 90.985 mm
Nominal piston clearance (new)	0.015 to 0.043 mm
B204 and B234:	
Standard A......................................	89.971 to 89.980 mm
Standard AB	89.980 to 89.989 mm
Standard B:	
B234i up to 1993	89.989 to 90.000 mm
B204/B234 from 1994 on	89.989 to 90.000 mm
B234 Turbo up to 1993	89.989 to 89.997 mm
Standard C:	
B234i up to 1993	90.000 to 90.013 mm
B204/B234 from 1994	90.000 to 90.013 mm
B234 Turbo up to 1993	89.997 to 90.013 mm
First oversize (0.5 mm)	90.482 to 90.488 mm
Second oversize (1.0 mm)	90.972 to 90.988 mm
Nominal piston clearance (new):	
Models up to 1993	0.006 to 0.041 mm
Models from 1994 on	0.011 to 0.041 mm

Connecting rods

Maximum weight difference between any two connecting rods:	
B202	9.0 g
B204/B234	6.0 g

Crankshaft

Endfloat (all engines)	0.06 to 0.31 mm
Main bearing journal diameter:	
Standard	57.981 to 58.000 mm
First undersize	57.731 to 57.750 mm
Second undersize	57.481 to 57.500 mm
Third undersize	57.237 to 57.250 mm
Fourth undersize	56.987 to 57.000 mm
Big-end bearing journal diameter:	
Standard	51.981 to 52.000 mm
First undersize	51.731 to 51.750 mm
Second undersize	51.481 to 51.500 mm
Third undersize	51.237 to 51.250 mm
Fourth undersize	50.987 to 51.000 mm

Maximum bearing journal out-of-round (all engines):
    New . . . . 0.005 mm
    Service . . . . 0.050 mm
Main bearing running clearance:
    B202 . . .0.020 to 0.062 mm
    B204/B234 (up to 1993) . . . . 0.020 to 0.062 mm
    B204/B234 (from 1994) . . . . 0.014 to 0.062 mm
Big-end bearing running clearance:
    Up to 1993 . . . . 0.026 to 0.062 mm
    From 1994 . . . . 0.020 to 0.068 mm

Piston rings

End gaps:
    Top compression ring:
        B202 . . . . 0.35 to 0.48 mm
        B204/B234 . . . . 0.30 to 0.50 mm
    Second compression ring:
        B202 . . . . 0.25 to 0.38 mm
        B234 up to 1993 . . . . 0.30 to 0.45 mm
        B204/B234 from 1994 . . . . 0.15 to 0.65 mm
    Oil control ring (segment where applicable) . . . . 0.38 to 1.40 mm
Side clearance in groove:
    Top compression ring:
        All engines . . . . 0.050 to 0.082 mm
    Second compression ring:
        Up to 1993 . . . . 0.034 to 0.070 mm
        1994 on . . . . 0.040 to 0.072 mm
    Oil control ring . . . . Not applicable

Torque wrench settings

Refer to Chapter 2A Specifications.

1 General information

Included in this Part of Chapter 2 are details of removing the engine from the vehicle, and general overhaul procedures for the cylinder head, cylinder block/crankcase, and all engine internal components.

The information given ranges from advice concerning preparation for an overhaul and the purchase of replacement parts, to detailed step-by-step procedures covering removal, inspection, renovation and refitting of engine internal components.

After Section 8, all instructions are based on the assumption that the engine has been removed from the vehicle. For information concerning in-car engine repair, as well as the removal and refitting of those external components necessary for full overhaul, refer to Part A of this Chapter. Ignore any preliminary dismantling operations described in Part A that are no longer relevant once the engine has been removed from the vehicle.

2 Engine overhaul - general information

It is not always easy to determine when, or if, an engine should be completely overhauled, as a number of factors must be considered.

High mileage is not necessarily an indication that an overhaul is needed, while low mileage does not preclude the need for an overhaul.

Frequency of servicing is probably the most important consideration. An engine which has had regular and frequent oil and filter changes, as well as other required maintenance, should give many thousands of miles of reliable service. Conversely, a neglected engine may require an overhaul very early in its life.

Excessive oil consumption is an indication that piston rings, valve seals and/or valve guides are in need of attention. Make sure that oil leaks are not responsible before deciding that the rings and/or guides are worn. Perform a compression test, as described in Part A of this Chapter, to determine the likely cause of the problem.

Check the oil pressure with a gauge fitted in place of the oil pressure switch, and compare it with that specified. If it is extremely low, the main and big-end bearings, and/or the oil pump, are probably worn out.

Loss of power, rough running, knocking or metallic engine noises, excessive valve gear noise, and high fuel consumption may also point to the need for an overhaul, especially if they are all present at the same time. If a complete service does not remedy the situation, major mechanical work is the only solution.

An engine overhaul involves restoring all internal parts to the specification of a new engine. During an overhaul, the cylinders are rebored (where necessary) and the pistons and the piston rings are renewed. New main and big-end bearings are generally fitted; if necessary, the crankshaft may be renewed or reground, to restore the journals. The valves

are also serviced as well, since they are usually in less-than-perfect condition at this point. While the engine is being overhauled, other components, such as the distributor (where applicable), starter and alternator, can be overhauled as well. The end result should be an as-new engine that will give many trouble-free miles.

Note: *Critical cooling system components such as the hoses, thermostat and water pump should be renewed when an engine is overhauled. The radiator should be checked carefully, to ensure that it is not clogged or leaking. Also, it is a good idea to renew the oil pump whenever the engine is overhauled.*

Before beginning the engine overhaul, read through the entire procedure, to familiarise yourself with the scope and requirements of the job. Overhauling an engine is not difficult if you follow carefully all of the instructions, have the necessary tools and equipment, and pay close attention to all specifications. It can, however, be time-consuming. Plan on the car being off the road for a minimum of two weeks, especially if parts must be taken to an engineering works for repair or reconditioning. Check on the availability of parts, and make sure that any necessary special tools and equipment are obtained in advance. Most work can be done with typical hand tools, although a number of precision measuring tools are required for inspecting parts to determine if they must be renewed. Often the engineering works will handle the inspection of parts, and will offer advice concerning reconditioning and renewal.

4.2 Remove the right-hand front wing moulding, followed by the wheelarch liner

4.3 Removing the splash guard panel from under the radiator

4.7 Removing the battery clamp

Note: *Always wait until the engine has been completely dismantled, and until all components (especially the cylinder block/crankcase and the crankshaft) have been inspected, before deciding what service and repair operations must be performed by an engineering works. The condition of these components will be the major factor to consider when determining whether to overhaul the original engine, or to buy a reconditioned unit. Do not, therefore, purchase parts or have overhaul work done on other components until they have been thoroughly inspected.* As a general rule, time is the primary cost of an overhaul, so it does not pay to fit worn or sub-standard parts.

As a final note, to ensure maximum life and minimum trouble from a reconditioned engine, everything must be assembled with care, in a spotlessly-clean environment.

3 Engine removal - methods and precautions

If you have decided that the engine must be removed for overhaul or major repair work, several preliminary steps should be taken.

Locating a suitable place to work is extremely important. Adequate workspace, along with storage space for the vehicle, will be needed. If a workshop or garage is not available, at the very least, a flat, level, clean worksurface is required.

Cleaning the engine compartment and engine/transmission before beginning the removal procedure will help keep tools clean and organised.

An engine hoist or A-frame will also be necessary. Make sure the equipment is rated in excess of the combined weight of the engine and transmission. Safety is of primary importance, considering the potential hazards involved in lifting the engine/transmission out of the vehicle.

If this is the first time you have removed an engine, an assistant should ideally be available. Advice and aid from someone more experienced would also be helpful. There are many instances when one person cannot simultaneously perform all of the operations

required when lifting the engine out of the vehicle.

Plan the operation ahead of time. Before starting work, arrange for the hire of, or obtain, all of the tools and equipment you will need. Some of the equipment necessary to perform engine/transmission removal and installation safely and with relative ease (in addition to an engine hoist) is as follows: a heavy-duty trolley jack, complete sets of spanners and sockets as described in the front of this manual, wooden blocks, and plenty of rags and cleaning solvent for mopping up spilled oil, coolant and fuel. If the hoist must be hired, make sure that you arrange for it in advance, and perform all of the operations possible without it beforehand. This will save you money and time.

Plan for the vehicle to be out of use for quite a while. An engineering works will be required to perform some of the work which the do-it-yourselfer cannot accomplish without special equipment. These places often have a busy schedule, so it would be a good idea to consult them before removing the engine, in order to accurately estimate the amount of time required to rebuild or repair components that may need work.

Always be extremely careful when removing and refitting the engine/transmission. Serious injury can result from careless actions. Plan ahead and take your time, and a job of this nature, although major, can be accomplished successfully.

The engine and transmission is removed by lifting upwards from the engine compartment.

4 Engine and transmission - removal, separation and refitting

Removal

Note: *The engine can be removed from the car only as a complete unit with the transmission; the two are then separated for overhaul. The engine/transmission is lifted upwards out of the engine compartment.*

1 Park the vehicle on firm, level ground. Chock the rear wheels, then firmly apply the handbrake. Jack up the front of the vehicle,

and securely support it on axle stands (see *"Jacking, towing and wheel changing"*).

2 Remove both front wheels, then unbolt the wing moulding and front wheelarch liner from the right-hand side for access to the engine **(see illustration)**.

3 Unbolt and remove the centre splash guard panel from under the radiator. The panel is secured by clips at its rear edge **(see illustration)**.

4 Position a suitable container beneath the radiator, then unscrew the drain plug and drain the coolant. **Note:** *The engine should be cold before draining the coolant.* Also drain the cylinder block by unscrewing the drain plug. Save the coolant if it is fit for re-use.

5 With the coolant drained, refit and tighten the drain plugs.

6 Remove the bonnet as described in Chapter 11. Alternatively, disconnect the support struts from the bonnet, and support it in the fully-open position.

> **HAYNES HiNT** *Saab technicians fit extensions to the top of the struts in order to open the bonnet further.*

7 Remove the battery with reference to Chapter 5A **(see illustration)**.

Models with LH-Jetronic fuel injection system

8 Release the strap from the fuel filter, and position the filter to one side on the bulkhead.

9 Unscrew the bolts securing the steady bar to the ABS brake unit.

10 Disconnect all wiring from the battery tray, and unplug the wiring connector for the ABS unit.

11 Disconnect the battery positive cable at the terminal block on the battery tray, and unbolt the battery negative cable from the earthing point on the front wing.

12 Move the wiring to one side, then unbolt the battery tray from the engine compartment.

13 On the left-hand side of the engine compartment, disconnect the wiring from the washer fluid level sensor and pump.

14 Disconnect the washer tube from the

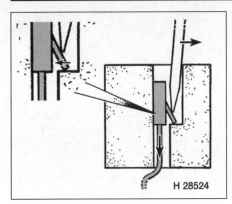

4.33 Method of removing the leads from the TSI socket

4.42 Upper hose on the coolant expansion tank

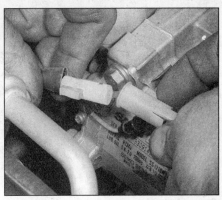

4.44a Disconnect the wiring for the air conditioning compressor . . .

4.44b . . . then unscrew the mounting bolts

reservoir, and plug the reservoir to prevent spillage.

15 Unscrew the mounting screws, and remove the washer reservoir from the engine compartment.

16 Disconnect the wiring plug from the airflow meter.

17 Release the toggle clips securing the air cleaner to the airflow meter, then disconnect the turbo inlet hose (where applicable) and withdraw the airflow meter from the engine compartment, together with the air cleaner top.

18 Where applicable, release the connector from the turbo solenoid valve. Loosen the clips and disconnect the hoses, then unscrew the fixing screws and remove the valve.

19 Carefully disconnect the coil HT lead at the distributor cap, and position it to one side.

20 Disconnect the Hall sensor wiring connector from the side of the distributor.

21 Release the cable-tie securing the knock detector lead, then loosen the clips and disconnect the top hose from the radiator and thermostat housing.

22 On Turbo models, loosen the clips on the turbo delivery hose, disconnect the bypass valve/pressure and transmission hoses, and remove the delivery hose from its location on the transmission.

23 Disconnect the accelerator cable from the throttle valve housing and bracket, with reference to Chapter 4A.

24 Loosen the clip and disconnect the fuel return hose from the fuel pressure regulator. Tie the hose to the bulkhead.

25 Loosen the clip and disconnect the fuel supply hose from the fuel filter from the fuel distribution rail. Position the hose behind the false bulkhead.

26 Remove the cover from the left-hand end of the heater air inlet plenum chamber at the rear of the engine compartment. At the same time, release the wiring loom and knock detector lead from the cable-tie.

27 Prise the rubber moulding from the top edge of the false bulkhead panel, then unscrew the bolts and lift out the panel.

28 On models with ABS, release the strap

and lift out the braking system ECU. Place the unit to one side.

29 Unbolt and remove the bracket for the ABS ECU.

30 Release the connector from the Bosch LH fuel injection ECU, and position the ECU on the left-hand wing panel.

31 Unbolt and remove the bracket for the Bosch LH fuel injection ECU.

32 Make a note of the position of all wiring in the engine compartment, to ensure correct refitting. Unplug all wiring from the engine.

33 Remove the TSI (diagnostic) socket as follows. Insert a small screwdriver in turn in the grey/red lead (pin 1) socket, and the violet/white lead (pin 2) socket, then depress the retaining tab and pull out the leads **(see illustration)**. Make a note of the lead positions for future reference.

34 Remove the remaining cable-tie for the knock detector, then unplug the connector and position the lead on the front wing.

35 Position the main wiring loom on top of the engine.

36 Disconnect the vacuum hose between the inlet manifold and the pressure sensor at the T-piece connector.

37 Loosen the clips and disconnect the heater hoses at the engine - to ensure correct refitting, identify each hose for position. Release the cable-tie for the airflow meter wiring, and position the heater hoses to one side.

38 On the bulkhead, disconnect the wiring for the electronic speedometer, then pull the wire through the rubber grommet in the bottom of the bulkhead panel, and position it on top of the engine.

39 On automatic transmission models, release the clip securing the kickdown cable to the gear selector cable, then release the cable-tie securing the cable to the steering servo pump pipe.

40 On automatic transmission models, clean the area around the transmission fluid cooler connections, then unscrew the union bolts and disconnect the fluid hoses from the transmission fluid cooler. Recover the copper washers, and store them in a safe place. Wrap

masking tape around the ends of the hoses, and similarly cover the apertures of the transmission, to prevent the entry of dust and dirt. Tie the hoses to the engine subframe.

41 Disconnect the gearchange rod (manual transmission models) or the selector control (automatic transmission models) from the transmission. The selector control is removed as follows. Unscrew the nut from the gear selector linkage and outer cable, then prise the cable from the clip, together with the rubber bush, using a screwdriver. Retain the cable behind the brake fluid reservoir.

42 Loosen the clips and disconnect the hoses from the coolant expansion tank **(see illustration)**. Unscrew the mounting bolt, release the cable-tie, then disconnect the wiring and remove the expansion tank from the right-hand side of the engine compartment.

43 Where fitted, remove the air conditioning drivebelt by loosening the tension locknut, moving the compressor towards the engine and slipping the drivebelt from the pulleys.

44 Position a suitable piece of cardboard over the right-hand side of the radiator and crossmember to prevent damage, then disconnect the wiring from the air conditioning compressor and unscrew the mounting bolts **(see illustrations)**.

45 Loosen the clip and disconnect the hose from the water pump, then lift the compressor and hose, and place them on the radiator

4.45 Lifting the air conditioning compressor from its mounting

4.56a Unscrew the nuts securing the exhaust downpipe to the exhaust manifold . . .

4.56b . . . and recover the gaskets

crossmember **(see illustration)**. Tie them onto the crossmember with a piece of string. **Do not** disconnect the refrigerant lines from the compressor (refer to the warnings given in Chapter 3).

46 Where applicable, release the clips and cable-tie securing the lambda wiring to the engine, then separate the connector at the inlet manifold, and lower the wiring onto the engine subframe.

47 Unscrew the bolts from the torque arm and upper right-hand engine mounting, and remove the mounting from the engine.

48 Loosen the clips and disconnect the radiator bottom hose.

49 Where applicable, loosen the clip and remove the turbo delivery hose.

50 Unscrew the nuts securing the exhaust downpipe to the exhaust manifold or turbocharger, then position the downpipe to one side.

51 Where applicable, unscrew and remove the top mounting bolt for the engine oil cooler, then loosen the bottom mounting bolts.

52 Release the oil cooler hose cable-ties, then lift the oil cooler from the lower mounting bolts, and place it on the engine. Use a piece of string to tie the oil cooler to the engine.

53 Syphon the fluid from the power steering fluid reservoir, using a poultry baster. Unscrew the reservoir mounting bolt, then lower it and disconnect the hose by loosening the clip. Be prepared for loss of fluid by positioning a suitable container beneath the reservoir. Remove the reservoir from the engine compartment, and position the fluid hose to one side.

54 Unscrew the union nut and disconnect the delivery hose from the power steering pump. Seal the end of the hose with masking tape or a rubber end cap, and tie the hose to the bulkhead.

55 Where applicable, disconnect the charcoal canister vacuum hose from the inlet manifold, and place the hose to one side.

Models with Trionic engine management system

56 Unscrew the nuts securing the exhaust downpipe to the exhaust manifold or turbocharger, then position the downpipe to one side. Recover the gaskets **(see illustration)**.

57 Remove the fusebox from the front of the battery tray.

4.58a Remove the battery positive cable support (retaining screw arrowed). . .

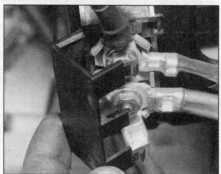

4.58b . . . then pull off the plastic cover . . .

4.58c . . . and disconnect the upper cable (arrowed)

4.59a Removing the terminal block

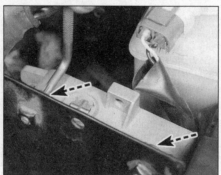

4.59b Unscrew the mounting screws . . .

4.59c . . . and remove the ABS ECU

4.60a Unscrew the battery tray mounting bolts . . .

4.60b . . . and remove the battery tray

4.61a Disconnecting the air inlet trunking from the throttle housing

58 Unscrew the battery positive cable support at the battery tray. Pull the plastic cover from the terminal block, and disconnect the upper cable by unscrewing the nut **(see illustrations)**.

59 Unscrew the screws and remove the terminal block, then remove the ABS ECU. Unbolt the battery negative cable from the earthing point on the front wing **(see illustrations)**.

60 Unbolt and remove the battery tray **(see illustrations)**.

61 Disconnect the air inlet trunking from the air cleaner assembly/turbo unit (as applicable) and throttle housing. Disconnect the wiring from the air inlet temperature sensor **(see illustrations)**.

62 Disconnect the accelerator cable from the throttle valve housing and bracket, with reference to Chapter 4A.

63 Remove the auxiliary drivebelt with reference to Chapter 1.

64 Unbolt the power steering pump with reference to Chapter 10, but do not disconnect the hydraulic hoses. To provide additional working room, remove the rear section of wheelarch liner, and unbolt the strut between the subframe and inner wing panel **(see illustrations)**. Position the pump to one side.

65 Unbolt the earth cable from the upper right-hand engine mounting, then unscrew the bolts and remove the torque arm/mounting from the engine **(see illustrations)**.

4.61b Removing the air inlet trunking

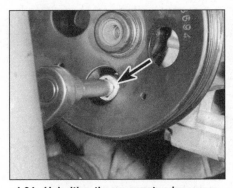

4.64a Unbolting the power steering pump

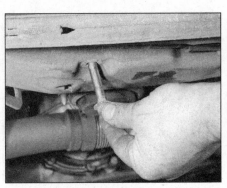

4.64b Unscrew the bolt . . .

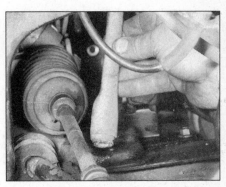

4.64c . . . and remove the strut

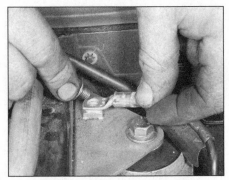

4.65a Unbolt the earth cable . . .

4.65b . . . then unscrew the bolts . . .

4.65c . . . and remove the torque arm/mounting

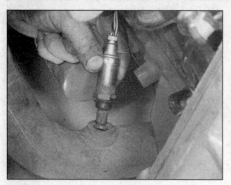

4.68 Removing the lambda sensor from the exhaust downpipe

4.69 Disconnecting the wiring main connector from the bulkhead

4.70a Detach the moulding . . .

66 Unbolt the power steering pump bracket, then remove the alternator with reference to Chapter 5A.

67 Unbolt the power steering pump pipe support from the right-hand driveshaft bearing bracket.

68 Where applicable, disconnect the lambda sensor wiring with reference to Chapter 4B. Access to the connector beneath the inlet manifold is quite restricted, and it is easier to unscrew the sensor from the exhaust downpipe; take care not to damage the wiring **(see illustration)**. Tie the sensor to the engine.

69 The engine wiring must now be disconnected at the bulkhead. To do this, unscrew the cap from the main connector, and pull out the plug **(see illustration)**.

70 Detach the moulding and remove the

cover(s) from the bulkhead. Remove the washer tube and drain hose **(see illustrations)**.

71 Release the clips, and remove the wiring loom extension leading to the manifold absolute pressure (MAP) sensor on the right-hand side of the bulkhead. Remove the MAP sensor **(see illustration)**. Note the routing of the loom under the heater assembly and behind the windscreen wiper motor bracket.

72 Unbolt and remove the false bulkhead panel **(see illustration)**.

73 Lift the ABS fusebox from its mounting, and position to one side **(see illustration)**

74 Release the wiring loom from the ABS fusebox mounting **(see illustration)**

75 Lift the brake/clutch hydraulic fluid

reservoir from its mounting, then release the wiring loom from the holder in the false bulkhead. Disconnect the wiring connector on the left-hand side of the bulkhead **(see illustration)**.

76 Remove the Trionic system ECU with reference to Chapter 4A.

77 Unbolt the earth cable from the left-hand side of the transmission **(see illustration)**.

78 Loosen the clips, and disconnect the radiator top hose from the radiator and thermostat housing.

79 Disconnect the wiring from the reversing light switch **(see illustration)** and electronic speedometer sender.

80 Position the main wiring loom on top of the engine.

81 Disconnect the charcoal canister and

4.70b . . . and remove the drain hose

4.71 Removing the manifold absolute pressure (MAP) sensor

4.72 Removing the false bulkhead panel

4.73 Lifting the ABS fusebox from its mounting

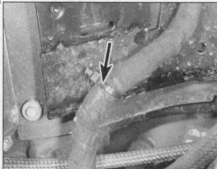

4.74 Release the wiring loom from the ABS fusebox mounting

4.75 Wiring connector located on the left-hand side of the bulkhead

4.77 Unbolt the earth cable from the transmission

4.79 Disconnecting the reversing light switch wiring

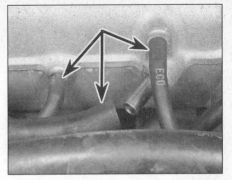

4.81 Disconnecting the vacuum hoses from the inlet manifold

crankcase ventilation vacuum hoses from the inlet manifold **(see illustration)**.

82 Disconnect the brake servo vacuum hose from the inlet manifold.

83 Where necessary, disconnect the expansion tank small hose from the radiator **(see illustration)**.

84 Loosen the clips, and disconnect the radiator bottom hose and lower expansion tank hose from the water pump.

85 Similarly, loosen the clips and disconnect the heater hoses from the cylinder head and coolant pipe located on the rear of the cylinder block **(see illustrations)**. Tie the hoses to one side. If necessary, identify each hose for position, to ensure correct refitting.

86 On manual transmission models, fit a hose clamp to the clutch hydraulic hose leading to

the transmission. Unscrew the union, and disconnect the hose from the slave cylinder pipe leading into the clutch bellhousing **(see illustration)**.

87 Position a suitable piece of cardboard over the right-hand side of the radiator and crossmember to prevent damage, then disconnect the wiring from the air conditioning compressor, and unscrew the mounting bolts. Lift the compressor, and place it on the radiator crossmember. **Do not** disconnect the refrigerant lines from the compressor (refer to the warnings given in Chapter 3).

88 Disconnect the fuel inlet union and return hose from the fuel rail and pressure regulator **(see illustrations)**. Position the hoses to one side.

89 On manual transmission models,

disconnect the gearchange rod from the transmission by unscrewing the 10 mm clamp bolt.

90 If required, the manual transmission oil may be drained at this stage, but this is not essential as the differential output shafts remain in the transmission.

91 On Turbo models, loosen the clips on the turbo delivery hose, then disconnect the bypass valve/pressure and transmission hoses, and remove the delivery hose from its location on the transmission.

92 On automatic transmission models, release the clip securing the kickdown cable to the gear selector cable, then release the cable-tie securing the cable to the steering servo pump pipe. Also disconnect the selector control from the transmission.

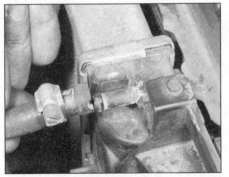

4.83 Disconnecting the expansion tank hose from the radiator

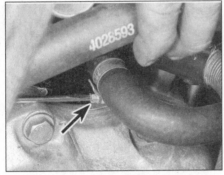

4.85a Heater hose connection to the coolant pipe

4.85b Heater hose connection to the cylinder head

4.86 Disconnecting the clutch hydraulic hose from the slave cylinder pipe

4.88a Fuel inlet hose union on the fuel rail

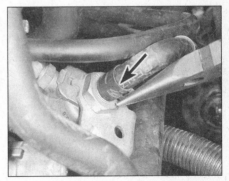

4.88b Releasing the clip on the fuel return hose to the pressure regulator

4.95 Unscrewing the engine right-hand mounting front nut

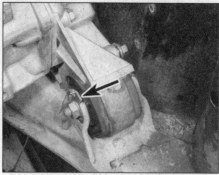

4.102 The left-hand engine mounting - slotted portion arrowed

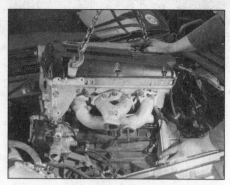

4.104 Removing the engine

93 On automatic transmission models, clean the area around the transmission oil cooler connections, then unscrew the union bolts and disconnect the fluid hoses from the transmission fluid cooler. Recover the copper washers, and store them in a safe place. Tie the hoses to the engine subframe.

 HAYNES HINT *Wrap masking tape around the ends of the hoses, and similarly cover the apertures of the transmission, to prevent the entry of dust and dirt.*

94 On automatic transmission models, disconnect the selector control from the side of the transmission as follows. Unscrew the nut from the gear selector linkage and outer cable, then prise the cable from the clip, together with the rubber bush, using a screwdriver. Retain the cable behind the brake fluid reservoir.

All models

95 Using a socket, unscrew the two engine right-hand mounting nuts **(see illustration)**. Access may be gained by using an extension from the top right-hand side of the engine compartment

96 Loosen and remove the clips securing the driveshaft rubber gaiters to the inner joints, in order to allow the joints to separate when the front suspension struts are moved outwards. If crimped-type clips are fitted, use snips to cut through them.

97 Working on each side of the car in turn, loosen (but do not remove) the bottom bolts securing the struts to the steering knuckles, and completely remove the upper bolts. This will allow the knuckles to move outwards sufficiently to disconnect the driveshaft inner joints. It will also be helpful to disconnect one of the steering track rod ends, to allow the suspension struts to move more freely.

98 Working on each side of the car in turn, pull out the steering knuckles; at the same time, disconnect the rubber gaiters to allow the inner ends of the driveshafts to separate from the inner joints. Cover the exposed ends of the driveshaft joints with polythene or masking tape, to prevent the entry of dust and dirt.

99 Unscrew and remove the lower mounting screw for the electric cooling fan assembly.
100 Unscrew the upper mounting screws for the electric cooling fan unit. Unplug the wiring connector, and withdraw the cooling fan unit from the engine compartment. Take care not to damage the radiator matrix.
101 If necessary, lower and support the car to the height necessary to operate the hoist. Manoeuvre the engine hoist into position, and attach it to the lifting brackets bolted onto the cylinder head.
102 Raise the hoist until it is supporting the weight of the engine. Unscrew the left-hand engine mounting nut - there is no need to completely remove the bolt, as the mounting is slotted **(see illustration)**.
103 Make a final check that any components which would prevent the removal of the engine/transmission from the car have been removed or disconnected. Ensure that components such as the gearchange selector rod are secured so that they cannot be damaged on removal.
104 Slowly raise the engine/transmission assembly from the engine compartment, making sure that it clears the components on the surrounding panels **(see illustration)**. In particular, make sure that it clears the ABS unit, the kickdown cable (automatic transmission models) and the radiator. With the assembly raised above the front crossmember, pull the hoist away from the car, and lower the assembly onto the ground.

Enlist the help of an assistant during this procedure, as it may be necessary to tilt the assembly slightly to clear the body panels.

Separation of transmission from engine

105 It is not essential to drain the oil, as driveshaft flanges are fitted to each side. If preferred, drain the transmission oil/fluid as described in Chapter 7A or 7B. Refit the drain and filler plugs, and tighten them securely.
106 If the engine is to be dismantled, working as described in Chapter 1, drain the oil and if required remove the oil filter. Clean and refit the drain plug, tightening it securely.
107 Support the engine/transmission assembly on suitable blocks of wood, on a workbench (or failing that, on a clean area of the workshop floor).
108 Remove the starter motor with reference to Chapter 5A.
109 Disconnect the electronic speedometer wiring at the connector, by inserting a screwdriver and pulling out the clip. If necessary, the complete engine wiring loom can be disconnected at this stage **(see illustrations)**.
110 Where the alternator has not yet been removed (on early models), unscrew the nut and disconnect the lead from the rear of the alternator. Also disconnect the charge warning light lead (green/white) from the alternator. Unscrew the alternator mounting bolts from the driveshaft bearing support bracket and

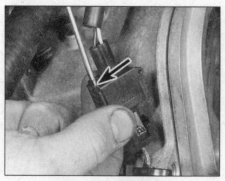

4.109a Insert a screwdriver . . .

4.109b . . . and pull out the clip

4.109c Releasing the wiring connector at the rear of the engine

4.109d Release all wiring from plastic cable-ties - this one is located on the oil filler tube

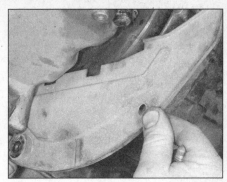

4.115 Removing the transmission housing bottom cover

power steering pump bracket, and withdraw the alternator from the engine.

111 Unbolt the driveshaft bearing support bracket from the rear of the cylinder block, at the same time sliding the splined shaft from the driveshaft extension.

112 Unbolt and remove the rear engine mounting bracket.

113 Position a suitable container beneath the oil filter, then unscrew and remove the oil filter from the bracket on the front or rear of the cylinder block (as applicable).

Manual transmission models

114 On Turbo models, unscrew the bolt securing the turbo oil pipe bracket to the transmission.

115 Unbolt the bottom cover from the transmission bellhousing **(see illustration)**.

116 Ensure that both engine and transmission are adequately supported, then unscrew the bolts securing the transmission housing to the engine **(see illustration)**. Note the correct fitted positions of each bolt as they are removed, to use as a reference on refitting. Withdraw the transmission directly from the engine. Take care not to allow the weight of the transmission to bear on the input shaft and clutch.

Automatic transmission models

117 Unscrew the top stud securing the transmission to the engine cylinder block, by approximately 10 mm. To do this, first

unscrew the nut a few threads, then tighten a further nut onto it, and unscrew both.

118 Disconnect the kickdown cable from the inlet manifold bracket. Extract the spring clip, and disconnect the accelerator cable from the lever on the throttle housing.

119 Remove the breather valve from the top of the transmission.

120 On Turbo models, unscrew the bolt securing the turbo oil pipe bracket to the transmission.

121 Working through the starter motor aperture, unscrew the three bolts securing the flywheel to the torque converter. To bring each bolt into view, turn the engine using a socket on the crankshaft pulley bolt **(see illustration)**.

122 Saab technicians use a special tool to hold the torque converter inside the transmission while the transmission is separated from the engine. The tool is quite basic, and consists of a plate which engages the torque converter through the timing hole in the top of the transmission. It is held in position using a pair of grips **(see illustration)**.

123 Support the weight of the transmission, preferably using a hoist.

124 Ensure that both engine and transmission are adequately supported, then unscrew the bolts securing the transmission housing to the engine. Note the correct fitted positions of each bolt as they are removed, to use as a reference on refitting. Withdraw the transmission directly from the engine. Make

sure that the torque converter stays inside the transmission bellhousing, otherwise it may fall out and be damaged.

Reconnection of transmission to engine

Automatic transmission models

125 Carefully offer the transmission to the engine. Make sure that the torque converter is held fully engaged with the transmission, using the special tool described in paragraph 122.

126 Insert and tighten the top mounting stud into the transmission, then unscrew and remove the second locknut, and tighten the mounting nut securely.

127 Insert and tighten to the specified torque the remaining bolts securing the transmission to the engine.

128 Remove the special tool, then insert and tighten to the specified torque the three bolts securing the flywheel to the torque converter. Turn the engine using a socket.

129 On Turbo models, insert and tighten the bolts securing the turbo oil pipe bracket to the transmission.

130 Refit the breather valve to the top of the transmission.

131 Reconnect the kickdown cable to the linkage on the throttle housing, then refit the outer cable to the inlet manifold bracket, and adjust with reference to Chapter 7B. Tighten the adjustment locknuts.

4.116 Unscrewing the bolts (two arrowed) securing the transmission to the engine

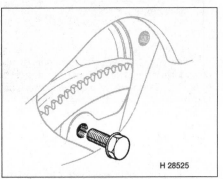

4.121 Removing one of the bolts securing the flywheel to the torque converter

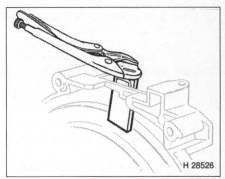

4.122 Tool (and grips) for holding the torque converter inside the transmission

Manual transmission models

132 Apply a smear of high-melting-point grease to the splines of the transmission input shaft. Do not apply too much, otherwise there is a possibility of the grease contaminating the clutch friction plate.

133 Carefully offer the transmission to the engine. Ensure that the weight of the transmission is not allowed to hang on the input shaft as it is engaged with the clutch friction disc. Insert and tighten to the specified torque the bolts securing the transmission to the engine.

134 Refit the bottom cover to the transmission bellhousing, and tighten the bolts.

135 On Turbo models, insert and tighten the bolts securing the turbo oil pipe bracket to the transmission.

All models

136 Wipe clean the contact surfaces, then refit and tighten the oil filter with reference to Chapter 1.

137 Refit the engine rear mounting bracket, and tighten the bolts.

138 Refit the driveshaft bearing support bracket to the rear of the cylinder block, while sliding the splined shaft onto the driveshaft extension. Insert and tighten the bolts.

139 On early models, refit the alternator to the driveshaft bearing support bracket and power steering pump bracket, and tighten the mounting bolts. Reconnect the starter motor lead, and tighten the nut. Reconnect the charge warning light lead to the rear of the alternator.

140 Refit the starter motor together with the steady bar with reference to Chapter 5A.

Refitting

141 Refitting is a reversal of removal, but note the following additional points:
a) Tighten all nuts and bolts to the specified torque.
b) Renew the copper washers on unions, as applicable.
c) Where applicable, tension the air conditioning compressor drivebelt with reference to Chapter 1.
d) Where applicable, bleed the clutch hydraulic system with reference to Chapter 6.
e) Reconnect and adjust the accelerator cable, with reference to Chapter 4A.
f) Ensure that all wiring has been reconnected, and all nuts and bolts have been tightened.
g) Refill the engine and transmission with the correct quantity and grade of oil/fluid, with reference to Chapter 1.
h) Refill the cooling system with reference to Chapter 1.
i) Check and if necessary top-up the power steering fluid, with reference to Chapter 1.

5 Engine overhaul - dismantling sequence

1 It is much easier to dismantle and work on the engine if it is mounted on a portable engine stand. These stands can often be hired from a tool hire shop. Before the engine is mounted on a stand, the flywheel/driveplate should be removed, so that the stand bolts can be tightened into the end of the cylinder block/crankcase.

2 If a stand is not available, it is possible to dismantle the engine with it blocked up on a sturdy workbench, or on the floor. Be extra-careful not to tip or drop the engine when working without a stand.

3 If you are going to obtain a reconditioned engine, all the external components must be removed first, to be transferred to the replacement engine (just as they will if you are doing a complete engine overhaul yourself). These components normally include the following, but check with your engine supplier first:
a) Alternator mounting bracket (Chapter 5A).
b) The distributor (where applicable), HT leads or Direct Ignition cartridge and spark plugs, as applicable (Chapter 1 and Chapter 5B).
c) Thermostat and housing (Chapter 3).
d) The dipstick tube, where applicable.
e) Air conditioning compressor mounting bracket (Chapter 3).
f) The fuel injection system and emission control components (Chapter 4A and 4B).
g) All electrical switches and sensors, and the engine wiring harness.
h) Inlet and exhaust manifolds (Chapter 4A).
i) Oil filter (Chapter 1).
j) Engine mounting brackets (Part A of this Chapter).
k) Flywheel/driveplate (Part A of this Chapter).

> **HAYNES HINT** When removing the external components from the engine, pay close attention to details that may be helpful or important during refitting. Note the fitted position of gaskets, seals, spacers, pins, washers, bolts, and other small items.

4 If you are obtaining a "short" engine (which consists of the engine cylinder block/crankcase, crankshaft, pistons and connecting rods all assembled), then the cylinder head and sump will have to be removed also.

5 If you are planning a complete overhaul, the engine can be dismantled, and the internal components removed, in the order given below, referring to Part A of this Chapter unless otherwise stated:
a) Inlet and exhaust manifolds (Chapter 4A).
b) Cylinder head (Chapter 2A).
c) Timing chain (and balance shaft chain

where applicable), sprockets and tensioner (Chapter 2A).
d) Flywheel/driveplate (Chapter 2A).
e) Balance shafts (where applicable) (Section 9).
f) Sump (Chapter 2A).
g) Piston/connecting rod assemblies (Section 10).
h) Crankshaft (Section 11).

6 Before beginning the dismantling and overhaul procedures, make sure that you have all of the correct tools necessary. Refer to "Tools and working facilities" for further information.

6 Cylinder head - dismantling

Note: New/reconditioned cylinder heads are obtainable from Saab, or from engine overhaul specialists. Be aware that some specialist tools are required for the dismantling and inspection procedures, and new components may not be readily available. It may therefore be more practical and economical for the home mechanic to purchase a reconditioned head, rather than dismantle, inspect and recondition the original head.

1 Remove the cylinder head as described in Part A, then unbolt the external components - these include the right-hand engine mounting bracket, the engine lifting eye, and the distributor blanking plug, according to model **(see illustrations)**.

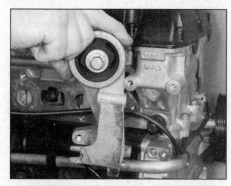

6.1a Removing the right-hand engine mounting bracket from the cylinder head

6.1b Unbolting the engine lifting eye from the front of the cylinder head

6.1c Unbolt the clamp . . .

6.1d . . . and remove the distributor blanking plug

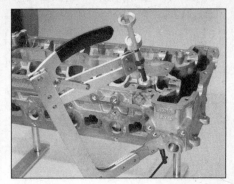

6.4a Using a compressor to compress the valve springs in order to remove the split collets

2 Remove the camshafts and hydraulic cam followers, with reference to Part A, Section 8.

3 Before removing the valves, consider obtaining plastic protectors for the hydraulic cam follower bores. When using certain valve spring compressors, the bores can easily be damaged, should the compressor slip off the end of the valve.

> **HAYNES HiNT** The cam follower bore protectors can be obtained from a Saab dealer; alternatively, a protector may be made out of plastic cut from a washing-up liquid container or similar.

4 Position the protector in the cam follower bore, then using a valve spring compressor, compress the valve spring until the split collets can be removed. Release the compressor, and lift off the spring retainer, spring and seat. Using a pair of pliers, carefully extract the valve stem seal from the top of the guide **(see illustrations)**.

5 If, when the valve spring compressor is screwed down, the spring retainer refuses to free and expose the split collets, gently tap the top of the tool, directly over the retainer, with a light hammer. This will free the retainer.

6 Withdraw the valve through the combustion chamber.

7 It is essential that each valve is stored together with its collets, retainer, spring, and spring seat. The valves should also be kept in their correct sequence, unless they are so badly worn that they are to be renewed. If they are going to be kept and used again, place each valve assembly in a labelled polythene bag or similar small container **(see illustrations)**. Note that No 1 cylinder is nearest to the timing chain end of the engine.

8 With all the valves removed, use a pair of pliers to pull the valve seals from the tops of the guides.

6.4b Removing the spring retainer . . .

6.4c . . . valve spring . . .

6.4d . . . and seat

6.4e Valve stem seal location

6.4f Removing a valve stem seal

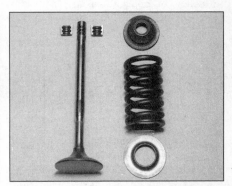

6.7a The valve spring components

6.7b Place each valve and its associated components in a labelled polythene bag

7.6 Checking the cylinder head gasket face for distortion

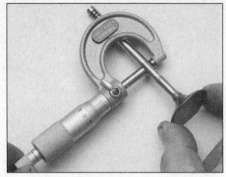

7.10 Measuring a valve stem diameter

7 Cylinder head and valves - cleaning and inspection

1 Thorough cleaning of the cylinder head and valve components, followed by a detailed inspection, will enable you to decide how much valve service work must be carried out during the engine overhaul. **Note:** *If the engine has been severely overheated, it is best to assume that the cylinder head is warped - check carefully for signs of this.*

Cleaning

2 Scrape away all traces of old gasket material from the cylinder head.
3 Scrape away the carbon from the combustion chambers and ports, then wash the cylinder head thoroughly with paraffin or a suitable solvent.
4 Scrape off any heavy carbon deposits that may have formed on the valves, then use a power-operated wire brush to remove deposits from the valve heads and stems.

Inspection

Note: *Be sure to perform all the following inspection procedures before concluding that the services of a machine shop or engine overhaul specialist are required. Make a list of all items that require attention.*

Cylinder head

5 Inspect the head very carefully for cracks, evidence of coolant leakage, and other damage. If cracks are found, a new cylinder head should be obtained.
6 Use a straight-edge and feeler blade to check that the cylinder head surface is not distorted **(see illustration)**. If it is, it may be possible to have it machined, provided that the cylinder head is not reduced to less than the specified height.
7 Examine the valve seats in each of the combustion chambers. If they are severely pitted, cracked, or burned, they will need to be renewed or re-cut by an engine overhaul specialist. If they are only slightly pitted, this can be removed by grinding-in the valve heads and seats with fine valve-grinding compound, as described below. Note that the

exhaust valves have a hardened coating and, although they may be ground-in with paste, they must not be machined.
8 Check the valve guides for wear by inserting the relevant valve, and checking for side-to-side motion of the valve. A very small amount of movement is acceptable. If the movement seems excessive, remove the valve. Measure the valve stem diameter (see below), and renew the valve if it is worn. If the valve stem is not worn, the wear must be in the valve guide, and the guide must be renewed. The renewal of valve guides is best carried out by a Saab dealer or engine overhaul specialist, who will have the necessary tools available.

Valves

9 Examine the head of each valve for pitting, burning, cracks, and general wear. Check the valve stem for scoring and wear ridges. Rotate the valve, and check for any obvious indication that it is bent. Look for pits and excessive wear on the tip of each valve stem. Renew any valve that shows any such signs of wear or damage.
10 If the valve appears satisfactory at this stage, measure the valve stem diameter at several points using a micrometer **(see illustration)**. Any significant difference in the readings obtained indicates wear of the valve stem. Should any of these conditions be apparent, the valve(s) must be renewed.
11 If the valves are in satisfactory condition, they should be ground (lapped) into their respective seats, to ensure a smooth, gas-tight seal. If the seat is only lightly pitted, or if it has been re-cut, fine grinding compound should be used to produce the required finish. Coarse valve-grinding compound should *not* be used, unless a seat is badly burned or deeply pitted. If this is the case, the cylinder head and valves should be inspected by an expert, to decide whether seat re-cutting, or even the renewal of the valve or seat insert (where possible) is required.
12 Valve grinding is carried out as follows. Place the cylinder head upside-down on a bench.
13 Smear a trace of (the appropriate grade of) valve-grinding compound on the seat face, and press a suction grinding tool onto the

valve head. With a semi-rotary action, grind the valve head to its seat, lifting the valve occasionally to redistribute the grinding compound. A light spring placed under the valve head will greatly ease this operation.
14 If coarse grinding compound is being used, work only until a dull, matt even surface is produced on both the valve seat and the valve, then wipe off the used compound, and repeat the process with fine compound. When a smooth unbroken ring of light grey matt finish is produced on both the valve and seat, the grinding operation is complete. *Do not grind-in the valves any further than absolutely necessary, or the seat will be prematurely sunk into the cylinder head.*
15 When all the valves have been ground-in, carefully wash off *all* traces of grinding compound using paraffin or a suitable solvent, before reassembling the cylinder head.
16 To ensure that the hydraulic cam followers operate correctly, the depth of the valve stems below the camshaft bearing surface must be within certain limits. It may be possible to obtain a Saab checking tool from a dealer, but if not, the check may be made using a steel rule and straight-edge. Check that the dimension is within the limits given in the Specifications by inserting each valve it its guide in turn, and measuring the dimension between the end of the valve stem and the camshaft bearing surface **(see illustration)**.

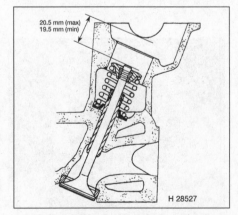

7.16 Check the depth of the valve stems below the camshaft bearing surface

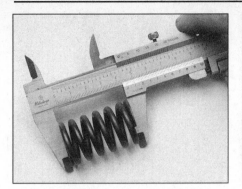

7.18 Checking the valve spring free length

7.19 Checking the valve springs for squareness

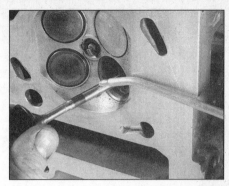

8.1 Inserting a valve in the cylinder head

17 If the dimension is not within the specified limits, adjustment must be made either to the end of the valve stem or to the valve seat height. If lower than the minimum amount, the length of the valve stem must be reduced, and if more than the maximum amount, the valve seat must be milled. Seek the advice of a Saab dealer or engine reconditioning specialist.

Valve components

18 Examine the valve springs for signs of damage and discoloration, and measure their free length **(see illustration)**.
19 Stand each spring on a flat surface, and check it for squareness **(see illustration)**. If any of the springs are less than the minimum free length, or are damaged, distorted or have lost their tension, obtain a complete new set of springs.
20 Obtain new valve stem oil seals, regardless of their apparent condition.

8 Cylinder head - reassembly

1 Lubricate the stems of the valves, and insert the valves into their original locations **(see illustration)**. If new valves are being fitted, insert them into the locations to which they have been ground.
2 Working on the first valve, dip the new valve stem seal in fresh engine oil. Carefully locate it over the valve and onto the guide. Take care not to damage the seal as it is passed over the

valve stem. Use a suitable socket or metal tube to press the seal firmly onto the guide **(see illustration)**.
3 Refit the valve spring followed by the spring retainer, then locate the plastic protector in the hydraulic cam follower bore.
4 Compress the valve spring, and locate the split collets in the recess in the valve stem. Release the compressor and remove the protector, then repeat the procedure on the remaining valves.

HAYNES HINT

Use a little dab of grease to locate the collets on the valve stems, and to hold them in place while the spring compressor is released

5 With all the valves installed, place the cylinder head flat on the bench and, using a hammer and interposed block of wood, tap

the end of each valve stem to settle the components.
6 Refit the hydraulic cam followers and camshafts with reference to Part A, Section 8.
7 Refit the external components removed in Section 6. When refitting the distributor blanking plug, check and if necessary renew the O-ring seal.
8 The cylinder head may now be refitted as described in Part A of this Chapter.

9 Balance shafts - removal, inspection and refitting

Removal

1 Position the crankshaft at TDC compression for No 1 piston (timing chain end of the engine) as described in Chapter 2A, Section 3.
2 Remove the timing cover as described in Chapter 2A, Section 5.
3 The balance shafts are "timed" at TDC, but since they rotate at twice the speed of the crankshaft, they may also be correctly "timed" at BDC. Check that the timing marks on the shafts are correctly aligned with the marks on the bearing brackets. As an extra precaution, apply dabs of paint to the chain and sprockets, to ensure correct refitting. Note that the balance shaft sprockets are marked "inlet" and "exhaust" for position, but the front bearings are marked identically. However, as the bearings are located with single bolts, the "inlet" and "exhaust" marks will always be correctly located at the top of the bearings.
4 Unbolt the balance shaft chain upper guide, then remove the tensioner and side guide.
5 Unscrew the retaining bolt and remove the idler from the block.
6 Release the chain from the balance shaft sprockets and crankshaft sprocket.
7 Unscrew the bearing retaining bolts, and withdraw the balance shafts from the cylinder block **(see illustrations)**. Keep the shafts identified for position.
8 Unscrew the retaining bolts, and remove the sprockets from the ends of the balance shafts, while holding each shaft in a soft-jawed vice.

8.2 Using a socket to fit the valve stem seals

9.7a Unscrew the bearing retaining bolts . . .

9.7b . . . and withdraw the exhaust balance shaft from the cylinder block

9.7c Removing the inlet balance shaft from the cylinder block

9.7d The two balance shafts removed from the engine

Inspection

9 Clean the balance shafts and examine the bearing journals for wear and damage. The bearings inside the cylinder block should also be examined. If these are excessively worn or damaged, get advice from a Saab dealer or engine reconditioner.

Refitting

10 Fit the sprockets to the ends of the balance shafts, and tighten the retaining bolts.

11 Lubricate the bearing journals with clean engine oil, then insert the balance shafts in the cylinder block in their correct positions.

12 Locate the balance shaft chain sprocket on the front of the crankshaft, with the word "Saab" facing outwards.

13 Fit the chain to the sprockets, and refit the idler to the front of the block, making sure that the timing marks remain aligned correctly.

14 Refit the side guide, tensioner and upper guide to the balance shaft chain.

15 Rotate the crankshaft one turn, and check that the balance shaft sprockets are still correctly aligned.

16 Refit the timing cover with reference to Chapter 2A, Section 5.

10 Piston/connecting rod assembly - removal

1 Remove the cylinder head, sump and oil pump pick-up/strainer as described in Part A of this Chapter.

2 If there is a pronounced wear ridge at the top of any bore, it may be necessary to remove it with a scraper or ridge reamer, to avoid piston damage during removal. Such a ridge indicates excessive wear of the cylinder bore.

3 Using a hammer and centre-punch, paint or similar, mark each connecting rod big-end bearing cap with its respective cylinder number on the flat machined surface provided; if the engine has been dismantled before, note carefully any identifying marks made previously. Note that No 1 cylinder is at the transmission (flywheel/driveplate) end of the engine.

4 Turn the crankshaft to bring pistons 1 and 4 to BDC (bottom dead centre).

5 Unscrew the nuts from No 1 piston big-end bearing cap. Take off the cap, and recover the bottom half bearing shell. If the bearing shells are to be re-used, tape the cap and the shell together (see illustrations).

6 To prevent the possibility of damage to the crankshaft bearing journals, tape over the connecting rod stud threads.

7 Using a hammer handle, push the piston up through the bore, and remove it from the top of the cylinder block. Recover the bearing shell, and tape it to the connecting rod for safe-keeping.

8 Loosely refit the big-end cap to the connecting rod, and secure with the nuts - this will help to keep the components in their correct order.

9 Remove No 4 piston assembly in the same way.

10 Turn the crankshaft through 180° to bring pistons 2 and 3 to BDC (bottom dead centre), and remove them in the same way.

11 Crankshaft - removal

1 Remove the timing chain and sprocket, the sump and oil pump pick-up/strainer/transfer tube, and the flywheel/driveplate, as described in Part A of this Chapter.

2 Remove the pistons and connecting rods, as described in Section 10. **Note:** *If no work is to be done on the pistons and connecting rods, there is no need to remove the cylinder head, or to push the pistons out of the cylinder bores. The pistons should just be pushed far enough up the bores that they are positioned clear of the crankshaft journals.*

3 Check the crankshaft endfloat with reference to Section 14, then proceed as follows.

4 Unbolt and remove the crankshaft rear oil seal housing from the end of the cylinder block, noting the correct fitted locations of the locating dowels. If the locating dowels are a loose fit, remove them and store them with the housing for safe-keeping. Remove the gasket.

5 Identification numbers should already be cast onto the base of each main bearing cap (see illustration). If not, number the cap and crankcase using a centre-punch, as was done for the connecting rods and caps.

10.5a Removing a big-end bearing cap

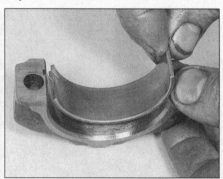

10.5b Removing a bearing shell from a big-end bearing cap

11.5 The main bearing caps are numbered from the timing chain end of the engine

11.6a Unscrew and remove the main bearing cap bolts . . .

11.6b . . . and remove the main bearing caps

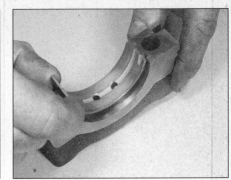

11.7 Removing a main bearing shell from its cap

6 Unscrew and remove the main bearing cap retaining bolts, and withdraw the caps, complete with bearing shells **(see illustrations)**. Tap the caps with a wooden or copper mallet if they are stuck.

7 Remove the bearing shells from the caps, but keep them with their relevant caps and identified for position to ensure correct refitting **(see illustration)**.

8 Carefully lift the crankshaft from the crankcase **(see illustration)**.

9 Remove the upper bearing shells from the crankcase, keeping them identified for position. Also remove the thrustwashers at each side of the centre main bearing, and store them with the bearing cap **(see illustrations)**.

10 With the crankshaft removed on B204 and B234 engines, the crankshaft position sensor reluctor may be removed if necessary, by unscrewing the screws and withdrawing the reluctor over the end of the crankshaft **(see illustration)**. Note that the screws are arranged so that it is only possible to refit the reluctor in one position.

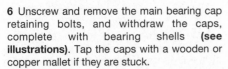

12 Cylinder block/crankcase - cleaning and inspection

Cleaning

1 Remove all external components and electrical switches/sensors from the block. For complete cleaning, the core plugs should ideally be removed, as follows. Drill a small hole in the plugs, then insert a self-tapping screw into the hole. Pull out the plugs by pulling on the screw with a pair of grips, or by using a slide hammer. Also unbolt the four oil jets from the crankcase on B204/B234 engines **(see illustration)**.

2 Scrape all traces of sealant from the cylinder block/crankcase, taking care not to damage the gasket/sealing surfaces.

3 Remove all oil gallery plugs (where fitted). The plugs are usually very tight - they may have to be drilled out, and the holes re-tapped. Use new plugs when the engine is reassembled.

4 If the cylinder block/crankcase is extremely dirty, it should be steam-cleaned.

5 Clean all oil holes and oil galleries, and flush all internal passages with warm water until the water runs clear. Dry thoroughly, and apply a light film of oil to all mating surfaces, to prevent rusting. Also oil the cylinder bores. If you have access to compressed air, use it to speed up the drying process, and to blow out all the oil holes and galleries.

> ⚠ *Warning: Wear eye protection when using compressed air!*

6 If the cylinder block is not very dirty, you can do an adequate cleaning job with hot (as hot as you can stand!), soapy water and a stiff brush. Take plenty of time, and do a thorough job. Regardless of the cleaning method used,

11.8 Lifting the crankshaft from the crankcase

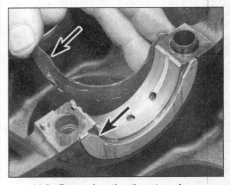

11.9a Removing the thrustwashers (arrowed) . . .

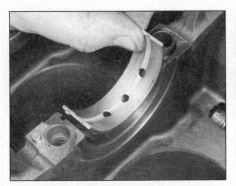

11.9b . . . and main bearing shells

11.10 Location of the screws securing the crankshaft position sensor reluctor

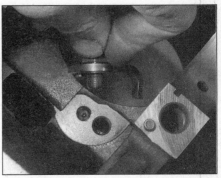

12.1 Removing an oil jet from the crankcase

12.7 Cleaning a cylinder head bolt hole in the cylinder block using a tap

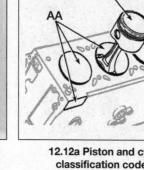

12.12a Piston and cylinder bore classification code locations

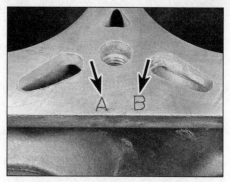

12.12b Cylinder bore classification on the front of the block

12.12c Piston classification on the piston crown

be sure to clean all oil holes and galleries very thoroughly, and to dry all components well. On completion, protect the cylinder bores as described above, to prevent rusting.

7 All threaded holes must be clean, to ensure accurate torque readings during reassembly. To clean the threads, run the correct-size tap into each of the holes to remove rust, corrosion, thread sealant or sludge, and to restore damaged threads **(see illustration)**. If possible, use compressed air to clear the holes of debris produced by this operation.

 HAYNES HiNT *A good alternative to compressed air is to inject aerosol-applied water-dispersant lubricant into each hole, using the long tube usually supplied.*

> ⚠ **Warning: Wear eye protection when cleaning out these holes in this way!**

8 Apply suitable sealant to the new oil gallery plugs, and insert them into the holes in the block. Tighten them securely. Refit and tighten the oil jets to the bottom of the crankcase on B204/B234 engines.

9 If the engine is not going to be reassembled right away, cover it with a large plastic bag to keep it clean; protect all mating surfaces and the cylinder bores as described above, to prevent rusting.

Inspection

10 Visually check the cylinder block for cracks and corrosion. Look for stripped threads in the threaded holes. If there has been any history of internal water leakage, it may be worthwhile having an engine overhaul specialist check the cylinder block/crankcase with special equipment. If defects are found, have them repaired if possible; otherwise, a new block will be needed.

11 Check each cylinder bore for scuffing and scoring. Check for signs of a wear ridge at the top of the cylinder, indicating that the bore is excessively worn.

12 The cylinder bores and pistons are matched and classified according to five codes - AB, B, C, 1 (0.5 mm oversize), and 2 (1.0 mm oversize). The code is stamped on the piston crowns, and on the front of the cylinder block **(see illustrations)**. Note that all

classifications may occur in the same cylinder block.

13 Wear of the cylinder bores and pistons can be measured by inserting the relevant piston (without piston rings) in its bore and using a feeler blade. Make the check with the piston near the top of its bore. If the clearance is more than the nominal (new) amount given in the Specifications, a rebore should be considered, and the opinion of an engine reconditioner sought.

13 Piston/connecting rod assembly - inspection

1 Before the inspection process can begin, the piston/connecting rod assemblies must be cleaned, and the original piston rings removed from the pistons **(see illustration)**.

2 Carefully expand the old rings over the top of the pistons. The use of two or three old feeler blades will be helpful in preventing the rings dropping into empty grooves **(see illustrations)**. Be careful not to scratch the piston with the ends of the ring. The rings are brittle, and will snap if they are spread too far. They're also very sharp - protect your hands and fingers. Note that the third ring incorporates an expander. Always remove the rings from the top of the piston. Keep each set of rings with its piston, if the old rings are to be re-used.

3 Scrape away all traces of carbon from the top of the piston. A hand-held wire brush (or a

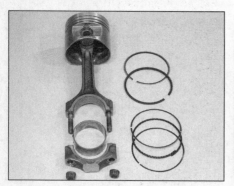

13.1 Piston/connecting rod assembly components

13.2a Removing a piston compression ring with the aid of a feeler blade

13.2b Removing the oil control ring

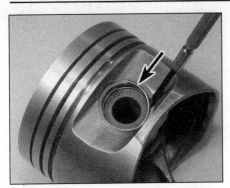

13.13a Prise out the gudgeon pin circlip . . .

13.13b . . . then withdraw the gudgeon pin, and separate the piston from the connecting rod

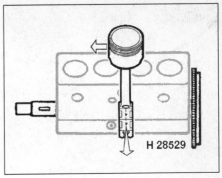

13.17 Relationship of the piston and connecting rod

piece of fine emery cloth) can be used, once the majority of the deposits have been scraped away.

4 Remove the carbon from the ring grooves in the piston, using an old ring. Break the ring in half to do this (be careful not to cut your fingers - piston rings are sharp). Be careful to remove only the carbon deposits - do not remove any metal, and do not nick or scratch the sides of the ring grooves.

5 Once the deposits have been removed, clean the piston/connecting rod assembly with paraffin or a suitable solvent, and dry thoroughly. Make sure that the oil return holes in the ring grooves are clear.

6 If the pistons and cylinder bores are not damaged or worn excessively, and if the cylinder block does not need to be rebored, the original pistons can be refitted. Normal piston wear shows up as even vertical wear on the piston thrust surfaces, and slight looseness of the top ring in its groove.

7 Carefully inspect each piston for cracks around the skirt, around the gudgeon pin holes, and at the piston ring "lands" (between the ring grooves).

8 Look for scoring and scuffing on the piston skirt, holes in the piston crown, and burned areas at the edge of the crown. If the skirt is scored or scuffed, the engine may have been suffering from overheating, and/or abnormal combustion which caused excessively high operating temperatures. The cooling and lubrication systems should be checked thoroughly. Scorch marks on the sides of the pistons show that blow-by has occurred. A hole in the piston crown, or burned areas at the edge of the piston crown, indicates that abnormal combustion (pre-ignition, knocking, or detonation) has been occurring. If any of the above problems exist, the causes must be investigated and corrected, or the damage will occur again. The causes may include incorrect ignition timing and/or fuel/air mixture.

9 Corrosion of the piston, in the form of pitting, indicates that coolant has been leaking into the combustion chamber and/or the crankcase. Again, the cause must be corrected, or the problem may persist in the rebuilt engine.

10 Where needed, pistons can be purchased from a Saab dealer.

11 Examine each connecting rod carefully for signs of damage, such as cracks around the big-end and small-end bearings. Check that the rod is not bent or distorted. Damage is highly unlikely, unless the engine has been seized or badly overheated. Detailed checking of the connecting rod assembly can only be carried out by a Saab dealer or engine repair specialist with the necessary equipment.

12 The gudgeon pins are of the floating type, secured in position by two circlips, and the pistons and connecting rods can be separated and reassembled as follows.

13 Using a small flat-bladed screwdriver, prise out the circlips, and push out the gudgeon pin **(see illustrations)**. Hand pressure should be sufficient to remove the pin. Identify the piston, gudgeon pin and rod to ensure correct reassembly.

14 Examine the gudgeon pin and connecting rod small-end bearing for signs of wear or damage. Wear can be cured by renewing both the pin and bush. Bush renewal, however, is a specialist job - press facilities are required, and the new bush must be reamed accurately.

15 The connecting rods themselves should not be in need of renewal, unless seizure or some other major mechanical failure has occurred. Check the alignment of the connecting rods visually, and if the rods are not straight, take them to an engine overhaul specialist for a more detailed check.

16 Examine all components, and obtain any new parts from your Saab dealer. If new pistons are purchased, they will be supplied complete with gudgeon pins and circlips. Circlips can also be purchased individually.

17 Position the piston so that the notch on the edge of the crown faces the timing end of the engine, and the numbers on the connecting rod and big-end cap face the exhaust side of the cylinder block. With the piston held in your hand and the notch facing the left, the connecting rod numbering should face towards you **(see illustration)**. Apply a smear of clean engine oil to the gudgeon pin. Slide it into the piston and through the connecting rod small-end. Check that the

piston pivots freely on the rod, then secure the gudgeon pin in position with the circlips. Ensure that each circlip is correctly located in its groove in the piston.

18 Measure the piston diameters, and check that they are within limits for the corresponding bore diameters. If the piston-to-bore clearance is excessive, the block will have to be rebored, and new pistons and rings fitted.

19 Examine the mating surfaces of the big-end caps and connecting rods, to see if they have ever been filed, in a mistaken attempt to take up bearing wear. This is extremely unlikely, but if evident, the offending connecting rods and caps must be renewed.

14 Crankshaft - inspection

Checking crankshaft endfloat

1 If the crankshaft endfloat is to be checked, this must be done when the crankshaft is still installed in the cylinder block/crankcase, but is free to move (see Section 11).

2 Check the endfloat using a dial gauge in contact with the end of the crankshaft. Push the crankshaft fully one way, and then zero the gauge. Push the crankshaft fully the other way, and check the endfloat **(see illustration)**. The result can be compared with the specified amount, and will give an indication as to whether new thrustwashers are required.

14.2 Using a dial gauge to check the crankshaft endfloat

14.3 Using feeler blades to check the crankshaft endfloat

14.10 Measuring a crankshaft big-end bearing journal diameter

15.1 "STD" marking on the backing of a big-end bearing shell

3 If a dial gauge is not available, feeler blades can be used. First push the crankshaft fully towards the flywheel end of the engine, then use feeler blades to measure the gap between the No 3 crankpin web and the centre main bearing thrustwasher **(see illustration)**.

Inspection

4 Clean the crankshaft using paraffin or a suitable solvent, and dry it, preferably with compressed air if available. Be sure to clean the oil holes with a pipe cleaner or similar probe, to ensure that they are not obstructed.

 Warning: Wear eye protection when using compressed air!

5 Check the main and big-end bearing journals for uneven wear, scoring, pitting and cracking.

6 Big-end bearing wear is accompanied by distinct metallic knocking when the engine is running (particularly noticeable when the engine is pulling from low speed), and some loss of oil pressure.

7 Main bearing wear is accompanied by severe engine vibration and rumble - getting progressively worse as engine speed increases - and again by loss of oil pressure.

8 Check the bearing journal for roughness by running a finger lightly over the bearing surface. Any roughness (which will be accompanied by obvious bearing wear) indicates that the crankshaft requires regrinding (where possible) or renewal. Note that it is permissible to regrind the crankshaft to the first undersize without rehardening, however further regrinding will necessitate rehardening by Tenifer treatment.

9 If the crankshaft has been reground, check for burrs around the crankshaft oil holes (the holes are usually chamfered, so burrs should not be a problem, unless regrinding has been carried out carelessly). Remove any burrs with a fine file or scraper, and thoroughly clean the oil holes as described previously.

10 Using a micrometer, measure the diameter of the main and big-end bearing journals, and compare the results with the Specifications **(see illustration)**. By measuring the diameter at a number of points around each journal's

circumference, you will be able to determine whether or not the journal is out-of-round. Take the measurement at each end of the journal, near the webs, to determine if the journal is tapered. Compare the results obtained with those given in the Specifications.

11 Check the oil seal contact surfaces at each end of the crankshaft for wear and damage. If the seal has worn a deep groove in the surface of the crankshaft, consult an engine overhaul specialist; repair may be possible, but otherwise a new crankshaft will be required.

15 Main and big-end bearings - inspection

1 Even though the main and big-end bearings are renewed during the engine overhaul, the old bearings should be retained for close examination, as they may reveal valuable information about the condition of the engine. The bearing shells are graded by thickness, the grade of each shell being indicated by the colour code marked on it - they may also have markings on their backing faces **(see illustration)**. Note that the following table only applies up to the second undersize - for the third and fourth undersizes, only one shell thickness is available.

B202/B234 up to 1993	Thin	Thick
Standard	Red	Blue
First undersize	Yellow	Green
Second undersize	White	Brown

B204/B234 from 1994	Colour
Thinnest	Red
Standard	Yellow (only size stocked as spare part)
First undersize	Blue

2 Bearing failure can occur due to lack of lubrication, the presence of dirt or other foreign particles, overloading the engine, or corrosion **(see illustration)**. Regardless of the cause of bearing failure, the cause must be corrected (where applicable) before the engine is reassembled, to prevent it from happening again.

3 When examining the bearing shells, remove them from the cylinder block/crankcase, the main bearing caps, the connecting rods and the connecting rod big-end bearing caps. Lay them out on a clean surface in the same general position as their location in the engine. This will enable you to match any bearing problems with the corresponding crankshaft journal. *Do not* touch any shell's bearing surface with your fingers while checking it, or the delicate surface may be scratched.

4 Dirt and other foreign matter gets into the

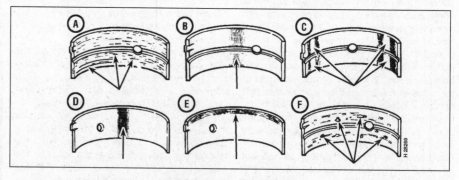

15.2 Typical bearing failures

A *Scratched by dirt; dirt embedded into bearing material*
B *Lack of oil; overlay wiped out*
C *Improper seating; bright (polished) sections*

D *Tapered journal; overlay gone from entire surface*
E *Radius ride*
F *Fatigue failure; craters or pockets*

engine in a variety of ways. It may be left in the engine during assembly, or it may pass through filters or the crankcase ventilation system. It may get into the oil, and from there into the bearings. Metal chips from machining operations and normal engine wear are often present. Abrasives are sometimes left in engine components after reconditioning, especially when parts are not thoroughly cleaned using the proper cleaning methods. Whatever the source, these foreign objects often end up embedded in the soft bearing material, and are easily recognised. Large particles will not embed in the bearing, and will score or gouge the bearing and journal. The best prevention for this cause of bearing failure is to clean all parts thoroughly, and keep everything spotlessly-clean during engine assembly. Frequent and regular engine oil and filter changes are also recommended.

5 Lack of lubrication (or lubrication breakdown) has a number of interrelated causes. Excessive heat (which thins the oil), overloading (which squeezes the oil from the bearing face) and oil leakage (from excessive bearing clearances, worn oil pump or high engine speeds) all contribute to lubrication breakdown. Blocked oil passages, which usually are the result of misaligned oil holes in a bearing shell, will also oil-starve a bearing, and destroy it. When lack of lubrication is the cause of bearing failure, the bearing material is wiped or extruded from the steel backing of the bearing. Temperatures may increase to the point where the steel backing turns blue from overheating.

6 Driving habits can have a definite effect on bearing life. Full-throttle, low-speed operation (labouring the engine) puts very high loads on bearings, tending to squeeze out the oil film. These loads cause the bearings to flex, which produces fine cracks in the bearing face (fatigue failure). Eventually, the bearing material will loosen in pieces, and tear away from the steel backing.

7 Short-distance driving leads to corrosion of bearings, because insufficient engine heat is produced to drive off the condensed water and corrosive gases. These products collect in the engine oil, forming acid and sludge. As the oil is carried to the engine bearings, the acid attacks and corrodes the bearing material.

8 Incorrect bearing installation during engine assembly will lead to bearing failure as well. Tight-fitting bearings leave insufficient bearing running clearance, and will result in oil starvation. Dirt or foreign particles trapped behind a bearing shell result in high spots on the bearing, which lead to failure.

9 *Do not* touch any shell's bearing surface with your fingers during reassembly; there is a risk of scratching the delicate surface, or of depositing particles of dirt on it.

> **HAYNES HiNT** *Bearing shells should be renewed as a matter of course during engine overhaul; to do otherwise is false economy. Refer to Section 18 for details of bearing shell selection.*

16 Engine overhaul - reassembly sequence

1 Before reassembly begins, ensure that all new parts have been obtained, and that all necessary tools are available. Read through the entire procedure, to familiarise yourself with the work involved, and to ensure that all items necessary for reassembly of the engine are at hand. In addition to all normal tools and materials, thread-locking compound will be needed. A suitable tube of sealant will also be required for the joint faces that are fitted without gaskets.

2 In order to save time and avoid problems, engine reassembly can be carried out in the following order:

a) Crankshaft (Section 18).
b) Piston/connecting rod assemblies (Section 19).
c) Sump (Chapter 2A).
d) Balance shafts on B204/B234 engines (Section 9).
e) Flywheel/driveplate (Chapter 2A).
f) Timing chain (and balance shaft chain where applicable), sprockets and tensioner, (Chapter 2A).
g) Cylinder head (Chapter 2A).
h) Inlet and exhaust manifolds (Chapter 4A).
i) Engine external components.

3 At this stage, all engine components should be absolutely clean and dry, with all faults repaired. The components should be laid out (or in individual containers) on a completely clean work surface.

17 Piston rings - refitting

1 Before fitting new piston rings, the ring end gaps must be checked as follows.

2 Lay out the piston/connecting rod assemblies and the new piston ring sets, so that the ring sets will be matched with the same piston and cylinder during the end gap measurement and subsequent engine reassembly.

3 Insert the top ring into the first cylinder, and push it down the bore using the top of the piston **(see illustration)**. This will ensure that the ring remains square with the cylinder walls. Position the ring near the bottom of the cylinder bore, at the lower limit of ring travel. Note that the top and second compression rings are different.

4 Measure the end gap using feeler blades, and compare the measurements with the figures given in the Specifications **(see illustration)**.

5 If the gap is too small (unlikely if genuine Saab parts are used), it must be enlarged, or the ring ends may contact each other during engine operation, causing serious damage. Ideally, new piston rings providing the correct end gap should be fitted. As a last resort, the end gap can be increased by filing the ring ends very carefully with a fine file. Mount the file in a vice with soft jaws, slip the ring over the file with the ends contacting the file face, and slowly move the ring to remove material from the ends. Take care, as piston rings are sharp, and are easily broken.

6 With new piston rings, it is unlikely that the end gap will be too large. If the gaps are too large, check that you have the correct rings for your particular engine.

7 Repeat the checking procedure for each ring in the first cylinder, and then for the rings in the remaining cylinders. Remember to keep rings, pistons and cylinders matched up.

8 Once the ring end gaps have been checked

17.3 Using the top of a piston to push a piston ring into the bore

17.4 Measuring a piston ring end gap

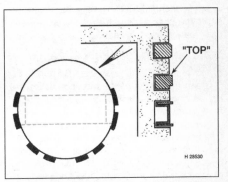

17.9 Piston ring cross-section and gap positioning

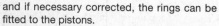

18.8 Plastigauge in place on the crankshaft main bearing journal

18.9 Tightening a main bearing cap bolt

18.11 Measuring the width of the deformed Plastigauge using the card gauge

and if necessary corrected, the rings can be fitted to the pistons.

9 Fit the piston rings using the same technique as for removal. Fit the bottom (oil control) ring first, and work up. When fitting the oil control ring, first insert the expander, then fit the lower and upper rings with the ring gaps both on the non-thrust side of the piston, with approximately 60° between them. Ensure that the second compression ring is fitted the correct way up, with the word "TOP" uppermost. Arrange the gaps of the top and second compression rings on opposite sides of the piston, above the ends of the gudgeon pin **(see illustration)**. **Note:** *Always follow any instructions supplied with the new piston ring sets - different manufacturers may specify different procedures. Do not mix up the top and second compression rings, as they have different cross-sections.*

18 Crankshaft -
refitting and main bearing running clearance check

Selection of new bearing shells

1 The main bearing shells are classified for thickness as described in Section 15. Note that up to the second undersize, it is possible to mix different thicknesses of shell in order to obtain the correct running clearance. Commence the procedure with the two thinnest shells, then if the clearance is too great, fit one thick shell with one thin shell, and make the check again. If the clearance is still too great, fit two thick shells.

Main bearing running clearance check

2 Clean the backs of the bearing shells, and the bearing locations in both the cylinder block and the main bearing caps.

3 Press the bearing shells into their locations, ensuring that the tab on each shell engages in the notch in the cylinder block or main bearing cap location. Take care not to touch any shell's bearing surface with your fingers.

4 The running clearance may be checked using one of two methods.

5 One method (which will be difficult to achieve without a range of internal micrometers or internal/external expanding calipers) is to refit the main bearing caps to the cylinder block/crankcase, with the bearing shells in place. With the cap retaining bolts correctly tightened, measure the internal diameter of each assembled pair of bearing shells. If the diameter of each corresponding crankshaft journal is measured and then subtracted from the bearing internal diameter, the result will be the main bearing running clearance.

6 The second (and more accurate) method is to use a product known as "Plastigauge". This consists of a fine thread of perfectly-round plastic, which is compressed between the bearing shell and the journal. When the cap and shell are removed, the plastic is deformed, and can be measured with a special card gauge supplied with the kit. The running clearance is determined from this gauge. Plastigauge may be available from your Saab dealer; otherwise, enquiries at one of the larger specialist motor factors should produce the name of a stockist in your area. The procedure for using Plastigauge is as follows.

7 With the main bearing upper shells in place, carefully lay the crankshaft in position. Do not use any lubricant at this stage; the crankshaft journals and bearing shells must be perfectly clean and dry.

8 Cut several lengths of the appropriate-size Plastigauge (they should be slightly shorter than the width of the main bearings), and place one length on each crankshaft journal axis **(see illustration)**. The length of Plastigauge should be placed approximately 6.0 mm to one side of the centre-line of the journal.

9 With the main bearing lower shells in position, refit the main bearing caps, then insert the bolts and tighten them progressively to the specified torque **(see illustration)**. Take care not to disturb the Plastigauge, and *do not* rotate the crankshaft at any time during this operation.

10 Unscrew the bolts and remove the main bearing caps, again taking great care not to disturb the Plastigauge or rotate the crankshaft.

11 Compare the width of the crushed Plastigauge on each journal to the scale printed on the Plastigauge envelope, to obtain the main bearing running clearance **(see illustration)**. Compare the clearance measured with that given in the Specifications at the start of this Chapter.

12 If the clearance is significantly different from that expected, the bearing shells may be the wrong size (or excessively worn, if the original shells are being re-used). Before deciding that different-size shells are required, make sure that no dirt or oil was trapped between the bearing shells and the main bearing caps or block when the clearance was measured. If the Plastigauge was wider at one end than at the other, the crankshaft journal may be tapered.

13 If the clearance is not as specified, use the reading obtained, along with the shell thicknesses quoted above, to calculate the necessary grade of bearing shells required. When calculating the bearing clearance required, bear in mind that it is always better to have the running clearance towards the lower end of the specified range, to allow for wear in use.

14 Where necessary, obtain the required grades of bearing shell, and repeat the running clearance checking procedure as described above.

15 On completion, carefully scrape away all traces of the Plastigauge material from the crankshaft and bearing shells. Use your fingernail, or a wooden or plastic scraper which is unlikely to score the bearing surfaces.

Final crankshaft refitting

16 Carefully lift the crankshaft out of the cylinder block once more. On B204 and B234 engines, refit the crankshaft position sensor reluctor if removed, and tighten the screws.

17 Using a little grease, stick the upper thrustwashers to each side of the centre main bearing upper location; ensure that the oilway grooves on each thrustwasher face outwards (away from the cylinder block)

18 Place the bearing shells in their locations in the caps as described earlier. If new shells are being fitted, ensure that all traces of protective grease are cleaned off, using

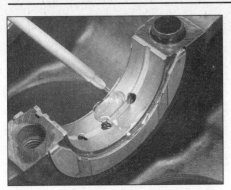

18.18 Lubricating the main bearing shells

18.25a Driving the crankshaft rear oil seal into the housing

18.25b Fitting the crankshaft rear oil seal using a block of wood in a vice

paraffin. Wipe dry the shells and connecting rods with a lint-free cloth. Liberally lubricate each bearing shell in the cylinder block/crankcase with clean engine oil **(see illustration)**.

19 Lower the crankshaft into position so that Nos 2 and 3 cylinder crankpins are at TDC. In this position, Nos 1 and 4 cylinder crankpins will be at BDC, ready for fitting No 1 piston. Check the crankshaft endfloat as described in Section 14.

20 Lubricate the lower bearing shells in the main bearing caps with clean engine oil. Make sure that the locating lugs on the shells engage with the corresponding recesses in the caps.

21 Fit the main bearing caps to their correct locations, ensuring that they are fitted the correct way round (the bearing shell lug recesses in the block and caps must be on the same side). Insert the bolts loosely.

22 Progressively tighten the main bearing cap bolts to the specified torque wrench setting.

23 Check that the crankshaft rotates freely.

24 Refit the piston/connecting rod assemblies to the crankshaft, as described in Section 19.

25 Before refitting the crankshaft rear oil seal housing, fit a new rear oil seal in the housing, with reference to Chapter 2A. Use a mallet and block of wood to drive it into the housing, or alternatively, use the block of wood in a vice **(see illustrations)**.

26 Apply suitable sealant to the contact faces

of the rear oil seal housing, then smear a little oil on the oil seal lips, and refit the locating dowels where necessary. Locate the housing on the rear of the cylinder block. To prevent damage to the oil seal as it locates over the crankshaft, make up a guide out of a plastic container, or alternatively use adhesive tape. Once the housing is in position, remove the guide or tape, then insert the bolts and tighten them to the specified torque **(see illustrations)**.

27 Refit the flywheel/driveplate, oil pick-up/strainer/transfer tube and sump, with reference to Part A of this Chapter.

28 Where removed, refit the cylinder head as described in Part A.

29 Refit the timing chain and sprocket as described in Part A of this Chapter.

19 Piston/connecting rod assembly - refitting and big-end bearing running clearance check

Selection of bearing shells

1 The big-end bearing shells are classified for thickness as described in Section 15. Note that up to the second undersize, it is possible to mix different thicknesses of shell, in order to obtain the correct running clearance. Commence the procedure with the two thinnest shells, then if the clearance is too

great, fit one thick shell with one thin shell, and make the check again. If the clearance is still too great, fit two thick shells.

Big-end bearing running clearance check

2 The clearance can be checked in either of two ways.

3 One method is to refit the big-end bearing cap to the connecting rod before refitting the pistons to the cylinder block, ensuring that they are fitted the correct way round, with the bearing shells in place. With the cap retaining nuts correctly tightened, use an internal micrometer or vernier caliper to measure the internal diameter of each assembled pair of bearing shells. If the diameter of each corresponding crankshaft journal is measured and then subtracted from the bearing internal diameter, the result will be the big-end bearing running clearance.

4 The second, and more accurate, method is to use Plastigauge (see Section 18) after refitting the pistons to the cylinder block. The following paragraphs describe the latter method, together with the refitting of the pistons to the cylinder block.

5 Position the cylinder block either on its side or on the flywheel/driveplate end.

6 Lay out the assembled pistons and rods in order, with the bearing shells, connecting rod caps and nuts.

7 Clean the backs of the bearing shells, and the bearing locations in both the connecting

18.26a Adhesive tape over the end of the crankshaft will prevent damage to the oil seal when refitting

18.26b Applying sealant to the rear oil seal housing

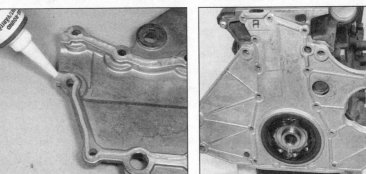

18.26c Refitting the rear oil seal housing (engine backplate)

19.10 Piston ring compressor fitted over the piston rings

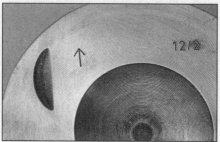

19.11a The arrow on the piston crown must point towards the timing chain end of the engine

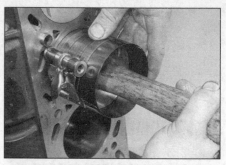

19.11b Using a hammer handle to tap the piston down the cylinder bore

rod and bearing cap. If new shells are being fitted, ensure that all traces of protective grease are cleaned off, using paraffin.

8 Press the bearing shells into their locations, ensuring that the tab on each shell engages in the notch in the connecting rod and cap. Take care not to touch any shell's bearing surface with your fingers. If the original bearing shells are being used for the check, ensure that they are refitted in their original locations.

9 Lubricate the cylinder bores, pistons and piston rings with clean engine oil, then lay out each piston/connecting rod assembly in its respective position. Do not lubricate the bearing shells at this stage.

10 Start with assembly No 1. Make sure that the piston rings are still spaced as described in Section 17, then clamp them in position with a piston ring compressor **(see illustration)**.

11 Insert the piston/connecting rod assembly into the top of cylinder No 1. Ensure that the notch or arrow on the piston crown is pointing towards the timing chain end of the engine. Using a block of wood or hammer handle against the piston crown, tap the assembly into the cylinder bore until the piston crown is flush with the top of the cylinder **(see illustrations)**. Make sure that the ends of the big-end bearing cap bolts do not scratch the bore walls.

12 With the No 1 crankpin at the bottom of its stroke, guide the connecting rod onto it while tapping the top of the piston with the hammer handle.

13 Place a strand of Plastigauge on the crankpin journal.

14 Refit the big-end bearing cap, using the marks made or noted on removal to ensure that they are fitted the correct way round.

19.14 Tightening the big-end bearing cap nuts

Tighten the bearing cap nuts to the specified torque **(see illustration)**. Take care not to disturb the Plastigauge or rotate the crankshaft during the tightening sequence.

15 Dismantle the assembly, then use the scale printed on the Plastigauge envelope to obtain the big-end bearing running clearance.

16 If the clearance is significantly different from that specified, the bearing shells may be the wrong size (or excessively worn, if the original shells are being re-used). If necessary, select different shells as described in paragraph 1. Make sure that no dirt or oil was trapped between the bearing shells and the cap or connecting rod when the clearance was measured. If the Plastigauge was wider at one end than at the other, the crankpins may be tapered.

17 Push the No 1 piston/connecting rod assembly to the top of the cylinder, then refit the No 4 piston/connecting rod assembly and repeat the bearing running clearance check. With Nos 1 and 4 pistons at the top of their bores, refit Nos 2 and 3 pistons and repeat the bearing running clearance check on these.

18 On completion, carefully scrape away all traces of the Plastigauge material from the crankshaft and bearing shells. Use your fingernail, or some other object which is unlikely to score the bearing surfaces.

Final piston/connecting rod refitting

19 Position No 1 crankpin at the bottom of its stroke. Liberally lubricate the crankpin and both bearing shells. Taking care not to mark the cylinder bores, tap the piston/connecting rod assembly down the bore and onto the crankpin. Refit the big-end bearing cap, tightening its retaining nuts finger-tight at first. Note that the faces with the identification marks must match (which means that the bearing shell locating tabs abut each other).

20 Tighten the bearing cap retaining nuts evenly and progressively to the specified torque setting.

21 Rotate the crankshaft. Check that it turns freely; some stiffness is to be expected if new components have been fitted, but there should be no signs of binding or tight spots.

22 Refit the remaining three piston/connecting rod assemblies to their crankpins in the same way.

23 Refit the oil pump pick-up/strainer, sump and cylinder head with reference to Part A of this Chapter.

20 Engine - initial start-up after overhaul

1 With the engine refitted in the vehicle, double-check the engine oil and coolant levels. Make a final check that everything has been reconnected, and that there are no tools or rags left in the engine compartment.

2 Remove the spark plugs. On models with a distributor, disable the ignition system by disconnecting the ignition HT coil lead from the distributor cap, and earthing it on the cylinder block. Use a jumper lead or similar wire to make a good connection. On models with Direct Ignition, disconnect the wiring plug from the ignition cartridge (refer to Chapter 5B if necessary).

3 Turn the engine on the starter until the oil pressure warning light goes out. Refit the spark plugs, and reconnect the coil lead to the distributor cap or DI cartridge wiring (as applicable).

4 Start the engine, noting that this may take a little longer than usual, due to the fuel system components having been disturbed.

5 While the engine is idling, check for fuel, water and oil leaks. Don't be alarmed if there are some odd smells and smoke from parts getting hot and burning off oil deposits.

6 Assuming all is well, keep the engine idling until hot water is felt circulating through the top hose then switch off the engine.

7 Check the ignition timing and the idle speed settings (as appropriate), then switch off the engine.

8 After a few minutes, recheck the oil and coolant levels as described in Chapter 1, and top-up as necessary.

9 There is no requirement to re-tighten the cylinder head bolts once the engine has first run after reassembly.

10 If new pistons, rings or crankshaft bearings have been fitted, the engine must be treated as new, and run-in for the first 500 miles (800 km). *Do not* operate the engine at full-throttle, or allow it to labour at low engine speeds in any gear. It is recommended that the oil and filter be changed at the end of this period.

Chapter 3
Cooling, heating and ventilation systems

Contents

Degrees of difficulty

Easy, suitable for novice with little experience		**Fairly easy,** suitable for beginner with some experience		**Fairly difficult,** suitable for competent DIY mechanic		**Difficult,** suitable for experienced DIY mechanic		**Very difficult,** suitable for expert DIY or professional	

Specifications

General

Expansion tank cap opening pressure	0.9 to 1.2 bars

Thermostat

Opening temperature	89°C ± 2°C

Electric cooling fan

Cut-in temperature:
  Speed 1:
1985 to 1988 models	92°C
1989 to 1994 models	90°C
1995 models	100°C

  Speed 2:
1989 to 1991 models	110°C
1992 to 1994 models	106°C
1995 models	111°C

Cut-out temperature:
  Speed 1:
1985 to 1988 models	88°C
1989 to 1994 models	86°C
1995 models	96°C

  Speed 2:
1985 to 1988 models	106°C
1989 to 1994 models	102°C
1995 models	107°C

LH-Jetronic temperature sensor

Resistance:
At 0°C	5800 ohms
At 20°C	2600 ohms
At 80°C	320 ohms

Trionic engine management system temperature sensor

Resistance:

At -30°C	20 000 to 30 000 ohms
At -10°C	7000 to 11 400 ohms
At 20°C	2100 to 2900 ohms
At 40°C	1000 to 1300 ohms
At 60°C	565 to 670 ohms
At 80°C	295 to 365 ohms
At 90°C	24 to 26 ohms
At 110°C	14 to 16 ohms

Torque wrench settings

	Nm	lbf ft
Automatic transmission fluid hose to radiator	25	19
Coolant temperature sensor (Trionic system)	13	10
Thermostat housing:		
B202/B204 engines	18	13
B234 engine	22	16
Water pump	22	16
Water pump pulley	8	6

1 General information and precautions

General information

1 The cooling system is of pressurised type, comprising a water pump driven by the auxiliary drivebelt, a crossflow radiator, electric cooling fan, a thermostat, heater matrix, and all associated hoses. The expansion tank is located on the right-hand side of the engine compartment.

2 The system functions as follows. Cold coolant in the bottom of the radiator passes through the bottom hose to the water pump, where it is pumped around the cylinder block and head passages. After cooling the cylinder bores, combustion surfaces and valve seats, the coolant reaches the underside of the thermostat, which is initially closed. The coolant passes through the heater, and is returned via the cylinder block to the water pump.

3 When the engine is cold, the coolant circulates only through the cylinder block, cylinder head, throttle housing (Trionic system) and heater. When the coolant reaches a predetermined temperature, the thermostat opens, and the coolant passes through the top hose to the radiator. As the coolant circulates through the radiator, it is cooled by the inrush of air when the car is in forward motion, and also by the action of the electric cooling fan when necessary. Upon reaching the bottom of the radiator, the coolant has now cooled, and the cycle is repeated.

4 When the engine is at normal operating temperature, the coolant expands, and some of it is displaced into the expansion tank. Coolant collects in the tank, and is returned to the radiator when the system cools.

5 The electric cooling fan mounted on the rear of the radiator is controlled by a thermostatic switch. At a predetermined coolant temperature, the switch/sensor actuates the fan.

Precautions

 Warning: Do not attempt to remove the expansion tank filler cap, or to disturb any part of the cooling system, while the engine is hot, as there is a high risk of scalding. If the expansion tank filler cap must be removed before the engine and radiator have fully cooled (even though this is not recommended), the pressure in the cooling system must first be relieved. Cover the cap with a thick layer of cloth, to avoid scalding, and slowly unscrew the filler cap until a hissing sound is heard. When the hissing has stopped, indicating that the pressure has reduced, slowly unscrew the filler cap until it can be removed; if more hissing sounds are heard, wait until they have stopped before unscrewing the cap completely. At all times, keep well away from the filler cap opening, and protect your hands.

 Warning: Do not allow antifreeze to come into contact with your skin, or with the painted surfaces of the vehicle. Rinse off spills immediately, with plenty of water. Never leave antifreeze lying around in an open container, or in a puddle in the driveway or on the garage floor. Children and pets are attracted by its sweet smell, but antifreeze can be fatal if ingested.

Warning: If the engine is hot, the electric cooling fan may start rotating even if the engine is not running. Be careful to keep your hands, hair, and any loose clothing well clear when working in the engine compartment.

Warning: Refer to Section 10 for precautions to be observed when working on models with air conditioning.

2 Cooling system hoses - disconnection and renewal

1 The number, routing and pattern of hoses will vary according to model, but the same basic procedure applies. Before commencing work, make sure that the new hoses are to hand, along with new hose clips if needed. It is good practice to renew the hose clips at the same time as the hoses.

2 Drain the cooling system, as described in Chapter 1, saving the coolant if it is fit for re-use. Squirt a little penetrating oil onto the hose clips if they are corroded.

3 Unscrew the clips and release the hose clips from the hose concerned.

4 Unclip any wires, cables or other hoses which may be attached to the hose being removed. Make notes for reference when reassembling if necessary. The hoses can be removed with relative ease when new - on an older vehicle, they may have stuck.

5 If a hose proves stubborn, try to release it by rotating it on its unions before attempting to work it off. Gently prise the end of the hose with a blunt instrument (such as a flat-bladed screwdriver), but do not apply too much force, and take care not to damage the pipe stubs or hoses. Note in particular that the radiator hose unions are fragile; do not use excessive force when attempting to remove the hoses.

> **HAYNES HiNT** *If all else fails, cut hoses with a sharp knife, then slit them so that they can be peeled off in two pieces. While expensive, this is preferable to buying a new radiator. Check first, however, that new hoses are readily available.*

6 Before fitting the new hose, smear the stubs with washing-up liquid or a suitable rubber lubricant to aid fitting. Do not use oil or grease, which may attack the rubber.

7 Fit the hose clips over the ends of the hose,

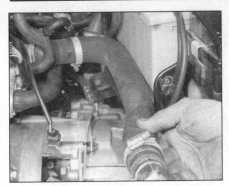

3.6 Disconnecting the top hose from the radiator

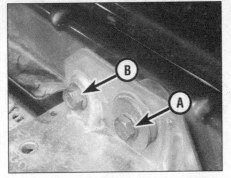

3.15 Radiator upper mounting bolt (A). Note air conditioning condenser mounting bolt (B)

4.4 Fuel pressure regulator and stay mounting bolts on the thermostat housing cover

then fit the hose over its stubs. Work the hose into position. When satisfied, locate and tighten the hose clips.

8 Refill the cooling system as described in Chapter 1. Run the engine, and check that there are no leaks.

9 Recheck the tightness of the hose clips on any new hoses after a few hundred miles.

10 Top-up the coolant level if necessary.

3 Radiator - removal, inspection and refitting

Note: *If the reason for removing the radiator is to cure a leak, it is worth trying the effect of a radiator sealing compound first - this is added to the coolant, and will often cure minor leaks with the radiator in situ.*

Removal

1 The radiator is removed upwards from the engine compartment, complete with the electric cooling fan. First apply the handbrake, then raise the front of the car and support on axle stands.

2 Disconnect the battery negative lead.

3 Unbolt and remove the centre air deflector from under the radiator. On early models, it may be necessary to remove the radiator grille with reference to Chapter 11.

4 Drain the cooling system as described in Chapter 1.

5 On models with air conditioning, where necessary, unscrew and remove the lower mounting bolts from the condenser.

6 Loosen the clip and disconnect the top hose from the radiator **(see illustration)**.

7 Where applicable, remove the air cleaner air inlet pipe.

8 On air conditioning models, unscrew and remove the upper mounting bolts from the condenser.

9 On Turbo models, disconnect the wiring from the boost pressure control valve, and detach it from the bracket on the fan cowling.

10 Disconnect the wiring from the radiator electric cooling fan and thermostatic switch.

11 On models fitted with an oil cooler, unscrew the upper mounting bolt and loosen

the lower mounting bolts from the oil cooler, then position the unit to one side.

12 Loosen the clips and disconnect the expansion tank hose and lower hose from the radiator.

13 Where applicable, unbolt the ignition coil mounting bracket from the radiator crossmember.

14 On automatic transmission models, loosen the unions and disconnect the fluid hoses from the radiator right-hand side tank. Plug or tape the ends of the hoses, to prevent dust and dirt entering the hydraulic system.

15 Unscrew and remove the radiator upper mounting bolt located centrally on top of the radiator **(see illustration)**, then lift the radiator up from the lower mounting rubbers, and remove it from the engine compartment.

16 If necessary, remove the lower mounting rubbers from the crossmember, and remove the electric cooling fan unit.

Inspection

17 If the radiator has been removed due to suspected blockage, reverse-flush it as described in Chapter 1. Clean dirt and debris from the radiator fins, using an air line (in which case, wear eye protection) or a soft brush. Be careful, as the fins are sharp, and easily damaged.

18 If necessary, a radiator specialist can perform a "flow test" on the radiator, to establish whether an internal blockage exists.

19 A leaking radiator must be referred to a specialist for permanent repair. Do not attempt to weld or solder a leaking radiator.

20 If the radiator is to be sent for repair, or is to be renewed, remove the cooling fan thermostatic switch.

21 Inspect the condition of the radiator mounting rubbers, and renew them if necessary.

Refitting

22 Refitting is a reversal of removal, bearing in mind the following points:

a) *Ensure that the lower lugs on the radiator are correctly engaged with the mounting rubbers in the body crossmember.*

b) *Reconnect the hoses with reference to Section 2.*

c) *On completion, refill the cooling system as described in Chapter 1.*

4 Thermostat - removal, testing and refitting

Removal

1 The thermostat is located on the left-hand (transmission) end of the cylinder head.

2 Drain the cooling system as described in Chapter 1.

3 On B204 and B234 engines, remove the airflow meter or air ducting (as applicable) with reference to Chapter 4A. Also disconnect the idle air control valve hose from the throttle housing.

4 On non-Turbo models, unscrew the fuel pressure regulator mounting bolts, then position the regulator to one side **(see illustration)**. Also remove the stay from the cover.

5 On B204 and B234 Turbo models, unbolt the stay from the thermostat housing cover. Also loosen the clip and disconnect the hose from the throttle housing preheater.

6 Unscrew the bolts from the thermostat housing cover, and lift off the cover **(see illustrations)**. If it is stuck, tap it carefully with a soft faced mallet to free the gasket.

4.6a Unscrew the mounting bolts . . .

4.6b . . . and remove the thermostat cover

4.7 Thermostat located in the cylinder head with the bleed hole at the top

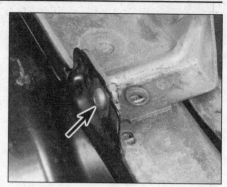

5.10 Electric cooling fan upper mounting screw (only one shown)

7 Note the fitted position of the thermostat (air bleed hole at the top), then prise it out of the housing **(see illustration)**.

Testing

8 A rough test of the thermostat may be made by suspending it with a piece of string in a container full of water. Heat the water to bring it to the boil - the thermostat must open by the time the water boils. If not, renew it.

9 If a thermometer is available, the precise opening temperature of the thermostat may be determined; compare with the figures given in the Specifications. The opening temperature is also marked on the thermostat.

9 A thermostat which fails to close as the water cools must also be renewed.

Refitting

10 Refitting is a reversal of removal, bearing in mind the following points:
 a) *Examine the sealing ring for signs of damage or deterioration, and if necessary, renew.*
 b) *Ensure that the thermostat is fitted the correct way round, as noted before removal. The air bleed hole should be uppermost.*
 c) *Where applicable, refit the air cleaner and/or the air inlet ducting, with reference to the relevant Part of Chapter 4.*
 d) *On completion, refill the cooling system as described in Chapter 1.*

6.2 The electric cooling fan thermostatic switch located in the bottom of the radiator

5 Electric cooling fan - testing, removal and refitting

Testing

1 Current supply to the cooling fan is direct from the battery (see Chapter 5), a fuse (see Chapter 12) and a cooling fan relay unit, located in front of the battery on the left-hand side of the engine compartment. The circuit is completed by the cooling fan thermostatic switch, which is mounted in the right-hand radiator tank. On models with air conditioning, the cooling fan is also controlled by the air conditioning control unit - see Section 6.

2 If the fan does not appear to work, run the engine until normal operating temperature is reached, then allow it to idle. The fan should cut in within a few minutes (just before the temperature gauge needle enters the red section). On air conditioning models, switching on the air conditioning will also operate the fan, since the same fan is used to draw air though the air conditioning condenser. If the fan does not operate, switch off the ignition, and disconnect the wiring plug from the cooling fan switch on the radiator. Bridge the two contacts in the wiring plug, using a length of spare wire. If the fan now operates, the switch is probably faulty, and should be renewed.

3 On models with a 2-speed fan, the resistor may be faulty if the fan only operates at one speed. Use an ohmmeter to check for continuity through the resistor, and if necessary renew the resistor as described later in this Section.

4 If the fan still fails to operate, check that battery voltage is available at the feed wire to the switch; if not, then there is a fault in the feed wire (possibly due to a blown fuse). If there is no problem with the feed, check that there is continuity between the switch earth terminal and a good earth point on the body; if not, then the earth connection is faulty, and must be re-made.

5 If the switch and the wiring are in good condition, the fault must lie in the motor itself. The motor can be checked by disconnecting it from the wiring loom, and connecting a 12-volt supply directly to it.

Removal

6 Disconnect the battery negative lead.

7 Disconnect the wiring for the electric cooling fan.

8 Where the ignition coil is located on the radiator crossmember, disconnect the HT lead from the distributor cap.

9 On Turbo models, disconnect the boost pressure control valve wiring, then remove the valve from its mounting on the cowling, and position it to one side.

10 Unscrew and remove the fan cowling upper mounting screws **(see illustration)**, pull the cowling out a little, then remove the cable clip.

11 Apply the handbrake, then jack up the front of the car and support on axle stands (see *"Jacking, towing and wheel changing"*).

12 Remove the centre air deflector from under the radiator.

13 Unscrew the lower mounting screw from the fan cowling, then lift the cowling complete with the motor and fan upwards from the engine compartment.

14 With the unit on the bench, unscrew the motor mounting nuts. On the 2-speed fan unit, detach the resistor by drilling out the pop-rivets. Remove the switches from the cowling, and take out the motor and fan.

Refitting

15 Refitting is a reversal of removal. Where applicable, fit new pop-rivets to secure the 2-speed fan unit resistor. The resistor can be renewed if necessary by cutting the wires and soldering on the new resistor wires.

6 Cooling system electrical switches - testing, removal and refitting

Electric cooling fan thermostatic switch

Testing

1 Testing of the switch is described in Section 5 as part of the electric cooling fan test procedure.

Removal

2 The switch is located in the bottom right-hand tank of the radiator **(see illustration)**.

The engine and radiator should be cold before removing the switch.

3 Drain the cooling system as described in Chapter 1. Alternatively, have ready a suitable bung to plug the switch aperture in the radiator when the switch is removed. If this method is used, take great care not to damage the radiator, and do not use anything which will allow foreign matter to enter the radiator.

4 Disconnect the wiring plug from the switch.

5 Carefully unscrew the switch from the radiator. If the system has not been drained, plug the switch aperture to prevent further coolant loss.

Refitting

6 Clean the switch threads thoroughly, then refit the switch using a reversal of the removal procedure. Make sure that the switch is tightened securely, then refill (or top-up) the cooling system as described in Chapter 1.

7 On completion, start the engine and run it until it reaches normal operating temperature. Continue to run the engine, and check that the cooling fan cuts in and out correctly.

Coolant temperature gauge sender

Testing

8 The sender is located in the left-hand end of the cylinder head, where the thermostat is located.

9 The temperature gauge is fed with voltage via the ignition switch and a fuse. The gauge earth is controlled by the sender. The sender contains a thermistor - an electronic component whose electrical resistance decreases at a predetermined rate as its temperature rises. When the coolant is cold, the sender resistance is high, current flow through the gauge is reduced, and the gauge needle points towards the blue (cold) end of the scale. As the coolant temperature rises and the sender resistance falls, current flow increases, and the gauge needle moves towards the upper end of the scale. If the sender is faulty, it must be renewed.

10 If the gauge develops a fault, first check the other instruments; if they do not work at all, check the instrument panel electrical feed. If the readings are erratic, there may be a fault in the voltage stabiliser, which will necessitate renewal of the stabiliser (the stabiliser is integral with the instrument panel printed circuit board - see Chapter 12). If the fault lies in the temperature gauge alone, check it as follows.

11 If the gauge needle remains at the "cold" end of the scale when the engine is hot, disconnect the sender wiring plug, and earth the relevant wire to the cylinder head. If the needle then deflects when the ignition is switched on, the sender unit is proved faulty, and should be renewed. If the needle still does not move, remove the instrument panel (Chapter 12) and check the continuity of the wire between the sender unit and the gauge, and the feed to the gauge unit. If continuity is

shown, and the fault still exists, then the gauge is faulty, and the gauge unit should be renewed.

12 If the gauge needle remains at the "hot" end of the scale when the engine is cold, disconnect the sender wire. If the needle then returns to the "cold" end of the scale, the sender unit is proved faulty, and should be renewed. If the needle still does not move, check the remainder of the circuit as described previously.

Removal and refitting

13 The procedure is similar to that described previously in this Section for the electric cooling fan thermostatic switch, but check and if necessary renew the copper sealing washers. On some models, access to the switch is poor, and other components may need to be removed (or hoses, wiring, etc moved to one side) before the sender unit can be reached.

Fuel injection system coolant temperature sensor (Bosch LH-Jetronic)

Testing

14 The coolant temperature sensor is screwed into the inlet manifold flange on the rear of the cylinder head.

15 The sensor is a thermistor (see paragraph 9). The fuel injection ECU supplies the sensor with a set voltage, and by measuring the current flowing in the sensor circuit, it determines the engine temperature. This information is then used, in conjunction with other inputs, to control the injector opening time (pulse width).

16 If the sensor circuit should fail to provide adequate information or if there is a break in the wiring, the ECU back-up facility will assume an engine temperature of 20°C. In this event, the fuel injection system will continue to run, albeit at reduced efficiency. When this occurs, the engine warning light on the instrument panel will come on, and the advice of a Saab dealer should be sought.

17 To check the sensor, disconnect the multi-plug from the fuel injection ECU (see Chapter 4A), then use a suitable ohmmeter connected to terminals 2 (yellow) and 11 (black) to check that the resistance of the sensor is as given in the Specifications.

18 If the resistance is more than specified, disconnect the wiring plug from the sensor, and use the ohmmeter to check the resistance of the actual sensor. If the correct reading is now obtained, either the connector terminals are corroded or the wiring is faulty. If the correct reading is not obtained, fit a new resistor. After checking the wiring and resistor, reconnect the wiring to the ECU and sensor.

Removal and refitting

19 The procedure is similar to that described previously in this Section for the electric cooling fan thermostatic switch. On some models, access to the switch is poor, and

other components may need to be removed (or hoses, wiring, etc moved to one side) before the sensor can be reached.

Fuel injection system coolant temperature sensor (Trionic)

Testing

20 The coolant temperature sensor is screwed into the inlet manifold on the rear of the cylinder head. On models with a normally-aspirated engine, access is gained by removing the upper inlet manifold as described in Chapter 4A.

21 The sensor operates in the same manner as the sensor on the LH-Jetronic system described in paragraphs 15 and 16.

22 To check the sensor, disconnect the wiring plug from the sensor on the rear of the cylinder head, and use an ohmmeter to check the resistance of the internal circuit. If necessary, the sensor may be removed and heated in a container of water. The resistance should be as given in the Specifications.

23 If the resistance is more than specified, either the connector terminals are corroded, or the wiring is faulty. After checking the wiring, refit the sensor (if removed) and reconnect the wiring.

Removal and refitting

24 The procedure is similar to that described in this Section for the electric cooling fan thermostatic switch.

7 Water pump - removal and refitting

B202 (non-balance shaft) engine

Removal

1 The water pump is driven by the auxiliary drivebelt, and is located on the front right-hand side of the engine **(see illustration)**.

2 Apply the handbrake, then jack up the front of the car and support on axle stands (see "Jacking, towing and wheel changing"). Remove the front right-hand wheel.

3 Remove the centre deflector from under the radiator, then drain the cooling system as described in Chapter 1.

7.1 Water pump location on the B202 engine

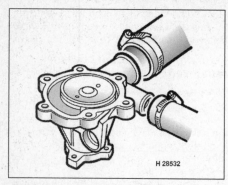

7.11 Water pump removed from the timing cover (B202 engine)

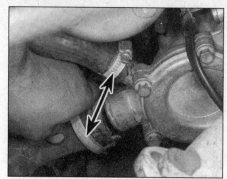

7.33 Disconnecting the hoses from the water pump

7.35 Removing the pulley from the water pump drive flange

4 Remove the plastic moulding and the front section of the wing liner from under the right-hand wheelarch.

5 Remove the auxiliary drivebelt(s) as described in Chapter 1.

6 Unscrew the bolts, and remove the pulley from the water pump drive flange.

7 Unbolt and remove the auxiliary drivebelt tensioner pulley.

8 Unscrew the bolt securing the oil cooler hoses to the timing cover.

9 Unscrew the bolt securing the water pipe to the cylinder block, and pull the pipe from the water pump. Remove the O-ring.

10 Loosen the clips and disconnect the hoses from the water pump.

11 Unscrew the mounting bolts, and remove the water pump from the timing cover (see illustration). Remove the gasket.

12 Clean all gasket and sealant from the contact surfaces of the water pump and timing cover.

Refitting

13 Ensure that all contact surfaces are clean. Locate a new gasket on the timing cover.

14 Locate the water pump on the gasket, then insert the mounting bolts and tighten them progressively to the specified torque.

15 Reconnect the hoses and tighten the clips.

16 Locate a new O-ring on the water pipe, and insert the pipe in the water pump. Insert and tighten the bolt securing the water pipe to the cylinder block.

17 Insert and tighten the bolt securing the oil cooler hoses to the timing cover.

18 Refit the auxiliary drivebelt tensioner pulley, making sure that the plate is located in the slot in the bracket.

19 Refit the pulley to the water pump drive flange, then insert the bolts and tighten to the specified torque.

20 Refit and tension the auxiliary drivebelt(s) with reference to Chapter 1.

21 Check that the radiator drain plug is tight, then refit the centre deflector.

22 Refill the cooling system with reference to Chapter 1.

23 Run the engine to normal temperature and check for leaks, then stop the engine.

24 Refit the plastic moulding and the front section of the wing liner under the right-hand wheelarch.

25 Refit the right-hand front wheel, and lower the car to the ground.

B204/B234 (balance shaft) engines

Removal

26 The water pump is driven by the auxiliary drivebelt, and is located on the front right-hand side of the engine.

27 Apply the handbrake, then jack up the front of the car and support on axle stands (see "Jacking, towing and wheel changing").

28 Remove the centre deflector from under the radiator, then drain the cooling system as described in Chapter 1.

29 Remove the coolant expansion tank from its mounting. On models up to 1991, unscrew the bolt; on later models, release the clip.

30 Loosen the clip and disconnect the lower hose from the expansion tank. Where applicable, disconnect the engine coolant level sensor from the expansion tank.

31 Pull on the multi-groove auxiliary drivebelt so that the automatic tensioner is retracted, then hold the tensioner in this position by fitting a home-made tool (see Chapter 1) in the special slots. Slip the drivebelt from the air conditioner compressor and water pump pulleys.

32 Place a piece of cardboard over the oil cooler and upper radiator crossmember (as applicable), then disconnect the wiring from the air conditioning compressor. Unbolt the compressor and move it to one side without disconnecting the refrigerant lines - also remove the bracket.

33 Loosen the clips and disconnect the hoses from the water pump (see illustration).

34 On Turbo models, remove the lambda wiring cable clips, then remove the coolant pipe from the turbocharger and water pump.

35 Unscrew the bolts, and remove the pulley from the water pump drive flange (see illustration).

36 Unscrew and remove the three mounting bolts securing the top of the water pump to the timing cover. Note that the upper bolt also secures the support for the lambda sensor wiring (see illustration).

7.36 Unscrew the upper water pump mounting bolt which secures the lambda wiring support

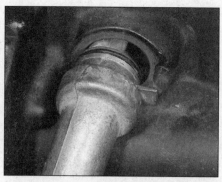

7.37a Removing the water pump and sleeve from the cylinder block

7.37b Releasing the coolant pipe from the aperture in the water pump

7.37c Remove the adapter from the water pump . . .

7.37d . . . and recover the O-rings

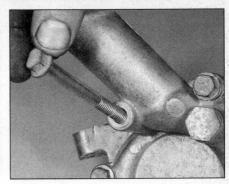

7.38a Unscrew the bolts . . .

37 Carefully prise out the water pump and sleeve from the cylinder block, at the same time releasing the coolant pump from the aperture in the water pump housing. Take care not to damage the lambda sensor (where fitted). Remove the adapter from the water pump, then recover the O-rings from the adapter and coolant pipe **(see illustrations)**.
38 Unscrew the bolts, and separate the water pump and cover. Remove the gasket **(see illustrations)**.
39 Clean all gasket and sealant from the contact surfaces of the water pump and housing.

Refitting

40 Ensure that all contact surfaces are clean. Locate the water pump in its housing together with a new gasket, then insert and tighten the bolts.
41 Apply a little petroleum jelly to the new O-rings, then locate them on the adapter sleeve, water pump and coolant pipe.
42 Locate the water pump on the timing cover; at the same time, locate the sleeve in the cylinder block and engage the end of the coolant pipe, then insert the bolts and tighten them to the specified torque. Remember to fit the lambda wiring support to the upper bolt.
43 Locate the pulley on the drive flange, then insert and tighten the bolts.
44 On Turbo models, refit the coolant pipes to the turbocharger and water pump, and refit the lambda wiring cable clips.
45 Reconnect the hoses to the water pump,

position the clips and tighten them.
46 Refit the air conditioning compressor and bracket, and reconnect the wiring.
47 Locate the multi-groove auxiliary drivebelt on the pulleys, then pull it to retract the automatic tensioner, and remove the locking tool. Release the drivebelt, and make sure that it is located correctly in the pulley grooves.
48 Where applicable, reconnect the engine coolant level sensor to the expansion tank.
49 Reconnect the lower hose to the expansion tank, and secure by tightening the clip.
50 Refit the coolant expansion tank, and tighten the bolt or reconnect the clip as applicable.
51 Check that the radiator drain plug is tight, then refit the centre deflector under the radiator.
52 Refill the cooling system with reference to Chapter 1.
53 Run the engine to normal temperature and check for leaks, then stop the engine.
54 Lower the car to the ground.

8 Heating/ventilation system - general information

1 Three types of heating/ventilation system are fitted - the Standard system controlled manually, the Standard system with air conditioning also controlled manually, and the Automatic Climate Control (ACC) system which maintains the temperature inside the car at a selected temperature, regardless of the

temperature outside the car. The basic heating/ventilation unit is common to all versions, and consists of air ducting from the centrally-located heater assembly to a central vent and two side vents, with an extension leading from the bottom of the heater through the centre console to the rear passenger footwell areas. A four-speed heater blower motor is fitted.
2 The heating and ventilation controls are mounted in the centre of the facia. Cable-controlled flap valves are contained in the air distribution housing, to divert the air to the various ducts and vents.
3 Cold air enters the system through the grille at the bottom of the windscreen. If required, the airflow is boosted by the blower, and then flows through the various ducts, according to the settings of the controls. Stale air is expelled through ducts at the rear of the vehicle. If warm air is required, the cold air is passed over the heater matrix, which is heated by the engine coolant.
4 On later models, air circulator blower motors are located in the rear doors **(see illustration)**.
5 On models fitted with air conditioning, a recirculation switch enables the outside air supply to be closed off, while the air inside the vehicle is recirculated. This can be useful to prevent unpleasant odours entering from outside the vehicle, but should only be used briefly, as the recirculated air inside the vehicle will soon become stale.

7.38b . . . separate the cover . . .

7.38c . . . and remove the gasket

8.4 Air circulator blower motor located in the rear door

9.13a Removing the wiper arms . . .

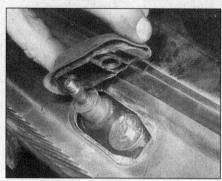

9.13b . . . and plastic covers

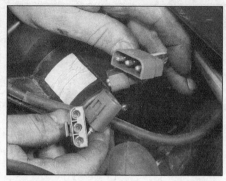

9.15 Disconnecting the heater blower and wiper wiring plugs

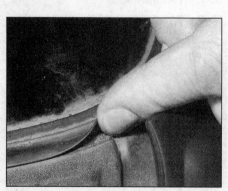

9.17a Removing the plastic end covers

---

9 Heating/ventilation components - removal and refitting

Heater blower motor (models without air conditioning or ACC)

Removal

1 Disconnect the battery negative lead.
2 Remove the ventilation air filter with reference to Chapter 1.
3 Disconnect the wiring for the heater blower motor and resistors.
4 Disconnect the inner cable from the temperature control flap on the heater box.
5 Using a screwdriver, release the retaining clips from each side of the heater blower motor housing.
6 Push the housing downwards, then remove it by moving it to the right-hand side of the car. Withdraw the housing from inside the car.
7 Unscrew the central screw, then release the clips and remove the grille from the discharge outlet.
8 Separate the blower motor housing halves.
9 Unscrew the motor mounting screw, lift the lead cover and remove the motor from the impeller.

Refitting

10 Refitting is a reversal of removal.

Heater blower motor (models with air conditioning and/or ACC)

Removal

11 Disconnect the battery negative lead.
12 Remove the bonnet with reference to Chapter 11.
13 Remove the wiper arms and plastic covers with reference to Chapter 12 **(see illustrations)**.
14 Where necessary, remove the covers from the evaporator and wiper motor.
15 Disconnect the wiring for the heater blower motor and wiper motor **(see illustration)**.
16 Unscrew the bolts and remove the false bulkhead panel from the rear of the engine compartment.
17 Carefully remove the plastic drainage moulding from just below the windscreen. To do this, first remove the plastic end covers, then prise the moulding up using a screwdriver at the positions of the retaining studs. Place the studs in a suitable container, and pull the moulding from under the windscreen moulding **(see illustrations)**.
18 Unscrew and remove the mounting bolts for the electronic control unit (ECU), and position the ECU to one side.
19 Prise free the linkage rod, then unscrew the mounting bracket screws, disconnect the wiring and remove the wiper motor assembly (refer to Chapter 12 if necessary).
20 Release the matrix coolant supply hoses from the clip on the bulkhead. Identify the hoses for position.

9.21 Disconnecting the hoses from the heater matrix

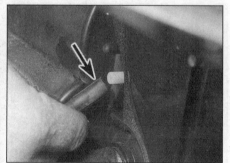

9.22a Disconnecting the hose from the cruise control vacuum adapter on the bulkhead

9.17b Remove the retaining studs . . .

9.17c . . . and pull the moulding from under the windscreen moulding

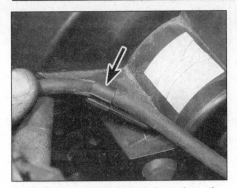

9.22b Releasing the vacuum hose from the clip on the heater motor housing

9.24a Unscrewing the evaporator body front . . .

9.24b . . . and rear securing screws . . .

21 Drain the cooling system with reference to Chapter 1 (or alternatively drain off a few litres of coolant), then loosen the clips retaining the hoses to the heater matrix. Disconnect the hoses from the matrix **(see illustration)**.

22 Where necessary, remove the throttle dashpot. Also disconnect the vacuum hose from the cruise control adapter tube on the bulkhead, and release the hose from the clip on the heater motor housing **(see illustrations)**.

23 Unscrew and remove the mounting screws for the cruise control system vacuum pump, and position the pump to one side. Disconnect the vacuum hose from the black outlet on the pump.

24 Unscrew the evaporator body securing screws, and release the refrigerant pipes from the plastic clips **(see illustrations)**.

25 Disconnect the inner control cable from the temperature control valve on the side of the heater blower housing **(see illustration)**.

26 Move the evaporator and housing as far to the right as possible, taking care not to damage the refrigerant pipes.

27 Release the retaining clips and unscrew the mounting screws (as applicable) and withdraw the complete heater blower motor unit **(see illustration)**. It will be necessary to turn the unit diagonally to do this in order to clear the bulkhead.

28 With the unit on the bench, unscrew the central screw, remove the plastic bracket, then release the clips and separate the two halves of the blower housing **(see**

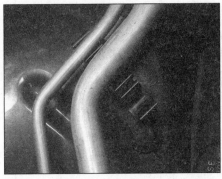

9.24c . . . and release the refrigerant pipes from the clips

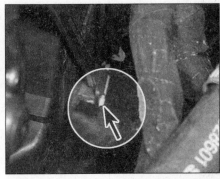

9.25 Disconnecting the temperature control valve cable on the side of the heater blower housing

9.27 Removing the heater blower motor

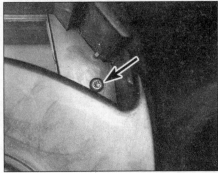

9.28a Unscrew the central screw (arrowed) . . .

9.28b . . . remove the plastic bracket . . .

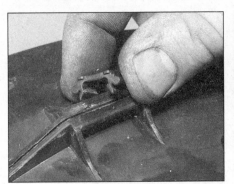

9.28c . . . release the clips . . .

9.28d . . . and separate the two halves of the blower housing

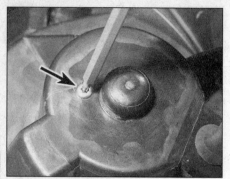

9.29a Unscrew the motor mounting screw . . .

9.29b . . . lift the lead cover . . .

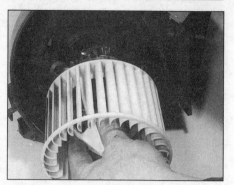

9.29c . . . and remove the motor from the housing

illustrations). Note how the two halves fit together, to facilitate reassembly.

29 Unscrew the motor mounting screw, lift the lead cover and remove the motor from the housing **(see illustrations)**.

Refitting

30 Refitting is a reversal of the removal procedure, but when refitting the false bulkhead panel, take care not to pull the wiring from the radiator fan control unit. When refitting the plastic drainage moulding, make sure that it locates under the windscreen moulding lower lip.

Heater matrix

Removal

31 Follow the procedure for removing the heater blower motor as previously described.

32 If not already done, drain the cooling system with reference to Chapter 1.

33 If not already done, loosen the clips and disconnect the hoses from the matrix.

34 Support the evaporator housing as high as possible, then withdraw the heater matrix from the heater housing **(see illustration)**. If necessary, the inlet and outlet stubs can be removed from the matrix, after removing the special clips. Recover the O-rings.

35 Examine the O-rings, and if necessary renew them.

Refitting

36 Refitting is a reversal of removal. After reconnecting the hoses and before refitting the

9.34 Removing the heater matrix from the heater housing

remaining components, refill the cooling system and check for leaks.

Heater box

Removal

37 Remove the heater blower motor and the matrix as described previously in this Section.

38 Remove the facia panel assembly as described in Chapter 11.

39 Remove the panel vents, air ducts, and the left-hand defroster vent, then disconnect the right-hand defroster vent.

40 Remove the air duct for the rear seat passengers from the heater box.

41 Disconnect the wiring for the servo motor and heater blower motor from the heater box.

42 Unscrew the heater box mounting bolts.

43 Unclip the wiring loom in the engine compartment, and pull the rubber grommet to one side.

44 Withdraw the heater box diagonally upwards. Note that the bottom of the heater box locates in a groove on the bulkhead and facia panel assembly.

Refitting

45 Refitting is a reversal of removal.

Heater control panel (except ACC models)

Removal

46 Remove the glovebox with reference to Chapter 11. Also remove the panel beneath the glovebox.

47 Reach up behind the heater control panel,

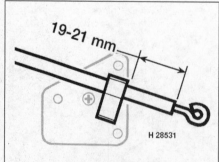

9.57 Heater temperature control cable refitting dimension

and release the four clips. Pull out the panel.

48 Disconnect the air distribution valve link rod, the bevel gear for the temperature control valve, and all connectors.

Refitting

49 Refitting is a reversal of removal, but note the following points:

a) When refitting the bevel gear for the temperature control valve, make sure that the valve in the engine compartment (as well as the control knob) is set to COLD.

b) When refitting the link rod, turn the pinion spindle anti-clockwise as far as possible, then set the air distribution control to position "O". Reconnect the link rod so that the orange part is towards the spindle on the control panel.

c) Check the operation of the heater controls on completion.

Heater temperature control cable

Removal

50 Remove the glovebox as described in Chapter 11. Also remove the panel from under the glovebox.

51 Remove the speaker grilles, then unscrew the screws from the top of the facia panel by prising up the front edge, and pulling it forwards so that the clip is released from the rear edge.

52 Unscrew the screws and lower the power distribution panel, then remove the side vent and defroster air ducts.

53 Reach up behind the heater control panel and release the clips. Pull the panel forwards.

54 Disconnect the air distribution valve link rod, and disconnect the bevel gear for the temperature control cable from the control panel.

55 Disconnect the inner control cable from the temperature valve in the engine compartment.

56 Release the clip securing the cable to the heater box, and remove the cable.

Refitting

57 Refitting is a reversal of removal, but note the following points:

a) When reconnecting the cable to the valve in the engine compartment, position the outer cable as shown **(see illustration)**.

b) *Refer to the refitting instructions given in paragraph 49.*

c) *Check the operation of the heater controls on completion.*

Climate control unit

Removal

58 Disconnect the battery negative lead.

59 Carefully pull out the ashtray, and leave it hanging on the wiring.

60 Push out the control panel complete with the control unit, and disconnect the multi-plug and earth.

Refitting

61 Refitting is a reversal of removal.

Climate control unit sensors

62 The climate control unit sensors are located as follows. The sun sensor is located either on the left-hand side of the facia, or on the top centre of the facia. The ambient air temperature sensor is located in the inlet air plenum to the heater assembly, and the interior air temperature sensor is located centrally on the facia. The mixed air sensor is also located centrally in the heater assembly.

Interior air temperature sensor

Removal

63 Disconnect the battery negative lead.

64 Remove the ashtray from the facia panel.

65 Remove the climate control unit as previously described.

66 Pull out the air sensor, and disconnect the wiring.

Refitting

67 Refitting is a reversal of removal, but make sure that the sensor hose is not twisted.

Ambient air temperature sensor

Removal

68 Disconnect the battery negative lead.

69 Working in the engine compartment, remove the bulkhead panel.

70 Disconnect the wiring and remove the sensor.

Refitting

71 Refitting is a reversal of removal, but make sure that the metallic surface of the sensor is facing upwards.

Mixed air sensor

Removal

72 Disconnect the battery negative lead.

73 Remove the glovebox with reference to Chapter 11.

74 Remove the sensor from the air distribution housing, and disconnect the wiring.

Refitting

75 Refitting is a reversal of removal.

Sun sensor

Removal

Note: *On later models the sensor was fitted to the glare shield on the dashboard.*

76 Disconnect the battery negative lead.

77 Remove the left-hand speaker grille.

78 Disconnect the wiring, and remove the sensor from the double-sided tape.

Refitting

79 Clean away all traces of the double-sided tape, then secure the new sensor with new tape. The remaining procedure is a reversal of removal.

Climate control system servo motors

Removal

80 On the control unit, press the red button until "HI" appears on the display.

81 Disconnect the battery negative lead.

82 Remove the glovebox as described in Chapter 11.

83 Unscrew the screws, and lower the power distribution panel.

84 Disconnect the wiring for the servo motors, heater blower motor and interior air sensor.

85 Disconnect the temperature control cable from the servo motor.

86 Unscrew the mounting screws, and pull out the bracket complete with the electric servo motors.

87 Disconnect the hose from the interior air sensor, and lift out the bracket complete with the motors.

Refitting

88 Pull out the control panel slightly from the facia, then refit the bracket with motors, making sure that the bevel gear is correctly located, and that the cable is reconnected on the correct side of the bracket. Insert and tighten the mounting screws.

89 Reconnect the wiring, and connect the hose to the interior air sensor.

90 Refit the power distribution panel, and tighten the screws.

91 Refit the glovebox with reference to Chapter 11.

92 Reconnect the battery negative lead.

Rear door air circulator blower motors

Removal

93 Remove the rear door interior trim panel, with reference to Chapter 11.

94 Disconnect the wiring, then unscrew the mounting screws and remove the motor from inside the door.

Refitting

95 Refitting is a reversal of removal.

10 Air conditioning system – general information and precautions

General information

1 Air conditioning is available on certain models. It enables the temperature of air inside the car to be lowered, and also dehumidifies the air, which makes for rapid demisting and increased comfort.

2 The cooling side of the system works in the same way as a domestic refrigerator. Refrigerant gas is drawn into a belt-driven compressor, and passes into a condenser mounted in front of the radiator, where it loses heat and becomes liquid. The liquid passes through a receiver and expansion valve to an evaporator, where it changes from liquid under high pressure to gas under low pressure. This change is accompanied by a drop in temperature, which cools the evaporator. The refrigerant returns to the compressor, and the cycle begins again **(see illustrations)**.

10.2a Air conditioning receiver is located in the front right-hand corner of the engine compartment (later models)

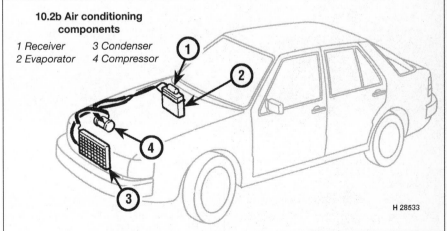

10.2b Air conditioning components

1 Receiver
2 Evaporator
3 Condenser
4 Compressor

H 28533

3 On certain non-UK models fitted with automatic climate control (ACC), a separate evaporator and fan unit is located in the boot.

4 Air drawn through the evaporator passes to the air distribution unit. The air conditioning system has two control buttons located to the left of the heater control panel - one button switches the air conditioning on, and the other operates the interior air recirculation system.

5 The heating side of the system works in the same way as on models without air conditioning (see Section 8).

6 The operation of the system is controlled by an electromagnetic clutch on the compressor drive pulley. Any problems with the system should be referred to a Saab dealer.

7 The air conditioning compressor will not operate if refrigerant pressure is below a satisfactory level.

Precautions

8 When working on the air conditioning system, it is necessary to observe special precautions. If for any reason the system must be disconnected, entrust this task to your Saab dealer or a refrigeration engineer.

⚠️ *Warning: The refrigeration circuit contains a liquid refrigerant under pressure, and it is therefore dangerous to disconnect any part of the system without specialised knowledge and equipment. The refrigerant is potentially dangerous, and should only be handled by qualified persons. If it is splashed onto the skin, it can cause frostbite. It is not itself poisonous, but in the presence of a naked flame (including a cigarette) it forms a poisonous gas. Uncontrolled discharging of the refrigerant is dangerous, and potentially damaging to the environment. Do not operate the air conditioning system if it is known to be short of refrigerant, as this may damage the compressor.*

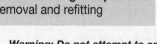

11 Air conditioning components
- removal and refitting

⚠️ *Warning: Do not attempt to open the refrigerant circuit. Refer to the precautions given in Section 10.*

1 The only operation which can be carried out easily without discharging the refrigerant is renewal of the compressor drivebelt. This is described in Chapter 1, Section 22. All other operations must be referred to a Saab dealer or an air conditioning specialist.

2 If necessary for access to other components, the compressor can be unbolted and moved aside, **without** disconnecting its flexible hoses, after removing the drivebelt.

3 Access to the condenser is gained by removing the radiator (and, where applicable, the intercooler).

Chapter 4 Part A: Fuel and exhaust systems

Contents

Degrees of difficulty

Easy, suitable for novice with little experience	Fairly easy, suitable for beginner with some experience	Fairly difficult, suitable for competent DIY mechanic	Difficult, suitable for experienced DIY mechanic	Very difficult, suitable for expert DIY or professional 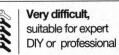

Specifications

System type

1985 cc models (1986 to 1993)	LH-Jetronic fuel injection system
1985 cc models (1994-on)	Saab Trionic SFi engine management system
2290 cc models (1990 to 1992)	LH-Jetronic fuel injection system
2290 cc non-Turbo models (1993)	LH-Jetronic fuel injection system
2290 cc Turbo models (1993-on)	Saab Trionic SFi engine management system

Fuel system data (LH-Jetronic fuel injection system)

Auxiliary air valve winding resistance (at 20°C)	40 to 60 ohms
Idle air control valve resistance (at 20°C):	
LH version 2.2	20 ± 5 ohms
LH version 2.4, LH version 2.4.1	7 ± 5 ohms
LH version 2.4.2	12 ± 3 ohms
Fuel pump capacity	900 cc/30 sec (minimum)
Fuel gauge sender unit winding resistance:	
Full tank	350 ohms
Empty tank	35 ohms
Idle speed:	
LH-Jetronic fuel injection system without automatic idle control (AIC) . .	850 ± 75 rpm
LH-Jetronic fuel injection system with AIC	Controlled by AIC valve at 850 ± 50 rpm (not adjustable)
Idle mixture CO content:	
B202 Turbo (1985)	1.3 ± 0.3 %
B202i (1986-on)	1.0 ± 0.5 %
B234i (1991-on)	1.0 ± 0.5 %

Fuel system data (Trionic engine management system)

Manifold absolute pressure sensor (expressed in **absolute** pressure):

Pressure	Voltage (approx)
-0.75 bar	0.48
-0.50 bar	0.95
0 bar	1.9
0.25 bar	2.4
0.50 bar	2.8
0.75 bar	3.3

Fuel system data (Trionic engine management system) (continued)

Inlet air temperature (AIC) sensor:

Temperature (°C)	Voltage (approx)
-30	4.5
-10	3.9
20	2.4
40	1.5
60	0.9
80	0.54
90	0.41

Throttle position switch:	Resistance	Voltage
Pins 1 and 2	1.6 to 2.4	5 ± 0.1
Pins 2 and 3 - idling	0.8 to 1.2	0.5 ± 0.4
Pins 2 and 3 - wide open	2.0 to 3.0	4.5 ± 0.4

Crankshaft position sensor:
Resistance (pins 1 and 2) .... 540 ± 55 ohms
Fuel pressure regulator:
Pressure .... 3.0 ± 0.1 bars
Injectors:
Resistance at 20°C:
Turbo engine .... 12.0 ± 0.35 ohms
Non-turbo engine .... 14.5 ± 0.35 ohms
Flow capacity:
Turbo engine .... 176 ± 14 ml/30 seconds
Non-turbo engine .... 127 ± 10 ml/30 seconds
Maximum flow difference between injectors:
Turbo engine .... 18 ml
Non-turbo engine .... 13 ml
Idle air control valve:
Resistance at 20°C .... 7.7 ± 1 ohms
Fuel pump:
Type .... Electric immersed in fuel tank
Capacity at 3.0 bars .... 700 ml/30 seconds (minimum)
Fuel gauge sender unit winding resistance .... 33 to 370 ohms
Idle speed .... Controlled by automatic idle control at 850 ± 50 rpm (not adjustable)
Idle mixture .... Controlled by lambda sensor

Turbocharger

Type:
Models from 1985 to 1988 .... Garrett T3
Models from 1989 to 1990 (without catalytic converter) .... Garrett TE05
1990 models (with catalytic converter) .... Garrett T25
1991 models (except 9000 Aero with manual gearbox) .... Garrett T25M
1993-on models .... Garrett TD04

Fuel tank

Capacity:
1985 to 1989 models .... 68 litres
1990 and 1992-on models .... 66 litres
1991 models .... 62 litres

Recommended fuel

Non-turbo models .... 95 RON Premium unleaded or 98 RON Super unleaded
Turbo models .... 98 RON Super unleaded

Torque wrench settings

	Nm	lbf ft
Crankshaft position sensor	8	6
Exhaust manifold to cylinder head	25	18
Exhaust manifold-to-turbocharger nuts:		
T3/TE05	40	30
T25/TD04	22	16
Exhaust system section flange joints	40	30
Front exhaust pipe to turbocharger	25	18
Inlet manifold:		
B202 engine	18	13
B234 engine	22	16
Intercooler-to-condenser mounting bolts	8	6
Lambda sensor	55	41
Oil cooler upper union bolt	18	13

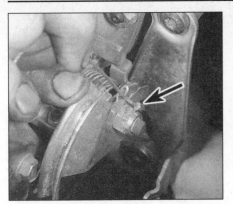

3.3 Disconnecting the inner cable (arrowed) from the throttle housing sector

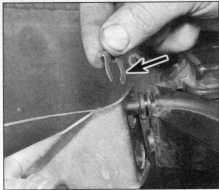

3.4 Removing the outer cable clip securing the accelerator cable to the throttle housing

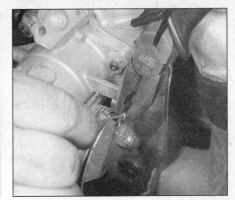

3.16 Using pliers to secure the end of the accelerator cable to the throttle housing sector

1 General information and precautions

The fuel system consists of a fuel tank mounted under the rear of the car (with an electric fuel pump immersed in it), a fuel filter, and the fuel feed and return lines. The fuel pump supplies fuel to the fuel rail, which acts as a reservoir for the four fuel injectors which inject fuel into the inlet tracts. A fuel filter is incorporated in the feed line from the pump to the fuel rail, to ensure that the fuel supplied to the injectors is clean. The filter is located between the battery and the false bulkhead on models with the LH-Jetronic fuel injection system, or adjacent to the fuel tank on models with the Trionic engine management system.

The fuel injection system is of Bosch LH-Jetronic type (models up to 1993) or Saab Trionic type (models from 1993 on). Refer to Section 8 for further information on the operation of the relevant fuel injection system, and to Section 22 for information on the exhaust system.

A cruise control system is fitted as standard equipment on most models. This system allows the driver to preselect the speed of the car, and then remove his foot from the accelerator pedal. The system is disengaged automatically when the clutch or brake pedals are depressed, or when the system is switched off.

A turbocharger is fitted to certain models. Refer to Section 17 for more information.

> ⚠️ **Warning: Many of the procedures in this Chapter require the removal of fuel lines and connections, which may result in some fuel spillage. Before carrying out any operation on the fuel system, refer to the precautions given in "Safety first!" and follow them implicitly. Petrol is a highly-dangerous and volatile liquid, and the precautions necessary when handling it cannot be overstressed.**

2 Air cleaner assembly - removal and refitting

Removal

1 Slacken the retaining clip, and disconnect the inlet duct hose from the air cleaner cover.
2 Release the toggle spring clips, and lift off the air cleaner cover.
3 Remove the air cleaner element (refer to Chapter 1 if necessary). On models with an LH-Jetronic fuel injection system, lift the element from the lower body. On models with the Trionic engine management system, pull the element out of the cylindrical body.
4 Unscrew the mounting screws, and withdraw the air cleaner body from the engine compartment, disconnecting the air inlet duct as necessary.

Refitting

5 Refitting is a reversal of the removal procedure.

3 Accelerator cable - removal, refitting and adjustment

Removal

1 Loosen the clips, and remove the inlet air duct from the throttle housing and inlet manifold.
2 Where applicable, remove the EGR pipe.
3 Release the accelerator inner cable from the throttle housing sector. The end of the inner cable may be clamped to the sector, in which case a small screwdriver will be required to prise the clamp apart (see illustration).
4 Pull out the clip, and disconnect the accelerator outer cable from the bracket on the throttle housing (see illustration).
5 Inside the car, pull back the insulation above the accelerator pedal. On left-hand drive models, remove the panel on the left-hand side of the centre console. On right-hand drive models, note that the pedal extends over to the left-hand side of the facia panel, and it

will be necessary to pull back the insulation from this side as well.
6 On 1994 models, detach the cruise control ball chain from the locking plate. Note the position of the plate, to ensure correct refitting.
7 While holding the accelerator pedal in the depressed position, disconnect the locking plate from the cable, and detach the cable and bushing from the accelerator pedal inside the car.
8 Attach a piece of string or wire to the end of the accelerator cable, then press the cable flange from the bulkhead with a screwdriver.
9 Pull the cable into the engine compartment, then disconnect the string and remove the cable.

Refitting

10 Apply a little petroleum jelly to the flange of the accelerator cable. Connect the string or wire to it, and draw it through the bulkhead. Press the flange into the bulkhead, using a large screwdriver.
11 Reconnect the cable and bushing to the accelerator pedal inside the car.
12 Untie the string, and refit the locking plate. Before releasing the pedal, secure the locking plate with insulating tape.
13 On 1994 models, reconnect the cruise control ball chain in its previously-noted position.
14 Refit the insulation and on left-hand drive models, refit the panel on the left-hand side of the centre console.
15 Refit the accelerator outer cable to the bracket on the throttle housing, and secure with the clip.
16 Reconnect the inner cable to the throttle housing sector, and where necessary compress the clamp using a pair of pliers (see illustration).
17 Turn the adjusting nut on the outer cable, until there is a little slack in the cable with the pedal released.
18 Where applicable, refit the EGR pipe.
19 Refit the air duct between the throttle housing and the inlet manifold, and tighten the clips.

4 Accelerator pedal - removal and refitting

Removal

1 Using a bolt or similar tool, hold the sector on the throttle housing slightly open, in order to relieve the tension of the cable when it is disconnected from the pedal.
2 Inside the car, remove the insulation above the pedals. On left-hand drive models, remove the panel from the left-hand side of the centre console. On right-hand drive models, remove the insulation above the passenger footwell.
3 Lift the pedal, and disconnect the inner cable after releasing the clip.
4 Unscrew the bolts on the pedal bracket, and remove the pedal.

Refitting

5 Refitting is a reversal of removal, but make sure that the mounting bolts are tightened securely. If necessary, adjust the accelerator cable as described in Section 3.

5 Cruise control system - description and component renewal

Description

1 The cruise control system allows the driver to preselect the speed of the car, then remove his foot from the accelerator pedal. The system is deactivated when the clutch or brake pedals are depressed, or when the main cruise control switch is switched off. There are two versions of cruise control fitted to the models covered by this manual. Both versions have their own electronic control unit, but the early version uses vacuum to move the accelerator pedal cable, whereas the later version uses a stepper motor to move the throttle lever on the throttle housing.
2 In the event of a fault in the cruise control system, first check all relevant wiring for security. Further testing is best left to a Saab dealer, who will have the necessary diagnostic equipment to find the fault quickly.

Early models

3 The main components of the system fitted to early models are as follows:
a) **Electronic control unit**: the electronic control unit (ECU) is located below the facia panel on the right-hand side (right-hand-drive models) or on the left-hand side (left-hand-drive models). The ECU stores the speed transmitted by the speed transducer when the "Set" button is depressed. The system is not operative at speeds below 23 mph, nor above 112 mph.
b) **Speed transducer**: the speed transducer is located on the rear of the instrument panel. It monitors the speed of the car, and sends signals to the vacuum pump to raise or reduce the vacuum in order to adjust the speed of the car.
c) **Cruise control switch**: the main control switch for the cruise control system is located on the left-hand side of the steering wheel, and is incorporated in the direction indicator switch.
d) **Vacuum pump and vacuum valve**: the vacuum pump is located on the right-hand side of the bulkhead in the engine compartment. When the cruise control system is activated, the pump runs, but the actual vacuum produced is regulated by the vacuum valve. In certain circumstances the vacuum pump will stop, in order to reduce the vacuum in the vacuum regulator.
e) **Vacuum regulator**: the vacuum regulator is located on a bracket near the accelerator pedal. It incorporates a ball-link chain, which is clipped to the accelerator cable at the top of the accelerator pedal. On right-hand-drive models, the accelerator pedal is extended into the left-hand footwell, and the vacuum regulator is located under the facia behind the glovebox position.
f) **Pedal switches**: switches are provided on the brake and clutch pedals, in order to disengage the system when either pedal is depressed. Each switch has a double function - electrical and vacuum. If either pedal is depressed, the electrical connection will be broken, and the vacuum pump will stop. At the same time,
the system vacuum will be dissipated by the switch's internal port.

Later models

4 The main components of the system fitted to later models are as follows:
a) **Control module**: the control module incorporates an electric stepper motor, which operates the control cable attached to the throttle butterfly lever on the throttle housing. The module is supplied with the speed of the car by signals sent from the speedometer in the instrument panel. The system is not operative at speeds below 20 mph, nor above 137 mph. When the cruise control system is active, the engine management ECU is informed of this fact by a signal, to ensure smoother control of the car's speed.
b) **Switches**: the main control switch for the cruise control system is located on the left-hand side of the steering wheel. Switches are provided on the brake and clutch pedals, in order to deactivate the system when either pedal is depressed. The brake pedal cruise control switch is earthed through the brake stop-light bulbs, via the main stop light switch - if this circuit develops a fault, the cruise control system will not operate.
c) **Indicator light**: the indicator light on the instrument panel is illuminated when the cruise control system is operating.

Component renewal - early models

Cruise control switch

5 The switch is integral with the direction indicator switch. Refer to Chapter 12 for the removal and refitting procedure.

Speed transducer

6 Remove the instrument panel as described in Chapter 12, then remove the upper section of the panel for access to the transducer.

Vacuum pump

7 The pump is located on the right-hand side of the engine compartment, on the bulkhead. Disconnect the wiring and vacuum hoses, then unscrew the mounting bracket bolts (**see illustrations**). The pump can be removed from the bracket after unscrewing the bolt.

5.7a Disconnecting the wiring . . .

5.7b . . . and vacuum hoses . . .

5.7c . . . then unscrew the mounting bolts (arrowed) and remove the cruise control vacuum pump

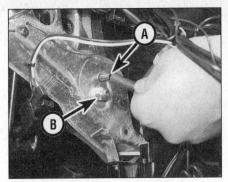

5.9a Disconnect the vacuum hose (A), then unscrew the mounting nut (B) . . .

5.9b . . . and remove the vacuum regulator (arrowed)

5.12 Cruise control module on later right-hand-drive models (removed from its mounting bracket)

ECU

8 Remove the lower panel from under the facia panel. The ECU is mounted on the same bracket as the APC system module. On right-hand drive models, the ECU is located on a bracket to the right of the steering column.

Vacuum regulator

9 The vacuum regulator is located on a bracket near the left-hand end of the accelerator pedal. Access is gained by removing the glovebox (right-hand drive models) or lower facia panel (left-hand drive models). Take care not to damage the rubber gaiter when removing and refitting the regulator. The ball-link chain should be fitted to the accelerator cable clip near the top of the accelerator pedal, so that all slack is taken up without moving the cable **(see illustrations)**.

Pedal switches

10 The switches are located on the same bracket as the stop-light switch. Access is gained by removing the lower facia panel. When refitting the switches, adjust them so that there is a clearance of 1.0 mm between the threaded part of the switch and the actuator tip. Make sure that the pedals are fully released before adjusting the switches.

Component renewal - later models

Control module

11 The control module is located beneath the right-hand side of the facia on right-hand-drive models, or behind the battery on left-hand-drive models.
12 On right-hand drive models, remove the module from its bracket, and disconnect the wiring **(see illustration)**. On left-hand-drive models, first remove the battery as described in Chapter 5A, then disconnect the wiring plug from the control module. Unscrew the three mounting bolts, then lift the module from its location as far as the throttle cable will allow. Open the throttle butterfly lever, then disconnect the cable from the sector on the throttle housing, and release it from the holder.
13 Refitting is a reversal of removal

Clutch and brake pedal switches

Note: *Refer to Chapter 9 for details of the stop-light switch.*

14 Remove the lower panel from under the facia. Disconnect the wiring from the switch, then prise the switch from the pedal bracket using a screwdriver.
15 Refitting is a reversal of removal.

Cruise control switch

16 Remove the upper and lower steering column shrouds with reference to Chapter 10, then disconnect the wiring plug. Unbolt and remove the switch.
17 Refitting is a reversal of removal.

6 Traction control system (TCS) - description and component renewal

Description

1 Fitted as an option on earlier models, and as standard on later high-specification models, the Traction Control System (TCS) prevents uncontrolled wheelspin under acceleration and on slippery surfaces. The TCS works in conjunction with the Anti-lock Braking System (ABS) described in Chapter 9. The main components of the TCS are as follows.

a) *Electronic Throttle System: The TCS uses an electronic throttle system (ETS) in addition to a cable to operate the throttle butterfly in the throttle housing. The ETS comprises a pedal potentiometer and a throttle potentiometer/motor. When the driver depresses the accelerator pedal with the system in operation, the potentiometer sends an output signal to the ETS electronic control module. Under normal conditions, the control module will activate the throttle motor, and position the throttle butterfly directly in relation to the pedal position. When wheelspin is detected within the pre-programmed operational speeds, the control module determines how much the throttle butterfly should be closed in order to reduce the torque from the engine until the wheel regains traction. Throttle repositioning is normally applied only at speeds above approximately 30 mph. The throttle potentiometer informs the control module of the throttle butterfly position.*

b) *ETS control module: the ETS control module is located on a bracket beneath the left-hand front seat, and on automatic transmission models, the traction control ASR (anti-spin) module is mounted on top of the ETS control module. On manual transmission models, the traction control module is integrated into the ABS control unit. The ETS control module uses information from the TCS/ABS control unit (manual models) or ASR module (automatic models) to determine when wheelspin is occurring.*

c) *TCS/ABS hydraulic actuator: the TCS/ABS hydraulic actuator **(see illustration)** consists of a unit containing solenoid valves and a pump, integrated into the front brake hydraulic circuits. The system uses the ABS wheel sensors to detect wheelspin via the ABS control unit mounted on the battery tray. The ABS control unit is specific to TCS models, and outputs a signal to the ETS control module when wheelspin is detected. At speeds below approximately 30 mph, the actuator solenoid valves are activated, to allow the pump to pressurise the relevant front brake circuit until the spinning wheel slows to a rotational speed corresponding*

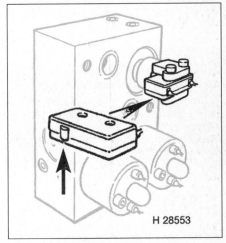

H 28553

6.1 TCS/ABS hydraulic actuator

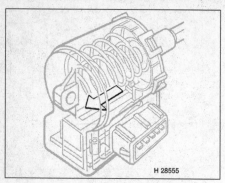

6.3 ETS accelerator pedal potentiometer

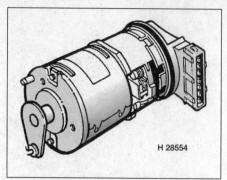

6.7 ETS Throttle potentiometer/motor

to the speed of the vehicle. This has the effect of transferring torque to the wheel with most traction.

d) **System switches:** a pressure switch in the TCS actuator is activated at a pressure of 6.0 bars, and this illuminates a TCS function light on the instrument panel, informing the driver that the TCS system is operating and attempting to counteract wheelspin. If the system develops a fault, the "TCS CTRL" warning light will be illuminated permanently. However, if the TCS system has been in operation for a long time, the "TCS CTRL" warning light will flash, to inform the driver that the TCS system is temporarily inoperative, in order to prevent overheating of the brakes.

e) **Main control switch:** the main control switch is located on the facia panel.

2 In the event of a fault in the traction control system, first check all relevant wiring for security. If a fault arises on the road, a back-up mode can be engaged by fully releasing the accelerator pedal, then depressing it again. In this mode, the throttle is operated by a cable. In back-up mode, engine performance will be limited, the accelerator pedal will be stiffer, and the cruise control and air conditioning systems will be inoperative. Further testing of the system is best left to a Saab dealer, who will have the necessary diagnostic equipment to find the fault quickly. It is not possible to make any adjustment to the system.

Component renewal

Accelerator pedal potentiometer

3 Working inside the car, disconnect the wiring plug from the potentiometer **(see illustration)**.
4 Disconnect the potentiometer arm from the accelerator pedal.
5 Unbolt and remove the unit.
6 Refitting is a reversal of removal.

Throttle potentiometer/motor

7 Disconnect the wiring plug from the throttle potentiometer/motor **(see illustration)**.
8 Disconnect the throttle lever.
9 Unbolt and remove the unit.
10 Refitting is a reversal of removal.

ETS control module

⚠ **Warning: If a new control module is to be fitted, note that it must be programmed (manual or automatic transmission) by a Saab dealer before connecting the wiring plug (new modules are supplied unprogrammed). Also note that the module is extremely sensitive to static electricity, and it is important to "earth" yourself before (and while) working on it.**

11 Move the left-hand front seat as far forwards as possible.
12 Lift the carpet, then unbolt and remove the cover.
13 Disconnect the wiring plug, and remove the control module from inside the car. On automatic transmission models, remove the ASR module from the top of the ETS control module.
14 Refitting is a reversal of removal.

Warning light

15 Remove the automatic climate control panel, with reference to Chapter 3.
16 Press out the warning light, and disconnect the wiring plug.
17 Refitting is a reversal of removal.

7 Unleaded petrol - general information and usage

Note: The information given in this Chapter is correct at the time of writing, and applies only to petrols currently available in the UK. If updated information is thought to be required, check with a Saab dealer. If travelling abroad, consult one of the motoring organisations (or a similar authority) for advice on the petrols available, and their suitability for your vehicle.

1 The fuel recommended by Saab is given in the Specifications at the start of this Chapter, followed by the equivalent petrol currently on sale in the UK.
2 RON and MON are different testing standards; RON stands for Research Octane Number (also written as RM), while MON stands for Motor Octane Number (also written as MM).

3 All Saab 9000 models are designed to run on fuel with a minimum octane rating of 91 (RON), but are more efficient with the higher octane fuels listed in the specifications.

8 Fuel injection system - general information

LH-Jetronic fuel injection system

The LH-Jetronic fuel injection system is a microprocessor-controlled fuel management system, which continuously monitors the engine using various sensors, and provides the correct amount of fuel necessary for complete combustion under all engine conditions **(see illustration)**. Data from the sensors is processed in the fuel system electronic control unit (ECU) in order to determine the opening period of the injectors for the exact amount of fuel to be injected into the inlet manifold. The system is of the simultaneous type, which means that all injectors open and close at the same time. They open once for each revolution of the crankshaft, except during cold starting, when they open twice for each revolution. On Turbo models manufactured up to 1989, a separate ECU is used to control the turbocharging function; from this date onwards, however, the function is incorporated in the Direct Ignition ECU. Where a catalytic converter is fitted (later models), a lambda sensor is incorporated in the LH-Jetronic system.

The main components of the system are as follows:

a) **ECU:** the electronic control unit controls the entire operation of the fuel injection system.

b) **Injectors:** each fuel injector consists of a solenoid-operated needle valve, which opens under the commands from the ECU. Fuel from the fuel rail is then delivered through the injector nozzle into the inlet manifold.

c) **Airflow meter:** the airflow meter measures the amount of air entering the engine by means of a hot wire.

d) **Temperature sensor:** the coolant temperature sensor monitors the engine temperature.

e) **Auxiliary air valve:** the auxiliary air valve provides additional air when the engine is cold. It is only fitted to 1985 models.

f) **Idle air control valve:** the idle air control valve controls the volume of air bypassing the throttle butterfly. It is fitted to 1986-on models.

g) **Throttle position switch:** the throttle position switch informs the ECU of the throttle butterfly position.

h) **Fuel pump:** the fuel pump is housed in the fuel tank. The pump housing

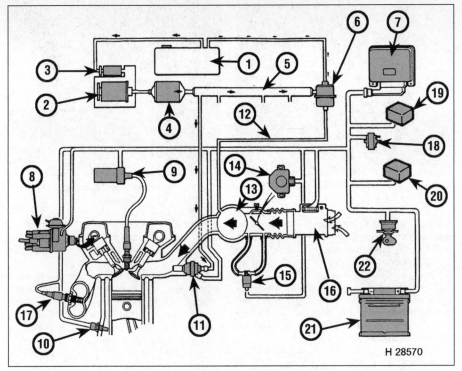

H 28570

8.1 LH-Jetronic fuel injection system layout

1 Fuel tank	9 Ignition coil	17 Lambda sensor (catalytic
2 Fuel pump	10 Temperature sensor	converter models)
3 Feed pump	11 Injection valve	18 Pressure switch (Turbo
4 Fuel filter	12 Vacuum line	models)
5 Fuel injection manifold	13 Inlet manifold	19 System relay
6 Fuel pressure regulator	14 Throttle position sensor	20 Fuel pump relay
7 Electronic control unit	15 Idle speed control valve	21 Battery
8 Distributor	16 Airflow meter	22 Ignition switch

incorporates a separate feed pump which supplies the main fuel pump with pressurised fuel, free of air bubbles.

i) **Fuel filter**: the fuel filter is located behind the battery in the engine compartment.

j) **Lambda sensor**: the lambda sensor provides the ECU with constant feedback on the oxygen content of the exhaust gases. The lambda sensor is fitted to later models with a catalytic converter.

k) **Cold start injector**: a cold start injector is fitted to certain models, and it injects additional fuel into the inlet manifold for a limited period during starting.

Trionic engine management system

The Saab Trionic engine management system controls three functions of the engine from a single electronic control unit (ECU). The three functions comprise the fuel injection system, ignition system, and (where applicable) the turbocharging system. Details of the ignition function are given in Chapter 5B. The system is microprocessor-controlled, and the fuel system provides the correct amount of fuel necessary for complete combustion under all engine conditions. Data from various sensors is processed in the ECU,

in order to determine the opening period of the injectors for the exact amount of fuel to be injected into the inlet manifold. The system is of sequential type, where fuel is injected according to the engine's firing order. When the ignition is initially switched on and after the fuel pump is operating, all the injectors operate for a short period, in order to supply a small amount of fuel in the vicinity of the inlet valves. This helps the engine to start quickly.

The main components of the system are as follows:

a) **ECU**: the electronic control unit controls the entire operation of the fuel injection system, ignition system and turbocharging system.

b) **Crankshaft position sensor**: the crankshaft position sensor provides a datum for the ECU to calculate the position of the crankshaft in relation to TDC.

c) **Manifold absolute pressure (MAP) sensor**: the MAP sensor provides a voltage to the ECU, proportional to the pressure in the inlet manifold.

d) **Inlet air temperature sensor**: the inlet air temperature sensor provides the ECU with signals which enable it to calculate the density of the air entering the engine.

e) **Engine coolant temperature sensor**: the engine coolant temperature sensor informs the ECU of the engine temperature.

f) **Throttle position switch**: the throttle position switch informs the ECU of the throttle butterfly position.

g) **Lambda sensor**: the lambda sensor provides the ECU with constant feedback on the oxygen content of the exhaust gases. The lambda sensor is of Bosch manufacture.

h) **Ignition discharge module**: the ignition discharge module (or cartridge) contains four HT coils connected directly to the spark plugs.

i) **Injectors**: each fuel injector consists of a solenoid-operated needle valve, which opens under the commands from the ECU. Fuel from the fuel rail is then delivered through the injector nozzle into the inlet manifold. The injectors are of Bosch manufacture.

j) **Boost pressure control (solenoid) valve**: the boost pressure control valve (also referred to as the solenoid valve) controls the operation of the turbocharger. Under certain conditions (ie in 1st gear), boost pressure is reduced.

k) **Idle air control valve**: the idle air control valve controls the volume of air bypassing the throttle butterfly. The system maintains the engine idle speed under all conditions of load imposed by the alternator, air conditioning compressor, or when a gear other than P or N is selected on automatic transmission models. If there is a break in the idle air control valve circuit, the valve opening is set by an internal spring, to control the engine speed at approximately 1000 rpm.

l) **EVAP canister-purge valve**: the EVAP canister-purge valve is operated when the engine is started, to purge fuel accumulated in the canister. In order to allow the lambda sensor to compensate for the additional fuel, the system is operated in short phases.

m) **Fuel pump**: the fuel pump is housed in the fuel tank. The pump housing incorporates a separate feed pump which supplies the main fuel pump with pressurised fuel, free of air bubbles.

n) **Fuel filter**: the fuel filter is located beneath the rear of the car adjacent to the fuel tank, and filters all fuel from the fuel pump.

If the system warning light comes on, the car should be taken to a Saab dealer at the earliest opportunity. A complete test of the engine management system can then be carried out, using a special electronic diagnostic test unit which is simply plugged into the system's diagnostic connector.

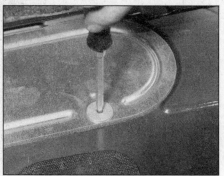

10.6a Use an Allen key to unscrew . . .

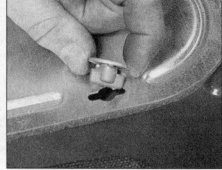

10.6b . . . and remove the retainers . . .

10.6c . . . then remove the cover from over the pump

9 Fuel injection system - precautions and depressurisation

Note: *Refer to the warning at the end of Section 1 before proceeding.*

⚠ *Warning: The following procedure will merely relieve the pressure in the fuel system - remember that fuel will still be present in the system components, and to take precautions accordingly before disconnecting any of them.*

1 The fuel system referred to in this Section is defined as the tank-mounted fuel pump, the fuel filter, the fuel injectors, the fuel rail and the pressure regulator, and the metal pipes and flexible hoses of the fuel lines between these components. All these contain fuel, which will be under pressure while the engine is running and/or while the ignition is switched on. The pressure may remain for some time after the ignition has been switched off, and must be relieved before any of these components are disturbed for servicing work.

2 Open the fusebox, and remove fuse 14 (the fuel pump fuse).

3 Start the engine (if possible) and run it until it stops. Try to start it twice more, to ensure that all pressure has been relieved.

4 Disconnect the battery negative terminal, then refit fuse 14.

5 Place a suitable container beneath the relevant connection/union to be disconnected, and have a large rag ready to soak up any escaping fuel not being caught by the container.

6 Slowly loosen the connection or union nut (as applicable) to avoid a sudden release of pressure, and position the rag around the connection to catch any fuel spray which may be expelled. Once the pressure is released, disconnect the fuel line.

> **HAYNES HiNT** *Plug or cap the fuel line/union, to minimise fuel loss and to prevent the entry of dirt into the fuel system.*

10 Fuel pump - testing, removal and refitting

Note: *Refer to the warning note at the end of Section 1 before proceeding. On models with Trionic engine management, the fuel pump also incorporates the fuel gauge sender unit; on models with LH-Jetronic fuel injection, the fuel pump and sender are separate units (see Section 12)*

Testing

1 To test the fuel pump without removing it, obtain a graduated container with a capacity of at least 900 cc. The pump is located in the fuel tank.

2 In the engine compartment, disconnect the return line at the fuel pressure regulator, and connect a hose between the regulator and the container.

3 Remove fuses 14 and 22 from the fusebox with reference to Chapter 12, then connect a bridging wire between the two terminals to run the fuel pump. Run the pump for 30 seconds exactly, then stop it. Check that the pump delivers a minimum of 900 cc of fuel.

4 Note that a more comprehensive test may be carried out to ascertain the actual pressure of the fuel. This test should be carried out by your Saab dealer, as it involves the use of a pressure gauge.

Removal

5 Disconnect the battery negative lead.

6 Remove the rear floor panel, then use an Allen key to remove the cover from over the fuel pump **(see illustrations)**.

Models with LH-Jetronic fuel injection

7 Disconnect the wiring plugs from the fuel pump, feed pump and fuel gauge sender unit, then move the cover to one side.

8 Unscrew the banjo union, and disconnect the fuel delivery pipe from the pump. Recover the sealing washers.

9 Loosen the clip on the pump rubber collar.

10 Lift out the fuel pump and the suction reservoir, then disconnect the fuel line from the reservoir, and pull the wiring from the rubber grommet in the tank. Remove the pump from inside the car. Cover the aperture in the top of the fuel tank.

11 With the pump on the bench, separate the suction reservoir from the pump, and remove the strainer. Recover the O-ring.

12 Loosen the clip, and disconnect the pump from the rubber grommet.

Models with Trionic engine management

13 Where necessary, remove the light plastic cover from the wiring plugs **(see illustration)**.

14 Disconnect the wiring plug from the top of the fuel pump **(see illustration)**.

15 Disconnect the fuel delivery and return

10.13 Remove the light plastic cover

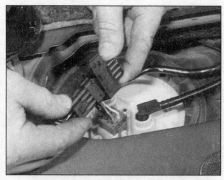

10.14 Disconnecting the wiring plug

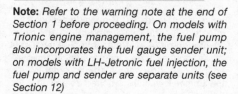

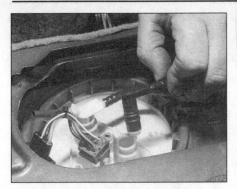

10.15 Disconnecting the fuel pipes from the pump

10.16 Using a pair of water pump pliers to unscrew the retaining ring

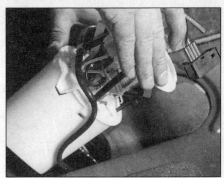

10.17a Removing the fuel pump from the fuel tank

pipes from the pump **(see illustration)**, noting which is which.

16 The unit is secured by a screwed ring. Saab technicians use a special tool to unscrew the ring, but a large pair of grips (water pump pliers) inserted between the serrations inside the ring will achieve the same result. Unscrew and remove the ring **(see illustration)**. Note the location arrows on the top of the pump and tank.

17 Carefully lift the pump from the fuel tank, taking care not to bend the sender arm **(see illustrations)**.

18 Remove the sealing O-ring from the neck of the fuel tank **(see illustration)**.

Refitting

Models with LH-Jetronic fuel injection

19 Locate the pump in the rubber grommet, so that the lip of the grommet is 50 mm above the top edge of the pump **(see illustration)**. Tighten the clip.

20 Refit the strainer to the pump, then refit the suction reservoir, using a new O-ring. Make sure that the relief valve is positioned at 45° from the front-facing mark, as shown **(see illustration)**. Also check that the overall length of the assembly is as in illustration 10.19.

21 Insert the fuel pump in the fuel tank, so that the mark on the rubber collar is 45° to the right when looking towards the front of the car. Locate the collar on the fuel tank, then refit and tighten the clip.

22 Refit the fuel delivery pipe and banjo

union, together with new sealing washers, and tighten securely.

23 Reconnect the wiring, making sure that each wire is correctly located.

Models with Trionic engine management

24 Check the sealing O-ring, and if necessary renew it. Wipe clean the fuel tank neck, then locate the O-ring.

25 Carefully lower the fuel pump into the tank, making sure that the location arrows are correctly aligned with each other.

26 Refit and tighten the screwed ring. Make sure it is tight enough, otherwise the joint may leak.

27 Reconnect the fuel delivery and return pipes.

28 Reconnect the wiring plugs to the top of the fuel pump in their previously-noted positions.

29 Reconnect the battery negative lead. Run the engine and check for leaks.

30 Refit the light plastic cover.

All models

31 Refit the fuel pump cover and the rear floor panel.

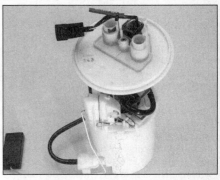

10.17b Fuel pump removed from the fuel tank

11 Fuel pump relay - testing and renewal

Testing

LH-Jetronic fuel injection system

1 Disconnect the wiring plugs from the airflow meter and the ECU.

2 Using a bridging wire, connect terminal 21 (yellow/white) and 17 (violet) on the ECU multi-plug, then use a voltmeter to check that battery voltage is present at the blue/red

10.18 Removing the sealing O-ring from the neck of the fuel tank

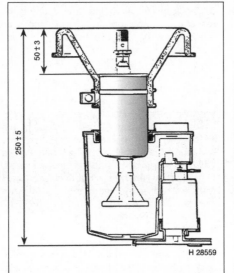

10.19 Correct fitted position of the rubber grommet above the top edge of the fuel pump

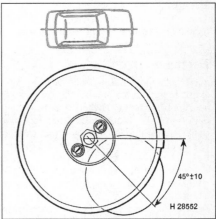

10.20 Fuel pump relief valve positioning

wiring loom lead in the engine compartment. Also check that battery voltage is present at one of the terminals for fuse 14. Check the wiring if voltage is not present.

3 Remove the glovebox with reference to Chapter 11, then remove the fuse panel (without disconnecting the wiring) with reference to Chapter 12.

4 Using a voltmeter, check that battery voltage is reaching terminal 30 on the panel.

5 Check that voltage is reaching terminal 87 on the fuel pump relay. If not, check the wiring for a fault. If all else is in good order, renew the relay.

Trionic engine management system

6 The fuel pump relay is located in the relay holder on the left-hand side of the facia. Switch on the ignition, and listen for a buzzing sound from the relay. Also listen for a buzzing sound from the fuel pump in the fuel tank below the rear luggage compartment.

7 If neither the relay nor the pump can be heard, check fuse 14 in the fusebox. If this is in order, remove the relay from the holder, and connect an LED tester to terminals 85 and 86 in the holder. With the ignition switched on, the tester should flash, proving that current is reaching the relay. If current is reaching the relay, but the pump is not running, the relay is suspect, and a new one should be fitted.

8 If the relay can be heard to click when current is supplied, connect a jumper lead across fuses 14 and 22 in the fusebox. The pump should now be receiving current. If the pump still refuses to operate, check for current at the pump wiring under the rear luggage floor. If the pump is receiving current but still refuses to operate, it must be faulty.

Renewal

9 To renew the relay, pull it direct from the relay panel.

10 Push the new relay firmly into the relay panel.

12 Fuel gauge sender unit (LH-Jetronic models) - removal and refitting

Note: *Refer to the warning note at the end of Section 1 before proceeding.*

Removal

1 Disconnect the battery negative lead.

2 For access to the sender unit, fold the rear seat cushions forward (where necessary).

3 Remove the luggage compartment floor panel, then remove the cover from over the fuel tank by turning the fasteners a quarter-turn, using an Allen key.

4 Disconnect the wiring plugs from the fuel gauge sender unit, noting their fitted positions.

5 The unit is secured by a screw cap. Saab technicians use a special tool to unscrew the cap, but a large pair of grips will achieve the same result.

6 Withdraw the sender unit from the top of the

fuel tank, taking care not to spill fuel onto the interior of the car. Recover the rubber sealing ring. Check the sealing ring, and if necessary obtain a new one.

Refitting

7 Refitting is a reversal of the removal procedure.

13 Fuel tank - removal, repair and refitting

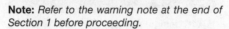

Note: *Refer to the warning note at the end of Section 1 before proceeding.*

Removal

1 Before removing the fuel tank, it is preferable that all the fuel is removed from the tank. Since a fuel tank drain plug is not provided, carry out the removal operation when the tank is nearly empty. If it is not possible to syphon or hand-pump the remaining fuel from the tank, use the following procedure. Remove the luggage compartment floor panel and the cover from the fuel pump, then disconnect the wiring from the pump. Disconnect the delivery hose from the pump, and connect a suitable plastic tube to the pump using a banjo union. Position the free end of the plastic tube in a suitable container. Remove fuses 14 and 22 from the fusebox with reference to Chapter 12, then connect a bridging wire between the two terminals to start the fuel pump. Pump all of the fuel out of the tank, then reconnect all components. Keep the fuel in a safe place, observing the precautions given in Section 1.

2 Disconnect the battery negative lead.

3 Remove the rear luggage compartment floor panels, and the cover from the fuel pump (using an Allen key).

4 Disconnect the fuel lines and wiring from the fuel pump.

5 Chock the front wheels, then jack up the rear of the car and support on axle stands (see *"Jacking, towing and wheel changing"*). Make sure that the stands will not obstruct the removal of the tank. Remove the right-hand rear wheel.

6 Loosen the clips and disconnect the inlet hose from the tank. Also disconnect the breather hose.

7 Working beneath the car, detach the handbrake cable (refer to Chapter 9).

8 Support the weight of the fuel tank using a trolley jack with an interposed block of wood, then unscrew the tank mounting nuts. Start with the right-hand mounting, so that the handbrake cable can be tied to one side. Remove both mounting straps.

9 With the help of an assistant, lower the fuel tank and remove it from under the car.

10 If the tank is contaminated with sediment or water, remove the sender unit (models with LH-Jetronic fuel injection - Section 12) and swill the tank out with clean fuel. In certain cases, it may be possible to have small leaks

or minor damage repaired. Seek the advice of a suitable specialist before attempting to repair the fuel tank.

Refitting

11 Refitting is the reverse of the removal procedure, noting the following points:

a) *When lifting the tank back into position, make sure that the mounting straps are correctly positioned, and take great care to ensure that none of the hoses become trapped between the tank and vehicle body.*

b) *Ensure that all pipes and hoses are correctly routed, and securely held in position with their retaining clips.*

c) *When refitting the anti-splash device, make sure that the butterfly spindle is vertical.*

d) *On completion, refill the tank with fuel, and check for signs of leakage prior to taking the vehicle out on the road.*

14 Fuel injection system - testing, checking and adjustment

Testing

1 If a fault appears in the fuel injection system, first ensure that all the system wiring connectors are securely connected and free of corrosion. Then ensure that the fault is not due to poor maintenance - ie, check that the air cleaner filter element is clean, the spark plugs are in good condition and correctly gapped, the cylinder compression pressures are correct, the ignition timing is correct (where this is adjustable), and that the engine breather hoses are clear and undamaged, referring to Chapters 1, 2 and 5 for further information.

2 If these checks fail to reveal the cause of the problem, the car should be taken to a Saab dealer for testing. A diagnostic connector is incorporated in the wiring circuit, into which a Saab special electronic diagnostic tester can be plugged. The tester will locate the fault quickly and simply, alleviating the need to test all the system components individually.

Checking and adjustment

3 The following **adjustments** are only possible on certain models fitted with the LH-Jetronic fuel injection system. The idle speed may be adjusted on engines not fitted with idle control, and the idle mixture may be adjusted on engines not fitted with a catalytic converter. On models with the Trionic engine management system, the idle speed and mixture are automatically controlled by the ECU. The **checking** of idle speed and mixture is possible on all models by using a tachometer and exhaust gas analyser, but some difficulty may be experienced connecting a conventional tachometer to the engine on cars fitted with Direct Ignition. Most models are in fact fitted with an engine tachometer on the instrument panel.

4 Before checking and adjusting the idle speed or mixture settings, always check the following first:

a) *Check the ignition timing (models with Hall-effect ignition) (Chapter 5B).*
b) *Check that the spark plugs are in good condition and correctly gapped (Chapter 1).*
c) *Check that the accelerator cable is correctly adjusted (Section 3).*
d) *Check that the crankcase breather hoses are secure, with no leaks or kinks (Chapter 1).*
e) *Check that the air cleaner filter element is clean (Chapter 1).*
f) *Check that the exhaust system is in good condition (Chapter 1).*
g) *If the engine is running very roughly, check the compression pressures (Chapter 2A).*

5 Take the car on a journey of sufficient length to warm the engine to normal operating temperature. **Note:** *Checking/adjustment should be completed as soon as possible so that the engine is still at its normal operating temperature. If the radiator electric cooling fan operates, first wait for the cooling fan to stop. Clear any excess fuel from the inlet manifold by racing the engine two or three times to between 2000 and 3000 rpm, then allow it to idle again.*

6 Ensure that all electrical loads are switched off, then stop the engine and connect a tachometer to it, following its manufacturer's instructions. Where a tachometer is fitted to the instrument panel, this may be used instead. If the idle mixture is to be checked, connect an exhaust gas analyser in accordance with its manufacturer's instructions.

Models with LH-Jetronic fuel injection (except models with idle air control and catalytic converter)

7 The idle speed adjustment screw is located on the throttle housing. Start the engine and allow it to idle, then check that the idle speed is as given in the Specifications. If adjustment is necessary, loosen the locknut. Adjust the screw in to reduce the speed, or out to increase the speed. Tighten the locknut after making the adjustment.

8 The idle mixture adjustment screw is located on the airflow meter, and may be hidden under a tamperproof cap. First remove the cap. With the engine idling at the correct idling speed, check that the CO level is as given in the Specifications. If adjustment is necessary, use an Allen key or screwdriver to turn the mixture adjustment screw in or out (in very small increments) until the CO level is as given in the Specifications. Turning the screw in (clockwise) richens the mixture and increases the CO level, turning it out will weaken the mixture and reduce the CO level.

9 If necessary, readjust the idle speed.

10 Temporarily increase the engine speed, then allow it to idle and recheck the settings.

11 When adjustments are complete, stop the engine and disconnect the test equipment.

Other models with LH-Jetronic and Trionic systems

12 The idle speed is controlled by an idle air control valve, in conjunction with the system ECU. With the engine at normal operating temperature, check that the idle speed is as given in the Specifications. No adjustment is possible.

13 The idle mixture is controlled by the lambda sensor, in conjunction with the system ECU. With the engine at normal operating temperature, check that the idle mixture is as given in the Specifications. No adjustment is possible.

14 If incorrect readings are obtained, take the car to a Saab dealer and have the system checked with the special tester.

15 Fuel injection system components (LH-Jetronic) - removal and refitting

Electronic control unit
Removal

1 Disconnect the battery negative lead.

2 With the bonnet open, remove the cover behind the bulkhead panel on the left-hand side of the engine compartment.

3 Unscrew the mounting screws, and withdraw the electronic control unit from the bulkhead.

4 Release the clip and disconnect the multi-plug connector from the ECU.

Refitting

5 Refitting is a reversal of the removal procedure.

Coolant temperature sensor
Removal and refitting

6 The procedure is described in Chapter 3, Section 6.

Throttle position switch
Removal

7 Disconnect the wiring plug from the throttle

position switch on the throttle housing (**see illustration**).

8 Mark the position of the switch on the throttle housing.

9 Unscrew the mounting screws and remove the switch.

Refitting and adjustment

10 Refit the switch to the throttle housing, and insert the mounting screws finger-tight.

11 If the original switch is being refitted, align the previously-made marks and tighten the screws.

12 If there is any doubt that the throttle housing butterfly valve stop position is incorrect, loosen the locknut and back off the adjustment screw until it is clear of the stop. Now screw it in until it just touches the stop. Turn the screw in a further quarter-turn, and lock it in this position.

13 With the throttle valve at its rest position, turn the throttle position switch until it touches the internal stop for the idling position, then tighten the mounting screws.

14 Connect a ohmmeter to the terminals on the switch. With the throttle valve at its rest position, the meter should register zero ohms (ie continuity). Open the throttle valve, and check that the internal contacts open immediately the throttle is moved. With the throttle valve close to the fully-open position (72° from rest position), the internal contacts should close again.

Throttle housing
Removal

15 Referring to Chapter 1, drain off approximately 2 litres of coolant, so that the coolant level is below the throttle housing.

16 Loosen the clip and disconnect the air inlet hose from the throttle housing (**see illustration**).

17 Disconnect the accelerator cable, and remove it from the throttle housing - refer to Section 3.

18 Disconnect the wiring plug from the throttle position switch.

19 Loosen the clips and disconnect the coolant hoses (**see illustration**). Plug the hoses to prevent loss of coolant.

20 On 1985 models only, disconnect the air hoses from the auxiliary air valve.

15.7 Disconnecting the wiring plug from the throttle position switch

15.16 Loosen the clip and disconnect the air inlet hose from the throttle housing

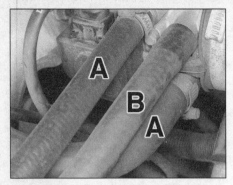

15.19 Coolant hoses (A) and vacuum hose (B) on the throttle housing

15.23 One of the mounting nuts securing the throttle housing to the inlet manifold

15.26 Airflow meter wiring plug

21 Where necessary, remove the turbo pressure (discharge) pipe.
22 Disconnect the vacuum hose from the throttle housing.
23 Unscrew the three mounting nuts and remove the throttle housing from the inlet manifold (see illustration).

Refitting

24 Refitting is a reversal of the removal procedure. On completion, check and if necessary adjust the throttle position switch and the accelerator cable. Top-up the cooling system with reference to Chapter 1.

Airflow meter

Removal

25 Loosen the clips and disconnect the hoses from each end of the airflow meter.
26 Disconnect the wiring multi-plug from the airflow meter (see illustration).
27 Release the toggle spring clips, then lift the airflow meter assembly from the air cleaner lower body.

Refitting

28 Refitting is a reversal of the removal procedure, but align the slot with the air cleaner body.

Fuel supply rail and injectors

Note: *Refer to the warning at the end of Section 1 before proceeding.*

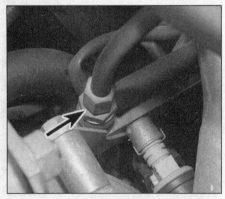

15.32 The connector (arrowed) for the fuel supply line at the supply rail

Removal

Note: *If a faulty injector is suspected, before condemning the injector, it is worth trying the effect of one of the proprietary injector-cleaning treatments.*

29 Clean the area surrounding the fuel supply rail, to prevent entry of dust and dirt into the fuel system.
30 Unbolt and remove the false bulkhead at the rear of the engine compartment.
31 Loosen the clip and disconnect the fuel return hose from the fuel pressure regulator - anticipate loss of fuel by placing a cloth beneath the regulator. Also disconnect the vacuum hose from the regulator. On some early models, the fuel pressure regulator may be located on a bracket secured to the cylinder head.
32 Unscrew the connector, and disconnect the fuel supply line for the supply rail (see illustration).
33 Disconnect the wiring plugs from the injectors.
34 Unscrew the mounting bolts, and withdraw the supply rail from the inlet manifold. Do not remove the injectors from the rail at this stage.
35 Remove the rubber O-rings from the inlet manifold.
36 Withdraw the fuel supply rail through the space between the inlet manifold and the bulkhead.
37 To remove the injectors from the rail, remove the clips and pull out the injectors.

Refitting

38 Refitting is a reversal of the removal procedure. Before locating the rubber O-rings in the inlet manifold, apply a little petroleum jelly to them, to facilitate entry of the injectors.

Fuel pressure regulator

Note: *Refer to the warning at the end of Section 1 before proceeding.*

Removal

39 Clean the area surrounding the fuel pressure regulator, to prevent entry of dust and dirt into the fuel system.

40 Unbolt and remove the false bulkhead at the rear of the engine compartment.
41 Loosen the clip and disconnect the fuel return hose from the fuel pressure regulator - anticipate loss of fuel by placing a cloth beneath the regulator. Also disconnect the vacuum hose from the regulator.
42 Unscrew the mounting bolts, and withdraw the supply rail from the inlet manifold sufficiently to gain access to the fuel pressure regulator.
43 Unbolt the regulator from the inlet manifold.
44 Unscrew the regulator from the bracket.

Refitting

45 Refitting is a reversal of removal

Auxiliary air valve

Removal

46 Disconnect the wiring plug from the auxiliary air valve.
47 Loosen the clips and disconnect the two hoses from the valve.
48 Unscrew the mounting bolts and remove the auxiliary air valve from the engine.

Refitting

49 Refitting is a reversal of removal.

Pressure switch (Turbo models)

Removal

50 Working under the facia on the left-hand side, unscrew the screws and remove the lower cover.
51 Remove the APC mounting panel.
52 Loosen the clips and disconnect the hoses, then remove the pressure switch.

Refitting

53 Refitting is a reversal of removal.

Automatic idle control (AIC) valve (B202 models)

Removal

54 The automatic idle control is located

15.54 Automatic idle control on B202 models

15.55 Disconnecting the wiring plug from the idle air control valve

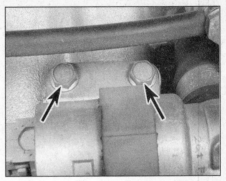

15.57 Idle air control valve mounting bolts

centrally over the inlet manifold **(see illustration)**.
55 Disconnect the wiring plug **(see illustration)**.
56 Loosen the clips and disconnect the hoses.
57 Unscrew the retaining bolts, then slide the valve from the clip **(see illustration)**.

Refitting

58 Refitting is a reversal of removal.

Cold start injector

Removal

59 A cold start injector is fitted to certain models. It is located on top of the inlet manifold.
60 Disconnect the wiring plug **(see illustration)**.
61 Unscrew the union bolt, and disconnect the fuel supply from the injector
62 Unscrew the mounting bolts, and remove the injector from the inlet manifold. Recover the gasket.

Refitting

63 Refitting is a reversal of removal, but renew the gasket.

16 Fuel injection system components (Trionic) - removal and refitting

Control module

Removal

1 With the ignition switched off, remove the cover from the false bulkhead.
2 Unscrew the bolt and disconnect the control module earth cable from the bulkhead **(see illustration)**.
3 Release the clip then lift the control module from its mounting **(see illustration)**.
4 Pull up the plastic cover, then unhook and release the multi-plug connector from the control module **(see illustration)**. Remove the module from the bulkhead.

Refitting

5 Refitting is a reversal of removal. Make sure that the correct module is fitted, and give the car a road test to check for operation.

Inlet air temperature sensor

Removal

6 Disconnect the wiring from the sensor, which is located in the main air inlet duct to the throttle housing.

15.64 Disconnecting the wiring plug from the cold start injector

7 Unscrew the sensor from the air inlet duct, and recover the sealing washer.

Refitting

8 Refitting is a reversal of removal, but check and if necessary renew the sealing washer.

Manifold absolute pressure (MAP) sensor

Removal

9 Lift the weatherstrip from the right-hand side of the false bulkhead.
10 Disconnect the wiring plug and vacuum hose, then lift the sensor from the false

16.2 Unbolting the earth cable from the bulkhead

16.3 Lifting the control module from its mounting

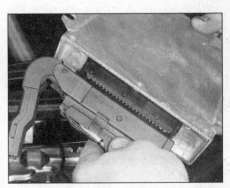

16.4 Disconnecting the multi-plug connector from the module

16.10 Removing the manifold absolute pressure (MAP) sensor

16.22a Crankshaft position sensor wiring support clip (arrowed) on the left-hand end of the engine

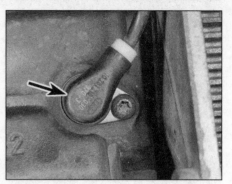

16.22b Crankshaft position sensor location

16.22c Removing the crankshaft position sensor

bulkhead and remove it (see illustration). If necessary, unscrew the mounting screws, and separate the sensor from the mounting bracket.

Refitting

11 Refitting is a reversal of removal.

Engine coolant temperature sensor

Removal

12 The sensor is located on the inlet manifold lower section. First drain the cooling system as described in Chapter 1.
13 Remove the upper inlet manifold with reference to Section 20.
14 Disconnect the wiring connector from the sensor.
15 Unscrew the sensor from the lower inlet manifold.

Refitting

16 Clean the threads, then insert the sensor in the lower inlet manifold, and tighten securely.
17 Refit the connector.
18 Refit the upper inlet manifold with reference to Section 20.
19 Refill the cooling system with reference to Chapter 1.

Crankshaft position sensor (non-turbo engine)

Removal

20 Remove the upper and lower sections of

the inlet manifold, with reference to Section 20.
21 Note the routing of the wiring for the crankshaft position sensor. Disconnect the wiring at the connector located below the inlet manifold. Note that access is very limited.
22 Release the wiring from the plastic cable-ties, and unscrew the support clips from the left-hand end of the engine. Remove the retaining screw and remove the sensor from its location on the front left-hand side of the cylinder block (see illustrations). Recover the O-ring, noting how it is fitted. Clean the seating in the cylinder block.

Refitting

23 Refitting is a reversal of removal, but tighten the sensor to the specified torque.

Crankshaft position sensor (turbo engine)

Removal

24 Disconnect the crankshaft position sensor wiring plug, located below the inlet manifold. Note that access is restricted.
25 Release the wiring from the plastic cable-ties, then unscrew the retaining screw and remove the sensor from its location on the front left-hand side of the cylinder block. Recover the O-ring, noting how it is fitted. Clean the seating in the cylinder block.

Refitting

26 Refitting is a reversal of removal, but tighten the sensor to the specified torque.

Throttle position sensor (not Electronic Throttle System)

Removal

27 The throttle position sensor is located on the throttle housing on the left-hand end of the inlet manifold.
28 Disconnect the wiring plug from the sensor.
29 Disconnect the large crankcase ventilation hose from the throttle housing
30 Unscrew the retaining screws, and remove the sensor from the housing. Remove the O-ring from the throttle spindle. Examine the O-ring, and obtain a new one if necessary.

Refitting

31 Refitting is a reversal of removal.

Idle air control valve (B204/B234 models without turbo)

Removal

32 The idle air control valve is located beneath the upper section of the inlet manifold. First disconnect the battery negative lead.
33 Disconnect the inlet hose from the throttle housing, and disconnect the wiring plug from the throttle position sensor.
34 Disconnect the crankcase ventilation hose from the throttle housing, and also disconnect the idle air control valve hose (under the throttle housing).
35 Using hose clamps, clamp the coolant hoses connected to the throttle housing. Careful use of grips and suitable packing will also achieve the same result. Loosen the clips and disconnect the hoses from the throttle housing.
36 Detach the accelerator cable (and where applicable, the automatic transmission kickdown cable).
37 Disconnect the fuel pressure regulator and crankcase ventilation vacuum hoses from the inlet manifold.
38 Disconnect the evaporative control canister-purge hose from the inlet manifold, then unscrew the outer screws from the inlet manifold.
39 Unscrew and remove the bolts from the oil filler pipe bracket.
40 Disconnect the manifold absolute pressure sensor hose.
41 Remove the upper section of the inlet manifold, then turn it over and disconnect the wiring plug from the idle air control valve.
42 Loosen the clips and disconnect the hoses.
43 Detach the idle air control valve from its mounting.

Refitting

44 Refitting is a reversal of removal, but adjust the accelerator cable (and where applicable, the automatic transmission kickdown cable) with reference to Section 3 of this Chapter and Chapter 7B.

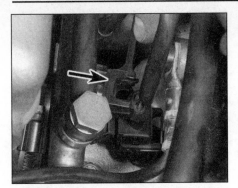

16.54a Removing a plastic locating rail (arrowed) from the injectors

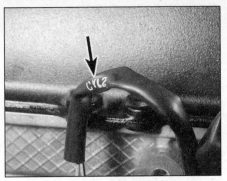

16.54b The injector wiring is marked according to the cylinder

16.54c Disconnecting the injector wiring plugs

Idle air control (IAC) valve (B204/B234 Turbo models, non-ETS engines)

Removal

45 Loosen the clips and disconnect the air duct from the throttle housing.

46 Prise out the circlip, and move the accelerator cable to one side.

47 On automatic transmission models, disconnect the kickdown cable with reference to Chapter 7B.

48 Loosen the clips and disconnect the idle air control valve hoses from the throttle housing.

49 Remove the valve from the mounting bracket, and disconnect the wiring pug.

50 Disconnect the hoses from the valve.

Refitting

51 Refitting is a reversal of removal, but delay fully tightening the hose clips until the valve is positioned correctly.

Fuel supply rail and Injectors (normally-aspirated engine)

Note: *Refer to the warning at the end of Section 1 before proceeding.*

Removal

Note: *If a faulty injector is suspected, before condemning the injector, it is worth trying the effect of one of the proprietary injector-cleaning treatments.*

52 Remove the upper section of the inlet manifold as described in Section 20.

53 Clean the area around the injectors and fuel connections to prevent entry of dust and dirt into the fuel system.

54 Remove the plastic locating rails, and disconnect the wiring plugs from the injectors. Note that the plug wiring is marked for position according to cylinder (**see illustrations**).

55 Depressurise the fuel system with reference to Section 9. Place a cloth beneath the fuel rail, to soak up fuel which will escape as the fuel rail is removed.

56 Unscrew the mounting screws, and lift out the fuel rail complete with the injectors.

57 Prise out the retaining clips, and pull the injectors from the fuel rail.

Refitting

58 Refitting is a reversal of the removal procedure. Before locating the rubber O-rings in the inlet manifold, apply a little petroleum jelly to them, to facilitate entry of the injectors. Make sure that the correct wiring plugs are attached to the injectors.

Fuel supply rail and Injectors (Turbo engine)

Note: *Refer to the warning at the end of Section 1 before proceeding.*

Removal

Note: *If a faulty injector is suspected, before condemning the injector, it is worth trying the effect of one of the proprietary injector-cleaning treatments.*

59 Depressurise the fuel system with reference to Section 9. Place a cloth beneath the fuel rail, to soak up fuel which will escape as the fuel rail is removed.

60 Unscrew the fuel rail mounting screws, and lift off the rail together with the injectors.

61 Remove the locating rails, and disconnect the wiring plugs from the injectors. Note that the plugs are marked for position.

62 Prise out the retaining clips, and pull the injectors from the fuel rail.

Refitting

63 Refitting is a reversal of the removal procedure. Before locating the rubber O-rings in the inlet manifold, apply a little petroleum jelly to them, to facilitate entry of the injectors. Make sure that the correct wiring plugs are attached to the injectors.

Throttle housing

Note: *The following paragraphs describe removal and refitting procedures for models not fitted with the Electronic Throttle System (as fitted to models with traction control), although the procedure will be very similar. Refer to Section 6 if necessary.*

Removal

64 Loosen the clip, and disconnect the rubber connecting hose from the throttle housing.

65 Disconnect the wiring plug from the throttle position sensor.

66 With the engine cold, unscrew the filler cap on the coolant expansion tank, then refit and tighten the cap.

67 Loosen the clips, then disconnect and plug the coolant hoses from the throttle housing.

68 Disconnect the crankcase breather hose from the throttle housing.

69 Disconnect the IAC valve hose from the throttle housing.

70 Disconnect the accelerator cable (and where necessary, the cruise control cable) with reference to Section 3.

71 On automatic transmission models, disconnect the kickdown cable with reference to Chapter 7B.

72 Unscrew the mounting nuts, and remove the throttle housing from the inlet manifold. Recover the O-ring.

Refitting

73 Clean the contact surfaces of the throttle housing and inlet manifold, then refit the throttle housing together with a new O-ring. Tighten the mounting bolts.

74 On automatic transmission models, reconnect and adjust the kickdown cable with reference to Chapter 7B.

75 Reconnect and adjust the accelerator cable (and where necessary, the cruise control cable) with reference to Section 3.

76 Reconnect the IAC valve hose and the crankcase breather hose.

77 Reconnect the coolant hoses and tighten the clips.

78 Reconnect the wiring plug to the throttle position sensor.

79 Reconnect the rubber connecting hose to the throttle housing, and tighten the clip.

80 Top-up the cooling system with reference to Chapter 1.

17 Turbocharger - description and precautions

Description

1 The turbocharger fitted to certain models increases engine efficiency by raising the pressure in the inlet manifold above atmospheric pressure. Instead of the air simply being sucked into the cylinder, it is forced in.

2 Energy for the operation of the turbocharger comes from the exhaust gas. The gas flows through a specially-shaped housing (the turbine housing) and in so doing, spins the turbine wheel. The turbine wheel is attached to a shaft, at the end of which is another vaned wheel, known as the compressor wheel. The compressor wheel spins in its own housing, and compresses the inlet air on the way to the inlet manifold.

3 Between the turbocharger and the inlet manifold, the compressed air passes through an intercooler. This is an air-to-air heat exchanger, mounted in front of the radiator. The purpose of the intercooler is to remove from the inlet air some of the heat gained in being compressed. Because cooler air is denser, removal of this heat further increases engine efficiency.

4 Boost pressure (the pressure in the inlet manifold) is limited by a wastegate, which diverts the exhaust gas away from the turbine wheel in response to a pressure-sensitive control valve. In the event of excess pressure in the inlet manifold (ie if the wastegate malfunctions), a safety cut-out system will switch off the fuel pump, and the engine will stop.

5 On models prior to 1987, the turbocharger is cooled only by the engine oil. From 1987 on, it is also water-cooled, in order to reduce the temperature of the bearing housing

6 All Turbo models are fitted with an Automatic Performance Control (APC) system. Its basic purpose is to adjust the ignition timing and turbocharger operation so that the engine runs at peak efficiency and economy, regardless of the quality and octane rating of fuel being used. This is necessary because fuels of the same grade can sometimes give different engine characteristics.

7 On models manufactured up to 1989, the APC system incorporates its own separate electronic control unit (ECU), located under the left-hand side of the facia panel. On this system, the APC only controls the turbocharger and not the ignition timing.

8 From 1989 to 1993, the APC system is incorporated into the Direct Ignition ECU located beneath the left-hand front seats. From 1994 onwards, the system is incorporated into the Trionic engine management ECU, located behind the engine compartment false bulkhead on the left-hand side. On both the latter systems, the ignition timing is retarded as and when necessary in addition to the control of the turbocharger. The APC system monitors the onset of pre-ignition ("pinking" or "knocking") in the engine by means of a knock detector. Also included in the system is a pressure transducer (which monitors pressure in the inlet manifold) and a solenoid valve (which controls the turbocharger wastegate).

9 The turbo shaft is pressure-lubricated by an oil feed pipe from the main oil gallery. The shaft "floats" on a cushion of oil. A drain pipe returns the oil to the sump.

Precautions

10 The turbocharger operates at extremely high speeds and temperatures. Certain precautions must be observed, to avoid premature failure of the turbo, or injury to the operator.

11 Do not operate the turbo with any of its parts exposed, or with any of its hoses removed. Foreign objects falling onto the rotating vanes could cause excessive damage, and (if ejected) personal injury.

12 Do not race the engine immediately after start-up, especially if it is cold. Give the oil a few seconds to circulate.

13 Always allow the engine to return to idle speed before switching it off - do not blip the throttle and switch off, as this will leave the turbo spinning without lubrication.

14 Allow the engine to idle for several minutes before switching off after a high-speed run.

15 Observe the recommended intervals for oil and filter changing, and use a reputable oil of the specified quality. Neglect of oil changing, or use of inferior oil, can cause carbon formation on the turbo shaft, leading to subsequent failure.

18 Turbocharger - removal and refitting

T3/TE05 turbocharger
Removal

1 Apply the handbrake, then jack up the front of the car and support on axle stands (see *"Jacking, towing and wheel changing"*).

2 Remove the centre air deflector from beneath the radiator, then, on models where the turbocharger is cooled by the coolant (ie models from 1987 on), drain the cooling system as described in Chapter 1.

3 Where applicable, remove the air conditioning compressor drivebelt and tensioner device.

4 Position a suitable container beneath the oil cooler, then unscrew the upper union and unscrew the mounting bolt on the oil cooler. Position the oil line to one side.

5 Unscrew the air conditioning compressor mounting bolts, protect the oil cooler with a piece of cardboard, then lift the compressor towards the expansion tank. **Do not** disconnect the refrigerant lines from the compressor - refer to the warnings in Chapter 3, Section 10.

6 Disconnect the remove the boost pressure control valve from its mounting on the fan cowling, and disconnect the wiring.

7 Disconnect the wiring from the electric cooling fan motor, then unscrew the bolts and remove the fan cowling complete with the radiator fan.

8 Disconnect the wiring from the airflow meter, then release the toggle clips from the air cleaner, and disconnect the rubber elbow from the turbocharger. Remove the airflow meter.

9 Loosen the clip and disconnect the delivery (pressure) pipe from the turbocharger.

10 Unscrew the flange bolts and disconnect the oil supply line from the turbocharger, then unscrew the oil line clamp bolt from the cylinder head. Unscrew the oil line banjo union from the cylinder block, and release the oil line from the clamp on the inlet manifold. Remove the oil line.

11 On models where the turbocharger is cooled by water, unscrew the union nuts and disconnect the coolant pipes from the turbocharger.

12 Unscrew the nuts and disconnect the exhaust front pipe from the turbocharger.

13 Release the front rubber mountings from the exhaust pipe.

14 Unbolt and remove the bracket between the turbocharger and the sump.

15 Unscrew the mounting bolts, and remove the oil return pipe from the turbocharger and sump. Recover the gasket and O-ring. Cover the holes with tape, to prevent entry of dirt and debris.

16 Unscrew and remove the exhaust manifold mounting nuts, then lift out the exhaust manifold from the cylinder head, complete with the turbocharger unit. Recover the gasket.

17 Unscrew the nuts, and separate the turbocharger unit from the exhaust manifold **(see illustration)**. Note that the nuts have a special locking flange on them, and should be renewed whenever removed. New locking nuts are pre-coated with lubricant. Recover the gasket.

Refitting

18 Clean the contact surfaces, then locate the exhaust manifold on the turbocharger studs with a new gasket, and tighten the **new** nuts to the specified torque. The locking flange on the nuts should face inwards.

19 Clean the contact surfaces, then fit the exhaust manifold complete with turbocharger to the cylinder head. Use a new gasket, and tighten the mounting nuts progressively to the specified torque.

20 Secure the oil line clamp to the inlet

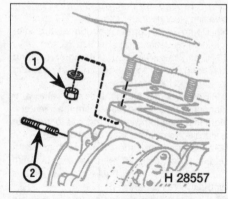

18.17 Removing the turbocharger from the exhaust manifold

1 Nut   2 Stud

manifold. Check that the copper washers are in good condition and renew if necessary, then tighten the banjo union to the cylinder block.

21 Fill the turbocharger inter-chamber with clean engine oil, through the oil supply union on the turbocharger. **Note:** *This is important, as the turbocharger must have oil in it when the engine is started.*

22 Reconnect the oil supply line to the turbocharger, and tighten the flange bolts. Refit and tighten the oil line clamp bolt in the cylinder head.

23 Where applicable, reconnect the coolant pipes to the turbocharger, and tighten the union nuts.

24 Refit the oil return pipe to the turbocharger and sump, together with a new gasket and O-ring, and tighten the bolts.

25 Refit the front rubber mountings to the exhaust pipe.

26 Reconnect the exhaust pipe to the turbocharger, using new locking nuts (the locking flanges should face outwards).

27 Reconnect the delivery (pressure) pipe to the turbocharger, and tighten the clip.

28 Refit the airflow meter, and reconnect the rubber elbow to the turbocharger and air cleaner. Refit the toggle clips, and reconnect the wiring to the airflow meter.

29 Refit the electric cooling fan cowling, complete with the radiator fan, and tighten the mounting bolts. Reconnect the wiring for the fan motor.

30 Refit the boost pressure control valve to its mounting on the fan cowling, and reconnect the return hose.

31 Where applicable, refit the air conditioning compressor, and tighten the mounting bolts.

32 Reconnect the oil line to the oil cooler, and tighten the upper union. Insert and tighten the mounting bolt on the oil cooler. Remove the cardboard protector.

33 Refit the air conditioning compressor tensioner device and drivebelt, and tension the belt with reference to Chapter 1.

34 Check that the radiator drain plug is tight, then refit the centre air deflector beneath the radiator.

35 Lower the car to the ground, then check and if necessary top-up the engine oil level. It is strongly recommended that the engine oil is changed before starting the engine if a new turbocharger has been fitted, as this will protect the turbo bearings during the "running-in" period.

36 On models where the turbocharger is cooled by coolant, check and if necessary top-up the cooling system.

37 It is recommended that the basic charging pressure is checked by a Saab dealer at the earliest opportunity.

T25/TD04 turbocharger
Removal

38 Apply the handbrake, then jack up the front of the car and support on axle stands (see *"Jacking, towing and wheel changing"*).

39 Remove the centre air deflector from beneath the radiator, then drain the cooling system as described in Chapter 1.

40 Disconnect the remove the boost pressure control valve from its mounting on the fan cowling, and disconnect the wiring.

41 Disconnect the wiring from the electric cooling fan motor, then unscrew the bolts and remove the fan cowling complete with the radiator fan.

42 Release the lambda sensor wiring from the retaining clips.

43 Unscrew the nuts and disconnect the exhaust front pipe from the turbocharger.

44 Loosen the clips and disconnect the air hose between the turbocharger and airflow meter.

45 Loosen the clips and disconnect the short hose between the coolant pipe and the turbocharger.

46 Unscrew the union bolts, and remove the coolant pipe between the turbocharger and water pump.

47 Where applicable, unscrew the coolant pipe and oil pipe mounting from the cylinder head.

48 Unscrew the union bolt, then detach the oil line from the turbocharger and position it to one side.

49 Unscrew the union bolts, and remove the coolant pipe between the turbocharger and the cylinder head.

50 Release the clips and disconnect the boost pressure control valve hoses from the turbocharger and wastegate.

51 Loosen the clip and disconnect the delivery (pressure) pipe from the turbocharger.

52 Unbolt and remove the bracket between the turbocharger and sump (B202 engine) or cylinder block (B204/B234 engines).

53 Unscrew the mounting bolts, and remove the oil return pipe from the turbocharger and sump/block. Recover the gasket and O-ring. Cover the holes with tape, to prevent entry of dirt and debris.

54 Unscrew the mounting nuts, and withdraw the turbocharger from the exhaust manifold. Recover the gasket. Remove the turbocharger from the engine compartment.

Refitting

55 Clean the contact surfaces, then refit the turbocharger to the exhaust manifold, together with a new gasket. Tighten the mounting nuts to the specified torque.

56 Refit the oil return pipe to the turbocharger and sump/block, together with a new gasket and O-ring, and tighten the bolts.

57 Refit the bracket between the turbocharger and sump (B202 engine) or cylinder block (B204/B234 engines), and tighten the bolts.

58 Apply a little anti-seize compound to the studs on the turbocharger, then refit the exhaust front pipe and tighten the mounting nuts to the specified torque.

59 Reconnect the delivery (pressure) pipe and tighten the clips.

60 Reconnect the boost pressure control valve hoses to the turbocharger and wastegate.

61 Refit the coolant pipe between the turbocharger and the cylinder head, and tighten the union bolts.

62 Fill the turbocharger inter-chamber with clean engine oil, through the oil supply union on the turbocharger. **Note:** *This is important, as the turbocharger must have oil in it when the engine is started.*

63 Refit the oil supply line to the turbocharger, and tighten the union bolt.

64 Where applicable, refit the coolant pipe and oil pipe mountings to the cylinder head.

65 Refit the coolant pipe between the turbocharger and water pump, and tighten the union bolts.

66 Reconnect the short hose between the coolant pipe and the turbocharger, and tighten the clips.

67 Reconnect the air hose between the turbocharger and airflow meter, and tighten the clips.

68 Locate the lambda sensor wiring in the clips.

69 Refit the electric cooling fan cowling, complete with the radiator fan, and tighten the mounting bolts. Reconnect the wiring.

70 Refit the boost pressure control valve to its mounting on the fan cowling, and reconnect the wiring.

71 Check that the radiator drain plug is tight, then refit the centre air deflector.

72 Lower the car to the ground, then check and if necessary top-up the engine oil level. It is strongly recommended that the engine oil is changed before starting the engine if a new turbocharger has been fitted, as this will protect the turbo bearings during the "running-in" period.

73 Refill the cooling system with reference to Chapter 1.

74 It is recommended that the basic charging pressure is checked by a Saab dealer at the earliest opportunity.

19 Intercooler - removal and refitting

Removal

1 Remove the radiator as described in Chapter 3.

2 Where applicable, remove the plastic guard from under the intercooler.

3 Loosen the clips and disconnect the hoses from each end of the intercooler.

4 Unscrew and remove the bolts securing the intercooler to the air conditioning condenser.

5 Remove the upper mounting bracket and grommets from the studs on the top of the intercooler and condenser.

6 Move the intercooler away from the front panel, lift it from its mountings, and withdraw it from the engine compartment.

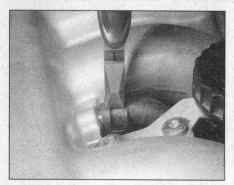

20.16 Disconnecting the brake servo vacuum hose from the inlet manifold

20.22 Removing the right-hand stay (arrowed) from the lower inlet manifold

20.23a Coolant temperature sensor wiring plug

Refitting

7 Check the upper mounting bracket grommets, and renew them if necessary.

8 Lower the intercooler onto its mountings.

9 Move the intercooler forwards against the condenser, then locate the upper mounting bracket and grommets on the studs on the intercooler and condenser. The radiator mounting end must be facing to the rear.

10 Refit the bolts securing the intercooler to the air conditioning condenser, and tighten to the specified torque.

11 Reconnect the hose to each end of the intercooler, and tighten the clips.

12 Where applicable, refit the plastic guard under the intercooler.

13 Refit the radiator with reference to Chapter 3.

20 Inlet manifold - removal and refitting

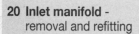

LH-Jetronic fuel injection models
Removal

1 Disconnect the battery negative lead.

2 Loosen the clip and disconnect the air supply hose from the inlet manifold.

3 Refer to Section 15 or 16 (as applicable) and remove the throttle housing from the inlet manifold. If preferred, the hoses and accelerator cable may remain attached, and the housing positioned to one side.

4 Remove the fuel supply rail from the inlet manifold as described in Section 15 or 16 (as applicable).

5 On models with automatic transmission, disconnect the kickdown cable from the bracket on the inlet manifold.

6 Release the turbo oil supply pipe from the clip on the inlet manifold.

7 Disconnect the brake servo vacuum hose from the inlet manifold.

8 Unscrew the mounting bolts securing the inlet manifold to the cylinder head. Also unscrew the lower bolt from the steady bar.

9 Withdraw the inlet manifold from the cylinder head. Recover the gasket.

Refitting

10 Refitting is a reversal of removal, but fit a new gasket and tighten the mounting bolts to the specified torque.

Trionic engine management models
Removal

11 Disconnect the battery negative lead.

Upper inlet manifold

12 To remove the upper section of the inlet manifold, first disconnect the plastic duct between the throttle housing and the inlet resonator.

13 Disconnect the idle air control valve hose from the throttle housing.

14 Disconnect the cruise control cable.

15 Unscrew the mounting nuts, and remove

the throttle housing from the inlet manifold. Position the housing to one side.

16 Loosen the clip and disconnect the vacuum hoses for the fuel pressure regulator and the brake servo **(see illustration)**. Also disconnect the small crankcase breather hose.

17 Disconnect the EVAP hose from the inlet manifold, and also disconnect the hose leading to the pressure sensor.

18 Unscrew and remove the upper retaining screws from the bracket on the side of the upper inlet manifold, and loosen the lower screws.

19 Unbolt and remove the oil filler pipe bracket.

20 Unscrew the remaining screws securing the upper inlet manifold to the lower manifold, and remove the upper manifold. Also disconnect the idle air control valve wiring.

21 Check the rubber hoses between the upper and lower inlet manifolds, and renew if necessary.

Lower inlet manifold

22 Unscrew the bolts securing the two stays to the inlet manifold **(see illustration)**. Where necessary, also loosen the stay bottom bolt/nut.

23 Disconnect the plug from the coolant temperature sensor. Also remove the screws securing the earth wires and wiring support to the inlet manifold **(see illustrations)**.

24 Disconnect the fuel supply and return hoses from the fuel rail and pressure regulator.

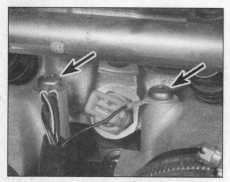

20.23b Earth wire screws (arrowed) on the lower inlet manifold

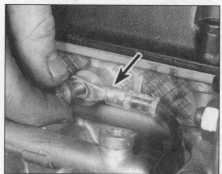

20.23c Detaching the earth wire at the timing chain end of the engine

20.23d Removing the wiring support from the inlet manifold

20.25 Wiring connector for the injectors

20.26 Removing the lower inlet manifold from the cylinder head

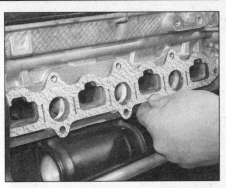

20.28 Removing the inlet manifold gasket from the cylinder head

25 Disconnect the wiring to the injectors (see illustration).
26 Unscrew the mounting bolts and remove the lower inlet manifold from the cylinder head (see illustration).
27 Loosen the clips, and separate the two halves of the lower inlet manifold. Recover the connecting hoses.
28 Remove the gasket from the cylinder head (see illustration).

Refitting

Upper and lower inlet manifolds

29 Refitting is a reversal of removal, but fit a new gasket and tighten the mounting bolts to the specified torque. Check and if necessary renew the connecting hoses and the O-ring between the throttle housing and the inlet manifold. Check and adjust the accelerator cable (and where necessary, the kickdown cable) with reference to Section 3 of this Chapter and Section 5 of Chapter 7B.

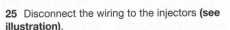

21 Exhaust manifold - removal and refitting

Non-turbo models

Removal

1 Apply the handbrake, then jack up the front of the car and support on axle stands (see *"Jacking, towing and wheel changing"*).
2 Remove the centre air deflector from beneath the radiator.

3 Where applicable, disconnect the lambda sensor wiring with reference to Chapter 4B.
4 Remove the exhaust front pipe with reference to Section 22.
5 Where air conditioning is fitted, the compressor must be moved aside. On B204 and B234 models, pull the auxiliary drivebelt upwards so that the tensioner spring is compressed, then retain the tensioner in this position by positioning a piece of bent metal rod over the tensioner bracket (refer to Chapter 1, Section 22). On B202 models, loosen the tensioner pulley and remove the compressor drivebelt. Unbolt the compressor, and position it to one side **without** disconnecting the refrigerant lines. Recover the washer on the lower mounting bolt on B202 models.
6 Unscrew and remove the exhaust manifold mounting nuts, then lift the manifold from the cylinder head. Where the manifold is in two sections, the centre section should be removed first, noting that on the remaining section, sleeves are fitted beneath all the mounting nuts **(see illustrations)**. On the single-section manifold, sleeves are only fitted beneath the nuts at each end of the manifold.
7 Remove the gasket from the studs on the cylinder head **(see illustration)**.

Refitting

8 Clean the contact surfaces of the cylinder head and exhaust manifold.
9 Refit the exhaust manifold to the studs on the cylinder head together with a new gasket,

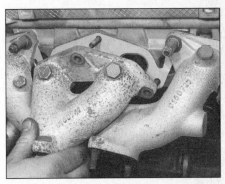

21.6a Removing the centre section of the exhaust manifold

21.6b Removing the sleeves from the outer section of the exhaust manifold

21.6c Removing the outer section of the exhaust manifold

21.7 Removing the exhaust manifold gasket

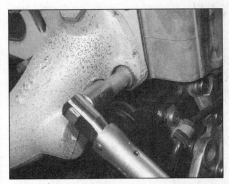

21.9 Tightening the exhaust manifold mounting nuts

then tighten the mounting nuts to the specified torque **(see illustration)**. Make sure that the sleeves are correctly located, as previously described. Where the manifold is in two sections, refit the outer section first, and tighten the mounting nuts to the specified torque, then refit the centre section and tighten the nuts.

10 On air conditioning models, refit the compressor, making sure that the washer is located on the lower mounting bolt on B202 models. On B204 and B234 models, pull up the auxiliary drivebelt and remove the metal rod, then release the drivebelt to allow the tensioner to apply the correct tension. On B202 models, adjust the drivebelt tension as described in Chapter 1, Section 22.

11 Refit the exhaust front pipe with reference to Section 22.

12 Where applicable, reconnect the lambda sensor wiring with reference to Chapter 4B.

13 Refit the centre air deflector beneath the radiator.

14 Lower the car to the ground.

T3/TE05 Turbo models

Removal and refitting

15 Refer to Section 18 - the procedure is identical to the removal and refitting of the turbocharger.

T25/TD04 Turbo models

Removal

16 Remove the turbocharger as described in Section 18.

17 Where air conditioning is fitted, the compressor must be moved aside. On B204 and B234 models, pull the auxiliary drivebelt upwards so that the tensioner spring is compressed, then retain the tensioner in this position by positioning a piece of bent metal rod over the tensioner bracket (see Chapter 1, Section 22). On B202 models, loosen the tensioner pulley and remove the compressor drivebelt. Unbolt the compressor, and position it to one side **without** disconnecting the refrigerant lines. Recover the washer on the lower mounting bolt on B202 models.

18 Unscrew and remove the exhaust manifold mounting nuts, then lift the manifold from the cylinder head. Note that sleeves are only fitted beneath the nuts at each end of the manifold.

19 Remove the gasket from the studs on the cylinder head.

Refitting

20 Clean the contact surfaces of the cylinder head and exhaust manifold.

21 Refit the exhaust manifold to the studs on the cylinder head together with a new gasket, then tighten the mounting nuts to the specified torque. Make sure that the sleeves are correctly located, as previously described.

22 On air conditioning models, refit the compressor, making sure that the washer is located on the lower mounting bolt on B202 models. On B204 and B234 models, pull up the auxiliary drivebelt and remove the metal rod, then release the drivebelt to allow the tensioner to apply the correct tension. On B202 models, adjust the drivebelt tension as described in Chapter 1, Section 22.

23 Refit the turbocharger with reference to Section 18.

22 Exhaust system - general information and component removal

General information

1 The exhaust system consists of four sections:
a) *The front pipe (incorporating a three-way catalytic converter on certain models).*
b) *The front silencer and pipe (incorporating a three-way catalytic converter on certain models).*
c) *The intermediate silencer and pipe.*
d) *The rear silencer and tailpipe.*

2 The exhaust system sections are joined by flanges with internal flared tube ends. The front pipe-to-manifold joint is gasketed, and is secured by studs and nuts. The front pipe and the connector pipes between the silencers are aluminium-plated. The silencers are made of chrome steel plate.

3 On models with a catalytic converter, the lambda sensor is located in the front pipe. The catalytic converter is located either in the front pipe or in the front silencer and pipe.

4 On non-Turbo models, the front pipe is of twin-branch type. On Turbo models, the single front pipe incorporates an elbow at its front end which is connected to the turbocharger.

5 On all models, the system is suspended throughout its entire length by rubber mountings.

Removal

6 Each exhaust section can be removed individually, but because the rear section of the system is located over the rear anti-roll bar, it is not possible to remove the complete exhaust system in one piece.

7 To remove a section of the system, first jack up the front or rear of the car and support it on axle stands (see *"Jacking, towing and wheel changing"*). Alternatively, position the car over an inspection pit, or on car ramps.

Front pipe (and catalytic converter where applicable)

Note: *Where a catalytic converter is fitted, do not drop the unit, as it contains a fragile ceramic element.*

8 On models with a catalytic converter, remove the lambda sensor as described in Chapter 4B.

9 Unscrew the nuts, and separate the flange joint between the front pipe and the front silencer and pipe.

10 Unhook the mounting rubber from the underbody.

11 Unscrew the nuts securing the front pipe to the turbocharger or exhaust manifold (as applicable), then lower the pipe between the engine and the front subframe crossmember. Recover the gaskets.

Front silencer/catalytic converter and pipe

Note: *Where a catalytic converter is fitted, do not drop the unit, as it contains a fragile ceramic element.*

12 Unscrew the nuts, and separate the flange joints connecting the front silencer and pipe to the front pipe, and the intermediate silencer and pipe.

13 Unhook the mounting rubbers from the underbody, and lower the front silencer and pipe to the ground.

Intermediate silencer and pipe

14 Unscrew the nuts/bolts, and separate the flange joints connecting the intermediate silencer and pipe to the front silencer and pipe, and the rear silencer and tailpipe.

15 Unhook the mounting rubbers from the underbody, and lower the intermediate silencer and pipe to the ground.

Rear silencer and tailpipe

16 Unscrew the bolts, and separate the flange joint connecting the rear silencer and tailpipe to the intermediate silencer and pipe.

17 Unhook the mounting rubbers from the underbody, and lower the rear silencer and tailpipe to the ground.

Heat shields

18 The heat shields are secured to the underbody by bolts. Each shield can be removed once the relevant exhaust section has been removed.

Refitting

19 Each section is refitted by a reversal of the removal sequence, noting the following points:
a) *Ensure that all traces of corrosion have been removed from the flared tube ends in the flanges, and renew the front pipe-to-exhaust manifold/turbocharger gasket(s).*
b) *Inspect the rubber mountings for signs of damage or deterioration, and renew as necessary.*
c) *On models with a catalytic converter, refit the lambda sensor with reference to Chapter 4B.*
d) *Make sure that all rubber mountings are correctly located, and that there is adequate clearance between the exhaust system and underbody.*

Chapter 4 Part B: Emissions control systems

Contents

Degrees of difficulty

| Easy, suitable for novice with little experience | | Fairly easy, suitable for beginner with some experience | | Fairly difficult, suitable for competent DIY mechanic | | Difficult, suitable for experienced DIY mechanic | | Very difficult, suitable for expert DIY or professional | |

Specifications

EGR system (models without a catalytic converter)

EGR valve colour coding:
Turbo	Blue
Non-turbo	Black

EGR thermostatic valve:
Opening temperature	30°C
Closing temperature	20°C

Evaporative emissions control system

Evaporative-loss control device (ELCD) canister-purge valve:
Resistance at 20°C	40 ± 20 ohms

Lambda sensor:
Resistance at 20°C (pins 1 and 2)	3.5 ± 0.4 ohms

Torque wrench setting

	Nm	lbf ft
Lambda sensor	55	41

1 General information

All models have the ability to use unleaded petrol, although Super unleaded is specified for early B202i and B202 Turbo models (see Chapter 4A). Various other features are built into the fuel system to help minimise harmful emissions. All models have a crankcase emissions control system, and all later models are equipped with a three-way catalytic converter. Some models are also fitted with exhaust gas recirculation and evaporative emissions control systems.

In certain non-UK territories having strict emissions laws, a secondary air injection system is fitted.

The emissions control systems function as follows.

Crankcase emissions control

To reduce emissions of unburned hydrocarbons from the crankcase into the atmosphere, the engine is sealed. The blow-by gases and oil vapour are drawn from inside the crankcase, through a double outlet on the camshaft cover, to the throttle housing and also via the turbocharger to the inlet manifold. On non-turbo models, the arrangement is slightly different, in that the connection to the turbocharger is taken direct to the inlet manifold.

Under conditions of high manifold depression (idling, deceleration) the gases will be sucked positively out of the crankcase to the throttle housing. Under conditions of low manifold depression (acceleration, full-throttle running) the gases are forced out of the crankcase by the (relatively) higher crankcase pressure; if the engine is worn, the raised crankcase pressure (due to increased blow-by) will cause some of the flow to return under all manifold conditions.

Exhaust emissions control

To minimise the amount of pollutants which escape into the atmosphere, some models are fitted with a catalytic converter in the exhaust system. The catalytic converter system is of the "closed-loop" type, in which a lambda sensor in the exhaust system provides the fuel-injection/ignition system ECU with constant feedback on the oxygen content of the exhaust gases. This enables the ECU to adjust the mixture to provide the best possible conditions for the converter to operate.

The lambda sensor has a built-in heating element, controlled by the ECU through the lambda sensor relay, to quickly bring the sensor's tip to an efficient operating temperature. The sensor's tip is sensitive to oxygen, and sends the ECU a varying voltage depending on the amount of oxygen in the exhaust gases; if the inlet air/fuel mixture is too rich, the sensor sends a high-voltage signal. The voltage falls as the mixture weakens. Peak conversion efficiency of all major pollutants occurs if the inlet air/fuel mixture is maintained at the chemically-correct ratio for the complete combustion of petrol - 14.7 parts (by weight) of air to 1 part of fuel (the "stoichiometric" ratio).

The sensor output voltage alters in a large step at this point, the ECU using the signal change as a reference point, and correcting the inlet air/fuel mixture accordingly by altering the fuel injector pulse width (injector opening time).

Exhaust gas recirculation system

This system circulates a proportion of the exhaust gas back into the combustion chambers during certain operating conditions, in order to reduce harmful exhaust gas emissions. This is achieved by effectively reducing the peak temperatures reached in the combustion chambers by the introduction of the inert exhaust gas. Two systems were fitted - a mechanical system, and an electronic system controlled by the LH-Jetronic ECU.

If a fault occurs in the EGR system, the "CHECK ENGINE" warning light on the instrument panel will be lit, and the corresponding fault code will be stored in the LH-Jetronic ECU.

Evaporative emissions control system

To minimise the escape into the atmosphere of unburned hydrocarbons, an evaporative emissions control system is fitted to certain models. The system is referred to as the "evaporative-loss control device" (ELCD). The fuel tank filler cap is sealed, and a charcoal canister is mounted on the front right-hand side of the car beneath the right-hand wing, to collect the petrol vapours generated in the tank when the car is parked. The vapours are stored until they can be cleared from the canister (under the control of the fuel system ECU via the purge valve, into the inlet tract, to be burned by the engine during normal combustion.

To ensure that the engine runs correctly when it is cold and/or idling, and to protect the catalytic converter from the effects of an over-rich mixture, the purge control valve is not opened by the ECU until the engine has warmed up, and the engine is under load; the valve solenoid is then modulated on and off, to allow the stored vapour to pass into the inlet tract.

Deceleration device

A deceleration dashpot (or "throttle damper") is fitted to the throttle lever on the throttle housing on some models. Its purpose is to control the deceleration of the engine during overrun, in order to prevent the emission of unburned hydrocarbons. If the accelerator pedal is released with the engine running at a speed of 3000 rpm, the engine should take approximately 4 seconds to decelerate to a speed of 875 rpm.

Automatic idling control (AIC)

Some models are fitted with an automatic idling control system, which provides smoother idling, improved cold and warm-up running, idle speed compensation (to allow for the operation of the air conditioning compressor, alternator or power steering pump), and engine deceleration control.

The AIC valve controls the flow of air bypassing the throttle valve. The valve is operated by the ECU.

Pulse-air system

Some models have a pulse-air system, which supplies air to the downstream side of the exhaust valves, in order to complete oxidation of any unburned hydrocarbons present in the exhaust gases. The system uses the pressure pulses in the exhaust manifold to draw the air from the air cleaner.

Secondary air injection

On this system, air is injected into the exhaust manifold before the lambda sensor and catalytic converter have reached working temperature, in order to assist in the combustion of hydrocarbons. The system is activated when the engine is started, and its running time depends on the engine temperature and the point when the lambda sensor begins to operate.

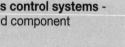

2 Emissions control systems - testing and component renewal

Crankcase emissions control

1 The components of this system require no attention, other than to check at regular intervals that the hose(s) are clear and undamaged.

EGR system

Testing

2 If a fault occurs in the EGR system, a fault code is stored in the LH-Jetronic ECU, and a warning light is lit on the instrument panel. Check all wiring and hose connections on the EGR valve for security. If this does not rectify the fault, the advice of a Saab dealer should be sought.

Removal and refitting

Air temperature sensor
3 To remove the inlet air temperature sensor, disconnect the wiring and unscrew the sensor from the inlet manifold. Refitting is a reversal of removal.

Vacuum tank
4 The vacuum tank is located on the left-hand front of the engine compartment. First, remove the airflow meter as described in Chapter 4A.
5 Disconnect the vacuum hoses, and remove the vacuum tank together with the mounting bracket.
6 Remove the mounting bracket, and fit it to the new vacuum tank.
7 Refitting is a reversal of removal.

Timing valve
8 The timing valve is located in the line between the vacuum tank and the EGR valve.

9 Disconnect the wiring and the hoses, noting their location, and remove the valve.
10 Refitting is a reversal of removal.

Lambda sensor

Testing

11 The lambda sensor may be tested with a multi-meter by disconnecting the wiring at the connector, either near the right-hand end of the inlet manifold (models with LH-Jetronic system) or on the right-hand side of the bulkhead (models with Trionic system).
12 Connect an ohmmeter between terminals 1 and 2 on the sensor wiring plug. **Do not** connect the ohmmeter to the ECU wiring. The resistance should be between 2.9 and 4.0 ohms for a 12-watt lambda sensor (unleaded petrol), or approximately 2.1 ohms for an 18-watt lambda sensor (leaded petrol and turbo class 1). The resistance varies with temperature, and can be as high as 10 ohms.
13 Reconnect the wiring after making the test.

Removal

Note: *The lambda sensor is DELICATE. It will not work if it is dropped or knocked, if its power supply is disrupted, or if any cleaning materials are used on it. The sensor should be renewed every 60 000 miles/90 000 km.*

Early models
14 Disconnect the wiring plug at the right-hand side of the inlet manifold.
15 Unclip the wiring from the cylinder head, and feed it through to the front of the engine.

Later models
16 Remove the weatherstrip and cover from the false bulkhead at the rear of the engine compartment. Lift the right-hand part of the cover, and disconnect the lambda sensor wiring plug.
17 Unscrew the screws from the bulkhead plate, then pull the lambda sensor wiring to the front of the engine compartment, lifting the air conditioning pipe where necessary.
18 Where necessary, release the wiring from the clamp on the coolant pipe, and unscrew the wiring support bolts as necessary **(see illustration)**.
19 Where necessary, release the clip near the lower air conditioning compressor mounting bolt.

All models
20 Unscrew the sensor from the exhaust system downpipe, and remove it. The sensor may be tight, in which case it will help if it is turned back and forth on its threads as it is being removed. Note that it is possible to obtain a special slotted socket, which locates on the sensor without causing any damage to the wiring.

Refitting

21 Refitting is a reverse of the removal procedure. Prior to installing the sensor, apply a smear of high-temperature grease to the sensor threads. Tighten the sensor to the specified torque **(see illustration)**. The wiring must be correctly routed, and in no danger of contacting the exhaust system.

2.18 Removing the lambda wiring support from the front of the cylinder block

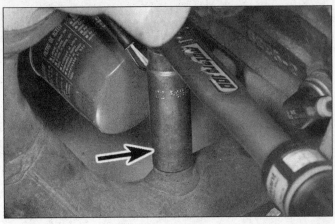

2.21 Tightening the lambda sensor (hidden beneath the deep socket) with a torque wrench

Throttle damper

Testing

22 Run the engine to normal temperature, and check the CO content setting and idling speed (where applicable).

23 Disconnect and plug the distributor vacuum hose and the EGR hoses, where fitted.

24 Start the engine, and increase its speed to between 2500 and 2700 rpm. With the engine held at this speed, make sure that the damper plunger is just touching the throttle stop pin. If not, loosen the locknut and adjust the position of the damper as necessary. Tighten the locknut after making the adjustment.

25 Increase the engine speed to 3000 rpm, then use a stopwatch to check that it takes between 3 and 5 seconds to return to normal idling speed when the throttle is released.

26 If adjustment is necessary, the retardation time may be shortened by screwing the damper away from the throttle, or lengthened by screwing the damper towards the throttle.

Removal

27 Unscrew the locknut, and remove the damper from the bracket on the throttle housing.

Refitting

28 Refitting is a reversal of removal, but adjust it with reference to paragraphs 22 to 26.

Evaporative emission canister and purge valve

Testing

29 If the system is thought to be faulty, first follow the procedure given in paragraphs 30 to 32. Check that the hoses from the charcoal canister and purge control valve are clear by blowing through them. If the purge control valve or charcoal canister are thought to be faulty, they must be renewed.

Removal

30 Apply the handbrake, then jack up the front of the car and support on axle stands

(see *"Jacking, towing and wheel changing"*). Remove the right-hand front wheel.

31 Remove the right-hand front wing plastic moulding, followed by the front section of the wheelarch liner.

32 Identify the positions of the hoses on the canister, then disconnect them **(see illustration)**.

33 Unhook the canister from its mounting bracket and remove from under the wing.

34 Disconnect and remove the purge valve, noting that the arrow points towards the connector end of the canister **(see illustration)**.

Refitting

35 Refitting is a reversal of the removal procedure, but make sure that the hoses are reconnected to their original positions, and that the purge valve arrow points in the correct direction.

Catalytic converter

Testing

36 The performance of the catalytic converter can be checked only by measuring the exhaust gases using a good-quality, carefully-calibrated exhaust gas analyser as described in Chapter 1.

37 If the CO level at the tailpipe is too high, the vehicle should be taken to a Saab dealer

so that the fuel injection and ignition systems, including the lambda sensor, can be thoroughly checked using special diagnostic equipment. Once these have been checked and are known to be free from faults, the fault must be in the catalytic converter, which must be renewed as described in Part A of this Chapter.

38 A temperature sensor is incorporated in the catalytic converter on some models, together with a warning light on the instrument panel.

Removal and refitting

39 Removal and refitting of the catalytic converter is described in Chapter 4A, as part of the exhaust system procedures.

Catalytic converter temperature sensor

Removal

40 To remove the temperature sensor, first push the right-hand front seat fully forwards, then disconnect the sensor wiring plug.

41 Tie a piece of string to the wiring, as an aid to refitting.

42 Apply the handbrake, then jack up the car and support on axle stands (see *"Jacking, towing and wheel changing"*).

43 Unbolt and remove the heat shield from beneath the catalytic converter.

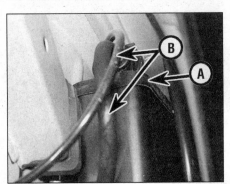

2.32 Evaporative emissions canister (A) and hoses (B) beneath the right-hand front wing

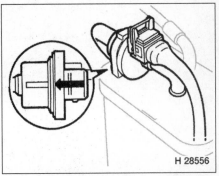

2.34 Purge valve location on the evaporative emissions canister

44 Unscrew the sensor from the catalytic converter, then pull the wiring through the floor and untie the string. Leave the string in place, to pull the wiring back through on refitting.

Refitting

45 Refitting is a reversal of removal, using the string to pull the wiring through the floor.

3 Catalytic converter - general information and precautions

1 The catalytic converter is a reliable and simple device which needs no maintenance in itself, but there are some facts of which an owner should be aware if the converter is to function properly for its full service life.

a) *DO NOT use leaded petrol in a car with a catalytic converter - the lead will coat the precious metals, reducing their converting efficiency, and may eventually destroy the converter.*

b) *Always keep the ignition and fuel systems well-maintained in accordance with the manufacturer's schedule (see Chapter 1).*

c) *If the engine develops a misfire, do not drive the car at all (or at least as little as possible) until the fault is cured.*

d) *DO NOT push- or tow-start the car - this will soak the catalytic converter in unburned fuel, causing it to overheat when the engine does start.*

e) *DO NOT switch the engine off at high engine speeds - ie do not "blip" the throttle before switching off. Allow it to return to idle first.*

f) *DO NOT use fuel or engine oil additives - these may contain substances harmful to the catalytic converter.*

g) *DO NOT continue to use the car if the engine burns oil to the extent of leaving a visible trail of blue smoke.*

h) *Remember that the catalytic converter operates at very high temperatures. DO NOT, therefore, park the car in dry undergrowth, over long grass, or over piles of dead leaves, after a long run.*

i) *Remember that the catalytic converter is FRAGILE - do not strike it with tools during servicing work.*

Chapter 5 Part A:
Starting and charging systems

Contents

Degrees of difficulty

Easy, suitable for novice with little experience	Fairly easy, suitable for beginner with some experience	Fairly difficult, suitable for competent DIY mechanic	Difficult, suitable for experienced DIY mechanic	Very difficult, suitable for expert DIY or professional

Specifications

System type .... 12-volt, negative earth

Battery
Type .... Lead-acid, "low-maintenance" or "maintenance-free" (sealed for life)
Battery capacity .... 60/62 amp/hr
Charge condition:
  Poor .... 12.5 volts
  Normal .... 12.6 volts
  Good .... 12.7 volts

Alternator
Type .....Bosch
Output current .... 70, 80 or 115 amps
Minimum brush protrusion from holder .... 5.0 mm
Minimum slip ring diameter:
  70 and 80 amp .... 26.8 mm
  115 amp .... 27.2 mm

Starter motor
Type .... Bosch
Output .... 1.4 kW

Torque wrench settings

	Nm	lbf ft
Starter solenoid to starter	5	4
Starter through-bolts	3	2

1 General information and precautions

General information

Because of their engine-related functions, the components of the starting and charging systems are covered separately from the body electrical devices such as the lights, instruments, etc (which are covered in Chapter 12). Refer to Part B of this Chapter for information on the ignition system.

The electrical system is of the 12-volt negative earth type.

The battery fitted as original equipment is of low-maintenance or "maintenance-free" (sealed for life) type. The battery is charged by the alternator, which is belt-driven from the crankshaft pulley. During the life of the car, the original battery may have been replaced by a standard type battery.

The starter motor is of the pre-engaged type, incorporating an integral solenoid. On starting, the solenoid moves the drive pinion into engagement with the flywheel/driveplate ring gear before the starter motor is energised. Once the engine has started, a one-way clutch prevents the motor armature being driven by the engine until the pinion disengages from the ring gear. Unlike some modern starter motors, it incorporates epicyclic reduction gears between the armature and the pinion.

Precautions

Further details of the various systems are given in the relevant Sections of this Chapter. While some repair procedures are given, the usual course of action is to renew the component concerned. The owner whose interest extends beyond mere component renewal should obtain a copy of the *"Automobile Electrical & Electronic Systems Manual"*, available from the publishers of this manual.

It is necessary to take extra care when working on the electrical system, to avoid damage to semi-conductor devices (diodes and transistors), and to avoid the risk of personal injury. In addition to the precautions given in *"Safety first!"* observe the following when working on the system:

Always remove rings, watches, etc before working on the electrical system. Even with the battery disconnected, capacitive discharge could occur if a component's live terminal is earthed through a metal object. This could cause a shock or nasty burn.

Do not reverse the battery connections. Components such as the alternator, electronic control units, or any other components having semi-conductor circuitry, could be irreparably damaged.

If the engine is being started using jump leads and a slave battery, connect the batteries *positive-to-positive* and *negative-to-negative* (see *"Booster battery (jump) starting"*). This also applies when connecting a battery charger.

Never disconnect the battery terminals, the alternator, any electrical wiring, or any test instruments, when the engine is running.

Do not allow the engine to turn the alternator when the alternator is not connected.

Never "test" for alternator output by "flashing" the output lead to earth.

Never use an ohmmeter of the type incorporating a hand-cranked generator for circuit or continuity testing.

Always ensure that the battery negative lead is disconnected when working on the electrical system.

Before using electric-arc welding equipment on the car, disconnect the battery, alternator, and components such as the fuel injection/ignition electronic control unit, to protect them from the risk of damage.

The radio/cassette unit fitted as standard equipment by Saab from 1994-on has a built-in security code, to deter thieves. If the power source to the unit is cut, the anti-theft system will activate. Even if the power source is immediately reconnected, the radio/cassette unit will not function until the correct security code has been entered. Therefore, if you do not know the correct security code for the radio/cassette unit, **do not** disconnect the battery negative terminal of the battery, nor remove the radio/cassette unit from the vehicle. Refer to *"Radio/cassette unit anti-theft system - precaution"* for further information.

2 Electrical fault-finding - general information

Refer to Chapter 12.

3 Battery - testing and charging

Standard and low-maintenance battery - testing

1 If the vehicle covers a small annual mileage, it is worthwhile checking the specific gravity of the electrolyte every three months, to determine the state of charge of the battery. Use a hydrometer to make the check, and compare the results with the following table. Note that the specific gravity readings assume an electrolyte temperature of 15°C (60°F); for every 10°C (18°F) below 15°C (60°F), subtract 0.007. For every 10°C (18°F) above 15°C (60°F), add 0.007. However, for convenience, the temperatures quoted in the following table are **ambient** (outdoor air) temperatures, above or below 25°C (77°F):

	Above 25°C (77°F)	Below 25°C (77°F)
Fully-charged	1.210 to 1.230	1.270 to 1.290
70% charged	1.170 to 1.190	1.230 to 1.250
Fully-discharged	1.050 to 1.070	1.110 to 1.130

2 If the battery condition is suspect, first check the specific gravity of electrolyte in each cell. A variation of 0.040 or more between any cells indicates loss of electrolyte or deterioration of the internal plates.

3 If the specific gravity variation is 0.040 or more, the battery should be renewed. If the cell variation is satisfactory but the battery is discharged, it should be charged as described later in this Section.

Maintenance-free battery - testing

4 In cases where a "sealed for life" maintenance-free battery is fitted, topping-up and testing of the electrolyte in each cell is not possible. The condition of the battery can therefore only be tested using a battery condition indicator or a voltmeter.

5 A battery with a built-in charge condition indicator may be fitted. The indicator is located in the top of the battery casing, and indicates the condition of the battery from its colour. If the indicator shows green, then the battery is in a good state of charge. If the indicator turns darker, eventually to black, then the battery requires charging, as described later in this Section. If the indicator shows clear/yellow, then the electrolyte level in the battery is too low to allow further use, and the battery should be renewed. **Do not** attempt to charge, load or jump-start a battery when the indicator shows clear/yellow.

6 If testing the battery using a voltmeter, connect the voltmeter across the battery, and compare the result with those given in the Specifications under "charge condition". The test is only accurate if the battery has not been subjected to any kind of charge for the

previous six hours, including charging by the alternator. If this is not the case, switch on the headlights for 30 seconds, then wait four to five minutes after switching off the headlights before testing the battery. All other electrical circuits must be switched off, so check (for instance) that the doors and tailgate or bootlid are fully shut when making the test.

7 If the voltage reading is less than 12.2 volts, then the battery is discharged. A reading of 12.2 to 12.4 volts indicates a partially-discharged condition.

8 If the battery is to be charged, remove it from the vehicle (Section 4) and charge it as described in the following paragraphs.

Standard and low-maintenance battery - charging

Note: *The following is intended as a guide only. Always refer to the manufacturer's recommendations (often printed on a label attached to the battery) before charging a battery.*

9 Charge the battery at a rate of 3.5 to 4 amps, and continue to charge the battery at this rate until no further rise in specific gravity is noted over a four-hour period.

10 Alternatively, a trickle charger charging at the rate of 1.5 amps can safely be used overnight.

11 Specially rapid "boost" charges which are claimed to restore the power of the battery in 1 to 2 hours are not recommended, as they can cause serious damage to the battery plates through overheating.

12 While charging the battery, note that the temperature of the electrolyte should never exceed 37.8°C (100°F).

Maintenance-free battery - charging

Note: *The following is intended as a guide only. Always refer to the manufacturer's recommendations (often printed on a label attached to the battery) before charging a battery.*

13 This battery type requires a longer period to fully recharge than the standard type, the time taken being dependent on the extent of discharge, but it can take anything up to three days.

14 A constant-voltage type charger is required, to be set, where possible, to 13.9 to 14.9 volts with a charger current below 25 amps. Using this method, the battery should be usable within three hours, giving a voltage reading of 12.5 volts, but this is for a partially-discharged battery and, as mentioned, full charging can take considerably longer.

15 Use of a normal trickle charger should not be detrimental to the battery, provided excessive gassing is not allowed to occur, and the battery is not allowed to become hot.

4 Battery - removal and refitting

Removal

1 The battery is located on the left-hand side of the engine compartment.
2 Loosen the clamp nut and disconnect the lead at the negative (earth) terminal. Disconnect the lead at the positive terminal in the same way.
3 Unscrew the bolt and remove the battery retaining clamp which secures the battery to the mounting bracket. On early models, just release the battery clamp.
4 Lift the battery out of the engine compartment (take care not to tilt it excessively).

Refitting

5 Refitting is a reversal of removal. Smear petroleum jelly on the terminals when reconnecting the leads, and always reconnect the positive lead first, and the negative lead last. On models up to 1994, the battery terminals are located nearest the engine, with the positive terminal at the front; from 1995 on, the terminals are located nearest the left-hand front wing, with the negative terminal at the front.

5 Charging system - testing

Note: *Refer to the warnings given in "Safety first!" and in Section 1 of this Chapter before starting work.*
1 If the ignition/no-charge warning light does not come on when the ignition is switched on, first check the alternator wiring connections for security. If satisfactory, check that the warning light bulb has not blown, and that the bulbholder is secure in its location in the instrument panel. If the light still fails to illuminate, check the continuity of the warning light feed wire from the alternator to the bulbholder. If all is satisfactory, the alternator is at fault, and should be taken to an auto-

electrician for testing and repair, or else renewed.
2 If the ignition warning light comes on when the engine is running, stop the engine. Check that the drivebelt is intact and correctly tensioned (see Chapter 1), and that the alternator connections are secure. If all is satisfactory, check the alternator brushes and slip rings as described in Section 8. If the fault persists, the alternator should be taken to an auto-electrician for testing and repair, or else renewed.
3 If the alternator output is suspect even though the warning light functions correctly, the regulated voltage may be checked as follows.
4 Connect a voltmeter across the battery terminals, and start the engine.
5 Increase the engine speed until the voltmeter reading remains steady; the reading should be approximately 12 to 13 volts, and no more than 14 volts.
6 Switch on as many electrical accessories (eg, the headlights, heated rear window and heater blower) as possible, and check that the alternator maintains the regulated voltage at around 13 to 14 volts.
7 If the regulated voltage is not as stated, the fault may be due to worn brushes, weak brush springs, a faulty voltage regulator, a faulty diode, a severed phase winding, or worn or damaged slip rings. The brushes and slip rings may be checked (see Section 8), but if the fault persists, the alternator should be taken to an auto-electrician for testing and repair, or else renewed.

6 Alternator drivebelt - removal, refitting and tensioning

Refer to the procedure given for the auxiliary drivebelt in Chapter 1, Section 22.

7 Alternator - removal and refitting

Removal

1 Disconnect the battery negative lead.
2 Apply the handbrake, then jack up the front

of the car and support on axle stands (see *"Jacking, towing and wheel changing"*). Remove the right-hand front wheel.
3 Remove the right-hand front wing plastic moulding, followed by the front section of the wheelarch liner, for access to the engine.
4 Remove the auxiliary drivebelt as described in Chapter 1, Section 22.
5 Unscrew the alternator upper and lower mounting bolts **(see illustration)**. On balance shaft (B204/B234) engines, the upper mounting is slotted.
6 Withdraw the alternator from under the right-hand wing, until it is possible to access the wiring connections. On balance shaft (B204/B234) engines, unbolt the power steering mounting bracket from the rear of the cylinder block - note that this bracket includes a pulley for the auxiliary drivebelt **(see illustrations)**.
7 Note the position of the wires on the rear of the alternator, then unscrew the terminal nuts (where applicable) and disconnect the wires.
8 Withdraw the alternator from under the wing.

Refitting

9 Refitting is a reversal of removal. Ensure that the alternator mountings are securely tightened, and refit the auxiliary drivebelt as described in Chapter 1.

8 Alternator brushes and regulator - inspection and renewal

1 Remove the alternator as described in Section 7.
2 Unscrew the large terminal nut and the screws securing the cover to the rear of the alternator **(see illustrations)**.
3 Using a screwdriver, lever off the cover, and remove it from the rear of the alternator **(see illustrations)**.
4 Unscrew and remove the two retaining screws, and remove the regulator/brush holder from the rear of the alternator **(see illustrations)**.
5 Measure the protrusion of each brush from

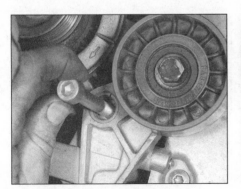

7.5 Removing the alternator lower mounting bolt

7.6a On B204/B234 engines, unbolt the power steering mounting bracket . . .

7.6b . . . and remove the alternator for access to the wiring terminals

8.2a Unscrew the large terminal nut . . .

8.2b . . . and the screws securing the cover to the rear of the alternator

8.3a Lever off the cover . . .

its holder, using a steel rule or vernier calipers **(see illustration)**. If less than 5.0 mm, the brushes should be renewed, or a new assembly obtained. On early models, the brushes can be unsoldered and renewed, but on later models, this may not be the case.

6 Using a soldering iron, unsolder the brush wires from the terminals on top of the holder. **Note:** *Take care not to overheat the regulator.* Remove the brushes from the holder, complete with the tension springs.

7 Remove excess solder from the terminals, and clean the holders. It is important that the new brushes move freely in the holders.

8 Insert the new brushes in the holder, one at a time, and hold them against the spring tension with a pair of pliers while the wires are

soldered onto the terminals. Do not release the brushes until the solder has cooled.

9 If the original brushes were in good condition, clean them and check that they move freely in their holders.

10 Clean the alternator slip-rings with a fuel-moistened cloth. Check for signs of scoring or burning on the surface of the slip-rings. It may be possible to have the slip rings renovated by an electrical specialist.

11 Refit the regulator/brush holder assembly, and securely tighten the retaining screws.

12 Refit the cover, then insert and tighten the retaining screws and refit the large terminal nut.

13 Refit the alternator with reference to Section 7.

9 Starting system - testing

Note: *Refer to the precautions given in "Safety first!" and in Section 1 of this Chapter before starting work.*

1 If the starter motor fails to operate when the ignition key is turned to the appropriate position, the following possible causes may apply:
a)   *The battery is faulty.*
b)   *The electrical connections between the switch, solenoid, battery and starter motor are somewhere failing to pass the*

necessary current from the battery through the starter to earth.
c)   *The solenoid is faulty.*
d)   *The starter motor is mechanically or electrically defective.*

2 To check the battery, switch on the headlights. If they dim after a few seconds, this indicates that the battery is discharged - recharge (see Section 3) or renew the battery. If the headlights glow brightly, operate the starter on the ignition switch, and observe the lights. If they dim, this indicates that current is reaching the starter motor - therefore, the fault must lie in the starter motor. If the lights continue to glow brightly (and no clicking sound can be heard from the starter motor solenoid), this indicates that there is a fault in the circuit or solenoid - see the following paragraphs. If the starter motor turns slowly when operated, but the battery is in good condition, then this indicates that either the starter motor is faulty, or that there is considerable resistance somewhere in the circuit.

3 If a fault in the circuit is suspected, disconnect the battery leads, the starter/solenoid wiring and the engine/transmission earth strap. Thoroughly clean the connections, and reconnect the leads and wiring, then use a voltmeter or test light to check that full battery voltage is available at the battery positive lead connection on the solenoid, and that the earth is sound.

8.3b . . . and remove it from the alternator

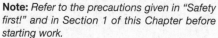

8.4a Remove the screws (arrowed) . . .

8.4b . . . and withdraw the regulator/brush holder from the rear of the alternator

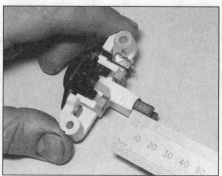

8.5 Measuring the brush protrusion from the holder

10.3 Disconnecting the battery supply lead from the starter motor terminal

10.4 Removing the positive cable support from the inlet manifold stay

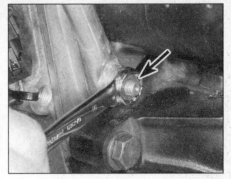

10.5a Unscrew the starter motor lower mounting nut . . .

HAYNES HiNT *Smear petroleum jelly around the battery terminals to prevent corrosion - corroded connections are amongst the most frequent causes of electrical system faults.*

4 If the battery and all connections are in good condition, check the circuit by disconnecting the wire from the solenoid terminal. Connect a voltmeter or test light between the wire end and a good earth (such as the battery negative terminal), and check that the wire is live when the ignition switch is turned to the "start" position. If it is, then the circuit is sound - if not, the circuit wiring can be checked as described in Chapter 12.

5 The solenoid contacts can be checked by connecting a voltmeter or test light between the terminal on the starter side of the solenoid, and earth. When the ignition switch is turned to the "start" position, there should be a reading or lighted bulb, as applicable. If there is no reading or lighted bulb, the solenoid or contacts are faulty and the solenoid should be renewed.

6 If the circuit and solenoid are proved sound, the fault must lie in the starter motor. Begin checking the starter motor by removing it (see Section 10), and checking the brushes (see Section 11). If the fault does not lie in the brushes, the motor windings must be faulty. In this event, it may be possible to have the starter motor overhauled by a specialist, but

check on the availability and cost of spares before proceeding, as it may prove more economical to obtain a new or exchange motor.

10 Starter motor - removal and refitting

Removal

1 The starter motor is located on the left-hand rear side of the engine, and is bolted to the engine backplate and transmission. First disconnect the battery negative lead.

2 Apply the handbrake, then jack up the front of the car and support on axle stands (see *"Jacking, towing and wheel changing"*).

3 Unscrew the nut and disconnect the battery positive supply lead from the terminal on the solenoid **(see illustration)**.

4 On B204 and B234 engines unbolt the positive cable support from the inlet manifold stay **(see illustration)**.

5 Unscrew the starter motor lower mounting nut, then unbolt and remove the inlet manifold stay **(see illustrations)**. The top of the stay is slotted, so it is not necessary to completely remove the bolt on the manifold.

6 Unscrew the nut and disconnect the solenoid trigger wire from the terminal blade.

7 Unscrew the upper starter motor mounting bolt, then lower the starter motor from the engine compartment **(see illustration)**.

Refitting

8 Refitting is a reversal of removal. Tighten all wire connections securely.

11 Starter motor - brush renewal

Note: *No minimum brush length is specified by the manufacturers, but it should be self-evident if the brushes are worn to the extent where renewal is required.*

1 Remove the starter motor as described in Section 10.

2 Unscrew the nut and disconnect the starter motor feed cable from the solenoid terminal **(see illustrations)**.

10.5b . . . then remove the inlet manifold stay

10.7 Removing the starter motor from the engine backplate

11.2a Unscrew the nut . . .

11.2b . . . and disconnect the motor feed cable from the solenoid terminal

11.3a Remove the screws . . .

11.3b . . . lift off the cover . . .

11.3c . . . and remove the seal

11.4 Removing the circlip and shims

11.5 Unscrew the through-bolts . . .

11.6 . . . and remove the commutator end bracket

11.7 Removing the brush holder assembly

11.9 Fitting the brush holders

3 Unscrew and remove the two screws securing the cover to the end bracket. Lift off the cover and remove the seal **(see illustrations)**.
4 Extract the circlip, and remove the shim(s) and O-ring seal **(see illustration)**.
5 Unscrew the through-bolts securing the commutator end bracket and yoke to the pinion end bracket **(see illustration)**. Mark the end bracket in relation to the yoke.
6 Remove the commutator end bracket **(see illustration)**.
7 Withdraw the brush holder assembly, at the same time releasing the feed cable grommet from the yoke. If the commutator/armature requires attention or cleaning, withdraw it from the yoke at this stage, then remove the brush holder assembly **(see illustration)**. As the holder assembly is removed, the brushes will be pushed out of their holders by the springs, but will be retained by the leads.
8 Check the brushes for wear, and renew as necessary. It may be possible to obtain

individual brushes from a motor factor, otherwise the complete brush holder may have to be renewed. Clean all the components before reassembly. Clean the commutator using fine glasspaper. If it is worn excessively, it may be possible to have it machined by an auto-electrician. Make sure that the brush holders are thoroughly cleaned, so that the new brushes will move freely in them.
9 Locate the brush plate without the brush holders part-way onto the commutator, then centralise the brushes, and fit the holders and springs over the brushes **(see illustration)**.
10 If removed, refit the armature inside the yoke.
11 Slide the complete bush holder assembly onto the armature commutator, while guiding the feed cable grommet in the yoke slot.
12 Locate the commutator end bracket on the armature, followed by the O-ring seal, shim(s) and circlip. Make sure that the O-ring seal is correctly fitted.
13 Refit the end bracket, making sure that the

mark is aligned with the previously-made mark on the yoke. Insert and tighten the through-bolts.
14 Refit the shims and circlip, then refit the cover and seal to the end bracket, and tighten the two screws.
15 Reconnect the feed cable to the solenoid terminal, and tighten the nut.
16 Refit the starter motor with reference to Section 10.

12 Ignition switch -
removal and refitting

Removal

1 Refer to Chapter 10 and remove the ignition switch/steering column lock.
2 To remove the ignition switch, unscrew the socket-headed screws, and withdraw the switch from the lock housing.
3 The lock cylinder may be removed by first inserting the ignition key and turning it to position "1". Using a suitable instrument through the hole provided, depress the locking tab, then withdraw the lock cylinder from the housing.

Refitting

4 To refit the lock cylinder, push it into the housing until the locking tab is engaged.
5 Locate the ignition switch on the housing, and tighten the two socket-headed screws.
6 Refer to Chapter 10 for details of refitting the ignition switch/steering column lock.

Chapter 5 Part B: Ignition system

Contents

Degrees of difficulty

Easy, suitable for novice with little experience	**Fairly easy,** suitable for beginner with some experience	**Fairly difficult,** suitable for competent DIY mechanic	**Difficult,** suitable for experienced DIY mechanic	**Very difficult,** suitable for expert DIY or professional

Specifications

System type

Models manufactured up to approx 1989 . . . . Hall-effect ignition system with Bosch LH-Jetronic
Models manufactured from approx 1989 to 1993 (1985 cc)
  or to 1992 (2290 cc) . . . . Direct Ignition (DI) system with Bosch LH-Jetronic
Models manufactured from 1994 (1985 cc) or from 1993 (2290 cc) . . . . Direct Ignition (DI) system incorporated in Trionic engine management system

Hall-effect ignition system

Ignition HT coil winding resistances:
  Primary . . . . 0.52 to 0.76 ohms
  Secondary:
    Up to approx 1986 . . . . 2400 to 3500 ohms
    From approx 1986 . . . . 7200 to 8200 ohms
HT lead resistances:
  Coil-to-distributor . . . . 500 to 1500 ohms
  Distributor-to-spark plug . . . . 2000 to 4000 ohms
Ignition timing (vacuum control disconnected):
  Non-turbo models . . . . 14° BTDC @ 850 rpm
  Turbo models . . . . 16° BTDC @ 850 rpm
Rotor arm resistance . . . . 1000 ohms

Direct Ignition (DI) system

Ignition discharge cartridge:
  Capacitor voltage . . . . 400 volts
  Ignition voltage (maximum) . . . . 40 000 volts
Ignition timing . . . . Pre-programmed in ECU

Firing order . . . . 1-3-4-2 (No 1 cylinder at timing chain end)

Torque wrench settings

	Nm	lbf ft
Crankshaft pulley bolt	190	140
Ignition cartridge (discharge module)	12	9
Knock detector	13 ± 2	10 ± 1.5
Spark plugs	28	21

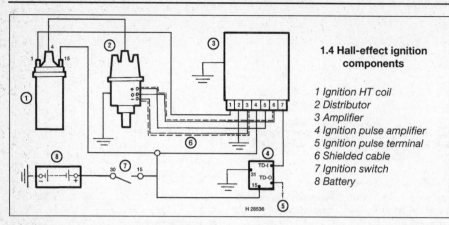

1.4 Hall-effect ignition components

1 Ignition HT coil
2 Distributor
3 Amplifier
4 Ignition pulse amplifier
5 Ignition pulse terminal
6 Shielded cable
7 Ignition switch
8 Battery

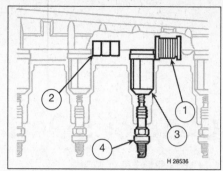

1.7 Direct Ignition cartridge
1 Transformer (12 volts/400 volts)
2 Capacitor   3 Ignition coil   4 Spark plug

1 General information

Models manufactured up to approximately 1989 are fitted with a Hall-effect breakerless ignition system, and these models are fitted with the Bosch LH-Jetronic fuel injection system described in Chapter 4. The Hall-effect ignition and the LH-Jetronic fuel injection systems operate independently of each other.

Models manufactured from approximately 1989 to 1993 (1985 cc) or from 1992 (2290 cc) are fitted with a Direct Ignition (DI) system. This system has its own electronic control unit (ECU), but additionally uses information from the Bosch LH-Jetronic fuel injection system ECU to control ignition timing.

Models manufactured from 1993 (2290 cc) or from 1994 (1985 cc) onwards have a Direct Ignition system which is incorporated into the Trionic engine management system. With this system, a single electronic control unit (ECU) controls both the fuel injection and ignition functions. The Trionic system was originally fitted to Turbo models only, but from 1994 it is also fitted to non-turbo engines. More information on the Trionic system is given in Chapter 4.

Hall-effect ignition system

The system is a breakerless electronic ignition system **(see illustration)**, and comprises an impulse generator (Hall sensor in the distributor), an amplifier, the coil and spark plugs. The impulse generator uses the Hall-effect method to send signals to the amplifier, which then switches the low-tension circuit by means of transistors. The amplifier also monitors and regulates the ignition dwell angle.

A separate ignition pulse amplifier (located behind the glovebox) was introduced in 1986, to reduce the effects of radio interference, and to provide better control of the system.

The distributor incorporates centrifugal advance weights, to automatically advance the ignition timing according to the engine speed. On some models (depending on country), the distributor also incorporates a double-acting vacuum capsule, which adjusts the ignition timing according to the load on the engine. The conventional vacuum control advances the ignition timing under light throttle conditions, but on Turbo models, it will retard the ignition timing when the turbocharger is in operation.

Direct Ignition (DI) system

The Direct Ignition system uses a separate HT coil for each spark plug **(see illustration)**. The system electronic control unit (ECU) monitors the engine by means of various sensors, in order to determine the most efficient ignition timing.

The components of the system are a crankshaft position/speed sensor, ignition cartridge with one coil per plug, diagnostic socket, ECU, pressure sensor in the inlet manifold (to determine engine load), knock detector, and a solenoid valve (to regulate the turbocharger operation).

During starting at a crankshaft speed in excess of 150 rpm, HT sparks are triggered in the cylinder pair with the pistons at TDC. Under difficult conditions, multi-sparking occurs during this period, to aid starting. The ECU determines in which cylinder combustion is taking place by monitoring the flow of current across the spark plug electrodes, and then uses this information to determine the firing order.

When the engine starts, the ignition timing is always set to 10° BTDC, and will remain at this setting until the engine speed exceeds 850 rpm. The ECU will regulate the ignition timing at engine speeds above 850 rpm.

When the ignition is switched off and the engine stops, the main relay remains operational for a further 6 seconds. During this period, the Trionic control module earths all the trigger leads 210 times a second for 5 seconds, in order to burn off impurities from the spark plug electrodes.

Because the system does not use any HT leads, radio suppression must be incorporated in the actual spark plugs, so resistor-type plugs must always be used.

The Direct Ignition system uses the capacitive discharge method of producing an HT spark. Approximately 400 volts is stored in a capacitor **(see illustration)**, and at the time of ignition, this voltage is discharged through the primary circuit of the relevant coil. Approximately 40 000 volts is induced in the

1.13 Direct Ignition capacitor (arrowed) located in the cartridge

HT secondary coil, and this is discharged across the spark plug electrodes.

Should a fault occur in the system, a fault code is stored in the ECU. This code can only be accessed by a Saab dealer, using dedicated equipment.

Note that the starter motor must never be operated with the ignition cartridge disconnected from the spark plugs but still connected to the wiring loom. This can cause irreversible damage to the cartridge.

Automatic Performance Control (APC)

All Turbo models are fitted with an Automatic Performance Control system. The APC system controls the turbo wastegage. If pinking is detected, the APC system opens the wastegate to reduce boost pressure, thus eliminating the pinking. On models from 1989 the APC and DI operations were control by the one ECU. With this sytem, when pinking is detected, the ignition timing and wastegate position are adjusted. Refer to Chapter 4 for more information.

Trionic ignition system

The Saab Trionic engine management system uses the Direct Ignition and Automatic Performance Control systems described above, but integrated into its own ECU.

With the Trionic system, the spark plugs themselves are used as knock sensors, instead of employing a separate knock detector in the cylinder block.

2 Ignition system - testing

⚠ *Warning: Voltages produced by an electronic ignition system are considerably higher than those produced by conventional ignition systems. Extreme care must be taken when working on the system with the ignition switched on. Persons with surgically-implanted cardiac pacemaker devices should keep well clear of the ignition circuits, components and test equipment. Refer to the precautions in Chapter 5A, Section 1 before starting work. Always switch off the ignition before disconnecting or connecting any component, and when using a multi-meter to check resistances.*

Hall-effect ignition system

1 The components of the Hall-effect ignition system are normally very reliable; most faults are far more likely to be due to loose or dirty connections, or to "tracking" of HT voltage due to dirt, dampness or damaged insulation, than to the failure of any of the system's components. **Always** check all wiring thoroughly before condemning an electrical component, and work methodically to eliminate all other possibilities before deciding that a particular component is faulty.

2 The old practice of checking for a spark by holding the live end of an HT lead a short distance away from the engine is **not** recommended; not only is there a high risk of a powerful electric shock, but the HT coil or amplifier unit may be damaged. Similarly, **never** try to "diagnose" misfires by pulling off one HT lead at a time.

Engine will not start

3 If the engine either will not turn over at all, or only turns very slowly, check the battery and starter motor. Connect a voltmeter across the battery terminals (meter positive probe to battery positive terminal). Disconnect the ignition coil HT lead from the distributor cap, and earth it. Note the voltage reading obtained while turning over the engine on the starter for (no more than) ten seconds. If the reading obtained is less than approximately 9.5 volts, first check the battery, starter motor and charging system as described in Part A of this Chapter.

4 If the engine turns over at normal speed but will not start, check the HT circuit by connecting a timing light (following its manufacturer's instructions) and turning the engine over on the starter motor; if the light flashes, voltage is reaching the spark plugs, so these should be checked first. If the light does not flash, check the HT leads themselves, followed by the distributor cap, carbon brush and rotor arm **(see illustration)**, using the information given in Chapter 1.

5 If there is a spark, check the fuel system for faults, referring to Chapter 4A for further information.

6 If there is still no spark, check the voltage at the ignition HT coil "+" terminal; it should be the same as the battery voltage (ie, at least 11.7 volts). If the voltage at the coil is more than 1 volt less than that at the battery, check the feed from the battery until the fault is found.

7 If the feed to the HT coil is sound, check the coil's primary and secondary winding resistance as described later in this Chapter; renew the coil if faulty, but be careful to check carefully the condition of the LT connections themselves before doing so, to ensure that the fault is not due to dirty or poorly-fastened connectors.

8 If the HT coil is in good condition, the fault is probably within the amplifier unit or Hall generator circuit inside the distributor. Testing of these components should be entrusted to a Saab dealer.

Engine misfires

9 An irregular misfire suggests either a loose connection or intermittent fault on the primary circuit, or an HT lead fault.

10 With the ignition switched off, check carefully through the system, ensuring that all connections are clean and securely fastened.

11 Check that the HT coil, the distributor cap and the HT leads are clean and dry. Check the leads themselves and the spark plugs (by substitution, if necessary), then check the distributor cap, carbon brush and rotor arm as described in Chapter 1.

12 Regular misfiring is almost certainly due to a fault in the distributor cap, HT leads or spark plugs. Use a timing light (paragraph 4 above) to check whether HT voltage is present at all leads.

13 If HT voltage is not present on any particular lead, the fault will be in that lead, or in the distributor cap. If HT is present on all leads, the fault will be in the spark plugs; check and renew them if there is any doubt about their condition.

14 If no HT is present, check the HT coil; its secondary windings may be breaking down under load.

Direct Ignition system

15 If a fault appears in the Direct Ignition system, first check that all wiring is secure and in good condition. If necessary, individual components of the Direct Ignition system may be removed for visual investigation as described later in this Chapter. Coils are best checked by substituting a suspect one with a known good coil, and checking if the misfire is cured.

16 Due to the location of the spark plugs beneath the DI cartridge, it is not possible to easily check the HT circuit for faults. Further testing should be carried out by a Saab dealer, who will have equipment to access fault codes stored in the system ECU.

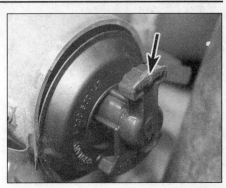

2.4 Rotor arm inside the distributor cap

3.1 Ignition coil located on the front crossmember

3 Ignition HT coil (Hall-effect system) - removal, testing and refitting

Removal

1 The ignition HT coil is located at the front of the engine compartment, above the radiator on the front crossmember **(see illustration)**. First roll back the rubber dust cover and disconnect the HT lead.

2 Identify the low-tension leads for position, then disconnect them from the terminals on the coil.

3 Unscrew the mounting clamp bolts, and remove the coil from the crossmember.

Testing

4 Testing of the coil is carried out using a multi-meter set to its resistance function, to check the primary (LT "+" to "-" terminals) and secondary (LT "+" to HT lead terminal) windings for continuity. Compare the results obtained to those given in the Specifications at the start of this Chapter. The resistance of the coil windings will vary slightly according to the coil temperature.

Refitting

5 Refitting is a reversal of removal, but make sure that the mounting clamp and coil are thoroughly cleaned, and that the wiring connectors are fitted correctly.

4.1 Releasing the distributor cap clips

5.1 The ignition system amplifier unit (Hall-effect ignition)

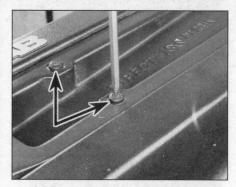

6.2 Removing the ignition cartridge retaining screws (two arrowed)

4 Distributor (Hall-effect system) - removal, overhaul and refitting

Removal

1 Mark the spark plug HT leads to aid refitting, and pull them from the distributor cap. If it is required to remove them from the spark plugs, it will be necessary to remove the inspection cover from the centre of the cylinder head. Release the clips from each side of the distributor cap, and place the cap to one side **(see illustration)**. If the clips are tight, use a screwdriver to prise them off carefully.

2 Apply the handbrake, then jack up the front of the car and support on axle stands (see *"Jacking, towing and wheel changing"*). On manual transmission models, the engine may be rotated by turning the front right-hand wheel with 4th gear engaged. On automatic transmission models, it will be necessary to remove the right-hand wheel and also the front section of the wheelarch liner, in order to use a socket or spanner on the crankshaft pulley.

3 Remove No 1 spark plug (nearest the timing chain end of the engine).

4 Place a finger over the plug hole, and turn the engine in the normal direction of rotation (clockwise, viewed from the crankshaft pulley end) until pressure is felt in No 1 cylinder. This indicates that the piston is commencing its compression stroke.

5 Continue turning the engine until the "0°" mark on the flywheel/driveplate is aligned with the timing mark on the bellhousing. Check also that the rotor arm is pointing towards the position where the No 1 HT lead segment would be if the distributor cap were fitted. If there is no mark on the rim of the distributor body, make a mark with a small file.

6 Using a dab of paint or a small file, make a reference mark between the distributor base and the cylinder head.

7 Disconnect the wiring plug for the Hall-effect sensor.

8 Where applicable, disconnect the vacuum hose from the double-acting vacuum capsule.

9 Unscrew the distributor clamp retaining bolt, and remove the clamp.

10 Withdraw the distributor from the end of

the cylinder head. Note that the distributor driveshaft incorporates an off-centre drive dog, which engages a slot in the end of the exhaust camshaft.

Overhaul

11 It is not possible to renew the Hall sensor or the slotted vane, and if either of these components is found to be faulty, the complete distributor should be renewed. The only components which may be renewed are the vacuum capsule (where fitted) and the rotor arm.

12 To remove the vacuum capsule, unscrew the retaining screws, and unhook the operating arm. When refitting the vacuum capsule, turn the Hall sensor clockwise as far as possible, then move it backwards and forwards while locating the operating arm on the pin.

13 Take care not to touch the Hall sensor with metal tools, as it may be damaged.

14 The rotor arm is bonded onto the distributor shaft, and must be crushed and destroyed in order to remove it. Secure the new rotor arm to the shaft using locking fluid.

Refitting

15 Check that the distributor is still at TDC with No 1 cylinder on compression. Check the condition of the O-ring seal on the distributor shoulder, and renew it if necessary.

16 Turn the rotor arm so that it is pointing towards the No 1 TDC position on the rim of the distributor.

17 Slide the distributor into the cylinder head, with the previously-made marks aligned. When nearly fully entered, it may be necessary to move the rotor arm slightly, so that the dog engages the slot in the exhaust camshaft. If a new distributor is being fitted, position the distributor body so that the rotor arm points towards the No 1 spark plug HT lead segment position in the cap.

18 Refit the clamp and tighten the retaining bolt.

19 Where applicable, reconnect the vacuum hose to the double-acting vacuum capsule.

20 Reconnect the wiring to the Hall-effect sensor.

21 Refit No 1 spark plug, and tighten to the specified torque.

22 Make sure that the socket or spanner is removed from the crankshaft pulley bolt (where

applicable). On automatic transmission models, refit the wheelarch liner and roadwheel.

23 Lower the car to the ground, and tighten the roadwheel bolts (where applicable)

24 Refit the distributor cap, then reconnect the HT leads.

25 Check and, if necessary, adjust the ignition timing as described in Section 14.

5 Ignition system amplifier unit (Hall-effect system) - removal and refitting

Removal

1 The ignition system amplifier unit is located on a cooling plate on the left-hand inner wing **(see illustration)**.

2 With the ignition switched off, disconnect the wiring plug from the amplifier unit.

3 Unscrew the retaining screws, and remove the amplifier unit from the inner wing.

Refitting

4 Refitting is a reversal of removal.

6 Ignition cartridge (DI/APC system) - removal and refitting

Note: *The individual coils sit in canisters which are filled with oil. The canister wall is translucent to allow the oil level to be checked. If the oil level is low, this could be the cause of loss of performance. There is no facility for replenishing the oil, replacement of all four canisters is the only option. Should replacement be required on an early model it is necessary to purchase an adapter lead to connect the loom to the later unit.*

Removal

1 Disconnect the battery negative lead.

2 Unscrew the four screws securing the ignition cartridge to the top of the cylinder head. An Allen key will be required for this **(see illustration)**.

3 Where applicable, unscrew the bolt and release the cartridge wiring support clip.

4 Where applicable, unscrew the bolt and disconnect the earth lead.

5 Disconnect the system wiring plug(s), located either behind the battery (non-Trionic

6.5 Disconnecting the wiring plug from the ignition cartridge

6.7a Unscrew the screws . . .

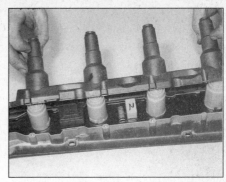

6.7b . . . and separate the black lower shroud from the cartridge

system) or on the left-hand end of the cartridge (Trionic system) **(see illustration)**.

6 Lift the ignition cartridge, at the same time releasing it from the tops of the spark plugs.

7 If necessary, the shroud may be removed from the bottom of the cartridge, by inverting it and removing the screws using an Allen key. Separate the black (lower) shroud from the cartridge **(see illustrations)**.

8 The HT springs may be removed from the shroud by careful use of a screwdriver.

Refitting

9 Refitting is a reversal of removal, but tighten the mounting bolts to the specified torque.

7 Ignition HT coils (DI/APC system) - removal and refitting

Removal

1 Remove the shroud from the ignition cartridge as described in Section 6.

2 Carefully remove the HT coils from the upper part of the cartridge.

Refitting

3 Refitting is a reversal of removal.

8 Knock detector (DI/APC system) - removal and refitting

Removal

1 The knock detector is located on the rear of the cylinder block, beneath the inlet manifold. First jack up the front of the car, and support on axle stands (see *"Jacking, towing and wheel changing"*).

2 Disconnect the wiring from the knock detector.

3 Unscrew the knock detector from the cylinder block.

Refitting

4 Wipe clean the threads of the knock detector, and the aperture in the cylinder block.

5 Insert the knock detector, and tighten it to the specified torque. **Note:** *It is important to*

tighten the unit to the correct torque, otherwise it may send incorrect signals to the system ECU.

6 Reconnect the wiring, and lower the car to the ground.

9 Solenoid valve (DI/APC system) - removal and refitting

Note: *The solenoid valve is only fitted to Turbo models.*

Removal

1 The solenoid valve is located on a bracket on the front left-hand side of the engine compartment, beneath the ignition coil on the non-Trionic system, or on the engine compartment front crossmember on the Trionic system.

2 Disconnect the wiring plug.

3 Disconnect the hoses from the solenoid valve.

4 Unscrew the mounting screws, and remove the valve from the engine compartment.

Refitting

5 Refitting is a reversal of removal.

10 Crankshaft sensor (DI/APC system) - removal and refitting

Note: *For models with the Trionic engine management system, refer to Chapter 4A, Section 16.*

Removal

1 Disconnect the battery negative lead.

2 Apply the handbrake, then jack up the front of the car and support on axle stands (see *"Jacking, towing and wheel changing"*). Remove the right-hand front wheel.

3 Unscrew the screws and remove the plastic moulding and front section of the wheelarch liner from under the right-hand front wheelarch.

4 Where applicable, remove the air conditioning compressor drivebelt.

5 Remove the auxiliary drivebelt as described in Chapter 1.

6 The crankshaft must now be held stationary while the crankshaft pulley bolt is loosened. Have an assistant insert a wide-bladed screwdriver through the timing aperture on the top of the transmission, and engage it with the starter ring gear.

7 Unscrew and remove the crankshaft pulley bolt. The bolt is tightened to a high torque, and a socket extension bar will be required. In extreme cases, it may help to heat the bolt to facilitate its removal, but take suitable precautions if this course of action is taken. With the bolt removed, slide the pulley off the front of the crankshaft.

8 Remove the screws and withdraw the sensor from the timing cover.

9 Disconnect the wiring plug located behind the battery, and remove the sensor from the engine compartment. Where necessary, release the wiring from the cable-tie.

Refitting

10 Refitting is a reversal of removal, but apply a little locking fluid to the threads of the sensor retaining screws before inserting and tightening them.

11 Slotted rotor for crankshaft sensor (DI/APC system) - removal and refitting

Removal

Non-Trionic models

1 Remove the crankshaft pulley as described in Section 10, paragraphs 1 to 7 inclusive.

2 Using an Allen key, unscrew the retaining screws, and remove the slotted rotor from the crankshaft pulley.

Trionic models

3 The slotted rotor is located on the flywheel/driveplate end of the crankshaft. Remove the crankshaft as described in Chapter 2B.

4 Using a Torx key, unscrew the four screws securing the slotted rotor to the crankshaft, then remove the rotor over the end of the crankshaft.

Refitting

Non-Trionic models

5 Refitting is a reversal of removal.

Trionic models

6 Refitting is a reversal of removal. Note that the rotor can only be fitted in one position, since the bolt holes are unequally-spaced.

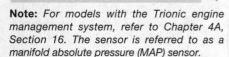

12 Pressure sensor (DI/APC system) - removal and refitting

Note: *For models with the Trionic engine management system, refer to Chapter 4A, Section 16. The sensor is referred to as a manifold absolute pressure (MAP) sensor.*

Removal

1 The pressure sensor is located beneath the left-hand side of the facia. First disconnect the battery negative lead.
2 Remove the lower trim panel from under the facia panel.
3 Unscrew the screws and remove the heating air duct.
4 Unscrew the mounting screws, lower the pressure sensor from the bulkhead, then disconnect the wiring.

Refitting

5 Refitting is a reversal of removal.

13 Electronic control unit (DI/APC system) - removal and refitting

Note: *Refer to Chapter 4A, Section 16 for the Trionic control module removal procedure.*

Removal

1 Disconnect the battery negative lead.

2 Remove the left-hand front seat as described in Chapter 11.
3 Unscrew the two scuffplate screws.
4 Unscrew the screws and remove the cover from the ECU.
5 Disconnect the wiring, and remove the ECU from inside the car.

Refitting

6 Refitting is a reversal of removal.

14 Ignition timing - checking and adjustment

Models with Hall-effect ignition

1 To check the ignition timing, a stroboscopic timing light will be required. Note that a socket is provided in the engine compartment or near the timing aperture on top of the transmission, for connection of a dedicated Saab test instrument; this instrument will not normally be available to the home mechanic.
2 Start the engine, allow it to warm up to normal operating temperature, then switch it off.
3 Disconnect the vacuum hose from the vacuum capsule on the distributor, and plug the hose.
4 Connect the timing light to No 1 cylinder plug HT lead (nearest the timing chain end of the engine) in accordance with its manufacturer's instructions. Ideally, a timing light which has a sensor clamp is to be preferred, as the clamp can then be clipped to the HT lead near the distributor cap. Where the timing light lead must be attached to No 1 spark plug, it will be necessary to remove the inspection cover from the top of the cylinder head for access to the spark plugs.
5 Start the engine, allowing it to idle at the specified speed, and point the timing light

through the transmission housing timing aperture.
6 The relevant timing mark on the flywheel/driveplate should appear to be aligned with the timing mark on the transmission housing.
7 If adjustment is necessary, loosen the distributor clamp bolt, then slowly rotate the distributor body as required until the correct timing marks are brought into alignment. Turning the distributor body clockwise will advance the timing, and turning it anti-clockwise will retard it. Once the marks are correctly aligned, hold the distributor stationary, and tighten the clamp bolt. Recheck that the timing marks are still correctly aligned and, if necessary, repeat the adjustment procedure.
8 With the timing correctly set at idle speed, progressively increase the engine speed and check that the timing is advanced - the timing marks should move further out of alignment as the speed is increased. This check shows that the centrifugal advance mechanism is at least functioning - a more thorough check should be left to a Saab dealer.
9 Reconnect the vacuum hose to the capsule, and check that the timing is advanced at light throttle - again a more thorough check should be left to a Saab dealer.
10 With the ignition timing set correctly, stop the engine and disconnect the timing light.

Models with Direct Ignition (including Trionic)

11 On models with Direct Ignition the ignition timing is pre-programmed into the system ECU, and cannot be adjusted or even checked with any accuracy. If the timing is thought to be incorrect, the car should be taken to a Saab dealer, who will have the necessary equipment to extract any fault codes stored in the ECU.

Chapter 6 Clutch

Contents

Degrees of difficulty

Easy, suitable for novice with little experience	Fairly easy, suitable for beginner with some experience	Fairly difficult, suitable for competent DIY mechanic	Difficult, suitable for experienced DIY mechanic	Very difficult, suitable for expert DIY or professional

Specifications

General

Make	AP, Fichtel & Sachs
Type	Single dry plate, diaphragm spring with spring-loaded hub
Operation	Hydraulic, via slave and master cylinders
Diameter	215 or 240 mm

Torque wrench settings

	Nm	lbf ft
Clutch pedal-to-pivot bolt locknut	42	31
Master cylinder-to-bulkhead bolts (pre-1994 model year, all models) ..	22	16
Master cylinder-to-delivery pipe union	16	12
Master cylinder-to-pedal assembly nuts (post-1994 model year, left-hand-drive models)	22	16
Pressure plate retaining screws	22	16
Pressure plate-to-flywheel bolts	22	16
Slave cylinder delivery pipe clip	22	16
Slave cylinder-to-transmission screws	22	16

1 General information

Vehicles with manual transmission are fitted with a hydraulically-operated, single dry plate clutch system. Unlike cable-operated systems, no adjustment is possible or necessary.

The clutch system main components comprise the clutch pedal, master cylinder, hydraulic pipes, slave cylinder, release bearing and fork, driven plate, and pressure plate.

The driven plate is mounted on the gearbox splined input shaft. It has minimal free radial movement, and must rotate with the shaft, but is free to slide axially along it. The pressure plate is bolted directly to the flywheel, and encompasses the driven plate. A diaphragm spring thrusts the friction lining of the pressure plate towards the flywheel, sandwiching the driven plate, and allowing drive to be transmitted from the crankshaft to the gearbox input shaft.

The clutch pedal is connected to the master cylinder piston by a link rod. When the pedal is depressed, the hydraulic fluid in the master cylinder is pressurised and displaced along the hydraulic pipes to the slave cylinder, which is mounted over the gearbox input shaft, inside the transmission bellhousing. As pressure builds up, the piston is forced along the slave cylinder, and actuates the clutch release bearing, via a forked lever.

The clutch release bearing tensions the diaphragm spring, which it turn causes it to relax the force exerted on the pressure plate and driven plate. The driven plate is then free to slide away from the flywheel, along the splined shaft, and the two can rotate independently, disconnecting drive to the gearbox input shaft.

This control over the diaphragm spring pressure allows the clutch to be partially engaged/disengaged, or "slipped", allowing smooth release and take-up of drive during gear shifting.

In addition, the driven plate is made up of two halves that are connected by a spring-loaded layer. When compressed, this sprung layer allows a small amount of movement between the plates, which serves to dampen the clutch operation, reducing vibration and juddering. Furthermore, the hub of the driven plate is radially spring-loaded, to provide damping against torsional shocks.

The hydraulic fluid employed in the clutch system is the same as that used in the braking system, hence fluid is supplied to the master cylinder from a tapping on the brake fluid reservoir. The clutch hydraulic system must be sealed before work is carried out on any of its components and then on completion, topped-up and bled to remove any air bubbles. Details of these procedures are given in Section 6 of this Chapter.

The layout of the Saab 9000 clutch control system has undergone a number of revisions, although the basic operation of the system has remained the same. In particular, the mounting location of the master cylinder differs between pre- and post-1994 model year vehicles, and between left- and right-hand-drive models. Accordingly, the link arrangement between the clutch pedal and the master cylinder is also dependent on the vehicle's age and type.

2 Master cylinder -
removal and refitting

> **Warning: Hydraulic fluid is poisonous; thoroughly wash off spills from bare skin without delay. Seek immediate medical advice if any fluid is swallowed or gets into the eyes. Certain types of hydraulic fluid are inflammable, and may ignite when brought into contact with hot components. When servicing any hydraulic system, it is safest to assume that the fluid IS inflammable, and to take precautions against the risk of fire as though it is petrol that is being handled. It is hygroscopic (it can absorb moisture from the air); excess moisture content lowers the fluid boiling point to an unacceptable level, resulting in a loss of hydraulic pressure. Old fluid may have suffered contamination, and should not be re-used. When topping-up or renewing the fluid, always use the recommended grade, and ensure that it comes from a freshly-opened sealed container.**

 HAYNES HINT *Hydraulic fluid is an effective paint stripper, and will also attack many plastics. If spillage occurs onto painted bodywork or fittings, it should be washed off immediately, using copious quantities of fresh water.*

Right-hand-drive models

Removal

1 Referring to Chapter 11 for guidance, remove the sound insulating trim panel from underneath the facia, on the driver's side.
2 At the connection point between the master cylinder link rod and the clutch pedal, use a pair of long-nosed pliers to remove the clip from the spigot, then pull off the link rod **(see illustration)**.
3 As a precaution, place a dust sheet under the clutch pedal in the footwell, to catch any hydraulic fluid spillage.
4 From the engine bay, seal the flexible supply hose from the fluid reservoir, using a proprietary brake hose clamp. Release the hose clip, and pull the supply hose off the master cylinder port **(see illustration)**. Be prepared for a small amount of hydraulic fluid loss; position a container or a wad of rags underneath the joint to catch any spillage.

 Warning: Observe the warning given at the beginning of this Section, regarding the hazards of handling hydraulic fluid.

5 Slacken the rigid delivery pipe union at the end of the master cylinder, and disconnect the pipe; again be prepared for some hydraulic fluid loss.

2.2 At the connection point between the master cylinder link rod and the clutch pedal, use a pair of long-nosed pliers to remove the clip from the spigot (arrowed)

6 Remove the two nuts from the retaining bolts, and lift the master cylinder away from the bulkhead, guiding the link rod through the aperture. Recover the gasket and inspect it for damage; renew it if necessary.

Refitting

7 Refit the master cylinder by following the removal procedure in reverse. On completion, refer to Section 6 and bleed the hydraulic system.

Pre-1994 model year left-hand-drive models

Removal

8 Referring to Chapter 11 for guidance, remove the sound insulating trim panel from underneath the facia, on the driver's side.
9 At the connection point between the master cylinder link rod and the clutch pedal, use a pair of long-nosed pliers to remove the clip from the clevis pin. Withdraw the pin, and pull off the link rod.
10 As a precaution, place a dust sheet under the clutch pedal in the footwell, to catch any hydraulic fluid spillage.
11 From the engine bay, remove the cover from the compartment behind the false bulkhead panel. The master cylinder is mounted vertically, directly above the clutch pedal, on the upper surface of the bulkhead.
12 Seal the flexible supply hose from the fluid reservoir, using a proprietary brake hose clamp. Release the hose clip, and pull the supply hose off the master cylinder port. Be prepared for a small amount of hydraulic fluid loss; position a container or a wad of rags underneath the joint to catch any spillage.

 Warning: Observe the warning given at the beginning of this Section, regarding the hazards of handling hydraulic fluid.

13 Slacken the rigid delivery pipe union at the end of the master cylinder, and disconnect the pipe; again be prepared for some hydraulic fluid loss.
14 Remove the two nuts from the retaining bolts, and lift the master cylinder up away from

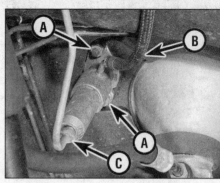
2.4 Clutch master cylinder
A Retaining nuts   C Delivery pipe union
B Supply hose

the bulkhead, guiding the link rod through the aperture. Recover the gasket and inspect it for damage; renew it if necessary.

Refitting

15 Refit the master cylinder by following the removal procedure in reverse. On completion, refer to Section 6 and bleed the hydraulic system.

Post-1994 model year left-hand-drive models

General

16 The master cylinder is mounted under the facia, on the brake/clutch pedal bracket, rather than in the engine bay. Although the removal process is no more involved than that for the pre-1994 model year vehicles, extra care is needed to avoid spilling hydraulic fluid inside the car as the supply and delivery hoses are disconnected.

Removal

17 Referring to Chapter 11 for guidance, remove the sound insulating trim panel from underneath the facia, on the driver's side.
18 Remove the clip from the end of the shaft between the clutch pedal and the master cylinder link rod. Extract the shaft.
19 Fit a proprietary brake hose clamp to the supply hose (this is the hose connected to the uppermost port on the side of the master cylinder). Expand the clip by hand, and disconnect the hose from the master cylinder. Be prepared for the loss of some hydraulic fluid at this point; position a container underneath the joint, to catch any spillage and prevent it from contaminating the footwell carpet.
20 At the lower port on the master cylinder body, slacken the delivery pipe union and unplug the pipe; again, be prepared for some hydraulic fluid leakage - reposition the container to catch the spillage.
21 Slacken and remove the retaining nuts, then lift master cylinder off the pedal bracket.

Refitting

22 Refit the master cylinder by following the removal procedure in reverse. Observe the specified torque wrench setting when

tightening the master cylinder-to-pedal bracket nuts.
23 On completion, refer to Section 6 and bleed the hydraulic system.

3 Clutch pedal - removal and refitting

Right-hand-drive models, and pre-1994 model year left-hand-drive models

Removal

1 Remove the sound insulating panel from underneath the facia, below the steering column; refer to Chapter 11 for guidance.
2 Referring to the relevant paragraphs of Section 2, disconnect the clutch master cylinder pushrod from the clutch pedal.
3 To improve access to the pedal mountings, remove the screw and lift off the bracket that supports the cruise control switches.
4 Depress the pedal to the end of its travel, then remove the locknut from the end of the pedal pivot bolt.
5 Unhook the spring from the pedal mounting bracket and slide it off, together with the plastic bobbin.

Refitting

6 Refit the pedal by reversing the removal procedure. Fit a new pivot bolt locknut, and tighten it to the correct torque.

Post-1994 model year left-hand-drive models

Removal

7 Remove the sound insulating panel from underneath the facia, below the steering column; refer to Chapter 11 for guidance.
8 Referring to the relevant paragraphs of Section 2, disconnect the clutch master cylinder from the pedal mounting bracket.
Note: There is no need to disconnect the hydraulic hoses from the master cylinder.
9 To improve access to the pedal mountings, remove the screw and lift off the bracket that supports the cruise control switches.
10 Depress the pedal, and remove the locknut from the end of the pivot bolt.
11 At the point where the return spring is linked to the pedal shaft, remove the clip from the end of the pin and lift off the spring, together with its bracket.
12 Detach the central locking ECU from its mounting position under the facia by releasing the clip from the facia moulding. Position it to one side, away from the work area.
13 Push the pedal upwards towards the facia, then slide it off the pivot bolt and remove from the vehicle.

Refitting

14 Refit the pedal by reversing the removal procedure, noting the following points:

a) Observe the specified torque wrench setting when refitting the master cylinder to the pedal mounting bracket.
b) Fit a new pivot bolt locknut, and tighten it to the correct torque.

4 Clutch assembly - removal and refitting

Removal

⚠ **Warning: Dust created by clutch wear and deposited on the clutch components may contain asbestos, which is a health hazard. DO NOT blow it out with compressed air, nor inhale any of it. DO NOT use petrol or petroleum-based solvents to clean off the dust. Brake system cleaner or methylated spirit should be used to flush the dust into a suitable receptacle. After the clutch components are wiped clean with clean rags, dispose of the contaminated rags and cleaner in a sealed, marked container.**

Note: Although some friction materials may no longer contain asbestos, it is safest to assume that they DO, and to take precautions accordingly

1 Unless the complete engine/transmission is to be removed from the car and separated for major overhaul (see Chapter 2B), the clutch can be accessed by removing the transmission, as described in Chapter 7A.
2 Before disturbing any of the clutch components, mark the relationship between the pressure plate, driven plate and flywheel.
3 To aid the removal of the pressure plate, the flywheel should ideally be locked in position by bolting a locking tool to one of the transmission mounting holes, and engaging it with the flywheel ring gear. If a universal flywheel locking tool is not available, the crankshaft (and hence the flywheel) can be held stationary using a wrench and socket on the crankshaft sprocket bolt. The help of an assistant will be required to complete this task.
4 Working diagonally across the pressure plate, progressively slacken the mounting screws, half a turn at a time, until they can be removed by hand.
5 Lift off the pressure plate, then recover the driven plate, noting its orientation **(see illustration)**.

Inspection

Note: Due to the amount of work necessary to remove and refit clutch components, it is usually considered good practice to renew the clutch friction plate, pressure plate assembly and release bearing as a matched set, even if only one of these is actually worn enough to require renewal.

4.5 Lift off the pressure plate, then recover the driven plate, noting its orientation

6 When cleaning clutch components, observe the warning at the beginning of this Section regarding the hazards of handling the friction materials contained in clutch components; remove dust using a clean, dry cloth, and working in a well-ventilated atmosphere.
7 Check the driven plate facings for signs of wear, damage or oil contamination. If the friction material is cracked, burnt, scored or damaged, or if it is contaminated with oil or grease (shown by shiny black patches), the friction plate must be renewed.
8 If the friction material is still serviceable, check that the centre boss splines are unworn, that the torsion springs are in good condition and securely fastened, and that all the rivets are tightly fastened. If any wear or damage is found, the friction plate must be renewed.
9 If the friction material is fouled with oil, this must be due to an oil leak from the crankshaft left-hand oil seal, from the sump-to-cylinder block joint, or from the transmission input shaft; renew the seal or repair the joint, as appropriate, as described in Chapter 2 or 7 before installing the new friction plate.
10 Check the pressure plate assembly for obvious signs of wear or damage; shake it to check for loose rivets or worn or damaged fulcrum rings, and check that the drive straps securing the pressure plate to the cover do not show signs of overheating (such as a deep yellow or blue discoloration). If the diaphragm spring is worn or damaged, or if its pressure is in any way suspect, the pressure plate assembly should be renewed.
11 Examine the machined bearing surfaces of the pressure plate and of the flywheel; they should be clean, completely flat and free from scratches or scoring. If either is discoloured from excessive heat or shows signs of cracks it should be renewed, although minor damage of this nature can sometimes be polished away using emery paper.
12 Check that the release bearing contact surface rotates smoothly and easily, with no sign of noise or roughness, and that the surface itself is smooth and unworn, with no signs of cracks, pitting or scoring. If there is any doubt about its condition, the bearing must be renewed; refer to Section 5 for guidance.

4.17 Progressively tighten the pressure plate bolts in a diagonal sequence and to the specified torque setting

5.5 Using a pair of screwdrivers, prise the release bearing off the slave cylinder guide sleeve

5.8 Slackening the union (arrowed) at the base of the hydraulic supply pipe

Refitting

13 On reassembly, ensure that the bearing surfaces of the flywheel and pressure plate are completely clean, smooth and free from oil or grease. Use solvent to remove any protective grease from new components.

14 Offer up the driven plate so that its spring hub assembly faces away from the flywheel; observe any manufacturers' markings which show which way around the plate should be fitted.

15 Refit the pressure plate assembly to the flywheel, engaging it with its locating dowels; align the marks made on dismantling if the original pressure plate is being re-used. Fit the pressure plate screws, hand-tightening them only at this stage, so that the friction plate can be rotated to aid alignment, if necessary.

16 The driven plate must now be centralised inside the pressure plate assembly, so that when the transmission is refitted, the input shaft will pass through the splines at the centre of the driven plate. This can be achieved by passing a large screwdriver or wrench extension bar through the driven plate and into the hole in the crankshaft; the driven plate can then be moved around until it is centred over the crankshaft hole. Alternatively, a universal clutch alignment tool can be used; these can be obtained from most car accessory shops.

> **HAYNES HINT** A clutch alignment device can be made up from a length of metal rod or wooden dowel which is either tapered at one end, or fits closely inside the crankshaft hole, and has insulating tape wound around it, to match the internal diameter of the driven plate splined hole.

Ensure that the driven plate alignment is correct before proceeding any further.

17 When the friction plate is centralised, progressively tighten the pressure plate bolts in a diagonal sequence and to the specified torque setting **(see illustration)**.

18 Where applicable, remove the flywheel locking tool.

19 Apply a thin smear of high-melting point grease to the splines of the friction plate and the transmission input shaft.

20 Refit the transmission as described in Chapter 7A.

5 Clutch release mechanism - removal, inspection and refitting

Release bearing

Inspection

1 Remove the transmission as described in Chapter 7A, and rest it securely on a worksurface.

2 Spin the release bearing whilst it is mounted on its guide sleeve, and listen to the sound it makes; any rattling or crunching noises indicates that either dirt has contaminated the internal bearings, or that the bearings themselves have failed. In either case, the release bearing should be renewed as described in the following sub-section.

3 Similarly, if the release bearing is stiff to rotate or is excessively loose in its mounted position, this indicates that it is worn and in need of renewal.

4 Note that, due to the comparatively low cost of the release bearing and the large expenditure of effort required to gain access to it, it is prudent to renew the bearing regardless of its condition, whenever the transmission is removed for clutch inspection or renewal.

Removal

5 Using a pair of screwdrivers, prise the release bearing off the slave cylinder guide sleeve, at the gearbox input shaft **(see illustration)**. Note its orientation, to ensure correct refitting.

Refitting

6 Refit the bearing by pushing back the dust cover bellows, and simply pressing it over the slave cylinder guide sleeve.

Slave cylinder housing

Removal

7 Remove the transmission as described in Chapter 7A, and rest it securely on a worksurface.

8 At the side of the slave cylinder housing, slacken the unions at the base of the hydraulic supply and bleed pipes. Disconnect both pipes from the cylinder housing **(see illustration)**.

9 Slacken and remove the three screws that secure the cylinder housing to the inside of the bellhousing. Lift the housing away from the bellhousing, over the gearbox input shaft **(see illustration)**. Recover and discard the O-ring seal; a new one must be fitted on reassembly.

10 Retract the dust cover bellows, prise the release bearing off the guide sleeve, and then lift off the dust cover bellows **(see illustrations)**.

5.9 Lift the slave cylinder housing away from the bellhousing, over the gearbox input shaft

5.10a Retract the dust cover bellows, prise the release bearing off the guide sleeve . . .

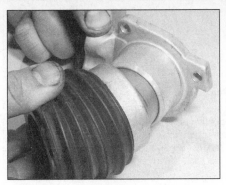

5.10b . . . and then lift off the dust cover bellows

5.12 Fit the new O-ring seal (arrowed) in the channel at the rear of the slave cylinder housing

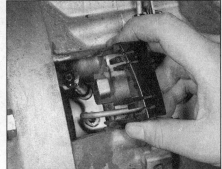

6.4 Remove the inspection cover from the top of the transmission bellhousing, to expose the bleed pipe and nipple

Refitting

11 Press the dust cover bellows over the guide sleeve, and fit the release bearing.

12 Fit the new O-ring seal in the channel at the rear of the slave cylinder housing **(see illustration)**; use a light smear of multi-purpose grease to hold the seal in place during refitting.

13 Offer up the slave cylinder housing to the bellhousing. Apply thread-locking compound to the three securing screws, then refit and tighten them.

14 Refit the hydraulic supply and bleed pipes, and tighten the unions securely.

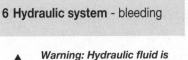

6 Hydraulic system - bleeding

> **Warning: Hydraulic fluid is poisonous; thoroughly wash off spills from bare skin without delay. Seek immediate medical advice if any fluid is swallowed or gets into the eyes. Certain types of hydraulic fluid are inflammable, and may ignite when brought into contact with hot components. When servicing any hydraulic system, it is safest to assume that the fluid IS inflammable, and to take precautions against the risk of fire as though it is petrol that is being handled. Hydraulic fluid is an effective paint stripper, and will also attack many plastics. If spillage occurs onto painted bodywork or fittings, it should be washed off immediately, using copious quantities of fresh water. It is also hygroscopic (it can absorb moisture from the air); excess moisture content lowers the fluid boiling point to an unacceptable level, resulting in a loss of hydraulic pressure. Old fluid may have suffered contamination, and should not be re-used. When topping-up or renewing the fluid, always use the recommended grade, and ensure that it comes from a freshly-opened sealed container.**

General information

1 Whenever the clutch hydraulic lines are disconnected for service or repair, a certain amount of air will enter the system. The presence of air in any hydraulic system will introduce a degree of elasticity and in the clutch system, this will translate into poor pedal feel and reduced travel, leading to inefficient gear changes, and even clutch failure. For this reason, the hydraulic lines must be sealed using hose clamps before any work is carried out; on completion, the fluid should be topped up and bled to remove any air bubbles.

2 To seal off the hydraulic supply to the clutch slave cylinder, trace the rigid pipe from its point of entry at the transmission bellhousing, back to the point where it connects to the flexible hydraulic hose. Fit a proprietary brake hose clamp to the flexible hose, and tighten it securely.

3 Unlike the braking system, the clutch hydraulic system cannot be bled by simply pumping the clutch pedal and catching the ejected fluid in a receptacle connected to the bleed pipe. The system must be pressurised externally; the most effective way of achieving this is to use a pressure brake bleeding kit. These are readily available in motor accessory shops and are extremely effective; the following sub-section describes bleeding the clutch system using such a kit.

Bleeding

4 Remove the inspection cover from the top of the transmission bellhousing, to expose the bleed pipe and nipple **(see illustration)**.

5 Fit a ring spanner over the bleed nipple head, but do not slacken it at this point. Connect a length of clear plastic hose over the nipple, and insert the other end into a clean container **(see illustration)**. Pour hydraulic fluid into the container, such that the end of the hose is covered.

6 Following the kit manufacturer's instructions, pour hydraulic fluid into the bleeding kit vessel.

7 Unscrew the vehicle's fluid reservoir cap,

6.5 Ring spanner, bleed hose and fluid receiving container connected to the clutch bleed nipple

then connect the bleeding kit fluid supply hose to the reservoir.

8 Connect the pressure hose to a supply of compressed air - a spare tyre is convenient source **(see illustration)**.

> **Caution: Check that the pressure in the tyre does not exceed the maximum quoted by the kit manufacturer, let some air escape to reduce the pressure, if necessary. Gently open the air valve, and allow the air and fluid pressures to equalise. Check that there are no leaks before proceeding.**

9 Using the spanner, slacken the bleed pipe nipple until fluid and air bubbles can be seen to flow through the tube, into the container. Maintain a steady flow until the emerging fluid is free of air bubbles; keep a watchful eye on the level of fluid in the bleeding kit vessel and the vehicle's fluid reservoir - if it is allowed to drop too low, air may be forced into the system, defeating the object of the exercise. To refill the vessel, turn off the compressed air supply, remove the lid, and pour in an appropriate quantity of clean fluid from a new container - do not re-use the fluid collected in the receiving container. Repeat as

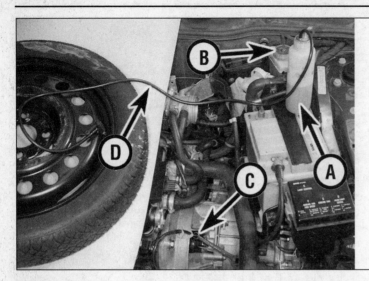

6.8 Clutch pressure bleeding kit in use

A Bleeding kit vessel
B Fluid supply connection at vehicle's fluid reservoir
C Receiving container connection at bleed nipple
D Compressed air supply from spare tyre

necessary until the ejected fluid is bubble-free.

10 On completion, pump the clutch pedal several times to assess its feel and travel. If firm, constant pedal resistance is not felt throughout the pedal stroke, it is probable that air is still present in the system - repeat the bleeding procedure until the pedal feel is restored.

11 Depressurise the bleeding kit, and remove it from the vehicle. At this point, the fluid reservoir will be "over-full"; the excess should be removed using a *clean* pipette to reduce the level to the "MAX" mark.

12 Tighten the bleed pipe nipple using the spanner, and remove the receiving container.

Refit the inspection cover at the transmission bellhousing.

13 Finally, road-test the vehicle and check the operation of the clutch changing up and down through the gears, pulling away from a standstill, and from a hill start.

Chapter 7 Part A: Manual transmission

Contents

Degrees of difficulty

Easy, suitable for novice with little experience		**Fairly easy,** suitable for beginner with some experience		**Fairly difficult,** suitable for competent DIY mechanic		**Difficult,** suitable for experienced DIY mechanic		**Very difficult,** suitable for expert DIY or professional	

Specifications

General

Type	Transversely-mounted, front-wheel-drive layout, with integral transaxle differential/final drive. Five forward speeds, one reverse, all with synchromesh
Oil type/capacity	See *"Lubricants, fluids and capacities"*

Gear ratios (typical)

Pre-1994 models, transmission code GM:

1st	3.31 : 1
2nd	1.76 : 1
3rd	1.18 : 1
4th	0.85 : 1
5th	0.68 : 1
Reverse	3.21 : 1
Final drive	4.45 : 1

1994-on models, transmission code FM:

1st	3.38 : 1
2nd	1.76 : 1
3rd	1.12 : 1
4th	0.89 : 1
5th	0.70 : 1
Reverse	3.17 : 1
Final drive	3.61 : 1

Torque wrench settings

	Nm	lbf ft
Bellhousing-to-engine block bolts	70	52
Gear lever-to-selector rod bolt	20	15
Gear lever housing-to-floorpan bolts	9	7
Left-hand bearing housing-to-differential screws	24	18
Reversing light switch	22	16
Right-hand bearing housing-to-differential screws	24	18
Selector rod pinch-bolt	33	24
Subframe front mounting bolts	50	37
Subframe rear mounting bolts	55	41
Transmission-to-subframe mounting bracket bolt	70	52

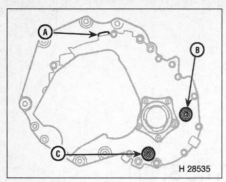

1.2 Plug locations, post-1994 model year vehicles

A Filler plug   B Level plug   C Drain plug

1 General information

The manual transmission is mounted transversely in the engine bay, bolted directly to the engine. This layout has the advantage of providing the shortest possible drive path to the front wheels, as well as locating the transmission in the airflow through the engine bay, optimising cooling.

The unit is cased in aluminium alloy, and has oil filler, drain and level plugs **(see illustration)**. Earlier derivatives included a dipstick integrated into the filler plug to facilitate level checking; refer to Section 2 for greater detail on their usage. The case has two mating faces; one to the bellhousing, which is sealed with "liquid gasket" compound, and one to the gearbox end cover, which sealed with a solid gasket. A "labyrinth" vent at the top of the gearcase allows for air expansion, and permits gases produced by the lubricant to escape. The vent is fitted with a filter plug, that prevents the ingress of water and dirt.

Drive from the crankshaft is transmitted via the clutch to the gearbox input shaft, which is splined to accept the clutch driven plate. All six driving gears (pinions) are mounted on the input shaft; reverse, first and second speed pinions are journalled on sliding contact bearings, and the third, fourth and fifth speed pinions are carried on needle bearings.

The driven gears for all five forward speeds are mounted on the output shaft, again with third, fourth and fifth speed gears carried on needle bearings. Reverse gear is integral with the first/second speed synchromesh sleeve.

The pinions are in constant mesh with their corresponding driven gears, and are free to rotate independently of the gearbox shafts until a speed is selected. The difference in diameter and number of teeth between the pinions and gears provides the necessary shaft speed reduction and torque multiplication. Drive is then transmitted to the final drive gears/differential through the output shaft.

All gears are fitted with syncromeshes, including reverse. When a speed is selected,

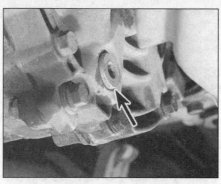

2.5 Transmission oil drain plug (arrowed)

the movement of the floor-mounted gear lever is communicated to the gearbox by a selector rod. This in turn actuates a series of selector forks inside the gearbox, which are slotted onto the synchromesh sleeves. The sleeves, which are locked to the gearbox shafts, but can slide axially by means of splined hubs, press baulk rings into contact with the respective gear/pinion. The coned surfaces between the baulk rings and the pinion/gear act as a friction clutch, progressively matching the speed of the synchromesh sleeve (and hence the gearbox shaft) with that of the gear/pinion. The dog teeth on the outside of the baulk ring prevent the synchromesh sleeve ring from meshing with the gear/pinion until their speeds are exactly matched; this allows gearchanges to be carried out smoothly, and greatly reduces the noise and mechanical wear caused by rapid gearchanges.

When reverse gear is engaged, an idler gear is brought into mesh between the reverse pinion and the teeth on the outside of the first/second speed synchromesh sleeve. This arrangement introduces the necessary speed reduction, and also causes the output shaft to rotate in the opposite direction, allowing the vehicle to be driven in reverse.

2 Manual transmission - draining and refilling

General information

1 The gearbox is filled with the correct quantity and grade of oil at manufacture. The level must be checked regularly, and if necessary topped-up, in accordance with the maintenance schedule (see Chapter 1). However, there is no requirement to drain and renew the oil during the normal lifetime of the gearbox, unless repair or overhaul is carried out.

Draining

2 Take the car on a road test of sufficient length to warm the engine/transmission up to normal operating temperature; this will speed up the draining process, and any sludge and debris will be more likely to be drained out.

3 Park the car on level ground, switch off the ignition, and apply the handbrake firmly. For improved access, jack up the front of the car

and support it securely on axle stands. **Note:** *The car must be lowered to the ground and parked on a level surface, to ensure accuracy when refilling and checking the oil level.*

4 Wipe clean the area around the filler plug, which is situated on the top surface of the transmission. Unscrew the plug from the casing, and recover the sealing washer.

5 Position a container with a capacity of at least 2 litres (ideally with a large funnel) under the drain plug **(see illustration)**. The drain plug is located on the right-hand end of the transmission, under the driveshaft; use a wrench to unscrew the plug from the casing. Note that the drain plug contains an integral magnet, designed to catch the metal fragments produced as the transmission components wear. If the plug is clogged with a large amount of metal debris, this may be an early indication of component failure.

6 Allow all the oil to drain completely into the container. If the oil is still hot, take precautions against scalding. Clean both the filler and drain plugs thoroughly, paying particular attention to the threads. Discard the original sealing washers; they should be always renewed whenever they are disturbed.

Refilling

7 When the oil has drained out completely, clean the plug hole threads in the transmission casing. Fit a new sealing washer to the drain plug. Coat the thread with thread-locking compound, and tighten it into the transmission casing. If the car was raised for the draining operation, lower it to the ground.

8 When refilling the transmission, allow plenty of time for the oil level to settle completely before attempting to check it. Note that the car must be parked on a flat, level surface when checking the oil level. Use a funnel if necessary to maintain a gradual, constant flow and avoid spillage.

9 Refill the transmission with the specified grade and quantity of oil, then check the oil level as described in Chapter 1. If a large quantity flows out when the level checking plug is removed, or if the level is over the "MAX" graduation on the dipstick (as applicable) refit both the filler and level plugs, then drive the car for a short distance so that the new oil is distributed fully around the transmission components. Re-check the level again upon your return.

10 On completion, fit the filler and level plugs with new sealing washers. Coat their threads with thread-locking compound and tighten them securely.

3 Gearchange linkage - adjustment

1 If the action of the gearchange linkage is stiff, slack or vague, the alignment between the gearchange linkage and the gearbox selector rod may be incorrect. The operations in the following paragraphs describe how to

3.4 Transmission alignment hole plug (arrowed) - post-1994 model year vehicles

3.5 Insert a screwdriver into the alignment hole in the side of the lever housing

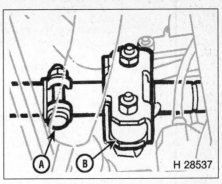

3.8 At the selector rod, slacken the pinch-bolt, adjacent to the rubber coupling

A Selector rod pinch-bolt   B Rubber coupling

check and, if necessary, adjust this alignment.
2 Park the vehicle, apply the handbrake and switch off the ignition.

Pre-1994 models only

3 Select reverse gear.

Post-1994 models only

4 Locate the alignment hole at the top of the gearbox casing, adjacent to the part number plate **(see illustration)**. Prise out the plug to expose the alignment hole. Select fourth gear, then take a screwdriver with a shaft diameter of approximately 4 mm, and insert it into the alignment hole; this will lock the gearbox in fourth gear - the screwdriver handle will prevent the screwdriver from falling into the gearbox.

All models

5 Inside the car, remove the gear lever gaiter and mounting frame to expose the gearchange lever housing. Take a screwdriver with a shaft diameter of approximately 4 mm, and insert it into the alignment hole in the side of the lever housing **(see illustration)**.
6 If the screwdriver can be inserted without difficulty, then the gearchange linkage alignment is correct, and hence cannot be blamed for the poor gearchange quality; the best course of action now is to remove the gearchange linkage and inspect it for wear or damage - refer to Section 4 for details.
7 If the screwdriver cannot be inserted into the alignment hole, then the gearchange linkage is incorrectly adjusted.
8 From the engine bay, at the point where the selector rod passes through the bulkhead, slacken the pinch-bolt adjacent to the rubber coupling, to allow movement between the two halves of the selector rod **(see illustration)**.
9 Move the gearchange lever such that the screwdriver shaft can be inserted into the alignment hole in the lever housing; ensure that the lever is still in the 4th gear position.
10 In the engine bay, tighten the pinch-bolt on the selector rod, observing the correct torque.
11 Remove the screwdriver from the gearbox alignment hole, and fit the plastic plug.
12 Remove the screwdriver from the gear

lever housing alignment hole.
13 Refit the gear lever gaiter and mounting frame.
14 Before moving the vehicle, check that the gear lever can be moved from neutral to all six gear positions. Finally, road test the vehicle, and check that all gears can be obtained smoothly and precisely.

4 Gearchange linkage - removal, inspection and refitting

Gear lever and housing

Removal

1 Park the vehicle, switch off the ignition, and apply the handbrake. If the selector rod is to be removed as well, select reverse gear (pre-1994 models) or 4th gear (post-1994 model year vehicles). Otherwise, move the gearchange lever to the neutral position.
2 Referring to Chapter 11, remove the gear lever gaiter, centre console and side carpet trim panels.

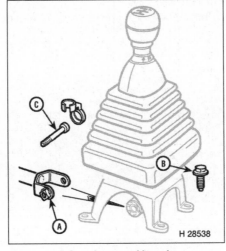

4.6 Gear lever and housing

A Selector rod
B Gear lever housing-to-floorpan bolts
C Gear lever-to-selector rod bolt

3 On left-hand-drive vehicles fitted with an airbag, a steering column restraining cable is anchored to the floorpan in front of, and to the right of, the gearchange lever. Release the cable by sliding it out of the anchoring bracket.
4 Extract the rear air duct retaining screw, and push the duct towards the rear of the vehicle.
5 Extract the clip to release the front air duct from the heater housing, then push the duct towards the bulkhead.
6 Slacken and remove the four bolts that secure the gearchange lever housing to the floorpan. Lift the housing up as far as possible, without damaging the console trim, and unbolt the gear lever from the selector shaft **(see illustration)**. Recover all bushes, washers and spacers, and remove the housing.

Inspection

7 It is possible to remove the gear lever from its housing, to allow the bearings to be inspected and renewed. It is most likely, however, that any slack found in the mechanism will be caused by worn bushes between the gear lever and the selector rod. Extract the bushes from the gear lever linkage **(see illustration)** and inspect them; if they appear worn or corroded, renew them.

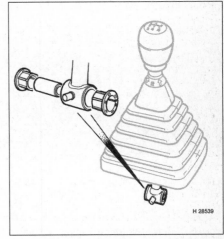

4.7 Gear lever-to-selector rod bushes (inset)

Refitting

8 Refit the gearchange lever and housing by reversing the removal sequence, noting the following:

a) *Observe the correct torque for the gear lever-to-selector rod bolt and the gear lever housing-to-floorpan bolts.*

b) *Refit the electric window control panel harness connectors using the notes made during removal.*

c) *On completion, check that the gear lever can be moved from neutral to all six gear positions. Finally, road test the vehicle, and check that all gears can be obtained smoothly and precisely.*

Selector rod

Removal

9 Refer to the previous sub-section, and remove the gear lever and housing. Ensure that the appropriate gear is selected before removal. On post-1994 model year vehicles, remove the plug from the alignment hole in the top of the gearbox casing, and lock the gearbox in 4th gear using a suitable screwdriver, as described in Section 3.

10 From within the engine bay, at the point where the selector rod passes through the bulkhead, slacken the pinch-bolt collar to detach the selector rod from the gearbox (refer to illustration 3.8)

11 From inside the cabin, carefully withdraw the selector rod through the bulkhead, taking care to avoid damaging the rubber grommet in the bulkhead.

Refitting

12 Lubricate the selector rod with silicone grease, and push it through the grommet in the bulkhead; do not tighten the pinch-bolt collar at the gearbox at this stage.

13 Refit the gear lever and housing as described earlier in this Section. Fit the bushes, and bolt the gear lever to the selector rod.

14 Lock the gear lever in 4th gear (post-1994 model year vehicles) or reverse gear (pre-1994 model year vehicles) by inserting a screwdriver

with a 4 mm shaft into the alignment hole on the gear lever housing.

15 Tighten the pinch-bolt collar on the selector rod at the gearbox, observing the specified torque.

16 Remove the screwdriver from the housing, and refit the gear lever gaiter.

17 Before moving the vehicle, check that the gear lever can be moved from neutral to all six gear positions. Finally, road test the vehicle, and check that all gears can be obtained smoothly and precisely.

5 Oil seals - renewal

Right-hand driveshaft oil seal

Pre-1994 models

1 On these models, the right-hand driveshaft oil seals cannot easily be serviced without dismantling the transmission.

Post-1994 models

Note: *This sub-section describes the renewal of the O-ring oil seal in the bearing casing only. Renewal of the driveshaft oil seal is a more complex task, requiring access to a hydraulic press, and as such should be entrusted to a Saab dealer.*

2 Park the vehicle on a level surface, apply the handbrake, and chock the rear wheels. Remove the wheel centre caps, and slacken the wheel bolts.

3 Apply the handbrake, then raise the front of the vehicle, rest it securely on axle stands and remove the roadwheels; refer to *"Jacking, towing and wheel changing"* for guidance.

4 Refer Section 2 and drain the transmission oil. Clean and refit the drain plug as described in Section 2.

5 Working from Chapter 8, remove the intermediate driveshaft and bearing assembly.

6 Remove the four retaining screws from the driveshaft bearing housing **(see illustration)**.

7 Thread a sliding hammer into the end of the driveshaft, and use its percussion action to

draw the shaft and bearing housing out of the differential casing.

8 Extract the O-ring seal from the bearing housing, and discard it.

9 Thoroughly clean the mating surfaces of the bearing housing and differential casing; take precautions to prevent debris entering the bearings of either assembly.

10 Lubricate the new O-ring seal with clean oil, and carefully fit it over the driveshaft bearing housing, ensuring that it is seated squarely.

11 Lightly lubricate the inboard splines of the driveshaft with multi-purpose grease. Offer up the driveshaft and bearing housing to the differential casing, and engage the splines of the driveshaft with the differential pinion. Using a light mallet, carefully tap the driveshaft into the differential, until the bearing housing is flush with the casing.

12 Ensure that the O-ring is seated squarely and not distorted, then refit the four retaining screws into the bearing housing, and tighten them to the correct torque.

13 Refer to Chapter 8 and refit the intermediate driveshaft and bearing assembly.

14 Refit the roadwheels, and lower the vehicle to the ground. Tighten the roadwheel bolts to the correct torque, and refit the wheel centre caps/trims.

15 Refer to Section 2 and refill the transmission with oil of the correct grade.

Left-hand driveshaft oil seal

Note: *This sub-section describes the renewal of the O-ring oil seal in the bearing casing only. Renewal of the driveshaft oil seal is a more complex task, requiring access to a hydraulic press, and as such should be entrusted to a Saab dealer.*

16 Park the vehicle on a level surface, apply the handbrake, and chock the rear wheels. Remove the wheel centre caps, and slacken the wheel bolts.

17 Apply the handbrake, then raise the front of the vehicle, rest it securely on axle stands and remove the **roadwheel**s; refer to *"Jacking, towing and wheel changing"* for guidance.

18 Refer to Section 2 and drain the transmission oil. Clean and refit the drain plug as described in Section 2.

19 Working from the relevant section of Chapter 8, disconnect the left-hand driveshaft from the transmission at the inboard universal joint.

20 Place a container beneath the driveshaft housing mating face, then slacken and withdraw the five retaining screws **(see illustration)**.

21 Using two large-diameter worm-drive hose clips, strap the shaft of a slide hammer to the outside of universal joint cup. Thread a nut onto the end of the slide hammer shaft to prevent it sliding off, then use the percussion action of the hammer to draw the universal cup, and hence the driveshaft, out of the differential housing.

5.6 Remove the four retaining screws (arrowed) from the right-hand driveshaft bearing housing

5.20 Slacken and withdraw the five retaining screws (arrowed) from the left-hand driveshaft bearing housing

22 As the driveshaft is withdrawn, recover the plunger and spring from the inboard end. Note their orientation and order of fitment, to aid reassembly.

23 Recover the shims from the driveshaft bearing housing, and then extract the O-ring. Thoroughly clean the mating surfaces of the bearing housing and differential casing; if a cleaning solvent is used, take care to prevent any entering the bearings of either assembly.

24 Refit the shims to the differential housing, then lubricate the new O-ring seal with clean engine oil, and carefully fit it over the driveshaft bearing housing, ensuring that it is seated squarely.

25 Lightly lubricate the inboard splines of the driveshaft with multi-purpose grease. Offer up the driveshaft and bearing housing to the differential casing, and engage the splines of the driveshaft with the differential pinion. Using a light mallet, carefully tap the driveshaft into the differential, until the bearing housing is flush with the casing.

26 Ensure that the O-ring is seated squarely and not distorted, then refit the five retaining screws into the bearing housing, and tighten them to the correct torque.

27 Refer to Chapter 8, and reconnect the right-hand driveshaft at the universal joint.

28 Refit the roadwheels, and lower the vehicle to the ground. Tighten the roadwheel bolts to the correct torque, and refit the wheel centre caps/trims.

29 Refer to Section 2 and refill transmission with oil of the correct grade.

Input shaft oil seal

30 Referring to Section 8, remove the transmission and rest it securely on a worksurface.

31 Working from Chapter 6, remove the clutch slave cylinder assembly.

32 Prise the seal from its housing in the slave cylinder; use a blunt-ended instrument that will not damage the mating surfaces of the housing, and cause seal to fail when the transmission is refitted.

33 Examine the input shaft sealing surface, to identify any imperfections that may have caused the seal to fail in the first place. Minor burrs can be removed using fine abrasive paper, but more serious wear or damage will mean that the input shaft has to be renewed.

34 Clean the mating surfaces thoroughly using a clean rag, then lightly lubricate the new oil seal with clean engine oil, and press it squarely into its housing.

35 Refit the clutch slave cylinder, referring to Chapter 6 for guidance.

36 Refer to Section 8 and refit the transmission.

Selector rod oil seal

37 Renewal of the selector rod oil seal can only be carried out as part of a complete transmission overhaul and as such, should be entrusted to a Saab dealer.

6 Reversing light switch - testing, removal and refitting

Testing

1 Disconnect the battery negative cable, and position it away from the terminal.

2 Unplug the wiring harness from the reversing light switch at the connector. On pre-1994 models, the switch is located on the endplate of the transmission, adjacent to the filler plug. On post-1994 models, the switch is located on the rear of the transmission casing, to the right of the differential casing **(see illustration)**.

3 Connect the probes of a continuity tester, or a multi-meter set to the resistance function, across the terminals of the reversing light switch.

4 The switch contacts are normally open, so with any gear other than reverse selected, the tester/meter should indicate an open-circuit. When reverse gear is then selected, the switch contacts should close, causing the tester/meter to indicate a short-circuit.

5 If the switch appears to be constantly open- or short-circuit, or is intermittent in its operation, it should be renewed.

Removal

6 If not already done, disconnect the battery negative cable, and position it away from the terminal.

7 Unplug the wiring harness from the reversing light switch at the connector.

8 Using a suitable spanner, unscrew the switch from the endplate, recovering any washers that may be fitted; these **must** be refitted, to ensure that the correct clearance exists between the switch shaft and the reverse gear shaft.

Refitting

9 Refit the switch by reversing the removal procedure.

10 Note that on post-1994 model year vehicles, the reversing light switch harness connector must be fitted with a new sealing grommet, whenever the connector is disturbed.

11 Reconnect the battery negative cable.

7 Speedometer drive - removal and refitting

General information

1 Two types of speedometer drive mechanism have been fitted. Vehicles built before 1987 have a conventional cable drive, which consists of a helical-cut gear driven directly from the differential by a dedicated pinion gear. The gear drives the speedometer remotely, by means of a cable with a rotating, flexible inner shaft.

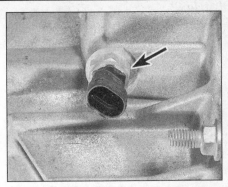

6.2 Reversing light switch location - post-1994 models

2 An erratic or inconsistent speedometer display, such as needle flickering or jumping, that cannot be cured by renewal of the speedometer drive cable, may be caused by gear wear; refer to the following sub-section for details of its removal and refitting.

3 Vehicles built after 1987 are fitted with an electronic transducer in place of the drive gear. This device measures the rotational speed of the transmission final drive, and converts the information into an electronic signal, which is then sent to the speedometer module in the instrument panel. The signal is also used as an input by the engine management system ECU (and where fitted, by the cruise control ECU, the trip computer and the traction control system ECU).

Mechanical speedometer drive
Removal

⚠️ *Caution: When removing the drive gear from transmissions built prior to serial number 310568, it is possible for the gear to accidentally drop down inside the transmission as the locating ring is removed; subsequent design changes have eliminated the possibility of this happening on later transmissions.*

4 Trace the speedometer drive cable back to the connection point on the right-hand side of the differential housing, at the rear of the transmission casing.

5 Unscrew the knurled nut by hand, and withdraw the end of the drive cable. Where fitted, recover the washer.

6 Wrap a length of thin copper wire around the thread of the gear, and secure the free end to a fixed point on the transmission; this will prevent the gear dropping down inside the transmission casing when the locating ring is removed.

7 Prise out the locating ring using a thin, flat-bladed instrument such as a watchmaker's screwdriver.

⚠️ *Caution: Do not allow the gear to fall into the transmission casing.*

8 Pull the gear out of its seat, then extract and discard the O-ring seal.

9 Clean the gear thoroughly, and examine the teeth for signs of wear or damage. Renew the component if necessary, but bear in mind that the drive pinion inside the differential casing is likely to be worn as well, and this can only be renewed as part of a complete transmission overhaul.

Refitting

10 Lubricate a new O-ring seal with clean oil, and fit it into the groove in the gear body.

11 Fit the gear into its seat, using the length of wire as before to prevent it from dropping into the transmission. Rotate the gear to ensure that the teeth engage with those on the drive pinion inside the transmission.

12 Snap the locating ring into the groove in the transmission housing, and remove the anchoring piece of wire.

13 Push the drive cable into the socket at the top of the gear, and screw on the knurled nut, tightening it securely. **Note:** *Where a washer was fitted between the nut and the gear body, ensure that it is fitted before the drive cable is reconnected.*

Electronic speedometer drive

Removal

14 Locate the speed transducer, which is on the differential housing, at the rear of the transmission case.

15 Unplug the wiring harness from the transducer, at the connector.

16 Remove the transducer retaining screw, and unscrew the unit from the transmission casing (**see illustration**).

17 Recover and discard the O-ring seal.

Refitting

18 Refit the transducer by following the removal procedure in reverse. **Note:** *A new O-ring seal must be used on refitting.*

7.16 Remove the speedometer transducer retaining screw (arrowed) - post-1994 models

8 Manual transmission - removal and refitting

Removal

Note: *Refer to Chapter 2B for details on removal of the engine and transmission as a complete assembly.*

1 Park the vehicle on a level surface, apply the handbrake and chock the rear wheels. Remove the wheel centre caps, and slacken the wheel bolts.

2 Apply the handbrake, then raise the front of the vehicle, rest it securely on axle stands and remove the roadwheels; refer to *"Jacking, towing and wheel changing"* for guidance.

3 If the transmission is to be removed as a complete assembly and then refitted without dismantling, there is no need to drain the transmission oil. If repairs or an overhaul are to be carried out, refer to Section 2 of this Chapter and drain the oil from the transmission. Refit and tighten the drain plug as described in Section 2.

4 Refer to Section 3, and set the gearchange linkage (and the transmission, where applicable) in a reference condition, to ensure correct alignment of the linkage on refitting.

5 Referring to Chapter 5A, disconnect both battery cables and then remove the battery.

6 Unbolt the battery tray from the side of the engine bay, unplugging the ABS ECU connector where applicable. Remove the positive supply distribution block, but do not disconnect the supply cables from it.

Pre-1994 models

7 Working from Chapter 4A, remove the fuel filter from the bulkhead, then remove the air cleaner.

8 Disconnect and plug the hoses from the washer fluid reservoir, then remove the retaining screws and remove it from the engine bay.

9 Unplug the cable connector, then remove the airflow meter, referring to Chapter 4A for guidance.

 Caution: The airflow meter is a delicate component, handle it with great care.

10 Unplug the LT connections from the distributor (where applicable), referring to Chapter 5B for guidance.

11 With reference to Chapter 8, remove the clip, and slide the intermediate driveshaft dust cover away from the differential housing.

Post-1994 models

12 With reference to Chapter 4A, disconnect the accelerator cable from the guide bracket on the inlet manifold. Tie the cable back against the bulkhead, away from the work area.

All models

13 Where applicable, unplug the wiring

connector from the air temperature sensor at the turbocharger delivery hose. Slacken the hose clips and remove the bypass valve, then disconnect the delivery hose from the turbocharger and the throttle body.

14 Unplug the wiring harness from the reversing light switch at the transmission; refer to Section 6 of this Chapter for guidance.

15 Still working from Section 6, disconnect the speedometer drive cable/transducer wiring connector, as applicable.

16 Working from Chapter 6, seal off the clutch hydraulic system by fitting a clamp to the flexible section of the slave cylinder supply hose. Place a container underneath the union between the rigid and flexible clutch hoses, to catch any spilt hydraulic fluid, then slacken and separate the union. Unbolt the rigid hose from the clamp at the top of the bellhousing. Tie back the free end of the flexible supply hose, away from the work area.

17 Remove the electrical earth strap from the transmission casing.

18 At the gearchange selector rod, locate the rubber coupling in the engine bay, between the bulkhead and the transmission. Slacken and withdraw the two bolts, and separate the two halves of the coupling.

19 Working under the front valance, remove the plastic undertray and brake cooling ducts, referring to Chapter 11 for guidance.

20 Remove the liner from the left-hand inner wheelarch, again referring to Chapter 11.

21 Refer to Chapter 10 and remove the pinch-bolt that secures the ball joint at the suspension lower arm to the base of the left-hand steering swivel member.

22 Still working from Chapter 10, unbolt the front anti-roll bar from the left-hand clamp bracket on the subframe, then unbolt the left-hand anti-roll bar link from the suspension lower arm.

23 Remove the nut and washers from the bolt that secures the inner wing stay bar to the subframe.

24 Referring to the relevant Sections of Chapter 2B, release the transmission from the mounting at the subframe by slackening and withdrawing the through-bolt; recover the dished washer, noting its orientation.

25 Position a lifting beam across the engine bay, locating the support legs securely in the sills at either side, in line with the strut top mountings. Hook the jib onto the engine lifting eyelet and raise it, so that the weight of the engine is taken off the transmission mounting. Most people won't have access to an engine lifting beam, but it may be possible to hire one. Alternatively, an engine hoist may be used to support the engine, but when using this method, bear in mind that if the vehicle is lowered on its axle stands to adjust the working height, for example, then the hoist will have to be lowered accordingly, to avoid straining the engine mountings.

26 With reference to Chapter 5A, remove the starter motor from the engine block, unbolting the inlet manifold stay bar at the same time.

27 To allow the transmission to be lowered out of the engine bay, the left-hand section of the front subframe must be partially unbolted and lowered; the following paragraphs describe this procedure **(see illustration)**.

28 At the front crossmember underneath the radiator, slacken the pivot link through-bolt, then remove the two link retaining bolts (refer to illustration 8.27).

29 At the front left-hand corner of the subframe, remove the two retaining bolts (refer to illustration 8.27).

30 Slacken the through-bolt at the pivot link in the rear crossmember, below the steering rack, then remove the two retaining bolts; one of these bolts also retains the steering rack. Note the orientation and order of assembly of all washers removed (refer to illustration 8.27).

31 At the rear left-hand corner of the subframe, remove the four retaining bolts that pass through the mounting bracket for the suspension lower arm rear bearing. Recover the bearing plate beneath the mounting bracket, noting its orientation (refer to illustration 8.27). As the lower arm bearing is released, tie the rear of the suspension arm to the vacated bolt hole in the subframe, using a cable-tie - this will prevent the front bearing from being strained.

32 Support the subframe as the last retaining bolt is removed, and allow it to pivot downwards to the end of its travel. Withdraw the front and rear pivot bolts, and remove the left-hand side of the subframe from the vehicle.

33 With reference to Chapter 8, separate the left-hand driveshaft from the transmission, at the inboard universal joint.

34 Work around the circumference of the bellhousing, and remove all but the uppermost transmission retaining bolts. Unbolt the flywheel cover plate from the lower edge of the bellhousing.

35 Position a jack underneath the transmission, and raise it to take the weight of the unit. Check that nothing remains connected to the transmission before attempting to separate it from the engine.

36 Remove the last retaining bolt from the bellhousing, and pull the transmission away from the engine. This involves simultaneously extracting the input shaft from the clutch driven plate whilst disconnecting the intermediate driveshaft from the differential - a task which should only be attempted with the help of an assistant. If difficulty is experienced, refer to Chapter 8 and remove the intermediate driveshaft and bearing bracket from the engine as an assembly, before progressing any further.

> ⚠️ **Warning: Maintain firm support on the transmission, to ensure that it remains steady on the jack head..**

37 When all the locating dowels are clear of their mounting holes, lower the transmission out of the engine bay using the jack.

Refitting

All models

38 Refit the transmission by reversing the removal procedure, noting the following points:

a) *Apply a smear of high-melting point grease to the transmission input shaft. Do not apply an excessive amount, as there is a possibility of the clutch driven plate being contaminated.*

b) *When securing the transmission at its mounting on the subframe, ensure that the dished washer is fitted the correct way around - convex side facing outwards, with the tang seated in the slot at the top of the mounting bracket.*

c) *Observe the specified torque wrench settings (where applicable) when tightening all nuts and bolts after refitting.*

d) *Bleed the clutch hydraulic system, referring to Chapter 6 for reference.*

e) *On completion, if the transmission was drained, refill with the specified type and quantity of oil as described in Section 2.*

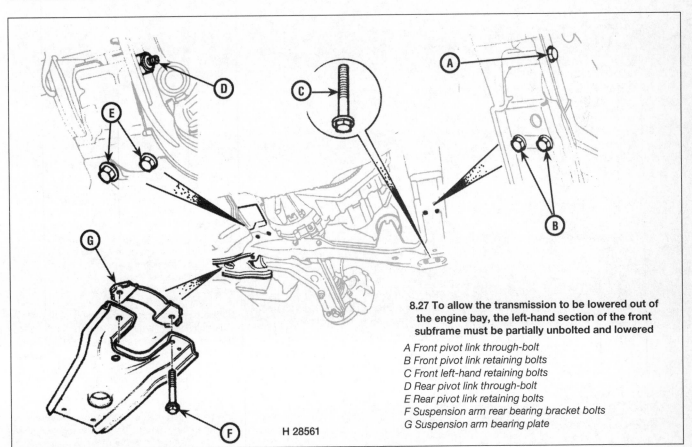

8.27 To allow the transmission to be lowered out of the engine bay, the left-hand section of the front subframe must be partially unbolted and lowered

A Front pivot link through-bolt
B Front pivot link retaining bolts
C Front left-hand retaining bolts
D Rear pivot link through-bolt
E Rear pivot link retaining bolts
F Suspension arm rear bearing bracket bolts
G Suspension arm bearing plate

H 28561

9 Manual transmission overhaul - general information

The overhaul of a manual transmission is a complex (and often expensive) engineering task for the DIY home mechanic to undertake, which requires access to specialist equipment. It involves dismantling and reassembly of many small components, measuring clearances precisely, and if necessary adjusting them by the selection shims and spacers. Internal transmission components are also often difficult to obtain, and in many instances extremely expensive. Because of this, if the transmission develops a fault or becomes noisy, the best course of action is to have the unit overhauled by a specialist repairer, or to obtain an exchange reconditioned unit.

Nevertheless, it is not impossible for the more experienced mechanic to overhaul the transmission, if the special tools are available and the job is carried out in a deliberate step-by-step manner, to ensure that nothing is overlooked.

The tools necessary for an overhaul include internal and external circlip pliers, bearing pullers, a slide hammer, a set of pin punches, a dial test indicator (dial gauge), and possibly a hydraulic press. In addition, a large, sturdy workbench and a vice will be required.

During dismantling of the transmission, make careful notes of how each component is fitted, to make reassembly easier and accurate.

Before dismantling the transmission, it will help if you have some idea of where the problem lies. Certain problems can be closely related to specific areas in the transmission, which can make component examination and renewal easier. Refer to *"Fault finding"* at the end of this manual for more information.

Chapter 7 Part B: Automatic transmission

Contents

Degrees of difficulty

Easy, suitable for novice with little experience	**Fairly easy,** suitable for beginner with some experience	**Fairly difficult,** suitable for competent DIY mechanic	**Difficult,** suitable for experienced DIY mechanic	**Very difficult,** suitable for expert DIY or professional

Specifications

General

Type	ZF automatic with planetary gearbox, providing four forward speeds and one reverse speed. Drive transmitted through hydrokinetic torque converter
Designation	4 HP 18
Fluid type/capacity	See "Lubricants, fluids and capacities"

Torque wrench settings

	Nm	lbf ft
Filter housing cover bolts	8	6
Selector lever-to-cable clamp nut	8	6

1 General information

The 4 HP 18 automatic transmission is a four-speed unit, incorporating a hydrokinetic torque converter with an integral torsional damper and a planetary gearbox.

The transmission is controlled by a floor-mounted, seven-position selector lever. The transmission operates in different modes, depending on the position of the selector lever.

In "Park", the transmission is mechanically locked, thus preventing the roadwheels from turning. For this reason, "Park" must only be selected when the vehicle has come to a complete standstill.

In "Neutral", the transmission disconnects drive between the engine and the driven wheels, in the same manner as a manual transmission. This selection should not be made if the vehicle is moving. Apply the handbrake when parking with the transmission in this position.

In "Drive", the transmission will automatically shift between the four forward gears, according to road speed and accelerator position. First gear is always selected when pulling away from standstill, and as the vehicle accelerates, higher-ratio gears are sequentially selected at pre-defined road speed thresholds, to provide optimum comfort, fuel consumption and driveability.

Before selecting "Reverse", the vehicle must first be allowed to come to a standstill; selection is prevented by a hydraulic latching mechanism in the transmission, if the vehicle's road speed has not dropped to zero.

The engine can only be started with either "Park" or "Neutral" selected.

The transmission shifting range can be limited to the first three gears, the first two, or even just first gear, if driving conditions require it. Selecting "3" allows automatic shifting between the first three gears, but the upshift to fourth gear is prevented. If "3" is selected whilst the transmission is in fourth gear (with "Drive" selected) the downshift to third takes place immediately. To avoid engine and transmission damage, do not select "3" at speeds above 80 mph.

Selecting "2" allows automatic shifting between the first two gears, but the upshift to higher-ratio gears is prevented, providing improved performance and control when ascending or descending steep hills. If "2" is selected whilst the transmission is in third gear (with "Drive" or "3" selected) the downshift to second takes place only when the road speed has dropped to a preset threshold, to avoid engine and transmission damage.

Selecting "1" locks the transmission in first gear, preventing the upshift to higher-ratio gears. This provides optimum performance and control when ascending or descending very steep hills, particularly when towing. It also prevents repeated automatic up and downshifts between first and second gear, which could otherwise overheat the transmission fluid. If "2" is selected whilst the transmission is in third, second or fourth gear (with "Drive", "3" or "2" selected) the downshift to first takes place sequentially when the road speed has dropped to the preset thresholds for third and second gear. This avoids engine and transmission damage, and sudden, unexpected engine braking.

To provide maximum acceleration for overtaking, pressing the accelerator to the end of its travel, past the full-throttle position, will cause the transmission to "kickdown". At this point, if the gear currently selected is not the optimum gear for maximum acceleration at the current road speed, the transmission will automatically downshift to a lower-ratio gear. Selection of that gear will then be maintained either until the accelerator is released from the kickdown position, or until the maximum road speed for the gear is reached; upshift to a higher-ratio gear will then occur.

Due to the complexity of the transmission, major repairs and overhaul operations should be left to a Saab dealer, who will have the necessary tools for fault diagnosis and repair. The information in this Chapter is therefore limited to descriptions of servicing operations that can be carried out without the need for specialised test or repair equipment.

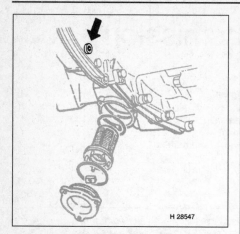

2.4 Filter element and transmission fluid drain plug (arrowed)

2 Fluid filter element - renewal

General

1 It is vitally important that the transmission fluid filter element is changed at the specified interval (see Chapter 1), to maintain the transmission in efficient working order.

Renewal

2 Refer to Chapter 1 and drain the transmission fluid.

3 Slacken and withdraw the three bolts, then lower the filter housing cover away from the transmission casing.

4 Remove the retaining nut, then withdraw the filter element. Recover and discard the O-ring seals **(see illustration)**.

5 Clean the area around the filter housing thoroughly, using a lint-free rag.

6 Lubricate a new O-ring seal with clean transmission fluid, and fit it to the filter element. Push the element into its housing, and refit the retaining nut.

7 Lubricate a new O-ring seal with clean transmission fluid, and fit it to the filter housing cover. Locate the cover over the housing, and fit the retaining bolts, ensuring that they are tightened to the correct torque.

8 Refer to Chapter 1, and refill the transmission with the correct type and quantity of fluid.

3 Selector cable - adjustment

1 Park the vehicle on a level surface, then release the handbrake and select "Neutral". With the engine running, ensure that drive to the roadwheels is fully disconnected (increase the engine speed to approximately 2000 rpm, and make sure that the car does not move). Apply the handbrake, then switch off the ignition.

2 From inside the car, remove the retaining screws, and lift off the cover panel from the base of the selector lever.

3 At the point where the selector cable is connected to the selector lever, slacken the adjusting nut to allow free movement of the cable **(see illustration)**.

4 Move the selector lever to the "Neutral" position.

5 Tighten the adjustment nut to the specified torque wrench setting.

6 Refit the cover panel and retaining screws.

7 Check the cable adjustment as follows. Move the selector lever first to "Park", then to "1", and check that no freeplay exists in the cable at these positions. Move the selector lever to "Drive", and check that no freeplay exists as the lever is moved to the "3" position. Move the selector lever to "Reverse" and check that no freeplay exists as the lever is moved to the "Park" position. Finally, check that when the lever is moved to the "Neutral" position, the transmission selects neutral smoothly.

8 Road test the vehicle, and verify that the transmission can be set in all gear positions smoothly and easily.

4 Kickdown cable - adjustment

1 Ensure that the throttle cable is correctly adjusted, as described in Chapter 4A.

2 Park the vehicle on a level surface, apply the handbrake and select "Neutral". Ensure that the ignition is switched off.

3 The kickdown cable terminates at the throttle actuating lever, on the side of the throttle body. The cable outer is secured to a mounting bracket by a locknut, in a similar arrangement to the throttle cable.

4 Operate the throttle actuating lever manually, until significant resistance can be felt through the kickdown cable; the resistance corresponds to the kickdown mechanism in the transmission beginning to engage. Hold the throttle actuating lever in this position, and measure the distance between the crimped ring on the kickdown cable inner, and the end of the threaded section of the cable outer **(see illustration)**. If the distance is not 39mm, move the ring along the cable to the obtain the correct setting.

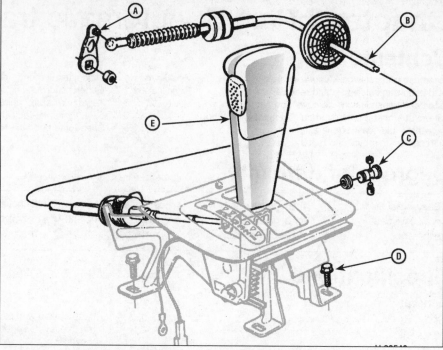

3.3 Selector lever and cable layout

A Selector lever   B Selector cable   C Adjustment nut
D Selector lever housing bolts   E Transmission selector lever

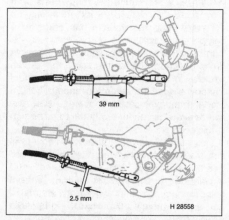

4.4 Adjustment of kickdown cable

5 Release the throttle actuating lever, and allow it to return to its rest position. Measure the distance between the crimped ring and the threaded end of the cable outer, as before. If the measurement is not 2.5mm, it can be brought into specification by slackening the inner and outer locknuts at the mounting bracket, and screwing the cable outer clockwise or anti-clockwise, as appropriate. When the distance is within specification, tighten the two locknuts.

6 Road test the vehicle, and verify that kickdown can be induced by pressing the accelerator pedal past the full-throttle position.

5 Driveshaft fluid seals - general information

To renew the driveshaft fluid seals without causing damage to the bearings, access to a hydraulic press is necessary. For this reason, it is recommended that this operation should be entrusted to a Saab dealer.

6 Fluid cooler - general information

The layout of the transmission fluid cooling system depends on vehicle model. In general, turbocharged European-specification vehicles are fitted with an fluid cooler that is integrated into the engine cooling radiator. Refer to Chapter 3, Section 3 for details.

7 Speedometer drive - removal and refitting

Refer to the information given in Chapter 7A.

8 Automatic transmission - removal and refitting

Removal

Note: *Refer to Chapter 2B for details of removal of the engine and transmission as a complete assembly.*

1 Park the vehicle on a level surface, apply the handbrake and chock the rear wheels. Remove the wheel centre caps, and slacken the wheel bolts.

2 Apply the handbrake, then raise the front of the vehicle, rest it securely on axle stands and remove the roadwheels; refer to *"Jacking, towing and wheel changing"* for guidance.

3 Refer to Chapter 1, and drain the fluid from the transmission. Refit the drain plug and tighten it securely.

4 Referring to Chapter 5A, disconnect both battery cables and then remove the battery.

5 Unbolt the battery tray from the side of the engine bay, unplugging the ABS ECU connector where applicable. Remove the

positive supply distribution block, but do not disconnect the supply cables from it.

Pre-1994 models

6 Working from Chapter 4A, remove the fuel filter from the bulkhead, then remove the air cleaner.

7 Disconnect and plug the hoses from the washer fluid reservoir, then remove the retaining screws and remove the reservoir from the engine bay.

8 Unplug the cable connector, then remove the airflow meter, referring to Chapter 4A for guidance.

 Caution: The airflow meter is a delicate component, handle it with great care.

9 Unplug the LT connections from the distributor (where applicable), referring to Chapter 5B for guidance.

10 With reference to Chapter 8, remove the clip, and slide the intermediate driveshaft dust cover away from the differential housing.

Post-1994 models

11 With reference to Chapter 4A, disconnect the throttle cable from the guide bracket on the inlet manifold. Tie the cable back against the bulkhead, away from the work area.

All models

12 Where applicable, unplug the wiring connector from the air temperature sensor at the turbocharger delivery hose. Slacken the hose clips and remove the bypass valve, then disconnect the delivery hose from the turbocharger and the throttle body.

13 Unplug the wiring harness from the reversing light/starter inhibitor switch at the transmission.

14 Working from Chapter 7A, disconnect the speedometer drive cable/transducer wiring connector, as applicable.

15 Remove the electrical earth strap from the transmission casing.

16 Mark the position of the locknuts, then disconnect the kickdown cable from the bracket at the throttle body.

17 Unbolt the selector cable from the selector lever at the transmission - do not split the balljoint.

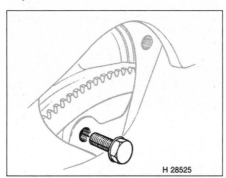

8.25 The torque converter-to-flywheel bolts (one shown) are accessible through the starter motor aperture

18 Slacken the union, and disconnect the fluid cooler inlet hose from the transmission.

19 Slacken and remove the locknut, and free the selector cable outer from the transmission casing.

20 Unbolt the union, and disconnect the fluid cooler return hose from the front of the transmission. Be prepared for an amount of fluid leakage; position a container underneath the joint to catch the spillage.

21 Unbolt the clamp that secures the turbocharger oil supply pipe to the transmission casing.

22 Working under the front bumper/valance, remove the plastic undertray and brake cooling ducts, referring to Chapter 11 for guidance.

23 With reference to Chapter 5A, remove the starter motor from the engine block, unbolting the inlet manifold stay bar at the same time.

24 Remove the liner from the left-hand inner wheelarch, again referring to Chapter 11.

25 Remove the bolts that secure the torque converter to the flywheel - these are accessible through the starter motor aperture. As each bolt is removed, rotate the crankshaft by means of a spanner at the crankshaft sprocket, to bring the next bolt into line **(see illustration)**.

26 To prevent the torque converter from falling off as the transmission is removed, insert a length of metal bar into the slot at the top of the torque converter casing, and secure it in position using a pair of self-locking pliers **(see illustration)**.

27 Refer to Chapter 10, and remove the pinch-bolt that secures the balljoint at the suspension lower arm to the base of the left hand steering swivel member.

28 Still working from Chapter 10, unbolt the front anti-roll bar from the left-hand clamp bracket on the subframe, then unbolt the left-hand anti-roll bar link from the suspension lower arm.

29 Remove the nut and washers from the bolt that secures the inner wing stay bar to the subframe.

30 Referring to the relevant Sections of

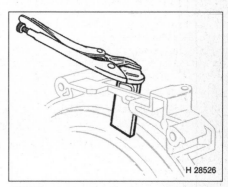

8.26 To prevent the torque converter from falling off as the transmission is removed, insert a length of metal bar into the slot at the top of the torque converter casing, and secure it in position using a pair of self-locking pliers

Chapter 2B, release the transmission from the mounting at the subframe by slackening and withdrawing the through-bolt; recover the dished washer, noting its orientation.

31 Position a lifting beam across the engine bay, locating the support legs securely in the sills at either side, in line with the strut top mountings. Hook the jib onto the engine lifting eyelet and raise it, so that the weight of the engine is taken off the transmission mounting. Most people won't have access to an engine lifting beam, but it may be possible to hire one. Alternatively, an engine hoist may be used to support the engine, but when using this method, bear in mind that if the vehicle is lowered on its axle stands to adjust the working height, for example, then the hoist will have to be lowered accordingly, to avoid straining the engine mountings.

32 To allow the transmission to be lowered out of the engine bay, the left-hand section of the front subframe must be partially unbolted and lowered; the following paragraphs describe this procedure.

33 At the front crossmember underneath the radiator, slacken the pivot link through-bolt, then remove the two link retaining bolts (refer to Chapter 7A, illustration 8.27).

34 At the front left-hand corner of the subframe, remove the two retaining bolts (refer to Chapter 7A, illustration 8.27).

35 Slacken the through-bolt at the pivot link in the rear crossmember, below the steering rack, then remove the two retaining bolts; one of these bolts also retains the steering rack. Note the orientation and order of assembly of all washers removed (refer to Chapter 7A, illustration 8.27).

36 At the rear left-hand corner of the subframe, remove the four retaining bolts that pass through the mounting bracket for the suspension lower arm rear bearing. Recover the bearing plate beneath the mounting bracket, noting its orientation (refer to Chap-

ter 7A, illustration 8.27). As the lower arm bearing is released, tie the rear of the suspension arm to the vacated bolt hole in the subframe, using a cable-tie - this will prevent the front bearing from being strained.

37 Support the subframe as the last retaining bolt is removed, and allow it to pivot downwards to the end of its travel. Withdraw the front and rear pivot bolts, and remove the left-hand side of the subframe from the vehicle.

38 With reference to Chapter 8, separate the left-hand driveshaft from the transmission, at the inboard universal joint.

39 Work around the circumference of the transmission-to-engine mating surface, and remove all but the uppermost retaining bolt.

40 Position a jack underneath the transmission, and raise it to take the weight of the unit. Check that nothing remains connected to the transmission before attempting to separate it from the engine.

41 Remove the last retaining bolt from the mating surface, and pull the transmission away from the engine. This involves simultaneously pulling the transmission away from the engine block locating dowels, whilst disconnecting the intermediate driveshaft from the differential - a task which should only be attempted with the help of an assistant. If difficulty is experienced at this stage, refer to Chapter 8 and remove the intermediate driveshaft and bearing bracket from the engine as an assembly, before progressing any further.

 Warning: Maintain firm support of the transmission, to ensure that it remains steady on the jack head.

42 When all the locating dowels are clear of their mounting holes, lower the transmission out of the engine bay using the jack.

Refitting

43 Refit the transmission by following the

removal procedure in reverse, noting the following points:

a) When refitting the torque converter-to-flywheel bolts, coat the threads with thread-locking compound, and then tighten them to the specified torque.

b) When securing the transmission at its mounting on the subframe, ensure that the dished washer is fitted the correct way around - convex side facing outwards, with the tang seated in the slot at the top of the mounting bracket.

c) Observe the specified torque wrench settings (where applicable) when tightening all nuts and bolts after refitting.

d) Adjust the selector and kickdown cables, as described in Sections 3 and 4 of this Chapter.

e) On completion, refill the transmission with the specified type and quantity of fluid, as described in Chapter 1.

9 Automatic transmission overhaul -general information

In the event of a fault occurring, it will be necessary to establish whether the fault is electrical, mechanical or hydraulic in nature, before repair work can be contemplated. Diagnosis requires detailed knowledge of the transmission's operation and construction, as well as access to specialised test equipment, and so is deemed to be beyond the scope of this manual. It is therefore essential that problems with the automatic transmission are referred to a Saab dealer for assessment.

Note that a faulty transmission should not be removed before the vehicle has been assessed by a dealer, as fault diagnosis is carried out with the transmission *in situ*.

Chapter 8 Driveshafts

Contents

Degrees of difficulty

Easy, suitable for novice with little experience	**Fairly easy,** suitable for beginner with some experience	**Fairly difficult,** suitable for competent DIY mechanic	**Difficult,** suitable for experienced DIY mechanic	**Very difficult,** suitable for expert DIY or professional

Specifications

General

Lubrication (overhaul or repair only) .... Use only special grease supplied in sachets with gaiter/overhaul kits; joints are otherwise pre-packed with grease and sealed

Torque wrench settings

	Nm	lbf ft
Driveshaft nut	280	207
Intermediate driveshaft bracket-to-engine bolts (post-1994 model year)	30	22
Intermediate driveshaft bracket-to-engine bolts (pre-1994 model year) .	27	20
Roadwheel bolts	115	85
Suspension strut lower mounting bolts	90	66

1 General information

Power is transmitted from the gearbox output shafts to the roadwheels by the driveshafts, via inboard plunge-type universal joints and outboard Rzeppa-type constant velocity (CV) joints.

An intermediate driveshaft, with its own support bearing, is fitted between the gearbox output and right-hand driveshafts - a layout which equalises driveshaft angles at all suspension positions, and reduces driveshaft flexing, improving directional stability under hard acceleration.

Note that the inboard joint is referred to throughout this section as a "universal joint", to distinguish it from the outboard "constant velocity joint", although technically, they are both constant velocity joints.

The CV joints allow smooth transmission of drive to the wheels at all steering and suspension angles. Drive is transmitted by means of six radially-static steel balls that run in grooves between the two halves of the joint. The joints are protected by rubber gaiters, and are packed with grease, to provide permanent lubrication. In the event of wear being detected, the joint can be removed from the driveshaft, but must be renewed with the hub, bearings and outboard driveshaft as a matched assembly. Normally, the CV joints do not require additional lubrication, unless they have been renovated or the rubber gaiters have been damaged, allowing the grease to become contaminated. Refer to Chapter 1 for guidance in checking the condition of the driveshaft gaiters.

The inboard universal joints are of the plunge-cup type; drive is transmitted across the joint by means of three rollers, mounted on the driveshaft in a tripod arrangement; they are radially-static, but are free to slide in grooves. This arrangement permits lateral movement of the driveshaft, which in turn allows the effective length of the driveshaft to alter with suspension travel, without the need for spline joints along the driveshaft itself. As with the CV joints, the universal joints are permanently lubricated by grease, packed into the gaiters, which only requires replenishment in the event of joint renewal or gaiter damage.

To check for driveshaft wear, road test the vehicle, driving it slowly in a circle on full steering lock (carry out the test on both left and right lock), while listening for a metallic clicking sound coming from the area behind the front wheels. An assistant in the passenger seat can listen for the clicking sound from the nearside joint. If such a sound is heard, this indicates wear in the outer constant velocity joint. If vibration proportional to road speed is felt through the car when accelerating or on over-run, there is a possibility of wear in the inner universal joints.

To check the joints for wear, remove and dismantle the driveshafts as described in Sections 2 and 3. The CV joints may be renewed, but note that the outer CV joints must be renewed as a complete assembly with the outboard driveshaft. Refer to a Saab dealer for information on the availability of driveshaft components.

2.9 Grasp the driveshaft with one hand, and tilt the steering swivel member away from the vehicle; the driveshaft can now be pulled out of the inboard universal joint, with the gaiter still attached

2 Driveshafts - removal, inspection and refitting

Removal

1 Park the vehicle on a level surface, apply the handbrake and chock the rear wheels. Disconnect the battery negative cable, and position it away from the terminal.

2 At the applicable roadwheel, remove the wheel trim (or wheel centre cap for vehicles fitted with alloy wheels). Slacken the driveshaft

2.13a Use a pair of circlip pliers to expand the circlip that holds the driveshaft in place . . .

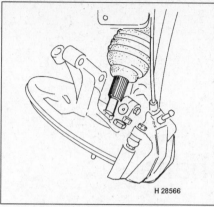

H 28566

2.10 Pull the splined section of the driveshaft out of the hub

nut, bearing in mind the high torque to which this nut is tightened - select a sturdy wrench and close-fitting socket to remove it.

3 Loosen the roadwheel bolts, then raise the front of the vehicle, rest it securely on axle stands and remove the roadwheel; refer to "*Jacking, towing and wheel changing* for guidance.

4 Remove the screws and drop the liner away from the inner wing; refer to Chapter 11 for further information.

5 Release the clips from the inboard driveshaft gaiter by snipping through the crimped section using a stout pair of cutters - note that the clips cannot be refitted once they have been removed; new items must be used on refitting.

6 Slide the rubber gaiter along the driveshaft, away from the inboard universal joint; be prepared for the loss of some lubricant as you do this - the viscosity of driveshaft joint grease reduces to that of gear oil after it has been in use for some time. Position some rags underneath the joint to catch any spillage.

7 Referring to Chapter 10 for guidance, unbolt the strut from its lower mounting bracket at the hub assembly. Extract the flexible brake hose from the clip on the strut body. Note that on models with ABS, the wheel sensor cable is clipped into a bracket that shares a mounting bolt with the suspension strut.

8 Remove the hub centre nut and thrustwasher. Note that on later models, the nut and washer are replaced by a single flange nut. In both cases, the nuts and washers must be discarded and renewed once disturbed.

9 Grasp the driveshaft with one hand, and tilt the steering swivel member away from the vehicle; the driveshaft can now be pulled out of the inboard universal joint, with the gaiter still attached **(see illustration)**. Again, be prepared for some lubricant loss.

10 Pull the splined section of the driveshaft out of the hub **(see illustration)**.

> **HAYNES HiNT** *The driveshaft may be difficult to extract, due to the locking compound applied to the spines. If this is the case, refit the old driveshaft nut to protect the threads, then tap the end of the driveshaft with a soft-faced mallet, to drive it out through the hub. Alternatively, a suitable three-legged puller may be used.*

11 Loosely refit one of the strut lower mounting bolts, to support the steering swivel member whilst the driveshaft is out of the vehicle. Cover the open universal joint cup on the vehicle, to prevent the ingress of dirt; use a plastic bag secured with elastic bands.

Inspection

12 Remove the remainder of the clips that secure the second rubber gaiter to the driveshaft. Slide the gaiters along the shaft, away from the joints. Wipe off the majority of the old grease with a rag.

13 At the CV joint, use a scribe or a dab of paint to mark the relationship between the joint and the driveshaft. Then, using pair of circlip pliers, expand the circlip that holds the driveshaft in place, and withdraw the shaft from the CV joint. Note that the circlip is captive in the joint, and need not be removed, unless it appears damaged or worn **(see illustrations)**.

14 At the inboard end of the driveshaft, use a hammer and centre-punch to mark the

2.13b . . . then withdraw the shaft from the CV joint

2.13c The circlip (arrowed) is captive in the joint and need not be removed, unless it appears damaged or worn

2.14a At the inboard end of the driveshaft, use a pair of circlip pliers to remove the circlip (arrowed) . . .

2.14b . . . then use a three-legged puller to draw the tripod joint off the end of the driveshaft

2.21 Fit a new rubber gaiter to the outboard end of the driveshaft, and secure it place with a clip

2.22 Pack the CV joint with grease from the service kit

relationship between the shaft and joint. Remove the circlip with a pair of circlip pliers, then using a three-legged puller, draw the tripod joint off the end of the driveshaft. Ensure that the legs of the puller bear upon the cast centre section of the joint, not the roller bearings **(see illustrations)**.

15 Slide both rubber gaiters off the driveshaft and discard them; it is recommended that new ones are fitted on reassembly as a a matter of course. Thoroughly clean the driveshaft splines, CV joint and tripod joint components with paraffin or a suitable solvent, taking care not to obliterate the alignment marks made during removal.

16 Examine the CV joint components for wear and damage; in particular, check the balls and corresponding grooves for pitting and corrosion. If evidence of wear is visible, then the joint must be renewed. Note that the CV joint, balls and outboard driveshaft must be renewed as a matched set.

17 Examine the tripod joint components for wear. Check that the three rollers are free to rotate without resistance, and that they are not worn, damaged or corroded. The rollers are supported by arrays of needle bearings; wear or damage will be manifested as axial play in the rollers, and/or roughness in rotation. If any such wear is discovered, the tripod joint must be renewed.

18 Fit a new rubber gaiter to the inboard end of the driveshaft, and secure it in place on the shaft with a clip.

19 Using the alignment marks made during removal, fit the tripod joint onto the splines of the driveshaft. Tap it into position using a soft-faced mallet - to ensure that the tripod joint rollers and driveshaft splines are not damaged, use a socket with an internal diameter slightly larger than that of the driveshaft as a drift. Refit the circlip.

20 Slide the gaiter over the tripod joint, and pack the gaiter with grease from the service kit.

> ⚠ *Caution: Do not allow grease to come into contact with the paintwork, as discolouring may result.*

21 Fit a new rubber gaiter to the outboard end of the driveshaft, and secure it place with a clip **(see illustration)**.

22 Pack the CV joint with grease from the service kit, pushing it into the ball grooves, and expelling any air that may be trapped underneath **(see illustration)**.

23 Lubricate the splines of the driveshaft with a smear of grease, then whilst splaying the retaining circlip open with a pair of circlip pliers, insert it into CV joint, observing the alignment marks made during removal. Ensure that the circlip snaps into the groove in the driveshaft; pull on the shaft to check that it is held securely in position.

24 Pack additional grease into the joint to displace any air pockets, then slide the rubber gaiter over the joint. Briefly lift the lip of the

gaiter to expel all the air from the joint, then secure it in place with a clip **(see illustrations)**.

Refitting

25 Ensure that the splines at the outboard end of the driveshaft are clean, then apply a suitable locking compound (eg Loctite 641) to the outer 10 mm of the splines.

26 After removing the temporarily-fitted bolt from the strut mounting, pivot the steering swivel member away from the vehicle, and push the splined end of the driveshaft into the hub.

27 Fit a new driveshaft thrustwasher and nut (or flange nut, as applicable), but do not fully tighten them at this point.

28 Align the suspension strut lower mounting with the bracket on the steering swivel member, and refit the two bolts, tightening them to the correct torque. On models with ABS, remember to fit the uppermost strut mounting bolt through the wheel sensor cable bracket. Press the flexible brake hose and grommet into the clip on the strut body.

29 Support the shaft with one hand, and push the steering swivel member back towards the vehicle, re-engaging the tripod in the universal joint. Slide the gaiter into position over the joint, and briefly lift the lip of the gaiter to expel any air trapped inside. Ensure that the gaiter is seated squarely over the universal joint, then fit a new clip around the centre of the joint to secure it in place.

2.24a Pack additional grease into the joint to displace any air pockets . . .

2.24b . . . then slide the rubber gaiter over the joint . . .

2.24c . . . securing it in place with a clip

30 Refit the inner wing liner, then the roadwheel and bolts.
31 Lower the vehicle to the ground, and tighten the driveshaft nut to the specified torque.
32 Tighten the roadwheel bolts to the specified torque, and refit the wheel trim/centre cap, as applicable.
33 Note: *The vehicle must not be brought back into service for at least one hour, to allow time for the driveshaft locking compound to harden.*

3 Driveshaft rubber gaiters - renewal

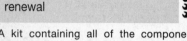

1 A kit containing all of the components needed when renewing the driveshaft gaiters can be obtained from Saab dealers.
2 Refer to Section 2 and remove the applicable driveshaft.
3 Referring to the *Inspection* sub-section of Section 2, remove the circlip and tripod joint from the inboard end of the driveshaft.
4 Remove the remaining clip from the inboard gaiter, and slide it off the driveshaft. Remove both clips from the outboard gaiter, then slide it along the length of the driveshaft, and remove it from the inboard end.
5 Thoroughly clean the driveshaft and joint components, using paraffin or a suitable solvent. If the gaiters are being renewed due to wear or damage, assume that the CV and universal joints need re-packing with grease as a matter of course.
6 Take the opportunity to examine the CV and universal joints for early signs of wear; refer to Section 2 for guidance.
7 Fit the first rubber gaiter over the inboard end of the driveshaft. Slide it along the shaft to the CV joint, taking care not to damage the sealing surface. Pack the CV joint with grease of the correct grade, from the service kit.

 Caution: Do not allow grease to come into contact with the paintwork, or discolouring may result.

8 Secure the gaiter over the CV joint and the driveshaft with clips.
9 Fit the second gaiter to the inboard end of the driveshaft, and secure it in place with a clip.
10 Slide the tripod joint onto the splines of the driveshaft, and refit the circlip. Pack the gaiter with grease from the service kit.
11 Support the driveshaft with one hand, and pivot the steering swivel member towards the vehicle. Guide the tripod joint into the universal joint cup, ensuring that the rollers can slide freely in their grooves. Seat the gaiter squarely over the universal joint, then secure it in place with a clip.
12 Refit the suspension strut to the steering swivel member, and tighten the bolts to the specified torque; refer to Chapter 10 for details. On vehicles with ABS, remember to fit

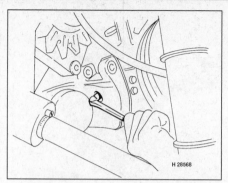

4.7a Remove the four bolts, and free the bearing bracket from the engine block

the wheel sensor cable bracket onto the lower strut mounting bolt.
13 Press the brake hose into the clip on the strut body.
14 Fit the inner wing liner in position, and tighten the retaining screws.
15 Refit the roadwheel and bolts, then lower the vehicle to the ground.
16 Tighten the roadwheel bolts to the correct torque, and refit the wheel trim / centre cap, as applicable.

4 Intermediate driveshaft and support bearing assembly - removal and refitting

Removal

Pre-1994 model year vehicles

1 Disconnect the battery negative cable, and position it away from the terminal.
2 With the vehicle parked on a level surface, apply the handbrake and chock the rear wheels. Slacken the right-hand roadwheel bolts, then rest the front of the vehicle, rest it securely on axle stands and remove the roadwheel; refer to *"Jacking, towing and wheel changing"* for guidance.
3 Referring to Chapter 10 and the relevant paragraphs of Section 2 for guidance, unbolt the strut lower mountings, then pivot the steering swivel member away from the vehicle, to separate the right-hand driveshaft from the intermediate driveshaft at the inner universal joint. The outboard end of the right-hand driveshaft need not be removed from the wheel hub; use a length of wire or cable-ties to support the inboard end - this will keep it away from the working area, and also prevent the CV joint from being strained. Cover the separated halves of the universal joint with plastic bags, to prevent the ingress of dirt.
4 Refer to Chapter 1 and slacken the auxiliary drivebelt.
5 Remove the lower alternator mounting bolt, then slacken the upper mounting bolt, and pivot the alternator away from the engine. Retighten the upper mounting bolt to hold the alternator in position.
6 Remove the clip from the dust cover on the

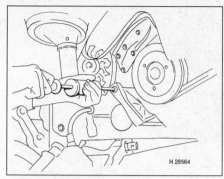

4.7b Using a suitable adapter, attach a slide hammer to the bearing bracket at the alternator mounting hole, and tap the entire bearing/driveshaft assembly off the gearbox output shaft splines

intermediate driveshaft, at the differential housing.
7 Remove the four bolts, and free the bearing bracket from the engine block. Using a suitable adapter, attach a slide hammer to the bearing bracket at the alternator mounting hole, and tap the entire bearing/driveshaft assembly off the gearbox output shaft splines **(see illustrations)**. Alternatively, a soft-faced mallet may be used - tap on the rear of the bearing bracket to draw the driveshaft off. Avoid using excessive force, as the bearing may be damaged.
8 Support the driveshaft as it nears release, to prevent it from dropping onto the floor. Note the position of the O-ring seal on the gearbox output shaft; recover and discard it, as a new one must be fitted on reassembly.

Post-1994 model year vehicles

9 Disconnect the battery negative cable, and position it away from the terminal.
10 To avoid damage when the engine is raised, it is recommended that the following procedures are carried out:
a) Disconnect the exhaust front pipe from the manifold, referring to Chapter 4A for guidance.
b) Remove the crankcase ventilation hose from the clips on the camshaft cover.
c) Remove the engine torque arm bracket; refer to Chapter 2A for more details.
11 With the vehicle parked on a level surface, apply the handbrake and chock the rear wheels. Slacken the right-hand roadwheel bolts, then raise the front of the vehicle, rest it securely on axle stands and remove the roadwheel; refer to *"Jacking, towing and wheel changing"* for guidance.
12 Refer to Chapter 11 and remove the front section of the inner wheel arch liner.
13 Working at the right-hand side of the vehicle (and referring to Chapter 10 and the relevant paragraphs of Section 2), unbolt the lower strut mountings, then pivot the steering swivel member away from the vehicle, to separate the right-hand driveshaft from the intermediate driveshaft at the inner universal joint.

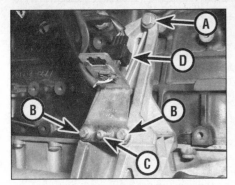

4.20 Intermediate driveshaft bearing bracket (post-1994 model year vehicles)

A Upper mounting bolt
B Lower mounting bolts
C Screw for power steering hose clip
D Oxygen sensor harness connector

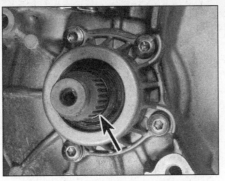

4.25 Note the position of the O-ring seal (arrowed) on the gearbox output shaft

4.45 Fit the intermediate shaft over the gearbox output shaft splines, by rotating the two shafts against each other until they are felt to engage

14 The outboard end of the right-hand driveshaft need not be removed from the wheel hub; use a length of wire or cable-ties to support the inboard end - this will keep it away from the working area, and prevent the CV joint from being strained.

15 Cover the separated halves of the universal joint with plastic bags, secured with elastic bands, to prevent the ingress of dirt.

16 Remove the single bolt that secures the intermediate bearing bracket to the mounting on the subframe.

17 Unbolt the engine earth cable from the connection on the cylinder head. Unbolt the engine lifting eye from the opposite end of the cylinder head. Transfer it to the earth cable mounting hole, and bolt it in position.

18 Fit a lifting beam transversely across the engine bay, ensuring that the legs rest securely in the sills on the inner wings.

19 Engage the jib hook with the engine lifting eye, and raise the engine and gearbox just enough to separate the intermediate bearing bracket from the mounting on the subframe.
Note: *If a lifting beam is not available, an engine hoist can be used instead. However, take care when the engine is raised, as a floor-standing hoist will tend to pull the engine towards the front of the vehicle.*

20 Remove the screw from the clamp that retains the power steering hydraulic fluid pipe at the bearing bracket **(see illustration)**.

21 Remove the two lower bolts that secure the intermediate bearing bracket to the engine block (refer to illustration 4.20). Note that these bolts also retain a mounting bracket for the oxygen sensor connector.

22 Remove the upper retaining bolt (refer to illustration 4.20), and draw the support bearing bracket off its guide pins and away from the engine. If the bracket sticks on the guide pins, carefully prise it off.

23 When the bracket is free, pull the intermediate driveshaft off the splined gearbox output shaft. If the shaft sticks, tap the bearing bracket from behind with a soft-faced mallet

to free it - do not use excessive force, as this may damage the bearing.

24 The driveshaft is sleeved with an aluminium pipe that has rubber seals at each end; it can be removed by simply twisting and pulling it away from the bearing bracket.

25 Note the position of the O-ring seal on the gearbox output shaft **(see illustration)**; recover and discard it, as a new one must be fitted on reassembly.

26 Lower the driveshaft and intermediate bearing bracket assembly away from the vehicle.

Inspection

All models

27 Clean all traces of old grease from the universal joint cup, using paraffin or a suitable solvent.

28 Examine the roller grooves in the cup for signs of wear, in the form of scuffing or scoring. If evidence of wear is found, the cup must be renewed.

29 Examine the intermediate bearing assembly for wear - excessive axial or radial play, or any roughness in rotation, indicates that it is in need of renewal. The assembly can be dismantled into its basic components, which can then be renewed individually. However, this procedure requires access to a bench-mounted hydraulic press, and is therefore deemed to be beyond the scope of this manual. Hence, it is recommended that the intermediate bearing be renewed as complete assembly.

Refitting

Pre-1994 model year vehicles

30 Ensure that the universal joint cup is completely clean, then pack it with suitable grease.

31 At the differential housing, fit a new O-ring seal on the gearbox output shaft in the same position as the original seal, and check that the dust cover is correctly seated.

32 Before refitting the intermediate bearing bracket, insert the inner lower mounting bolt into its hole, as access to it is difficult once the bracket is in place on the engine block.

33 Check that the bracket locating dowels

have not been damaged, and are still correctly aligned.

34 Lubricate the gearbox output shaft splines with a smear of molybdenum-based grease. Align the intermediate driveshaft with the end of the output shaft by twisting the two against each other, until the splines are felt to engage. Tap the edge of the bearing bracket with a soft-faced mallet, to drive the intermediate shaft over the output shaft.

35 Align the bearing bracket with its mounting holes on the engine block. Insert the remaining bolts, but only hand-tighten them at this stage.

36 Slacken the upper mounting bolt, and pivot the alternator back towards the engine. Fit the alternator lower mounting bolt through the bearing bracket.

37 Tighten the bearing bracket bolts to the correct torque, then tighten both alternator mounting bolts.

38 Fit a new clip onto the driveshaft dust cover, at the differential housing.

39 Re-engage the right-hand driveshaft with the intermediate driveshaft, and refit the suspension strut mounting bolts, referring to Section 2 and Chapter 10 for details.

40 Refer to Chapter 1 and check the tension of the auxiliary drivebelt, adjusting it as necessary.

41 Reconnect the battery negative cable.

Post-1994 model year vehicles

42 Ensure that the universal joint cup is completely clean, then pack it with suitable grease.

43 Slide the aluminium sleeve over the driveshaft, and seat it securely in the intermediate bearing bracket.

44 At the differential housing, fit a new O-ring seal on the gearbox output shaft, in the same position as the original seal.

45 Offer up the shaft and support bearing assembly to the engine block. Fit the intermediate shaft over the gearbox output shaft splines, by rotating the two shafts against each other until they are felt to engage **(see illustration)**. Push the shaft on as far as possible by hand, then tap the bearing bracket with a soft-faced mallet to push the shaft through the remainder of its travel. This will

4.49 Insert the bolt that secures the bearing bracket to the mounting on the subframe

also allow the bearing bracket to align it with its guide pins and mounting holes.

46 Refit the bearing bracket upper mounting bolt.

47 Refit the two bearing bracket lower mounting bolts, ensuring that the oxygen sensor connector bracket is correctly refitted. Fit the screw that secures the power steering hydraulic hose clamp.

48 Re-engage the right-hand driveshaft with intermediate driveshaft universal joint, referring to Section 2 for guidance. Ensure that the rubber gaiter fits squarely over the joint, then fit a new clip to secure it in place. Refer to Chapter 10 and refit the suspension strut lower mounting bolts. On vehicles fitted with ABS, remember to fit the wheel sensor cable bracket to the suspension strut lower mounting bolt.

49 Insert the bolt that secures the bearing bracket to the mounting on the subframe, and tighten it to the specified torque **(see illustration)**.

50 Refit the inner wing liner and tighten the retaining screws; refer to Chapter 11 for details.

51 Refit the roadwheel, and hand-tighten the bolts. Lower the vehicle to the ground, and tighten the wheel bolts to the specified torque.

52 Lower the lifting beam jib hook, then unbolt the engine lifting eye and move it back to its original position at the opposite end of the cylinder head, bolting it in place. Bolt the engine earth cable to the vacated mounting hole.

53 Refit the engine torque arm bracket, referring to Chapter 2A for guidance.

54 Fit the crankcase ventilation hose into the clips on the camshaft cover.

55 Refer to Chapter 4A and reconnect the exhaust front pipe.

56 Reconnect the battery negative cable.

Chapter 9 Braking system

Contents

Degrees of difficulty

Easy, suitable for novice with little experience	**Fairly easy,** suitable for beginner with some experience	**Fairly difficult,** suitable for competent DIY mechanic	**Difficult,** suitable for experienced DIY mechanic	**Very difficult,** suitable for expert DIY or professional

Specifications

General

Brake system type and layout::

Footbrake . . . . Diagonally-split dual hydraulic circuits; front right/rear left primary) and front left/rear right (secondary). Outboard discs fitted front and rear, ventilated at the front. Single-piston,sliding calipers fitted front and rear. Anti-lock Braking System ABS) fitted as an option on certain models, with individual circuits for front wheels and single circuit for both rear wheels. Non-ABS models vacuum servo-assisted, ABS models hydraulic servo-assisted. Traction control system fitted as option on certain models, integrated with ABS

Handbrake . . . . Dual-cable, lever-operated, acting on rear discs

Front brakes

Turbo models to 1987, and non-Turbo models to 1989:

Discs:

Type	Ventilated
Outside diameter	278 mm
Thickness (new disc)	23.5 ± 0.2 mm
Minimum thickness after grinding	21.5 mm
Maximum grinding depth (each side)	1.0 mm
Maximum runout	0.08 mm (with disc fitted)
Maximum variation in disc thickness	0.015 mm

Calipers:

Make	Girling
Type	Colette 54
Piston diameter	54 mm

Pads:

Friction material thickness:

New	16.7 mm
Minimum	4.0 mm

Front brakes (continued)

Turbo models from 1987, and non-Turbo models from 1989:

Discs:

Type	Ventilated
Outside diameter	278 mm
Thickness (new disc)	25.0 ± 0.2 mm
Minimum thickness after grinding	23.5 mm
Maximum grinding depth (each side)	1.0 mm
Maximum runout	0.08 mm (with disc fitted)
Maximum variation in disc thickness	0.015 mm

Calipers:

Make	ATE
Type	FN 57
Piston diameter	57 mm

Pads:

Friction material thickness:

New	19.5 mm
Minimum	4.0 mm

Rear brakes (all models)

Discs:

Type	Solid
Outside diameter	258 mm
Thickness (new disc)	9.0 ± 0.1 mm
Minimum thickness after grinding	7.5 mm
Maximum grinding depth (each side)	0.7 mm
Maximum runout	0.08 mm (with disc fitted)
Maximum variation in disc thickness	0.015 mm

Calipers:

Make	ATE
Piston diameter	33 mm

Pads:

Friction material thickness:

New	11.0 mm
Minimum	4.0 mm
Handbrake actuator lever-to-end stop clearance	1.0 ± 0.5 mm

Brake servo unit (non-ABS models)

Make/type	Girling, vacuum-assisted
Diameter	203 mm

Master cylinder (non-ABS models)

Make/type	Girling, tandem cylinder
Diameter	22.2 mm

ABS components (1987 to 1990 models only)

Hydraulic unit:

Make	ATE
Operating pressure, brake circuits	0 to 180 bars

Brake fluid reservoir:

Fluid level indicator resistance	10 ohms (reservoir empty)
ABS warning switch resistance	1 ohm (reservoir full)

Solenoid valves:

Electrical resistance	5 to 7 ohms

Wheel sensors:

Resistance	800 to 1400 ohms
Sensor-to-toothed disc clearance	0.65 mm

Torque wrench settings

	Nm	lbf ft
ABS accumulator retaining bolt	40	30
ABS hydraulic unit-to-bulkhead bolts	26	19
ABS pressure switch	23	17
ABS pump delivery hose unions	20	15
Front caliper carrier retaining bolts	90	66
Rear caliper carrier retaining bolts	80	59
Roadwheel bolts	115	85
Vacuum servo unit-to-bulkhead bolts	26	19

1 General information

Models with conventional braking system

Braking is achieved by a dual-circuit hydraulic system, assisted by a vacuum servo unit. All models have outboard discs fitted at the front and rear. The front discs are ventilated, to improve cooling and reduce brake fade.

The dual hydraulic circuits are diagonally-split; one circuit operates the front right and rear left brakes, the other operates the front left and rear right brakes. This design ensures that at least 50% of the vehicle's braking capacity will be available, should pressure be lost in one of the hydraulic circuits. Under these circumstances, the diagonal layout should prevent the vehicle from becoming unstable if the brakes are applied when only one circuit is operational.

The brake calipers are of the floating single-piston type - a design which occupies minimal space, and also lessens the amount of heat transferred to the brake fluid, reducing brake fade. Each caliper houses two asbestos-free brake pads, one inboard and one outboard of the disc. During braking, hydraulic pressure supplied to the caliper forces the piston along its cylinder, and presses the inboard brake pad against the disc. The caliper body reacts to this effort by sliding along its guide pins, bringing the outboard pad into contact with the disc. In this manner, equal pressure is applied to either side of the disc by the brake pads. When braking is ceased, the hydraulic pressure behind the piston drops and the piston is retracted back into the cylinder, releasing the inboard pad from the disc. The caliper body then slides back along its guide pins, and releases the outboard pad. Note that the rear caliper cylinders are smaller in diameter than those in the front caliper; the resulting difference in braking power between front and rear calipers prevents rear wheel lock-up during hard braking, eliminating the need for pressure-regulating valves. In addition, the rear calipers house a lever-and-return spring arrangement that allows them to be actuated mechanically by the handbrake.

The master cylinder converts footbrake pedal effort into hydraulic pressure. Its tandem construction incorporates two cylinders, one for each circuit, which operate in parallel. Each cylinder houses a piston and a corresponding return spring. The movement of the pistons along the cylinders causes brake fluid to flow through the brake lines in each circuit, and transfers pressure from the brake pedal to the caliper pistons. The two (master cylinder) pistons are partially-linked, an arrangement which allows equal pressure to be applied to all four calipers under normal operation, and also allows full pedal effort to be transferred to the working circuit in the event of the other

circuit failing, albeit with increased pedal travel.

A constant supply of brake fluid to the master cylinder is maintained by the brake fluid reservoir. It is divided in to three separate chambers; one for each brake circuit, and on manual transmission vehicles, one for the clutch circuit. This construction ensures that a supply of fluid for at least one of the brake circuits is retained in the reservoir, even if the other circuit loses all its fluid through leakage. A consequence of this feature is that the reservoir cannot be drained completely. The reservoir is semi-transparent, to allow visual inspection of the fluid level, and a screw-fit cap allows the level to be topped-up. A level detection switch is incorporated into the filler cap; this causes a light to illuminate on the dashboard when the level of fluid in the reservoir becomes too low.

The vacuum servo unit uses engine manifold vacuum to amplify the effort applied to the master cylinder by the brake pedal.

Models with anti-lock braking system (ABS)

Available as an option on certain models, the anti-lock braking system prevents wheel lock-up (skidding) under heavy braking, which not only optimises stopping distances (under most conditions), but also allows full steering control to be maintained under maximum braking.

By electronically monitoring the speed of each roadwheel in relation to the other wheels, the system can detect when a wheel is about to lock-up, before control is actually lost. The brake fluid pressure applied to that wheel's brake caliper is then decreased and restored ("modulated") several times a second until control is regained. The system is split into three circuits, giving control over each front wheel individually, and both rear wheels together.

The system components comprise an Electronic Control Unit (ECU), four wheel speed sensors, a hydraulic unit, brake lines, a dedicated relay/fuse box and dashboard-mounted warning lights.

The hydraulic unit incorporates the following components:

a) A tandem master cylinder, which operates the two front brake calipers under normal braking.

b) A valve block, which modulates the pressure in the three brake circuits during ABS operation.

c) An accumulator, which provides a supply of highly-pressurised brake fluid.

d) A hydraulic pump to charge the accumulator.

e) A servo cylinder, which regulates the pressurised fluid supply from the accumulator, to provide hydraulic power assistance (replacing the vacuum servo unit used in conventional braking systems) as well as pressure to operate the rear brakes.

f) A fluid reservoir.

The four wheel sensors are mounted on the wheel hubs. Each wheel has a rotating toothed disc mounted in the hub; the wheel speed sensors are mounted in close proximity to these discs. The teeth on the surface of the discs excite the sensors, causing them to produce a voltage waveform whose frequency varies with the speed of the discs' rotation. These waveforms are transmitted to the ECU, which uses them to calculate the rotational speed of each wheel.

The fuse/relay box is mounted in the engine bay, close to the ABS ECU. Inside are fuses for the ECU, as well as the main system relay, and a relay for the hydraulic pump.

The ECU has a self-diagnostic facility, and will inhibit the operation of the ABS if a fault is detected, lighting the dashboard-mounted warning light. The braking system will then revert to conventional, non-ABS operation. If the nature of the fault is not immediately obvious upon inspection, the vehicle *must* be taken to a Saab dealer, who will have the diagnostic equipment required to interrogate the ABS ECU electronically and pin-point the problem; refer to Section 19.

2 Hydraulic system - bleeding

 Warning: Hydraulic fluid is poisonous; thoroughly wash off spills from bare skin without delay. Seek immediate medical advice if any fluid is swallowed or gets into the eyes. Certain types of hydraulic fluid are inflammable, and may ignite when brought into contact with hot components. When servicing any hydraulic system, it is safest to assume that the fluid IS inflammable, and to take precautions against the risk of fire as though it is petrol that is being handled. It is hygroscopic (it can absorb moisture from the air); excess moisture content lowers the fluid boiling point to an unacceptable level, resulting in a dangerous loss of braking effectiveness. Old fluid may have suffered contamination, and should never be re-used. When topping-up or renewing the fluid, always use the recommended grade, and ensure that it comes from a freshly-opened sealed container.

> **HAYNES HiNT** *Hydraulic fluid is an effective paint stripper, and will also attack many plastics. If spillage occurs onto painted bodywork or fittings, it should be washed off immediately, using copious quantities of fresh water.*

Models with conventional braking systems

General

1 The correct operation of any hydraulic system relies on the fact that the fluid used in it is incompressible, otherwise the effort exerted at the brake pedal and master cylinder will not be fully transmitted to the brake calipers or wheel cylinders. The presence of contaminants in the system will allow the fluid to compress - this results in a "spongy" feel to the brakes, and unpredictable performance, in the form of brake fade (or at worst, brake failure). In addition, brake fluid deteriorates with age through oxidation and moisture absorption. This lowers its boiling point, and may cause vaporisation under hard braking, again affecting brake performance. For this reason, old or contaminated fluid must be renewed - this is achieved by bleeding the system.

2 When refilling the system, use only clean, new hydraulic fluid of the recommended type and grade; *never* re-use fluid that has already been bled from the system. Ensure that sufficient fluid is available before starting work.

3 If there is any possibility of there being incorrect fluid in the system already, the brake components and circuits must be flushed completely with new fluid of the correct type and grade, and new seals should be fitted throughout the system.

4 If hydraulic fluid has been lost from the system, or air has entered because of a leak, ensure that the fault is corrected before proceeding further.

5 Park the vehicle on level ground, switch off the engine, and select first or reverse gear (manual transmission) or "Park" (automatic transmission). Chock the wheels, and release the handbrake.

6 Check that all pipes and hoses are secure, unions tight, and bleed screws closed. Remove the dust caps, and clean off all dirt from around the bleed screws.

7 Unscrew the master cylinder reservoir cap, and top the master cylinder reservoir up to the "MAX" level line; refit the cap loosely, and remember to maintain the fluid level at least above the "MIN" level line throughout the procedure, otherwise there is a risk of further air entering the system, as the level drops.

8 There are a number of one-man, do-it-yourself brake bleeding kits currently available from motor accessory shops. It is recommended that one of these kits is used whenever possible, as they greatly simplify the bleeding operation, and also reduce the risk of expelled air and fluid being drawn back into the system. If such a kit is not available, the basic (two-man) method must be used, which is described in detail below.

9 If a kit is to be used, prepare the vehicle as described previously, and follow the kit manufacturer's instructions, as the procedure may vary slightly according to the type being used. Generally, they are as outlined below in the relevant sub-section.

10 It is possible to partially bleed the system (ie just one brake line and caliper at a time). This may be all that is necessary, if only one brake circuit has been opened for repair work, but it is far safer to bleed the entire system.

11 Refer to Chapter 1 for a description of the brake fluid renewal procedure.

Bleeding sequence

12 The order in which the brakes lines are dealt with is not important, as each caliper has its own connection to the master cylinder.

Bleeding - basic (two-man) method

13 Obtain a clean glass jar, a suitable length of plastic or rubber tubing which is a tight fit over the bleed screw, and a ring spanner to fit the screw. Alternatively, a proprietary brake bleeding kit can be obtained. **Note:** *The help of an assistant will also be required.*

14 Remove the dust cap from the first caliper's bleed screw. Fit the spanner over the bleed screw, and push the tube onto the bleed screw nipple **(see illustrations)**. Place the other end of the tube in the jar, and pour in sufficient fluid to cover the end of the tube.

15 Throughout the procedure, keep an eye on the reservoir fluid level, and ensure that it is maintained above the "MIN" level line as the brakes are bled; top it up before starting if necessary.

16 Have the assistant fully depress the brake pedal several times to build up pressure - then on the final downstroke, keep it depressed.

17 While pedal pressure is maintained, slacken the bleed screw (approximately one turn) and allow the brake fluid to flow into the jar. Pedal pressure should be maintained throughout; follow the pedal down to the end of its travel if necessary, but do not release it. When the flow stops, tighten the bleed screw again, then have your assistant release the pedal slowly. Re-check the reservoir fluid level, and top it up if necessary.

18 If air is present in the brake lines, it will appear as bubbles in the expelled fluid. Repeat the steps given in the two previous paragraphs, until the fluid emerging from the bleed screw is free from air bubbles. If the master cylinder has been drained and refilled, and air is being bled from the first brake line, allow approximately five seconds between cycles for the master cylinder passages to refill.

19 When no more air bubbles appear, tighten the bleed screw securely, then remove the tube and spanner and refit the dust cap.

⚠ *Caution: Do not overtighten the bleed screw.*

20 Repeat the procedure on the remaining brake lines to be bled, until all air is removed from the system and the brake pedal feels firm again.

Bleeding - using a one-way valve kit

21 As their name implies, these kits consist of a length of tubing with a one-way valve fitted, to prevent expelled air and fluid being drawn back into the system; some kits include a translucent container, which can be positioned so that the air bubbles can be more easily seen flowing from the end of the tube.

22 The kit is connected to the bleed screw, which is then opened. The user returns to the driver's seat, depresses the brake pedal with a smooth, steady stroke and slowly releases it; this process is repeated until the expelled fluid is free of air bubbles.

23 Note that the use of these kits can simplify the bleed operation so much, that it is easy to forget the reservoir fluid level. Ensure that it is maintained at least above the "MIN" level line at all times, or air may be drawn into the system.

Bleeding - using a pressure-bleeding kit

24 These kits are usually powered by the reservoir of pressurised air contained in the spare tyre. However, note that it will probably be necessary to reduce the tyre pressure to a lower level than normal; refer to the instructions supplied with the kit.

25 The method involves connecting a pressurised, fluid-filled container to the master cylinder reservoir. Bleeding can then be carried out simply by opening each bleed screw in turn, and allowing the fluid to flow out under moderate pressure until no more air bubbles can be seen in the expelled fluid.

26 This method has the advantage that the large reservoir of fluid provides an additional safeguard against air being drawn into the system during bleeding.

27 Pressure-bleeding is particularly effective

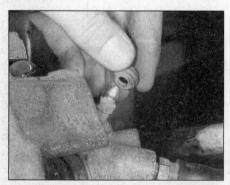

2.14a Remove the dust cap from the first caliper's bleed screw (rear left-hand caliper shown)

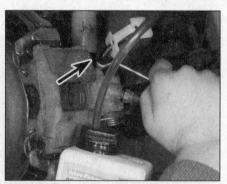

2.14b Fit the spanner over the bleed screw, and push the tube onto the bleed screw nipple

when bleeding "difficult" systems, or when bleeding the complete system at the time of routine fluid renewal.

All methods

28 When bleeding is complete, and firm pedal feel is restored, wash off any spilt fluid, tighten the bleed screws securely, and refit their dust caps (where applicable).

29 Check the hydraulic fluid level in the master cylinder reservoir; top it up if necessary.

30 Dispose of any hydraulic fluid that has been bled from the system; it cannot be re-used. *Bear in mind that brake fluid is poisonous and highly-flammable.*

31 Check the feel of the brake pedal. If it feels at all spongy, it is probable that air is still present in the system; further bleeding will therefore be required. If the bleeding procedure has been repeated several times and brake feel has still not been restored, the problem may be caused by worn master cylinder seals (this is confirmed if excessive air bubbles are seen in the fluid reservoir as the brake pedal is depressed). See Section 10 for a description of the master cylinder overhaul procedure.

Models with ABS

Note: *The front wheel brake circuits must always be bled before the rear circuit.*

Front wheel brake circuits

32 Follow one of the methods described above for non-ABS models.

Rear wheel brake circuits

33 Top-up the level of fluid in the reservoir to the "MAX" mark. Maintain the level at least above the "MIN" mark throughout the bleeding process.

34 Fit one end of a length of tubing to the rear brake caliper bleed screw, and immerse the other end of the tubing in brake fluid, contained in a clean jar.

35 Have an assistant turn the ignition switch to the second position, then depress and hold the brake pedal; this will power the hydraulic pump and pressurise the rear brake circuit.

36 Using a ring spanner, slacken the caliper bleed screw by about one turn, and allow brake fluid to flow through the tube into the jar. Ensure that pedal pressure is maintained whilst the bleed screw is open.

> ⚠ **Caution: Do not allow the hydraulic pump to run for more than two minutes at a time. After this period, switch off the ignition, and allow the pump to cool for ten minutes before restarting. Under no circumstances must the pump be allowed to run dry.**

37 Any air present in the system will be expelled as bubbles in the brake fluid. When no more bubbles can be seen escaping, tighten the bleed screw, release the brake pedal, and switch off the ignition.

38 Clean off any excess brake fluid from around the bleed screw, and refit the dust cap.

39 The above process can be repeated at the other rear wheel caliper, if necessary.

40 When the system has been bled, top-up the level of fluid in the reservoir to the "MAX" mark, and refit the cap.

---

3 Front brake pads - renewal

> ⚠ **Warning: Brake pads must be renewed as a complete set, ie BOTH left and right brake pad sets must be renewed at the same time. DO NOT renew the pads on just one roadwheel, as unbalanced braking may occur, making the car unstable. Although standard Saab brake pads do not contain asbestos, it is still wise to take safety precautions when cleaning the brake components. Do not use compressed air to blow out brake dust and debris - use a brush. Avoid inhaling any of the dust; wear an approved filtration mask. Use only proprietary brake cleaner fluid or methylated spirit to cleanse the brake components, DO NOT use petrol or any other petroleum-based product.**

Note: *As the handbrake and footbrake systems are self-adjusting, it is not possible to assess brake pad wear from the amount of* pedal or lever travel - a visual inspection must be carried out, as described in Chapter 1.

1 The specification of the Saab 9000's front brakes has been revised during the car's production life; refer to the Specifications for details, and establish which components are fitted to your model.

2 Park the vehicle on a firm, level surface, then chock the rear wheels and apply the handbrake. Raise the front of the vehicle, rest it securely on axle stands, and remove both front roadwheels - refer to *"Jacking, towing and wheel changing"* for guidance.

Pad removal - Girling caliper

3 At the first caliper, use a socket wrench and spanner to unscrew the lower guide pin bolt.

4 Grasp the hydraulic body of the caliper and pivot it upwards, taking care not to strain brake hose or union. Draw out both brake pads; if they bind against the disc, apply pressure to the inboard pad with a pair of grips to retract the piston back into the caliper.

> ⚠ **Caution: Keep an eye on the level in the brake fluid reservoir as you retract the pads, to ensure that the displaced fluid does not cause it to overflow.**

5 Remove the pads from the second caliper in the same manner.

6 Clear the dust and debris from the carrier surfaces, using a wire brush and brake cleaner fluid. Avoid inhaling the airborne dust.

7 Examine piston seals for signs of leaking or deterioration, and the piston itself for signs of wear or damage.

Pad removal - ATE caliper

8 At the first caliper, remove the dust caps, then use a 7 mm hex bit to slacken and remove the guide pins **(see illustrations)**.

9 Carefully prise off the spring clip using a screwdriver **(see illustration)**; support the caliper hydraulic body as you do this.

10 Take the weight of the hydraulic body, and lift it away from the carrier. If the pads bind against the disc, apply pressure to the inboard pad with a pair of grips to retract the piston back into the caliper. Remove the inboard

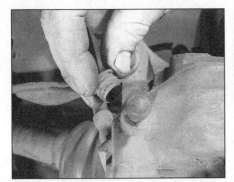

3.8a At the first caliper, remove the dust caps . . .

3.8b . . . then use a 7 mm hex bit to slacken and remove the guide pins

3.9 Carefully prise off the spring clip (arrowed) using a screwdriver

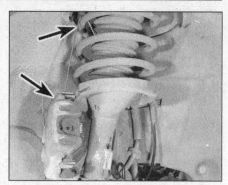

3.10a Take the weight of the hydraulic body, and lift it away from the carrier

3.10b Remove the inboard brake pad from the hydraulic body by prising the anti-rattle spring attached to its backplate out of the piston

3.11 Hydraulic body suspended from the coil spring on a length of wire

brake pad from the hydraulic body, by prising the anti-rattle spring attached to its backplate out of the piston. Lift out the outboard brake pad **(see illustrations)**.

11 Attach a cable-tie or a length of welding rod to a part of the hydraulic body casting, and suspend it from a convenient point on the suspension (see illustration).

 Caution: Do not let the hydraulic body dangle by the brake hose.

12 Remove the pads from the second caliper in the same manner.

13 Clear the dust and debris from the caliper surfaces, using a brush and brake cleaner fluid. Avoid inhaling the airborne dust.

14 Examine piston seals for signs of leaking or deterioration, and the piston itself for signs of wear or damage. With the hydraulic body removed, check that the guide pins slide freely in their bores, without excessive play.

Pad inspection - all calipers

15 Measure the depth of the friction material remaining on each pad. If any of the pads has worn down below its service limit (see "Specifications"), then the complete set of four pads (both roadwheels) must be renewed. Similarly, if any of the pads has been contaminated with grease or oil, it is not possible to clean and re-use it; the whole set

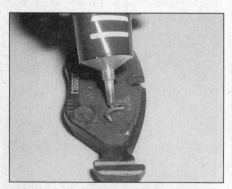

3.16 Apply a small quantity of copper-based brake grease to the metal backing plates of the pads; but *do not* allow any to come into contact with the friction material

must be renewed. If the pads have been contaminated, identify and rectify the cause before fitting new pads. If all the pads are still serviceable, clean them thoroughly using a brush (ideally, a fine wire brush) and brake cleaning fluid. Pay particular attention to the metal backplate, where the pad contacts the caliper. Examine the surface of the friction material; carefully prise out any fragments that have become embedded in it.

16 Apply a small quantity of copper-based brake grease to the metal backing plates of the pads; *do not* allow any to come into contact with the friction material **(see illustration)**.

17 It is good practice to examine the condition of the brake discs when inspecting or renewing the pads; refer to Section 7 for guidance.

Pad fitting - Girling caliper

18 At the first caliper, slide the pads into position with the friction material facing the brake disc.

19 Pivot the caliper hydraulic body down into position. If the pads bind against the disc, apply pressure to the inboard pad with a pair of grips to retract the piston back into the caliper.

20 Refit and tighten the guide pin retaining bolt.

21 Fit the brake pads to the second caliper in the same manner.

22 Depress the brake pedal several times; this will pressurise the braking system and bring the pads into contact with the disc. If the pedal has a developed a spongy feel, air may have entered the system when the pads were being removed - refer to Section 2 for guidance in bleeding the system.

23 Refit the roadwheels, lower the vehicle to the ground and tighten the bolts to the correct torque.

24 Top-up level of brake fluid in the reservoir to the "MAX" mark, and refit the cap.

Pad fitting - ATE caliper

25 Fit the outboard pad to the first caliper by sliding the backplate locating lugs into the corresponding grooves in the carrier. Ensure

that the friction material surface rests squarely against the disc surface.

26 Fit the inboard pad to the hydraulic body by pressing the tangs of its anti-rattle spring into the hollow piston.

27 Using G-clamps or pipe grips, force the piston and inboard pad back into the hydraulic body. With the pad retracted, the hydraulic body can be refitted to the carrier.

 Caution: Keep an eye on the level in the brake fluid reservoir as you retract the pads, to ensure that the displaced fluid does not cause it to overflow.

28 Slacken and remove the G-clamps/grips, allowing the piston and pads settle in position. Lightly lubricate the guide pins with a smear of anti-seize grease and refit them, tightening them to the correct torque (refer to Specifications). Refit the dust caps.

29 Fit the spring clip in position, locating the ends of it in the holes provided in the hydraulic body.

30 Fit the pads to the second caliper in the same manner.

31 Depress the brake pedal several times; this will pressurise the braking system and bring the pads into contact with the disc. If the pedal has a developed a spongy feel, air may have entered the system when the pads were being removed - refer to Section 2 for guidance in bleeding the system.

32 Refit the roadwheels, lower the vehicle to the ground and tighten the bolts to the correct torque.

33 Top-up level of brake fluid in the reservoir to the "MAX" mark and refit the cap.

4 Rear brake pads - renewal

 Warning: Refer to the warning at the start of Section 3 before starting work.

Note: *As the handbrake and footbrake are self-adjusting, it is not possible to assess brake pad wear from the amount of pedal or lever travel - a visual inspection must be carried out, as described in Chapter 1.*

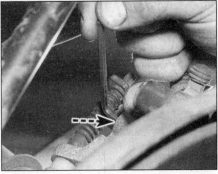

4.2a At the first caliper, remove the dust plug from the adjusting screw drilling on the hydraulic body

4.2b Using an Allen key, turn the adjusting screw anti-clockwise to the end of its travel

4.3a Prise out the two dust caps . . .

1 Park the vehicle on a firm, level surface. Chock the front wheels, and select first gear (manual transmission) or "Park" (automatic transmission) - do not apply the handbrake. Raise the rear of the vehicle, rest it securely on axle stands, and remove both rear roadwheels - refer to "Jacking, towing and wheel changing" for guidance.

2 At the first caliper, unscrew the dust plug from the adjusting screw drilling on the hydraulic body. Using an Allen key, turn the adjusting screw anti-clockwise to the end of its travel - this will cause the piston to be retracted fully into the hydraulic body, drawing the brake pad away from the disc **(see illustrations)**.

3 Prise out the two dust caps, then using a 7 mm hex bit and socket wrench, slacken and withdraw the caliper guide pins **(see illustrations)**.

4 Using a screwdriver, lever the retaining spring clip off the caliper **(see illustration)**.

5 Lift the hydraulic body away from the carrier, then relieve the spring tension on the handbrake lever, and release the handbrake cable from it **(see illustration)**.

6 Extract the brake pads from the hydraulic body. Note that the inboard pad must be prised away from the piston, as it is retained by an anti-rattle spring, attached to the pad backplate **(see illustration)**.

7 Hang the hydraulic body casting from a rigid point on the vehicle's suspension, using cable-ties or wire (see illustration 3.11). Do not

allow it to dangle by the brake hose, as this will undoubtedly cause damage to the hose.

8 Remove the pads from the caliper at the other roadwheel in the same manner.

9 Examine the caliper piston seals for signs of leaking or deterioration, and the piston itself for signs of wear or damage. Clear the dust and debris from the hydraulic body and carrier surfaces, using a brush and brake cleaner fluid. Avoid inhaling the airborne dust by wearing an approved filtration mask.

10 With the hydraulic body removed, check that the guide pins slide freely in their bores, without excessive play.

11 Measure the depth of the friction material remaining on each pad. If any of the pads has worn down below its service limit (see "Specifications"), then the complete set of four pads (both roadwheels) must be renewed. Similarly, if any of the pads has been contaminated with grease or oil, it is not possible to clean and re-use it; the whole set must be renewed. If the pads have been contaminated, or have worn unevenly, identify and rectify the cause before fitting new pads.

12 If all the pads are still serviceable, clean them thoroughly using a brush (ideally, a fine wire brush) and brake cleaning fluid. Pay particular attention to the metal backplate, where the pad contacts the carrier/piston. Examine the surface of the friction material; carefully prise out any fragments that have

4.3b . . . then using a 7 mm hex bit and socket wrench, slacken . . .

4.3c . . . and withdraw the caliper guide pins

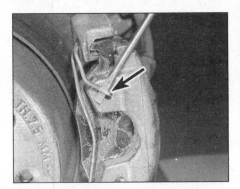

4.4 Using a screwdriver, lever the retaining spring clip (arrowed) off the caliper

4.5 Lift the hydraulic body away from the carrier, then relieve the spring tension on the handbrake lever, and release the handbrake cable from it

4.6 Extract the brake pads from the hydraulic body. Note that the inboard pad must be prised away from the piston, as it is retained by an anti-rattle spring, attached to the pad backplate

become embedded in it. Brush out the grooves if they are clogged

13 It is good practice to examine the condition of the brake discs when inspecting or renewing the pads; refer to Section 7 for guidance.

14 Apply a small quantity of copper-based brake grease to the metal backing plates of the pads; do not allow any to come into contact with the friction material (refer to illustration 3.16).

15 Fit the pads to the hydraulic body, pressing the inboard pad anti-rattle spring into the hollow of the piston. Fit the hydraulic body to the carrier.

16 Lubricate the guide pins with a smear of anti-seize grease, and refit them. Tighten them securely using a 7 mm hex bit, then refit the dust caps.

17 Fit the spring clip into place, locating the ends into the holes provided in the hydraulic body casting.

18 Using an Allen key, screw in the adjusting screw until the inboard pad is almost touching the brake disc.

19 Refit the plug and washer but make sure that they are thoroughly cleaned before doing so.

20 Operate the handbrake lever against the return spring tension and reconnect the handbrake cable, then refer to Chapter 1 and adjust the operation of the handbrake.

21 Depress the brake pedal several times; this will pressurise the braking system and bring the pads into contact with the disc. If the pedal has a developed a spongy feel, air may have entered the system when the pads were being removed - refer to Section 2 for guidance in bleeding the system.

22 Refit the roadwheels, lower the vehicle to the ground, and tighten the roadwheel bolts to the correct torque.

23 Top-up level of brake fluid in the reservoir to the "MAX" mark, and refit the cap.

---

5 Front brake caliper - removal, overhaul and refitting

 Warning: Refer to the warning notes at the start of Sections 2 and 3 regarding the safe handling of brake system components and fluids.

5.2 Brake hose clamp in use

1 Park the vehicle on a firm, level surface, then chock the rear wheels and apply the handbrake. Apply the handbrake, then raise the front of the vehicle, rest it securely on axle stands, and remove the appropriate front roadwheel to expose the caliper requiring attention. Refer to "*Jacking, towing and wheel changing*" for guidance.

2 To allow the caliper to be removed, the brake hose must be disconnected from it - this will entail some brake fluid loss. The amount of fluid lost can be minimised by clamping the flexible brake hose using a proprietary hose clamp **(see illustration)**. These are designed to constrict hoses without pinching the walls and causing damage - they can be obtained from motor accessory shops at minimal cost.

 Caution: The unprotected jaws of a G-clamp should not be used, as they may damage the hose, leading to premature failure.

Removal

3 Clean the caliper in the area around the brake hose union with a clean rag. Slacken the hose union, but do not attempt to unscrew it completely at this stage, or the hose will become twisted.

4 Remove the brake pads as described in Section 3.

5 On models fitted with Girling calipers (see "*Specifications*"), prise out the dust cap, and unscrew the upper guide pin bolt using a spanner and socket wrench. The hydraulic body can then be lifted away from the carrier.

6 The hydraulic body can now be detached from the brake hose; hold the hose still, and rotate the hydraulic body until the hose union unscrews from the tapping. Be prepared for some brake fluid loss - have a small container or a clean rag ready to catch spills. If the flow of fluid does not stop after the initial discharge, check the security and tightness of the hose clamp.

7 Wipe clean the end of the brake hose and the tapping in the hydraulic body, and fit them with dust caps.

HAYNES HiNT *If dust caps are not available, cut the fingers out of an old rubber glove, and stretch them over the open end of the brake pipe, securing them with elastic bands.*

8 Slacken and remove the retaining bolts, then lower the carrier away from the steering swivel member.

Overhaul

9 The cleanliness of the work area is of great importance when dismantling brake system components. Dirt entering the hydraulic system may adversely affect the system's performance, and possibly cause failure. Select a clean, uncluttered surface to work on; laying a sheet of plain paper or card on the

surface may help to keep things clean and easily visible.

10 Clean off all traces of dirt and dust from the hydraulic body, using a brush.

 Warning: Take great care to avoid inhaling the airborne dust.

11 The piston can be removed from the cylinder by applying compressed air to the hydraulic hose tapping. Only low pressure is required, so that produced by a bicycle or foot pump should be sufficient. Remove the dust cap, and couple the pump to the tapping with an old piece of vacuum or fuel hose to make a good seal - do not use anything that may damage the thread inside the tapping. Use a block of wood as padding to protect the end of the piston as it is ejected under pressure.

12 Carefully prise the dust cover out from the cylinder bore, leaving it attached to the piston - use a plastic instrument that will not damage the surface of the cylinder. Put the piston and dust cover to one side.

13 Using the same plastic instrument, lever out the piston seal from its seat in the cylinder bore. Avoid scoring the inside of the bore or the seal seat.

14 Clean all components thoroughly, using only methylated spirit, isopropyl alcohol or clean hydraulic fluid as a cleaning agent. **Do not** use mineral-based solvents such as petrol or paraffin, as they will attack the hydraulic system's rubber components. Dry the components straight after cleaning, using compressed air or a clean, lint-free cloth. Use compressed air to blow the fluid passages clear. If reassembly is not going to be carried out immediately, remember to refit a dust cap to the brake hose tapping.

15 Examine all components closely, and renew any that are worn or damaged. Check particularly the cylinder bore and piston; if they are scratched, worn or corroded in any way, they should be renewed (note that this means the renewal of the whole hydraulic body assembly). Check also the condition of the guide pins and their bores in the hydraulic body; both pins should be free from damage and corrosion. After cleaning, they should form a reasonably tight sliding fit in their corresponding bores. Renew any component whose condition is dubious.

16 If the assembly is fit for further use, obtain an appropriate repair kit; the components are available from Saab dealers in various combinations.

17 Renew all rubber seals, dust covers and caps disturbed on dismantling as a matter of course; the old items should *never* be re-used.

18 Before reassembly, ensure that all components are completely clean and dry.

19 Lubricate the new piston seal with the grease provided in the kit. Use the same grease to lubricate the new dust cap.

20 Fit the new piston seal into its seat in the cylinder; do not use any tools when doing this.

21 Fit the new dust cap to the piston; slide it

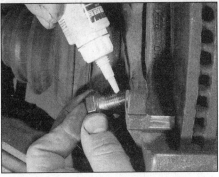

5.25a Refit the carrier to the steering swivel member

5.25b Apply a quantity of thread-locking compound to the retaining bolts . . .

5.25c . . . then tighten them to the specified torque

over the end that contacts the brake pad, then pull it down to the other end of the piston.

22 With the hydraulic body laid on the work surface, offer up the piston to the cylinder bore. Starting at the lower edge, press the collar of the dust cap into the cylinder bore, working around its circumference until the collar is firmly seated all the way around.

23 The piston can now be pressed into the cylinder - use care as the piston engages with the new seal. Note that it may be necessary to remove the dust cap from the brake hose tapping as you do this, to allow the air in the cylinder to escape.

Refitting

24 Reconnect the hydraulic body to the brake hose by threading the hose union into the tapping, holding the hose stationary and rotating the hydraulic body. Do not fully tighten the union at this stage.

25 Refit the carrier to the steering swivel member - apply a quantity of thread-locking compound to the retaining bolts, then insert and tighten them to the specified torque **(see illustrations)**. On models fitted with Girling calipers, lift the hydraulic body into position on the carrier and fit the upper guide pin bolt, tightening it securely.

26 For all calipers, follow the brake pad refitting sequence at the end of Section 3, but do not refit the roadwheel at this stage.

27 With the brake pads fitted, fully tighten the brake pipe union.

28 Remove the brake pipe clamp tool.

Referring to Section 2, bleed the system to expel the air that will have entered the brake hose when the caliper was removed. If suitable precautions were taken to minimise fluid loss, it should only be necessary to bleed the system at that caliper.

29 Refit the roadwheel, lower the vehicle to the ground and tighten the bolts to the specified torque.

---

6 Rear brake caliper - removal, overhaul and refitting

> ⚠ *Warning: Refer to the warning notes at the start of Sections 2 and 3 regarding the safe handling of brake system components and fluids.*

1 Park the vehicle on a firm, level surface. Chock the front wheels, and select first gear (manual transmission) or "Park" (automatic transmission). Release the handbrake. Raise the rear of the vehicle, rest it securely on axle stands, and remove the appropriate rear roadwheel to expose the caliper requiring attention. Refer to *"Jacking, towing and wheel changing"* for guidance.

2 To allow the caliper to be removed, the brake hose must be disconnected from it - this will entail some brake fluid loss. The amount of fluid lost can be minimised by clamping the flexible brake hose using a proprietary hose clamp (refer to illustration 5.2). These are designed to constrict hoses without pinching the walls and causing damage - they can be obtained from motor accessory shops at minimal cost.

> ⚠ *Caution: The unprotected jaws of a G-clamp should not be used, as they may damage the hose, leading to premature failure.*

Removal

3 Clean the caliper in the area around the brake hose union with a clean rag. Slacken the hose union, but do not attempt to unscrew it completely at this stage, or the hose will become twisted.

4 Remove the brake pads as described in Section 4.

5 Fit a brake hose clamp tool over the brake hose, and tighten it. Hold the brake hose stationary with one hand, and rotate the hydraulic body with the other, until the hose union unscrews from its tapping. Be prepared for some brake fluid leakage; have a small container or rag ready to catch spills. If the flow of fluid does not stop after the initial discharge, check the security and tightness of the hose clamp.

6 Wipe clean the end of the brake hose and the tapping in the hydraulic body, and fit them with dust caps.

> **HAYNES HiNT** *If dust caps are not available, cut the fingers out of an old rubber glove, and stretch them over the open brake pipe end, securing them with elastic bands.*

7 Slacken and remove the retaining bolts, then lower the carrier away from the hub assembly.

Overhaul

8 The cleanliness of the work area is of great importance when dismantling brake system components. Dirt entering the hydraulic system may adversely affect the system's performance, and possibly cause failure. Select a clean, uncluttered surface to work on; laying a sheet of plain paper or card on the surface may help to keep things clean and easily visible.

9 Clean off all traces of dirt and dust from the hydraulic body, using a brush.

> ⚠ *Warning: Take great care to avoid inhaling the airborne dust.*

10 Lay the hydraulic body on the work surface. Using a blunt screwdriver, lever out the guide pin spacer sleeves, together with the dust covers. Avoid scratching the internal surfaces of the spacer sleeves.

11 Lift the handbrake lever return spring off its pivot, and put it to one side.

12 Prise off the dust cover retaining ring; avoid damaging the piston by using a plastic implement, or a small screwdriver with its blade wrapped in tape. Pull the dust cover away from the piston.

13 Using 4 mm Allen key, rotate the adjusting screw clockwise to force the piston out of the cylinder. It may be necessary to remove the dust cap from the brake hose tapping at this point, to allow air into the cylinder as the piston is pushed out.

14 Lever the piston seal out of its seat using the plastic instrument; take care not to score the surface of the cylinder bore.

15 Clean all components thoroughly, using only methylated spirit, isopropyl alcohol or clean hydraulic fluid as a cleaning medium. **Do not** use mineral-based solvents such as petrol or paraffin, as they will attack the hydraulic system's rubber components.

6.26a Refit the carrier to the hub assembly

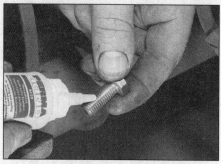

6.26b Apply a quantity of thread-locking compound to the retaining bolts, then tighten them to the specified torque

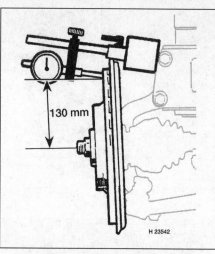

7.11 Brake disc runout measurement - DTI gauge method

16 Dry the components straight after cleaning, using compressed air or a clean, lint-free cloth. Use compressed air to blow the fluid passages clear. If reassembly is not going to be carried out immediately, remember to refit a dust cap to the brake hose tapping.

17 Examine all components closely, and renew any that are worn or damaged. Check particularly the cylinder bore and piston; if they are scratched, worn or corroded in any way, they should be renewed (note that this means the renewal of the whole hydraulic body assembly). Check also the condition of the guide pins and their bores in the hydraulic body; both pins should be free from damage and corrosion. After cleaning, they should form a reasonably tight sliding fit in their corresponding bores. If they cause the caliper to jam or stick, they may have distorted through overheating - check them for warpage against a straight edge. Renew any component whose condition is doubtful.

18 If the assembly is fit for further use, obtain an appropriate repair kit; the components are available from Saab dealers in various combinations.

19 Renew all rubber seals, dust covers and caps disturbed on dismantling as a matter of course; the old items should *never* be re-used.

20 Before reassembly, ensure that all components are completely clean and dry.

21 Lubricate the new piston seal and dust cap with the grease provided in the kit.

22 Fit the new piston seal into its seat in the cylinder - do not use any tools when doing this.

23 Fit the new dust cap to the piston; slide it over the end that contacts the brake pad, then pull it down to the other end of the piston.

24 Push the piston into the cylinder bore, and retract it fully by turning the adjusting screw anti-clockwise with a 4 mm Allen key.

25 Push the skirt of the dust cap over the lip on the edge of the cylinder. Ensure that it is firmly seated, then fit the retaining ring.

26 Refit the handbrake lever return spring onto its pivot. Ensure that one end engages with the lever itself, and the other braces against the casting.

27 Fit the two rubber bushes and guide pin spacer sleeves.

Refitting

28 Refit the carrier to the hub assembly - apply a quantity of thread-locking compound to the retaining bolts, then insert and tighten them to the specified torque **(see illustrations)**.

29 Reconnect the hydraulic body to the brake hose by threading the hose union into the tapping (after removing the dust cap), holding the hose stationary and rotating the hydraulic body. Do not fully tighten the union at this stage.

30 Refer to Section 4 for details of fitting the brake pads and reconnecting the handbrake cable. Do not refit the roadwheel at this point.

31 Tighten the brake pipe union securely. Remove the brake hose clamp tool. Referring to Section 2, bleed the system to expel the air that will have entered the brake hose when the caliper was removed. If suitable precautions were taken to minimise fluid loss, it should only be necessary to bleed the system at that caliper.

32 Refer to Chapter 1 and adjust the operation of the handbrake.

33 Refit the roadwheel, lower the vehicle to the ground, and tighten the bolts to the specified torque.

7 Front brake disc - inspection, removal and refitting

> **Warning: Refer to the warning notes at the start of Sections 2 and 3 regarding the safe handling of brake system components.**

Inspection

1 Park the vehicle on a firm, level surface, then chock the rear wheels and apply the handbrake. Raise the front of the vehicle, rest it securely on axle stands, and remove the front roadwheels. Refer to *"Jacking, towing and wheel changing"* for guidance.

2 Rotate the brake disc by hand, and examine the whole of the surface area swept by the brake pads, on both sides of the disc. **Note:** *It will be necessary to remove the caliper hydraulic body to allow an adequate*

inspection of the disc's rear surface; refer to Section 5 for details. Typically, the surface will have a polished appearance, and should be free from heavy scoring. Smooth rippling is produced by normal operation, and does not indicate excessive wear. Deep scoring and cracks, however, are indications of more serious damage in need of correction.

3 If deep scoring is discovered, it may be possible to have the disc reground to restore the surface, depending on the extent of the damage. To determine whether this is a feasible course of action, it will be necessary to measure the thickness of the disc, as described later.

4 Check the whole surface of the disc for cracks, particularly around the roadwheel bolt holes. A cracked disc must be renewed.

5 Inspect the cooling vents between the two friction surfaces of the disc, and clear out any traces of dirt and brake dust; blocked vents will impair the cooling efficiency, and reduce brake performance. Use a piece of rag wrapped around a length of wire, soaked in brake cleaning fluid to clear the vents. Do not use compressed air, as this will propel the harmful brake dust into the air.

6 A ridge of rust and brake dust at the inner and outer edges of the disc, beyond the pad contact area, is normal - this can be scraped away quite easily.

7 Raised ridges caused by the brake pads eroding the disc material, however, are an indication of excessive wear. If close examination reveals such ridges, the thickness of the disc must be measured, to assess whether it is still fit for use.

8 To measure the thickness of the disc, take readings at several points on the surface using a micrometer, in the area swept by the brake pads. Include any points where the disc has been scored; align the jaws of the micrometer with the deepest area of scoring, to get a true indication of the extent of the wear. Compare these measurements with the limits listed in Specifications. If the disc has worn below its

7.17 Slacken off the disc locating stud (A) and retaining screw (B) - these are on the same radius as the wheel bolt holes

8.3 Slackening the rear brake disc locating stud

minimum thickness, at any point, it must be renewed.

9 If the discs are suspected of causing brake judder, check the disc runout, using one of the following methods:-

Runout measurement - DTI method

10 Refit the four roadwheel bolts, together with one M14 plain washer per stud - this will ensure adequate disc-to-hub contact. Tighten the studs to 5 Nm (4 lbf ft).
11 Clamp the DTI to a stand, and attach the stand (preferably via a magnetic base) to the strut mounting bracket. Align the gauge so that its pointer rests upon the area of the disc swept by the brake pads, on an arc 130 mm from the centre of the hub **(see illustration)**.
12 Zero the gauge, and slowly rotate the disc through one revolution, observing the pointer movement. Note the maximum deflection recorded, and compare the figure with that listed in Specifications.

Runout measurement - feeler blade method

13 Use the gauges to measure the clearance between the disc and a convenient fixed point, such as the disc backplate. Rotate the disc, and measure the variation in clearance at several points around the disc. Compare the maximum figure with that listed in the Specifications.
14 If the disc runout is outside of tolerance, first check that the hub is not worn - refer to Chapter 10 for guidance. If the hub is in good condition, remove the disc (as described later in this Section), rotate it through 180° and refit it. This may improve the seating and eradicate the excessive runout.
15 If the runout is still unacceptable, then it may be possible to restore the disc by regrinding; consult your Saab dealer or a machine shop for a professional opinion - it may prove more economical to purchase a new disc. If the disc cannot be reground, then it must be renewed.
16 Measure the thickness of the disc at several points using a micrometer; compare the figures with those listed in Specifications.

Removal

17 Mark the relationship between the disc and the hub, using chalk or a marker pen. Slacken off the disc locating stud and retaining screw - these are on the same radius as the wheel bolt holes - but do not remove them at this stage **(see illustration)**.
18 To allow the disc to be removed, the brake caliper must be unbolted from the hub assembly, but does not need to be dismantled - the brake pads and hydraulic hose can be left in place. Retract the inboard brake pad and piston back into the cylinder, using a pair of grips or G-clamps - check that the displaced brake fluid does not overflow from the fluid reservoir.
19 Slide the hydraulic body along the guide pins, so that both brake pads are clear of the disc. Referring to the relevant paragraphs of Section 5, remove the hydraulic body from the carrier; hang it from a rigid point on the suspension, using wire or a cable-tie (see illustration 3.11). Do not allow it to dangle freely, as this will strain the brake hose.
20 Again referring to Section 5, remove the carrier from the steering swivel member.
21 Remove the disc locating stud and retaining screw completely. Support the disc as you do this, and lift it off as it comes free. If it sticks, tap the rear face lightly with a soft-faced mallet to release it.
22 Remove the polished glaze from the surface of the disc with sand/emery paper. Use small, circular motions, to avoid producing a directional finish on the surface.

Refitting

23 If a new disc is being fitted, remove the protective coating from the surface, using an appropriate solvent.
24 Locate the disc on the hub so that the roadwheel bolt, retaining screw and locating stud holes are all correctly aligned; use the alignment marks made on removal, where applicable. If the disc is being removed in an attempt to improve seating and hence runout, turn the disc through 180° and then refit it.
25 Refit the locating stud and retaining screw, tightening them securely.

26 Refit the brake caliper carrier and hydraulic body, tightening the retaining bolts to the correct torque; refer to Section 5 for details.
27 Re-check the disc runout, using one of the methods described earlier.
28 Depress the brake pedal several times to advance the brake pads towards the disc.
29 Refit the roadwheel, and lower the vehicle to the ground. Tighten the roadwheel bolts to the correct torque.

8 Rear brake disc - inspection, removal and refitting

 Warning: Refer to the warning notes at the start of Sections 2 and 3 regarding the safe handling of brake system components.

Inspection

1 Park the vehicle on a firm, level surface, then chock the rear wheels and apply the handbrake. Raise the front of the vehicle, rest it securely on axle stands, and remove the appropriate front roadwheel. Refer to *"Jacking, towing and wheel changing"* for guidance.
2 Refer to the beginning of Section 7 for a description of the disc inspection procedure, noting that the rear discs are not ventilated. **Note:** *It will be necessary to remove the caliper hydraulic body to allow an adequate inspection of the disc's rear surface; refer to Section 6 for details.*

Removal

3 Mark the relationship between the disc and the hub, using chalk or a marker pen. Slacken off the locating stud and retaining screw - these are on the same radius as the wheel bolt holes **(see illustration)** - but do not remove them at this point.
4 To allow the disc to be removed, the brake caliper must be unbolted from the hub assembly, but does not need to be dismantled - the brake pads and hydraulic hose can be left in place. Retract the inboard brake pad and piston back into the cylinder, using a pair of grips or G-clamps - check that the displaced brake fluid does not overflow from the fluid reservoir. Slide the hydraulic body along the guide pins, so that both brake pads are clear of the disc.
5 Remove the guide pins, then lift the hydraulic body away from the disc. Hang it from a rigid point on the suspension, using wire or a cable-tie (see illustration 3.11). Unbolt and remove the carrier casting from the hub assembly; refer to Section 6 for details.
6 Remove the disc locating stud and retaining screw completely. Support the disc as you do this, and lift it off as it comes free **(see illustration)**. If it sticks, tap the rear face lightly with a soft faced mallet to release it.
7 Remove the polished glaze from the surface of the disc with sand/emery paper. Use small,

8.6 Removing the rear brake disc

circular motions, to avoid producing a directional finish on the surface.

Refitting

8 If a new disc is being fitted, remove the protective coating from the surface, using an appropriate solvent.

9 Locate the disc on the hub so that the roadwheel bolt, retaining screw and locating stud holes are all correctly aligned, using the alignment marks made on removal, where applicable. If the disc is being removed in an attempt to improve seating and runout, turn the disc through 180° and then refit it.

10 Refit the locating stud and retaining screw, tightening them securely.

11 Refit the brake caliper carrier and hydraulic body, tightening the retaining bolts to the correct torque; refer to Section 6 for details.

12 Re-check the disc runout, using one of the methods described earlier.

13 Depress the brake pedal several times to advance the brake pads towards the disc.

14 Check and adjust the operation of the handbrake as described in Chapter 1.

15 Refit the roadwheel, and lower the vehicle to the ground. Tighten the roadwheel bolts to the correct torque.

9 Hydraulic pipes and hoses - renewal

Note: *Before starting work, refer to the warning at the beginning of Section 2 concerning the hazards of working with hydraulic fluid.*

1 If any pipe or hose is to be renewed, minimise fluid loss as far as is possible. Flexible hoses can be sealed using a proprietary brake hose clamp; metal brake pipe unions can be plugged (if care is taken not to allow dirt into the system) or capped immediately they are disconnected. Place a small container or a wad of rag under any union that is to be disconnected, to catch any spilt fluid. In addition, before starting work, remove the fluid reservoir cap, then tighten it down over a piece of polythene, to obtain an airtight seal.

2 If a flexible hose is to be disconnected,

unscrew the brake pipe union nut before removing the hose from its mounting bracket.

3 To unscrew the union nuts, it is preferable to obtain a brake pipe spanner of the correct size; these are available from most large motor accessory shops. Failing this, a close-fitting open-ended spanner will be required, though if the nuts are tight or corroded, their flats may be rounded-off if the spanner slips. In this case, a self-locking wrench is often the only way to unscrew a stubborn union, but it follows that the pipe and the damaged nuts must be renewed on reassembly. Always clean a union and surrounding area before disconnecting it.

 HAYNES HiNT *If disconnecting a component with more than one union, make a careful note of the connections before disturbing any of them.*

4 If a brake pipe is to be renewed, it can be obtained, cut to length and with the union nuts and end flares in place, from Saab dealers. All that is then necessary is to bend it to shape, following the line of the original, before fitting it to the vehicle. Alternatively, most motor accessory shops can make up brake pipes from kits, but this requires very careful measurement of the original, to ensure that the replacement is of the correct length. The safest answer is usually to take the original to the shop as a pattern.

5 On refitting, do not overtighten the union nuts. It is not necessary to use excessive force to obtain a sound joint.

6 Ensure that the pipes and hoses are correctly routed, with no kinks, and that they are properly secured in the clips or brackets provided. Ensure that they do not chafe against the vehicle's body or any other components; bounce the vehicle down on its suspension, and turn the steering from lock to lock, to check that the lines or pipes will not contact any moving components when the car is driven.

7 After fitting, bleed the hydraulic system as described in Section 2. Wash off any spilt fluid, and check carefully for fluid leaks.

10 Master cylinder - removal, overhaul and refitting

⚠ *Warning: Before starting work, refer to the warning at the beginning of Section 2 concerning the hazards of working with hydraulic fluid.*
Caution: Refer to Section 9 for background information regarding the correct handling of brake lines and hoses.

Removal - models with ABS

1 On models fitted with ABS, the master cylinder is part of the hydraulic unit; refer to Sections 19 and 20.

Removal - models without ABS

2 Disconnect both battery cables, and remove the battery; refer to Chapter 5A for details.

3 On pre-1990 model-year vehicles, free the fuel filter from its retaining strap and move it to one side; refer to Chapter 4A for details.

4 Remove the brake fluid reservoir cap, and drain all the fluid out of the two brake circuit chambers (it is not necessary to drain the fluid from the clutch circuit chamber, on manual transmission models). This can be done in a number of ways - one method is to siphon the fluid directly from the reservoir, using an old syringe. Another method is to pump the fluid out through a bleed screw, at one of the brake calipers. Connect one end of a length of tubing to the bleed screw, and insert the other end into a container large enough to hold at least 1.0 litre of fluid. Open the bleed screw with a spanner, and using regular, steady strokes, pump the brake pedal until all the fluid has drained from the reservoir brake circuit chambers into the container. Retighten the bleed screw

⚠ *Warning: Do not attempt to siphon the fluid out with your mouth and a piece of tube - brake fluid is highly poisonous, and it may be ingested accidentally.*

5 Wipe clean the areas around the brake pipe unions and hose connection ports. Two braided hoses lead from the bottom of the reservoir to the master cylinder. Disconnect these by prising the end connectors out of the ports on the master cylinder - exercise care when doing this, to avoid damaging the plastic connectors. Make a note of the port each hose is connected to. Be prepared for spillage - position a wad of rag under the connectors, to absorb any fluid that may leak out. Plug the disconnected hoses and ports, to prevent the ingress of dirt and excessive fluid loss.

6 Detach all four brake pipes from the master cylinder, after slackening the unions. Make a note of the port each pipe is connected to.

7 Remove the two securing nuts, then lift the master cylinder away from the vacuum servo unit and out of the engine bay.

Overhaul

8 Select a clean flat worksurface upon which to carry out the overhaul. It may help to lay down a sheet of paper or card - this will aid visibility, and absorb any brake fluid that drains from the dismantled components.

9 Clamp the master cylinder lightly in a soft-jawed vice. Use blocks of wood to protect the cylinder, if the vice has bare metal jaws. Remove the rubber seals from the pipe and hose connection ports, and discard them; new ones must be fitted on reassembly.

10 Push the primary plunger along the cylinder bore, far enough to allow the secondary plunger stop-pin to be removed. To avoid scratching the cylinder bore, use a blunt implement, such as a wooden dowel, when pushing out the primary plunger.

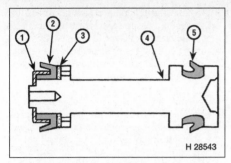

10.11 Secondary plunger assembly

1 Seal retainer 4 Plunger
2 Recuperating seal 5 Plunger seal
3 Washer

11 Allow the plunger to spring back to rest, then withdraw the entire primary and secondary plunger assembly from the cylinder, together with the loose plastic bleed cup **(see illustration)**. As the components emerge, note their order of assembly, and lay them in that order on a clean worksurface. If the plunger proves difficult to extract, careful application of compressed air to the brake pipe ports will force it out of the cylinder - pad the open end of the cylinder with a wad of rag, in case the plunger ejects faster than expected.

 Warning: Wear eye protection when using compressed air in this manner.

12 When cleaning any of the brake system components, only use approved brake cleaning fluid, methylated spirit or new hydraulic fluid as a cleaning medium. Never use mineral-based solvents such as petrol or paraffin, as they will attack the hydraulic system's rubber components.
13 Thoroughly clean all the components, and dry them off with a lint-free cloth or compressed air. Pay particular attention to the inside of the cylinder bore and the brake pipe and hose ports.
14 Examine the inside of the cylinder bore. The surface should be shiny and smooth; if there are signs of corrosion, pitting or scoring, then the master cylinder must be renewed. Similarly, if the plunger pistons are scored or corroded, they should also be renewed as a complete assembly.
15 If the cylinder and plunger assemblies can be re-used, obtain a master cylinder service kit from a Saab dealer. This will contain replacements for all those components which are likely to have worn out in the course of normal operation.
16 Before rebuilding the assembly, soak the plunger components and the new seals from the service kit in new brake fluid. Coat the inside of the cylinder bore with fluid in the same manner.
17 Reassemble the plunger assembly using the new seals; refer to the notes made during dismantling, to ensure that the correct order is maintained. Insert the plunger into the cylinder

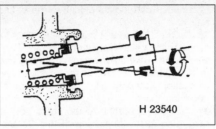

10.17 Insert the secondary plunger into the cylinder bore at an angle initially, feeding the lip of the first seal into the bore using a twisting motion

bore at an angle initially, feeding the lip of the first seal into the bore using a twisting motion, to ensure that it is not folded back on itself **(see illustration)**. When the first seal is fully inserted, push the remainder of the plunger squarely into the cylinder; use a blunt instrument such as a wooden dowel, to avoid scratching the surface of the cylinder bore.
18 Push the plunger against the force of the secondary chamber return spring, and insert the stop-pin. Allow the spring to push the plunger back, and check that the stop-pin holds it in position.

Refitting

19 Wipe clean the vacuum servo unit mating surface, and lift the assembled master cylinder onto the mounting studs, ensuring that the pushrod is correctly aligned with the master cylinder plunger. Refit the nuts, and tighten them securely.
20 Remove the plugs from the rigid brake pipes and, referring to the notes made during removal, fit them to their respective ports on the master cylinder. Tighten the unions securely, but do not overtighten them.
21 Press the reservoir hose connectors into their respective ports on the master cylinder; refer to the notes made during removal to ensure that they are connected the right way around. Take care to ensure that the port seals are not dislodged as the connectors are pressed home.
22 Fill the reservoir to the "MAX" mark with brake fluid of the correct grade.
23 Bleed the entire brake system to eliminate all trapped air pockets - refer to Section 2 for details.
24 On pre-1990 model-year vehicles, refit the fuel filter.
25 Refit the battery, and reconnect the battery cables.

11 Vacuum servo unit non-return valve -
removal, testing and refitting

Removal

1 Slacken the retaining clip (where fitted), and disconnect the vacuum hose from the servo unit check valve.
2 Withdraw the valve from its rubber sealing

grommet, using a twisting motion. Remove the grommet from the servo.

Testing

3 Examine the check valve for signs of damage, and renew if necessary. The valve may be tested by blowing through it in both directions. Air should flow through the valve in one direction only - when blown through from the servo unit end of the valve. Renew the valve if this is not the case.
4 Examine the rubber sealing grommet and flexible vacuum hose for signs of damage or deterioration, and renew as necessary.

Refitting

5 Fit the sealing grommet into position in the servo unit.
6 Carefully ease the check valve into position, taking great care not to displace or damage the grommet. Reconnect the vacuum hose to the valve and, where necessary, securely tighten its retaining clip.
7 On completion, start the engine and check the check valve-to-servo unit connection for signs of air leaks.

12 Vacuum servo unit - testing, removal and refitting

Testing

1 To test the operation of the servo unit, depress the footbrake several times with the engine switched off, to exhaust the vacuum. Start the engine, keeping the pedal firmly depressed; as the engine speed rises to normal idle, there should be a slight drop in the brake pedal resistance as the manifold vacuum builds up. Allow the engine to run for at least two minutes, then switch it off. If the brake pedal is now depressed, it should feel normal, but further applications should result in the pedal feeling firmer, with the pedal stroke decreasing with each application.
2 If the servo does not operate as described, first check the operation the servo unit non-return valve, as described in Section 11.
3 If the operation of the servo is still unsatisfactory, then the fault must lie within the unit itself. As it is not serviceable, it must be renewed.

Removal

4 In the front left-hand footwell, remove the trim panel from underneath the facia.
5 Identify the link rod that connects the pedal linkage to the vacuum servo unit. At the point where the link rod attaches to the linkage, remove the retaining clip and extract the clevis pin.
6 Disconnect both battery cables, and remove the battery from the engine bay - refer to Chapter 5A for a more detailed description.
7 On pre-1990 model year vehicles, slacken the fuel filter securing strap, lift out the filter (without disconnecting the fuel lines) and position it away from the battery tray.

8 Remove the terminal blocks from the battery tray. Unbolt the battery tray from the inner wing, and lift it out of the engine bay.

9 Refer to Chapter 1 and drain the brake fluid from the system.

10 Refer to Section 10 and remove the master cylinder.

11 Refer to Section 11 and extract the non-return valve from the vacuum servo unit, but leave it connected to the vacuum hose leading to the inlet manifold.

12 Working in the cabin, from the left-hand side footwell, remove the four servo unit retaining nuts, located behind the brake linkage bracket.

> ⚠ **Caution: Get an assistant to support the servo unit as you do this, to prevent it from dropping out as the last nut is removed.**

Refitting

13 Clean the mating surfaces of the servo unit and the bulkhead. Fit a new gasket over the servo mounting studs.

14 Offer up the servo unit to its mounting location. Insert the link rod through the bulkhead, ensuring that it aligns correctly with the brake linkage.

15 Refit the clevis pin and retaining clip. Refit the four retaining nuts to the servo unit studs protruding through the bulkhead, and tighten them to the correct torque. Press the trim back into place behind the pedals.

16 Reconnect the vacuum hose by pressing the non-return valve back into the grommet on the servo unit; refer to Section 11 for details.

17 Refit the master cylinder, brake lines and hoses, referring to Section 10 for guidance.

18 Refit the battery tray, battery and battery cables by reversing their removal sequence.

Reconnect the terminal blocks to the battery tray.

19 On pre-1990 model year vehicles, refit the fuel filter and its retaining strap.

20 Fill the brake fluid reservoir to the "MAX" mark and bleed the entire brake system; refer to Section 2 for a detailed description of this operation.

21 Test the operation of the servo unit, as described at the beginning of this Section, before bringing the vehicle back into service.

13 Handbrake - checking and adjustment

> ⚠ **Warning: Adjustment of the handbrake should be carried out after the brake discs have been allowed to cool completely, and not immediately after driving the vehicle, when the discs may still be hot. The expansion of the discs at high temperatures may give rise to an inaccurate adjustment.**

1 If the handbrake has to be pulled through an excessive degree of travel before it takes effect, or if the rear wheels appear to be binding, the handbrake may be in need of adjustment **(see illustration)**.

2 Park the vehicle on a level surface, with the engine and ignition switched off. Select first gear (manual transmission) or "Park" (automatic transmission). Do not apply the handbrake.

3 Chock the front wheels, raise the rear of the vehicle and rest it securely on axle stands - refer to "Jacking, towing and wheel changing" for guidance.

4 Remove both rear roadwheels to gain access to the brake calipers.

5 Remove the retaining screw and prise the brush seal out of the centre console, and slide it off the handbrake lever. This will expose two adjusting nuts, at the base of the lever; remove the plastic lockplate from them, and put it to one side **(see illustration)**.

6 At the right-hand rear caliper, unscrew the plug from the adjusting screw hole. Use a 4 mm Allen key to turn the adjusting screw clockwise until it reaches the end of its travel, then back it off half a turn. This should set the brake pads just clear of the disc - rotate the disc by hand, and check that it still turns freely. If it binds, back off the adjusting screw by a further quarter-turn and check the disc again. Refit the adjusting screw plug.

7 At the caliper, slide a 1.0 mm feeler blade between the handbrake actuator lever and its end stop. Inside the car, turn the right-hand adjusting nut at the base of the handbrake lever to decrease or increase the clearance at the caliper. The clearance is set correctly when the feeler blade will just slide between the lever and end stop, with slight resistance **(see illustration)**.

8 If the correct clearance cannot be obtained, or if it can be set correctly but the brake disc still binds on the pads, after the handbrake is applied and released, check the handbrake actuator lever and return spring on the caliper for signs of corrosion or damage. If no problems exist there, the handbrake cables may be sticking internally due to corrosion - refer to Section 14 for more information.

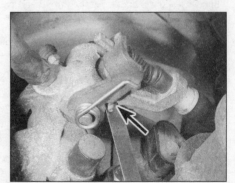

13.5 Removing the plastic lockplate, to expose the handbrake cable adjusting nuts

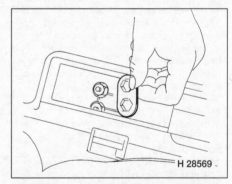

13.7 At the caliper, slide a 1.0 mm feeler blade between the handbrake actuator lever and its end stop

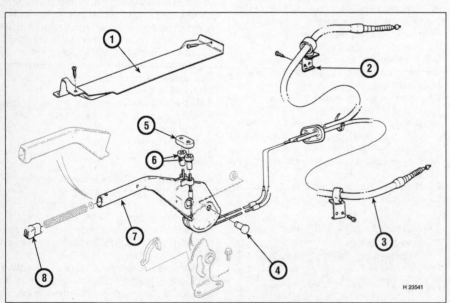

13.1 Handbrake cable layout and adjustment mechanism

1 Cover	3 Cable	5 Plastic locking plate	7 Handbrake lever
2 Cable guide	4 Pivot pin	6 Adjusting nuts	8 Pawl release button

9 Repeat the above procedure at the left-hand caliper, this time using the left-hand adjusting screw at the handbrake lever to set the clearance.

10 Upon completion, press the lockplate over the adjusting screws at the base of the handbrake lever.

11 Slide the brush seal over the handbrake lever, and refit it to the centre console. Secure the brush seal by refitting its retaining screw.

12 Refit the roadwheels, and after lowering the vehicle to the ground, tighten the wheel bolts.

13 Before bringing the vehicle back into service, thoroughly check the operation of the handbrake.

14 Handbrake cables - removal and refitting

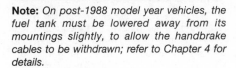

Note: *On post-1988 model year vehicles, the fuel tank must be lowered away from its mountings slightly, to allow the handbrake cables to be withdrawn; refer to Chapter 4 for details.*

Removal

1 Park the vehicle on a level surface, with the engine and ignition switched off. Select first gear (manual transmission) or "Park" (automatic transmission). Do not apply the handbrake.

2 Refer to Chapter 11 and remove the front left-hand seat.

3 Prise the brush seal out of the centre console, and slide it off the handbrake lever. Unscrew the bezel, and slide the gaiter off the gear change/selector lever. Remove the four retaining screws, and lift off the rear section of the centre console. Refer to Chapter 11 for more detail.

4 Remove the sill anti-scuff plates, after extracting the retaining screws.

5 Fold back the carpet to expose the cable channel, and unscrew the cover.

6 Remove the lockplate from the handbrake cable adjusting nuts, and put it to one side; refer to Section 13 for details.

7 Fully slacken both the adjusting screws, detaching them from the bracket on the handbrake lever and the handbrake cables.

8 Chock the front wheels, raise the rear of the vehicle and rest it securely on axle stands - refer to *"Jacking, towing and wheel changing"* for guidance.

9 Remove both rear roadwheels to gain access to the brake calipers.

10 At the first caliper, unhook the handbrake cable from the actuator lever, and recover the rubber gaiter; refer to Section 4.

11 Unscrew/prise out the cable guide from the suspension lower arm, as applicable.

12 Free the remainder of the cable by pulling it through the grommet in the floorpan - the cable assembly can now be withdrawn from the vehicle.

13 Repeat the above procedure for the remaining cable.

Refitting

14 Guide the end of the first new cable through the grommet in the floorpan.

15 Screw/press the other end of the cable into the spring guide on the suspension lower arm, as applicable

16 From inside the car, pull the cable through to the bracket on the base of the handbrake lever. Thread the adjusting screw onto the end of the cable, but do not tighten it fully.

17 Working at the caliper, pack the rubber gaiter with grease, and thread the handbrake cable inner through it. Hook the cable outer into the slotted bracket affixed to the caliper, and engage the inner cable nipple with the handbrake actuator lever.

18 Repeat the above the procedure to fit the second cable.

19 On post-1988 model year vehicles, raise the fuel tank back into place and secure the mountings; refer to Chapter 4 for details.

20 Apply and release the handbrake several times, to allow the cables to stretch and settle.

21 Refer to Section 13 and adjust the operation the handbrake.

22 Refit the roadwheels, then lower the vehicle to the ground and tighten the wheel bolts to the specified torque.

23 Screw down the cable covers inside the car, and lay the carpet back in position. Refit the sill anti-scuff plates.

24 Refer to Chapter 11 and refit the centre console, handbrake lever brush seal, and the seat.

25 Perform a full check of the handbrake operation, as described in Section 13, before bringing the vehicle back into service.

15 Handbrake lever - removal and refitting

Removal

1 Park the vehicle on a level surface, with the engine and ignition switched off. Select first gear (manual transmission) or "Park" (automatic transmission). Do not apply the handbrake.

2 Prise the brush seal out of the centre console, and slide it off the handbrake lever. Unclip the bezel, and slide the gaiter off the gear change/selector lever. Remove the four retaining screws, and lift off the rear section of the centre console; refer to Chapter 11 for more detail.

3 Prise the lockplate off the two handbrake cable adjusting nuts, and retain it for refitting later. Slacken and remove the adjusting nuts, then free the two cables from the brackets on the sides of the handbrake lever.

4 Remove the circlip from the end of the handbrake lever pivot pin, then draw the pin out.

5 Lift the handbrake lever away from its mounting bracket.

Refitting

6 Refit the lever to its mounting bracket, then push the pivot pin through, engaging it with the mounting bracket / ratchet plate.

7 Guide the handbrake cables through the brackets on the side of the lever, and refit the adjusting nuts.

8 Refer to Section 13, and adjust the operation of the handbrake. Remember to fit the adjusting nut lockplate upon completion.

9 Refit the centre console, handbrake lever brush seal and gear change/selector lever gaiter by reversing the removal procedure - refer to Chapter 11 for guidance.

16 Handbrake "ON" warning light switch - removal, testing and refitting

Removal

1 The handbrake "ON" warning light switch is mounted on a bracket bolted to the floorpan, directly underneath the handbrake lever. Refer to Chapter 11 and remove the rear section of the centre console to expose it.

2 Park the vehicle on a level surface, and apply the handbrake.

3 Remove the bolt securing the mounting bracket to the floorpan, and unplug the switch at the cable connector. Lift the assembly out of the vehicle.

Testing

4 The switch is a single-pole device, and has normally-closed (NC) contacts. The operation of the switch can be tested using either a multimeter (switched to the resistance measurement function), or a continuity tester made up of a flashlight bulb, dry cell battery and two pieces of wire. Connect the meter/tester to the switch connector terminals (the order of connection is immaterial) with the switch in its rest position. A healthy switch will show a short-circuit reading (no more than 1 or 2 ohms) on the meter, and will light the continuity tester light.

5 Press the switch plunger down, and repeat the measurement. The reading on the meter should be open-circuit (very high resistance), and the continuity tester light should go out.

6 If the switch does not behave as described, or is intermittent in its operation, then it must be replaced; the unit is not serviceable.

Refitting

7 Bolt the switch mounting bracket to the floorpan, and plug in the cable connector.

8 Ensure that the vehicle is parked on a level surface. Select first gear (manual transmission) or "Park" (automatic transmission), apply the footbrake and switch on the ignition - but do not start the engine.

9 Release the handbrake, and check that in its rest position, the metal tab protruding from the handbrake lever contacts the switch plunger squarely and pushes it down. The handbrake

"ON" warning light on the dashboard should go out.

10 Reapply the handbrake, and check that the metal tab now clears the switch plunger, allowing it to extend fully. The handbrake "ON" warning light on the dashboard should now be lit.

11 Refer to Chapter 11 and refit the rear section of the centre console.

17 Brake pedal - removal and refitting

General information

1 The vehicle's braking system is laid out principally to serve the left-hand drive market. In this configuration, the brake pedal acts directly on the master cylinder via a single pushrod linkage. Right-hand drive vehicles are fitted with a mechanism that transfers effort from the brake pedal across the bulkhead, to a bracket directly behind the master cylinder/ vacuum servo/ABS hydraulic unit on the left of the vehicle.

Removal

2 Park the vehicle on a level surface, and apply the handbrake. Working in the right-hand footwell, remove the soundproofing panel from the underside of the dashboard, to expose the pedal assemblies. Refer to Chapter 11 for guidance in removing trim panel fixings without damaging them.

3 Where applicable, refer to Chapter 4A and remove the cruise control cancel switches.

4 Remove the retaining clip, and extract the clevis pin from the point where the pedal is joined to the servo unit pushrod.

5 Refer to Chapter 6 and remove the clutch pedal (vehicles with manual transmission only).

6 Note the position of the brake pedal return spring - push the hooked ends off the bracket, and allow the brake pedal to drop out of the bracket. Recover the plastic bushes.

7 Extract the two smaller plastic bushes and the metal pivot pin bush from the pedal - note their order of assembly.

Refitting

8 Refit the components by reversing the removal process. For vehicles fitted with manual transmission, refer to Chapter 6 for details of refitting the clutch pedal.

18 Stop-light switch - adjustment, removal and refitting

Removal

1 On right-hand drive vehicles, the stop-light switch is mounted on the brake linkage bracket, on the bulkhead at the left-hand side of the vehicle; refer to Section 17, *General Information*. It is a single-pole switch, whose contacts are normally closed. When operating

correctly, the stop-lights should come on after the brake pedal has been depressed by 10 mm.

2 Working from the left-hand footwell, remove the sound insulation panel from underneath the facia; refer to Chapter 11 for details.

3 Ensure that the ignition switch is turned to the "off" position, then unplug the electrical cables from the switch terminals.

4 At the end of the stop-light switch body, squeeze together the plastic tangs, and pull the switch back through the mounting bracket.

Testing

5 The switch is a single-pole device, and has normally-closed (NC) contacts. The operation of the switch can be tested using either a multimeter (switched to the resistance measurement function), or a continuity tester made up of a flashlight bulb, dry cell battery and two pieces of wire. Connect the meter/tester to the switch connector terminals (the order of connection is immaterial) with the switch in its rest position. A healthy switch will show a short-circuit reading (no more than 1 or 2 ohms) on the meter, and will light the continuity tester light.

6 Press the switch plunger down, and repeat the measurement. The reading on the meter should be open-circuit (very high resistance), and the continuity tester light should go out.

7 If the switch does not behave as described, or is intermittent in its operation, then a new switch must be fitted; the unit is not serviceable.

Refitting

8 Refit the brake light switch by reversing the removal procedure.

19 Anti-lock Braking System (ABS) components - general information

The Anti-lock Braking System (ABS) is managed by an Electronic Control Unit (ECU), which has the capacity to monitor the status and condition of all the components in the system, including itself. If the ECU detects a fault, it responds by shutting down the ABS and illuminating the dashboard-mounted ABS warning light. Under these circumstances, conventional non-ABS braking is maintained. If the nature of the fault detected is such that it may interfere with the operation of the conventional braking system as well, the ECU also illuminates the normal brake warning light.

As a consequence, if the ABS warning lights indicate that all is not well, it is very difficult to diagnose problems with the system, without the equipment and expertise to electronically "interrogate" the ECU. Hence, this Section is limited firstly to a list of the basic checks that should be carried out, to establish the integrity of the system, (eg - is there enough brake fluid?, is anything leaking?, etc). Section 20 is

limited to a description of the removal and refitting of the ABS wheel sensors and ECU only, as in certain instances, it will be necessary to remove these components to gain access to other assemblies on the vehicle.

If the cause of the fault cannot be immediately identified using the check list described, the *only* course of action open is to take the vehicle to a Saab dealer for examination. Dedicated test equipment is needed to interrogate ABS ECU, to determine the nature and incidence of the fault. For safety reasons, owners are strongly advised against attempting to diagnose complex problems with the ABS using standard workshop equipment.

Basic fault-finding checks

Brake fluid level

1 Check the brake fluid level with the vehicle parked on a flat surface, and the accumulator fully charged. To ensure that the accumulator is fully charged, switch on the ignition and listen to the hydraulic pump, which is part of the hydraulic unit assembly. The sound made by the pump will be quite audible; when it stops, the accumulator will be fully charged. Switch off the ignition, and without touching the brake pedal, check the brake fluid level in the reservoir. If necessary, top it up to the "MAX" mark with brake fluid of the correct grade.

2 If the level is exceptionally low, there may be leak somewhere in the hydraulic system. Refer to Chapter 1 and carry out a check of the brake hoses and pipes throughout the vehicle. If no leaks are apparent, remove each roadwheel in turn, and check for leaks at the brake caliper pistons - refer to Sections 5 and 6 for details of the front and rear caliper layout.

Fuses and relays

3 The fuses (and relays) for the ABS are situated in a separate protective box, in the engine bay adjacent to the brake fluid reservoir (see illustration). Remove the cover and pull out each fuse, one by one. Visually check the fuse filament; if it is difficult to see

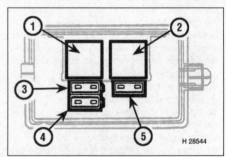

19.3 ABS fuses and relays

1 Hydraulic pump motor relay
2 ECU relay
3 ECU fuse, 10A
4 ECU fuse, 30A
5 Hydraulic pump motor fuse, 30A

whether or not it has blown, use a multimeter or continuity tester to check the electrical continuity of the fuse. If any of the fuses are blown, do not fit a new one, until the fault that caused the fuse to blow has been found and rectified; have the vehicle inspected by a Saab dealer, and inform him of your findings.

> ⚠️ *Caution: Fuses are there to protect equipment and people from damage; a blown fuse is an indication of a problem. Simply fitting a new fuse, or even bypassing the old one before the problem is corrected, will increase the risk of damage, and may result in a fire.*

4 The system relays can be found in the same protective box as the fuses. In general, relays are difficult to test conclusively without an electrical specification. However, the metal contacts inside a relay can usually be felt (and often heard) to open or close as it operates - if the relay in question does behave in this way when the ignition switch is turned on, it may be faulty. It should be noted that this is not a conclusive test; substitution with a known good relay *of the same type* is the only way to verify the component operation. If any of the relays is suspected of being faulty, it can be renewed by pulling it out of its socket - noting its orientation - and pushing in a new unit.

Electrical connections and earthing points

5 The engine bay is a hostile environment for electrical connections, and even the best seals can sometimes be penetrated. Water, chemicals and air will induce corrosion on the connector's contacts and prevent good continuity, sometimes intermittently. Disconnect the battery negative cable, then check the security and condition of all connectors at the ABS hydraulic unit, situated in the engine bay on the rear bulkhead. Unplug each connector, and examine the contacts inside.

6 Clean contacts that are found to be dirty or corroded using a proprietary contact cleaning oil, obtainable in most garages and car accessory shops. Avoid scraping the contacts clean with a blade, as this will accelerate

corrosion later. Use a piece of lint-free cloth in conjunction with the cleaning oil to produce a clean, shiny contact surface that will result in good electrical continuity.

7 In addition, check the security and condition of the electrical earthing point, on the front of the hydraulic unit.

20 Anti-lock Braking System (ABS) components - removal and refitting

1 Due to the complexity of the ABS, and the fact that specialised test equipment is needed to diagnose faults with it, this Section is limited to a description of the removal and refitting of the ABS wheel sensors and ECU only, as in certain instances, it will be necessary to remove these components to gain access to other assemblies on the vehicle. Section 19 contains a list of the basic checks that should be carried out, to establish the integrity of the ABS system, and to help identify any prominent faults.

Wheel sensors
General

2 Two different types of ABS wheel sensor have been fitted to the Saab 9000 to date, although both versions are very similar in appearance and operation.

3 The most significant difference between the types of sensor is the method of installation and adjustment. Sensors fitted to pre-1990 model year vehicles have two fixings built into the sensor housing; a bolt to secure the sensor to the wheel hub assembly, and a set screw to adjust the protrusion depth of the sensor tip. The set screw has been deleted from sensors fitted to post-1990 model year vehicles, as these have a fixed protrusion depth, and require no adjustment once installed.

4 The later type of sensor can be retro-fitted to pre-1990 model year vehicles, by transferring the set screw and adjustment sleeve from the old sensor to the new one. A self-adhesive fibre spacer 0.65 mm thick (available from Saab dealers) is then pressed onto the end of the sensor tip, to give the

correct clearance when it is fitted; this procedure is described in more detail later in this Section.

Front wheel sensors - removal

5 Locate the harness connectors in the engine bay, behind the false bulkhead panel. They are bayonet-type connectors, released by squeezing together the finger grips and twisting the two halves of the connector apart.

6 Where applicable, raise the air conditioning coolant pipe clips by slackening the pipe clips, to allow the connector to pass underneath.

7 Slacken the retaining bolts, and raise the false bulkhead panel to allow the sensor cable and connector to pass underneath.

8 Ensure that the vehicle is parked on a level surface, then apply the handbrake and chock the rear wheels. Raise the front of the vehicle, resting it securely on axle stands, and remove the front roadwheel(s). Refer to *"Jacking, towing and wheel changing"* for guidance.

9 Refer to Chapter 11, and remove the rear section of the inner wheelarch liners.

10 Use a pair of cable shears to cut through the cable-tie that secures the sensor cable to its mounting bracket.

11 Carefully guide the sensor cable and connector through the grommet in the wheelarch.

12 Slacken and withdraw the sensor retaining bolt, extract the cable from the bracket at the base of the strut mounting, and remove the sensor from the hub assembly, together with its protective sleeve **(see illustrations)**.

Front wheel sensors - refitting

13 Push the sensor into the drilling in the hub assembly, then refit and tighten the retaining bolt.

14 Using a feeler blade inserted between the sensor tip and the toothed disc, set the clearance to the value listed in Specifications. When the clearance is correct, tighten the set screw.

15 Pass the sensor connector and cable through the grommet in the wheelarch, then secure the cable to the mounting bracket on the suspension strut, using a new cable-tie.

16 Refit the remainder of the components by reversing the removal sequence.

Rear wheel sensors - removal

17 Tilt the rear seat forwards to expose the cable covers in the floorpan. Remove the right or left-hand cover, as applicable.

18 Unplug the sensor cable at the connector. Note that the connectors are of the bayonet type, released by squeezing together the finger grips and twisting the two halves of the connector apart.

19 Ensure that the vehicle is parked on a level surface, then chock the front wheels and select first gear (manual transmission) or "Park" (automatic transmission). Raise the rear of the vehicle, rest it securely on axle stands and remove the right or left-hand rear roadwheel, as appropriate. Refer to *"Jacking, towing and wheel changing"* for guidance.

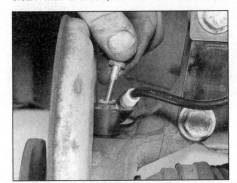

20.12a Slacken and withdraw the sensor retaining bolt . . .

20.12b . . . and remove the sensor from the hub assembly, together with its protective sleeve

20.21 Rear wheel ABS sensor (arrowed)

20 Extract the sensor cable from the clip, and carefully guide the connector through the grommet in the wheelarch.
21 Slacken and withdraw the sensor retaining bolt **(see illustration)**, then extract the sensor from the hub assembly.

Rear wheel sensors - refitting

22 Push the sensor into the drilling in the hub assembly, then refit and tighten the retaining bolt.
23 Using a feeler blade inserted between the sensor tip and the toothed disc, set the clearance to the value listed in Specifications. When the clearance is correct, tighten the set screw.
24 Refit the remainder of the components by reversing the removal sequence.

Rear wheel sensors (later type) - retro-fitting to pre-1990 models

Note: *Vehicles from 1990 model year onwards are fitted with a different type of wheel sensor*

and toothed disc. The sensors can be retro-fitted to pre-1990 model year cars, as follows.
25 Slide the adjusting sleeve off the old sensor, after slackening the set screw.
26 If renewing the fibre spacer on a used sensor, ensure that all traces of the old spacer are removed, using a fine wire brush and a rag moistened with a suitable solvent. Once the tip of the sensor is clean, peel the backing film from the rear of the new 0.65 mm thick fibre spacer, and press it onto the tip.
27 Slowly turn the brake disc by hand, and using a fine wire brush, clean off any traces of dirt and old fibre spacer from the toothed disc.
28 Insert the sensor into the drilling in the hub assembly, and tighten the retaining bolt. Gently push the spacer against the surface of the toothed disc, and tighten the set screw.

 Caution: Do not rotate the toothed disc until the sensor has been secured in position, or the disc teeth may gouge the fibre spacer, giving an incorrect sensor clearance.

Electronic control unit (ECU)
Removal

29 Disconnect the battery negative cable, and position it away from the terminal.
30 The ECU is mounted in the engine bay, behind the false bulkhead panel. Remove the left-hand cover to expose it.
31 Open the clips that secure the ECU in position. Lift the ECU slightly to allow access to the multi-plug connector, then unplug it by releasing the clamp bar.

 Caution: The ECU contains components that are sensitive to the levels of static electricity generated by a person during normal activity. Once the multi-plug harness connector has been unplugged, the exposed ECU pins can freely conduct stray static electricity to these components, damaging or even destroying them - the damage will be invisible, and may not manifest itself immediately. Expensive repairs can be avoided by observing the following basic handling rules:
a) *Handle a disconnected ECU by its case only; do not allow fingers or tools to come into contact with the pins.*
b) *When carrying an ECU around, "ground" yourself from time to time, by touching a metal object such as an unpainted water pipe; this will discharge any static that may have built up.*
c) *Do not leave the ECU unplugged from its connector for any longer than is absolutely necessary.*

Refitting

32 Refit the ECU by reversing the removal procedure.

 Warning: After working on any part of the braking system, test the vehicle exhaustively before bringing it back into service. Make sure that all warning lights go out, check all disturbed joints and unions for leaks, and top-up the fluid level in the reservoir to the "MAX" mark. Finally, repeatedly check that the braking system is capable of stopping the vehicle normally, before taking it out onto public roads.

Chapter 10 Suspension and steering

Contents

Degrees of difficulty

Easy, suitable for novice with little experience	**Fairly easy,** suitable for beginner with some experience	**Fairly difficult,** suitable for competent DIY mechanic	**Difficult,** suitable for experienced DIY mechanic	**Very difficult,** suitable for expert DIY or professional

Specifications

General

Front suspension type	Independent with MacPherson struts and anti-roll bar. Struts incorporate oil/gas combination dampers and coil springs
Rear suspension type	Dead beam axle, supported in Watts linkage with trailing lower arm/spring link, leading upper arm/torque bar, Panhard rod, anti-roll bar, coil springs and gas/oil combination shock absorbers
Steering type	Rack-and-pinion, hydraulic power assistance on all models

Coil springs

Front suspension:
  Free length .... 455 mm
  Rod diameter:
    Brown/violet colour-code .... 12.86 mm
    Orange/pink colour-code .... 12.97 mm
    Black/white colour-code .... 13.09 mm
Rear suspension:
  Free length .... 321 mm
  Rod diameter:
    Brown/blue colour-code .... 12.86 mm
    Black/white colour-code .... 12.97 mm

Roadwheels

	Aluminium alloy	Steel (spare)
Size	6J x 15 H2	4J x 15H2
Maximum radial runout	0.5 mm	-
Maximum lateral runout	0.5 mm	-
Wheel alignment (vehicle unladen):		
Rear:		
Toe-in	2.5 ± 1.5 mm	
Camber	-0.25 ± 0.25°	
Front:		
Toe-in	1.5 ± 0.5 mm (measured between inner rims)	
Camber	-0.65 ± 0.5°	
Castor	1.65 ± 0.5°	
Kingpin inclination	11.3 ± 0.5°	
Steering angle:		
Outer wheel	20.0°	
Inner wheel	21.0 ± 0.5°	

Tyres

For sizes and recommended pressures, see Chapter 1 Specifications

Track rod balljoints

Wear limits in inner balljoints:	
Axial play	2.0 mm
Radial play	1.0 mm
Wear limits in track rod ends:	
Axial play	2.0 mm
Radial play	1.0 mm

Power steering

Steering wheel turns, lock to lock	3.21
Servo fluid capacity	0.75 litres
Hydraulic servo pump:	
Belt tension:	
New belt	800 ± 45 N
After adjustment	535 ± 45 N
Minimum	355 N

Torque wrench settings

	Nm	lbf ft
Front suspension		
Front anti-roll bar link-to-anti-roll bar	30	22
Strut damper rod nut (after fitting to vehicle)	75	55
Strut-to-wing securing bolts	25	18
Suspension lower arm rear mounting nut	65	48
Suspension lower arm-to-anti-roll bar link	25	18
Suspension lower arm-to-balljoint	30	22
Suspension lower arm-to-front bush mounting bolts	50	37
Suspension lower arm-to-rear bush mounting bolts	50	37
Rear suspension		
Rear anti-roll bar mounting bolts	85	63
Rear brake caliper securing bolts	80	59
Rear shock absorber lower mounting bolt	85	63
Steering		
Power steering rack damper yoke locknut	80	59
Power steering rack hydraulic hose unions	27	20
Power steering rack inner balljoint	90	66
Power steering rack pinion locknut	30	22
Power steering rack retaining bolts	70	52
Power steering rack track rod end locknut	70	52
Steering column bracket mounting bolts, standard	23	17
Steering column bracket mounting bolts, green chromatised	18	13
Steering column universal joint intermediate shaft pinch-bolt	27	20
Steering column universal joint pinch-bolt	27	20
Steering swivel member to balljoint	50	37
Steering swivel member to brake caliper	90	66
Steering swivel member to hub	57	42
Steering swivel member to strut, lubricated threads	65	48
Steering swivel member to strut, unlubricated threads	80	59
Steering swivel member to track rod end	55	41
Steering wheel centre nut	30	22
Hubs		
Hub centre nut (front and rear)	280	207
Roadwheel bolts	115	85

1 General information

The front suspension is fully independent, utilising MacPherson struts and an anti-roll bar. The struts incorporate coil springs and double-acting gas/oil combination dampers, as a single assembly. The dampers are an integral part of the strut body, rather than an insert, but can easily be renewed after dismantling the assembly using a spring compression tool. The struts are mounted between the inner wings and the tops of the steering swivel members, which are in turn located by transverse lower suspension arms.

The front hubs are bolted to the steering swivel members, and house a double race of permanently-lubricated, non-serviceable ball bearings. The outboard driveshafts are secured in the hubs by a single nut and thrustwasher.

The front lower suspension arms are fabricated from pressed-steel, and are connected to the vehicle's subframe by bracketed rubber bushes. Bolt-on balljoints connect the suspension arms to the steering swivel members.

The rear suspension is arranged in a Watts

linkage configuration, employing a rigid, tubular axle located by upper and lower suspension arms - the trailing lower arms also serving as carriers for the coil springs. The leading upper arms provide positive axle location without limiting suspension travel, opposing the torsional reaction caused when the rear brakes are applied. Lateral axle location is achieved by means of a Panhard rod, bolted between the axle tube and a hanging bracket on the vehicle body. The anti-roll bar and shock absorbers are anchored by common brackets at the ends of the axle tube.

The rear hub carriers are mounted at either end of the axle tube, housing the stub axles onto which the wheel hubs are mounted.

A power-assisted, rack-and-pinion steering system is fitted to all variants. The steering rack is essentially a hydraulic ram, which is actuated mechanically by a pinion gear, and hydraulically by pressurised hydraulic fluid, supplied by the power steering pump. A two-stage steering column, coupled by universal joints, transmits effort applied at the steering wheel to the pinion and a control valve, which manages the supply of hydraulic fluid to the steering rack. When the steering wheel is turned, the valve directs fluid to the appropriate side of the ram, moving it linearly - extending and retracting the track rods attached to the ends of the rack. The track rods, connected to the steering swivel members by balljoints, then alter the steering angle of the roadwheels.

The design and mounting position of the steering column are such that, in the event of a head-on collision, it will absorb impact by crumpling longitudinally, and will also be deflected away from the driver.

The power steering pump is mounted externally on the engine block, and is driven by the auxiliary drivebelt.

2 Front suspension strut - removal, overhaul and refitting

Note: *A coil spring compression tool will be required during the course of this operation.*

 Warning: If renewing the strut damper during overhaul, BOTH dampers (left and right-hand) should be renewed as a pair, to preserve the handling characteristics of the vehicle.

Removal

1 Park the vehicle on a level surface, apply the handbrake, and chock the rear wheels. At the relevant roadwheel, remove the wheel centre cap and slacken the wheel bolts.
2 Apply the handbrake, then raise the front of the vehicle, rest it securely on axle stands and remove the roadwheel; refer to *"Jacking, towing and wheel changing"* for guidance.
3 Position a trolley jack underneath the suspension lower arm and raise it, so that it just takes the combined weight of the arm and steering swivel member.
4 Extract the flexible brake hose from the clip on the strut body, then slacken and withdraw the strut lower mounting bolts, recovering the ABS wheel sensor cable bracket.

 HAYNES HINT *Leave one of the lower bolts loosely inserted temporarily, to support the strut when the upper mounting bolts are removed.*

5 As the damper rod nut is difficult to slacken with the strut on the bench, it is recommended that it is slackened by half a turn whilst the strut is still fitted to the vehicle. The damper rod must be prevented from rotating as the nut is slackened - this can be achieved by fitting a 13/16" spark plug socket with a hex head to the damper rod nut, and inserting the hex Allen bit through the top of the socket. The socket can then be turned with a spanner, whilst the damper rod is held stationary **(see illustration)**.

 Warning: Slacken the nut by half a turn only - do not remove the it completely at this stage.

6 From the engine bay, detach the top of the strut from the wing by removing the three securing bolts; make a note their fitted locations to ensure correct refitting, as there are several possible mounting holes **(see illustration)**.
7 Lower the jack as necessary, to allow the strut to clear the steering swivel member, but avoid straining the suspension lower arm mountings.
8 Remove the strut from the wheelarch.

Overhaul

 Warning: Before attempting to dismantle the front suspension strut, the coil spring must be first held in compression, using a suitable tool. Adjustable coil spring compressors are readily-available, and are essential for this operation. DO NOT attempt to dismantle the strut without such a tool, as damage and/or personal injury is likely.

Note: *A new damper rod nut must be used on reassembly.*

9 Support the strut by clamping it in a vice; avoid damaging the surface of the strut by lining the vice jaws with aluminium or wooden blocks. Avoid distorting the mounting bracket.
10 Using the spring compressor, contract the coils of the spring just enough to relieve all pressure from the upper spring seat **(see illustration)**.
11 Prise out the dust cap from the top of the strut, to expose the retaining nut. Using the method described in *"Removal"* to keep the damper rod stationary, slacken the nut until it can be removed by hand.

 Warning: Ensure that the upper spring seat has been completely relieved of spring pressure before removing the retaining nut.

12 Lift off the top bearing plate, upper spring seat, coil spring (still compressed), lower spring seat, compression stop and rubber gaiter. Carefully release the spring compression tool.
13 Examine the coil spring for signs of general wear, deterioration or damage. In particular, look for cracking and serious

2.5 Using a 13/16" spark plug socket and hex Allen bit to slacken the strut damper rod nut

2.6 Detach the top of the strut from the wing by removing the three securing bolts

2.10 Using the spring compressor, contract the coils of the spring just enough to relieve all pressure from the upper spring seat

2.16 Pass the lower spring seat over the damper rod and fit it to the cup on the strut body

2.17a Pass the rubber gaiter over the piston rod, and push it into position

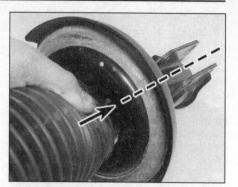

2.17b Rotate the gaiter to align the mark on its lower edge (arrowed) with the strut lower mounting bracket

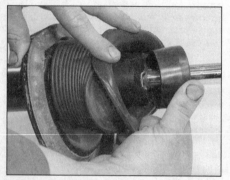

2.18 Press the dust cap onto the top of the damper unit

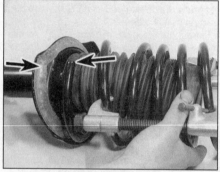

2.19 Fit the coil spring onto the lower spring seat, rotating it to engage the end of the coil with the step in the lower spring seat (arrowed)

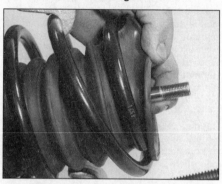

2.20 Fold the upper lip of the gaiter over the top of the coil spring

corrosion; renew the spring if either are found. Check the squareness by resting the spring vertically on a flat surface, and placing an engineer's square against it. A specific tolerance is not quoted, but if the spring is obviously distorted, renew it.

14 Prise off the dust cap, and inspect the damper section for signs of fluid leakage, particularly from the piston rod seal. Test the action of the damper by pushing the piston rod firmly through two or three full-length strokes, then rapidly through several short strokes. Smooth, consistent resistance should be felt; if the action is at all uneven, weak or unduly noisy, then the damper unit should be renewed. Check the piston rod for signs of corrosion or distortion and again, renew the

damper unit if its condition is unsatisfactory.
15 Examine the compression stop, rubber gaiter and spring seats; renew those that are damaged, worn or corroded. Note that a split or perished gaiter will admit dirt into the damper, and possibly cause it to fail.
16 Pass the lower spring seat over the damper rod, and fit it to the cup on the strut body (see illustration).
17 Pass the rubber gaiter over the piston rod, and push it into position; the lower edge of the gaiter must be 12 mm above the surface of the lower spring seat cup. Rotate the gaiter to align the mark on its lower edge with the strut lower mounting bracket (see illustrations).

18 Press the dust cap onto the top of the damper unit (see illustration).
19 Contract the coil spring using the compression tool. Fit it onto the lower spring seat, rotating it to engage the end of the coil with the step in the lower spring seat (see illustration). Ensure that the compression is sufficient to allow the top fixings to be installed.
20 Fold the upper lip of the gaiter over the top of the coil spring (see illustration).
21 Fit the compression stop over the piston rod, and slide it into position (see illustration).
22 Refit the upper spring seat, aligning the notch in its edge with the mark on the lower edge of the gaiter and the strut lower mounting bracket (see illustration).

2.21 Fit the compression stop over the piston rod, and slide it into position

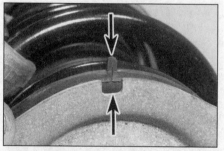

2.22 Refit the upper spring seat, aligning the notch in its edge with the mark on the lower edge of the gaiter and the strut lower mounting bracket (arrowed)

2.23a Refit the top bearing plate . . .

2.23b . . . and fit the new damper rod nut

2.24 Lift the strut assembly into the wheelarch

2.25 Align the three mounting holes at the top of the strut with those on the inner wing, making reference to the notes made during removal. Insert the retaining bolts, but hand-tighten them only at this stage

23 Refit the top bearing plate, and fit the new damper rod nut **(see illustrations)**. Using the method described in *"Removal"*, partially tighten the retaining nut. **Note:** *It is recommended that the nut is tightened to the final torque* **after** *the strut has been refitted to the vehicle, as this is difficult to achieve with the strut on the bench.* Check that the assembly marks are still aligned, before removing the compression tool.

Refitting

24 Lift the strut assembly into the wheelarch, and insert the top through the mounting hole in the inner wing **(see illustration)**.
25 Align the three mounting holes at the top of the strut with those on the inner wing,

making reference to the notes made during removal. Insert the retaining bolts, but hand-tighten them only at this stage **(see illustration)**.
26 Using the method described in *"Removal"*, use a socket and hex Allen bit to tighten the damper rod nut to the specified torque.
27 Align the mounting holes at the base of the strut with those on the steering swivel member, raising the jack as necessary, then refit the retaining bolts. On vehicles with ABS, remember to fit the wheel sensor cable bracket to the upper of the two mounting bolts. Tighten the bolts to the specified torque **(see illustrations)**.
28 Press the flexible brake hose into the clip at the base of the strut body **(see illustration)**.
29 Tighten the three strut upper mounting bolts to the specified torque.
30 Refit the roadwheel and bolts, then lower the vehicle to the ground. Tighten the roadwheel bolts to the correct torque.

3 Front suspension lower arm - removal and refitting

Removal

1 Park the vehicle on a level surface, apply the handbrake, and chock the rear wheels. At the relevant roadwheel, remove the wheel centre cap, and slacken the wheel bolts.
2 Raise the front of the vehicle, rest it securely

on axle stands and remove the roadwheel; refer to *"Jacking, towing and wheel changing"* for guidance.
3 Slacken and remove the three nuts that secure the lower suspension arm to the balljoint at the base of the steering swivel member.
4 Remove the nut that secures the anti-roll bar link to the lower suspension arm, referring to Section 4 for details. Recover the washers and bushes.
5 Again referring to Section 4, slacken the nut between the anti-roll bar link and anti-roll bar just enough to allow movement between them; do not remove the nut completely.
6 Pull the hub assembly away from the vehicle slightly, then push down on the lower suspension arm, and extract the anti-roll bar link from it.

⚠ *Caution: Do not deflect the suspension arm more than is necessary to remove the link, as this may damage the mountings.*

7 At the front mounting, remove the two nuts from the bolts that secure the suspension arm to the subframe **(see illustration)**. Using a narrow screwdriver, push the ends of the bolt threads back into the subframe, to allow the bearing bracket to clear the bolt threads.
8 At the rear mounting, remove the retaining

2.27a Refit the strut lower mounting bolts, then tighten them to the specified torque

2.27b On vehicles with ABS, remember to fit the wheel sensor cable bracket to the upper of the two mounting bolts

2.28 Press the flexible brake hose into the clip at the base of the strut body

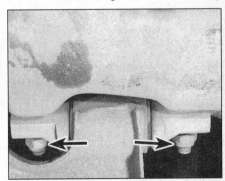

3.7 At the front mounting, remove the two nuts from the bolts that secure the suspension arm to the subframe

4.3 Slacken and remove the bolts (arrowed) at the U-clamps on the subframe, then release the anti-roll bar

4.5 Remove the nut (arrowed) that secures the anti-roll bar link rod to the suspension arm

4.6 Slacken the nut (arrowed) at the end of the anti-roll bar to allow the link rod to move freely

bolts and screws, then lower the reinforcement plate away from the subframe.

Refitting

10 Offer the suspension arm up to its mounting position on the vehicle. Line up the front bearing mounting bracket with the mounting holes on the subframe, then from the engine side of the subframe, push the mounting bolts through the bracket holes. Refit the nuts, but leave them loose at this stage.

11 At the rear mounting, line up the bearing bracket with the mounting holes on the subframe. Refit the reinforcement plate and the retaining bolts and screws.

12 Securely tighten the front bearing retaining nuts and reinforcement plate bolts and screws.

13 Pull the hub assembly away from the vehicle slightly, and engage the anti-roll bar link with the mounting hole in the suspension arm. Refit the bushes and washers, ensuring that the convex sides of the washers face the bush. Refit the retaining nut and tighten it to the specified torque.

14 Tighten the nut that secures the anti-roll bar to the link rod, observing the specified torque figure.

15 Engage the three balljoint mounting bolts with the holes in the end of the suspension arm, fit new nuts and tighten them to the specified torque.

16 Refit the roadwheel and bolts, then lower the vehicle to the ground and tighten the bolts to the correct torque. Refit the wheel centre cap.

17 Check and if necessary adjust the front toe setting; refer to Section 23.

4 Front anti-roll bar - removal and refitting

Removal

1 Park the vehicle on a level surface, apply the handbrake, and chock the rear wheels. Remove the wheel centre caps and slacken the wheel bolts.

2 Raise the front of the vehicle, rest it securely on axle stands and remove the roadwheels;

refer to "*Jacking, towing and wheel changing*" for guidance.

3 Slacken and remove the bolts at the U-clamps on the subframe, then release the anti-roll bar **(see illustration)**.

4 Working on one side of the vehicle at a time, remove the three nuts that secure the suspension lower arm to the balljoint at the base of the steering swivel member.

5 Remove the nut that secures the anti-roll bar link rod to the suspension arm **(see illustration)**; recover the bushes and washers.

6 Slacken the nut at the end of the anti-roll bar to allow the link rod to move freely **(see illustration)**, then push down on the suspension arm and extract the link rod from it.

7 Repeat the above operations at the other suspension arm.

8 Carefully withdraw the anti-roll bar from the vehicle.

9 Inspect the rubber bushes at the subframe U-clamps and at the anti-roll bar link mounting for signs of wear or deterioration; renew bushes that are perished, deformed or split.

10 Inspect the anti-roll bar itself for cracks, particularly around the mounting points.

Refitting

11 Manoeuvre the anti-roll bar into position on the subframe.

12 Insert the anti-roll bar link into the mounting hole in the suspension arm. Ensure that the bushes and washers are correctly arranged on the thread - the bushes fit either side of the suspension arm, and the washers fit outside of the bushes, convex side facing the suspension arm.

13 Fit the retaining nuts and tighten them to the specified torque.

14 Lift the suspension arm to engage the balljoint bolts in their mounting holes. Fit new retaining nuts, and tighten them to the specified torque.

15 Repeat the above operations at the other suspension arm.

16 Fit the anti-roll bar into the two U-clamps on the subframe, and tighten the retaining bolts.

17 Refit the roadwheels and bolts, then lower the vehicle and tighten the roadwheel bolts to the specified torque. Refit the wheel centre cap.

5 Steering swivel member - removal and refitting

Removal

1 Park the vehicle on a level surface, apply the handbrake, and chock the rear wheels.

2 At the relevant roadwheel, remove the wheel centre cap, then slacken the wheel bolts.

3 Slacken and remove the hub centre nut (recover the thrustwasher, where fitted).

4 Raise the front of the vehicle, rest it securely on axle stands and remove the roadwheel; refer to "*Jacking, towing and wheel changing*" for guidance.

5 Refer to the relevant Sections of Chapter 9 and remove the brake caliper, carrier and disc from the steering swivel member. Do not disconnect the caliper from the brake hose; hang it inside the wheelarch from the coil spring, using a cable-tie or wire, so that the hose is not strained.

6 On vehicles with ABS, refer to Chapter 9 and disconnect the wheel sensor from the steering swivel member. Tie it back using wire or a cable-tie.

7 Referring to Section 22, detach the track rod end balljoints from the steering swivel member, using a balljoint splitter.

8 Slacken and remove the two bolts that secure the bottom of the suspension strut to the steering swivel member, referring to Section 2 for details. On vehicles with ABS, position the wheel sensor cable away from the work area.

9 Remove the locking clip, then slacken and completely withdraw the pinch-bolt from the balljoint spigot at the underside of the steering swivel member **(see illustrations)**.

10 Separate the suspension lower arm from the steering swivel member - if necessary, refer to Section 4 unbolt the anti-roll bar link rod from it, to allow a greater degree of

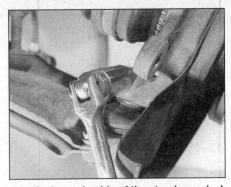

5.9a At the underside of the steering swivel member, remove the locking clip then slacken . . .

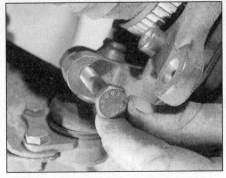

5.9b . . . and completely withdraw the pinch-bolt from the balljoint spigot

5.12 Support the driveshaft, and lift off the steering swivel member

movement. Do not allow the arm to hang unsupported, as this may damage the bush bearings - position a jack underneath the arm and raise it to provide support.

11 Push the splined section of the driveshaft out of the hub. The driveshaft may be difficult to extract, due to the locking compound applied to the spines. If this is the case, refit the old driveshaft nut to protect the threads, then tap the end of the shaft with a soft-faced mallet, to drive it out through the hub. Alternatively, a suitable three-legged puller may be used.

12 Support the driveshaft, and lift off the steering swivel member **(see illustration)**. To avoid straining the CV joints, allow the driveshaft to rest on the suspension lower arm, or alternatively support it from the coil spring using wire or a cable-tie.

13 Refer to Section 6 for details of the inspection, removal and refitting of the hub assembly.

14 Use a suitable cleaning agent to remove all traces of grease and locking compound from the outboard driveshaft splines and bearing contact surface.

Refitting

15 Apply a smear of grease to the balljoint spigot, then fit the steering swivel member over it. Loosely refit the pinch-bolt and nut,

ensuring that it engages with the slot machined in the spigot.

16 Apply thread-locking compound to the outer 10 mm of the outboard driveshaft splines **(see illustration)**, then rotate the steering swivel member to allow the outboard driveshaft and CV joint to be inserted. Loosely fit the new driveshaft flange nut (or nut and thrustwasher, where applicable).

17 Refit the bolts that secure the bottom of the suspension strut to the bracket on the top of the steering swivel member, and tighten them to the specified torque; refer to Section 2 for details.

18 On vehicles fitted with ABS, refit (and where applicable, adjust) the wheel sensor; refer to Chapter 9 for details.

19 Tighten the balljoint pinch-bolt to the specified torque and refit the locking clip **(see illustrations)**.

20 Insert the track rod end into the mounting hole in the steering swivel member, and tighten the nut to the specified torque; refer to Section 22 for details.

21 Refit the brake disc and caliper, referring to Chapter 9 for guidance. Press the brake hose into the clip on the strut body.

22 Refit the roadwheel, and partially tighten the bolts.

23 Lower the vehicle to the ground, then tighten the roadwheel bolts to the specified torque.

24 Tighten the driveshaft nut to the specified torque, referring to Chapter 8 for details, then refit the wheel centre cap.

25 Allow at least an hour for the thread-locking compound on the driveshaft to harden, before bringing the vehicle back into service.

6 Front hub assembly -
removal and refitting

Note: *The hub is a sealed, permanently-lubricated unit, designed to last the life of the vehicle without maintenance or servicing. The bearings are not adjustable, and if wear is discovered, the hub should be renewed as a complete assembly. The hub and driveshaft nuts should not be tightened beyond their recommended torques in an attempt to adjust the bearings.*

Removal

1 Refer to Section 5 and remove the steering swivel member.

2 Lay the assembly flat on a worksurface, then with a scribe or marker pen, mark the relationship between the hub and the steering swivel member. Note that on earlier models, the hub flange has a cut-out on its upper surface to aid alignment.

3 Remove the four bolts that secure the hub

5.16 Apply thread-locking compound to the outer 10 mm of the outboard driveshaft splines

5.19a Tighten the balljoint pinch-bolt to the specified torque . . .

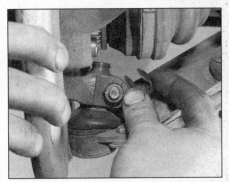

5.19b . . . and refit the locking clip

6.3 Remove the four bolts that secure the hub to the steering swivel member

6.4a Lift off the steering swivel member . . .

6.4b . . . and brake disc backplate

to the steering swivel member **(see illustration)**.

4 Lift off the steering swivel member and brake disc backplate **(see illustrations)**.

Refitting

5 Reassemble the hub and brake disc backplate to the steering swivel member by reversing the removal procedure, observing the specified torque wrench settings. Use the marks made during removal to ensure that the hub is aligned correctly.

6 Refer to Section 5 and refit the steering swivel member to the vehicle.

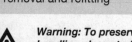

7 Rear shock absorber - removal and refitting

⚠️ *Warning: To preserve the handling characteristics of the vehicle, BOTH rear dampers (left and right-hand) should be renewed as a pair.*

Removal

1 Park the vehicle on a level surface, chock the front wheels and select first gear (manual transmission) or "PARK" (automatic transmission). At the applicable rear roadwheel, remove the centre cap and slacken the bolts.

2 Raise the rear of the vehicle, rest it securely on axle stands and remove the roadwheel; refer to *"Jacking, towing and wheel changing"*.

7.4 Remove the nut, locknut, cup and bush from the damper rod

3 Reposition the jack, so that it is positioned under the joint between the axle tube and the lower suspension arm. Raise the jack just enough to relieve the load on the shock absorbers and anti-roll bar.

4 From within the load space, remove the spare wheel protective panel, then fold back the carpet and side trim panel, to expose the shock absorber top mounting; refer to Chapter 11 for guidance. Remove the nut, locknut, cup and bush from the damper rod **(see illustration)**.

5 From underneath the vehicle, remove the bolt that secures the shock absorber and anti-roll bar to the mounting bracket on the axle tube **(see illustration)**.

6 Lower the jack slightly, and separate the shock absorber bottom mounting from the axle tube.

7 Withdraw the shock absorber from the wheelarch, noting the positions of the remaining bush and washer at the top mounting.

8 Inspect the shock absorber for signs of fluid leakage, particularly from the piston rod seal. Test the action of the shock absorber by pushing the piston rod firmly through two or three full length strokes, then rapidly through several short strokes. Smooth, consistent resistance should be felt; if the action is at all uneven, weak or unduly noisy, then the shock absorber unit should be renewed.

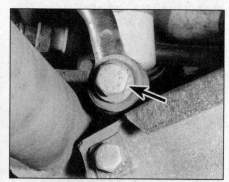

7.5 From underneath the vehicle, remove the bolt (arrowed) that secures the shock absorber and anti-roll bar to the mounting bracket on the axle tube

9 Check the piston rod for signs of corrosion or distortion; renew the shock absorber unit if its condition is unsatisfactory.

Refitting

10 Refit the shock absorber by following the removal sequence in reverse order, noting the following:

a) *Ensure that the shock absorber top mounting components are refitted in the correct order (see illustration).*

b) *Tighten the lower mounting bolt to the specified torque.*

c) *Refit the roadwheel, lower the vehicle to the ground and tighten the roadwheel bolts to the specified torque.*

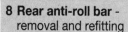

8 Rear anti-roll bar - removal and refitting

Removal

1 Park the vehicle on a level surface, chock the front wheels and select first gear (manual transmission) or "PARK" (automatic transmission). At the rear roadwheels, remove the centre caps and slacken the bolts.

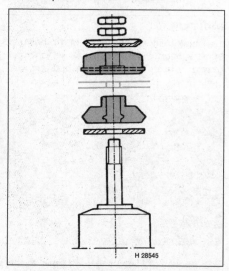

H 28545

7.10 Correct assembled order of rear shock absorber top mounting components

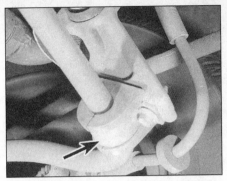

8.5 Free the anti-roll bar from the inboard mountings by removing the two bolts that secure the U-clamps (arrowed) to the hanging brackets

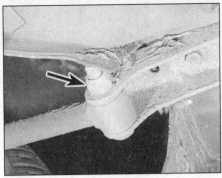

10.3a Unbolt the fixings at either end of the torque arm, at the floorpan (arrowed) . . .

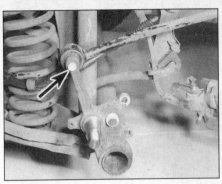

10.3b . . . and the top of the hub carrier (arrowed; hub removed for clarity)

2 Raise the rear of the vehicle, rest it securely on axle stands and remove the roadwheels; refer to *"Jacking, towing and wheel changing"*.
3 On one side of the vehicle, reposition the jack, so that it is positioned under the joint between the axle tube and the lower suspension arm. Raise the jack just enough to relieve the load on the shock absorber and anti-roll bar.
4 Referring to the relevant paragraphs of Section 7, unbolt the anti-roll bar from the mounting on the axle tube (see illustration 7.5). Repeat the procedure at the other side of the vehicle.
5 Free the anti-roll bar from the inboard mountings by removing the two bolts that secure the U-clamps to the hanging brackets **(see illustration)** .
6 Lower the anti-roll bar away from the vehicle, and recover the bushes from the inboard mountings.
7 Inspect the rubber bushes for signs of wear or deterioration; renew bushes that are perished, deformed or split. Examine the anti-roll bar for cracks, particularly around the mounting points.

Refitting

8 Refit the anti-roll bar by following the removal sequence in reverse order, noting the following:
a) *Tighten the lower mounting bolt to the specified torque.*
b) *Refit the roadwheel, lower the vehicle to the ground and tighten the roadwheel bolts to the specified torque.*

9 Rear coil spring - removal and refitting

Removal

1 Park the vehicle on a level surface, chock the front wheels and select first gear (manual transmission) or "PARK" (automatic transmission). At the applicable roadwheel, remove the centre cap and slacken the bolts.

2 Raise the rear of the vehicle, and rest it securely on axle stands.
3 Detach the handbrake cable from the suspension lower arm, by prising out the press-stud clip.
4 Position a jack underneath the trailing end of the suspension lower arm, then remove the bolt that secures the arm to the axle tube; refer to Section 12 for details.
5 Use the jack to lower the suspension arm, until the coil spring can be removed from its mounting position. Recover the rubber seat.

Refitting

6 Place the spring and rubber seat in their mounting positions on the suspension lower arm; ensure that the stepped lower edge of the spring engages with the ridge on the suspension arm.
7 Use the jack to raise the suspension arm; ensure that the top of the spring sits squarely on its upper seat.
8 Refit the bolt that secures the trailing end of the suspension arm to the axle tube, and tighten it securely.
9 Screw the handbrake cable bracket back in position on the edge of the suspension arm.
10 Refit the roadwheel and bolts, then lower the vehicle to the ground and tighten the roadwheel bolts to the specified torque. Refit the wheel centre cap.

10 Rear suspension torque arm - removal and refitting

Removal

1 Park the vehicle on a level surface, chock the front wheels and select first gear (manual transmission) or "PARK" (automatic transmission). At the applicable roadwheel, remove the centre cap and slacken the bolts.
2 Raise the rear of the vehicle, and rest it securely on axle stands. Remove the roadwheel.
3 Unbolt the fixings at either end of the torque arm, at the floorpan, and at the top of the hub carrier **(see illustrations)**.
4 Lower the leading end of the arm away from the bracket on the floorpan, and then push the

trailing end off the hub carrier. Recover the bushes as the arm is released.
5 Examine the bushes for signs of wear or deterioration, and renew them if necessary.

Refitting

6 Refit the torque arm by following the removal process in reverse.

11 Rear suspension Panhard rod - removal and refitting

Removal

1 Park the vehicle on a level surface, chock the front wheels and select first gear (manual transmission) or "PARK" (automatic transmission).
2 Raise the rear of the vehicle, and rest it securely on axle stands. Removal of the roadwheels will improve access, but is not essential.
3 Slacken and withdraw the two Panhard rod mounting bolts, first at the axle tube and then at the hanging bracket at the vehicle's underside **(see illustrations)**.
4 Remove the Panhard rod from the vehicle, recovering the bushes.
5 Check the rod for distortion, damage and serious corrosion. Examine the bushes for signs of wear or damage; renew them if they appear perished, deformed or age-hardened.

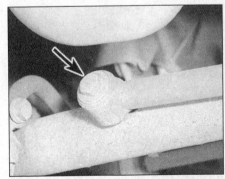

11.3a Slacken and withdraw the two Panhard rod mounting bolts, first at the axle tube (arrowed) . . .

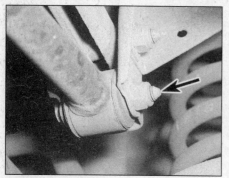

11.3b . . . and then at the hanging bracket at the vehicle's underside (arrowed)

12.3 Detach the handbrake cable from the suspension lower arm, by prising out the press-stud clip

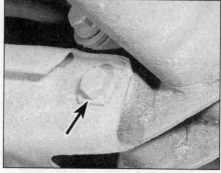

12.4 Remove the bolt (arrowed) that secures the arm to the axle tube

Refitting

6 Refit the Panhard rod by following the removal process in reverse.

12 Rear suspension lower arm - removal and refitting

Removal

1 Park the vehicle on a level surface, chock the front wheels and select first gear (manual transmission) or "PARK" (automatic transmission). At the applicable roadwheel, remove the centre cap and slacken the bolts.

2 Raise the rear of the vehicle, rest it securely on axle stands and remove the roadwheel; refer to *"Jacking, towing and wheel changing"*.

3 Detach the handbrake cable from the suspension lower arm, by prising out the press-stud clip **(see illustration)**.

4 Position a jack underneath the trailing end of the suspension lower arm, then remove the bolt that secures arm to the axle tube **(see illustration)**.

5 Use the jack to lower the suspension arm, until the coil spring can be removed from its mounting position - refer to Section 9 for details.

6 Detach the leading-end mounting bracket and bush from the vehicle's floorpan by removing the two retaining bolts **(see illustration)**.

7 Withdraw the suspension arm from under the vehicle. Check it for damage, corrosion and distortion. Examine the leading-end bush for signs of wear or damage; if it is at all perished, deformed or age-hardened, renew it. Likewise, if the trailing-end bush shows signs of wear, it should be renewed. The bush renewal procedures are described in the following paragraphs.

Leading-end bush - renewal

8 Slacken the nut and withdraw the centre bolt. Lift out the bush and bracket assembly.

9 Fit a new bush assembly, and refit the centre bolt.

⚠️ **Caution: Do not tighten the centre bolt until the suspension arm has been refitted to the vehicle.**

Trailing-end bush - renewal

10 Hold the suspension arm firmly in a vice; pad the jaws of the vice to protect the anti-corrosive surface of the arm. The bush can be removed by driving it out using a socket (with an external diameter just smaller than that of the bush) as a drift. Ensure that the socket bears squarely on the bush, then tap it out with a light mallet.

11 Lubricate the new bush with washing-up liquid, then carefully drive it into suspension arm, using the same method employed during removal.

Refitting

12 Lift the suspension arm up to the subframe, and refit the bolts that secure the leading-end bush and bracket to the vehicle's floorpan.

13 Seat the coil spring and rubber seat in their mounting positions on the suspension lower arm, referring to Section 9 for details.

14 Using the jack, raise the suspension arm to engage the top of the spring with the upper seat on the floorpan.

15 Refit the bolt that secures the trailing end of the suspension arm to the axle tube, and tighten it securely.

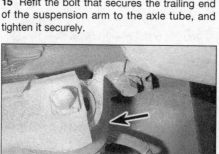

12.6 Detach the leading-end mounting bracket and bush (arrowed) from the vehicle's floorpan by removing the two retaining bolts

16 Press the handbrake cable clip back in position on the edge of the suspension arm.

17 Refit the roadwheel and bolts, then lower the vehicle to the ground and tighten the roadwheel bolts to the specified torque. Refit the wheel centre cap.

13 Rear hub assembly - removal and refitting

Removal

1 Park the vehicle on a level surface, select first gear (manual transmission) or "PARK" (automatic transmission) and chock the front wheels. Slacken the bolts at the applicable rear roadwheel.

2 Raise the rear of the vehicle, support it securely on axle stands and remove the roadwheel.

3 Refer to Chapter 9 and remove the brake caliper, carrier and disc. Note that there is no need to disconnect the caliper from the brake hose; use wire or a cable-tie to suspend it from the coil spring, to avoid straining the hose.

4 Using a mallet and a stout screwdriver or chisel, prise off the hub dust cap ; if it is stiff, work around the perimeter of the cap, and tap it off progressively **(see illustration)**. Do not use excessive force, as this may damage the cap, necessitating its renewal.

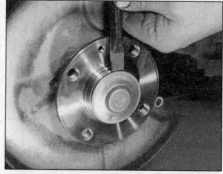

13.4 Using a mallet and a stout screwdriver or chisel, prise off the hub dust cap

13.6a Remove the hub nut (and thrustwasher, where fitted) . . .

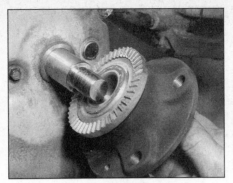

13.6b . . . then lift off the hub

13.10 Fit a new nut (and thrustwasher, where applicable) and tighten it to the specified torque

5 Fit a socket and breaker bar over the wheel hub nut. Loosely refit two of the roadwheel bolts to the hub flange, and insert a lever bar between; use it to brace the wheel hub, as the hub nut is slackened.

 Caution: On earlier models, the flange of the hub nut is deformed into a groove in the stub axle, to lock it in position. Before attempting to slacken the nut, bend back the nut flange to release it from the stub axle, using a punch and hammer.

6 Remove the hub nut (and thrustwasher, where fitted), then lift off the hub **(see illustrations)**.
7 Clean the stub axle using a suitable degreasing agent, paying particular attention to the thread and bearing contact surface.

 Caution: Take care to ensure that the delicate tip of the ABS wheel sensor is not damaged during the cleaning process.

8 Examine the stub axle for evidence of wear, in the form of channelling or gouging where the bearings contact the axle surface; a polished ring is normal, but excessive erosion or cracks indicate that the stub axle and hub carrier are in need of renewal. These are an integral part of the rear axle and must be renewed as a complete assembly; a description of this procedure is detailed in Section 14.

Refitting

9 Apply a smear of multi-purpose grease to the stub axle, then fit the hub over the stub axle.
10 Ensure that the hub is seated squarely, then fit a new nut (and thrustwasher, where applicable), tightening it to the specified torque **(see illustration)**. Note: *On earlier models, the flange of the nut should be deformed into the groove in the stub axle thread, using a hammer and punch, to lock it into position.*
11 Refit the dust cap **(see illustration)**, and tap it back into place using a soft-faced mallet.
12 Refit the brake disc, carrier and caliper, referring to Chapter 9 for details.

13 Refit the roadwheel and bolts, then lower the vehicle to the ground. Tighten the roadwheel bolts to the specified torque and refit the roadwheel centre cap.

14 Rear axle tube - removal and refitting

Removal

1 Park the vehicle on a level surface, select first gear (manual transmission) or "PARK" (automatic transmission) and chock the front roadwheels; do not apply the handbrake. Remove the centre caps and slacken the rear roadwheel bolts.
2 Raise the rear of the vehicle, support it securely on axle stands and remove the roadwheels; refer to *"Jacking, towing and wheel changing"* for guidance.
3 Unbolt the handbrake cable brackets from the lower suspension arms.
4 Remove the brake calipers, as described in Chapter 9. There is no need to disconnect the caliper from the brake hose; use wire or a cable-tie to suspend it from the suspension coil spring, to avoid straining the hose.
5 Unbolt the Panhard rod from the axle tube; tie the free end to the underside if the body, to keep it out of the way.
6 Manoeuvre a jack under the centre point of the axle tube. Protect the axle tube by inserting a block of wood between it and the jack head. Raise it just enough to relieve the suspension of the axle's weight, but no more.
7 Remove the bolt that secures the shock absorber and anti-roll bar to the bracket on the axle tube; refer to Section 7 for more detail.
8 Slowly lower the jack, and allow the axle tube to drop away from the vehicle. As the suspension lower arms deflect, retrieve the coil springs and store them out of the way; refer to Section 9 for details.
9 Refer to Section 10 and unbolt the leading ends of the torque arms from the tops of the hub carriers; tie them up inside the wheelarch, clear of the work area.
10 Remove the bolts that secure the trailing ends of the suspension lower arms to the bases of the hub carriers. Place a wooden

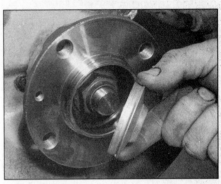

13.11 Refit the dust cap, and tap it back into place using a soft-faced mallet

block underneath the end of the suspension arm, to provide support whilst it is disconnected.

Refitting

11 Balance the axle tube on the jack head, and manoeuvre it underneath the vehicle.
12 Raise the axle up to its mounting position, and loosely refit the hub carrier-to-suspension lower arm and torque arm securing bolts.
13 Locate the coil springs squarely on the lower arm, referring to Section 9 for more detail.
14 Slowly raise the axle, ensuring that the coil springs contact their upper seats squarely; support the anti-roll bar as the axle is raised, so that it falls on the correct side of its mountings.
15 Line up the shock absorber and anti-roll bar bushes with their mounting bracket on the axle tube, and engage the retaining bolt through them. Fit the nuts, and tighten them to the specified torque.
16 Tighten the hub carrier-to-suspension lower arm and torque arm bolts securely. The jack can now be lowered away from the axle tube.
17 Lower the Panhard rod into position and refit the mounting bolt through the axle tube; refer to Section 11 for details.
18 Refit the brake calipers, referring to Chapter 9 for details.
19 Press the handbrake cable clips into the suspension lower arms.

15.8 Fit the new washer in place, then screw a new steering wheel nut on to the shaft thread, and tighten it to the specified torque (vehicle with SRS shown)

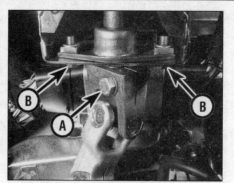

16.8 Steering column-to-intermediate shaft universal joint and lower bearing

A Upper pinch-bolt
B Lower bearing housing retaining bolts

16.10 On vehicles fitted with a driver's airbag/SRS, slacken and remove the transverse bolt from the support bracket (arrowed)

20 Fit the roadwheels and bolts, then lower the vehicle to the ground and tighten the roadwheel bolts to the specified torque. Refit the wheel centre caps.

15 Steering wheel -
removal and refitting

Removal

1 Park the vehicle with the front roadwheels pointing straight ahead. Turn the ignition switch to the "OFF" position, but keep the key in the barrel, to disarm the steering column lock

2 Disconnect the battery negative cable, and position it away from the terminal.

3 On vehicles fitted with a driver's airbag/SRS, refer to Chapter 11, Section 28 and remove the airbag module and rotary contact unit.

4 Remove the trim from non-airbag steering wheels as follows. On three-spoke steering wheels, prise out the triangular centre panel, unhooking the rubber flanges from the spokes. On four-spoke steering wheels, prise out the circular badge panel from the centre of the wheel.

5 Using a scribe or marker pen, mark the relationship between the steering wheel and steering column, then slacken, remove and discard the centre nut and washer, as new items must be used on refitting. Ensure that the steering wheel is kept in the straight ahead position throughout.

⚠️ **Caution: Do not use the ignition switch steering lock to brace the column whilst the nut is being removed, as this may cause damage.**

Refitting

6 Ensure that the front roadwheels are still pointing straight ahead.

7 Fit the steering wheel onto the shaft splines, aligning the marks made during removal, and engaging the direction indicator cancelling collar lug with the switch lever.

8 Fit the new washer in place, then screw a new nut on to the shaft thread, and tighten it to the specified torque **(see illustration)**.

⚠️ **Caution: Do not use the ignition switch steering lock to brace the column whilst the nut is being removed, as this may cause damage.**

9 On vehicles fitted with a driver's airbag/SRS, refer to Chapter 11, Section 28 and refit the rotary contact unit and airbag module.

10 On three-spoke steering wheels, press the wheel centre pad into place, ensuring that the rubber flanges hook over the spokes.

11 On four-spoke steering wheels, press the centre badge pad into place.

12 Road test the vehicle, to assess the steering wheel-to-roadwheel alignment. With the vehicle travelling in a straight line, the flat segment of the steering should be horizontal. Substantial misalignment means that the steering wheel has been refitted one or more splines adrift on the column; remove the wheel, rotate it as appropriate and refit it. Slight misalignment which cannot be eliminated by rotating the steering wheel to the adjacent spline can be corrected by adjusting the track rods by the same amount (but in opposite directions) on each side; refer to Sections 22 and 23 for details of track rod length adjustment.

16 Steering column, lock and ignition switch -
removal and refitting

Removal

1 Disconnect the battery negative cable, and position it away from the terminal.

2 Refer to Section 15 and remove the steering wheel.

3 Remove the screws, then lift off the upper and lower sections of the steering column cowling; refer to Chapter 11 for details.

4 Cut the wiring harness cable-tie to detach it from the steering column.

5 Refer to Chapter 12 and remove the column stalk switch assembly. Label the cables to aid refitting later, and tie them back out of the work area.

6 Remove the screws and drop the sound insulation panel away from the facia underside; referring to Chapter 11 for details.

7 Remove the floor ventilation duct from underneath the facia.

8 Locate the universal joint that connects the steering column shaft to the intermediate shaft. Slacken and remove the upper pinch-bolt from the steering column side of the joint, and pull it off the splined shaft **(see illustration)**.

9 Use circlip pliers to remove the circlip from the base of the steering column shaft.

10 On vehicles fitted with a driver's airbag/SRS, slacken and remove the transverse bolt from the support bracket **(see illustration)**.

11 On vehicles fitted with a steering column adjustment mechanism, use a centre-punch as a drift, and drive the tubular dowel out of the adjustment spindle. Make a note the orientation of the spindle with respect to the lock assembly casting, to aid the refitting process. Slacken the nut at the end of the spindle, then remove it together with the washer, and draw the spindle out. **Note:** *Use a wrench fitted with a hex Allen bit to hold the adjustment spindle stationary during this operation.*

12 Reach behind the facia, grasp the steering column, and push it up out of the lower bearing. The shaft, steering lock and ignition switch can now be withdrawn as a complete assembly.

⚠️ **Caution: Do not allow the two halves of the steering column splined joint to become separated. Unplug the multi-plug connector from the switch terminals.**

Refitting

13 Position the lock assembly over its mounting position in the facia. Engage the steering column with the lower bearing.

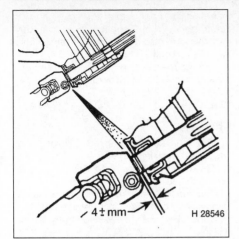

16.16 Adjust the upper pinch-bolt to give the correct clearance between the end of the universal joint flange and the column bracket

14 Where applicable, reassemble the steering wheel adjustment mechanism by inserting the spindle into the lock assembly, then fitting and tightening the washer and nut. Ensure that the adjustment spindle is correctly aligned, then use a centre-punch and mallet to drive the tubular dowel into the bore in the spindle.

15 To set the adjustment mechanism tension, set the clamp lever in the "unclamped" position, and slowly tighten the spindle nut. The tension is correct when resistance is just felt as the steering shaft is moved in and out. Set the lever in the "clamped" position, and check that the shaft is still free to rotate, but cannot be moved axially with reasonable force.

16 Refit the circlip to the bottom of the steering column shaft. Slide the universal joint onto both shafts, and refit the pinch-bolts and nuts. Ensure that the lower pinch-bolt is below the stop on the intermediate shaft. Adjust the upper pinch-bolt to give the correct clearance between the end of the universal joint flange and the column bracket **(see illustration)**. Finally, tighten the pinch-bolts to the specified torque.

17 Refit the remainder of the components in the following order:

a) *Refit the floor ventilation duct.*
b) *Refit the sound insulation panel to the underside of the facia.*
c) *Referring to Section 12, refit the stalk switch assembly to the steering column, and reconnect the wiring harness. Use the labels made during removal to ensure that the connectors are correctly coupled. Secure the harness with a cable-tie.*
d) *Refit the steering column cowling.*
e) *Referring to Section 15, refit the steering wheel. Check the steering wheel-to-roadwheel alignment by driving the vehicle.*
f) *Where applicable, refer to Chapter 11 and refit the rotary contact unit and airbag module.*

17 Steering column lower bearing - renewal

1 Refer to Section 16 and remove the ignition switch/steering lock and steering column assembly.
2 At the steering column bracket, remove the two bolts that retain the lower bearing housing; recover the serrated washers (refer to illustration 16.8).
3 Lift the housing away from the support bracket, and push out the bearing.
4 Lubricate the new bearing with a small quantity of multi-purpose grease, then push it into the housing.
5 Refit the housing to the support bracket, using new serrated washers, and tighten the bolts securely.
6 Refer to Section 16, and refit the ignition switch/steering lock and steering column assembly.

18 Power steering hydraulic system - draining, refilling and bleeding

Note: *The power steering hydraulic system must be bled if any part of the system has been disconnected.*

Draining

1 At the side of the fluid reservoir, thoroughly clean the area around the connection point for the fluid return hose (this is the smaller-diameter, uppermost hose). Slacken the clip, then disconnect the hose. Plug the open ends of the hose and reservoir port.
2 Insert the free end of the return hose into a clean, dry container, with a capacity of at least one litre.
3 Secure the container in the engine bay, away from any moving components and direct sources of heat.
4 Start the engine, and allow the hydraulic fluid to be pumped into the container. Turn the steering lock-to-lock twice, to purge the fluid from the steering rack.
5 When the flow of fluid ceases, turn off the engine immediately; do not allow the power steering pump to run dry for any length of time.

Refilling

6 Remove the fluid reservoir filler cap, and top-up to the maximum level mark with fluid of the specified type and grade; refer to Chapter 1 for guidance.

Bleeding

7 Park the vehicle on a level surface, apply the handbrake and chock the rear wheels. Raise the front of the vehicle, and rest it securely on axle stands; refer to *"Jacking, towing and wheel changing"* for guidance.
8 With the engine stopped, slowly move the steering from lock-to-lock several times to purge any trapped air, then top-up the level in the fluid reservoir. Repeat this procedure until the fluid level in the reservoir does not drop any further.
9 Start the engine, then slowly move the steering from lock-to-lock several times to purge out any remaining air in the system. Repeat this procedure until bubbles cease to appear in the fluid reservoir.
10 If an abnormal noise is heard from the pump or fluid pipes when the steering is operated, this is an indication that there is still air in the system. Confirm this by turning the wheels to the straight-ahead position and switching off the engine. If the fluid level in the reservoir rises, then air is present in the system, and further bleeding will be necessary. Repeat the above procedure as necessary.
11 Once all traces of air have been driven from the power steering hydraulic system, stop the engine and allow the system to cool. Finally, check that the fluid level is up to the maximum mark on the reservoir, and top-up if necessary.

19 Steering gear assembly - removal and refitting

Removal

1 Refer to Section 18 and drain the hydraulic fluid from the power steering system. Leave the fluid return hose disconnected from the power steering fluid reservoir.
2 Disconnect the battery negative cable, and position it away from the terminal.
3 To improve access to the steering gear, slacken the fixing bolt and move the engine oil filler/dipstick tube to one side.
4 At the power steering pump, clean the area around the delivery hose union. Disconnect the hose union from the pump body, then plug the exposed port and hose end, to prevent the ingress of dirt.
5 Refer to Chapter 11, and at the driver's footwell, remove the sound insulation panel from underneath the facia.
6 Peel back the carpet to expose the rubber gaiter at the base of the steering column intermediate shaft. Fold back the gaiter, and remove the lower pinch-bolt from the universal joint. At the point where the intermediate shaft is coupled to the upper steering column shaft, disconnect the lower pinch-bolt from the universal joint. Remove the intermediate shaft from under the facia.
7 At the point where the steering rack pinion shaft protrudes through the bulkhead, remove the retaining screws from the dished metal cover plate and lift it out, recovering the gasket, seal and rubber bush. Inspect the gasket for signs of wear or damage - renew it if necessary.
8 Remove the wheel centre caps, and slacken the wheel bolts. Apply the handbrake, then raise the front of the vehicle, rest it securely on

19.12a Steering rack left-hand retaining nut (arrowed)

19.12b Steering rack right-hand retaining nut (arrowed)

axle stands and remove the front roadwheels; refer to *"Jacking, towing and wheel changing"* for guidance.

9 Refer to Chapter 11 and remove the rear section of the right-hand wheelarch liner.

10 Refer to Section 22 and detach the track rod ends from the steering swivel members.

11 Where applicable, detach the subframe-to-wheelarch steady bar upper retaining bolt.

12 Working from underneath the vehicle, remove the two steering rack retaining bolts. It will be necessary to hold the corresponding nuts stationary with a spanner (or socket and wrench) by reaching between the bulkhead and subframe, into the engine bay **(see illustrations)**. Recover the washers and bushes, noting their order of assembly.

13 Where applicable, remove the subframe-to-wheelarch steady bar lower retaining bolt.

14 Pull down the free ends of the previously-disconnected hydraulic hoses, then lift the steering rack off its mounting points and withdraw it via the right-hand wheelarch, moving aside the wiring harness as necessary to prevent it from fouling the rack.

Refitting

15 The steering gear can be refitted by following the removal procedure in reverse, noting the following points:

a) *When refitting the steering rack mounting bolts on 1987 model year vehicles with chassis number* **H 1003410 or earlier,** *a 2 mm plain washer must be fitted to the left-hand bolt, between the rack assembly and the subframe.*

b) *Ensure that the steering rack retaining bolts are tightened to the specified torque.*

c) *When refitting new track rod ends, ensure that they are adjusted to the same length as the existing rods, as measured when they were removed.* **Note:** *Leave the locknuts loose initially, until the toe-setting is checked.*

d) *Refer to Section 22 and reconnect the track rod ends to the steering swivel members, observing the specified torque setting.*

e) *Tighten the pinch-bolts at the universal joints on the steering column intermediate shaft to the specified torque.*

f) *Referring to Section 18, refill and bleed the hydraulic system, using fluid of the specified grade.*

g) *Reconnect the battery negative cable and start the engine, then check the operation of the steering system.*

h) *Referring to Section 23, check the toe-setting and adjust it if necessary. On completion, tighten the track rod locknuts securely.*

i) *Make a final check of all unions and hoses that were disturbed, then re-check the reservoir fluid level.*

20 Power steering servo pump - removal and refitting

Removal

⚠️ **Caution: Avoid applying force to the servo pump shaft during removal/refitting, as this may damage the shaft bearings.**

1 Refer to Section 18, and drain the hydraulic fluid from the power steering system.

2 Disconnect the battery negative cable, and position it away from the terminal.

3 On pre-1994 model year vehicles, where the engine oil filler pipe is mounted to the side of the engine bay, withdraw the retaining screws and move it away, to improve access to the servo pump.

4 Refer to Chapter 2A and remove the engine upper mounting arm.

5 Thoroughly clean the area around the servo pump inlet hose - this is the larger-diameter hose that is connected between the hydraulic fluid reservoir and the servo pump. Plug the open ends of the hose and the pump port.

6 Remove the mounting screw, then lift off the hydraulic fluid reservoir, and position it towards the front of the engine bay to improve access to the servo pump.

7 Refer to Chapter 1, and slacken the auxiliary drivebelt. Remove the belt from the servo pump pulley.

8 Thoroughly clean the area around the servo pump delivery hose union, to avoid contamination of the hydraulic system. Disconnect the delivery hose at the union,

then plug the open end of the hose and the pump port. Where applicable, unclip the transmission kickdown cable (automatic transmission only).

9 Remove the servo pump-to-engine block bolts; the third bolt is accessible through the holes in the drive pulley.

10 Lift the servo pump out of the engine bay.

Refitting

11 Refit the servo pump by following the removal process in reverse.

12 On completion, refer to Chapter 1 and tension the auxiliary drivebelt correctly.

13 Reconnect the battery negative cable, then working from Section 18 of this Chapter, refill and bleed the power steering hydraulic system.

21 Steering rack rubber gaiters - renewal

1 Refer to Section 22 and remove the track rod ends from the track rods.

2 Unscrew the locknuts from the track rods.

3 Snip through the larger, inboard metal clips that retain the rubber gaiters, using a stout pair of cutters. The outboard clips can be expanded by pressing together the metal tags, allowing them to be slid off.

4 Slide the gaiters off the ends of the track rods.

5 If the gaiters are being renewed due to damage, check the condition of the track rods and balljoints beneath. Clean off all traces of dirt, and lubricate the balljoints with multi-purpose grease.

6 Fit the new gaiters over the track rods, and secure them in place with a new set of clips.

7 Refit the track rod end locknuts.

8 Referring to Section 22, refit and adjust the track rod ends.

22 Track rod end - removal and refitting

Removal

1 Park the vehicle on a level surface, apply the handbrake and chock the rear wheels. Remove the wheel centre caps and slacken the wheel bolts.

2 Raise the front of the vehicle, rest it securely on axle stands and remove the roadwheels; refer to *"Jacking, towing and wheel changing"* for guidance.

3 At each track rod, *accurately* measure and record the distance between the locknut and the machined groove in the inboard section of the track rod **(see illustration)**.

4 Slacken the locknuts.

5 Slacken the nut securing the track rod end to the steering swivel member, and unscrew it to the end of the stud thread; this will protect the thread, and prevent the track rod end from

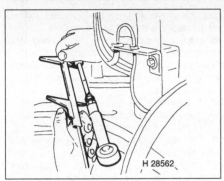

22.3 At each track rod, *accurately* measure and record the distance between the track rod end and the machined groove in the inboard section of the track rod

22.5a Slacken the nut securing the track rod end to the steering swivel member

22.5b Using a balljoint splitter to separate the joint

ejecting at high speed when the joint is split. Use a balljoint splitter to separate the joint, then remove the nut **(see illustrations)**.

6 Unscrew the track rod ends from the track rods.

7 Take the opportunity to inspect the steering rack gaiters, with reference to Section 20. Renew them if they are perished or worn.

Refitting

8 Lightly grease the threads of the track rod, and screw on the new track rod ends, such that the distances between their ends and the machined grooves in the track rods are exactly the same as the measurements made before removal.

9 Fit the outboard joint into the steering swivel member, then screw on and tighten the retaining nut, observing the specified torque wrench setting.

10 Refit the roadwheels and bolts, and lower the vehicle to the ground. Tighten the wheel bolts to the specified torque.

11 Refer to Section 23 and check the toe setting. On completion, tighten the locknuts securely.

23 Wheel alignment and steering angles - general information

Definitions

1 A vehicle's steering and suspension geometry is defined in four basic settings - all angles are expressed in degrees (toe settings are also expressed as a measurement); the steering axis is defined as an imaginary line drawn through the axis of the suspension strut, extended where necessary to contact the ground **(see illustration)**.

2 **Camber** is the angle between each roadwheel and a vertical line drawn through its centre and tyre contact patch, when viewed from the front or rear of the car. "Positive" camber is when the roadwheels are tilted outwards from the vertical at the top; "negative" camber is when they are tilted inwards.

3 Camber is not adjustable, and is given for reference only; while it can be checked using a

camber checking gauge, if the figure obtained is significantly different from that specified, the vehicle must be taken for careful checking by a professional, as the fault can only be caused by wear or damage to the body or suspension components.

4 **Castor** is the angle between the steering axis and a vertical line drawn through each roadwheel centre and tyre contact patch, when viewed from the side of the car. "Positive" castor is when the steering axis is tilted so that it contacts the ground ahead of the vertical; "negative" castor is when it contacts the ground behind the vertical.

5 Castor is not adjustable, and is given for reference only; while it can be checked using a castor checking gauge, if the figure obtained is significantly different from that specified, the vehicle must be taken for careful checking by a professional, as the fault can only be caused by wear or damage to the body or suspension components.

6 **Steering axis inclination/SAI** - also known as **kingpin inclination/KPI** - is the angle between the steering axis and a vertical line drawn through each roadwheel centre and tyre contact patch, when viewed from the front or rear of the car.

7 SAI/KPI is not adjustable, and is given for reference only.

8 **Toe** is the difference, viewed from above, between lines drawn through the roadwheel centres and the car's centre-line. "Toe-in" is when the roadwheels point inwards, towards each other at the front, while "toe-out" is when they splay outwards from each other at the front.

9 The front wheel toe setting is adjusted by screwing the balljoints in or out of their track rods, to alter the effective length of the track rod assemblies.

10 Rear wheel toe setting is not adjustable, and is given for reference only. While it can be checked, if the figure obtained is significantly different from that specified, the vehicle must be taken for careful checking by a professional, as the fault can only be caused by wear or damage to the body or suspension components.

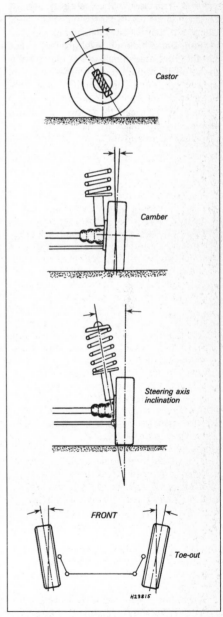

23.1 Wheel alignment and steering angle measurements

Checking - general

11 Due to the special measuring equipment necessary to check the wheel alignment, and the skill required to use it properly, the checking and adjustment of these settings is best left to a Saab dealer or similar expert. Note that most tyre-fitting shops now possess sophisticated checking equipment.

12 For **accurate** checking, the vehicle **must** be at the kerb weight, i.e. unladen and with a full tank of fuel, and the ride height must be correct (see Section 9).

13 Before starting work, check first that the tyre sizes and types are as specified, then check the tyre pressures and tread wear, the roadwheel run-out, the condition of the hub bearings, the steering wheel free play, and the condition of the front suspension components (Chapter 1). Correct any faults found.

14 Park the vehicle on level ground, check that the front roadwheels are in the straight-ahead position, then rock the rear and front ends to settle the suspension. Release the handbrake, and roll the vehicle backwards approximately 1 metre, then forwards again, to relieve any stresses in the steering and suspension components.

Toe setting - checking and adjusting

Front wheel toe setting

15 The front wheel toe setting is checked by measuring the distance between the front and rear inside edges of the roadwheel rims. Proprietary toe measurement gauges are available from motor accessory shops.

16 Prepare the vehicle as described in paragraphs 12 to 14 above.

17 A tracking gauge must now be obtained. Two types of gauge are available, and can be obtained from motor accessory shops. The first type measures the distance between the front and rear inside edges of the roadwheels, as described previously, with the car stationary. The second type, known as a "scuff plate", measures the actual position of the contact surface of the tyre in relation to the road surface, with the vehicle in motion. This is achieved by pushing or driving the front tyre over a plate, which then moves slightly according to the scuff of the tyre, and shows this movement on a scale. Both types have their advantages and disadvantages, but either can give satisfactory results if used correctly and carefully. Alternatively, a tracking gauge can be fabricated from a length of steel tubing, suitably cranked to clear the engine and gearbox assembly, with a set-screw and a locknut at one end.

18 Many tyre specialists will also check toe settings free, or for a small charge.

19 Make sure that the steering is in the straight-ahead position when taking measurements.

20 If adjustment is found to be necessary, clean the ends of the track rods in the areas of the adjustment pin locknuts.

21 Slacken the locknuts (one at the inner and outer end of each adjustment pin), and use a pair of grips to turn each track rod by equal amounts in the same direction. Only turn each track rod by a quarter of a turn at a time, before re-checking.

22 Check that the track rod end balljoints are centralised, and not forced to the limit of movement in any direction.

23 When adjustment is correct, tighten the locknuts.

24 Check that the track rod lengths are equal, and that the steering wheel spokes are in the straight-ahead position.

Rear wheel toe setting

25 The procedure for checking the rear toe setting is same as described for the front in paragraph 17. The setting is not adjustable - see paragraph 10.

Chapter 11 Bodywork and fittings

Contents

Degrees of difficulty

Easy, suitable for novice with little experience	Fairly easy, suitable for beginner with some experience	Fairly difficult, suitable for competent DIY mechanic	Difficult, suitable for experienced DIY mechanic	Very difficult, suitable for expert DIY or professional

Specifications

Torque wrench settings

	Nm	lbf ft
Passenger airbag lower panel screws	4	3
Passenger airbag retaining screws	4	3
Steering wheel airbag retaining screws	6	4

1 General information

The vehicle's body is constructed from overlapping pressed-steel sections that are either spot-welded or seam-welded together, depending on the position of the joint and the stresses it is expected to withstand, both in normal use and in the event of a collision. The overall rigidity of the body is increased by the use of stiffening beams built into the body panels, steel flanges in the window and door openings, and the application of adhesive in fixed glass joints.

A front subframe assembly provides mounting points for the engine, front suspension, transmission and steering gear. The rear suspension assembly is bolted directly to the system of beams that forms the vehicle's floorpan, and the doors are bolted to the structural A and B pillars. The front wings are also bolted on, rather than welded on, allowing accident damage to be repaired easily.

The vehicle's underside is coated with polyester underseal and an anti-corrosion compound. This treatment provides protection against the elements, and also serves as an effective sound insulation layer. The cabin, luggage area and engine compartment are also lined with bituminous felt and other sound-insulating materials, to provide further noise damping.

All models are fitted with electric windows front and rear. The window glass is raised and lowered by an electric motor, linked by a cable to the window regulator mechanism. A master switch panel is mounted in the centre console, from which all windows can be operated and locked. In addition, individual switch panels are mounted on the rear door trim panels.

Central locking is fitted to all models, and is actuated from the driver's door lock. It operates the locks on all four doors, the tailgate/boot, and the fuel filler cap. The front passenger door and tailgate/boot can be opened individually; in the event of a power failure, the driver's door, front passenger door and tailgate/boot locks can be opened manually, using the key. In addition, the fuel filler cap can be opened manually from inside the loadspace. The lock mechanisms are actuated by servo motor units that can be separated from the lock assemblies and renewed individually; refer to Section 17 for details. The system is controlled by an Electronic Control Unit (ECU), which is mounted on a bracket beneath the facia, on the driver's side of the cabin.

Vehicles built from 1988 model year onwards were available with an optional driver's airbag system, built into the centre of the steering wheel. This subsequently became standard equipment from 1993 model year onwards. In addition, passenger airbags built into the facia were fitted from 1994 model year onwards as an option, as were driver and front passenger seat belt tensioners. These components form part of the Supplementary Restraint System (SRS), activated centrally by an Electronic Control Unit (ECU). Sensors built into the ECU casing and the front of the engine bay are triggered in the event of a front-end collision, and prompt the ECU to activate the airbag(s) and the seat belt tensioners, reducing the risk of the front seat passengers striking the steering wheel, windscreen or steering column.

 Warning: Section 28 details the special precautions that need to be observed when working on vehicles with an airbag/SRS.

2 Maintenance - bodywork and underframe

The general condition of a vehicle's bodywork is the one thing that significantly affects its value. Maintenance is easy, but needs to be regular. Neglect, particularly after minor damage, can lead quickly to further deterioration and costly repair bills. It is important also to keep watch on those parts of the vehicle not immediately visible, for instance the underside, inside all the wheel arches, and the lower part of the engine compartment.

The basic maintenance routine for the bodywork is washing - preferably with a lot of water, from a hose. This will remove all the loose solids which may have stuck to the vehicle. It is important to flush these off in such a way as to prevent grit from scratching the finish. The wheel arches and underframe need washing in the same way, to remove any accumulated mud, which will retain moisture and tend to encourage rust. Paradoxically enough, the best time to clean the underframe and wheel arches is in wet weather, when the mud is thoroughly wet and soft. In very wet weather, the underframe is usually cleaned of large accumulations automatically, and this is a good time for inspection.

Periodically, except on vehicles with a wax-based underbody protective coating, it is a good idea to have the whole of the underframe of the vehicle steam-cleaned, engine compartment included, so that a thorough inspection can be carried out to see what minor repairs and renovations are necessary. Steam-cleaning is available at many garages, and is necessary for the removal of the accumulation of oily grime, which sometimes is allowed to become thick in certain areas. If steam-cleaning facilities are not available, there are some excellent grease solvents available which can be brush-applied; the dirt can then be simply hosed off. Note that these methods should not be used on vehicles with wax-based underbody protective coating, or the coating will be removed. Such vehicles should be inspected annually, preferably just prior to Winter, when the underbody should be washed down, and any damage to the wax coating repaired. Ideally, a completely fresh coat should be applied. It would also be worth considering the use of such wax-based protection for injection into door panels, sills, box sections, etc, as an additional safeguard against rust damage, where such protection is not provided by the vehicle manufacturer.

After washing paintwork, wipe off with a chamois leather to give an unspotted clear finish. A coat of clear protective wax polish will give added protection against chemical pollutants in the air. If the paintwork sheen has dulled or oxidised, use a cleaner/polisher combination to restore the brilliance of the shine. This requires a little effort, but such dulling is usually caused because regular washing has been neglected. Care needs to be taken with metallic paintwork, as special non-abrasive cleaner/polisher is required to avoid damage to the finish. Always check that the door and ventilator opening drain holes and pipes are completely clear, so that water can be drained out. Brightwork should be treated in the same way as paintwork. Windscreens and windows can be kept clear of the smeary film which often appears, by the use of proprietary glass cleaner. Never use any form of wax or other body or chromium polish on glass.

3 Maintenance - upholstery and carpets

Mats and carpets should be brushed or vacuum-cleaned regularly, to keep them free of grit. If they are badly stained, remove them from the vehicle for scrubbing or sponging, and make quite sure they are dry before refitting. Seats and interior trim panels can be kept clean by wiping with a damp cloth. If they do become stained (which can be more apparent on light-coloured upholstery), use a little liquid detergent and a soft nail brush to scour the grime out of the grain of the material. Do not forget to keep the headlining clean in the same way as the upholstery. When using liquid cleaners inside the vehicle, do not over-wet the surfaces being cleaned. Excessive damp could get into the seams and padded interior, causing stains, offensive odours or even rot.

HAYNES HiNT *If the inside of the vehicle gets wet accidentally, it is worthwhile taking some trouble to dry it out properly, particularly where carpets are involved. Do not leave oil or electric heaters inside the vehicle for this purpose.*

4 Minor body damage - repair

Note: *No body repairs should be attempted (other than by a Saab Approved repairers) on vehicles less than 6 years old, as this may invalidate the Saab corrosion guarantee.*

Repairs of minor scratches in bodywork

If the scratch is very superficial, and does not penetrate to the metal of the bodywork, repair is very simple. Lightly rub the area of the scratch with a paintwork renovator, or a very fine cutting paste, to remove loose paint from the scratch, and to clear the surrounding bodywork of wax polish. Rinse the area with clean water.

Apply touch-up paint to the scratch using a fine paint brush; continue to apply fine layers of paint until the surface of the paint in the scratch is level with the surrounding paintwork. Allow the new paint at least two weeks to harden, then blend it into the surrounding paintwork by rubbing the scratch area with a paintwork renovator or a very fine cutting paste. Finally, apply wax polish.

Where the scratch has penetrated right through to the metal of the bodywork, causing the metal to rust, a different repair technique is required. Remove any loose rust from the bottom of the scratch with a penknife, then apply rust-inhibiting paint to prevent the formation of rust in the future. Using a rubber or nylon applicator, fill the scratch with bodystopper paste. If required, this paste can be mixed with cellulose thinners to provide a very thin paste which is ideal for filling narrow scratches. Before the stopper-paste in the scratch hardens, wrap a piece of smooth cotton rag around the top of a finger. Dip the finger in cellulose thinners, and quickly sweep it across the surface of the stopper-paste in the scratch; this will ensure that the surface of the stopper-paste is slightly hollowed. The scratch can now be painted over as described earlier in this Section.

Repairs of dents in bodywork

When deep denting of the vehicle's bodywork has taken place, the first task is to pull the dent out, until the affected bodywork almost attains its original shape. There is little point in trying to restore the original shape completely, as the metal in the damaged area will have stretched on impact, and cannot be reshaped fully to its original contour. It is better to bring the level of the dent up to a point which is about 3 mm below the level of the surrounding bodywork. In cases where the dent is very shallow anyway, it is not worth trying to pull it out at all. If the underside of the dent is accessible, it can be hammered out gently from behind, using a mallet with a wooden or plastic head. Whilst doing this, hold a suitable block of wood firmly against the outside of the panel, to absorb the impact from the hammer blows and thus prevent a large area of the bodywork from being "belled-out".

Should the dent be in a section of the bodywork which has a double skin, or some other factor making it inaccessible from behind, a different technique is called for. Drill several small holes through the metal inside the area - particularly in the deeper section. Then screw long self-tapping screws into the holes, just sufficiently for them to gain a good purchase in the metal. Now the dent can be pulled out by pulling on the protruding heads of the screws with a pair of pliers.

The next stage of the repair is the removal of the paint from the damaged area, and from an inch or so of the surrounding "sound" bodywork. This is accomplished most easily by using a wire brush or abrasive pad on a power drill, although it can be done just as effectively by hand, using sheets of abrasive paper. To complete the preparation for filling, score the surface of the bare metal with a screwdriver or the tang of a file, or alternatively, drill small holes in the affected area. This will provide a really good "key" for the filler paste.

To complete the repair, see the Section on filling and respraying.

Repairs of rust holes or gashes in bodywork

Remove all paint from the affected area, and from an inch or so of the surrounding "sound" bodywork, using an abrasive pad or a wire brush on a power drill. If these are not available, a few sheets of abrasive paper will do the job most effectively. With the paint removed, you will be able to judge the severity of the corrosion, and therefore decide whether to renew the whole panel (if this is possible) or to repair the affected area. New body panels are not as expensive as most people think, and it is often quicker and more satisfactory to fit a new panel than to attempt to repair large areas of corrosion.

Remove all fittings from the affected area, except those which will act as a guide to the original shape of the damaged bodywork (eg headlight shells etc). Then, using tin snips or a hacksaw blade, remove all loose metal and any other metal badly affected by corrosion. Hammer the edges of the hole inwards, in order to create a slight depression for the filler paste.

Wire-brush the affected area to remove the powdery rust from the surface of the remaining metal. Paint the affected area with rust-inhibiting paint, if the back of the rusted area is accessible, treat this also.

Before filling can take place, it will be necessary to block the hole in some way. This can be achieved by the use of aluminium or plastic mesh, or aluminium tape.

Aluminium or plastic mesh, or glass-fibre matting, is probably the best material to use for a large hole. Cut a piece to the approximate size and shape of the hole to be filled, then position it in the hole so that its edges are below the level of the surrounding bodywork. It can be retained in position by several blobs of filler paste around its periphery.

Aluminium tape should be used for small or very narrow holes. Pull a piece off the roll, trim it to the approximate size and shape required, then pull off the backing paper (if used) and stick the tape over the hole; it can be overlapped if the thickness of one piece is insufficient. Burnish down the edges of the tape with the handle of a screwdriver or similar, to ensure that the tape is securely attached to the metal underneath.

Bodywork repairs - filling and respraying

Before using this Section, see the Sections on dent, deep scratch, rust holes and gash repairs.

Many types of bodyfiller are available, but generally speaking, those proprietary kits which contain a tin of filler paste and a tube of resin hardener are best for this type of repair. A wide, flexible plastic or nylon applicator will be found invaluable for imparting a smooth and well-contoured finish to the surface of the filler.

Mix up a little filler on a clean piece of card or board - measure the hardener carefully (follow the maker's instructions on the pack), otherwise the filler will set too rapidly or too slowly. Using the applicator, apply the filler paste to the prepared area; draw the applicator across the surface of the filler to achieve the correct contour and to level the surface. As soon as a contour that approximates to the correct one is achieved, stop working the paste - if you carry on too long, the paste will become sticky and begin to "pick-up" on the applicator. Continue to add thin layers of filler paste at 20-minute intervals, until the level of the filler is just proud of the surrounding bodywork.

Once the filler has hardened, the excess can be removed using a metal plane or file. From then on, progressively-finer grades of abrasive paper should be used, starting with a 40-grade production paper, and finishing with a 400-grade wet-and-dry paper. Always wrap the abrasive paper around a flat rubber, cork, or wooden block - otherwise the surface of the filler will not be completely flat. During the smoothing of the filler surface, the wet-and-dry paper should be periodically rinsed in water. This will ensure that a very smooth finish is imparted to the filler at the final stage.

At this stage, the "dent" should be surrounded by a ring of bare metal, which in turn should be encircled by the finely "feathered" edge of the good paintwork. Rinse the repair area with clean water, until all of the dust produced by the rubbing-down operation has gone.

Spray the whole area with a light coat of primer - this will show up any imperfections in the surface of the filler. Repair these imperfections with fresh filler paste or bodystopper, and once more smooth the surface with abrasive paper. Repeat this spray-and-repair procedure until you are satisfied that the surface of the filler, and the feathered edge of the paintwork, are perfect. Clean the repair area with clean water, and allow to dry fully.

 HAYNES HINT *If bodystopper is used, it can be mixed with cellulose thinners, to form a really thin paste which is ideal for filling small holes.*

The repair area is now ready for final spraying. Paint spraying must be carried out in a warm, dry, windless and dust-free atmosphere. This condition can be created artificially if you have access to a large indoor

working area, but if you are forced to work in the open, you will have to pick your day very carefully. If you are working indoors, dousing the floor in the work area with water will help to settle the dust which would otherwise be in the atmosphere. If the repair area is confined to one body panel, mask off the surrounding panels; this will help to minimise the effects of a slight mis-match in paint colours. Bodywork fittings (eg chrome strips, door handles etc) will also need to be masked off. Use genuine masking tape, and several thicknesses of newspaper, for the masking operations.

Before commencing to spray, agitate the aerosol can thoroughly, then spray a test area (an old tin, or similar) until the technique is mastered. Cover the repair area with a thick coat of primer; the thickness should be built up using several thin layers of paint, rather than one thick one. Using 400-grade wet-and-dry paper, rub down the surface of the primer until it is really smooth. While doing this, the work area should be thoroughly doused with water, and the wet-and-dry paper periodically rinsed in water. Allow to dry before spraying on more paint.

Spray on the top coat, again building up the thickness by using several thin layers of paint. Start spraying at one edge of the repair area, and then, using a side-to-side motion, work until the whole repair area and about 2 inches of the surrounding original paintwork is covered. Remove all masking material 10 to 15 minutes after spraying on the final coat of paint.

Allow the new paint at least two weeks to harden, then, using a paintwork renovator, or a very fine cutting paste, blend the edges of the paint into the existing paintwork. Finally, apply wax polish.

Plastic components

With the use of more and more plastic body components by the vehicle manufacturers (eg bumpers, spoilers, and in some cases major body panels), rectification of more serious damage to such items has become a matter of either entrusting repair work to a specialist in this field, or renewing complete components. Repair of such damage by the DIY owner is not really feasible, owing to the cost of the equipment and materials required for effecting such repairs. The basic technique involves making a groove along the line of the crack in the plastic, using a rotary burr in a power drill. The damaged part is then welded back together, using a hot-air gun to heat up and fuse a plastic filler rod into the groove. Any excess plastic is then removed, and the area rubbed down to a smooth finish. It is important that a filler rod of the correct plastic is used, as body components can be made of a variety of different types (eg polycarbonate, ABS, polypropylene).

Damage of a less serious nature (abrasions, minor cracks etc) can be repaired by the DIY owner using a two-part epoxy filler repair material. Once mixed in equal proportions, this is used in similar fashion to the bodywork filler used on metal panels. The filler is usually cured in twenty to thirty minutes, ready for sanding and painting.

If the owner is renewing a complete component himself, or if he has repaired it with epoxy filler, he will be left with the problem of finding a suitable paint for finishing which is compatible with the type of plastic used. At one time, the use of a universal paint was not possible, owing to the complex range of plastics encountered in body component applications. Standard paints, generally speaking, will not bond to plastic or rubber satisfactorily. However, it is now possible to obtain a plastic body parts finishing kit which consists of a pre-primer treatment, a primer and coloured top coat. Full instructions are normally supplied with a kit, but basically, the method of use is to first apply the pre-primer to the component concerned, and allow it to dry for up to 30 minutes. Then the primer is applied, and left to dry for about an hour before finally applying the special-coloured top coat. The result is a correctly-coloured component, where the paint will flex with the plastic or rubber, a property that standard paint does not normally posses.

5 Major body damage - repair

Where serious damage has occurred, or large areas need renewal due to neglect, it means that complete new panels will need welding-in, and this is best left to professionals. If the damage is due to impact, it will also be necessary to check completely the alignment of the bodyshell, and this can only be carried out accurately by a Saab dealer, using special jigs. If the body is left misaligned, it is primarily dangerous, as the car will not handle properly, and secondly, uneven stresses will be imposed on the steering, suspension and possibly transmission, causing abnormal wear, or complete failure, particularly to such items as the tyres.

6 Front bumper - removal and refitting

Removal

1 Park the vehicle on a level surface, apply the handbrake and chock the rear wheels. Raise the front of the vehicle and rest it securely on axle stands; refer to "Jacking, towing and wheel changing " for guidance.
2 Where applicable, remove the retaining screws, then lower the undertray and brake cooling ducts away from the vehicle; note that the front of the undertray is clipped onto the trailing edge of the valance moulding.
3 Remove the retaining screws, and separate the valance moulding from the bumper. Where fitted, disconnect the wiring for the

driving/foglights and ambient air temperature sensor.
4 Slacken the two through-bolts that secure the bumper to the front subframe.
5 Disengage the ends of the bumper from the body side mouldings, then pull the bumper away from the front of the vehicle.
6 The bumper outer moulding can then be separated from the inner metal core, by removing the securing screws.

Refitting

7 Refit the bumper by reversing the removal procedure; ensure that the lugs protruding from the front wing engage with the corresponding recesses in the ends of the bumper.

7 Rear bumper - removal and refitting

Removal

1 Park the vehicle on a level surface, and apply the handbrake.
2 Working directly behind the rear wheelarches, remove the two screws that secure the lower edges of the rear valance to the side bumper mouldings.
3 Open the boot/tailgate, and lift the panel above the spare wheel compartment, securing it in the raised position. Prise the rubber sealing strip away from the edge of the loadspace, to expose the edge of the carpet trim panel.
4 Pull the carpet away from the area behind the rear light cluster, guiding the luggage securing eyelet through the hole in the carpet.
5 The bumper assembly is secured by four bolts; two on either side of the vehicle, directly below the light clusters. The upper bolts also act as mounting points for the luggage securing eyelets. The lower bolts are concealed behind plastic panels in the floor of the loadspace, which can be prised out to expose the retaining nuts. Remove all four nuts, supporting the bumper as the last nut is removed.
6 Pull the bumper assembly squarely away from the body, and recover the rubber washers.

8.7 The inside bottom edge of the grille has plastic locating lugs at each end (arrowed)

Refitting

7 Refit the bumper assembly by reversing the removal procedure, tightening the mounting nuts securely.

8 Bonnet and front grille - removal and refitting

Bonnet

 Warning: It is essential that the help of an assistant is enlisted during this operation.

Removal

1 Open the bonnet, and prop it up with a stout pole.
2 Disconnect the washer jet hoses at the three-way joint.
3 Lever out the pins from the hinges on both sides of the bonnet; maintain a firm grip on the bonnet as the pins are released, to prevent it from tilting forwards.
4 Using a screwdriver, prise the clip from the joint at the top of each bonnet support strut. Separate the joint, and recover the washers. Allow the struts to swivel forward and rest on the wings.
5 With the help of your assistant, lift off the bonnet and set it down on its edge, using a dust sheet to protect the paintwork.

Refitting

6 Refit the bonnet by reversing the removal process.

Front grille

7 Remove the four screws that secure the grille to the front crossmember; these are accessed through the front of the grille, adjacent to the headlight units, and along the top edge of the grille. Note when refitting that the inside bottom edge of the grille has plastic locating lugs at each end, which engage with dowels, adjacent to the headlight units (see illustration).

9 Bonnet release cable - removal and refitting

Removal

1 Refer to Section 8 and remove the front grille.
2 Refer to Chapter 12 and remove the right-hand indicator light unit.
3 Working underneath the bonnet locks, release the stop nipples from the end of the release cable inner at each lock.
4 Unscrew the cable clip from above the right-hand headlight unit.
5 Remove the clips that secure the extension cable to the underside of the front crossmember.
6 Working inside the cabin, remove the driver's door sill scuff plate, and the trim panel

surrounding the bonnet release handle. Extract the fixings, and lower the sound insulation panel away from the underside of the steering column/facia.

7 Prise off the clip, and release the cable outer from the stop. Pull the cable towards the handle, and free the cable inner nipple from it.

8 Pull the entire cable through into the cabin area. If it proves difficult to remove, greater access to the cable run may be gained by jacking up the vehicle, removing the right-hand front roadwheel - refer to *"Jacking, towing and wheel changing"* - and removing the inner wing liner - refer to Section 22.

Refitting

9 Refit the cable by reversing the removal process. Adjust both cable stops at the bonnet locks, to ensure that the locks release correctly when the handle is operated. Check also that when the handle is at rest, the bonnet is held securely in closed position by the locks on *both* sides; pull up firmly at each corner of the bonnet to assess this. If necessary, adjust the striker pin lengths as described in Section 10.

10 Bonnet lock -
removal and refitting

Removal

1 Open the bonnet, then remove the four screws that secure the front grille in position.

2 Referring to the relevant paragraphs of Section 9, free the release cable from the bonnet lock actuator levers.

3 Remove the two securing bolts at either side of the lock unit, and withdraw it from the crossmember.

Refitting

4 Refit the locks by reversing the removal procedure; when refitting the release cable, adjust both cable stops at the bonnet locks, to ensure that the locks release correctly when the handle is operated. Check also that when the handle is at rest, the bonnet is held securely in closed position by the locks on *both* sides; pull up firmly at each corner of the bonnet to assess this. If necessary, adjust the striker pin lengths as described below.

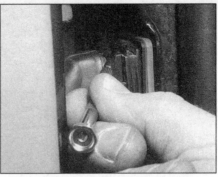

11.2a Using a small screwdriver, prise out the locking bar from the connector . . .

Striker pin adjustment

5 If the striker pin is badly adjusted such that it is too long, the bonnet will be loose in the closed position and may rattle; more importantly, there is the risk that the lock may burst open. Similarly, if the striker pin is too short, closing the bonnet may require excessive force, and the risk of damage or only partial engagement of the locks is potential hazard.

6 To adjust the length of the striker pin, slacken the locknut and turn the pin (clockwise to retract, anti-clockwise to extend) using a screwdriver inserted into the slotted end. When the desired length is achieved, re-tighten the locknut and re-check the security of the bonnet locks.

11 Doors - removal,
refitting and adjustment

Front doors

Removal

1 Disconnect the battery negative cable, and position it away from the terminal.

2 Open the door to gain access to the wiring harness connector. Using a small screwdriver, prise out the locking bar from the connector housing; this will allow the locking mechanism to compress, releasing it from the aperture in the body **(see illustrations)**.

3 Withdraw the connector from the aperture, together with the rubber seal, and unplug the

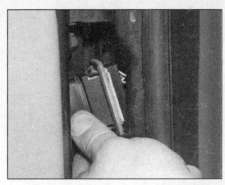

11.2b . . . this will allow the locking mechanism to compress, releasing it from the aperture in the body

two halves **(see illustration)**. Note: *On earlier models, it will be necessary to remove the door inner trim panel (refer to Section 12) and pull the harness through the grommet in the edge of the door, after unplugging the electrical connectors individually.*

4 Remove the screw and detach the restrainer bar from the anchoring point on the body **(see illustration)**. Note: *On earlier models, it will be necessary to tap out the roll pin from the restrainer bar, using a hammer and punch; a new roll pin must then be used on refitting.*

5 On later models, remove the grub screws from the upper and lower hinges **(see illustration)**.

6 Open the door wide, so that the notch and lug on the two sides of the hinge line up.

7 Lift the door squarely off its hinges, and set it down on a dust sheet to protect the edges.

Refitting

8 Refit the door by reversing the removal procedure.

Rear doors

Removal

9 Refer to Section 12, and remove the inner trim panel.

10 Unplug all the wiring harness connectors to the central locking servo, electric window motor and "door open" sensor (where fitted), labelling them to aid refitting later. Withdraw the harness through the grommet in the edge of the door.

11.3 Withdraw the connector from the aperture, together with the rubber seal, and unplug the two halves

11.4 Remove the screw (arrowed) and detach the restrainer bar from the anchoring point on the body

11.5 On later models, remove the grub screws from the upper and lower hinges

12.2a Remove the screw (arrowed) from the bi-colour courtesy lamp at the edge of the door

12.2b Lift off the lens, disengaging the leading edge from the rear of the door stowage bin

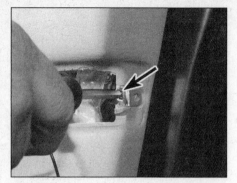

12.3 Remove the retaining screw (arrowed) from the courtesy light housing

12.4a Prise out the boot/tailgate release switch, using a flat-bladed screwdriver . . .

12.4b . . . then unplug the connector

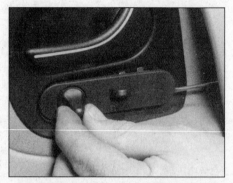

12.5a Prise out the plastic switch panel directly beneath the interior door handle . . .

11 Follow the procedure described for the removal of the front door.

Refitting

12 Refit the door by reversing the removal procedure.

12 Door inner trim panel -
removal and refitting

Front door

Removal

1 Disconnect the battery negative cable, and position it away from the terminal.

2 Remove the screw from the bi-colour courtesy light at the edge of the door. Lift off the lens, disengaging the leading edge from the rear of the door stowage bin **(see illustrations)**.

3 Remove the retaining screw from the courtesy light housing **(see illustration)**.

4 If the driver's door panel is being removed, prise out the boot/tailgate release switch, using a flat-bladed screwdriver. Unplug the connector, and label the cables on the harness side, to aid refitting later **(see illustrations)**.

5 Prise out the plastic switch panel directly beneath the interior door handle. On the driver's door, the panel houses the electric mirror switches; on both rear doors, it houses

the electric window switches; (a blank panel is fitted to the front passenger door). Where applicable, unplug the connectors, and label the cables on the harness side, to aid refitting later **(see illustrations)**.

6 Remove the screw beneath the switch panel, and lift out the door handle bezel **(see illustration)**.

7 Prise the plastic caps from the top and bottom of the door grab handle, then remove the retaining screws and lift off the handle **(see illustration)**. Note that on later models, the grab handle remains attached to the door panel, but the mounting screws still need to be removed.

8 Remove the plastic caps from both ends of

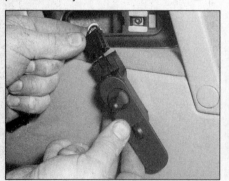

12.5b . . . then unplug the connectors (where applicable), labelling the cables on the harness side, to aid refitting later

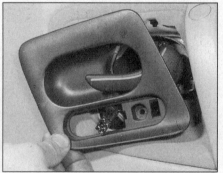

12.6 Remove the screw beneath the switch panel, and lift out the door handle bezel

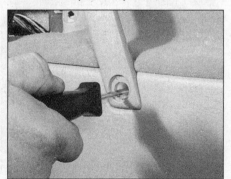

12.7 Remove the door grab handle retaining screws

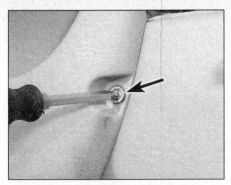

12.8 Slacken and remove the screws at either end of the door stowage bin

12.10 Lift the panel away from the door

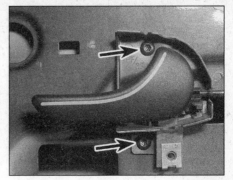

13.4 Remove the two handle assembly retaining screws

the door stowage bin, then slacken and remove the screws **(see illustration)**. Note that these screws actually secure the door trim panel to the door; the stowage bin itself remains attached to the door panel.

9 Use a wide-bladed flat instrument, such as a spatula or a filling knife padded with PVC tape, to release the press-stud fixings from the outer rim of the panel. Insert the instrument to one side of each fixing, between the trim panel and the door, and carefully lever out the panel until the press-stud disengages. (When the panel is refitted, these studs can simply be lined up with their mounting holes, and pressed back into position.)

10 Lift the panel away from the door, prising the trim strip out of the window aperture, and guiding the lock release button through the hole in the top of the panel **(see illustration)**.

11 On earlier models, there will be a plastic moisture-resistant film stretched over the door panel. Start at one corner, and carefully peel the film away from the door, keeping it taut to stop it sticking to itself and anything else. Ideally, the film should be renewed once disturbed. However, if the old one is to be re-used, find a suitable place to hang the film upright by its top edge, until it is refitted.

12 On later models, the door is lined with a combination of expanded foam sheeting, and wads of sound insulation material. Both are held in place with steel spring clips, which must be removed with care to avoid

scratching the paintwork and inducing corrosion.

Refitting

13 Refit the panel by reversing the removal procedure.

Rear door

14 The procedure for removing the rear door trim panel is essentially the same as that for the front doors, with the exception that later models have a window demister fan screwed to the inside of the panel; remember to unplug its cabling at the connector, as the trim panel is removed.

---

13 Door handle and lock components - removal and refitting

Interior door handles

Note: *This procedure is applicable to both the front and rear interior door handles.*

Removal

1 Ensure that the window glass is fully raised.
2 Disconnect the battery negative cable, and position it away from the terminal.
3 Refer to Section 12 and remove the door interior trim panel.
4 Remove the two retaining screws **(see**

illustration), then lift the handle assembly away from the door.
5 Release the link rod from the plastic clip at the rear of the interior handle assembly. If necessary, release the link rod from the intermediate guide clip first **(see illustration)**.

Refitting

6 Refit the handle assembly by reversing the removal procedure.

Exterior door handles

Note: *This procedure is applicable to both the front and rear exterior door handles, with the exception that references to the lock cylinder should be ignored when working on the rear doors.*

Removal

7 Ensure that the window glass is fully raised. Disconnect the battery negative cable, and position it away from the terminal.
8 Refer to Section 12 and remove the door interior trim panel.
9 Remove the two handle retaining screws; one at the rear edge of the door, adjacent to the outer lock mechanism, and one directly behind the handle assembly, accessible through the void in the door **(see illustrations)**.
10 Remove the window glass guide channel, after removing the retaining screws from the rear edge of the door. Unclip the central

13.5 Release the link rod from the plastic clip at the rear of the interior handle assembly

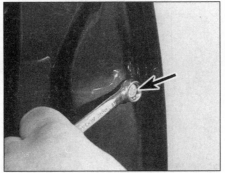

13.9a Remove the two handle retaining screws; one at the rear edge of the door, adjacent to the outer lock mechanism . . .

13.9b . . . and one directly behind the handle assembly, accessible through the void in the door

13.10a Remove the window glass guide channel

13.10b Unplug the central locking switch cable from the wiring harness at the connector

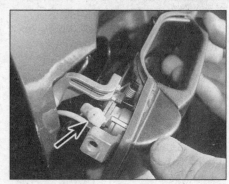

13.12 Separate the link rod balljoint at the lock cylinder (arrowed)

locking switch cable from the guide channel as it is withdrawn from the inside the door, and unplug it from the wiring harness at the connector **(see illustrations)**.

11 Lift the handle assembly away from the door, together with the rubber seal. Guide out the internal components carefully, to avoid scratching the paintwork.

12 A link rod connects the lock cylinder to the internal lock mechanism by means of plastic balljoints; use a screwdriver to separate the balljoint at the lock cylinder **(see illustration)**.

Refitting

13 Offer up the handle assembly to the door aperture, ensuring that the rubber seal is correctly seated.

14 Snap the link rod balljoint back onto the lock cylinder. Ensure at this point that the roller protruding from the back of the handle engages with the internal lock mechanism release lever

15 Refit the handle retaining screws. Operate the door handle to check that the door release functions correctly, before progressing any further.

16 Press the central locking switch cable into the clip at the top of the window glass guide channel, then bolt the strip in position inside the door, whilst pulling the slack in the cable through at the same time. Push the remainder of the cable into the clips on the guide channel, then plug together the harness connector.

17 Refer to Section 12 and refit the door interior trim panel.

18 Reconnect the battery negative cable, and test the operation of the electric window. If the window glass sticks, or is abnormally slow in its movement, slacken the guide channel screws at the edge of the door, to allow it adopt the correct position in relation to the window glass, then retighten the screws.

Lock cylinders

19 Remove the front door exterior handle, as described earlier in this Section.

20 The lock cylinder is secured to the handle assembly by two screws; remove these and withdraw the cylinder, recovering the sealing washer if it is loose **(see illustrations)**.

21 When refitting the cylinder, ensure that the sealing washer is correctly seated before re-tightening the retaining screws.

Lock mechanism

Note: *This procedure is applicable to both the front and rear door lock mechanisms, with the exception that references to the lock cylinder should be ignored when dealing with the rear door lock mechanism.*

Removal

22 The door lock mechanism is made up of two assemblies; one bolted externally on the rear edge of the door, containing the latch components, and one bolted inside the door void, housing the central locking servo and release mechanisms.

23 To remove the external assembly, open the door and remove the three screws that secure the assembly to the door **(see illustration)**. Note that additional location is provided by two dowels.

24 Ensure that the window glass is fully raised. Disconnect the battery negative cable, and position it away from the terminal.

25 Refer to Section 12 and remove the door interior trim panel.

26 Unplug the cables leading to the central locking servo and "door open" switch at the connectors; label them to aid refitting later **(see illustration)**.

27 Unbolt the window glass guide channel, and after unclipping the central locking cable,

13.20a Remove the lock cylinder retaining screws . . .

13.20b . . . and withdraw the cylinder, recovering the sealing washer if it is loose

13.23 Removing the external door lock assembly

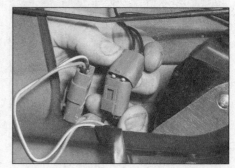

13.26 Unplug the cables leading to the central locking servo and "door open" switch at the connectors

13.30a Remove the two screws that retain the internal lock mechanism assembly, located on the rear edge of the door . . .

13.30b . . . and at the lower edge of the door, adjacent to the central locking servo

14.4 Carefully prise the rubber sealing strip from the outside edge of the window aperture

withdraw the guide channel from inside the door (refer to illustration 13.10).

28 The lock cylinder actuates the lock mechanism via a link rod, secured by plastic balljoints at each end. Use a screwdriver to separate the balljoint at the lock mechanism (refer to illustration 13.12).

29 At the door latch release lever on the lock mechanism, unhook the link rod that runs to the interior door handle.

30 Remove the two screws that retain the internal lock mechanism assembly, located on the rear edge of the door and at the lower edge of the door, adjacent to the central locking servo **(see illustrations)**.

31 Withdraw the lock assembly from the door, together with the link rod connected to the internal lock release knob.

Refitting

32 Offer up the lock mechanism to its mounting position inside the door, and refit the retaining screws. Ensure at this point that the lock mechanism release lever engages with the tab protruding from the back of the exterior door handle.

33 Attach the interior door handle link rod to the latch release lever on the lock mechanism.

34 Snap the lock cylinder linkage balljoint into place at the lock release lever.

35 Refit the window glass guide channel, feeding the central locking cable through the clips as the channel is fitted. Insert and tighten the retaining screws.

36 Plug together the connectors for the central locking servo and "door open" switch cables.

37 Operate the handle a couple of times to check that the exterior door release is functioning correctly, before progressing any further.

38 Fit the external lock mechanism into place, engaging the locating dowels with the corresponding holes. Refit and tighten the three retaining screws.

39 Refer to Section 12 and refit the door interior trim panel.

40 Reconnect the battery negative cable, and test the operation of the electric windows. If the glass sticks, or is abnormally slow in its movement, slacken the guide channel screws

at the edge of the door, to allow it adopt the correct position in relation to the window glass, then retighten the screws.

Striker plate

41 The striker plate posts are screwed into the B/C-pillars, and can removed using a spanner on the hex bolt heads at the base.

14 Door window glass and regulator - removal and refitting

⚠️ *Warning: If a glass panel is being removed to due to breakage, carefully dislodge all loose fragments of glass from the panel before attempting to remove it. Protect your eyes and hands with suitable goggles and gloves, and dispose of the glass safely, labelling any packages containing broken glass to warn others of the contents. Remember to remove any fragments of glass that may have dropped down inside the door panel.*

Front door window glass

Removal

1 Lower the window glass by approximately three-quarters of its travel.

2 Disconnect the battery negative cable, and position it away from the terminal.

3 Refer to Section 12 and remove the door interior trim panel.

4 Carefully prise the rubber sealing strip from the outside edge of the window aperture **(see illustration)**; if an implement is used as a lever, select one that will not scratch the paintwork. The rubber sealing strip has a mounting channel that contains a flexible metal core; avoid splaying out the sides of the channel excessively during removal, as a good seal will be hard to attain on refitting.

5 Working inside the door at the lower edge of the window glass, use a pen to mark the relationship between the window regulator bracket and the window glass support frame.

6 Remove the two flange screws that secure the glass in place; support the glass as the last screw is removed, to prevent it from dropping down inside the door **(see illustration)**.

> **HAYNES HINT** *Roll up a dust sheet and lay it inside the door, underneath the lower edge of the window glass. This will support the glass as it is released, and provide cushioning if it is accidentally dropped during the removal process.*

7 Push the glass up through the door, and lift it clear of the vehicle **(see illustration)**. Set it down on padded surface, to prevent the edges from chipping.

14.6 Remove the two flange screws (arrowed) that secure the glass in place

14.7 Push the glass up through the door, and lift it clear of the vehicle

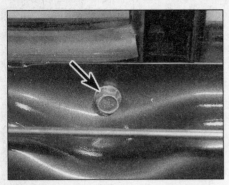

14.18 Free the window channel upright from the (rear) door frame by removing the retaining screw from the inside edge of the door panel (arrowed)

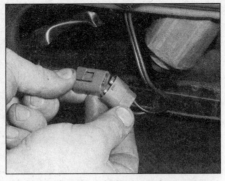

14.29 Unplug the window regulator motor from the wiring harness at the connector

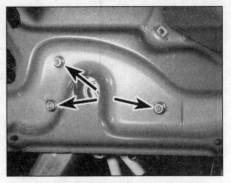

14.30a Remove the three nuts from the motor assembly mounting bolts (arrowed) . . .

Refitting

8 Lower the glass into the door, and align the frame mounting holes with those on the window regulator bracket. Refit the retaining flange screws, using the marks made during removal to achieve the correct alignment before tightening them; this should avoid the need to adjust the window after refitting.

9 Press the rubber sealing strip back onto the edge of the window aperture, ensure that it is level and secure.

10 Reconnect the battery negative cable, and test the operation of the electric window. If the window glass is not correctly aligned in the aperture, particularly in the closed position, slacken the window glass-to-regulator bracket screws, and manoeuvre the glass manually to achieve the desired fit, then retighten the screws. In addition, if the glass sticks or is abnormally slow in its movement, slacken the guide channel screws at the edge of the door, to allow it adopt the correct position in relation to the window glass, then retighten the screws.

11 Refit the door interior trim panel, referring to Section 12 for details.

Rear door window glass

Removal

12 Lower the window glass by approximately three-quarters of its travel.

13 Disconnect the battery negative cable, and position it away from the terminal.

14 Refer to Section 12 and remove the door interior trim panel.

15 Carefully prise the rubber sealing strip from the inside edge of the window aperture; if an implement is used as a lever, select one that will not scratch the paintwork. The rubber sealing strip has a mounting channel that contains a flexible metal core; avoid splaying out the sides of the channel excessively during removal, as a good seal will be hard to attain on refitting.

16 Carefully prise off the plastic moulding from the outside lower edge of the window aperture.

17 Pull the rubber sealing strip from the window channel upright.

18 Free the window channel upright from the door frame by removing the retaining screw from the inside edge of the door panel **(see illustration)**.

19 Working inside the door at the lower edge of the window glass, use a pen to mark the relationship between the window regulator bracket and the window glass support frame.

20 Remove the two flange screws that secure the glass to the window regulator bracket; support the glass as the last screw is removed, to prevent it from dropping down inside the door. **Note:** *Roll up a dust sheet and lay it inside the door, underneath the lower edge of the window glass. This will support the glass as it is released, and provide cushioning if it is accidentally dropped during the removal process.*

21 Push the glass up through the door, and lift it clear of the vehicle. Set it down on padded surface, to prevent the edges from chipping.

Refitting

22 Lower the glass into the door, and align the frame mounting holes with those on the window regulator bracket. Refit the retaining flange screws, using the marks made during removal to achieve the correct alignment before tightening them; this should avoid the need to adjust the window after refitting.

23 Refit the window channel upright in position, then insert and tighten the retaining screw. Press the rubber sealing strip into the channel.

24 Press the rubber sealing strip back onto the inside lower edge of the window aperture, ensuring that it is level and secure.

25 Press the plastic moulding back into place on the outside lower edge of the window aperture.

26 Reconnect the battery negative cable, and test the operation of the electric window. If the window glass is not correctly aligned in the aperture, particularly in the closed position, slacken the window glass-to-regulator bracket screws, and manoeuvre the glass manually to

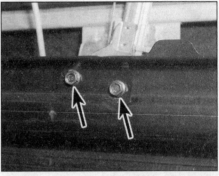

14.30b . . . then remove the three regulator assembly retaining screws; two at the lower edge of the door (arrowed) . . .

achieve the desired fit. Retighten the screws.

27 Refit the door interior trim panel, referring to Section 12 for details.

Window regulator assembly

Note: *This procedure is applicable to both the front and rear window regulators, but it should be noted that the mounting positions of some components will differ slightly between the front and rear doors.*

Removal

28 Refer to the previous sub-section, and separate the window glass from the window regulator bracket. At this stage, the glass can either be removed completely, lowered to rest at the bottom of the door, or temporarily suspended in position from the top of the door frame using several strips of packing tape; if the latter option is chosen, line the top of the door frame with a sheet of paper, to prevent the tape from damaging the paintwork.

29 Unplug the window regulator motor from the wiring harness at the connector **(see illustration)**.

30 Remove the three nuts from the motor assembly mounting bolts, then remove the three regulator assembly retaining screws **(see illustrations)**.

31 Lift the motor and regulator assembly out through the door aperture as a complete unit;

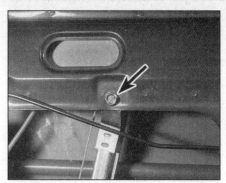

14.30c . . . and one at the upper edge (arrowed)

14.31 Lift the motor and regulator assembly out through the door aperture as a complete unit; note that the motor remains attached to the regulator assembly by the glass lift cable

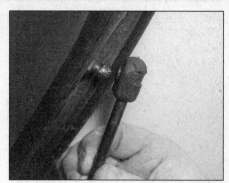

15.11 Carefully lever the support strut joint off the spigot on the tailgate

note that the motor remains attached to the regulator assembly by the glass lift cable **(see illustration)**.

Refitting

32 Refit the regulator assembly by reversing the removal procedure; refer to the previous sub-section for details of refitting the window glass.

Rear door quarter-light

33 Remove the rear door window glass, referring to the description given earlier in this Section.
34 Grasp the quarter-light panel, slide it towards the leading edge of the door, and lift it away from the door frame.
35 When refitting the panel, ensure that it is pushed firmly into the door frame before screwing the window channel upright in position.

15 Tailgate and support struts - removal and refitting

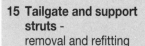

Tailgate
Removal

⚠ **Warning: It is essential that the help of an assistant is enlisted during this operation.**

1 Disconnect the battery negative cable, and position it away from the terminal.
2 Remove the tailgate interior trim panel, as described in Section 25.
3 Unplug the wiring connectors to the central locking servo motor, door "open" switch, fog, reversing and number plate lights, and rear window wiper. Label each connector, to avoid confusion on refitting.
4 Where applicable, refer to Chapter 12 and remove the cover from the high-level brake light; unplug the wiring at the connector. Disconnect the hose from the rear window washer jet. If the original tailgate is to be refitted, tie draw-strings to the ends of the cables, to aid the process of pulling them back into position later.

5 Lay a dust sheet on the rear edge of the roof. Prise out the rubber grommets, and withdraw the cables and washer hose from the tailgate, laying them on the dust sheet to avoid scratching the paintwork.
6 Support the weight of the tailgate using a stout prop of appropriate length. Prise off the retaining clips, then detach the upper ends of the support struts from the spigots on the tailgate.
7 At each hinge, slacken and remove the two grub screws, then remove the main retaining bolts and separate the two halves of the hinge. Maintain firm support of the tailgate, to prevent it from tilting.
8 With the help of your assistant, lift off the tailgate and lower it to ground, resting it on a dust sheet to protect the edges. If the original tailgate is to be refitted, leave the drawstrings tails in place, with enough slack to allow the cabling to be pulled through.

Refitting

9 Refit the tailgate by reversing the removal procedure. If the tailgate is being renewed, transfer all serviceable components from the old tailgate to the new one before fitting it. Close the tailgate, and check the operation of the catch/lock mechanism. If excessive force is required to engage it correctly, or if the catch appears loose when the tailgate is closed, then refer to Section 16 and adjust the striker plate.

Support struts
Removal

10 Support the weight of the tailgate using a stout prop of suitable length.
11 Prise the retaining clips from the balljoints at the upper ends of the support struts, then carefully lever the joint off the spigot on the tailgate **(see illustration)**. On earlier models, the strut joints are secured in position by steel spring clips, which can be prised off using a screwdriver.
12 Repeat this operation at the lower end of the struts, then remove them from the vehicle.

⚠ **Warning: Ensure that the struts are fully extended by keeping the tailgate propped open, otherwise they may expand suddenly when released from their mountings.**

Refitting

13 Refit the struts by reversing the removal procedure.

16 Tailgate/bootlid lock components - removal and refitting

Catch
Removal

1 Disconnect the battery negative cable, and position it away from the terminal.
2 Remove the tailgate interior trim panel, as described in Section 25.
3 Slacken and withdraw the three catch assembly retaining bolts **(see illustration)**.
4 Unplug the wiring at the multi-plug connector **(see illustration)**.
5 Disconnect the lock cylinder link cable from the catch assembly by twisting the metal hook at the end of the cable out of the actuator lever **(see illustration)**. Lift the catch assembly away from the tailgate.

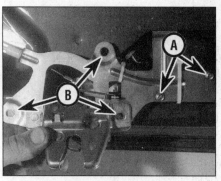

16.3 Tailgate catch assembly

A Servo motor retaining screws
B Catch assembly retaining screws

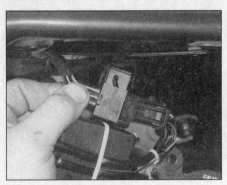

16.4 Unplug the wiring at the multi-plug connector

16.5 Disconnect the lock cylinder link cable from the catch assembly by twisting the metal hook at the end of the cable out of the actuator lever

16.8 Striker plate mounting bolts (arrowed)

Refitting

6 Refit the catch assembly by reversing the removal procedure. Upon completion, test the operation of the catch; if excessive force is required to engage the tailgate catch, or if the catch appears loose when the tailgate is closed, then refer to the following sub-section and adjust the striker plate.

Striker plate

Removal

7 Remove the retaining screws, and lift off the loadspace scuff plate.
8 Slacken and withdraw the two mounting bolts **(see illustration)**, then remove the striker plate.

Refitting

9 Refitting is a reversal of removal, adjusting the position of the striker as described below.

Adjustment

10 The mounting holes for the striker plate bolts are elongated, to allow a degree of adjustment. Slacken the bolts slightly, and move the striker plate to suit; slide the plate downwards to tighten the catch, or upwards to loosen it, then re-tighten the bolts, close the tailgate and check the security of the catch.

Lock cylinder

Removal

11 Remove the tailgate interior trim panel, as described in Section 25. Remove the two

retaining screws from the lock cylinder assembly **(see illustration)**. Turn the cylinder to allow it to be withdrawn through the hole in the tailgate.
12 Unhook the link cable nipple from the pulley, and remove the cylinder **(see illustration)**.

Refitting

13 Refit the lock cylinder by reversing the removal procedure.

17 Central locking servo motors - removal and refitting

Door lock servo motors

Note: *This procedure is applicable to both front and rear doors.*

Removal

1 Disconnect the battery negative cable, and position it away from the terminal.
2 Refer to Section 12 and remove the door interior trim panel.
3 Unplug the servo motor wiring from the wiring harness at the connector (refer to illustration 13.26).
4 Remove the two servo motor retaining screws **(see illustration)**.
5 Unhook the plunger from the lock mechanism, and lift out the servo motor.

Refitting

6 Refit the unit by reversing the removal procedure.

Tailgate/boot lock servo motor

Removal

7 Disconnect the battery negative cable, and position it away from the terminal.
8 Refer to Section 12 and remove the tailgate interior trim panel.
9 Unplug the servo motor wiring from the wiring harness at the connector.
10 Remove the two servo motor retaining screws (refer to illustration 16.3).
11 Unhook the plunger from the lock mechanism, and lift out the servo motor.

Refitting

12 Refit the unit by reversing the removal procedure.

Fuel filler lock servo motor

Removal

13 Disconnect the battery negative cable, and position it away from the terminal.
14 Refer to Section 25 and remove the loadspace side trim panels.
15 Unplug the servo motor wiring from the wiring harness at the connector.
16 The servo motor is mounted on a metal bracket, which is bolted to the inside of the wing. Remove the three retaining nuts to free the bracket, then separate the servo motor from it by extracting the two screws.

16.11 Remove the two retaining screws from the lock cylinder assembly (arrowed)

16.12 Unhook the link cable nipple from the pulley, and remove the cylinder

17.4 Remove the two servo motor retaining screws (arrowed)

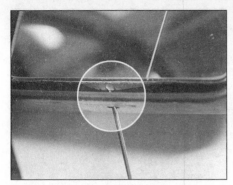

19.2 Insert a flat-bladed screwdriver into the hole in the underside of the mirror housing, and engage the blade with slotted plastic wheel

17 Unhook the plunger from the lock mechanism, and lift out the servo motor.

Refitting

18 Refit the unit by reversing the removal procedure. Ensure that the manual release cable is presented inside the loadspace when refitting the side trim panels.

18 Electric window components
- removal and refitting

Regulators and motors

1 The electric window motors and regulators are complete assemblies, and cannot be renewed individually; refer to Section 14 for details of removal and refitting.

Switches

2 Refer to Chapter 12 for details of switch removal and refitting.

19 Exterior door mirrors -
removal and refitting

Mirror glass

⚠️ **Warning: If the mirror glass is being removed to due to breakage, carefully dislodge all loose fragments of glass from the panel before attempting to remove it. Protect your eyes and hands with suitable goggles and gloves, and dispose of the glass safely, labelling any packages containing broken glass to warn others of the contents.**

Renewal

1 Using the mirror control switch, tilt the mirror glass upwards to the maximum extent of its travel.

2 Insert a flat-bladed screwdriver into the hole in the underside of the mirror housing, and engage the blade with slotted plastic wheel **(see illustration)**.

3 Turn the wheel two clicks to the right, to bring the third slot in line with the centre of the hole in the housing.

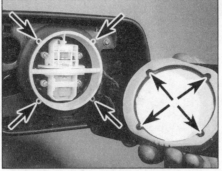

19.6 When refitting the mirror glass, ensure that the plastic slotted wheel is positioned such that plastic lugs on the back of the mirror are lined up with the cut-outs in the inside edge of the wheel (arrowed)

4 Lift the mirror glass out of the housing.

5 If the mirror glass is being removed due to breakage, remember to brush out any fragments of broken glass from inside the mirror housing, and check that none are wedged in the position adjustment mechanism.

6 When refitting the mirror glass, ensure that the plastic slotted wheel is positioned such that plastic lugs on the back of the mirror are lined up with the cut-outs in the inside edge of the wheel **(see illustration)**. Fit the mirror glass to the housing and, using a screwdriver inserted into the hole in the underside of the mirror, turn the slotted wheel two clicks to the left to secure the glass in place. On completion, check the operation of the electric position adjustment and demister.

Mirror assembly
Removal

7 Disconnect the battery negative cable, and position it away from the terminal.

8 Refer to Section 12 and remove the door interior trim panel.

9 Release the mirror cable bundle from the clip on the door panel, then unplug it from the wiring harness at the connectors - one for the mirror heater element, and one for the position adjustment motor **(see illustration)**.

10 Refer to the previous sub-section and remove the mirror glass.

19.12 Slacken and remove the three mounting screws (arrowed), recovering the metal plate from the lower mountings

19.9 Release the mirror cable bundle from the clip on the door panel, then unplug it from the wiring harness at the connectors

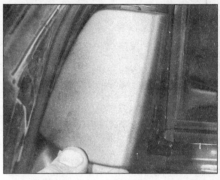

19.11 Unclip the plastic trim panel from inside the door, to expose the mirror mounting screws

11 Unclip the plastic trim panel from inside the door, to expose the mirror mounting screws **(see illustration)**.

12 Slacken and remove the three mounting screws, recovering the metal plate from the lower mountings **(see illustration)**.

13 Lift the mirror assembly away from the door, guiding out the wiring and connector **(see illustration)**. Recover the rubber gaiter from the mirror, and inspect it for wear or damage; renew it if necessary.

Refitting

14 Refit the mirror assembly by reversing the removal procedure. Refer to the previous sub-section for details of refitting the mirror glass.

19.13 Lift the mirror assembly away from the door, guiding out the wiring and connector

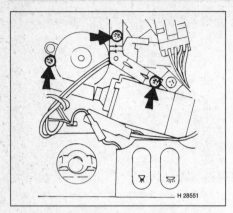

21.7 Slacken and withdraw the drive motor assembly retaining screws (arrowed)

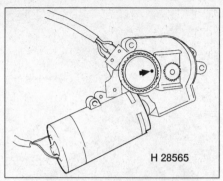

21.8 The alignment mark on the large drivegear should be adjacent to the smaller drivegear; this corresponds to the sunroof panel being in the "tilt" position

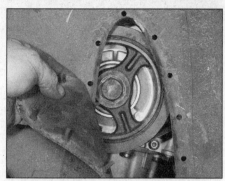

22.9 The right-hand front section (of the inner wheelarch liner) has a removable rubber pad that can be simply pulled out to gain access to the auxiliary drivebelt pulleys

20 Windscreen and fixed windows - general information

With the exception of the fixed quarter-light in the rear doors (see Section 14), these areas of glass are bonded in position with a special adhesive. Renewal of such fixed glass is a complex, messy and time-consuming task, which is deemed to be beyond the scope of the home mechanic; without the benefit of extensive practice, it is difficult to attain a secure, waterproof fit. Furthermore, the task carries a high risk of accidental breakage - this applies especially to the laminated glass windscreen. In view of this, owners are strongly advised to entrust work of this nature to a Saab dealer, or one of the many specialist windscreen fitters.

Note: *Vehicles fitted with airbags/SRS have windscreens that are cemented in differently to standard vehicles, to provide support during airbag detonation; bear this in mind when dealing with windscreen fitting companies.*

21 Sunroof assembly - removal and refitting

General information

1 Due to the complexity of the tilt/slide sunroof mechanism, considerable expertise is required to repair, renew or adjust the sunroof components successfully. Removal of the sunroof first requires that the headlining be removed, which is a tedious operation, not to be undertaken lightly (see Section 25). Therefore, this Section is limited to a description of the drive motor assembly removal/refitting, and it is recommended that any other problems related to the sunroof are referred to a Saab dealer.

Drive motor assembly
Removal

2 If the drive motor and its associated components are thought to be the cause of failure, first check the condition of the fuse; refer to Chapter 12 for details.

3 Operate the sunroof so that the trailing edge is tilted open; use the manual cranking spindle, located behind the panel in the overhead console, if the drive motor cannot be operated.
4 Turn the ignition switch to the "OFF" position, then disconnect the battery negative cable, and position it away from the terminal.
5 Referring to Chapter 12, Section 6, remove the retaining screw, and lower the overhead switch/light console away from the roof.
6 Unplug the wiring at the connectors, labelling them to aid refitting later.
7 Slacken and withdraw the three retaining screws **(see illustration)** and lower the drive motor assembly away from its mountings.

Refitting

8 Refit the drive motor assembly by reversing the removal procedure, noting that the alignment mark on the large drivegear should be adjacent to the smaller drivegear **(see illustration)**; this corresponds to the sunroof panel being in the "tilt" position. If the gears are not in this position, temporarily reconnect the battery negative cable; plug in the drive motor wiring, and using the sunroof operating switch, run the motor until the marks are aligned correctly.

22 Body exterior fittings - removal and refitting

Badges and trim mouldings
Removal

1 Side trim panels, rubbing strips, bonnet, bootlid and tailgate emblems are all secured in place by a combination of press-studs and adhesive tape.
2 To remove the fittings from the bodywork, select an implement to use as a lever that will not damage the paintwork, such as a plastic spatula, or a filling knife wrapped in PVC tape.
3 Insert the lever between the top edge of the fitting and the bodywork, and carefully prise it away to release the press-stud fixings; if more

than one stud is used, start at one end of the fitting and work along its length, releasing the studs one by one.
4 Progressively pull the lower edge of the fitting away from the bodywork, allowing the adhesive tape to peel off.
5 Clean the bodywork surface, removing all traces of dirt and the remains of any adhesive tape.

Refitting

6 Peel the backing strip from the new fitting. Offer it up to its mounting position, top edge first, and press the stud fixings into their holes. Smooth the lower edge of the fitting into place, then press down on it firmly to ensure that the tape adheres along its whole length.

Wheelarch trims

7 To remove, unscrew the flange nuts from the studs that protrude inside the wheelarch. Pull the trim away from the wheelarch, guiding the stud threads through their mounting holes.
8 Clean the surface of the wheelarch before refitting the trim, and brush out any dirt from around the mounting holes, inside the wheelarch.

Inner wheelarch liners

9 The front wheelarch liners consist of two moulded plastic panels that form the front and rear sections. Both are secured by means of flange screws and nuts, threaded into the bodywork. The right-hand front section has a removable rubber pad that can be simply pulled out to gain access to the auxiliary drivebelt pulleys **(see illustration)**.
10 To remove, first detach the wheelarch trim as described in the previous sub-section.
11 Both the front and rear sections of the wheelarch liners can be removed by simply extracting their retaining screws; the front section should be removed first **(see illustration)**. Note that on later models, the brake cooling ducts must be removed from under the front valance before the front section of the wheelarch liner can be withdrawn; these is achieved by simply removing the retaining screws.

22.11 Removing the front section of the
right-hand inner wheelarch liner

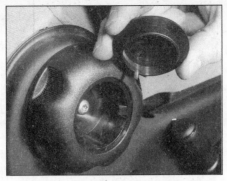

23.3a Prise out the plastic cap from the
rake adjustment knob

23.3b Remove the retaining screw . . .

23.3c . . . and lift off the knob

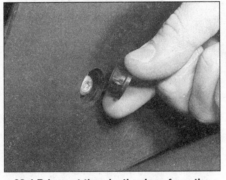

23.4 Prise out the plastic plugs from the
side trim panel, and remove the retaining
screws beneath

23.5 Unbolt the seat belt anchorage
bracket from the seat rail

23 Seats - removal and refitting

Front seats

Removal

1 Disconnect the battery negative cable, and
position it away from the terminal.
2 Where seat height adjusters are fitted,
ensure that these are set to the lowest
position.
3 Insert a small screwdriver into the slot
provided, and prise out the plastic cap from
the rake adjustment knob. Remove the
retaining screw, and lift off the knob **(see
illustrations)**.

4 Prise out the plastic plugs from the side trim
panel, and remove the retaining screws
beneath **(see illustration)**.
5 Unbolt the seat belt anchorage bracket from
the seat rail **(see illustration)**.
6 Slacken and withdraw the bolts that secure
both seat rails to the floorpan **(see illustrations)**.
7 Tilt the seat backwards and rest it against
the rear seat, taking care to avoid straining the
cables underneath. Unplug the wiring for the
seat heating elements at the connector,
located on the floor-mounted bracket **(see
illustration)**.
8 If the passenger seat is being removed,
unhook the switch from the bottom of the seat
cushion wire, noting its point of connection.
9 Lift the seat out of the cabin area.

Refitting

10 Refit the seat by reversing the removal
procedure, noting the following points:
a) *Ensure that all electrical wiring is
reconnected correctly; if the passenger
seat is being refitted, ensure that the
pressure switch is hooked onto the
underside of the cushion in the correct
position, as noted during removal.*
b) *When refitting the seat belt anchor
bracket, engage the tang with the slot on
the seat bracket. Although a torque
wrench setting for the retaining nut is not
specified by Saab, ensure that it is
securely tightened. Where self-locking
nuts are fitted, ideally these should be
renewed once disturbed.*

23.6a Removing seat rail-to-floorpan bolts
at the front . . .

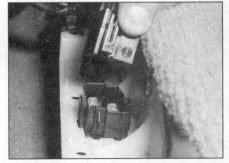

23.6b . . . and rear of the rail

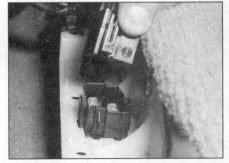

23.7 Unplug the wiring for the seat heating
elements at the connector, located on the
floor-mounted bracket

23.12a Unbolt the backrest mounting bracket from the floorpan . . .

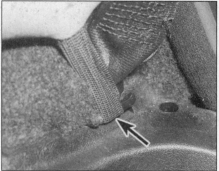

23.12b . . . and unhook the lower edge of the upholstery from the seat belt anchor brackets (arrowed)

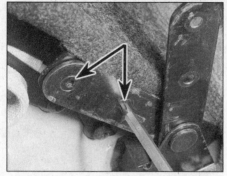

23.13 To separate the backrests, remove the retaining screws from the hinge at the edges

Rear seat backrests

Removal

11 Using the hand straps, raise the seat cushion, and tilt it fully forwards.

12 The rear seat backrests are mounted on brackets which are bolted to the floorpan at three points. To remove both backrests together, peel back the carpet, unbolt the mounting brackets from the floorpan, unhook the lower edge of the upholstery from the seat belt anchor brackets, and lift out the backrest (see illustrations).

13 To separate the backrests, remove the retaining screws from the hinge at the edges (see illustration).

Refitting

14 Refit the backrests by reversing the removal procedure.

Rear seat cushion

Removal

15 Using the hand straps, raise the seat cushion, and tilt it fully forwards.

16 Remove the screws that secure the metal backplate to the hinge bar, then lift out the cushion.

Refitting

17 Refit the seat cushion by reversing the removal procedure; ensure that the cushion is fitted evenly to the hinge bar and is not twisted, before tightening the retaining screws.

24 Seat belt components - removal and refitting

General information

1 The front seat belts are of the three-point inertia reel type. The fixed ends of the belts are anchored on the seat frames, as are the buckle stalks. The height of the B-pillar support is adjustable, to adapt to different driving positions.

2 The two outer rear seats are also fitted with inertia reel three point belts; the centre rear seat position is fitted with a lap restraint.

3 All models fitted with a Supplementary Restraint System (SRS) are equipped with seat belt tensioning devices; refer to Section 28 before disturbing any of the components associated with these devices.

4 Saab state that the seat belts are classed as components which must be renewed after a collision has occurred, regardless of apparent condition. Refer to your Saab dealer if you have doubts regarding the correct course of action under these circumstances.

Front seat belt buckles

Removal

5 Referring to Section 23, unbolt the applicable front seat from the floorpan, and slide it backwards to gain access to the seat belt buckle.

6 Free the wiring for the "buckle fastened" switch from the seat bracket, then reach underneath the seat and unplug the cable connector.

7 Slacken and withdraw the retaining nut, recover the washer, and lift off the buckle stalk.

Refitting

8 Refit the buckle by reversing the removal procedure. When refitting the buckle stalk retaining nut, although a torque wrench setting is not specified by Saab, ensure that the nut is securely tightened. Where self-locking nuts are fitted, ideally these should be renewed once disturbed.

Front seat belt anchor points

9 Refer to Section 23 (front seat removal) for details of removal and refitting.

Front seat belt height adjustment components

Removal

Note: Whilst not essential, the removal the applicable front seat will improve access, and hence ease the completion of this operation.

10 Using a flat-bladed screwdriver, carefully prise the plastic covers out from both the front and rear door sill scuff plates. Undo the retaining screws, lift off the metal plates, and remove the scuff plates (see illustrations).

24.10a Using a flat-bladed screwdriver, carefully prise the plastic covers out from the door sill scuff plates

24.10b Undo the retaining screws . . .

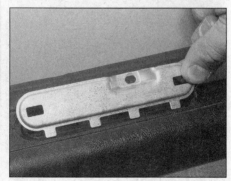

24.10c . . . and lift off the metal plates

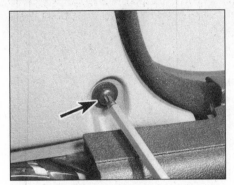

24.11 Remove the screws from the bottom of the B-pillar trim panel

24.12 Release the clips behind the height adjustment knob, and lift it off

24.13 Remove the retaining screw and lift off the adjustment knob bracket, belt support pulley and bush; note their orientation and order of fitment

11 Remove the screws from the bottom of the B-pillar trim panel **(see illustration)**.
12 Release the clips behind the height adjustment knob, and lift it off **(see illustration)**.
13 Remove the retaining screw, and lift off the adjustment knob bracket, belt support pulley and bush; note their orientation and order of fitment **(see illustration)**.
14 Working from the floor upwards, prise the rubber sealing strips away from the door apertures, then carefully release the press-stud fixings beneath the trim panel one at a time, by easing it away from the B-pillar. On vehicles fitted with a Safety Restraint System, take great care to avoid disturbing the seat belt tensioner components, situated above the inertia reel.

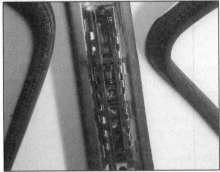

24.15 Seat belt height adjustment rack

24.19 Remove the single bolt (arrowed) that secures the inertia reel to the base of the B-pillar, and recover the washer

15 Remove the upper and lower retaining screws, then lift the adjustment rack away from the B-pillar **(see illustration)**.

Refitting

16 Refit the height adjustment components by reversing the removal procedure.

Front seat belt inertia reel assembly (vehicles with SRS)

17 On vehicles fitted with seat belt tensioning devices, removal of the seat belt inertia reel should be entrusted to a Saab dealer; refer to Section 28 for more detail.

Front seat belt inertia reel assembly (vehicles without SRS)

18 Proceed as described in paragraphs 10 to 12 inclusive.
19 Remove the single bolt that secures the inertia reel to the base of the B-pillar, and recover the washer **(see illustration)**. Lift off the reel assembly, together with the seat belt.

Rear seat belt anchorages and buckles

20 The rear seat belt buckles are mounted on spring-loaded stalks bolted directly to the floorpan, as is the anchor bracket for the centre lap belt **(see illustration)**.
21 The inertia reels for the outer rear seat belts are bolted in position behind the loadspace side trim panels. To gain access to them, refer to Section 25 and remove the loadspace side trim panel.

24.20 Mounting for rear seat belt buckle and centre lap belt anchorage

25 Interior trim panels- removal and refitting

A-pillar trim panels

1 Open the relevant front door, and prise the rubber sealing strip from the door aperture at the A-pillar.
2 Working from the headlining down, grasp the panel firmly and progressively ease it away from the pillar, allowing the press-studs beneath to disengage one at a time **(see illustration)**.
3 To refit, offer the panel up to its mounted position, and apply firm pressure over each press-stud until it engages. Press the door aperture sealing strip back into place.

B-pillar trim panels

4 The B-pillar trims form the cover for the seat belt inertia reel assemblies; refer to Section 24 for details of their removal.

C-pillar trim panels

5 Open the relevant rear door, and prise the rubber sealing strip from the door aperture at the C-pillar.
6 Remove the passenger reading light, referring to Chapter 12 for more detail.
7 Working around the outside edge, carefully ease the panel away from the C-pillar, allowing the press-stud fixings to disengage one at a time.

25.2 Removing the A-pillar trim panel

25.12 Remove the retaining screws, and lift off the internal grab handle

25.13 Unscrew the fixings from the ends of the rigid plastic trim panels

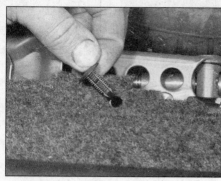

25.15a Prise out the press-studs . . .

25.15b . . . then remove the retaining screws, and lift off the scuff plate from the loadspace sill, together with the integral carpet panel

25.16 Remove the screws, and lift off the scuff panel at the front of the loadspace

8 To refit, offer the panel up to its mounted position, and apply firm pressure over each press-stud until it engages. Press the door aperture sealing strip back into place, then refit the passenger reading light.

Headlining

9 The headlining is clipped to the roof panel, and can only be lowered once all fittings such as the grab handles, sunvisors, sunroof (where fitted), pillar trim panels, and interior lights have been removed. The weatherstrip for the door apertures (and where applicable, the tailgate and sunroof apertures) will also have to be prised away from the bodywork.

10 Note that the removal of the headlining requires considerable skill and experience if it is to be carried out without damage, and is therefore best entrusted to an expert.

Tailgate interior trim panel

11 Open the tailgate, and remove the internal trim panel fixing studs by twisting each one anti-clockwise through a quarter-turn.

12 Remove the retaining screws, and lift off the internal grab handle (see illustration).

13 At the inside lower edge of the rear window glass, unscrew the fixings from the ends of the rigid plastic trim panels (see illustration). Carefully lower the interior trim panel away from the tailgate.

14 To refit, reverse the removal procedure.

Spare wheel cover

15 Prise out the press-studs, then remove the retaining screws and lift off the scuff plate from the loadspace sill, together with the integral carpet panel (see illustrations).

16 Tilt the rear seat backrest forward, then remove the screws and lift off the scuff panel at the front of the loadspace (see illustration).

17 Three screws, adjacent to the hinged joint, secure the spare wheel cover to the floorpan; remove these, and lift the cover out of the loadspace.

18 Refit the cover by reversing the removal procedure.

Loadspace side trim panels

19 Remove the spare wheel cover as described in the preceding sub-section.

20 Remove the plastic caps from the studs that secure the trim panel to the rear of the loadspace, then prise the rubber sealing strip away from the edge of the tailgate aperture (see illustrations).

21 Working from the tailgate aperture, carefully draw the panel away from the side of the loadspace. At the underside of the parcel shelf support/speaker bracket, use a screwdriver to release the plastic tangs from the cut-outs in the trim panel (see illustration).

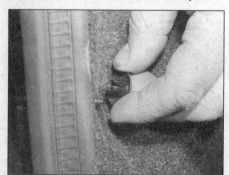

25.20a Remove the plastic caps from the studs that secure the trim panel to the rear of the load space . . .

25.20b . . . then prise the rubber sealing strip away from the edge of the tailgate aperture

25.21 Carefully draw the panel away from the side of the loadspace. At the underside of the parcel shelf support/speaker bracket, use a screwdriver to release the plastic tangs from the cut-outs in the trim panel

25.22 Unscrew the seat backrest locking spigot from the front of the wheelarch protrusion, and lift off the metal backing plate

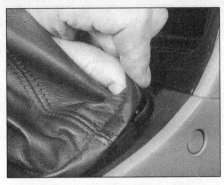

26.2a Prise off the gear lever gaiter to expose the mounting frame beneath

26.2b Remove the retaining screw, and lift off the frame

26.3a Release the electric window switch panel from the console, reaching through the gear lever orifice and pressing up on the underside of the panel to ease its release

26.3b Label the harness connector and cables to aid refitting, then unplug the connector and remove the panel

26.4 Prise out the plastic plugs, and remove the two retaining screws from the flanks of the gear lever console

22 Unscrew the seat backrest locking spigot from the front of the wheelarch protrusion, and lift off the metal backing plate **(see illustration)**.

23 Free the corner of the trim panel from the rear door aperture scuff panel by slackening the retaining screws.

24 Carefully ease the remainder of the trim panel away from the bodywork, and lift it out of the vehicle.

26 Centre console - removal and refitting

Removal

1 Disconnect the battery negative cable, and position it away from the terminal.

2 Prise off the gear lever/selector lever gaiter, to expose the mounting frame beneath. Remove the retaining screw, and lift off the frame **(see illustrations)**.

3 Release the electric window switch panel from the console, reaching through the gear lever orifice and pressing up on the underside of the panel to ease its release. Label the harness connector and cables to aid refitting, then unplug the connector and remove the panel **(see illustrations)**.

4 Prise out the plastic plugs, and remove the two retaining screws from the flanks of the gear lever console **(see illustration)**.

5 Extract the mounting screw, and remove the handbrake lever brush seal **(see illustration)**.

6 Slide both front seats fully forwards, then fold back the flaps in the carpet to expose the centre console rear retaining screws **(see illustrations)**. Remove the screws and lift out the entire console. Where applicable, unplug the wiring for rear passenger cigarette lighter/ashtray illumination.

7 Extract the fixings and remove the trim panels from either side of the forward section of the centre console. The fixings are of the press-stud type - these can be removed without damage by sliding the prongs of an

26.5 Extract the mounting screw, and remove the handbrake lever brush seal

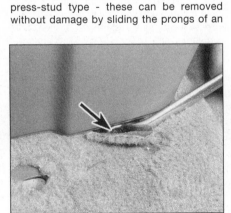

26.6a Slide both front seats fully forwards, then fold back the flaps in the carpet to expose the centre console rear retaining screws

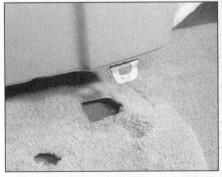

26.6b Remove the screws and lift out the entire console

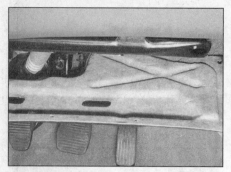

27.4 Carefully lower the sound insulation panels away from the facia, and pull them off the metal anchoring tabs at the bulkhead

27.6a Remove the three screws (arrowed) . . .

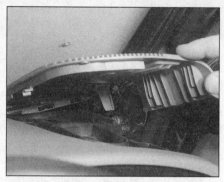

27.6b . . . lift off the speaker/ventilation grilles . . .

old fork underneath their heads and carefully levering them out. Do not attempt to remove the fixings by pulling on the trim panel; they may pull through the panel, or snap off completely.

Refitting

8 Refit the centre console by reversing the removal procedure.

---

27 Facia assembly -
removal and refitting

Removal

1 Disconnect the battery negative cable, and position it away from the terminal.

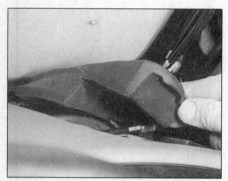

27.6c . . . and recover the rubber spacers

⚠️ **Warning: On vehicles fitted with airbags, allow 20 minutes to elapse after disconnecting the battery negative cable, before working on any component in the airbag system; refer to Section 28 for more details.**

2 Refer to Section 26 and remove the centre console.

3 Remove the carpeted trim panels from the sides of the driver and passenger footwells by extracting the crosshead screws and press-studs.

4 Prise out the press-studs from the front edges of the sound insulation panels, underneath the driver and passenger side of the facia. **Note:** *The press-studs are of the two-piece type, which can be removed as follows: press the rod at the centre of the stud in as far as it will go, using a narrow-bladed screwdriver. Slide the prongs of an old fork underneath the head of the stud, and prise it out of the panel. Carefully lower the panels away from the facia, and pull them off the metal anchoring tabs at the bulkhead* **(see illustration).**

5 Prise the rubber sealing strips away from the driver and passenger door apertures; just enough to allow access to the A-pillar trim panels. Grasp the panel firmly and working from the top, ease it away from the A-pillar to release the press-studs; refer to Section 25 for further details.

6 Remove the three screws, then lift off the

speaker/ventilation grilles, and recover the rubber spacers **(see illustrations).**

7 To release the upper facia panel, unscrew the fixings at the following locations: three at either end of the facia beneath the speaker/ventilation grilles, one in the glovebox housing - accessed by opening the glovebox door and prising out the rubber cap, and one at the front edge of the facia - directly above the tachometer dial.

8 Apply the handbrake, then raise the front edge of the upper facia panel, and extract the A-pillar restraint cable from its mounting clips. Where fitted, unplug the wiring from the sun sensor, at the connector. Lift the panel away from the facia and out of the cabin area **(see illustration).**

9 Remove the retaining screws and lift out the entire glovebox assembly; unplug the wiring for the internal switch and light as the connectors are revealed **(see illustrations).** **Note:** *Where a passenger airbag is fitted, refer to Section 28 for details of its removal.*

10 On vehicles fitted with Automatic Climate Control (ACC), reach through the glovebox aperture, and press the ACC unit out of the facia front panel. Unplug the connectors, labelling them to aid refitting later **(see illustrations).**

11 On vehicles with air conditioning and/or a conventional heating system, reach through the glovebox aperture, compress the four catches, and press the heater control panel out of the facia front panel. Separate the

27.8 Lift the upper facia panel away from the facia

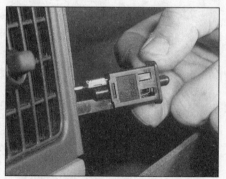

27.9a Unplug the wiring for the glovebox internal switch . . .

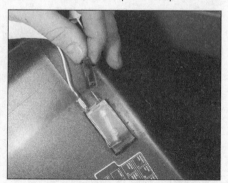

27.9b . . . and glovebox light, as the connectors are revealed

27.10a Reach through the glovebox aperture, and press the ACC unit out of the facia front panel

27.10b Unplug the connectors, labelling them to aid refitting later

27.12 Reach behind the facia, and press out the stowage bin moulding, directly beneath the ashtray

balljoint for the link rod in the air distribution valve, then detach the gear housing for the temperature control valve (refer to Chapter 3 for guidance). Unplug the electrical connectors, labelling them to aid refitting later.

12 Reach behind the facia, and press out the stowage bin moulding, directly beneath the ashtray **(see illustration)**.

13 Pull the ashtray drawer out of its housing. Use a small screwdriver to release the ashtray housing retaining clips, then lift it out of the facia front panel **(see illustrations)**. Unplug the cigarette lighter wiring as the connector is revealed.

14 Using the special key supplied with the vehicle, extract the radio/cassette unit from the facia front panel **(see illustration)**.

Unplug the connectors, label them, then feed them back through the facia aperture.

15 Remove the two screws, and lift the lower plastic cowling panel from the steering column.

16 On vehicles fitted with a driver's airbag, refer to Section 28 and remove the airbag module.

17 Refer to Chapter 10 and remove the steering wheel.

18 On vehicles fitted with a driver's airbag, refer to Section 28 and remove the airbag rotary contact unit. Ensure that the indicator stalk switch is in the neutral/off position, to prevent it fouling the contact unit.

19 Remove the two screws, and lift the upper plastic cowling panel from the steering

column.

20 Referring to Chapter 12 for details, slacken and remove the three retaining screws, and lift off the steering column stalk switch assembly. Unplug the multi-plug connectors from the assembly; label them carefully and note their fitted positions, as they are very similar in appearance.

21 To release the facia front panel, unscrew the fixings at the following locations: two inside the ashtray mounting aperture, and two behind clip-on plastic covers either side of the steering column, adjacent to the switch banks. Note that the fifth fixing doubles up as the retaining screw for the mounting frame, to which the gear lever gaiter is attached **(see illustrations)**.

27.13a Use a small screwdriver to release the ashtray housing retaining clips . . .

27.13b . . . then lift it out of the facia front panel

27.14 Using the special key supplied with the vehicle, extract the radio/cassette unit from the facia front panel

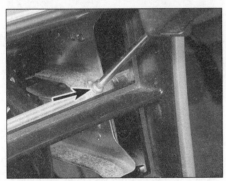

27.21a Facia front panel fixings: two inside the ashtray mounting aperture . . .

27.21b . . . two behind clip-on plastic covers adjacent to the switch banks, on the right-hand side . . .

27.21c . . . and left-hand side of the steering column . . .

27.21d . . . the fifth fixing doubles up as the retaining screw for the mounting frame, to which the gear lever gaiter is attached

27.30 Remove the screws that secure the front of the fuse panel/relay box to the facia (locations arrowed)

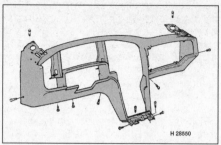

27.31 Locations of facia framework assembly retaining screws

22 On vehicles fitted with ACC, prise off the plastic cover from the cabin temperature sensor. Reach behind the facia front panel, and release the sensor body. Unlike all other components fitted into the facia, the sensor body is withdrawn from the rear of the panel, rather than from the front. Refer to Chapter 3 if necessary.

23 Refer to Chapter 12 and remove the hazard light switch, heated seat rheostats, instrument panel illumination rheostat, headlight leveller control, front and rear foglight switches, and headlight switch. Label all connectors, to aid refitting later.

24 Again referring to Chapter 12, remove the clock/trip computer module from the facia. Unplug the connector, and label the cables to aid refitting later.

25 Carefully draw the facia front panel away from the main framework, ensuring that nothing remains connected, before lifting the panel out of the cabin area.

26 Referring to Chapter 12, remove the four screws that secure the instrument panel in position. Note that the screw heads face the bulkhead, and so must be extracted from within the facia, using a short-handled screwdriver. Recover the rubber mounting bushes. Lift the instrument panel out through the top of the facia, and recover the rubber mounting feet.

27 Remove the screws that secure the side window demister ducts to the speaker mounting brackets.

28 Disconnect the cables from the speaker terminals.

29 At the lower right-hand side of facia, under the steering column, remove the screws that secure the cruise control ECU bracket (where applicable) to the facia. Refer to Chapter 4A for further details.

30 Remove the screws that secure the front of the fuse panel/relay box to the facia, and allow it to hang on its rear mounting bracket **(see illustration)**.

31 Work around the periphery of the facia framework assembly, and remove all the remaining fixings **(see illustration)**.

32 Finally, disengage the framework from the locating lug on the top of the steering column bracket, and pull it away from the bulkhead, disconnecting the ventilation ducts from the facia grilles and the heater unit casing. Check that nothing remains connected to the assembly, then lift it out of the cabin area.

Refitting

33 Refit the facia by following the removal procedure in reverse, noting the points in the following paragraphs.

34 When fitting the facia framework assembly, ensure that all the ventilation ducting locates correctly over the ports on the heater unit casing and the facia grilles, before inserting any of the retaining screws. In addition, ensure that where the framework passes over the steering column, it engages

with the lug fixed to the top of the steering column bracket **(see illustration)**.

35 As the instrument panel is refitted, check that the rubber feet locate in the indentations on the metal mounting brackets; refer to Chapter 12 for guidance.

36 Refer to Section 28 when refitting the driver's airbag rotary contact unit, and follow the instructions carefully. If the unit is refitted incorrectly, it can easily be damaged, rendering the airbag system inoperative.

37 Reinstate all electrical connections according to the notes made during removal.

38 When fitting the facia front panel, ensure that all the ventilation ducting locates correctly over the grilles before inserting any of the facia retaining screws.

39 When refitting the heater control panel on vehicles fitted with air conditioning and/or a conventional heating system (not ACC), set the heater unit flap valve in the engine bay to the "cold" position (away from the bulkhead), then reconnect the gear housing for the temperature control valve, with the control turned to the "cold" position. Refit the air distribution control with the knob is set to "0" and the distribution gear mechanism rotated fully anti-clockwise.

40 Ensure that as the facia top panel is refitted, the A-pillar restraint cable is clipped securely to its underside, and is not fouled by any other components or wiring.

41 Refit the two-piece press-studs at the front edge of the sound insulation panel under the facia, as follows. Pull the rod at the centre of the stud out to the end of its travel, insert

27.34 When fitting the facia framework assembly, ensure that it engages with the lug fixed to the top of the steering column bracket (arrowed)

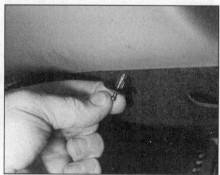

27.41a To refit the sound insulation panel, insert the stud into the panel . . .

27.41b . . . then lock it in position by pushing in the centre rod, until it is flush with the top of the stud head, using a narrow-bladed screwdriver

the stud into the panel, then lock it in position by pushing in the centre rod, until it is flush with top of the stud head, using a narrow-bladed screwdriver **(see illustrations)**.

42 On completion, reconnect the battery negative cable, and check the operation of all controls, gauges and instruments disturbed during the removal process, including the ventilation system. On vehicles with SRS, check that the instrument panel warning light extinguishes after the initial self-test period; refer to Section 28 for further details.

28 Supplementary Restraint System (SRS) components - removal and refitting

General information

The operation of the SRS is managed by an Electronic Control Unit (ECU). When the vehicle's ignition switch is turned to the "Start" or "Drive" position, the ECU performs its "housekeeping" self-test checks of the system's components; if a fault is detected, the ECU records it in memory as a "fault flag". Following this, the ECU flashes the instrument panel-mounted warning light in a sequence that depends on the results of the housekeeping checks, as follows:

1988-1991 model year vehicles: At start-up, the ECU will flash the SRS warning light for approximately six seconds, as a visual check of the bulb operation, and then extinguish. If the ECU has previously-set fault flags stored in memory, or if a fault is detected at start-up, the SRS warning light will flash for approximately 10 minutes, and then shine steadily. If the vehicle has been involved in a collision in which the SRS has been activated, the SRS warning light will flash for approximately five seconds, and then shine steadily.

Post-1991 model year vehicles: As an added safety measure, the SRS warning light is now illuminated by two bulbs that are fused independently. At start -up, if no faults are detected, both bulbs will illuminate the SRS warning light for approximately five seconds, and then extinguish. If the ECU has previously-set fault flags stored in memory, or if a fault is detected at start-up, bulb No 2 will shine continuously, whilst No 1 bulb will flash for approximately five minutes, and then shine steadily. If the vehicle has been involved in a collision in which the SRS has been activated, both bulbs will illuminate the SRS warning light continuously.

Once a fault has manifested itself in the manner described above, the *only* course of action open is to take the vehicle to a Saab dealer for examination. Dedicated test equipment is needed to interrogate SRS ECU, firstly to determine the nature and incidence of the fault, and secondly to clear the stored fault

flag, thus preventing the fault from being displayed by the warning light once the fault has been rectified.

For safety reasons, owners are strongly advised against attempting to diagnose problems with the SRS using standard workshop equipment. The information in this Section is therefore limited to those components in the SRS which must occasionally be removed to gain access to other components on the vehicle.

⚠ **Warning: A number of additional precautions must be observed when working on vehicles with airbags/SRS:**

a) *Disconnect the battery negative cable, and wait **at least twenty minutes** before disconnecting any of the SRS components' electrical wiring; this gives the ECU internal trigger capacitor time to discharge, and avoids accidental detonation.*

b) *Make no attempt to splice into any of the electric cables in the SRS wiring harness, as this may affect the operation of the SRS.*

c) *Avoid hammering or causing any harsh vibration at the front of the vehicle, particularly in the engine bay, as this may trigger the crash sensors and activate the SRS.*

d) *Do not use ohmmeters or any other device capable of supplying current on any of the SRS components, as this may cause accidental detonation.*

e) *Before working on the steering system, be sure to lock the steering column in the dead-ahead position before disconnecting it from the steering rack, as any misalignment caused when the column and rack are reunited may damage the steering wheel contact unit.*

f) *Airbags (and seat belt tensioners) are classed as pyrotechnical (explosive) devices, and must be stored and handled according to the relevant laws in the country concerned. In general, do not leave these components disconnected from their electrical wiring any longer than is absolutely necessary; in this state they*

28.4 Unplug the cable connector from the rear of the airbag

are unstable, and the risk of accidental detonation is introduced. Rest a disconnected airbag with the metal bracket facing downwards, away from flammable materials - never leave it unattended.

Driver's airbag module

Removal

1 Disconnect the battery negative cable, and wait *at least twenty minutes* before progressing any further; refer to the Warnings listed in the *"General Information"* sub-section above for more detail.

2 Remove the two airbag retaining screws; these are accessed from behind the steering wheel, at the rear of the spokes.

3 Carefully prise the airbag module away from the steering wheel, to gain access to the wiring behind.

4 Unplug the cable connector from the rear of the airbag **(see illustration)**.

Refitting

5 Refit the airbag by reversing the removal procedure; observe the torque wrench setting listed when tightening the airbag retaining screws.

6 Reconnect the battery negative cable, and turn the ignition switch to the "Drive" or "Start" position. Check the condition of the system by observing the SRS warning light; refer to the *"General Information"* sub-section to interpret the results obtained.

Passenger airbag module

Removal

7 The passenger airbag module is held in the facia by four retaining screws and a number of clips **(see illustration)**.

8 Disconnect the battery negative cable, and wait *at least twenty minutes* before progressing any further; refer to the Warnings listed in the *"General Information"* sub-section for more detail.

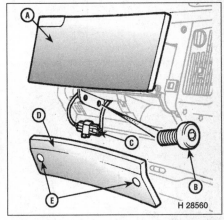

28.7 Passenger airbag module

A Passenger airbag module
B Airbag module retaining screws
C Wiring harness connector
D Cover panel
E Cover panel retaining screw locations

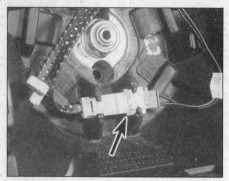

28.17a Prise the horn cable connector out of the mounting bracket on the steering wheel casting (arrowed) . . .

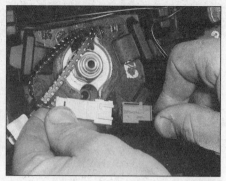

28.17b . . . and unplug it, labelling the cable to aid refitting later

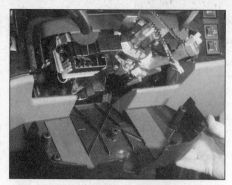

28.19 Removing the lower cowling panel from the steering column

9 Prise out the plastic caps from the retaining screws on the lower front panel, then remove the screws.

10 Pull the lower panel away from the facia, releasing the clips one at a time.

11 Unplug the airbag module wiring at the connector.

12 Remove the four airbag module retaining screws, then reach inside the facia, grasp the module from behind and carefully draw it out, whilst releasing it from the mounting clips.

Refitting

13 Refit the airbag by reversing the removal procedure; observe the specified torque wrench setting when tightening the airbag and lower cover panel retaining screws.

14 Reconnect the battery negative cable, and turn the ignition switch to the "Drive" or "Start" position. Check the condition of the system by observing the SRS warning light; refer to the *"General Information"* sub-section to interpret the results obtained.

Steering wheel rotary contact unit

Removal

15 Disconnect the battery negative cable, and wait *at least twenty minutes* before progressing any further; refer to the Warnings listed in the *"General Information"* sub-section for more detail.

16 Remove the driver's airbag module, as described earlier in this Section.

17 Prise the horn cable connector out of the mounting bracket on the steering wheel casting and unplug it, labelling the cable to aid refitting later **(see illustrations)**.

18 Set the steering in the straight-ahead position, then refer to Chapter 10 and remove the steering wheel, feeding the cable connectors through the hole in the steering wheel casting.

19 Remove the retaining screws, and lift the upper and lower cowling panels away from the steering column **(see illustration)**.

20 Unplug the contact unit and horn cables at the connectors, after cutting through the cable-tie securing them to the ignition switch/lock assembly **(see illustration)**. Label the cables, to aid refitting later.

21 Slacken and withdraw the retaining screws, then lift the contact unit off the steering column **(see illustration)**. Take great care to ensure that the two halves of the contact unit are not rotated whilst it is separated from the steering column.

Refitting

22 Guide the contact unit onto the steering column, then refit and tighten the retaining screws.

23 Plug the horn and contact unit connectors

together, then secure them to the ignition switch/lock assembly with a cable-tie.

24 Refit the upper and lower steering column cowling panels, and tighten the retaining screws.

25 Align the contact unit with the steering wheel as follows. Check that the front roadwheels are still in the straight-ahead position. Rotate the upper section of the contact unit fully anti-clockwise, until it is felt to touch its end stop. **Note:** *Ensure that the direction indicator stalk is in the "off" position, otherwise the cancelling mechanism may affect the alignment accuracy.*

> ⚠ **Caution: Do not apply excessive force during this operation; the contact unit has very fragile internal components. Now rotate the contact unit clockwise by the number of turns printed on the unit's label (either 2.5 or 3.5 turns) - ensure that the unit is now kept in this position until the steering wheel is refitted.**

26 Offer up the steering wheel to the steering column, and feed the cable connectors through the hole in the wheel casting. Engage the spigot protruding from the contact unit with the alignment hole in the steering wheel casting - ensure that the wheel is fitted squarely in the straight-ahead position; the contact unit may be rotated slightly to allow the alignment spigot to engage, if necessary.

27 Fit a new steering wheel centre nut and tighten it to the specified torque, referring to Chapter 10 for details.

28 Plug together the horn cable connector, and then press the connector housing into the mounting provided in the steering wheel casting.

29 Refit the airbag, as described earlier in this Section.

30 Reconnect the battery negative cable, and turn the ignition switch to the "Drive" or "Start" position. Check the condition of the system by observing the SRS warning light; refer to the *"General Information"* sub-section to interpret the results obtained.

28.20 Unplug the contact unit and horn cables at the connectors, after cutting through the cable-tie securing them to the ignition switch/lock assembly

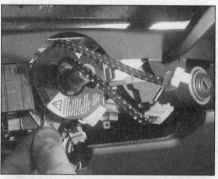

28.21 Slacken and withdraw the retaining screws, then lift the contact unit off the steering column

Chapter 12 Body electrical systems

Contents

Degrees of difficulty

Easy, suitable for novice with little experience	**Fairly easy,** suitable for beginner with some experience	**Fairly difficult,** suitable for competent DIY mechanic	**Difficult,** suitable for experienced DIY mechanic	**Very difficult,** suitable for expert DIY or professional

Specifications

Bulb ratings

	Watts
Courtesy lights	5
Direction indicator, rear	21
Direction indicator, front/parking light	21/5
Direction indicator side repeaters	5
Door courtesy/warning lights	5
Engine bay light	15
Facia light	5
Foglight, rear/tail light	21/4
Glovebox light	5
Headlight, H4 holder (single-reflector)	60/55
Headlight, H1 holder (double-reflector)	55

Bulb ratings

	Watts
High-level brake light:	
Inner pair of bulbs	3
Outer pair of bulbs	5
Luggage area light	10
Map reading lights	5
Number plate light	5
Parking light	4
Reversing lights	21
Seat belt warning light	5
Stop-lights	21
Tail light	4

1 General information

This Chapter covers all electrical systems not directly related to the vehicle's powertrain. The starting, charging and ignition systems are covered in Chapter 5, Parts A and B.

Refer to the precautions listed in "Safety first!", before commencing any of the operations detailed in this Chapter.

 Caution: Electronic Control Units (ECUs) contain components that are sensitive to the levels of static electricity generated by a person during normal activity. Once the multi-plug connector has been unplugged, the exposed ECU connector pins can freely conduct stray static electricity to these components, damaging or even destroying them - the damage will be invisible, and may not manifest itself immediately. Expensive repairs can be avoided by observing the following basic handling rules:

a) *Handle a disconnected ECU by its case only; do not allow fingers or tools to come into contact with the pins.*
b) *When carrying an ECU around, "earth" yourself from time to time, by touching a metal object such as an unpainted water pipe, this will discharge any potentially-damaging static that may have built up.*
c) *Do not leave the ECU unplugged from its connector for any longer than is absolutely necessary.*

2 Electrical fault-finding - general information

Note: *Refer to the precautions given in "Safety first!" and in Section 1 of this Chapter before starting work. The following tests relate to testing of the main electrical circuits, and should not be used to test delicate electronic circuits (such as anti-lock braking systems), particularly where an electronic control unit (ECU) is involved.*

General

1 A typical electrical circuit consists of an electrical component, any switches, relays, motors, fuses, fusible links or circuit breakers related to that component, and the wiring and connectors which link the component to both the battery and the chassis. To help to pinpoint a problem in an electrical circuit, wiring diagrams are included at the end of this manual.

2 Before attempting to diagnose an electrical fault, first study the appropriate wiring diagram, to obtain a more complete understanding of the components included in the particular circuit concerned. The possible sources of a fault can be narrowed down by noting whether other components related to the circuit are operating properly. If several components or circuits fail at one time, the problem is likely to be related to a shared fuse or earth connection.

3 Electrical problems usually stem from simple causes, such as loose or corroded connections, a faulty earth connection, a blown fuse, a melted fusible link, or a faulty relay (refer to Section 3 for details of testing relays). Visually inspect the condition of all fuses, wires and connections in a problem circuit before testing the components. Use the wiring diagrams to determine which terminal connections will need to be checked, in order to pinpoint the trouble-spot.

4 The basic tools required for electrical fault-finding include: a circuit tester or voltmeter (a 12-volt bulb with a set of test leads can also be used for certain tests), a self-powered test light (sometimes known as a continuity tester), an ohmmeter (to measure resistance), a battery and set of test leads, and a jumper wire, preferably with a circuit breaker or fuse incorporated, which can be used to bypass suspect wires or electrical components. Before attempting to locate a problem with test instruments, use the wiring diagram to determine where to make the connections.

5 To find the source of an intermittent wiring fault (usually due to a poor or dirty connection, or damaged wiring insulation), an integrity test can be performed on the wiring, which involves moving the wiring by hand, to see if the fault occurs as the wiring is moved. It should be possible to narrow down the source of the fault to a particular section of wiring. This method of testing can be used in conjunction with any of the tests described in the following sub-Sections.

6 Apart from problems due to poor connections, two basic types of fault can occur in an electrical circuit - open-circuit, or short-circuit.

7 Open-circuit faults are caused by a break somewhere in the circuit, which prevents current from flowing. An open-circuit fault will prevent a component from working, but will not cause the relevant circuit fuse to blow.

8 Short-circuit faults are caused by a "short" somewhere in the circuit, which allows the current flowing in the circuit to "escape" along an alternative route, usually to earth. Short-circuit faults are normally caused by a breakdown in wiring insulation, which allows a feed wire to touch either another wire, or an earthed component such as the bodyshell. A short-circuit fault will normally cause the relevant circuit fuse to blow. **Note:** *A short-circuit that occurs in the wiring between a circuit's battery supply and its fuse will not cause the fuse in that particular circuit to blow. This part of the circuit is unprotected - bear this in mind when fault-finding on the vehicle's electrical system.*

Finding an open-circuit

9 To check for an open-circuit, connect one lead of a circuit tester or voltmeter to either the negative battery terminal or a known good earth.

10 Connect the other lead to a connector in the circuit being tested, preferably nearest to the battery or fuse.

11 Switch on the circuit, bearing in mind that some circuits are live only when the ignition switch is moved to a particular position.

12 If voltage is present (indicated either by the tester bulb lighting or a voltmeter reading, as applicable), this means that the section of the circuit between the relevant connector and the battery is problem-free.

13 Continue to check the remainder of the circuit in the same fashion.

14 When a point is reached at which no voltage is present, the problem must lie between that point and the previous test point with voltage. Most problems can be traced to a broken, corroded or loose connection.

Finding a short-circuit

15 To check for a short-circuit, first disconnect the load(s) from the circuit (loads are the components which draw current from a circuit, such as bulbs, motors, heating elements, etc).

16 Remove the relevant fuse from the circuit, and connect a circuit tester or voltmeter to the fuse connections.

17 Switch on the circuit, bearing in mind that some circuits are live only when the ignition switch is moved to a particular position.

18 If voltage is present (indicated either by the tester bulb lighting or a voltmeter reading, as applicable), this means that there is a short-circuit.

19 If no voltage is present, but the fuse still blows with the load(s) connected, this indicates an internal fault in the load(s).

Finding an earth fault

20 The battery negative terminal is connected to "earth" - the metal of the engine/transmission and the car body - and most systems are wired so that they only receive a positive feed, the current returning via the metal of the car body. This means that the component mounting and the body form part of that circuit. Loose or corroded mountings can therefore cause a range of electrical faults, ranging from total failure of a circuit, to a puzzling partial fault. In particular, lights may shine dimly (especially when another circuit sharing the same earth point is in operation), motors (eg wiper motors or the radiator cooling fan motor) may run slowly, and the operation of one circuit may have an apparently-unrelated effect on another. Note that on many vehicles, earth straps are used between certain components, such as the engine/transmission and the body, usually where there is no metal-to-metal contact between components, due to flexible rubber mountings, etc.

21 To check whether a component is properly earthed, disconnect the battery, and connect one lead of an ohmmeter to a known good earth point. Connect the other lead to the wire or earth connection being tested. The resistance reading should be zero; if not, check the connection as follows.

22 If an earth connection is thought to be faulty, dismantle the connection, and clean back to bare metal both the bodyshell and the wire terminal, or the component's earth connection mating surface. Be careful to remove all traces of dirt and corrosion, then use a knife to trim away any paint, so that a clean metal-to-metal joint is made. On reassembly, tighten the joint fasteners securely; if a wire terminal is being refitted, use serrated washers between the terminal and the bodyshell, to ensure a clean and secure connection. When the connection is remade, prevent the onset of corrosion in the future by applying a coat of petroleum jelly or silicone-based grease, or by spraying on (at regular intervals) a proprietary ignition sealer or a water-dispersant lubricant.

3 Fuses and relays - general information

Fuses

1 Fuses are designed to break an electrical circuit when a predetermined current limit is reached, in order to protect the components and wiring which could be damaged by excessive current flow. Any excessive current flow will be due to a fault in the circuit, usually a short-circuit (see Section 2).

2 The main fuses are located in the fusebox, which is mounted behind a drop-down panel inside the glovebox. The fusebox also serves as a distribution board for the different sections of the vehicle's harness.

3 To gain access to the fusebox, open the glovebox, then press and release the top of the fusebox panel, allowing it to flip open.

4 Additional fuses are housed in the auxiliary fusebox, which is mounted in the engine bay, in front of the battery **(see illustration)**. On certain models, fuses specific to the ABS and TCS systems are housed in a dedicated fusebox, mounted in the engine bay on the bulkhead, adjacent to the brake fluid reservoir.

5 To remove a fuse, first ensure that the relevant circuit is switched off. If in doubt, disconnect the battery negative cable to isolate the supply.

6 Using the plastic tool provided in the fusebox, pull the fuse from its socket.

3.4 Auxiliary fusebox

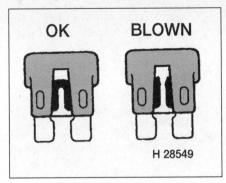

3.7 A blown fuse can be recognised by its melted or broken wire

3.12 Removing the main fusebox to gain access to the main relay panel

the substitute relay is of exactly the same type.

16 To remove a relay, first ensure that the relevant circuit is switched off. The relay can then simply be pulled out from the socket, and pushed back into position. Note that some of the more heavy-duty relays may be secured in position by a retaining screw.

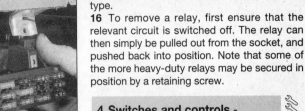

4 Switches and controls - removal and refitting

⚠ **Warning: To eliminate the risk of causing accidental short-circuits, disconnect the battery negative cable, and position it away from the terminal, before attempting any of the following operations.**

Ignition switch/steering column lock

1 Refer to Chapter 10.

Steering column combination switches
Removal

Note: *It is possible to remove the combination switches without having to remove the steering wheel – it is sufficient just to remove the column shrouds. However, we removed the steering wheel for clarity.*

2 Refer to Chapter 10 and remove the steering wheel.

3 Remove the three retaining screws, and lift the switch assembly away from the steering column **(see illustration)**.

4 Label the cables leading to the switch assembly to aid refitting later, then unplug the multi-plug connectors.

5 Remove the two screws at the base of each switch module, and separate them from the mounting bracket **(see illustrations)**.

Refitting

6 Refit the switches by reversing the removal procedure.

Headlight height adjustment switch, instrument panel illumination control, seat heater controls
Removal

7 These switches are all encased in modules

---

7 Inspect the fuse from the side, through the transparent plastic body - a blown fuse can be recognised by its melted or broken wire **(see illustration)**.

8 Spare fuses are provided in the blank terminal positions in the fusebox.

9 Before renewing a blown fuse, trace and rectify the cause, and always use a fuse of the correct rating. Never substitute a fuse of a higher rating, or make temporary repairs using wire or metal foil; more serious damage, or even a fire, could result.

10 Note that the fuses are colour-coded, as described below - refer to the wiring diagrams for details of the fuse ratings and the circuits protected.

Colour	Rating
Orange	5A
Red	10A
Blue	15A
Yellow	20A
Clear or white	25A
Green	30A

Relays

11 A relay is an electrically-operated mechanical switch, which may be used for the following reasons:

a) *A relay can switch a heavy current remotely from the circuit in which the current is flowing, therefore allowing the use of lighter-gauge wiring and switch contacts.*

b) *A relay can receive more than one control input, unlike a mechanically-operated switch.*

c) *Relays are available with internal timing components, to provide a time delay function - for example, the intermittent wiper relay and direction indicator flasher module.*

12 The main relays are mounted on a panel behind the main fusebox. To gain access to it, remove the glovebox as described in the relevant paragraphs of Chapter 11, Section 27, then remove the retaining screws and lift the fusebox away from the bulkhead mountings **(see illustration)**.

13 Additional relays are located in an auxiliary fusebox mounted in the engine bay, in front of the battery tray (refer to illustration 3.4).

14 Relays specific to the ABS and TCS systems are housed in a dedicated fusebox, mounted in the engine bay on the bulkhead, adjacent to the brake fluid reservoir.

15 If a circuit or system that is controlled by a relay develops a fault and the performance of the relay is in doubt, switch on the system in question. *In general*, if the relay is functioning, it should be possible to hear it "click" as it energises. If this is found to be the case, then it is probable that the fault lies with the system's components or wiring. If the relay cannot be heard to energise, then either the relay is not receiving a main supply or switching voltage, or the relay itself is faulty. Verification can be carried out by the substitution of a known good unit, but be careful - while some relays are identical in appearance and operation, others look similar but perform different functions - ensure that

---

4.3 Remove the three retaining screws, and lift the switch assembly away from the steering column

4.5a Remove the two screws (arrowed) at the base of each switch module . . .

4.5b . . . and separate them from the mounting bracket

4.8 To improve access to the side of the switch, remove the cover panel from the facia retaining screw

4.9 Unplug the connector from the rear of the switch (driver's seat heater control switch shown)

4.13 Removing the headlight switch (switch unit below removed to improve access)

of standard size, and each can be removed in a similar manner.

8 Insert small, flat-bladed instruments (such as a watchmaker's screwdriver) either side of the switch housing, and use them to prise it out of the facia. Pad the facia with a piece of card or insulating tape, to protect the surface. To improve access to the side of the switch, remove the cover panel from the facia retaining screw **(see illustration)**.

9 Unplug the connector from the rear of the switch; label the cable to avoid confusion if more than one switch is to be removed **(see illustration)**. **Note:** *On early models, the switch button must be removed before the switch housing can be pulled out.*

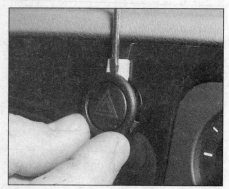

4.16 Removing the hazard light switch; note the use of a piece of card to protect the facia

Refitting

10 Plug in the connector securely, and push the switch housing back into the aperture in the facia, until the locking lugs are felt to engage.

Exterior light switches

Fog/driving light switches

11 The removal and refitting procedures are the same as those described for the headlight height adjustment switch, etc; refer to the previous sub-section for details.

Headlight switch

12 Remove the switch unit directly below the headlight rotary switch.

13 Using the method described in the previous sub-section, prise the switch from the facia. To ease its release, reach through vacated switch aperture below, and press on the rear of the switch housing **(see illustration)**.

14 Unplug the multi-plug connector from the rear of the switch housing.

15 Refit the switch by reversing the removal procedure.

Hazard light switch

16 Using the method described in the previous sub-section, prise the switch out of the facia front panel, using a small piece of card to protect the surface **(see illustration)**.

Heater blower motor switch (vehicles without ACC)

17 The blower motor switch is an integral part of the heater and air distribution control panel; refer to Chapter 3 for details of its removal.

ACC panel

18 The removal/refitting of the ACC panel is described in Chapter 11 as part of the facia removal procedure.

Seat belt warning switches

19 Switches in the seat belt buckles activate the "Fasten seat belts" warning panel when the vehicle is started, if the belts have not been fastened. However, they are not serviceable components, and can only be renewed as part of the stalk/buckle assembly.

Electric door mirror switch

20 The electric door mirror switch is housed in the driver's door inner trim panel. Chapter 11 describes the removal the switch as part of the trim panel removal procedure.

Overhead console switches

21 Remove the retaining screw, then unclip the overhead console from the headlining **(see illustrations)**.

22 Prise the switch from its socket, using a flat-bladed screwdriver **(see illustration)**.

23 Unplug the wiring connector from the rear of the switch.

24 Refit the switch by reversing the removal procedure.

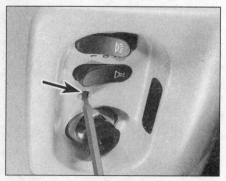

4.21a Remove the retaining screw . . .

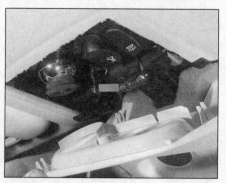

4.21b . . . then unclip the overhead console from the headlining

4.22 Prise the switch from its socket, using a flat-bladed screwdriver

5.2a Slacken and withdraw the three screws . . .

5.2b . . . then remove the map reading light lens

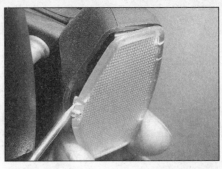

5.5 Using a small, flat-bladed screwdriver, prise the plastic lens from the facia light unit to expose the bulb

Door open/closed sensors

25 With reference to Chapter 11, remove the internal lock mechanism from inside the door panel.
26 Unclip the door sensor from the lock mechanism mounting bracket.
27 Unplug the sensor cabling at the connector.
28 Refit the sensor by reversing the removal procedure.

Courtesy light door switches

29 The switches that operate the courtesy lights as the doors open are located on the leading edges of the door frame, adjacent to the hinges.
30 Open the relevant door, and prise the rubber gaiter from the switch.
31 Remove the securing screw, then withdraw the switch from the door pillar. Disconnect the wiring connector as it becomes accessible.

> **HAYNES HiNT**
> Tape the wiring to the door, to prevent it falling back into the door pillar. Alternatively, tie a length of string to the wiring to retrieve it.

32 Refitting is a reversal of removal; ensure that the rubber gaiter is correctly seated on the switch, to prevent moisture ingress.

Glovebox light switch

33 The switch is located at the lower left-hand corner of the glovebox aperture.
34 Open the glovebox door, then prise the switch out of its mounting hole using a small flat-bladed screwdriver.
35 Unplug the cable connectors from the rear of the switch body.
36 Refit the switch by reversing the removal procedure.

Centre console-mounted switches (electric windows and sunroof)

Note: *The removal of the centre console and its associated switches is described in Chapter 11; where appropriate, references are made to relevant illustrations.*

37 Unscrew the handbrake lever gaiter from the centre console.
38 Use a suitable flat-bladed screwdriver to carefully prise the switch panel from the centre console. At the same time, reach through the handbrake lever aperture, and press on the switch panel from below to ease its release (refer to illustration 26.3a).
39 Release the clip, and unplug the switch wiring connector(s) (refer to illustration 26.3b).
40 Refit the switch panel by reversing the removal procedure.

5 Interior light bulbs - removal and refitting

> ⚠ **Warning: To eliminate the risk of causing accidental short-circuits, disconnect the battery negative cable, and position it away from the terminal, before attempting any of the following operations.**

Front courtesy lights
Map reading light

1 Remove the retaining screw, and lower the cover panel away from the overhead console.
2 Slacken and withdraw the three screws, then remove the map reading light lens **(see illustrations)**.
3 The bulb is a bayonet fit in the holder.
4 Refitting is a reversal of removal.

Facia light

5 Using a small, flat-bladed screwdriver, prise

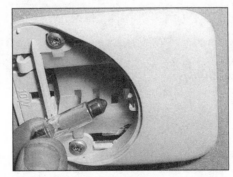

5.9 Unclip the bulb from the spring-loaded contacts

the plastic lens from the facia light unit to expose the bulb **(see illustration)**.
6 Unclip the bulb from the spring-loaded contacts.
7 Refitting is a reversal of removal.

Centre light

8 Using a small, flat-bladed screwdriver, prise the plastic lens from the centre light unit to expose the bulb **(see illustration)**.
9 Unclip the bulb from the spring-loaded contacts **(see illustration)**.
10 Refitting is a reversal of removal.

"Fasten seat belts" warning light

11 Remove the retaining screw, and lower the cover panel away from the overhead console.
12 Unclip the bulb from the spring-loaded contacts **(see illustration)**.
13 Refitting is a reversal of removal.

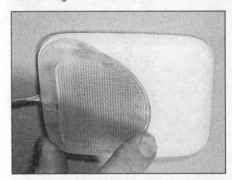

5.8 Unclipping the centre light unit lens

5.12 Removing the "Fasten seat belts" warning light bulb

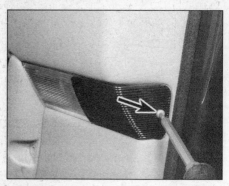

5.14 Remove the screw from the trailing edge of the light unit

5.16 Unclip the bulb from the spring-loaded contacts

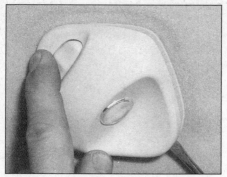

5.19 Prise the light unit from the aperture in the trim panel, using a wide flat-bladed screwdriver

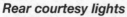

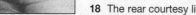

5.20 The bulb is bayonet fit in the holder bracket

5.26 Remove the screws, then lift the light unit out, and unclip the bulb from the spring-loaded contacts

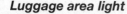

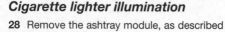

Door courtesy/warning lights

14 Open the relevant door, and remove the screw from the trailing edge of the light unit (**see illustration**).

15 Slide the unit backwards to free the trailing edge from the door bin, and turn it over to expose the bulbholder.

16 Unclip the bulb from the spring-loaded contacts (**see illustration**).

17 Refitting is a reversal of removal.

Rear courtesy lights

18 The rear courtesy lights are located on the C-pillar interior trim panels.

19 Prise the light unit from the aperture in the trim panel, using a wide flat-bladed screwdriver (**see illustration**).

20 The bulb is bayonet fit in the holder bracket (**see illustration**).

21 Refitting is a reversal of removal.

Glovebox light

22 Refer to Chapter 11, Section 27 and remove the glovebox, to gain access to the light unit.

23 Prise the light unit out of the aperture in the top of the glovebox interior, then unclip the bulb from the spring-loaded terminals.

24 Refitting is a reversal of removal.

Luggage area light

25 Remove the two screws that secure the light assembly to the trim panel, at the side of the load space.

26 Lift the light unit out, and unclip the bulb from the spring-loaded contacts (**see illustration**).

27 Refitting is a reversal of removal.

Cigarette lighter illumination

28 Remove the ashtray module, as described in the relevant paragraphs of Chapter 11, Section 27.

29 Unclip the cable connector, then draw the bulb out of its housing (**see illustration**).

30 Refit the bulb by reversing the removal procedure.

Instrument panel illumination

31 Remove the instrument panel, as described in Section 9 of this Chapter.

32 Illumination of the analogue gauges is provided by several bulbs, secured in the rear of the instrument panel by means of bayonet fittings (**see illustration**).

33 To remove a bulb, grasp the body, and twist it through quarter of a turn until the lugs disengage (**see illustration**).

34 Refit the bulb in a similar manner, using a twisting motion to engage the bulb in its mounting hole. Ensuring that the printed circuit contacts do not crease as the bulb is twisted into place.

35 To gain access to the pictogram segment bulbs and the warning panel bulbs, place the instrument panel face down on a worksurface, and remove the screws at the rear of both rigid printed circuit boards. Lift the circuit boards

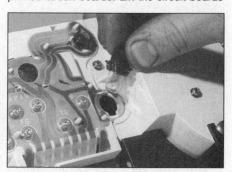

5.29 Unclip the cable connector, then draw the bulb out of its housing

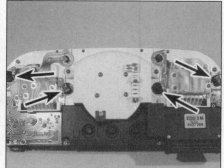

5.32 Instrument panel illumination bulbs (arrowed)

5.33 To remove a bulb, grasp the body, and twist it through quarter of a turn until the lugs disengage

6.3 Unplug the cable edge connector from the light cluster terminals

6.4a Remove the nuts from the four mounting bolts (arrowed) . . .

6.4b . . . then pull the light cluster away from the vehicle

away from the instrument panel; the bulbs can be removed by pulling them out of their sockets.

Heater control panel illumination

36 Remove the knobs from the heater controls, then extract the two screws beneath and remove the front panel.
37 The bulb is mounted in the rear panel by a push-fit holder.
38 Refitting is a reversal of removal.

ACC module light

39 Remove the ACC panel as described in relevant paragraphs of Chapter 11, Section 27.
40 Extract the bayonet-fit bulb from the mounting hole at the rear of the ACC panel, using a flat-bladed screwdriver.
41 Refitting is reversal of removal.

Instrument switch illumination

42 Early models are fitted with instrument switches that have no renewable internal light bulbs. Failure of the bulb means that the entire switch assembly will have to be renewed; refer to Section 4 for details.
43 Remove the switch assembly from the facia, as described in Section 4.
44 Press together the clips at the base of the bulb, and withdraw it from the switch body.
45 To refit the bulb, push the lens into the switch until the clips engage.

6 Exterior light units - removal and refitting

> **Warning: To eliminate the risk of causing accidental short-circuits, disconnect the battery negative cable, and position it away from the terminal, before attempting any of the following operations.**

Rear light clusters

Removal

1 With reference to Chapter 11, partially remove the load space interior trim panel, to gain access to the rear of the light cluster.
2 Refer to Section 7 and remove the bulbholder panel.
3 Unplug the cable edge connector from the light cluster terminals **(see illustration)**.
4 Remove the nuts from the four mounting bolts, then pull the light cluster away from the vehicle **(see illustrations)**.

Refitting

5 Align the mounting bolts with the holes in the body, then push the light cluster into position, ensuring that the rubber seal is correctly seated.
6 Refit the retaining nuts and tighten them securely.
7 Plug the edge connector onto the light cluster terminals, ensuring that the retaining clips engage.
8 Refit the load space trim panel, referring to Chapter 11 for guidance.

Front direction indicator units (later models)

9 Open the bonnet.
10 The leading edge of the indicator unit is retained by means of a spring clip. Unhook the spring clip from the web underneath the crossmember at the front of the engine bay, adjacent to the headlight unit **(see illustration)**.
11 Pivot the light unit out, and disengage the spigot at the trailing edge of the unit from the mounting hole in the wing.
12 Disconnect the bulbholder and remove the light unit **(see illustration)**.
13 Refitting is a reversal of removal.

Front light clusters (earlier models)

14 Unplug the cable connectors from the rear of the light cluster, labelling them to aid refitting later.
15 Remove the retaining screw at the upper edge of the crossmember at front of the engine bay, adjacent to the headlight unit fixing.
16 Slide the unit forward and out, to disengage the rear fixings from the rubber bushed mounting holes.
17 Refitting is a reversal of removal.

Direction indicator side repeaters

18 Slide the light unit towards the rear of the vehicle, then unclip the leading edge from the wing aperture, and lift the unit out **(see illustration)**. Recover the rubber seal.

6.10 The leading edge of the indicator unit is retained by means of a spring clip (arrowed)

6.12 Disconnect the bulbholder and remove the light unit

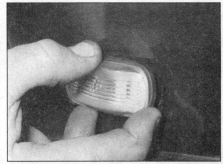

6.18 Slide the light unit towards the rear of the vehicle, then unclip the leading edge from the wing aperture, and lift the unit out

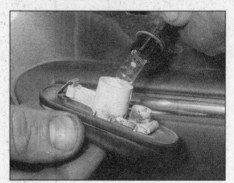

6.19 Withdraw the bulbholder from the light unit

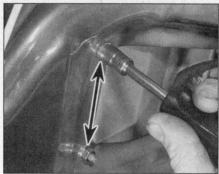

6.23 Removing two of the reflector panel retaining nuts (arrowed)

6.34 Unplug the bulb supply cable from the light unit at the multi-plug connector (arrowed)

6.35a Remove the retaining screws from the headlight unit - one on the left . . .

6.35b . . . one on the right-hand side . . .

19 Withdraw the bulbholder from the light unit (see illustration).
20 Refitting is a reversal of removal, ensuring that the rubber seal is evenly seated.

Reversing light/rear foglight/reflector panel assembly (later models only)

21 On later models, the rear fog and reversing lights are an integral part of the rear reflector bar, mounted between the rear light clusters. As such, they must be renewed as part of a complete assembly.
22 With reference to Chapter 11, remove the trim panel from the tailgate/boot to expose the reflector panel mounting nuts.
23 Remove the nuts and lift off the reflector panel (see illustration).
24 Refitting is a reversal of removal.

Headlight unit

Removal\

25 Open the bonnet, then with reference to Chapter 11, remove the front grille.

Earlier models

26 Where applicable, disconnect the washer jet hose at the connection to the wiper arm.
27 Unplug the wiper motor cable at the three-way connector.
28 With reference to Section 14, remove the nut and disconnect the wiper arm from the drive spindle.
29 Remove the retaining screw, and separate the wiper motor assembly from the headlight unit.
30 Unscrew the weatherproof cover from the rear of the headlight unit, then unplug the bulb supply cable at the connector.
31 Refer to the relevant sub-section, and remove the adjacent front light cluster.
32 Remove the retaining screws from the headlight unit; one on the lower edge behind the bumper moulding, and two along the upper edge.
33 Lift the headlight unit away from the vehicle.

Later models

34 Unplug the bulb supply cable from the light unit at the multi-plug connector (see illustration). Note: *Pull the red locking bar out of the male section of the connector body to unlock it from the female side.*
35 Remove the retaining screws from the headlight unit - one each on the left and right-hand sides, and two along the upper edge (see illustrations).
36 Where applicable, unplug the headlight levelling motor cable at the connector (see illustration).
37 Lift the headlight unit out of the vehicle (see illustration).

Dismantling

38 Refer to Section 7 for details of bulb removal.
39 To remove the lens, carefully prise off the metal spring clips; use a screwdriver as a

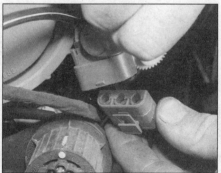

6.35c . . . and two along the upper edge (one shown)

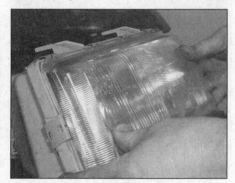

6.36 Unplug the headlight levelling motor cable at the connector

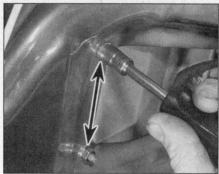

6.37 Lift the headlight unit out of the vehicle

6.39a To remove the lens, carefully prise off the metal spring clips

6.39b Removing the lens

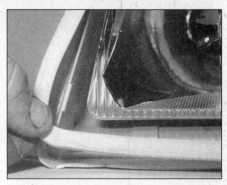

6.39c Recover the rubber seal beneath

lever, but ensure that it bears only on the plastic body of the light unit, not the glass lens itself. As the lens is freed, recover the rubber seal beneath **(see illustrations)**.

40 To remove the headlight levelling motor (where applicable), reach inside the rear cover aperture, and unclip the end of the servo motor shaft from the internal reflector. Twist the servo motor body until the locking lug is felt to disengage, and lift the motor out **(see illustration)**.

41 To remove the headlight wiper motor from the vehicle on later models, first unplug the supply cable at the three-way connector. Disconnect the washer jet hose, then remove the two retaining screws and lift the entire assembly away from the vehicle **(see illustrations)**.

Refitting

42 Refit the light unit by reversing the removal procedure.

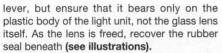

7 Exterior light bulbs - renewal

General

1 When renewing bulbs, note the following points:
a) To eliminate the risk of causing accidental short-circuits, disconnect the battery

negative cable, and position it away from the terminal.
b) When fitting a new bulb, avoid touching the glass lens - hold it by the metal flange, as deposits left by hand contact can shorten the bulb's service life.
c) Only fit new bulbs of the correct power rating (refer to the Specifications).
d) Before fitting a new bulb, first check the condition of the contacts in the bulbholder. Ensure that there is no corrosion or dirt that may cause a poor connection.
e) The Saab 9000 bulb filament monitoring system uses a balanced relay to detect bulb failure. It has been suggested that all bulbs (except headlamps) should be replaced in pairs, otherwise the monitoring systems may pick up the imbalance of current and indicate a bulbs has failed.

Headlight bulb

General

2 On earlier models, the main and dipped beam filaments for each headlight are contained in one bulb, at the centre of a single reflector.

3 Later models are fitted with dual-reflector headlight units, utilising separate bulbs for main and dipped beam.

Models with single-reflector headlights

4 Open the bonnet, and from within the engine bay, pull off the cover from the rear of the headlight unit.

6.40 Removing the headlight levelling motor

5 Unplug the cable connector, then unhook the retaining clip and pivot it back to release the bulb.

6 Fit the new bulb, ensuring that the three locating lugs on the bulbs metal flange engage with the housing. Press the retaining clip back into position.

Models with dual-reflector headlights

Dipped beam

7 Open the bonnet, and from within the engine bay, unscrew the circular cover from the rear of the headlight unit.

8 The dipped beam bulb is at the centre of the reflector. Pull off the cable connector, then unhook the metal retaining clip and lift out the bulb **(see illustration)**.

9 Refitting is a reversal of removal.

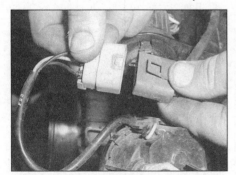

6.41a To remove the headlight wiper motor from the vehicle on later models, first unplug the supply cable at the three-way connector . . .

6.41b . . . disconnect the washer jet hose . . .

6.41c . . . then remove the two retaining screws (arrowed)

7.8 Removing the dipped beam bulb

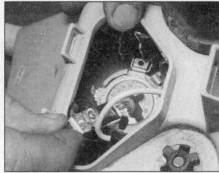

7.11 Removing the main beam bulb

7.22 Removing the direction indicator bulb

Main beam

10 Open the bonnet, and from within the engine bay, unclip the plastic cover from the rear of the headlight unit.

11 Unplug the cable connector, then unhook the metal retaining clip and lift out the bulb **(see illustration)**.

12 Refitting is a reversal of removal.

Parking light bulb

General

13 On earlier models, the parking light is part of the front light cluster, below the direction indicator light.

14 On later models, the parking light is integrated in the headlight unit, and shares the same reflector as the dipped beam bulb.

7.24 On later models, prise open the cut-out panel in the loadspace trim to gain access to the rear of the light cluster

Models with single-reflector headlights

15 At the rear of the light unit, unplug the cable connector, then twist the bulbholder through quarter of a turn and pull it out of the light unit. The bulb can then be withdrawn from the holder.

16 Refitting is a reversal of removal.

Models with dual-reflector headlights

17 Open the bonnet, and from within the engine bay, unscrew the circular cover from the rear of the headlight unit.

18 The parking light bulb is offset to one side of the centre of the reflector. Pull off the cable connector and lift out the bulbholder; the bulb can then be withdrawn from the holder.

19 Refitting is a reversal of removal.

Direction indicator bulb (including side repeaters)

Early models

20 Proceed as described for parking light bulb renewal.

Later models

21 Remove the direction indicator unit, as described Section 6.

22 Squeeze together the plastic tangs at the side of the bulbholder, and rotate it anti-clockwise through a quarter of a turn. Pull the bulbholder out of the light unit, then pull the bulb out of the holder **(see illustration)**.

23 Refitting is a reversal of removal.

Rear light cluster bulbs

24 Open the boot/tailgate to gain access to the rear of the light clusters. On later models, prise open the cut-out panel in the loadspace trim **(see illustration)**.

25 Squeeze together the plastic clips to release the bulbholder. The bulbs are a bayonet fit in the holder **(see illustration)**.

26 Refitting is a reversal of removal.

Rear foglight bulb

27 On earlier models, the rear foglight is an integral part of the rear light cluster; refer to the previous sub-section for details of its renewal.

28 On later models, open the boot/tailgate, then unclip the plastic panel from the rear of the light unit and withdraw the bulbholder; the bulb is a bayonet fit in the holder **(see illustrations)**.

29 Refitting is a reversal of removal.

Reversing light bulb

30 On earlier models, the reversing light is an integral part of the rear light cluster; refer to the previous sub-section for details of its renewal.

31 On later models, proceed as in the description given for the rear foglight renewal.

32 Refitting is a reversal of removal.

High-level brake light bulbs

33 Remove the two screws, and separate the

7.25 The bulbs are a bayonet fit in the holder

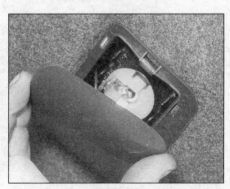

7.28a Unclip the plastic panel from the rear of the light unit

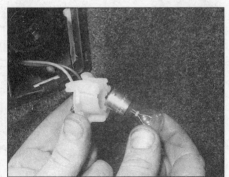

7.28b Removing the rear foglight bulb

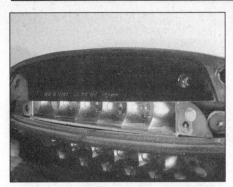

7.33 Remove the screws, and separate the lens and cover moulding from the bulbholder assembly

7.34 The bulbs are a push fit in the holder

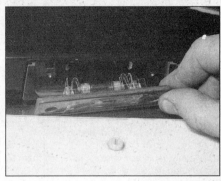

7.36 Removing the rear number plate light bulb

lens and cover moulding from the bulbholder assembly **(see illustration).**

34 The bulbs are push fit in the holder **(see illustration).**

35 Refitting is reversal of removal.

Rear number plate bulb

36 Remove the two screws from the lens, and lower the assembly away from the bodywork **(see illustration).**

37 Unclip the bulb from the spring-loaded terminals.

38 Refitting is a reversal of removal.

8 Headlight beam adjustment - general information

Accurate adjustment of the headlight beam is only possible using optical beam-setting equipment, and this work should therefore be carried out by a Saab dealer or suitably-equipped workshop.

Certain models have a headlight beam adjustment control, which allows the aim of the headlights to be adjusted to compensate for variation in the vehicle's payload. The aim is altered by means of facia-mounted switch, which controls electric adjuster motors located in the rear of the headlight assemblies. The switch should be positioned as follows, according to the load being carried in the vehicle:

Switch position	Vehicle load
0	Up to 3 occupants (no more than one in the rear seat), no luggage.
1	Up to 3 occupants in rear seats, up to 30 kg in luggage.
2	Up to 3 occupants in rear seats, up to 90 kg in luggage.
3	Up to 3 occupants in rear seats, luggage area full - OR up to 5 occupants, luggage area full, towing caravan/trailer.

9 Instrument panel - removal and refitting

General

1 The instrument panel is a single module, housing the speedometer, tachometer, gauges and warning lights, and EDU display.

2 The top panel of the facia can be removed, allowing access to the instrument panel without the need to remove the entire facia assembly.

Removal

3 Disconnect the battery negative cable, and position it away from the terminal.

4 Refer to the relevant paragraphs of Chapter 11, Section 27 and remove the panel from the top of the facia.

5 With reference to Chapter 3, remove the air ducting from above the instrument panel.

6 At the rear of the instrument panel, disconnect all the multi-plug cable connectors, labelling them to aid refitting later.

7 Where applicable, disconnect the speedometer drive cable from the rear of the instrument panel.

8 On turbocharged vehicles, unplug the boost gauge hose from the rear of the instrument panel.

9 Remove the two retaining screws from the top corners of the instrument panel. Note that the screw heads face the bulkhead, and so must be extracted from within the facia, using a short-handled screwdriver. Recover the rubber mounting bushes.

10 Lift the instrument panel out through the top of the facia, and recover the rubber mounting feet

11 Refer to Section 5 for guidance in renewing the instrument panel illumination and warning panel bulbs.

12 The instrument panel is modular in design, and as such, it is possible to renew individual gauges by simply removing the retaining screws and lifting the required gauge out.

Refitting

13 Refit the instrument panel by reversing the

removal procedure, noting the following points:

a) *As the instrument panel is lowered into position, ensure that the rubber mounting feet locate in the indentations on the metal mounting brackets **(see illustration)***

b) *Ensure that the multi-plug cable connectors are refitted according to the notes made during removal, and that they are firmly plugged in.*

c) *Make reference to the relevant paragraphs of Chapter 11, Section 27 when fitting the top panel of the facia; ensure that all retaining screws are correctly refitted.*

10 Clock/trip computer module - removal and refitting

General

1 The clock/trip computer module varies in function and appearance according to the specification of the vehicle, but the module housing (and hence the removal procedure) remains the same.

2 The top panel of the facia can be removed, allowing access to the module without the need to remove the entire facia assembly.

3 The EDU display panel is an integral part of the instrument panel, refer to Section 9 for details of its removal.

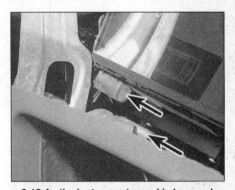

9.13 As the instrument panel is lowered into position, ensure that the rubber mounting feet locate in the indentations on the metal mounting brackets (arrowed)

Removal

4 Disconnect the battery negative cable, and position it away from the terminal.

5 Refer to the relevant paragraphs of Chapter 11, Section 27, and remove the panel from the top of the facia.

6 With reference to Chapter 3, remove the air ducting from above the instrument panel.

7 Apply light hand pressure at the rear of the module, to release it from the facia.

8 At the rear of the module, disconnect the multi-plug cable connectors, labelling them to aid refitting later.

Refitting

9 Refit the clock/trip computer module by reversing the removal procedure. Ensure that the multi-plug cable connectors are refitted according to the notes made during removal, and that they are firmly plugged in.

11 Cigarette lighter - removal and refitting

Removal

1 Disconnect the battery negative cable, and position it away from the terminal.

2 Refer to the relevant paragraphs of Chapter 11, Section 27, and remove the ashtray assembly from the facia front panel.

3 Unplug the cable connectors from the rear of the cigarette lighter body, labelling them to aid refitting later.

4 Using a small, flat-bladed screwdriver, prise off the metal retaining clip, then withdraw the cigarette lighter from the ashtray.

Refitting

5 Refit the cigarette lighter by reversing the removal procedure.

12 Speedometer drive cable - renewal

General

1 Two types of speedometer drive mechanism have been fitted. Vehicles built

before 1987 have a conventional speedometer cable, which drives the speedometer remotely, by means of a cable with a rotating, flexible inner shaft.

2 An erratic or inconsistent speedometer display, such as needle flickering or jumping, may be attributable to wear in the speedometer drive cable.

3 Vehicles built after 1987 are fitted with an electronic transducer in place of the drivegear. This device measures the rotational speed of the transmission final drive, and converts the information into an electronic signal, which is then sent to the speedometer module in the instrument panel. The signal is also used as an input by the engine management system ECU (and where fitted, the cruise control ECU, the trip computer, and the traction control system ECU).

Removal

4 Refer to the relevant paragraphs of Chapter 11, Section 27, and remove the panel from the top of the facia.

5 With reference to Chapter 3, remove the air ducting from above the instrument panel.

6 Disconnect the drive cable from the rear of the speedometer module.

7 Release the cable from the clips securing it to the inside of the facia, then pull the free end of cable through the bulkhead into the engine bay, noting the cable routing. Do not use excessive force, as this may damage the rubber grommet at the bulkhead.

8 At the gearbox, unscrew the knurled nut at the point where the speedometer cable enters the differential casing. Withdraw the cable inner from the drivegear.

9 Remove the speedometer cable from the vehicle.

Refitting

10 Refit the speedometer drive cable by reversing the removal process. Follow the same routing behind the facia as the original drive cable, ensuring that all moving components are avoided. Do not force the cable to follow tight curves, as this may adversely affect the rotation of the cable inner.

13 Horn components - removal and refitting

Horn push buttons

1 Disconnect the battery negative cable, and position it away from the terminal.

2 Using a thin plastic spatula, prise the horn button from the steering wheel spoke, and lift off the upper electrical contact **(see illustration)**.

3 Remove the retaining screw, and lift off the lower electrical contact **(see illustration)**.

4 Examine both the lower and upper contacts for signs of wear or corrosion; renew them if necessary.

5 Refitting is a reversal of removal.

Horns

Note: *On early models, the second horn is mounted in the engine bay, inside the left-hand wheelarch.*

6 Disconnect the battery negative cable, and position it away from the terminal.

7 Refer to Chapter 11, Section 8 and remove the front grille.

8 Unplug the wiring harness connector from the horn.

9 Slacken and withdraw the retaining nut at the bottom of the horn bracket, and lift off the horns **(see illustration)**.

14 Windscreen, tailgate and headlight wiper arms - removal and refitting

Windscreen wiper arms

1 Note the position on the windscreen at which wiper blades settle, when in the parked position. Mark this position on the screen with a strip of masking tape.

2 Flip up the hinged plastic cover at the base of the wiper arm, to expose the retaining nut.

3 Slacken and remove the nut, then lift off the wiper arm.

4 When refitting, ensure that the splined drive spindle engages with the wiper arm mounting

13.2 Prise the horn button from the steering wheel spoke (airbag removed for clarity)

13.3 Remove the retaining screw, and lift off the lower electrical contact (airbag removed for clarity)

13.9 Slacken and withdraw the retaining nut (arrowed) at the bottom of the horn bracket

14.5 Flip up the hinged plastic cover at the base of the tailgate wiper arm, to expose the retaining nut

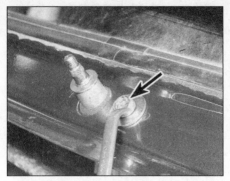

15.6 Using a ring spanner, slacken and remove the drive spindle extension shaft nuts

15.8a Separate the link rod from the left-hand wiper extension shaft at the balljoint

hole such that the blade falls in the same position on the windscreen as before, as marked by the strip of masking tape. Tighten the retaining nut, and flip down the plastic cover.

Tailgate wiper arm

5 The procedure is identical to that given for the windscreen wiper arms above **(see illustration)**.

Headlight wiper arms

6 Note the position on the headlight lens at which wiper blade settles, when in the parked position. Mark this position on the lens with a strip of masking tape.
7 Flip up the hinged plastic cover at the base of the wiper arm, to expose the retaining nut.
8 Hold the drive spindle stationary with a pair of grips, then slacken and remove the retaining nut, and lift off the wiper arm.
9 When refitting, ensure that the drive spindle engages with the wiper arm mounting hole such that the blade falls in the same position on the headlight lens as before, as marked by the strip of masking tape. Tighten the retaining nut securely, and flip down the plastic cover.

---

15 Windscreen, tailgate and headlight wiper motor and linkage - removal and refitting

⚠️ *Warning: To eliminate the risk of causing accidental short-circuits, disconnect the battery negative cable, and position it away from the terminal, before attempting any of the following operations*

Windscreen wiper motor and linkage

Removal

1 With reference to Section 14, remove both wiper arms.
2 Lift off the rubber grommets and plastic weather caps, as applicable, from the spindle shaft.
3 On later models, remove the plastic trim panel from the lower edge of the windscreen, by

releasing the press-stud fixings and then lifting off the bonnet hinge end caps at either side. Carefully lift the lower edge of the windscreen sealing strip, and slide out the trim panel.
4 Access to the wiper motor and linkage can be improved if the false bulkhead panel and cover are removed from the engine bay; remove the two retaining screws at either side and lift the panel out; refer to Chapter 2B, Section 4.
5 Unplug the wiper motor cables at the connectors - label them to aid refitting later.
6 Using a ring spanner, slacken and remove the wiper drive spindle nuts. Note that on later models, the wiper drive spindles are fitted with extension shafts, which are secured to the bodywork by separate retaining bolts **(see illustration)**.
7 Remove the four wiper motor assembly mounting bolts.
8 Using a screwdriver as a lever, separate the link rod from the left-hand wiper extension shaft at the balljoint. Separate the other end of the link rod from the wiper motor assembly at the drive arm balljoint **(see illustrations)**.
9 Lift out the wiper motor assembly and left-hand wiper link rod. Note the position of the drive arm in the "parked" position, to aid refitting later.
10 The right-hand wiper link rod can be removed in the same way. Note that on later models, where drive spindle extension shafts are fitted, a bracing bar is fitted between the two extension shafts. This must be detached

15.8b Separate the other end of the link rod from the wiper motor assembly at the balljoint

by unscrewing the through-bolt, before the extension shafts can be unbolted.

Refitting

11 Refit the wiper motor and linkage by reversing the removal process; ensure that the wiper motor drive arm is still in the "parked" position before attempting to reconnect the link rods.

Tailgate wiper motor

Removal

12 With reference to Section 14, remove the tailgate wiper arm.
13 Unscrew the spindle nut, then lift off the rubber grommet **(see illustrations)**.

15.13a Unscrew the tailgate wiper spindle nut . . .

15.13b . . . then lift off the rubber grommet

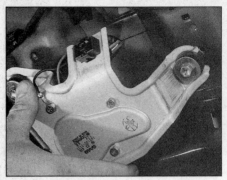

15.16 Slacken the retaining bolts, and lower the wiper motor assembly away from the tailgate

16.9 Disconnect the hose from the underside of the washer jet

16.13 Slide the washer jet moulding out of the housing in the bulbholder assembly

14 Open the tailgate and remove the trim panel from the inside of the tailgate, referring to Chapter 11 for details.

15 Unplug the wiper motor cable at the connector.

16 Slacken the retaining bolts and lower the wiper motor assembly away from the tailgate, guiding the drive spindle through the tailgate aperture **(see illustration)**.

Refitting

17 Refit the wiper motor assembly by reversing the removal procedure. Ensure that the three anti-vibration rubber bushes are correctly seated, before tightening the retaining bolts.

Headlight wiper motor

General

18 On earlier models fitted with single-reflector headlight units, the wiper motor assembly is bolted to the underside of the headlight unit.

19 On later models, where dual-reflector headlight units are fitted, the wiper motor assembly is bolted to the bodywork, directly underneath the headlight unit.

20 Removal of the wiper motor assembly is described in Section 6, as part of the headlight unit dismantling procedure.

16 Windscreen, tailgate and headlight washer system components - removal and refitting

General

1 The windscreen, tailgate and headlight washer jets are all supplied by one electric pump, which is mounted on the washer fluid reservoir.

2 The mounting position of the fluid reservoir depends on the age of the vehicle. On earlier vehicles, the reservoir is screwed to the left-hand inner wing, in front of the battery tray. On later models, the fluid reservoir is mounted inside the right-hand wing cavity, in front of the wheelarch.

Washer pump

Removal

3 Disconnect the battery negative cable, and position it away from the terminal.

4 On later models, refer to Chapter 11, Section 22 and remove the right-hand wheelarch liner.

5 Disconnect the fluid delivery hose from the port on the pump housing. Be prepared for fluid spillage as the hose is removed.

6 Unplug the motor cabling at the connector.

7 Remove the pump by easing it away from the reservoir slightly, and then pulling it up out of the rubber sealing grommet. If the level of fluid in the reservoir is above the level of the sealing grommet, be ready to catch the spillage by positioning a container under the reservoir.

Refitting

8 Refit the washer pump by reversing the removal procedure.

Windscreen washer jets

9 Open the bonnet, and disconnect the hose from the underside of the washer jet **(see illustration)**.

10 Using a plastic spatula, or a flat-bladed screwdriver wrapped in PVC to protect the paintwork, prise the washer jet from the bonnet aperture.

11 Refitting is a reversal of removal.

Tailgate washer jet

12 Refer to Section 7, and separate the high-level brake light lens and cover moulding from the bulbholder assembly.

13 Slide the washer jet moulding out of the housing in the bulbholder assembly **(see illustration)**.

14 Refitting is a reversal of removal.

Headlight washer jet

15 The headlight washer jets are integrated into the headlight lens wiper arms; refer to Section 14 for guidance in removing the wiper arm.

17 In-car entertainment components - general information

The make and type of radio/cassette/ compact disc player fitted depends on the age and specification of the vehicle, as does the method of removal. For specific instructions regarding the removal of the unit, refer to the manufacturer's documentation supplied with the vehicle, or seek advice from your Saab dealer.

18 Loudspeakers - removal and refitting

Front speakers

Removal

1 Ensure that the radio/cassette/CD player is switched off.

2 With reference to Chapter 11, Section 27, remove the top panel from the facia. Lift off the grille, and recover the rubber spacer beneath.

3 Remove the screws and lift out the speaker units, unplugging the cables and labelling them to aid refitting later.

Refitting

4 Refitting is a reversal of removal.

Rear speakers

Removal

5 Working from Chapter 11, remove the trim panel from side of the loadspace.

6 Remove the retaining nuts, and lower the speaker unit away from the parcel shelf support.

7 Unplug the cables, labelling them to aid refitting later **(see illustration)**.

Refitting

8 Refit the speaker unit by reversing the removal procedure.

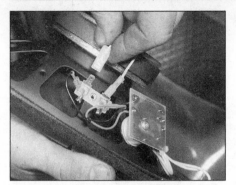

18.7 Unplug the speaker cables, labelling them to aid refitting later

19.3 Remove the locknut from the top of the aerial, then lift off the grommet

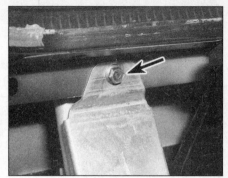

19.4a Remove the upper . . .

19 Radio aerial (electric) - removal and refitting

Removal

1 Switch off the radio, and ensure that the aerial returns to its fully-retracted position. Disconnect the battery negative cable, and position it away from the terminal.
2 Refer to Chapter 11 and remove the inner trim panel from the left-hand side of the loadspace.
3 Remove the locknut from the top of the aerial using a spanner, then lift off the grommet **(see illustration)**.
4 Remove the upper and lower retaining screws, and lift out the aerial assembly **(see illustrations)**.
5 Disconnect the power and coaxial cables from the aerial assembly **(see illustrations)**.

Refitting

6 Refit the aerial assembly by reversing the removal procedure.

20 Anti-theft alarm - general information

At the time of writing, very little detailed information was available regarding the anti-theft alarm. It is recommended that any problems or queries with the system should be referred to a Saab dealer.

21 Heated front seat components - general information

All models are fitted with thermostatically-regulated heated front seats. Individual control switches are provided for each seat, which allow the heating element temperature to be set to one of three levels, or switched off completely.

Two heating elements are fitted to each seat - one in the backrest, and one in the seat cushion. Access to the heating elements can only be gained by removing the upholstery from the seat - this is an operation which should be entrusted to a Saab dealer.

22 Tow bar - general information

All models have a wiring connector already wired up for a tow bar located in the luggage compartment. For further information regarding this component contact your local Saab dealer.

19.4b . . .and lower aerial assembly retaining screws

19.5a Disconnect the power cable . . .

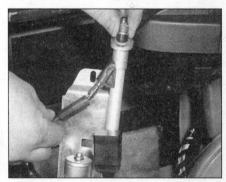

19.5b . . . and coaxial cable from the aerial assembly

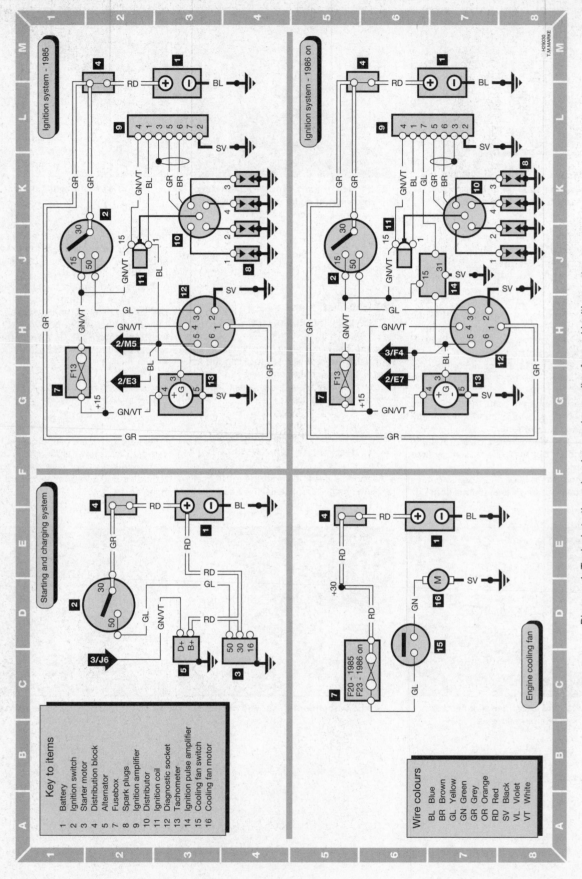

Diagram 1: Typical starting, charging, engine cooling fan and ignition systems

Key to items

1 Battery
2 Ignition switch
3 Starter motor
4 Distribution block
5 Alternator
7 Fusebox
8 Spark plugs
9 Ignition amplifier
10 Distributor
11 Ignition coil
12 Diagnostic socket
13 Tachometer
14 Ignition pulse amplifier
15 Cooling fan switch
16 Cooling fan motor

Wire colours

BL Blue
BR Brown
GL Yellow
GN Green
GR Grey
OR Orange
RD Red
SV Black
VL Violet
VT White

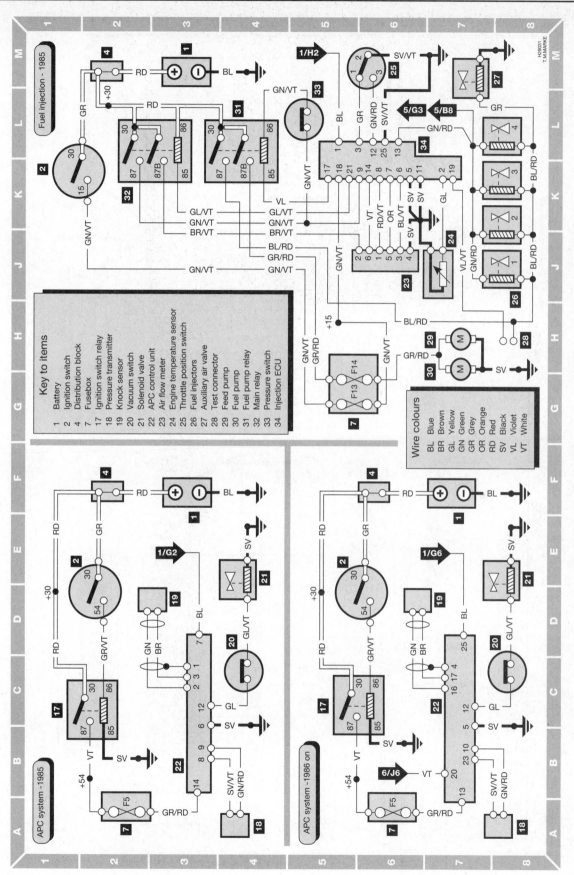

Diagram 2: Typical APC systems and LH-Jetronic fuel injection (1985)

Fuel injection - 1985

Key to items

1 Battery
2 Ignition switch
4 Distribution block
7 Fusebox
17 Ignition switch relay
18 Pressure transmitter
19 Knock sensor
20 Vacuum switch
21 Solenoid valve
22 APC control unit
23 Air flow meter
24 Engine temperature sensor
25 Throttle position switch
26 Fuel injectors
27 Auxiliary air valve
28 Test connector
29 Feed pump
30 Fuel pump
31 Fuel pump relay
32 Main relay
33 Pressure switch
34 Injection ECU

Wire colours

BL Blue
BR Brown
GL Yellow
GN Green
GR Grey
OR Orange
RD Red
SV Black
VL Violet
VT White

APC system -1985

APC system -1986 on

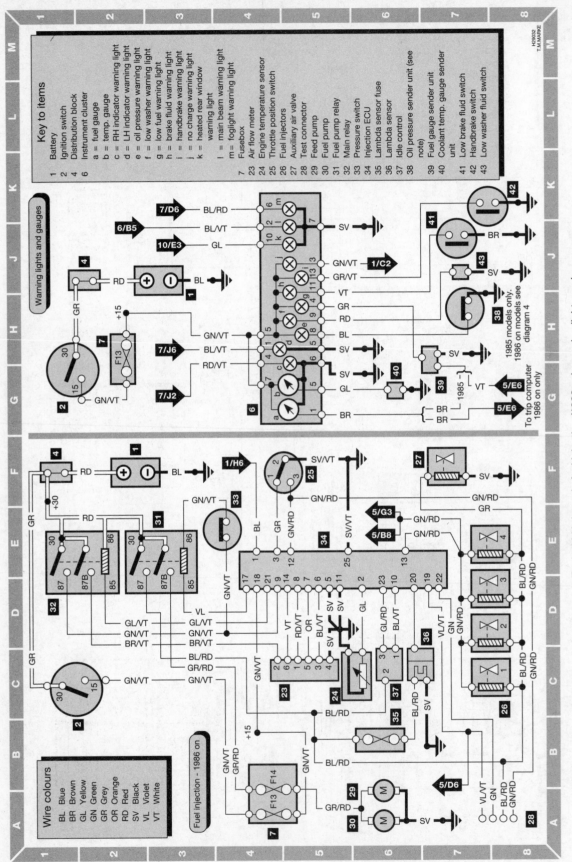

Key to items

1 Battery
2 Ignition switch
4 Distribution block
6 Instrument cluster
   a = fuel gauge
   b = temp. gauge
   c = RH indicator warning light
   d = LH indicator warning light
   e = oil pressure warning light
   f = low washer warning light
   g = low fuel warning light
   h = brake fluid warning light
   i = handbrake warning light
   j = no charge warning light
   k = heated rear window
       warning light
   l = main beam warning light
   m = foglight warning light
7 Fusebox
23 Air flow meter
24 Engine temperature sensor
25 Throttle position switch
26 Fuel injectors
27 Auxiliary air valve
28 Test connector
29 Feed pump
30 Fuel pump
31 Fuel pump relay
32 Main relay
33 Pressure switch
34 Injection ECU
35 Lambda sensor fuse
36 Lambda sensor
37 Idle control
38 Oil pressure sender unit (see
   note)
39 Fuel gauge sender unit
40 Coolant temp. gauge sender
   unit
41 Low brake fluid switch
42 Handbrake switch
43 Low washer fluid switch

Wire colours

BL Blue
BR Brown
GL Yellow
GN Green
GR Grey
OR Orange
RD Red
SV Black
VL Violet
VT White

Warning lights and gauges

Fuel injection – 1986 on

Diagram 3: Typical LH-Jetronic fuel injection (1986 on), warning lights and gauges

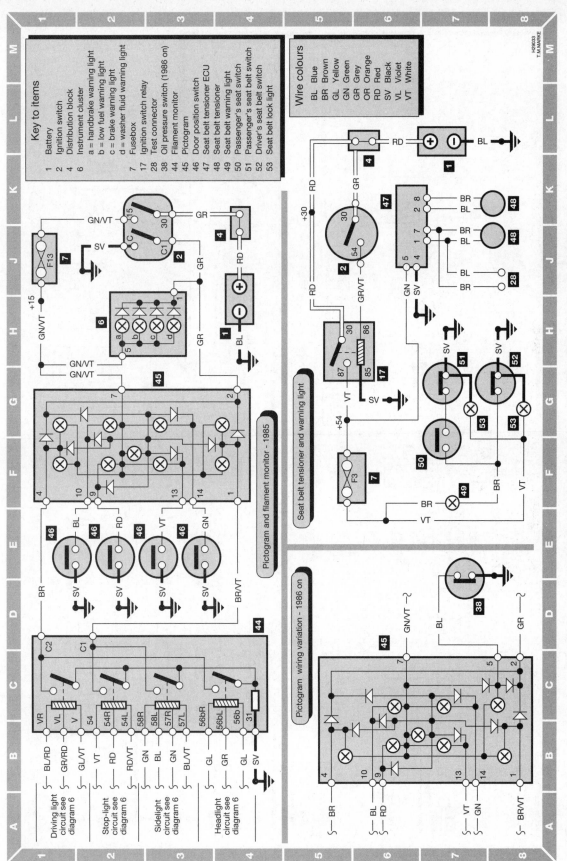

Key to items

1   Battery
2   Ignition switch
4   Distribution block
6   Instrument cluster
    a = handbrake warning light
    b = low fuel warning light
    c = brake warning light
    d = washer fluid warning light
7   Fusebox
17 Ignition switch relay
28 Test connector
38 Oil pressure switch (1986 on)
44 Filament monitor
45 Pictogram
46 Door position switch
47 Seat belt tensioner ECU
48 Seat belt tensioner
49 Seat belt warning light
50 Passenger's seat switch
51 Passenger's seat belt switch
52 Driver's seat belt switch
53 Seat belt lock light

Wire colours

BL Blue
BR Brown
GL Yellow
GN Green
GR Grey
OR Orange
RD Red
SV Black
VL Violet
VT White

Pictogram and filament monitor - 1985

Seat belt tensioner and warning light

Pictogram wiring variation - 1986 on

Diagram 4: Typical pictogram (filament monitor), seat belt tensioner and warning light

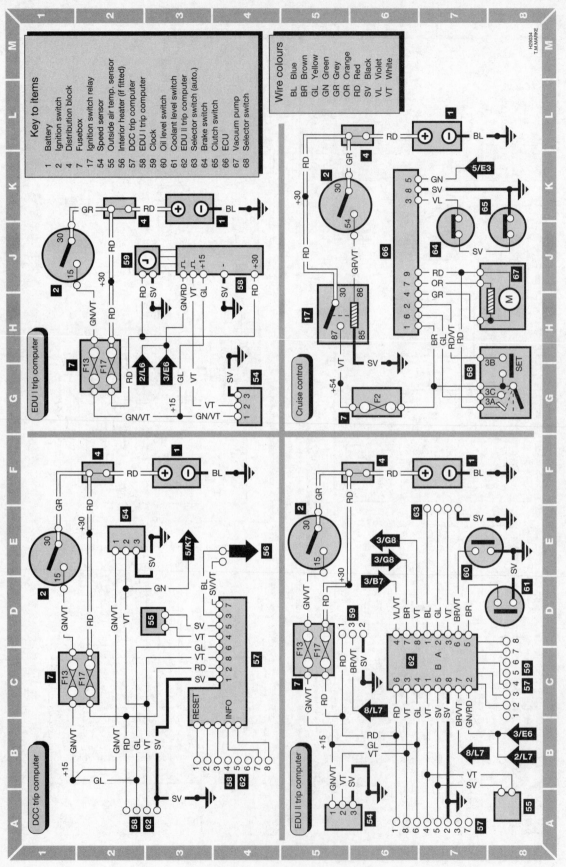

Diagram 5: Typical trip computers and cruise control

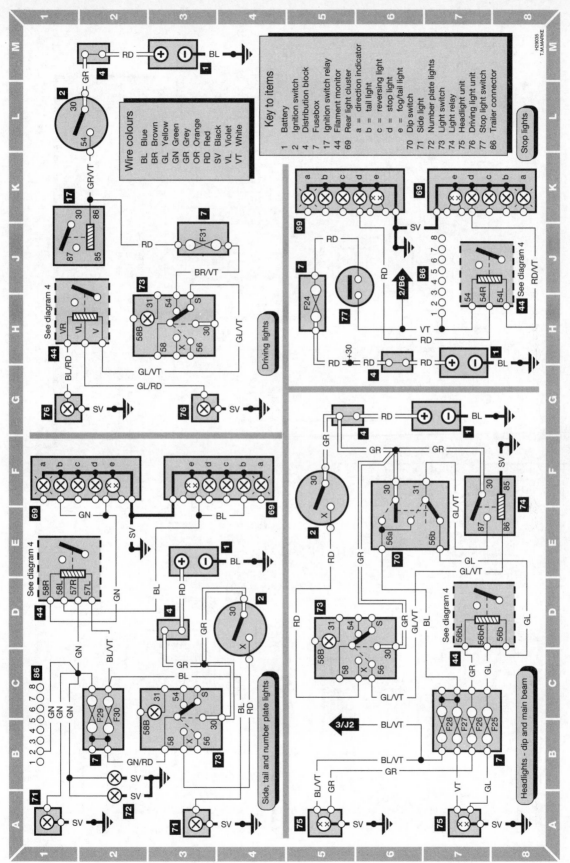

Key to items

1 Battery
2 Ignition switch
3 Distribution block
7 Fusebox
17 Ignition switch relay
44 Filament monitor
69 Rear light cluster
  a = direction indicator
  b = tail light
  c = reversing light
  d = stop light
  e = fog/tail light
70 Dip switch
71 Side light
72 Number plate lights
73 Light switch
74 Light relay
75 Headlight unit
76 Driving light unit
77 Stop light switch
86 Trailer connector

Wire colours

BL Blue
BR Brown
GL Yellow
GN Green
GR Grey
OR Orange
RD Red
SV Black
VL Violet
VT White

Stop lights

Driving lights

Side, tail and number plate lights

Headlights – dip and main beam

Diagram 6: Typical exterior lighting

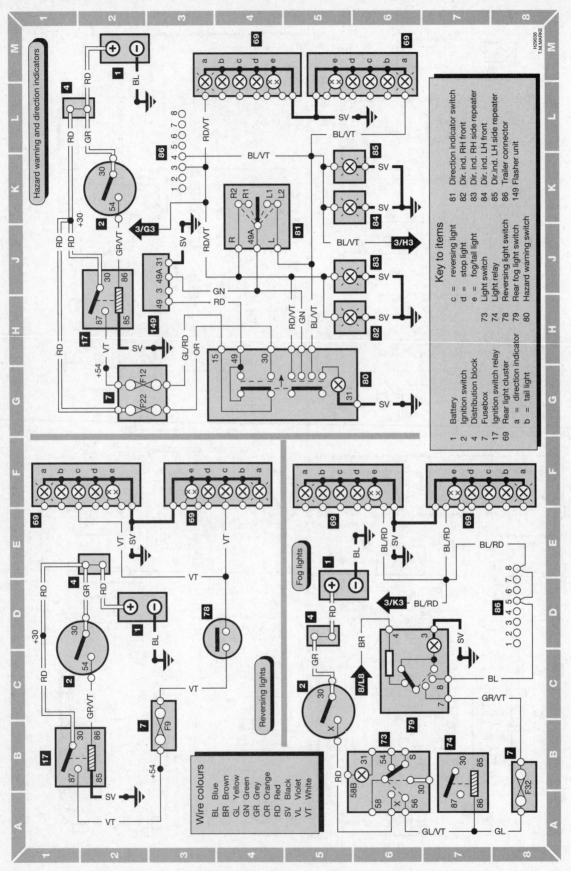

Diagram 7: Typical exterior lighting continued

Hazard warning and direction indicators

Reversing lights

Fog lights

Wire colours

BL	Blue
BR	Brown
GL	Yellow
GN	Green
GR	Grey
OR	Orange
RD	Red
SV	Black
VL	Violet
VT	White

Key to items

1 Battery
2 Ignition switch
4 Distribution block
7 Fusebox
17 Ignition switch relay
69 Rear light cluster
  a = direction indicator
  b = tail light
  c = reversing light
  d = stop light
  e = fog/tail light
73 Light switch
74 Light relay
78 Reversing light switch
79 Rear fog light switch
80 Hazard warning switch
81 Direction indicator switch
82 Dir. ind. RH front
83 Dir. ind. RH side repeater
84 Dir. ind. LH front
85 Dir. ind. LH side repeater
86 Trailer connector
149 Flasher unit

H29036
T.M.MARKE

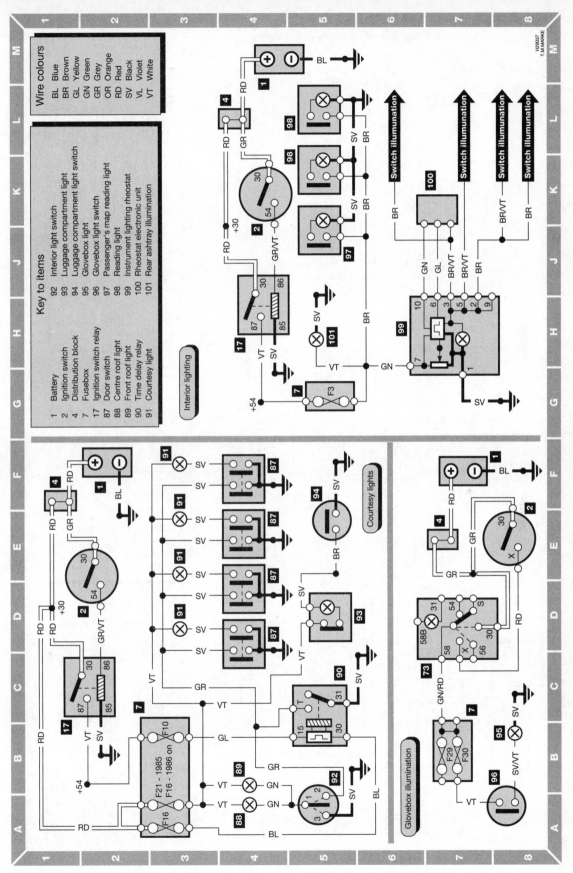

Wire colours

BL	Blue
BR	Brown
GL	Yellow
GN	Green
GR	Grey
OR	Orange
RD	Red
SV	Black
VL	Violet
VT	White

Key to items

1	Battery
2	Ignition switch
4	Distribution block
7	Fusebox
17	Ignition switch relay
87	Door switch
88	Centre roof light
89	Front roof light
90	Time delay relay
91	Courtesy light
92	Interior light switch
93	Luggage compartment light
94	Luggage compartment light switch
95	Glovebox light
96	Glovebox light switch
97	Passenger's map reading light
98	Reading light
99	Instrument lighting rheostat
100	Rheostat electronic unit
101	Rear ashtray illumination

Interior lighting

Courtesy lights

Glovebox illumination

Diagram 8: Typical interior lighting

H29037
T.M.MARKE

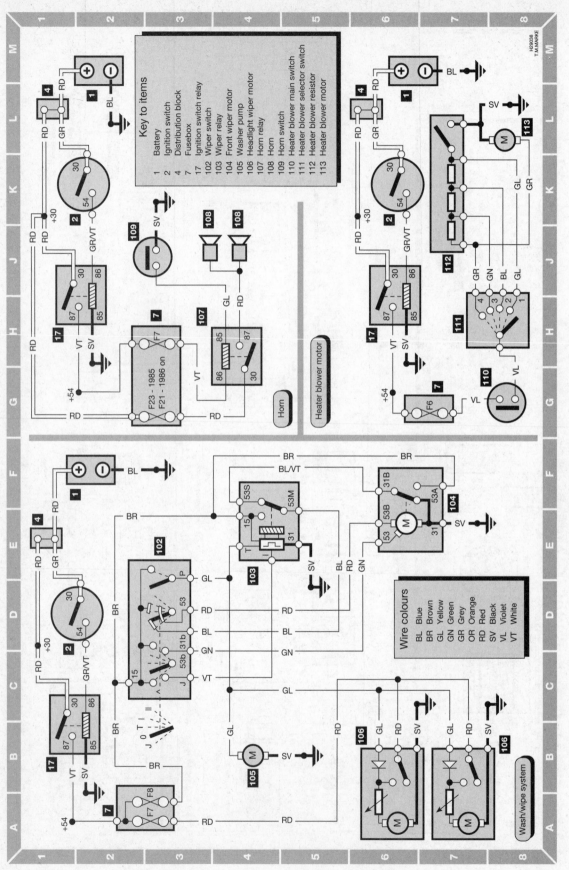

Key to items

1 Battery
2 Ignition switch
4 Distribution block
7 Fusebox
17 Ignition switch relay
102 Wiper switch
103 Wiper relay
104 Front wiper motor
105 Washer pump
106 Headlight wiper motor
107 Horn relay
108 Horn
109 Horn switch
110 Heater blower main switch
111 Heater blower selector switch
112 Heater blower resistor
113 Heater blower motor

Wire colours

BL Blue
BR Brown
GL Yellow
GN Green
GR Grey
OR Orange
RD Red
SV Black
VL Violet
VT White

Diagram 9: Typical wash/wipe, horn and heater blower

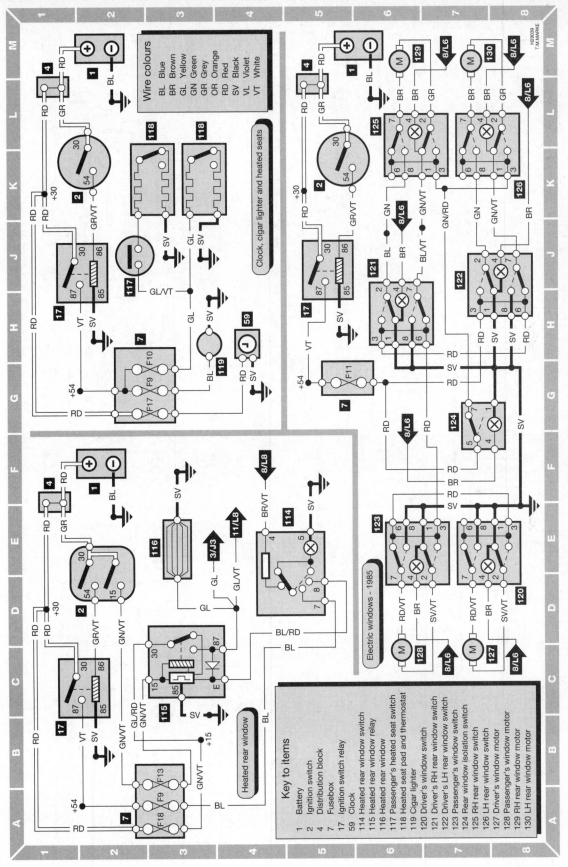

Wire colours

BL Blue
BR Brown
GL Yellow
GN Green
GR Grey
OR Orange
RD Red
SV Black
VL Violet
VT White

Clock, cigar lighter and heated seats

Electric windows – 1985

Heated rear window

Key to items

1 Battery
2 Ignition switch
4 Distribution block
7 Fusebox
17 Ignition switch relay
59 Clock
114 Heated rear window switch
115 Heated rear window relay
116 Heated rear window
117 Passenger's heated seat switch
118 Heated seat pad and thermostat
119 Cigar lighter
120 Driver's window switch
121 Driver's RH rear window switch
122 Driver's LH rear window switch
123 Passenger's window switch
124 Rear window isolation switch
125 RH rear window switch
126 LH rear window switch
127 Driver's window motor
128 Passenger's window motor
129 RH rear window motor
130 LH rear window motor

Diagram 10: Typical heated seats, heated rear window, clock, cigar lighter and electric windows (1985)

H29039
T.M.MARKE

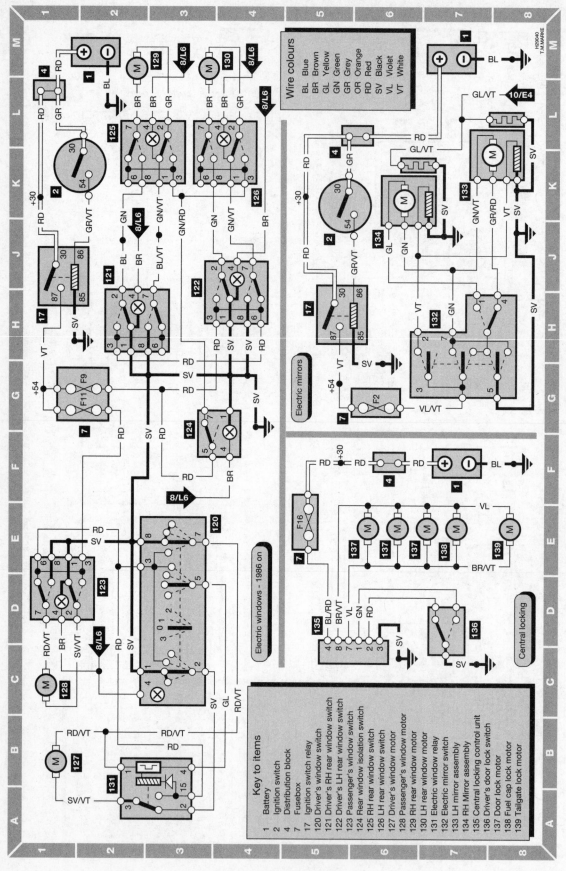

Wire colours

BL	Blue
BR	Brown
GL	Yellow
GN	Green
GR	Grey
OR	Orange
RD	Red
SV	Black
VL	Violet
VT	White

Electric mirrors

Electric windows – 1986 on

Central locking

Key to items

1 Battery
2 Ignition switch
4 Distribution block
7 Fusebox
17 Ignition switch relay
120 Driver's window switch
121 Driver's RH rear window switch
122 Driver's LH rear window switch
123 Passenger's window switch
124 Rear window isolation switch
125 RH rear window switch
126 LH rear window switch
127 Driver's window motor
128 Passenger's window motor
129 RH rear window motor
130 LH rear window motor
131 Electric window relay
132 Electric mirror switch
133 LH mirror assembly
134 RH Mirror assembly
135 Central locking control unit
136 Driver's door lock switch
137 Door lock motor
138 Fuel cap lock motor
139 Tailgate lock motor

Diagram 11: Typical electric windows (1986 on), central locking and electric mirrors

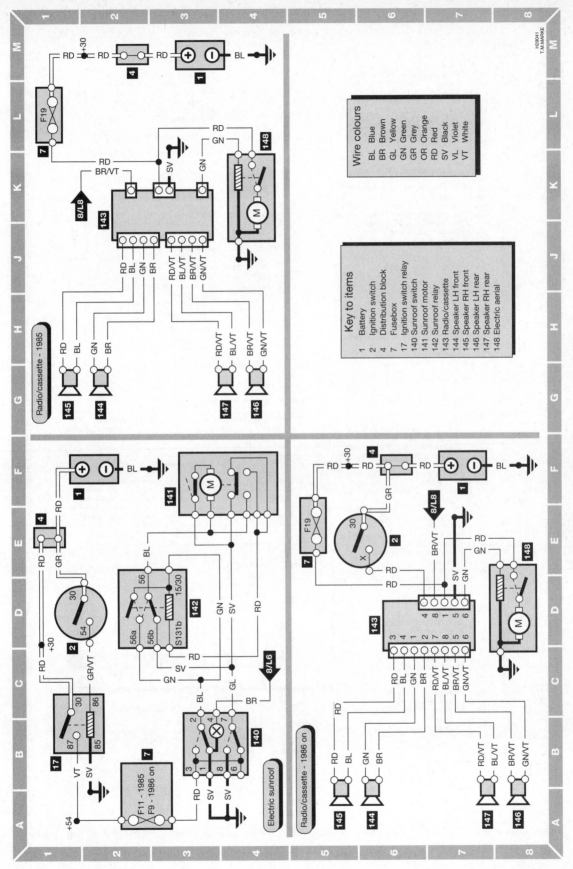

Wire colours

BL	Blue
BR	Brown
GL	Yellow
GN	Green
GR	Grey
OR	Orange
RD	Red
SV	Black
VL	Violet
VT	White

Key to items

1 Battery
2 Ignition switch
4 Distribution block
7 Fusebox
17 Ignition switch relay
140 Sunroof switch
141 Sunroof motor
142 Sunroof relay
143 Radio/cassette
144 Speaker LH front
145 Speaker RH front
146 Speaker LH rear
147 Speaker RH rear
148 Electric aerial

Radio/cassette - 1985

Radio/cassette - 1986 on

Electric sunroof

Diagram 12: Typical sunroof and radio/cassette

Fuses for 1985 models

Fuse	Rating	Circuit
1	10A	Automatic climate control (ACC)
2	10A	Cruise control, electric mirrors
3	10A	Seat belt warning light, seat belt lock lights and reading lights
4	30A	Air conditioning
5	10A	APC system
6	30A	Heater blower
7	10A	Headlight wipers and horn
8	15A	Wash/wipe
9	25A	Cigar lighter and reversing lights
10	15A	Heated seats
11	30A	Electric windows and sunroof
12	15A	Direction indicators
13	10A	Instruments, voltmeter, etc.
14	20A	Fuel pump
15	----	Spare
16	10A	Central locking and interior light delay
17	10A	Voltmeter, etc., ACC, clock
18	20A	Heated rear window
19	15A	Radio
20	30A	Radiator fan
21	10A	Interior lighting
22	15A	Hazard warning lights
23	25A	Horn
24	15A	Stop lights
25	15A	Headlight dipped beam
26	15A	Headlight dipped beam
27	15A	Headlight full beam
28	15A	Headlight full beam
29	10A	Side lights
30	10A	Side lights and instrument lighting
31	15A	Driving lights
32	15A	Rear fog lights

Fuses for 1986 models

Fuse	Rating	Circuit
1	10A	Automatic climate control (ACC)
2	10A	Cruise control, electric mirrors
3	10A	Seat belt warning light, seat belt lock lights and reading lights
4	30A	Air conditioning
5	10A	APC system
6	30A	Heater blower
7	10A	Headlight wipers and horn
8	15A	Wash/wipe
9	25A	Cigar lighter and reversing lights rear electric windows and sunroof
10	15A	Heated seats
11	30A	Electric windows and sunroof
12	15A	Direction indicators
13	10A	Instruments, voltmeter, etc.
14	20A	Fuel pump
15	10A	Extra foglights
16	10A	Central locking and interior light delay
17	10A	Voltmeter, etc., ACC, clock
18	30A	Heated rear window
19	15A	Radio
20	30A	Radiator fan
21	10A	Horn
22	15A	Hazard warning lights
23	25A	Engine cooling fan
24	15A	Stop lights
25	15A	Headlight dipped beam RH
26	15A	Headlight dipped beam LH
27	15A	Headlight full beam RH
28	15A	Headlight full beam LH
29	10A	Side lights
30	10A	Side lights and instrument lighting
31	15A	Driving lights
32	15A	Rear fog lights

Fuses for later models - typical

Fuse	Rating	Circuit
1	5A	Automatic climate control (ACC)
2	10A	Cruise control, electric mirrors
3	10A	Seat belt warning light, seat belt lock lights and reading lights
4	5A	Airbag
5	10A	APC system
6	30A	Heater blower
7	10A	Headlight wipers and horn
8	20A	Wash/wipe
9	25A	Cigar lighter and reversing lights rear electric windows and sunroof
10	25A	Heated seats
11	25A	Electric windows and sunroof
12	15A	Direction indicators
13	10A	Instruments, voltmeter, etc.
14	20A	Fuel pump
15	5A	Electronic throttle actuator
16	15A	Central locking and interior light delay
17	10A	Voltmeter, etc., ACC, clock
18	30A	Heated rear window
19	15A	Radio
20	30A	Radiator fan
21	25A	Electronic throttle actuator and horn
22	15A	Hazard warning lights
23	5A	Data link connectors, engine and car electronics
24	15A	Stop lights
25	30A	Electric seat LH
26	30A	Electric seat RH
27	10A	Radio, shift lock
28	10A	Heated lambda probe
29	15A	Side lights
30	10A	Side lights and instrument lighting
31	15A	Driving lights
32	15A	Rear fog lights

Ignition switch function

Connection between....	Locked position	Parked position	Running position	Test position	Start position
30-50					O
30-54		O——O			
30-15			O——O——O		
30-X		O——O——O			
30-B	O——O——O——O——O				
C-C1				O	

Key to symbols

Switch		In-line connector	——O
Fuse	F13	Termination connector	O—
Item no.	7	Connecting wires	
Pump/motor	M	Bulb	⊗
Earth		Connection to other circuits (e.g. diagram 3/grid location B2). Direction of arrow denotes current flow.	3/B2
Resistor		Solenoid actuator	
Variable resistor		Wire-battery positive potential (double line)	
Diode		Wire-battery negative potential (thick line)	
		Wire-interconnecting (thin line)	

H29029
T.M.MARKE

Fuses, ignition switch function and key to symbols

Many people see the words 'advanced driving' and believe that it won't interest them or that it is a style of driving beyond their own abilities. Nothing could be further from the truth. Advanced driving is straightforward safe, sensible driving - the sort of driving we should all do every time we get behind the wheel.

An average of 10 people are killed every day on UK roads and 870 more are injured, some seriously. Lives are ruined daily, usually because somebody did something stupid. Something like 95% of all accidents are due to human error, mostly driver failure. Sometimes we make genuine mistakes - everyone does. Sometimes we have lapses of concentration. Sometimes we deliberately take risks.

For many people, the process of 'learning to drive' doesn't go much further than learning how to pass the driving test because of a common belief that good drivers are made by 'experience'.

Learning to drive by 'experience' teaches three driving skills:

- ☐ Quick reactions. (Whoops, that was close!)
- ☐ Good handling skills. (Horn, swerve, brake, horn).
- ☐ Reliance on vehicle technology. (Great stuff this ABS, stop in no distance even in the wet...)

Drivers whose skills are 'experience based' generally have a lot of near misses and the odd accident. The results can be seen every day in our courts and our hospital casualty departments.

Advanced drivers have learnt to control the risks by controlling the position and speed of their vehicle. They avoid accidents and near misses, even if the drivers around them make mistakes.

The key skills of advanced driving are **concentration,** effective all-round **observation, anticipation** and **planning.** When **good vehicle handling** is added to these skills, all driving situations can be approached and negotiated in a safe, methodical way, leaving nothing to chance.

Concentration means applying your mind to safe driving, completely excluding anything that's not relevant. Driving is usually the most dangerous activity that most of us undertake in our daily routines. It deserves our full attention.

Observation means not just looking, but seeing and seeking out the information found in the driving environment.

Anticipation means asking yourself what is happening, what you can reasonably expect to happen and what could happen unexpectedly. (One of the commonest words used in compiling accident reports is 'suddenly'.)

Planning is the link between seeing something and taking the appropriate action. For many drivers, planning is the missing link.

If you want to become a safer and more skilful driver and you want to enjoy your driving more, contact the Institute of Advanced Motorists at www.iam.org.uk, phone 0208 996 9600, or write to IAM House, 510 Chiswick High Road, London W4 5RG for an information pack.

Tools and Working Facilities

Introduction

A selection of good tools is a fundamental requirement for anyone contemplating the maintenance and repair of a motor vehicle. For the owner who does not possess any, their purchase will prove a considerable expense, offsetting some of the savings made by doing-it-yourself. However, provided that the tools purchased meet the relevant national safety standards and are of good quality, they will last for many years and prove an extremely worthwhile investment.

To help the average owner to decide which tools are needed to carry out the various tasks detailed in this manual, we have compiled three lists of tools under the following headings: *Maintenance and minor repair, Repair and overhaul*, and *Special*. Newcomers to practical mechanics should start off with the *Maintenance and minor repair* tool kit, and confine themselves to the simpler jobs around the vehicle. Then, as confidence and experience grow, more difficult tasks can be undertaken, with extra tools being purchased as, and when, they are needed. In this way, a *Maintenance and minor repair* tool kit can be built up into a *Repair and overhaul* tool kit over a considerable period of time, without any major cash outlays. The experienced do-it-yourselfer will have a tool kit good enough for most repair and overhaul procedures, and will add tools from the *Special* category when it is felt that the expense is justified by the amount of use to which these tools will be put.

Maintenance and minor repair tool kit

The tools given in this list should be considered as a minimum requirement if routine maintenance, servicing and minor repair operations are to be undertaken. We recommend the purchase of combination spanners (ring one end, open-ended the other); although more expensive than open-ended ones, they do give the advantages of both types of spanner.

☐ *Combination spanners:*
   Metric - 8 to 19 mm inclusive
☐ *Adjustable spanner - 35 mm jaw (approx.)*
☐ *Spark plug spanner (with rubber insert) - petrol models*
☐ *Spark plug gap adjustment tool - petrol models*
☐ *Set of feeler gauges*
☐ *Brake bleed nipple spanner*
☐ *Screwdrivers:*
   Flat blade - 100 mm long x 6 mm dia
   Cross blade - 100 mm long x 6 mm dia
   Torx - various sizes (not all vehicles)
☐ *Combination pliers*
☐ *Hacksaw (junior)*
☐ *Tyre pump*
☐ *Tyre pressure gauge*
☐ *Oil can*
☐ *Oil filter removal tool*
☐ *Fine emery cloth*
☐ *Wire brush (small)*
☐ *Funnel (medium size)*
☐ *Sump drain plug key (not all vehicles)*

Repair and overhaul tool kit

These tools are virtually essential for anyone undertaking any major repairs to a motor vehicle, and are additional to those given in the *Maintenance and minor repair* list. Included in this list is a comprehensive set of sockets. Although these are expensive, they will be found invaluable as they are so versatile - particularly if various drives are included in the set. We recommend the half-inch square-drive type, as this can be used with most proprietary torque wrenches.

The tools in this list will sometimes need to be supplemented by tools from the *Special* list:

☐ *Sockets (or box spanners) to cover range in previous list (including Torx sockets)*
☐ *Reversible ratchet drive (for use with sockets)*
☐ *Extension piece, 250 mm (for use with sockets)*
☐ *Universal joint (for use with sockets)*
☐ *Flexible handle or sliding T "breaker bar" (for use with sockets)*
☐ *Torque wrench (for use with sockets)*
☐ *Self-locking grips*
☐ *Ball pein hammer*
☐ *Soft-faced mallet (plastic or rubber)*
☐ *Screwdrivers:*
   Flat blade - long & sturdy, short (chubby), and narrow (electrician's) types
   Cross blade – long & sturdy, and short (chubby) types
☐ *Pliers:*
   Long-nosed
   Side cutters (electrician's)
   Circlip (internal and external)
☐ *Cold chisel - 25 mm*
☐ *Scriber*
☐ *Scraper*
☐ *Centre-punch*
☐ *Pin punch*
☐ *Hacksaw*
☐ *Brake hose clamp*
☐ *Brake/clutch bleeding kit*
☐ *Selection of twist drills*
☐ *Steel rule/straight-edge*
☐ *Allen keys (inc. splined/Torx type)*
☐ *Selection of files*
☐ *Wire brush*
☐ *Axle stands*
☐ *Jack (strong trolley or hydraulic type)*
☐ *Light with extension lead*
☐ *Universal electrical multi-meter*

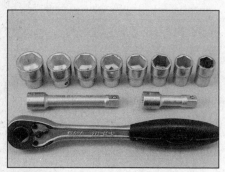

Sockets and reversible ratchet drive

Brake bleeding kit

Torx key, socket and bit

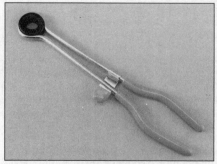

Hose clamp

Angular-tightening gauge

Special tools

The tools in this list are those which are not used regularly, are expensive to buy, or which need to be used in accordance with their manufacturers' instructions. Unless relatively difficult mechanical jobs are undertaken frequently, it will not be economic to buy many of these tools. Where this is the case, you could consider clubbing together with friends (or joining a motorists' club) to make a joint purchase, or borrowing the tools against a deposit from a local garage or tool hire specialist. It is worth noting that many of the larger DIY superstores now carry a large range of special tools for hire at modest rates.

The following list contains only those tools and instruments freely available to the public, and not those special tools produced by the vehicle manufacturer specifically for its dealer network. You will find occasional references to these manufacturers' special tools in the text of this manual. Generally, an alternative method of doing the job without the vehicle manufacturers' special tool is given. However, sometimes there is no alternative to using them. Where this is the case and the relevant tool cannot be bought or borrowed, you will have to entrust the work to a dealer.

- ☐ Angular-tightening gauge
- ☐ Valve spring compressor
- ☐ Valve grinding tool
- ☐ Piston ring compressor
- ☐ Piston ring removal/installation tool
- ☐ Cylinder bore hone
- ☐ Balljoint separator
- ☐ Coil spring compressors (where applicable)
- ☐ Two/three-legged hub and bearing puller
- ☐ Impact screwdriver
- ☐ Micrometer and/or vernier calipers
- ☐ Dial gauge
- ☐ Stroboscopic timing light
- ☐ Dwell angle meter/tachometer
- ☐ Fault code reader
- ☐ Cylinder compression gauge
- ☐ Hand-operated vacuum pump and gauge
- ☐ Clutch plate alignment set
- ☐ Brake shoe steady spring cup removal tool
- ☐ Bush and bearing removal/installation set
- ☐ Stud extractors
- ☐ Tap and die set
- ☐ Lifting tackle
- ☐ Trolley jack

Buying tools

Reputable motor accessory shops and superstores often offer excellent quality tools at discount prices, so it pays to shop around.

Remember, you don't have to buy the most expensive items on the shelf, but it is always advisable to steer clear of the very cheap tools. Beware of 'bargains' offered on market stalls or at car boot sales. There are plenty of good tools around at reasonable prices, but always aim to purchase items which meet the relevant national safety standards. If in doubt, ask the proprietor or manager of the shop for advice before making a purchase.

Care and maintenance of tools

Having purchased a reasonable tool kit, it is necessary to keep the tools in a clean and serviceable condition. After use, always wipe off any dirt, grease and metal particles using a clean, dry cloth, before putting the tools away. Never leave them lying around after they have been used. A simple tool rack on the garage or workshop wall for items such as screwdrivers and pliers is a good idea. Store all normal spanners and sockets in a metal box. Any measuring instruments, gauges, meters, etc, must be carefully stored where they cannot be damaged or become rusty.

Take a little care when tools are used. Hammer heads inevitably become marked, and screwdrivers lose the keen edge on their blades from time to time. A little timely attention with emery cloth or a file will soon restore items like this to a good finish.

Working facilities

Not to be forgotten when discussing tools is the workshop itself. If anything more than routine maintenance is to be carried out, a suitable working area becomes essential.

It is appreciated that many an owner-mechanic is forced by circumstances to remove an engine or similar item without the benefit of a garage or workshop. Having done this, any repairs should always be done under the cover of a roof.

Wherever possible, any dismantling should be done on a clean, flat workbench or table at a suitable working height.

Any workbench needs a vice; one with a jaw opening of 100 mm is suitable for most jobs. As mentioned previously, some clean dry storage space is also required for tools, as well as for any lubricants, cleaning fluids, touch-up paints etc, which become necessary.

Another item which may be required, and which has a much more general usage, is an electric drill with a chuck capacity of at least 8 mm. This, together with a good range of twist drills, is virtually essential for fitting accessories.

Last, but not least, always keep a supply of old newspapers and clean, lint-free rags available, and try to keep any working area as clean as possible.

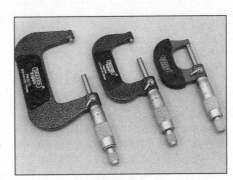
Micrometers

Dial test indicator ("dial gauge")

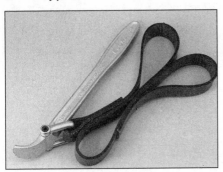
Strap wrench

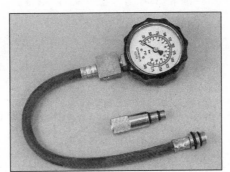
Compression tester

Fault code reader

General Repair Procedures

Whenever servicing, repair or overhaul work is carried out on the car or its components, it is necessary to observe the following procedures and instructions. This will assist in carrying out the operation efficiently and to a professional standard of workmanship.

Joint mating faces and gaskets

When separating components at their mating faces, never insert screwdrivers or similar implements into the joint between the faces in order to prise them apart. This can cause severe damage which results in oil leaks, coolant leaks, etc upon reassembly. Separation is usually achieved by tapping along the joint with a soft-faced hammer in order to break the seal. However, note that this method may not be suitable where dowels are used for component location.

Where a gasket is used between the mating faces of two components, ensure that it is renewed on reassembly, and fit it dry unless otherwise stated in the repair procedure. Make sure that the mating faces are clean and dry, with all traces of old gasket removed. When cleaning a joint face, use a tool which is not likely to score or damage the face, and remove any burrs or nicks with an oilstone or fine file.

Make sure that tapped holes are cleaned with a pipe cleaner, and keep them free of jointing compound, if this is being used, unless specifically instructed otherwise.

Ensure that all orifices, channels or pipes are clear, and blow through them, preferably using compressed air.

Oil seals

Oil seals can be removed by levering them out with a wide flat-bladed screwdriver or similar implement. Alternatively, a number of self-tapping screws may be screwed into the seal, and these used as a purchase for pliers or some similar device in order to pull the seal free.

Whenever an oil seal is removed from its working location, either individually or as part of an assembly, it should be renewed.

The very fine sealing lip of the seal is easily damaged, and will not seal if the surface it contacts is not completely clean and free from scratches, nicks or grooves.

Protect the lips of the seal from any surface which may damage them in the course of fitting. Use tape or a conical sleeve where possible. Lubricate the seal lips with oil before fitting and, on dual-lipped seals, fill the space between the lips with grease.

Unless otherwise stated, oil seals must be fitted with their sealing lips toward the lubricant to be sealed.

Use a tubular drift or block of wood of the appropriate size to install the seal and, if the seal housing is shouldered, drive the seal down to the shoulder. If the seal housing is unshouldered, the seal should be fitted with its face flush with the housing top face (unless otherwise instructed).

Screw threads and fastenings

Seized nuts, bolts and screws are quite a common occurrence where corrosion has set in, and the use of penetrating oil or releasing fluid will often overcome this problem if the offending item is soaked for a while before attempting to release it. The use of an impact driver may also provide a means of releasing such stubborn fastening devices, when used in conjunction with the appropriate screwdriver bit or socket. If none of these methods works, it may be necessary to resort to the careful application of heat, or the use of a hacksaw or nut splitter device.

Studs are usually removed by locking two nuts together on the threaded part, and then using a spanner on the lower nut to unscrew the stud. Studs or bolts which have broken off below the surface of the component in which they are mounted can sometimes be removed using a proprietary stud extractor. Always ensure that a blind tapped hole is completely free from oil, grease, water or other fluid before installing the bolt or stud. Failure to do this could cause the housing to crack due to the hydraulic action of the bolt or stud as it is screwed in.

When tightening a castellated nut to accept a split pin, tighten the nut to the specified torque, where applicable, and then tighten further to the next split pin hole. Never slacken the nut to align the split pin hole, unless stated in the repair procedure.

When checking or retightening a nut or bolt to a specified torque setting, slacken the nut or bolt by a quarter of a turn, and then retighten to the specified setting. However, this should not be attempted where angular tightening has been used.

For some screw fastenings, notably cylinder head bolts or nuts, torque wrench settings are no longer specified for the latter stages of tightening, "angle-tightening" being called up instead. Typically, a fairly low torque wrench setting will be applied to the bolts/nuts in the correct sequence, followed by one- or more stages of tightening through specified angles.

Locknuts, locktabs and washers

Any fastening which will rotate against a component or housing in the course of tightening should always have a washer between it and the relevant component or housing.

Spring or split washers should always be renewed when they are used to lock a critical component such as a big-end bearing retaining bolt or nut. Locktabs which are folded over to retain a nut or bolt should always be renewed.

Self-locking nuts can be re-used in non-critical areas, providing resistance can be felt when the locking portion passes over the bolt or stud thread. However, it should be noted that self-locking stiffnuts tend to lose their effectiveness after long periods of use, and in such cases should be renewed as a matter of course.

Split pins must always be replaced with new ones of the correct size for the hole.

When thread-locking compound is found on the threads of a fastener which is to be re-used, it should be cleaned off with a wire brush and solvent, and fresh compound applied on reassembly.

Special tools

Some repair procedures in this manual entail the use of special tools such as a press, two or three-legged pullers, spring compressors, etc. Wherever possible, suitable readily-available alternatives to the manufacturer's special tools are described, and are shown in use. Unless you are highly-skilled and have a thorough understanding of the procedures described, never attempt to bypass the use of any special tool when the procedure described specifies its use. Not only is there a very great risk of personal injury, but expensive damage could be caused to the components involved.

Environmental considerations

When disposing of used engine oil, brake fluid, antifreeze, etc, give due consideration to any detrimental environmental effects. Do not, for instance, pour any of the above liquids down drains into the general sewage system, or onto the ground to soak away. Many local council refuse tips provide a facility for waste oil disposal, as do some garages. If none of these facilities are available, consult your local Environmental Health Department for further advice.

With the universal tightening-up of legislation regarding the emission of environmentally-harmful substances from motor vehicles, most current vehicles have tamperproof devices fitted to the main adjustment points of the fuel system. These devices are primarily designed to prevent unqualified persons from adjusting the fuel/air mixture, with the chance of a consequent increase in toxic emissions. If such devices are encountered during servicing or overhaul, they should, wherever possible, be renewed or refitted in accordance with the vehicle manufacturer's requirements or current legislation.

OIL CARE
FOLLOW THE CODE

OIL BANK LINE
0800 66 33 66
www.oilbankline.org.uk

Note: It is antisocial and illegal to dump oil down the drain. To find the location of your local oil recycling bank, call this number free.

Engine 1

- [ ] Engine fails to rotate when attempting to start
- [ ] Engine rotates, but will not start
- [ ] Engine difficult to start when cold
- [ ] Engine difficult to start when hot
- [ ] Starter motor noisy or excessively-rough in engagement
- [ ] Engine starts, but stops immediately
- [ ] Engine idles erratically
- [ ] Engine misfires at idle speed
- [ ] Engine misfires throughout the driving speed range
- [ ] Engine hesitates on acceleration
- [ ] Engine stalls
- [ ] Engine lacks power
- [ ] Engine backfires
- [ ] Oil pressure warning light illuminated with engine running
- [ ] Engine runs-on after switching off
- [ ] Engine noises

Cooling system 2

- [ ] Overheating
- [ ] Overcooling
- [ ] External coolant leakage
- [ ] Internal coolant leakage
- [ ] Corrosion

Fuel and exhaust systems 3

- [ ] Excessive fuel consumption
- [ ] Fuel leakage and/or fuel odour
- [ ] Excessive noise or fumes from exhaust system

Clutch 4

- [ ] Pedal travels to floor - no pressure or very little resistance
- [ ] Clutch fails to disengage (unable to select gears)
- [ ] Clutch slips (engine speed increases, with no increase in vehicle speed)
- [ ] Judder as clutch is engaged
- [ ] Noise when depressing or releasing clutch pedal

Manual transmission 5

- [ ] Noisy in neutral with engine running
- [ ] Noisy in one particular gear
- [ ] Difficulty engaging gears
- [ ] Jumps out of gear
- [ ] Vibration
- [ ] Lubricant leaks

Automatic transmission 6

- [ ] Fluid leakage
- [ ] Transmission fluid brown, or has burned smell
- [ ] General gear selection problems
- [ ] Transmission will not downshift (kickdown) with accelerator fully depressed
- [ ] Engine will not start in any gear, or starts in gears other than Park or Neutral
- [ ] Transmission slips, shifts roughly, is noisy, or has no drive in forward or reverse gears

Driveshafts 7

- [ ] Clicking or knocking noise on turns (at slow speed on full-lock)
- [ ] Vibration when accelerating or decelerating

Braking system 8

- [ ] Vehicle pulls to one side under braking
- [ ] Noise (grinding or high-pitched squeal) when brakes applied
- [ ] Excessive brake pedal travel
- [ ] Brake pedal feels spongy when depressed
- [ ] Excessive brake pedal effort required to stop vehicle
- [ ] Judder felt through brake pedal or steering wheel when braking
- [ ] Brakes binding
- [ ] Rear wheels locking under normal braking

Suspension and steering systems 9

- [ ] Vehicle pulls to one side
- [ ] Wheel wobble and vibration
- [ ] Excessive pitching and/or rolling around corners, or during braking
- [ ] Wandering or general instability
- [ ] Excessively-stiff steering
- [ ] Excessive play in steering
- [ ] Lack of power assistance
- [ ] Tyre wear excessive

Electrical system 10

- [ ] Battery will not hold a charge for more than a few days
- [ ] Ignition/no-charge warning light remains illuminated with engine running
- [ ] Ignition/no-charge warning light fails to come on
- [ ] Lights inoperative
- [ ] Instrument readings inaccurate or erratic
- [ ] Horn inoperative, or unsatisfactory in operation
- [ ] Windscreen/tailgate wipers inoperative, or unsatisfactory in operation
- [ ] Windscreen/tailgate washers inoperative, or unsatisfactory in operation
- [ ] Electric windows inoperative, or unsatisfactory in operation
- [ ] Central locking system inoperative, or unsatisfactory in operation

Introduction

The vehicle owner who does his or her own maintenance according to the recommended service schedules should not have to use this section of the manual very often. Modern component reliability is such that, provided those items subject to wear or deterioration are inspected or renewed at the specified intervals, sudden failure is comparatively rare. Faults do not usually just happen as a result of sudden failure, but develop over a period of time. Major mechanical failures in particular are usually preceded by characteristic symptoms over hundreds or even thousands of miles. Those components which do occasionally fail without warning are often small and easily carried in the vehicle.

With any fault-finding, the first step is to decide where to begin investigations. Sometimes this is obvious, but on other occasions, a little detective work will be necessary. The owner who makes half a dozen haphazard adjustments or replacements may be successful in curing a fault (or its symptoms), but will be none the wiser if the fault recurs, and ultimately may have spent more time and money than was necessary. A calm and logical approach will be found to be more satisfactory in the long run. Always take into account any warning signs or abnormalities that may have been noticed in the period preceding the fault - power loss, high or low gauge readings, unusual smells, etc - and remember that failure of components such as fuses or spark plugs may only be pointers to some underlying fault.

The pages which follow provide an easy-reference guide to the more common problems which may occur during the operation of the vehicle. These problems and their possible causes are grouped under

Fault Finding

headings denoting various components or systems, such as Engine, Cooling system, etc. The Chapter and/or Section which deals with the problem is also shown in brackets. Whatever the fault, certain basic principles also apply. These are as follows:

Verify the fault. This is simply a matter of being sure that you know what the symptoms are before starting work. This is particularly important if you are investigating a fault for someone else, who may not have described it very accurately.

Don't overlook the obvious. For example, if the vehicle won't start, is there fuel in the tank? (Don't take anyone else's word on this particular point, and don't trust the fuel gauge either!) If an electrical fault is indicated, look for loose or broken wires before digging out the test gear.

Cure the disease, not the symptom. Substituting a flat battery with a fully-charged one will get you off the hard shoulder, but if the underlying cause is not attended to, the new battery will go the same way. Similarly, changing oil-fouled spark plugs for a new set will get you moving again, but remember that the reason for the fouling (if it wasn't simply an incorrect grade of plug) will have to be established and corrected.

Don't take anything for granted. Particularly, don't forget that a "new" component may itself be defective (especially if it's been rattling around in the boot for months), and don't leave components out of a fault diagnosis sequence just because they are new or recently-fitted. When you do finally diagnose a difficult fault, you'll probably realise that all the evidence was there from the start.

1 Engine

Engine fails to rotate when attempting to start

- [ ] Battery terminal connections loose or corroded (Chapter 1).
- [ ] Battery discharged or faulty (Chapter 5A).
- [ ] Broken, loose or disconnected wiring in the starting circuit (Chapter 5A).
- [ ] Defective starter solenoid or switch (Chapter 5A).
- [ ] Defective starter motor (Chapter 5A).
- [ ] Starter pinion or flywheel/driveplate ring gear teeth loose or broken (Chapters 2A or 5A).
- [ ] Engine earth strap broken or disconnected (Chapter 5A).

Starter motor turns engine slowly

- [ ] Partially-discharged battery (recharge, use jump leads, or push start) (Chapter 5A).
- [ ] Battery terminals loose or corroded (Chapter 1).
- [ ] Battery earth to body defective (Chapter 5A).
- [ ] Engine earth strap loose (Chapter 5A).
- [ ] Starter motor (or solenoid) wiring loose (Chapter 5A).
- [ ] Starter motor internal fault (Chapter 5A).

Engine rotates, but will not start

- [ ] Fuel tank empty.
- [ ] Battery discharged (engine rotates slowly) (Chapter 5A).
- [ ] Battery terminal connections loose or corroded (Chapter 1).
- [ ] Ignition components damp or damaged (Chapters 1 and 5B).
- [ ] Broken, loose or disconnected wiring in the ignition circuit (Chapters 1 and 5B).
- [ ] Worn, faulty or incorrectly-gapped spark plugs (Chapter 1).
- [ ] Fuel injection system fault (Chapter 4A).
- [ ] Major mechanical failure (eg broken timing chain) (Chapter 2A).

Engine difficult to start when cold

- [ ] Battery discharged (Chapter 5A).
- [ ] Battery terminal connections loose or corroded (Chapter 1).
- [ ] Worn, faulty or incorrectly-gapped spark plugs (Chapter 1).
- [ ] Fuel injection system fault (Chapter 4A).
- [ ] Other ignition system fault (Chapters 1 and 5B).
- [ ] Low cylinder compressions (Chapter 2A).

Engine difficult to start when hot

- [ ] Air filter element dirty or clogged (Chapter 1).
- [ ] Fuel injection system fault (Chapter 4A).
- [ ] Low cylinder compressions (Chapter 2A).

Starter motor noisy or excessively-rough in engagement

- [ ] Starter pinion or flywheel/driveplate ring gear teeth loose or broken (Chapters 2A or 5A).
- [ ] Starter motor mounting bolts loose or missing (Chapter 5A).
- [ ] Starter motor internal components worn or damaged (Chapter 5A).

Engine starts, but stops immediately

- [ ] Loose or faulty electrical connections in the ignition circuit (Chapters 1 and 5B).
- [ ] Vacuum leak at the throttle body or inlet manifold (Chapter 4A).
- [ ] Fuel injection system fault (Chapter 4A).

Engine idles erratically

- [ ] Incorrectly-adjusted idle speed (Chapter 4A).
- [ ] Air filter element clogged (Chapter 1).
- [ ] Vacuum leak at the throttle body, inlet manifold or associated hoses (Chapter 4A or 4B).
- [ ] Worn, faulty or incorrectly-gapped spark plugs (Chapter 1).
- [ ] Uneven or low cylinder compressions (Chapter 2A).
- [ ] Camshaft lobes worn (Chapter 2A).
- [ ] Fuel injection system fault (Chapter 4A).

Engine misfires at idle speed

- [ ] Worn, faulty or incorrectly-gapped spark plugs (Chapter 1).
- [ ] Faulty spark plug HT leads or DI cartridge as applicable (Chapter 1).
- [ ] Vacuum leak at the throttle body, inlet manifold or associated hoses (Chapter 4A or 4B).
- [ ] Fuel injection system fault (Chapter 4A).
- [ ] Distributor cap cracked or tracking internally, where applicable (Chapter 1).
- [ ] Uneven or low cylinder compressions (Chapter 2A).
- [ ] Disconnected, leaking, or perished crankcase ventilation hoses (Chapter 4B).

Engine misfires throughout the driving speed range

- [ ] Fuel filter choked (Chapter 1).
- [ ] Fuel pump faulty, or delivery pressure low (Chapter 4A).
- [ ] Fuel tank vent blocked, or fuel pipes restricted (Chapter 4A).
- [ ] Vacuum leak at the throttle body, inlet manifold or associated hoses (Chapter 4A).
- [ ] Worn, faulty or incorrectly-gapped spark plugs (Chapter 1).
- [ ] Faulty spark plug HT leads or DI cartridge, as applicable (Chapter 1).
- [ ] Distributor cap cracked or tracking internally, where applicable (Chapter 1).
- [ ] Faulty ignition coil (Chapter 5B).
- [ ] Uneven or low cylinder compressions (Chapter 2A).
- [ ] Fuel injection system fault (Chapter 4A).

Engine stalls

- [ ] Vacuum leak at the throttle body, inlet manifold or associated hoses (Chapter 4A or 4B).
- [ ] Fuel filter choked (Chapter 1).
- [ ] Fuel pump faulty, or delivery pressure low (Chapter 4A).
- [ ] Fuel tank vent blocked, or fuel pipes restricted (Chapter 4A).
- [ ] Fuel injection system fault (Chapter 4A).

Engine hesitates on acceleration

- [ ] Worn, faulty or incorrectly-gapped spark plugs (Chapter 1).
- [ ] Vacuum leak at the throttle body, inlet manifold or associated hoses (Chapter 4A or 4B).
- [ ] Fuel injection system fault (Chapter 4A).

Engine lacks power

- [ ] Fuel filter choked (Chapter 1).
- [ ] Fuel pump faulty, or delivery pressure low (Chapter 4A).
- [ ] Uneven or low cylinder compressions (Chapter 2A).
- [ ] Worn, faulty or incorrectly-gapped spark plugs (Chapter 1).
- [ ] Vacuum leak at the throttle body, inlet manifold or associated hoses (Chapter 4A or 4B).
- [ ] Fuel injection system fault (Chapter 4A).
- [ ] Faulty turbocharger, where applicable (Chapter 4A).
- [ ] Brakes binding (Chapters 1 and 9).
- [ ] Clutch slipping (Chapter 6).

Engine backfires

- [ ] Vacuum leak at the throttle body, inlet manifold or associated hoses (Chapter 4A or 4B).
- [ ] Fuel injection system fault (Chapter 4A).

Oil pressure warning light illuminated with engine running

- [ ] Low oil level, or incorrect oil grade (Chapter 1).
- [ ] Faulty oil pressure sensor (Chapter 2A).
- [ ] Worn engine bearings and/or oil pump (Chapter 2A or 2B).
- [ ] Excessively high engine operating temperature (Chapter 3).
- [ ] Oil pressure relief valve defective (Chapter 2A).
- [ ] Oil pick-up strainer clogged (Chapter 2A).

Note: *Low oil pressure in a high-mileage engine at tickover is not necessarily a cause for concern. Sudden pressure loss at speed is far more significant. In any event, check the gauge or warning light sender before condemning the engine.*

Engine runs-on after switching off

- [ ] Excessive carbon build-up in engine (Chapter 2A or 2B).
- [ ] Excessively high engine operating temperature (Chapter 3).

Engine noises

Pre-ignition (pinking) or knocking during acceleration or under load

- [ ] Ignition timing incorrect/ignition system fault (Chapters 1 and 5B).
- [ ] Incorrect grade of spark plug (Chapter 1).
- [ ] Incorrect grade of fuel (Chapter 1).
- [ ] Vacuum leak at throttle body, inlet manifold or associated hoses (Chapter 4A or 4B).
- [ ] Excessive carbon build-up in engine (Chapter 2A or 2B).
- [ ] Fuel injection system fault (Chapter 4A).

Whistling or wheezing noises

- [ ] Leaking inlet manifold or throttle body gasket (Chapter 4A).
- [ ] Leaking exhaust manifold gasket (Chapter 4A).
- [ ] Leaking vacuum hose (Chapters 4A, 4B and 9).
- [ ] Blowing cylinder head gasket (Chapter 2A).

Tapping or rattling noises

- [ ] Worn valve gear, timing chain, camshaft or hydraulic tappets (Chapter 2A).
- [ ] Ancillary component fault (water pump, alternator, etc) (Chapters 3, 5A, etc).

Knocking or thumping noises

- [ ] Worn big-end bearings (regular heavy knocking, perhaps less under load) (Chapter 2B).
- [ ] Worn main bearings (rumbling and knocking, perhaps worsening under load) (Chapter 2B).
- [ ] Piston slap (most noticeable when cold) (Chapter 2B).
- [ ] Ancillary component fault (water pump, alternator, etc) (Chapters 3, 5A, etc).

2 Cooling system

Overheating

- [ ] Auxiliary drivebelt broken - or, where applicable, incorrectly adjusted (Chapter 1).
- [ ] Insufficient coolant in system (Chapter 1).
- [ ] Thermostat faulty (Chapter 3).
- [ ] Radiator core blocked, or grille restricted (Chapter 3).
- [ ] Electric cooling fan or thermostatic switch faulty (Chapter 3).
- [ ] Pressure cap faulty (Chapter 3).
- [ ] Ignition timing incorrect, or ignition system fault (Chapters 1 and 5B).
- [ ] Inaccurate temperature gauge sender unit (Chapter 3).
- [ ] Airlock in cooling system (Chapter 1).

Overcooling

- [ ] Thermostat faulty (Chapter 3).
- [ ] Inaccurate temperature gauge sender unit (Chapter 3).

External coolant leakage

- [ ] Deteriorated or damaged hoses or hose clips (Chapter 1).
- [ ] Radiator core or heater matrix leaking (Chapter 3).
- [ ] Pressure cap faulty (Chapter 3).
- [ ] Water pump internal seal leaking (Chapter 3).
- [ ] Water pump-to-block O-ring or housing gasket leaking (Chapter 3).
- [ ] Boiling due to overheating (Chapter 3).
- [ ] Core plug leaking (Chapter 2B).

Internal coolant leakage

- [ ] Leaking cylinder head gasket (Chapter 2A).
- [ ] Cracked cylinder head or cylinder block (Chapter 2A or 2B).

Corrosion

- [ ] Infrequent draining and flushing (Chapter 1).
- [ ] Incorrect coolant mixture or inappropriate coolant type (Chapter 1).

3 Fuel and exhaust systems

Excessive fuel consumption

- [ ] Air filter element dirty or clogged (Chapter 1).
- [ ] Fuel injection system fault (Chapter 4A).
- [ ] Ignition timing incorrect or ignition system fault (Chapters 1 and 5B).
- [ ] Brakes binding (Chapter 9).
- [ ] Tyres under-inflated (Chapter 1).

Fuel leakage and/or fuel odour

- [ ] Damaged fuel tank, pipes or connections (Chapters 1 and 4A).

Excessive noise or fumes from exhaust system

- [ ] Leaking exhaust system or manifold joints (Chapters 1 and 4A).
- [ ] Leaking, corroded or damaged silencers or pipe (Chapters 1 and 4A).
- [ ] Broken mountings causing body or suspension contact (Chapter 4A).

4 Clutch

Pedal travels to floor - no pressure or very little resistance

☐ Leak in clutch hydraulic system (Chapter 6).
☐ Faulty hydraulic master or slave cylinder (Chapter 6).
☐ Broken clutch release bearing or fork (Chapter 6).
☐ Broken diaphragm spring in clutch pressure plate (Chapter 6).

Clutch fails to disengage (unable to select gears)

☐ Leak in clutch hydraulic system (Chapter 6).
☐ Faulty hydraulic master or slave cylinder (Chapter 6).
☐ Clutch disc sticking on gearbox input shaft splines (Chapter 6).
☐ Clutch disc sticking to flywheel or pressure plate (Chapter 6).
☐ Faulty pressure plate assembly (Chapter 6).
☐ Clutch release mechanism worn or incorrectly assembled (Chapter 6).

Clutch slips (engine speed increases, with no increase in vehicle speed)

☐ Clutch disc linings excessively worn (Chapter 6).
☐ Clutch disc linings contaminated with oil or grease (Chapter 6).
☐ Faulty pressure plate or weak diaphragm spring (Chapter 6).

Judder as clutch is engaged

☐ Clutch disc linings contaminated with oil or grease (Chapter 6).
☐ Clutch disc linings excessively worn (Chapter 6).
☐ Faulty or distorted pressure plate or diaphragm spring (Chapter 6).
☐ Worn or loose engine or gearbox mountings (Chapter 2A or 2B).
☐ Clutch disc hub or gearbox input shaft splines worn (Chapter 6).

Noise when depressing or releasing clutch pedal

☐ Worn clutch release bearing (Chapter 6).
☐ Worn or dry clutch pedal bushes (Chapter 6).
☐ Faulty pressure plate assembly (Chapter 6).
☐ Pressure plate diaphragm spring broken (Chapter 6).
☐ Broken clutch disc cushioning springs (Chapter 6).

5 Manual transmission

Difficulty engaging gears

☐ Clutch fault (Chapter 6).
☐ Worn or damaged gear linkage (Chapter 7A).
☐ Incorrectly-adjusted gear linkage (Chapter 7A).
☐ Worn synchroniser units (Chapter 7A).*

Jumps out of gear

☐ Worn or damaged gear linkage (Chapter 7A).
☐ Incorrectly-adjusted gear linkage (Chapter 7A).
☐ Worn synchroniser units (Chapter 7A).*
☐ Worn selector forks (Chapter 7A).*

Vibration

☐ Lack of oil (Chapter 1).
☐ Worn bearings (Chapter 7A).*

Noisy in neutral with engine running

☐ Input shaft bearings worn (noise apparent with clutch pedal released, but not when depressed) (Chapter 7A).*
☐ Clutch release bearing worn (noise apparent with clutch pedal depressed, possibly less when released) (Chapter 6).

Noisy in one particular gear

☐ Worn, damaged or chipped gear teeth (Chapter 7A).*

Lubricant leaks

☐ Leaking oil seal (Chapter 7A).
☐ Leaking housing joint (Chapter 7A).*

*Although the corrective action necessary to remedy the symptoms described is beyond the scope of the home mechanic, the above information should be helpful in isolating the cause of the condition, so that the owner can communicate clearly with a professional mechanic.

6 Automatic transmission

Note: Due to the complexity of the automatic transmission, it is difficult for the home mechanic to properly diagnose and service this unit. For problems other than the following, the vehicle should be taken to a dealer service department or automatic transmission specialist.

Fluid leakage

☐ Automatic transmission fluid is usually deep red in colour. Fluid leaks should not be confused with engine oil, which can easily be blown onto the transmission by air flow.
☐ To determine the source of a leak, first remove all built-up dirt and grime from the transmission housing and surrounding areas, using a degreasing agent or by steam-cleaning. Drive the vehicle at low speed, so that air flow will not blow the leak far from its source. Raise and support the vehicle, and determine where the leak is coming from. The following are common areas of leakage.
a) Fluid pan (transmission "sump").
b) Dipstick tube (Chapter 1).
c) Transmission-to-fluid cooler fluid pipes/unions (Chapter 7B).

Transmission fluid brown, or has burned smell

☐ Transmission fluid level low, or fluid in need of renewal (Chapter 1).

General gear selection problems

☐ The most likely cause of gear selection problems is a faulty or poorly-adjusted gear selector mechanism. The following are common problems associated with a faulty selector mechanism.
a) Engine starting in gears other than Park or Neutral.
b) Indicator on gear selector lever pointing to a gear other than the one actually being used.
c) Vehicle moves when in Park or Neutral.
d) Poor gear shift quality, or erratic gear changes.
☐ Refer any problems to a Saab dealer, or an automatic transmission specialist.

Transmission will not downshift (kickdown) with accelerator pedal fully depressed

☐ Low transmission fluid level (Chapter 1).
☐ Incorrect selector cable adjustment (Chapter 7B).

Engine will not start in any gear, or starts in gears other than Park or Neutral

☐ Incorrect starter inhibitor switch adjustment - where applicable (Chapter 7B).
☐ Incorrect selector cable adjustment (Chapter 7B).

Transmission slips, shifts roughly, is noisy, or has no drive in forward or reverse gears

☐ There are many probable causes for the above problems, but the home mechanic should be concerned with only one possibility -

fluid level. Before taking the vehicle to a dealer or transmission specialist, check the fluid level and condition of the fluid as described in Chapter 1. Correct the fluid level as necessary, or change the fluid and filter if needed. If the problem persists, professional help will be necessary.

7 Driveshafts

Clicking or knocking noise on turns (at slow speed on full-lock)

☐ Lack of constant velocity joint lubricant, possibly due to damaged gaiter (Chapter 8).
☐ Worn outer constant velocity joint (Chapter 8).

Vibration when accelerating or decelerating

☐ Worn inner constant velocity joint (Chapter 8).
☐ Bent or distorted driveshaft (Chapter 8).

8 Braking system

Note: *Before assuming that a brake problem exists, make sure that the tyres are in good condition and correctly inflated, that the front wheel alignment is correct, and that the vehicle is not loaded with weight in an unequal manner. Apart from checking the condition of all pipe and hose connections, any faults occurring on the anti-lock braking system should be referred to a Saab dealer for diagnosis.*

Vehicle pulls to one side under braking

☐ Worn, defective, damaged or contaminated front or rear brake pads on one side (Chapters 1 and 9).
☐ Seized or partially-seized front or rear brake caliper piston (Chapter 9).
☐ A mixture of brake pad lining materials fitted between sides (Chapter 9).
☐ Brake caliper mounting bolts loose (Chapter 9).
☐ Worn or damaged steering or suspension components (Chapters 1 and 10).

Noise (grinding or high-pitched squeal) when brakes applied

☐ Brake pad friction lining material worn down to metal backing (Chapters 1 and 9).
☐ Excessive corrosion of brake disc - may be apparent after the vehicle has been standing for some time (Chapters 1 and 9).

Brake pedal feels spongy when depressed

☐ Air in hydraulic system (Chapter 9).
☐ Deteriorated flexible rubber brake hoses (Chapters 1 and 9).
☐ Master cylinder mountings loose (Chapter 9).
☐ Faulty master cylinder (Chapter 9).

Excessive brake pedal travel

☐ Faulty master cylinder (Chapter 9).
☐ Air in hydraulic system (Chapter 9).
☐ Faulty vacuum servo unit (Chapter 9).

Excessive brake pedal effort required to stop vehicle

☐ Faulty vacuum servo unit (Chapter 9).
☐ Disconnected, damaged or insecure brake servo vacuum hose (Chapters 1 and 9).
☐ Primary or secondary hydraulic circuit failure (Chapter 9).
☐ Seized brake caliper piston(s) (Chapter 9).
☐ Brake pads incorrectly fitted (Chapter 9).
☐ Incorrect grade of brake pads fitted (Chapter 9).
☐ Brake pads contaminated (Chapter 9).

Judder felt through brake pedal or steering wheel when braking

☐ Excessive run-out or distortion of brake disc(s) (Chapter 9).
☐ Brake pad linings worn (Chapters 1 and 9).
☐ Brake caliper mounting bolts loose (Chapter 9).
☐ Wear in suspension or steering components or mountings (Chapters 1 and 10).

Brakes binding

☐ Seized brake caliper piston(s) (Chapter 9).
☐ Incorrectly-adjusted handbrake mechanism (Chapter 9).
☐ Faulty master cylinder (Chapter 9).

Rear wheels locking under normal braking

☐ Seized brake caliper piston(s) (Chapter 9).
☐ Faulty brake pressure regulator (Chapter 9).

9 Suspension and steering

Note: *Before diagnosing suspension or steering faults, be sure that the trouble is not due to incorrect tyre pressures, mixtures of tyre types, or binding brakes.*

Vehicle pulls to one side

☐ Defective tyre (Chapter 1).
☐ Excessive wear in suspension or steering components (Chapters 1 and 10).
☐ Incorrect front wheel alignment (Chapter 10).
☐ Accident damage to steering or suspension components (Chapters 1 and 10).

Wheel wobble and vibration

☐ Front roadwheels out of balance (vibration felt mainly through the steering wheel) (Chapter 10).
☐ Rear roadwheels out of balance (vibration felt throughout the vehicle) (Chapter 10).
☐ Roadwheels damaged or distorted (Chapter 10).
☐ Faulty or damaged tyre (Chapter 1).
☐ Worn steering or suspension joints, bushes or components (Chapters 1 and 10).
☐ Wheel bolts loose (Chapter 10).

Excessive pitching and/or rolling around corners, or during braking

- ☐ Defective shock absorbers (Chapters 1 and 10).
- ☐ Broken or weak coil spring and/or suspension component (Chapters 1 and 10).
- ☐ Worn or damaged anti-roll bar or mountings (Chapter 10).

Wandering or general instability

- ☐ Incorrect front wheel alignment (Chapter 10).
- ☐ Worn steering or suspension joints, bushes or components (Chapters 1 and 10).
- ☐ Roadwheels out of balance (Chapter 10).
- ☐ Faulty or damaged tyre (Chapter 1).
- ☐ Wheel bolts loose (Chapter 10).
- ☐ Defective shock absorbers (Chapters 1 and 10).

Excessively-stiff steering

- ☐ Lack of steering gear lubricant (Chapter 10).
- ☐ Seized track rod end balljoint or suspension balljoint (Chapters 1 and 10).
- ☐ Broken or incorrectly adjusted auxiliary drivebelt (Chapter 1).
- ☐ Incorrect front wheel alignment (Chapter 10).
- ☐ Steering rack or column bent or damaged (Chapter 10).

Excessive play in steering

- ☐ Worn steering column universal joint(s) (Chapter 10).
- ☐ Worn steering track rod end balljoints (Chapters 1 and 10).
- ☐ Worn rack-and-pinion steering gear (Chapter 10).
- ☐ Worn steering or suspension joints, bushes or components (Chapters 1 and 10).

Lack of power assistance

- ☐ Broken or incorrectly-adjusted auxiliary drivebelt (Chapter 1).
- ☐ Incorrect power steering fluid level (Chapter 1).
- ☐ Restriction in power steering fluid hoses (Chapter 1).
- ☐ Faulty power steering pump (Chapter 10).
- ☐ Faulty rack-and-pinion steering gear (Chapter 10).

Tyre wear excessive

Tyres worn on inside or outside edges

- ☐ Tyres under-inflated (wear on both edges) (Chapter 1).
- ☐ Incorrect camber or castor angles (wear on one edge only) (Chapter 10).
- ☐ Worn steering or suspension joints, bushes or components (Chapters 1 and 10).
- ☐ Excessively-hard cornering.
- ☐ Accident damage.

Tyre treads exhibit feathered edges

- ☐ Incorrect toe setting (Chapter 10).

Tyres worn in centre of tread

- ☐ Tyres over-inflated (Chapter 1).

Tyres worn on inside and outside edges

- ☐ Tyres under-inflated (Chapter 1).
- ☐ Worn shock absorbers (Chapters 1 and 10).

Tyres worn unevenly

- ☐ Tyres out of balance (Chapter 1).
- ☐ Excessive wheel or tyre run-out (Chapter 1).
- ☐ Worn shock absorbers (Chapters 1 and 10).
- ☐ Faulty tyre (Chapter 1).

10 Electrical system

Note: *For problems associated with the starting system, refer to the faults listed under "Engine" earlier in this Section.*

Battery will not hold a charge for more than a few days

- ☐ Battery defective internally (Chapter 5A).
- ☐ Battery electrolyte level low - where applicable (Chapter 1).
- ☐ Battery terminal connections loose or corroded (Chapter 1).
- ☐ Auxiliary drivebelt worn - or incorrectly adjusted, where applicable (Chapter 1).
- ☐ Alternator not charging at correct output (Chapter 5A).
- ☐ Alternator or voltage regulator faulty (Chapter 5A).
- ☐ Short-circuit causing continual battery drain (Chapters 5A and 12).

Ignition/no-charge warning light remains illuminated with engine running

- ☐ Auxiliary drivebelt broken, worn, or incorrectly adjusted (Chapter 1).
- ☐ Alternator brushes worn, sticking, or dirty (Chapter 5A).
- ☐ Alternator brush springs weak or broken (Chapter 5A).
- ☐ Internal fault in alternator or voltage regulator (Chapter 5A).
- ☐ Broken, disconnected, or loose wiring in charging circuit (Chapter 5A).

Ignition/no-charge warning light fails to come on

- ☐ Warning light bulb blown (Chapter 12).
- ☐ Broken, disconnected, or loose wiring in warning light circuit (Chapter 12).
- ☐ Alternator faulty (Chapter 5A).

Lights inoperative

- ☐ Bulb blown (Chapter 12).

- ☐ Corrosion of bulb or bulbholder contacts (Chapter 12).
- ☐ Blown fuse (Chapter 12).
- ☐ Faulty relay (Chapter 12).
- ☐ Broken, loose, or disconnected wiring (Chapter 12).
- ☐ Faulty switch (Chapter 12).

Instrument readings inaccurate or erratic

Instrument readings increase with engine speed

- ☐ Faulty voltage regulator (Chapter 12).

Fuel or temperature gauges give no reading

- ☐ Faulty gauge sender unit (Chapters 3 and 4).
- ☐ Wiring open-circuit (Chapter 12).
- ☐ Faulty gauge (Chapter 12).

Fuel or temperature gauges give continuous maximum reading

- ☐ Faulty gauge sender unit (Chapters 3 and 4).
- ☐ Wiring short-circuit (Chapter 12).
- ☐ Faulty gauge (Chapter 12).

Horn inoperative, or unsatisfactory in operation

Horn operates all the time

- ☐ Horn contacts permanently bridged or horn push stuck down (Chapter 12).

Horn fails to operate

- ☐ Blown fuse (Chapter 12).
- ☐ Cable or cable connections loose, broken or disconnected (Chapter 12).
- ☐ Faulty horn (Chapter 12).

Horn emits intermittent or unsatisfactory sound

- [ ] Cable connections loose (Chapter 12).
- [ ] Horn mountings loose (Chapter 12).
- [ ] Faulty horn (Chapter 12).

Windscreen/tailgate wipers inoperative, or unsatisfactory in operation

Wipers fail to operate, or operate very slowly

- [ ] Wiper blades stuck to screen, or linkage seized or binding (Chapters 1 and 12).
- [ ] Blown fuse (Chapter 12).
- [ ] Cable or cable connections loose, broken or disconnected (Chapter 12).
- [ ] Faulty relay (Chapter 12).
- [ ] Faulty wiper motor (Chapter 12).

Wiper blades sweep over too large or too small an area of the glass

- [ ] Wiper arms incorrectly positioned on spindles (Chapter 1).
- [ ] Excessive wear of wiper linkage (Chapter 12).
- [ ] Wiper motor or linkage mountings loose or insecure (Chapter 12).

Wiper blades fail to clean the glass effectively

- [ ] Wiper blade rubbers worn or perished (Chapter 1).
- [ ] Wiper arm tension springs broken, or arm pivots seized (Chapter 12).
- [ ] Insufficient windscreen washer additive to adequately remove road film (Chapter 1).

Windscreen/tailgate washers inoperative, or unsatisfactory in operation

One or more washer jets inoperative

- [ ] Blocked washer jet (Chapter 1).
- [ ] Disconnected, kinked or restricted fluid hose (Chapter 12).
- [ ] Insufficient fluid in washer reservoir (Chapter 1).

Washer pump fails to operate

- [ ] Broken or disconnected wiring or connections (Chapter 12).
- [ ] Blown fuse (Chapter 12).
- [ ] Faulty washer switch (Chapter 12).
- [ ] Faulty washer pump (Chapter 12).

Washer pump runs for some time before fluid is emitted from jets

- [ ] Faulty one-way valve in fluid supply hose (Chapter 12).

Electric windows inoperative, or unsatisfactory in operation

Window glass will only move in one direction

- [ ] Faulty switch (Chapter 12).

Window glass slow to move

- [ ] Regulator seized or damaged, or in need of lubrication (Chapter 11).
- [ ] Door internal components or trim fouling regulator (Chapter 11).
- [ ] Faulty motor (Chapter 11).

Window glass fails to move

- [ ] Blown fuse (Chapter 12).
- [ ] Faulty relay (Chapter 12).
- [ ] Broken or disconnected wiring or connections (Chapter 12).
- [ ] Faulty motor (Chapter 11).

Central locking system inoperative, or unsatisfactory in operation

Complete system failure

- [ ] Blown fuse (Chapter 12).
- [ ] Faulty relay (Chapter 12).
- [ ] Broken or disconnected wiring or connections (Chapter 12).

A

ABS (Anti-lock brake system) A system, usually electronically controlled, that senses incipient wheel lockup during braking and relieves hydraulic pressure at wheels that are about to skid.

Air bag An inflatable bag hidden in the steering wheel (driver's side) or the dash or glovebox (passenger side). In a head-on collision, the bags inflate, preventing the driver and front passenger from being thrown forward into the steering wheel or windscreen.

Air cleaner A metal or plastic housing, containing a filter element, which removes dust and dirt from the air being drawn into the engine.

Air filter element The actual filter in an air cleaner system, usually manufactured from pleated paper and requiring renewal at regular intervals.

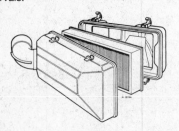

Air filter

Allen key A hexagonal wrench which fits into a recessed hexagonal hole.

Alligator clip A long-nosed spring-loaded metal clip with meshing teeth. Used to make temporary electrical connections.

Alternator A component in the electrical system which converts mechanical energy from a drivebelt into electrical energy to charge the battery and to operate the starting system, ignition system and electrical accessories.

Ampere (amp) A unit of measurement for the flow of electric current. One amp is the amount of current produced by one volt acting through a resistance of one ohm.

Anaerobic sealer A substance used to prevent bolts and screws from loosening. Anaerobic means that it does not require oxygen for activation. The Loctite brand is widely used.

Antifreeze A substance (usually ethylene glycol) mixed with water, and added to a vehicle's cooling system, to prevent freezing of the coolant in winter. Antifreeze also contains chemicals to inhibit corrosion and the formation of rust and other deposits that would tend to clog the radiator and coolant passages and reduce cooling efficiency.

Anti-seize compound A coating that reduces the risk of seizing on fasteners that are subjected to high temperatures, such as exhaust manifold bolts and nuts.

Asbestos A natural fibrous mineral with great heat resistance, commonly used in the composition of brake friction materials.

Asbestos is a health hazard and the dust created by brake systems should never be inhaled or ingested.

Axle A shaft on which a wheel revolves, or which revolves with a wheel. Also, a solid beam that connects the two wheels at one end of the vehicle. An axle which also transmits power to the wheels is known as a live axle.

Axleshaft A single rotating shaft, on either side of the differential, which delivers power from the final drive assembly to the drive wheels. Also called a driveshaft or a halfshaft.

B

Ball bearing An anti-friction bearing consisting of a hardened inner and outer race with hardened steel balls between two races.

Bearing The curved surface on a shaft or in a bore, or the part assembled into either, that permits relative motion between them with minimum wear and friction.

Bearing

Big-end bearing The bearing in the end of the connecting rod that's attached to the crankshaft.

Bleed nipple A valve on a brake wheel cylinder, caliper or other hydraulic component that is opened to purge the hydraulic system of air. Also called a bleed screw.

Brake bleeding Procedure for removing air from lines of a hydraulic brake system.

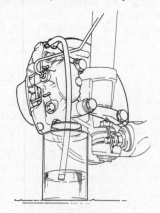

Brake bleeding

Brake disc The component of a disc brake that rotates with the wheels.

Brake drum The component of a drum brake that rotates with the wheels.

Brake linings The friction material which contacts the brake disc or drum to retard the vehicle's speed. The linings are bonded or riveted to the brake pads or shoes.

Brake pads The replaceable friction pads that pinch the brake disc when the brakes are applied. Brake pads consist of a friction material bonded or riveted to a rigid backing plate.

Brake shoe The crescent-shaped carrier to which the brake linings are mounted and which forces the lining against the rotating drum during braking.

Braking systems For more information on braking systems, consult the *Haynes Automotive Brake Manual*.

Breaker bar A long socket wrench handle providing greater leverage.

Bulkhead The insulated partition between the engine and the passenger compartment.

C

Caliper The non-rotating part of a disc-brake assembly that straddles the disc and carries the brake pads. The caliper also contains the hydraulic components that cause the pads to pinch the disc when the brakes are applied. A caliper is also a measuring tool that can be set to measure inside or outside dimensions of an object.

Camshaft A rotating shaft on which a series of cam lobes operate the valve mechanisms. The camshaft may be driven by gears, by sprockets and chain or by sprockets and a belt.

Canister A container in an evaporative emission control system; contains activated charcoal granules to trap vapours from the fuel system.

Canister

Carburettor A device which mixes fuel with air in the proper proportions to provide a desired power output from a spark ignition internal combustion engine.

Castellated Resembling the parapets along the top of a castle wall. For example, a castellated balljoint stud nut.

Castor In wheel alignment, the backward or forward tilt of the steering axis. Castor is positive when the steering axis is inclined rearward at the top.

Catalytic converter A silencer-like device in the exhaust system which converts certain pollutants in the exhaust gases into less harmful substances.

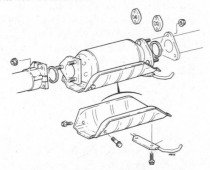

Catalytic converter

Circlip A ring-shaped clip used to prevent endwise movement of cylindrical parts and shafts. An internal circlip is installed in a groove in a housing; an external circlip fits into a groove on the outside of a cylindrical piece such as a shaft.

Clearance The amount of space between two parts. For example, between a piston and a cylinder, between a bearing and a journal, etc.

Coil spring A spiral of elastic steel found in various sizes throughout a vehicle, for example as a springing medium in the suspension and in the valve train.

Compression Reduction in volume, and increase in pressure and temperature, of a gas, caused by squeezing it into a smaller space.

Compression ratio The relationship between cylinder volume when the piston is at top dead centre and cylinder volume when the piston is at bottom dead centre.

Constant velocity (CV) joint A type of universal joint that cancels out vibrations caused by driving power being transmitted through an angle.

Core plug A disc or cup-shaped metal device inserted in a hole in a casting through which core was removed when the casting was formed. Also known as a freeze plug or expansion plug.

Crankcase The lower part of the engine block in which the crankshaft rotates.

Crankshaft The main rotating member, or shaft, running the length of the crankcase, with offset "throws" to which the connecting rods are attached.

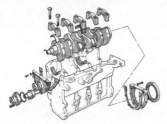

Crankshaft assembly

Crocodile clip See Alligator clip

D

Diagnostic code Code numbers obtained by accessing the diagnostic mode of an engine management computer. This code can be used to determine the area in the system where a malfunction may be located.

Disc brake A brake design incorporating a rotating disc onto which brake pads are squeezed. The resulting friction converts the energy of a moving vehicle into heat.

Double-overhead cam (DOHC) An engine that uses two overhead camshafts, usually one for the intake valves and one for the exhaust valves.

Drivebelt(s) The belt(s) used to drive accessories such as the alternator, water pump, power steering pump, air conditioning compressor, etc. off the crankshaft pulley.

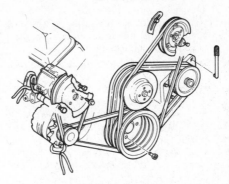

Accessory drivebelts

Driveshaft Any shaft used to transmit motion. Commonly used when referring to the axleshafts on a front wheel drive vehicle.

Drum brake A type of brake using a drum-shaped metal cylinder attached to the inner surface of the wheel. When the brake pedal is pressed, curved brake shoes with friction linings press against the inside of the drum to slow or stop the vehicle.

E

EGR valve A valve used to introduce exhaust gases into the intake air stream.

Electronic control unit (ECU) A computer which controls (for instance) ignition and fuel injection systems, or an anti-lock braking system. For more information refer to the *Haynes Automotive Electrical and Electronic Systems Manual*.

Electronic Fuel Injection (EFI) A computer controlled fuel system that distributes fuel through an injector located in each intake port of the engine.

Emergency brake A braking system, independent of the main hydraulic system, that can be used to slow or stop the vehicle if the primary brakes fail, or to hold the vehicle stationary even though the brake pedal isn't depressed. It usually consists of a hand lever that actuates either front or rear brakes mechanically through a series of cables and linkages. Also known as a handbrake or parking brake.

Endfloat The amount of lengthwise movement between two parts. As applied to a crankshaft, the distance that the crankshaft can move forward and back in the cylinder block.

Engine management system (EMS) A computer controlled system which manages the fuel injection and the ignition systems in an integrated fashion.

Exhaust manifold A part with several passages through which exhaust gases leave the engine combustion chambers and enter the exhaust pipe.

F

Fan clutch A viscous (fluid) drive coupling device which permits variable engine fan speeds in relation to engine speeds.

Feeler blade A thin strip or blade of hardened steel, ground to an exact thickness, used to check or measure clearances between parts.

Feeler blade

Firing order The order in which the engine cylinders fire, or deliver their power strokes, beginning with the number one cylinder.

Flywheel A heavy spinning wheel in which energy is absorbed and stored by means of momentum. On cars, the flywheel is attached to the crankshaft to smooth out firing impulses.

Free play The amount of travel before any action takes place. The "looseness" in a linkage, or an assembly of parts, between the initial application of force and actual movement. For example, the distance the brake pedal moves before the pistons in the master cylinder are actuated.

Fuse An electrical device which protects a circuit against accidental overload. The typical fuse contains a soft piece of metal which is calibrated to melt at a predetermined current flow (expressed as amps) and break the circuit.

Fusible link A circuit protection device consisting of a conductor surrounded by heat-resistant insulation. The conductor is smaller than the wire it protects, so it acts as the weakest link in the circuit. Unlike a blown fuse, a failed fusible link must frequently be cut from the wire for replacement.

G

Gap The distance the spark must travel in jumping from the centre electrode to the side electrode in a spark plug. Also refers to the spacing between the points in a contact breaker assembly in a conventional points-type ignition, or to the distance between the reluctor or rotor and the pickup coil in an electronic ignition.

Adjusting spark plug gap

Gasket Any thin, soft material - usually cork, cardboard, asbestos or soft metal - installed between two metal surfaces to ensure a good seal. For instance, the cylinder head gasket seals the joint between the block and the cylinder head.

Gasket

Gauge An instrument panel display used to monitor engine conditions. A gauge with a movable pointer on a dial or a fixed scale is an analogue gauge. A gauge with a numerical readout is called a digital gauge.

H

Halfshaft A rotating shaft that transmits power from the final drive unit to a drive wheel, usually when referring to a live rear axle.

Harmonic balancer A device designed to reduce torsion or twisting vibration in the crankshaft. May be incorporated in the crankshaft pulley. Also known as a vibration damper.

Hone An abrasive tool for correcting small irregularities or differences in diameter in an engine cylinder, brake cylinder, etc.

Hydraulic tappet A tappet that utilises hydraulic pressure from the engine's lubrication system to maintain zero clearance (constant contact with both camshaft and valve stem). Automatically adjusts to variation in valve stem length. Hydraulic tappets also reduce valve noise.

I

Ignition timing The moment at which the spark plug fires, usually expressed in the number of crankshaft degrees before the piston reaches the top of its stroke.

Inlet manifold A tube or housing with passages through which flows the air-fuel mixture (carburettor vehicles and vehicles with throttle body injection) or air only (port fuel-injected vehicles) to the port openings in the cylinder head.

J

Jump start Starting the engine of a vehicle with a discharged or weak battery by attaching jump leads from the weak battery to a charged or helper battery.

L

Load Sensing Proportioning Valve (LSPV) A brake hydraulic system control valve that works like a proportioning valve, but also takes into consideration the amount of weight carried by the rear axle.

Locknut A nut used to lock an adjustment nut, or other threaded component, in place. For example, a locknut is employed to keep the adjusting nut on the rocker arm in position.

Lockwasher A form of washer designed to prevent an attaching nut from working loose.

M

MacPherson strut A type of front suspension system devised by Earle MacPherson at Ford of England. In its original form, a simple lateral link with the anti-roll bar creates the lower control arm. A long strut - an integral coil spring and shock absorber - is mounted between the body and the steering knuckle. Many modern so-called MacPherson strut systems use a conventional lower A-arm and don't rely on the anti-roll bar for location.

Multimeter An electrical test instrument with the capability to measure voltage, current and resistance.

N

NOx Oxides of Nitrogen. A common toxic pollutant emitted by petrol and diesel engines at higher temperatures.

O

Ohm The unit of electrical resistance. One volt applied to a resistance of one ohm will produce a current of one amp.

Ohmmeter An instrument for measuring electrical resistance.

O-ring A type of sealing ring made of a special rubber-like material; in use, the O-ring is compressed into a groove to provide the sealing action.

Overhead cam (ohc) engine An engine with the camshaft(s) located on top of the cylinder head(s).

Overhead valve (ohv) engine An engine with the valves located in the cylinder head, but with the camshaft located in the engine block.

Oxygen sensor A device installed in the engine exhaust manifold, which senses the oxygen content in the exhaust and converts this information into an electric current. Also called a Lambda sensor.

P

Phillips screw A type of screw head having a cross instead of a slot for a corresponding type of screwdriver.

Plastigage A thin strip of plastic thread, available in different sizes, used for measuring clearances. For example, a strip of Plastigage is laid across a bearing journal. The parts are assembled and dismantled; the width of the crushed strip indicates the clearance between journal and bearing.

Plastigage

Propeller shaft The long hollow tube with universal joints at both ends that carries power from the transmission to the differential on front-engined rear wheel drive vehicles.

Proportioning valve A hydraulic control valve which limits the amount of pressure to the rear brakes during panic stops to prevent wheel lock-up.

R

Rack-and-pinion steering A steering system with a pinion gear on the end of the steering shaft that mates with a rack (think of a geared wheel opened up and laid flat). When the steering wheel is turned, the pinion turns, moving the rack to the left or right. This movement is transmitted through the track rods to the steering arms at the wheels.

Radiator A liquid-to-air heat transfer device designed to reduce the temperature of the coolant in an internal combustion engine cooling system.

Refrigerant Any substance used as a heat transfer agent in an air-conditioning system. R-12 has been the principle refrigerant for many years; recently, however, manufacturers have begun using R-134a, a non-CFC substance that is considered less harmful to the ozone in the upper atmosphere.

Rocker arm A lever arm that rocks on a shaft or pivots on a stud. In an overhead valve engine, the rocker arm converts the upward movement of the pushrod into a downward movement to open a valve.

Glossary of Technical Terms

Rotor In a distributor, the rotating device inside the cap that connects the centre electrode and the outer terminals as it turns, distributing the high voltage from the coil secondary winding to the proper spark plug. Also, that part of an alternator which rotates inside the stator. Also, the rotating assembly of a turbocharger, including the compressor wheel, shaft and turbine wheel.

Runout The amount of wobble (in-and-out movement) of a gear or wheel as it's rotated. The amount a shaft rotates "out-of-true." The out-of-round condition of a rotating part.

S

Sealant A liquid or paste used to prevent leakage at a joint. Sometimes used in conjunction with a gasket.

Sealed beam lamp An older headlight design which integrates the reflector, lens and filaments into a hermetically-sealed one-piece unit. When a filament burns out or the lens cracks, the entire unit is simply replaced.

Serpentine drivebelt A single, long, wide accessory drivebelt that's used on some newer vehicles to drive all the accessories, instead of a series of smaller, shorter belts. Serpentine drivebelts are usually tensioned by an automatic tensioner.

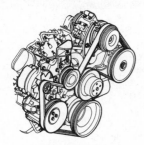

Serpentine drivebelt

Shim Thin spacer, commonly used to adjust the clearance or relative positions between two parts. For example, shims inserted into or under bucket tappets control valve clearances. Clearance is adjusted by changing the thickness of the shim.

Slide hammer A special puller that screws into or hooks onto a component such as a shaft or bearing; a heavy sliding handle on the shaft bottoms against the end of the shaft to knock the component free.

Sprocket A tooth or projection on the periphery of a wheel, shaped to engage with a chain or drivebelt. Commonly used to refer to the sprocket wheel itself.

Starter inhibitor switch On vehicles with an automatic transmission, a switch that prevents starting if the vehicle is not in Neutral or Park.

Strut See MacPherson strut.

T

Tappet A cylindrical component which transmits motion from the cam to the valve stem, either directly or via a pushrod and rocker arm. Also called a cam follower.

Thermostat A heat-controlled valve that regulates the flow of coolant between the cylinder block and the radiator, so maintaining optimum engine operating temperature. A thermostat is also used in some air cleaners in which the temperature is regulated.

Thrust bearing The bearing in the clutch assembly that is moved in to the release levers by clutch pedal action to disengage the clutch. Also referred to as a release bearing.

Timing belt A toothed belt which drives the camshaft. Serious engine damage may result if it breaks in service.

Timing chain A chain which drives the camshaft.

Toe-in The amount the front wheels are closer together at the front than at the rear. On rear wheel drive vehicles, a slight amount of toe-in is usually specified to keep the front wheels running parallel on the road by offsetting other forces that tend to spread the wheels apart.

Toe-out The amount the front wheels are closer together at the rear than at the front. On front wheel drive vehicles, a slight amount of toe-out is usually specified.

Tools For full information on choosing and using tools, refer to the *Haynes Automotive Tools Manual*.

Tracer A stripe of a second colour applied to a wire insulator to distinguish that wire from another one with the same colour insulator.

Tune-up A process of accurate and careful adjustments and parts replacement to obtain the best possible engine performance.

Turbocharger A centrifugal device, driven by exhaust gases, that pressurises the intake air. Normally used to increase the power output from a given engine displacement, but can also be used primarily to reduce exhaust emissions (as on VW's "Umwelt" Diesel engine).

U

Universal joint or U-joint A double-pivoted connection for transmitting power from a driving to a driven shaft through an angle. A U-joint consists of two Y-shaped yokes and a cross-shaped member called the spider.

V

Valve A device through which the flow of liquid, gas, vacuum, or loose material in bulk may be started, stopped, or regulated by a movable part that opens, shuts, or partially obstructs one or more ports or passageways. A valve is also the movable part of such a device.

Valve clearance The clearance between the valve tip (the end of the valve stem) and the rocker arm or tappet. The valve clearance is measured when the valve is closed.

Vernier caliper A precision measuring instrument that measures inside and outside dimensions. Not quite as accurate as a micrometer, but more convenient.

Viscosity The thickness of a liquid or its resistance to flow.

Volt A unit for expressing electrical "pressure" in a circuit. One volt that will produce a current of one ampere through a resistance of one ohm.

W

Welding Various processes used to join metal items by heating the areas to be joined to a molten state and fusing them together. For more information refer to the *Haynes Automotive Welding Manual*.

Wiring diagram A drawing portraying the components and wires in a vehicle's electrical system, using standardised symbols. For more information refer to the *Haynes Automotive Electrical and Electronic Systems Manual*.

Conversion Factors

Length (distance)

Inches (in)	25.4	= Millimetres (mm)	x 0.0394	=	Inches (in)
Feet (ft)	0.305	= Metres (m)	x 3.281	=	Feet (ft)
Miles	1.609	= Kilometres (km)	x 0.621	=	Miles

Volume (capacity)

Cubic inches (cu in; in³)	x 16.387	= Cubic centimetres (cc; cm³)	x 0.061	=	Cubic inches (cu in; in³)
Imperial pints (Imp pt)	x 0.568	= Litres (l)	x 1.76	=	Imperial pints (Imp pt)
Imperial quarts (Imp qt)	x 1.137	= Litres (l)	x 0.88	=	Imperial quarts (Imp qt)
Imperial quarts (Imp qt)	x 1.201	= US quarts (US qt)	x 0.833	=	Imperial quarts (Imp qt)
US quarts (US qt)	x 0.946	= Litres (l)	x 1.057	=	US quarts (US qt)
Imperial gallons (Imp gal)	x 4.546	= Litres (l)	x 0.22	=	Imperial gallons (Imp gal)
Imperial gallons (Imp gal)	x 1.201	= US gallons (US gal)	x 0.833	=	Imperial gallons (Imp gal)
US gallons (US gal)	x 3.785	= Litres (l)	x 0.264	=	US gallons (US gal)

Mass (weight)

Ounces (oz)	x 28.35	= Grams (g)	x 0.035	=	Ounces (oz)
Pounds (lb)	x 0.454	= Kilograms (kg)	x 2.205	=	Pounds (lb)

Force

Ounces-force (ozf; oz)	x 0.278	= Newtons (N)	x 3.6	=	Ounces-force (ozf; oz)
Pounds-force (lbf; lb)	x 4.448	= Newtons (N)	x 0.225	=	Pounds-force (lbf; lb)
Newtons (N)	x 0.1	= Kilograms-force (kgf; kg)	x 9.81	=	Newtons (N)

Pressure

Pounds-force per square inch (psi; lbf/in²; lb/in²)	x 0.070	= Kilograms-force per square centimetre (kgf/cm²; kg/cm²)	x 14.223	=	Pounds-force per square inch (psi; lbf/in²; lb/in²)
Pounds-force per square inch (psi; lbf/in²; lb/in²)	x 0.068	= Atmospheres (atm)	x 14.696	=	Pounds-force per square inch (psi; lbf/in²; lb/in²)
Pounds-force per square inch (psi; lbf/in²; lb/in²)	x 0.069	= Bars	x 14.5	=	Pounds-force per square inch (psi; lbf/in²; lb/in²)
Pounds-force per square inch (psi; lbf/in²; lb/in²)	x 6.895	= Kilopascals (kPa)	x 0.145	=	Pounds-force per square inch (psi; lbf/in²; lb/in²)
Kilopascals (kPa)	x 0.01	= Kilograms-force per square centimetre (kgf/cm²; kg/cm²)	x 98.1	=	Kilopascals (kPa)
Millibar (mbar)	x 100	= Pascals (Pa)	x 0.01	=	Millibar (mbar)
Millibar (mbar)	x 0.0145	= Pounds-force per square inch (psi; lbf/in²; lb/in²)	x 68.947	=	Millibar (mbar)
Millibar (mbar)	x 0.75	= Millimetres of mercury (mmHg)	x 1.333	=	Millibar (mbar)
Millibar (mbar)	x 0.401	= Inches of water (inH₂O)	x 2.491	=	Millibar (mbar)
Millimetres of mercury (mmHg)	x 0.535	= Inches of water (inH₂O)	x 1.868	=	Millimetres of mercury (mmHg)
Inches of water (inH₂O)	x 0.036	= Pounds-force per square inch (psi; lbf/in²; lb/in²)	x 27.68	=	Inches of water (inH₂O)

Torque (moment of force)

Pounds-force inches (lbf in; lb in)	x 1.152	= Kilograms-force centimetre (kgf cm; kg cm)	x 0.868	=	Pounds-force inches (lbf in; lb in)
Pounds-force inches (lbf in; lb in)	*x 0.113*	*= Newton metres (Nm)*	*x 8.85*	*=*	*Pounds-force inches (lbf in; lb in)*
Pounds-force inches (lbf in; lb in)	x 0.083	= Pounds-force feet (lbf ft; lb ft)	x 12	=	Pounds-force inches (lbf in; lb in)
Pounds-force feet (lbf ft; lb ft)	x 0.138	= Kilograms-force metres (kgf m; kg m)	x 7.233	=	Pounds-force feet (lbf ft; lb ft)
Pounds-force feet (lbf ft; lb ft)	x 1.356	= Newton metres (Nm)	x 0.738	=	Pounds-force feet (lbf ft; lb ft)
Newton metres (Nm)	x 0.102	= Kilograms-force metres (kgf m; kg m)	x 9.804	=	Newton metres (Nm)

Power

Horsepower (hp)	x 745.7	= Watts (W)	x 0.0013	=	Horsepower (hp)

Velocity (speed)

Miles per hour (miles/hr; mph)	x 1.609	= Kilometres per hour (km/hr; kph)	x 0.621	=	Miles per hour (miles/hr; mph)

Fuel consumption*

Miles per gallon, Imperial (mpg)	x 0.354	= Kilometres per litre (km/l)	x 2.825	=	Miles per gallon, Imperial (mpg)
Miles per gallon, US (mpg)	x 0.425	= Kilometres per litre (km/l)	x 2.352	=	Miles per gallon, US (mpg)

Temperature

Degrees Fahrenheit = (°C x 1.8) + 32   Degrees Celsius (Degrees Centigrade; °C) = (°F - 32) x 0.56

* It is common practice to convert from miles per gallon (mpg) to litres/100 kilometres (l/100km), where mpg (Imperial) x l/100 km = 282 and mpg (US) x l/100 km = 235

Note: *References throughout this index relate to Chapter•page number*

Preserving Our Motoring Heritage

< The Model J Duesenberg Derham Tourster. Only eight of these magnificent cars were ever built – this is the only example to be found outside the United States of America

Almost every car you've ever loved, loathed or desired is gathered under one roof at the Haynes Motor Museum. Over 300 immaculately presented cars and motorbikes represent every aspect of our motoring heritage, from elegant reminders of bygone days, such as the superb Model J Duesenberg to curiosities like the bug-eyed BMW Isetta. There are also many old friends and flames. Perhaps you remember the 1959 Ford Popular that you did your courting in? The magnificent 'Red Collection' is a spectacle of classic sports cars including AC, Alfa Romeo, Austin Healey, Ferrari, Lamborghini, Maserati, MG, Riley, Porsche and Triumph.

A Perfect Day Out

Each and every vehicle at the Haynes Motor Museum has played its part in the history and culture of Motoring. Today, they make a wonderful spectacle and a great day out for all the family. Bring the kids, bring Mum and Dad, but above all bring your camera to capture those golden memories for ever. You will also find an impressive array of motoring memorabilia, a comfortable 70 seat video cinema and one of the most extensive transport book shops in Britain. The Pit Stop Cafe serves everything from a cup of tea to wholesome, home-made meals or, if you prefer, you can enjoy the large picnic area nestled in the beautiful rural surroundings of Somerset.

John Haynes O.B.E., Founder and Chairman of the museum at the wheel of a Haynes Light 12.

< Graham Hill's Lola Cosworth Formula 1 car next to a 1934 Riley Sports.

The Museum is situated on the A357 Castle Cary to Frome road at Sparkford, just off the A303 in Somerset. It is about 40 miles south of Bristol, and 25 minutes drive from the M5 intersection at Taunton.

Open 9.30am - 5.30pm (10.00am - 4.00pm Winter) 7 days a week, *except Christmas Day, Boxing Day and New Years Day*

Special rates available for schools, coach parties and outings Charitable Trust No. 292048